BUTTERWORTHS

STONE'S JUSTICES' MANUAL 2022

One Hundred and Fifty–Fourth Edition

VOLUME 3

edited by

A J TURNER

Barrister, Chambers of Adrian Turner, Eastbourne

S E JONES

Barrister, Secretary JCS

A J KELLY

District Judge (Magistrates' Courts)

N J WATTAM

District Judge (Magistrates' Courts)

Contributors

B J LLOYD – Extradition

Barrister, 6KBW College Hill, London

A MORRIS – Human Rights

Barrister, Garden Court Chambers, London

LexisNexis® UK & Worldwide

United Kingdom	RELX (UK) Limited trading as LexisNexis®, 1–3 Strand, London WC2N 5JR and 9–10 St Andrew Square, Edinburgh EH2 2AF
LNUK Global Partners	LexisNexis® encompasses authoritative legal publishing brands dating back to the 19th century including: Butterworths® in the United Kingdom, Canada and the Asia-Pacific region; Les Editions du Juris Classeur in France; and Matthew Bender® worldwide. Details of LexisNexis® locations worldwide can be found at www.lexisnexis.com

ISBN 978-1-4743-2111-2

9 781474 321112

ISBN 978-1-4743-2108-2

9 781474 321082

ISBN for this volume: 9781474321112

ISBN for the set: 9781474321082

Printed and bound by CPI Group (UK) Ltd, Croydon, CR0 4YY

Visit LexisNexis at www.lexisnexis.co.uk

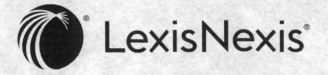

CONTENTS

(WITH REFERENCE TO PARAS)

KEY MATERIALS

CRIMINAL PRACTICE DIRECTIONS

CRIMINAL PROCEDURE RULES 2020

MAGISTRATES' COURTS SENTENCING GUIDELINES

Ready Reference

	Statutory provision		Narrative
Proof of service	CrimPR Pt 4, r 4.12	*KM* B.4	
Adjournment			1.210
Allocation and sending for trial – general	CDA 1998, s 50A-52	1.107	1.243
Plea before venue	MCA 1980, ss 17A–17C	1.566	1.247
Mode of trial	MCA 1980, s 18–22A	1.571	1.254
Guidelines	Sentencing Guidelines	*KM* C.1	
Adults and youths	CDA 1998, ss 50A, 51 & 51A	1.1084	1.260, 5.12
Criminal damage	MCA 1980, s 22	1.576	1.261
Low value shoplifting	MCA 1980, s 22A	1.577	1.242
Sending for trial	CDA 1998, ss 50A, 51 & 51A	1.1084	1.244 ff, 5.10 ff
Trial			1.280
Proceeding in absence of accused			1.186
Procedure	CrimPR Pt 24	*KM* B.23	1.313
Evidence			
Identification	PACE Code D	2.373	2.128
Exclusion of unfairly obtained	PACE 1984, s 78	2.244	2.46
Hearsay	CJA 2003, ss 114–134	2.347 2.364	2.104 ff
	CrimPR Pt 20	*KM* B.19	1.303
Bad character	CJA 2003, ss 98–112	2.332 2.346	2.83 ff
	CrimPR Pt 21	*KM* B.20	1.304
Oaths etc	Oaths Act 1978	2.200	1.316
Competence	YJCEA 1999, s 53	2.322	2.48
Compellability	PACE 1984, s 80	2.246	2.48
Hostile witness	Crim Proc Act 1865, s 3	1.412	1.322
Special measures	YJCEA 1999, Pt II, Ch I	2.282	2.55 ff 1.300
Extended use of live links	Coronavirus Act 2020		2.67
Protection from cross examination	YJCEA 1999, Pt II, Ch II	2.304	2.79
	Crim PR Pt 23	B.22	
Complainant's sexual history	YJCEA 1999, Pt II, Ch III	2.310	2.80
	Crim PR Pt 22	B.21	1.305
Refreshing memory	CJA 2003, s 139	2.367	1.324
Accused – effect of silence of at trial	CJPOA 1994, s 35	2.263	2.134
Submission of no case			1.331
Burden and standard of proof			1.340 1.344
Human Rights			
Fair Trial	ECHR, Art 6		7.6686
Private life	ECHR, Art 8		7.6686

	Statutory provision		Narrative
– *mandatory/special reasons*	RTOA 1988, s 34(1)	4.488	
– *discretionary*	RTOA 1988, s 34(2)	4.488	
– *penalty points/mitigating circumstances*	RTOA 1988, s 35	4.497	4.22
Dangerous and Prohibited Dogs			7.3062–7.3068

PART VII
MISCELLANEOUS OFFENCES AND CIVIL PROCEEDINGS (J–W)

JURIES

Juries Act 1974
(1974 c 23)

7.7401   20.   Offences: failure to attend, serving while disqualified etc   (1)   Subject to the provisions of subsections (2) to (4) below—

(*a*)   if a person duly summoned under this Act fails to attend (on the first or any subsequent day on which he is required to attend by the summons or by the appropriate officer) in compliance with the summons, or

(*b*)   if a person, after attending in pursuance of a summons, is not available when called on to serve as a juror, or is unfit for service by reason of drink or drugs,

he shall be liable to a fine not exceeding **level 3** on the standard scale.

(2)   An offence under subsection (1) above shall be punishable either on summary conviction or as if it were criminal contempt of court committed in the face of the court.

(3)   Subsection (1)(*a*) above shall not apply to a person summoned, otherwise than under s 6 of this Act[1], unless the summons was duly served on him on a date not later than fourteen days before the date fixed by the summons for his first attendance.

(4)   A person shall not be liable to be punished under the preceding provisions of this section if he can show some reasonable cause for his failure to comply with the summons, or for not being available when called on to serve, and those provisions have effect subject to the provisions of this Act about the withdrawal or alteration of a summons and about the granting of any excusal or deferral.

(5)   If any person—

(*a*)   having been summoned under this Act makes, or causes or permits to be made on his behalf, any false representation to the appropriate officer with the intention of evading jury service; or

(*b*)   makes or causes to be made on behalf of another person who has been so summoned any false representation to that officer with the intention of enabling the other to evade jury service; or

(*c*)   when any question is put to him in pursuance of section 2(5) of this Act, refuses without reasonable excuse to answer, or gives an answer he knows to be false in a material particular, or recklessly gives an answer which is false in a material particular; or

(*d*)   knowing that he is not qualified for jury service by reason of section 40 of the Criminal Justice and Public Order Act 1994,, serves on a jury, or

(*e*)   knowing that he is not qualified for jury service by reason of section 40 of the Criminal Justice and Public Order Act 1994, serves on a jury,

he shall be liable on summary conviction to a fine of not more than **level 5** on the standard scale in the case of an offence of serving on a jury when disqualified and, in any other case, a fine of not more than **level 3** on the standard scale.

[Juries Act 1974, s 20 as amended by the Criminal Justice Act 1982, ss 38 and 46, the Criminal Justice Act 1988, Sch 15, the Criminal Justice and Public Order Act 1994, Sch 10, the Criminal Justice Act 2003, Sch 33 and the Criminal Justice and Courts Act 2015, s 71.]

---

[1]   Section 6 contains a power to summon a person in exceptional circumstances without any written notice.

7.7402   20A.   Offence: research by jurors   (1)   It is an offence for a member of a jury that tries an issue in a case before a court to research the case during the trial period, subject to the exceptions in subsections (6) and (7).

(2)   A person researches a case if (and only if) the person—

(*a*)   intentionally seeks information, and

(*b*)   when doing so, knows or ought reasonably to know that the information is or may be relevant to the case.

(3)   The ways in which a person may seek information include—

(*a*)   asking a question,

(*b*)   searching an electronic database, including by means of the internet,

(*c*)   visiting or inspecting a place or object,

(*d*)   conducting an experiment, and

    (e)   asking another person to seek the information.

(4)   Information relevant to the case includes information about—

    (a)   a person involved in events relevant to the case,

    (b)   the judge dealing with the issue,

    (c)   any other person involved in the trial, whether as a lawyer, a witness or otherwise,

    (d)   the law relating to the case,

    (e)   the law of evidence, and

    (f)   court procedure.

(5)   "The trial period", in relation to a member of a jury that tries an issue, is the period—

    (a)   beginning when the person is sworn to try the issue, and

    (b)   ending when the judge discharges the jury or, if earlier, when the judge discharges the person.

(6)   It is not an offence under this section for a person to seek information if the person needs the information for a reason which is not connected with the case.

(7)   It is not an offence under this section for a person—

    (a)   to attend proceedings before the court on the issue;

    (b)   to seek information from the judge dealing with the issue;

    (c)   to do anything which the judge dealing with the issue directs or authorises the person to do;

    (d)   to seek information from another member of the jury, unless the person knows or ought reasonably to know that the other member of the jury contravened this section in the process of obtaining the information;

    (e)   to do anything else which is reasonably necessary in order for the jury to try the issue.

(8)   A person guilty of an offence under this section is liable, on conviction on indictment, to imprisonment for a term not exceeding 2 years or a fine (or both).

(9)   Proceedings for an offence under this section may only be instituted by or with the consent of the Attorney General.

[Juries Act 1974, s 20A as inserted by the Criminal Justice and Courts Act 2015, s 71.]

7.7403   20B.   Offence: sharing research with other jurors   (1)   It is an offence for a member of a jury that tries an issue in a case before a court intentionally to disclose information to another member of the jury during the trial period if—

    (a)   the member contravened section 20A in the process of obtaining the information, and

    (b)   the information has not been provided by the court.

(2)   Information has been provided by the court if (and only if) it has been provided as part of—

    (a)   evidence presented in the proceedings on the issue, or

    (b)   other information provided to the jury or a juror during the trial period by, or with the permission of, the judge dealing with the issue.

(3)   A person guilty of an offence under this section is liable, on conviction on indictment, to imprisonment for a term not exceeding 2 years or a fine (or both).

(4)   Proceedings for an offence under this section may not be instituted except by or with the consent of the Attorney General.

(5)   In this section, "the trial period" has the same meaning as in section 20A.

[Juries Act 1974, s 20B as inserted by the Criminal Justice and Courts Act 2015, s 72.]

7.7404   20C.   Offence: jurors engaging in other prohibited conduct   (1)   It is an offence for a member of a jury that tries an issue in a case before a court intentionally to engage in prohibited conduct during the trial period, subject to the exceptions in subsections (4) and (5).

(2)   "Prohibited conduct" means conduct from which it may reasonably be concluded that the person intends to try the issue otherwise than on the basis of the evidence presented in the proceedings on the issue.

(3)   An offence under this section is committed whether or not the person knows that the conduct is prohibited conduct.

(4)   It is not an offence under this section for a member of the jury to research the case (as defined in section 20A(2) to (4)).

(5)   It is not an offence under this section for a member of the jury to disclose information to another member of the jury.

(6)   A person guilty of an offence under this section is liable, on conviction on indictment, to imprisonment for a term not exceeding 2 years or a fine (or both).

(7)   Proceedings for an offence under this section may not be instituted except by or with the consent of the Attorney General.

(8)   In this section, "the trial period" has the same meaning as in section 20A.

[Juries Act 1974, s 20C as inserted by the Criminal Justice and Courts Act 2015, s 73.]

7.7405   20D.   Offence: disclosing jury's deliberations   (1)   It is an offence for a person intentionally—

    (a)   to disclose information about statements made, opinions expressed, arguments advanced or votes cast by members of a jury in the course of their deliberations in proceedings before a court, or

    (b)   to solicit or obtain such information,

subject to the exceptions in sections 20E to 20G.

(2)   A person guilty of an offence under this section is liable, on conviction on indictment, to imprisonment for a term not exceeding 2 years or a fine (or both).

(3)   Proceedings for an offence under this section may not be instituted except by or with the consent of the Attorney General.

[Juries Act 1974, s 20D as inserted by the Criminal Justice and Courts Act 2015, s 74.]

7.7406   20E.   Offence of disclosing jury's deliberations: initial exceptions   (1)   It is not an offence under section 20D for a person to disclose information in the proceedings mentioned in section 20D(1) for the purposes of enabling the jury to arrive at their verdict or in connection with the delivery of that verdict.

(2)   It is not an offence under section 20D for the judge dealing with those proceedings to disclose information—

(a)   for the purposes of dealing with the case, or

(b)   for the purposes of an investigation by a relevant investigator into whether an offence or contempt of court has been committed by or in relation to a juror in the proceedings mentioned in section 20D(1).

(3)   It is not an offence under section 20D for a person who reasonably believes that a disclosure described in subsection (2)(b) has been made to disclose information for the purposes of the investigation.

(4)   It is not an offence under section 20D to publish information disclosed as described in subsection (1) or (2)(a) in the proceedings mentioned in section 20D(1).

(5)   In this section—

"publish" means make available to the public or a section of the public;

"relevant investigator" means—

(a)   a police force;

(b)   the Attorney General;

(c)   any other person or class of person specified by the Lord Chancellor for the purposes of this section by regulations made by statutory instrument.

(6)   The Lord Chancellor must obtain the consent of the Lord Chief Justice before making regulations under this section.

(7)   A statutory instrument containing regulations under this section is subject to annulment in pursuance of a resolution of either House of Parliament.

[Juries Act 1974, s 20E as inserted by the Criminal Justice and Courts Act 2015, s 74.]

7.7407   20F.   Offence of disclosing jury's deliberations: further exceptions   (1)   It is not an offence under section 20D for a person to disclose information to a person listed in subsection (2) if—

(a)   the disclosure is made after the jury in the proceedings mentioned in section 20D(1) has been discharged, and

(b)   the person making the disclosure reasonably believes that—

(i)   an offence or contempt of court has been, or may have been, committed by or in relation to a juror in connection with those proceedings, or

(ii)   conduct of a juror in connection with those proceedings may provide grounds for an appeal against conviction or sentence.

(2)   Those persons are—

(a)   a member of a police force;

(b)   a judge of the Court of Appeal;

(c)   the registrar of criminal appeals;

(d)   a judge of the court where the proceedings mentioned in section 20D(1) took place;

(e)   a member of staff of that court who would reasonably be expected to disclose the information only to a person mentioned in paragraphs (b) to (d).

(3)   It is not an offence under section 20D for a member of a police force to disclose information for the purposes of obtaining assistance in deciding whether to submit the information to a judge of the Court of Appeal or the registrar of criminal appeals, provided that the disclosure does not involve publishing the information.

(4)   It is not an offence under section 20D for a judge of the Court of Appeal or the registrar of criminal appeals to disclose information for the purposes of an investigation by a relevant investigator into—

(a)   whether an offence or contempt of court has been committed by or in relation to a juror in connection with the proceedings mentioned in section 20D(1), or

(b)   whether conduct of a juror in connection with those proceedings may provide grounds for an appeal against conviction or sentence.

(5)   It is not an offence under section 20D for a judge of the Court of Appeal or the registrar of criminal appeals to disclose information for the purposes of enabling or assisting—

(a)   a person who was the defendant in the proceedings mentioned in section 20D(1), or

(b)   a legal representative of such a person,

to consider whether conduct of a juror in connection with those proceedings may provide grounds for an appeal against conviction or sentence.

(6)   It is not an offence under section 20D for a person who reasonably believes that a disclosure described in subsection (4) or (5) has been made to disclose information for the purposes of the investigation or consideration in question.

(7)   It is not an offence under section 20D for a person to disclose information in evidence in—

(a)   proceedings for an offence or contempt of court alleged to have been committed by or in relation to a juror in connection with the proceedings mentioned in section 20D(1),

(b)   proceedings on an appeal, or an application for leave to appeal, against a decision in the proceedings mentioned in section 20D(1) where an allegation relating to conduct of or in relation to a juror forms part of the grounds of appeal, or

(c)   proceedings on any further appeal or reference arising out of proceedings mentioned in paragraph (a) or (b).

(8)   It is not an offence under section 20D for a person to disclose information in the course of taking reasonable steps to prepare for proceedings described in subsection (7)(a) to (c).

(9)   It is not an offence under section 20D to publish information disclosed as described in subsection (7).

(10)   In this section—

"publish" means make available to the public or a section of the public;

"relevant investigator" means—

(a)   a police force;

(b)   the Attorney General;

(c)   the Criminal Cases Review Commission;

(d)   the Crown Prosecution Service;

(e)   any other person or class of person specified by the Lord Chancellor for the purposes of this section by regulations made by statutory instrument.

(11)   The Lord Chancellor must obtain the consent of the Lord Chief Justice before making regulations under this section.

(12)   A statutory instrument containing regulations under this section is subject to annulment in pursuance of a resolution of either House of Parliament.

[Juries Act 1974, s 20F as inserted by the Criminal Justice and Courts Act 2015, s 74.]

7.7408   20G.   Offence of disclosing jury's deliberations: exceptions for soliciting disclosures or obtaining information   (1)   It is not an offence under section 20D to solicit a disclosure described in section 20E(1) to (4) or section 20F(1) to (9).

(2)   It is not an offence under section 20D to obtain information—

(a)   by means of a disclosure described in section 20E(1) to (4) or section 20F(1) to (9), or

(b)   from a document that is available to the public or a section of the public.

[Juries Act 1974, s 20G as inserted by the Criminal Justice and Courts Act 2015, s 74.]

LIBEL

Contents

7.7409 Immunity for informants, witnesses, etc in criminal investigations and proceedings.—A witness has absolute privilege when giving evidence in court and in relation to prior statements made to the party calling the witness or to that party's lawyers: *Watson v M'Ewan* [1905] AC 480. Immunity for out of court statements is not confined to persons who are subsequently called as witnesses: *Taylor v Director of the Serious Fraud Office* [1999] 2 AC 177, [1998] 4 All ER 801, HL(E). Absolute immunity from suit also applies to those who participate in a criminal investigation whether as informants, investigators, or prosecutors. This is justified by the necessity for the due administration of criminal justice that complaints of alleged criminal conduct should always be capable of being made to the police free from fear that the person accused will subsequently involve the complainant in costly litigation. Such immunity is consistent with art 8 of the European Convention on Human Rights. A person who makes a complaint to the police, thereby instigating a police investigation which does not lead to a prosecution, can shelter behind the defence of absolute privilege if a claim is brought against her in defamation: *Westcott v Westcott* [2008] EWCA Civ 818, [2009] QB 407. The question is whether the oral statement made by a defendant to a libel action and her subsequent written statement can each fairly be said to be part of the process of investigating a crime or a possible crime with a view to a prosecution or possible prosecution in respect of the matter being investigated: *Evans v London Hospital Medical College (University of London)* [1981] 1 All ER 715, [1981] 1 WLR 184. Although immunity for defamatory statements extends to a malicious informer, where malice is established there may be a claim for the different tort of malicious prosecution. The different torts protect different public interests—the wider administration of justice in the case of the making of defamatory statements and the narrower need to prevent abuse of the process of the court in the case of malicious prosecution: *Martin v Watson* [1996] AC 74, [1995] 3 All ER 559.

Newspapers, Printers, and Reading Rooms Repeal Act 1869
(1869 c 24)

[12th July 1869]

7.7410 1.   Continuance of Acts in second schedule   . . . The provisions of the . . . Acts which are set out in the second schedule to this Act shall continue in force in the same manner as if they were enacted in the body of this Act; . . .

[Newspapers, Printers, and Reading Rooms Repeal Act 1869, s 1.]

7.7411 2.   Short title   This Act may be cited as "The Newspapers, Printers, and Reading Rooms Repeal Act 1869."

[Newspapers, Printers, and Reading Rooms Repeal Act 1869, s 2.]

7.7412

SCHEDULE 1	Section 1

7.7413 ...

SCHEDULE 2	Section 1

THE ENACTMENTS IN THIS SCHEDULE, WITH THE EXCEPTION OF SECTION 19 OF 6 & 7 WILL 4 c 76, DO NOT APPLY TO IRELAND

7.7414   39 Geo 3 c 79

Section twenty-eight

Not to extend to papers printed by authority of Parliament Nothing in this Act contained shall extend or be construed to extend to any papers printed by the authority and for the use of either House of Parliament.

Section twenty-nine

Printers to keep a copy of every paper they print, and write thereon the name and abode of their employer. Penalty of £20 for neglect or refusing to produce the copy within six months Every person who shall print any paper for hire, reward, gain, or profit, shall carefully preserve and keep one copy (at least) of every paper so printed by him or her, on which he or she shall write, or cause to be written or printed, in fair and legible characters, the name and place of abode of the person or persons by whom he or she shall be employed to print the same; and every person printing any paper for hire, reward, gain, or profit who shall omit or neglect to write, or cause to be written or printed as aforesaid, the name and place of his or her employer on one of such printed papers, or to keep or preserve the same for the space of six calendar months next after the printing thereof, or to produce and show the same to any justice of the peace who within the said space of six calendar months shall require to see the same, shall for every such omission, neglect, or refusal be liable on summary conviction to a fine of level 2 on the standard scale.

Section thirty-one

Not to extend to impressions of engravings or the printing names and addresses Nothing herein contained shall extend . . . to the printing . . . of the name, or the name and address, or business or profession, of any person, and the articles in which he deals, or to any papers for the sale of estates or goods by auction or otherwise.
Section thirty-four

Prosecutions to be commenced within three months after penalty is incurred No person shall be prosecuted . . . for any penalty imposed by this Act, unless such prosecution shall be commenced. . . within three calendar months next after such penalty shall have been incurred.
Part of section thirty-five
. . . Section thirty-six
. . . 51 Geo 3 c 65
Section three

Name and residence of printers not required to be put to bank notes, bills, etc, or to any paper printed by authority of any public board or public office Nothing in the Unlawful Societies Act 1799, or in this Act contained shall extend or be construed to extend to require the name and residence of the printer to be printed upon any bank note, . . . of the . . . Bank of England, upon any bill of exchange, or promissory note, or upon any bond or other security for payment of money, or upon any bill of lading, policy of insurance, letter of attorney, deed, or agreement, or upon any transfer or assignment of any public stocks, funds, or other securities, or upon any transfer or assignment of the stocks of any public corporation or company authorised or sanctioned by Act of Parliament, or upon any dividend warrant of or for any such public or other stocks, funds, or securities, or upon any receipt for money or goods, or upon any proceeding in any court of law or equity, or in any inferior court, warrant, order, or other papers printed by the authority of any public board or public officer in the execution of the duties of their respective offices, notwithstanding the whole or any part of the said several securities, instruments, proceedings, matters, and things aforesaid shall have been or shall be printed.
6 & 7 Will 4 c 76
Section nineteen

Discovery of proprietors, printers, or publishers of newspapers may be enforced by bill, etc If any person shall file any bill in any court for the discovery of the name of any person concerned as printer, publisher, or proprietor of any newspaper, or of any matters relative to the printing or publishing of any newspaper, in order the more effectually to bring or carry on any suit or action for damages alleged to have been sustained by reason of any slanderous or libellous matter contained in any such newspaper respecting such person, it shall not be lawful for the defendant to plead or demur to such bill, but such defendant shall be compellable to make the discovery required; provided always, that such discovery shall not be made use of as evidence or otherwise in any proceeding against the defendant, save only in that proceeding for which the discovery is made.
2 & 3 Vict c 12
Section two

Penalty upon printers for not printing their name and residence on every paper or book, and on persons publishing the same Every person who shall print any paper or book whatsoever which shall be meant to be published or dispersed, and who shall not print upon the front of every such paper, if the same shall be printed on one side only, or upon the first or last leaf of every paper or book which shall consist of more than one leaf, in legible characters, his or her name and usual place of abode or business, and every person who shall publish or disperse, or assist in publishing or dispersing, any printed paper or book on which the name and place of abode of the person printing the same shall not be printed as aforesaid, shall for every copy of such paper so printed by him or her be liable on summary conviction to a fine not exceeding level 1 on the standard scale: Provided always, that nothing herein contained shall be construed to impose any penalty upon any person for printing any paper excepted out of the operation of the Unlawful Societies Act 1799 either in the said Act or by any Act made for the amendment thereof.
Section three

As to books or papers printed at the university presses In the case of books or papers printed at the University Press of Oxford, or the Pitt Press of Cambridge, the printer, instead of printing his name thereon, shall print the following words, "Printed at the University Press, Oxford," or "The Pitt Press, Cambridge," as the case may be.
Section four

No actions for penalties to be commenced except in the name of the Attorney or Solicitor General in England or the Queen's Advocate in Scotland

Provided always, that it shall not be lawful for any person or persons whatsoever to commence, prosecute, enter, or file, or cause or procure to be commenced, prosecuted, entered, or filed, any action, bill, plaint, or information in any of Her Majesty's courts, or before any justice or justices of the peace, against any person or persons for the recovery of any fine, penalty, or forfeiture made or incurred or which may hereafter be incurred under the provisions of this Act, unless the same be commenced, prosecuted, entered, or filed in the name of Her Majesty's Attorney General . . . in . . . England, or Her Majesty's Advocate for Scotland (as the case may be respectively); and if any action, bill, plaint or information shall be commenced, prosecuted, or filed in the name or names of any other person or persons than is or are in that behalf before mentioned, the same and every proceeding thereupon had are hereby declared and the same shall be null and void to all intents and purposes. 9 & 10 Vict c 33
Section one

Proceedings shall not be commenced unless in the name of the law officers of the Crown It shall not be lawful for any person or persons to commence, prosecute, enter, or file, or cause or procure to be commenced, prosecuted, entered, or filed, any action, bill, plaint, or information in any of Her Majesty's courts, or before any justice or justices of the peace, against any person or persons for the recovery of any fine which may hereafter be incurred under the provisions of the Unlawful Societies Act 1799 set out in this Act, unless the same be commenced, prosecuted, entered, or filed in the name of Her Majesty's Attorney General . . . in England or Her Majesty's Advocate in Scotland, and every action, bill, plaint or information which shall be commenced, prosecuted, entered, or filed in the name or names of any other person or persons than is in that behalf before mentioned, and every proceeding thereupon had, shall be null and void to all intents and purposes.

Judicial Proceedings (Regulation of Reports) Act 1926
(16 & 17 Geo 5 c 61)

7.7415 1. Restriction on publication of reports of judicial proceedings (1) It shall not be lawful to print or publish, or cause or procure to be printed or published—

(a)   in relation to any judicial proceedings[1] any indecent matter or indecent medical, surgical or physiological details, being matter or details the publication of which would be calculated to injure public morals;

(b)   in relation to any judicial proceedings for dissolution of marriage, for nullity of marriage, or for judicial separation[2], or for the dissolution or annulment of a civil partnership or for the separation of civil partners, any particulars other than the following, that is to say:

(i)   the names, addresses and occupations of the parties and witnesses;

(ii)   a concise statement of the charges, defences and countercharges in support of which evidence has been given;

(iii)   submissions on any point of law arising in the course of the proceedings and the decision of the court thereon;

(iv)   the summing up of the judge and the finding of the jury (if any) and the judgment of the court and observations made by the judge in giving judgment:

Provided that nothing in this part of this subsection shall be held to permit the publication of anything contrary to the provisions of paragraph (a) of this subsection.[*]

(2) If any person acts in contravention of the provisions of this Act, he shall in respect of each offence be liable, on summary conviction, to imprisonment for a term not exceeding **four months**[**] or to a fine not exceeding **level 5** on the standard scale, or to both such imprisonment and fine: Provided that no person, other than a proprietor, editor, master printer or publisher, shall be liable to be convicted under this Act.

(3) No prosecution to be commenced without the Attorney-General's sanction.

(4) Nothing in this section shall apply to the printing of any pleading, transcript of evidence or other document for use in connection with any judicial proceedings or the communication thereof to persons concerned in the proceedings, or to the printing or publishing of any notice or report in pursuance of the directions of the court; or to the printing or publishing of any matter in any separate volume or part of any bona fide series of law reports which does not form part of any other publication and consists solely of reports of proceedings in courts of law, or in any publication of a technical character bona fide intended for circulation among members of the legal or medical professions.

(5) *Repealed.*

[Judicial Proceedings (Regulation of Reports) Act 1926, s 1 as amended by the Criminal Justice Act 1982, ss 38 and 46 and the Civil Partnership Act 2004, Sch 27.]

---

[*] **Amended by the Family Law Act 1996, Sch 8 from a date to be appointed.**
[**] **Words substituted by the Criminal Justice Act 2003, Sch 26 from a date to be appointed.**
[1] Not defined by this Act. Cf Perjury Act 1911, s 1(2), post.
[2] For newspaper reports of domestic proceedings, see the Magistrates' Courts Act 1980, s 71 in PART I: MAGISTRATES' COURTS, PROCEDURE, ante.

7.7416 Minors and Youth Courts Prohibition against publication of certain matter in newspapers. See Children and Young Persons Act 1933, ss 39, 49 in PART V: YOUTH COURTS.

Defamation Act 1996[1]
(1996 c 31)

Statutory privilege

7.7417 14. Reports of court proceedings absolutely privileged (1) A fair and accurate report of proceedings in public before a court to which this section applies, if published contemporaneously with the proceedings, is absolutely privileged.

(2) A report of proceedings which by an order of the court, or as a consequence of any statutory provision, is required to be postponed shall be treated as published contemporaneously if it is published as soon as practicable after publication is permitted.

(3) This section applies to—

(a)   any court in the United Kingdom,

(b)   any court established under the law of a country or territory outside the United Kingdom;

(c)   any international court or tribunal established by the Security Council of the United Nations or by an international agreement;

and in paragraphs (a) and (b) "court" includes any tribunal or body exercising the judicial power of the State.

[Defamation Act 1996, s 14 as amended by the Defamation Act 2013, s 7.]

---

[1] The Defamation Act 1996 amends the law of defamation and amends the law of limitation with respect to actions for defamation or malicious falsehood. Only those provisions of the Act which are relevant to the work of magistrates' courts are included in this manual.

7.7418   **15.   Reports, etc. protected by qualified privilege.** (1) The publication of any report or other statement mentioned in Schedule 1 to this Act is privileged unless the publication is shown to be made with malice, subject as follows.

(2) In defamation proceedings in respect of the publication of a report or other statement mentioned in Part II of that Schedule, there is no defence under this section if the plaintiff shows that the defendant—

(a)   was requested by him to publish in a suitable manner a reasonable letter or statement by way of explanation or contradiction, and

(b)   refused or neglected to do so.

For this purpose "in a suitable manner" means in the same manner as the publication complained of or in a manner that is adequate and reasonable in the circumstances.

(3) This section does not apply to the publication to the public, or a section of the public, of matter which is not of public interest and the publication of which is not for the public benefit.

(4) Nothing in this section shall be construed—

(a)   as protecting the publication of matter the publication of which is prohibited by law, or

(b)   as limiting or abridging any privilege subsisting apart from this section.

[Defamation Act 1996, s 15 as amended by the Defamation Act 2013, s 7.]

Supplementary provisions

7.7419   **17.   Interpretation** (1) In this Act—

"publication" and "publish", in relation to a statement, have the meaning they have for the purposes of the law of defamation generally, but "publisher" is specially defined for the purposes of section 1;

"statement" means words, pictures, visual images, gestures or any other method of signifying meaning; and

"statutory provision" means—

(a)   a provision contained in an Act or in subordinate legislation within the meaning of the Interpretation Act 1978, or

(aa)   a provision contained in an Act of the Scottish Parliament or in an instrument made under such an Act, or

(b)   a statutory provision within the meaning given by section 1 (*f*) of the Interpretation Act (Northern Ireland) 1954.

(2) In this Act as it applies to proceedings in Scotland—

"costs" means expenses; and

"plaintiff" and "defendant" mean pursuer and defender.

[Defamation Act 1996, s 17 as amended by the Scotland Act 1998, Sch 8.]

General provisions

7.7420   **20.   Short title and saving** (1)   This Act may be cited as the Defamation Act 1996.

(2) *Repealed.*

[Defamation Act 1996, s 20 as amended by the Coroners and Justice Act 2009, Sch 23.]

SCHEDULES

SCHEDULE 1
QUALIFIED PRIVILEGE   Section 15

(Amended by the Scotland Act 1998, Sch 8, SI 2001/2237, SI 2002/808 and 1057, the Government of Wales Act 2006, Sch 10, SI 2009/1941 and the Defamation Act 2013, s 7.)

PART I
STATEMENTS HAVING QUALIFIED PRIVILEGE WITHOUT EXPLANATION OR CONTRADICTION

7.7421   **1.**   A fair and accurate report of proceedings in public of a legislature anywhere in the world.

2.   A fair and accurate report of proceedings in public before a court anywhere in the world.

3.   A fair and accurate report of proceedings in public of a person appointed to hold a public inquiry by a government or legislature anywhere in the world.

4.   A fair and accurate report of proceedings in public anywhere in the world of an international organisation or an international conference.

5.   A fair and accurate copy of or extract from any register or other document required by law to be open to public inspection.

6.   A notice or advertisement published by or on the authority of a court, or of a judge or officer of a court, anywhere in the world.

7.   A fair and accurate copy of or extract from matter published by or on the authority of a government or legislature anywhere in the world.

8.   A fair and accurate copy of or extract from matter published anywhere in the world by an international organisation or an international conference.

PART II
STATEMENTS PRIVILEGED SUBJECT TO EXPLANATION OR CONTRADICTION

9.   (1)   A fair and accurate copy of, extract from or summary of a notice or other matter issued for the information of the public by or on behalf of—

(a)   a legislature or government anywhere in the world;

(b)   an authority anywhere in the world performing governmental functions;

(c)   an international organisation or international conference.

(2)   In this paragraph "governmental functions" includes police functions.

10.   A fair and accurate copy of, extract from or summary of a document made available by a court anywhere in the world, or by a judge or officer of such a court.

11.   (1)   A fair and accurate report of proceedings at any public meeting or sitting in the United Kingdom of—

(a)   a local authority or local authority committee;

(aa)   in the case of a local authority which are operating executive arrangements, the executive of that authority or a committee of that executive;

(b)   a justice or justices of the peace acting otherwise than as a court exercising judicial authority;

(c)   a commission, tribunal, committee or person appointed for the purposes of any inquiry by any statutory provision, by Her Majesty or by a Minister of the Crown a member of the Scottish Executive, the Welsh Ministers or the Counsel General to the Welsh Assembly Government or a Northern Ireland Department;

(d)   a person appointed by a local authority to hold a local inquiry in pursuance of any statutory provision;

(e)   any other tribunal, board, committee or body constituted by or under, and exercising functions under, any statutory provision.

(1A)   In the case of a local authority which are operating executive arrangements, a fair and accurate record of any decision made by any member of the executive where that record is required to be made and available for public inspection by virtue of section 22 of the Local Government Act 2000 or of any provision in regulations made under that section.

(2)   In sub-paragraphs (1)(a), (1)(aa) and (1A)—

"local authority" means

(a)   in relation to England and Wales, a principal council within the meaning of the Local Government Act 1972, any body falling within any paragraph of section 100J(1) of that Act or an authority or body to which the Public Bodies (Admission to Meetings) Act 1960 applies,

(b)   in relation to Scotland, a council constituted under section 2 of the Local Government etc. (Scotland) Act 1994 or an authority or body to which the Public Bodies (Admission to Meetings) Act 1960 applies,

(c)   in relation to Northern Ireland, any authority or body to which sections 23 to 27 of the Local Government Act (Northern Ireland) 1972 apply; and

"local authority committee" means any committee of a local authority or of local authorities, and includes—

(a)   any committee or sub-committee in relation to which sections 100A to 100D of the Local Government Act 1972 apply by virtue of section 100E of that Act (whether or not also by virtue of section 100J of that Act), and

(b)   any committee or sub-committee in relation to which sections 50A to 50D of the Local Government (Scotland) Act 1973 apply by virtue of section 50E of that Act.

(2A)   In sub-paragraphs (1) and (1A)—

"executive" and "executive arrangements" have the same meaning as in Part II of the Local Government Act 2000.

(3)   A fair and accurate report of any corresponding proceedings in any of the Channel Islands or the Isle of Man or in another member State.

11A.   A fair and accurate report of proceedings at a press conference held anywhere in the world for the discussion of a matter of public interest.]

12.   (1)   A fair and accurate report of proceedings at any public meeting held anywhere in the world.

(2)   In this paragraph a "public meeting" means a meeting bona fide and lawfully held for a lawful purpose and for the furtherance or discussion of a matter of public interest, whether admission to the meeting is general or restricted.

13.   (1)   A fair and accurate report of proceedings at a general meeting of a listed company.

(2)   A fair and accurate copy of, extract from or summary of any document circulated to members of a listed company—

(a)   by or with the authority of the board of directors of the company,

(b)   by the auditors of the company, or

(c)   by any member of the company in pursuance of a right conferred by any statutory provision.

(3)   A fair and accurate copy of, extract from or summary of any document circulated to members of a listed company which relates to the appointment, resignation, retirement or dismissal of directors of the company or its auditors.

(4)   In this paragraph "listed company" has the same meaning as in Part 12 of the Corporation Tax Act 2009 (see section 1005 of that Act).

14.   A fair and accurate report of any finding or decision of any of the following descriptions of association, formed anywhere in the world, or of any committee or governing body of such an association—

(a)   an association formed for the purpose of promoting or encouraging the exercise of or interest in any art, science, religion or learning, and empowered by its constitution to exercise control over or adjudicate on matters of interest or concern to the association, or the actions or conduct of any person subject to such control or adjudication;

(b)   an association formed for the purpose of promoting or safeguarding the interests of any trade, business, industry or profession, or of the persons carrying on or engaged in any trade, business, industry or profession, and empowered by its constitution to exercise control over or adjudicate upon matters connected with that trade, business, industry or profession, or the actions or conduct of those persons;

(c)   an association formed for the purpose of promoting or safeguarding the interests of a game, sport or pastime to the playing or exercise of which members of the public are invited or admitted, and empowered by its constitution to exercise control over or adjudicate upon persons connected with or taking part in the game, sport or pastime;

(d)   an association formed for the purpose of promoting charitable objects or other objects beneficial to the community and empowered by its constitution to exercise control over or to adjudicate on matters of interest or concern to the association, or the actions or conduct of any person subject to such control or adjudication.

14A.   A fair and accurate—

(a)   report of proceedings of a scientific or academic conference held anywhere in the world, or

(b)   copy of, extract from or summary of matter published by such a conference.

15.   (1)   A fair and accurate report or summary of, copy of or extract from, any adjudication, report, statement or notice issued by a body, officer or other person designated for the purposes of this paragraph by order of the Lord Chancellor.

(2)   An order under this paragraph shall be made by statutory instrument which shall be subject to annulment in pursuance of a resolution of either House of Parliament.

PART III
SUPPLEMENTARY PROVISIONS

16.   (1)   In this Schedule—

"court" includes—

(a)   any tribunal or body established under the law of any country or territory exercising the judicial power of the State;

(b)   any international tribunal established by the Security Council of the United Nations or by an international agreement;

(c)   any international tribunal deciding matters in dispute between States;

"international conference" means a conference attended by representatives of two or more governments;

"international organisation" means an organisation of which two or more governments are members, and includes any committee or other subordinate body of such an organisation;

"legislature" includes a local legislature; and

"member State" includes any European dependent territory of a member State.

LOCAL GOVERNMENT

Contents

FIXED PENALTIES ISSUED BY LOCAL AUTHORITIES

7.7422 The Environmental Offences (Fixed Penalties) (Miscellaneous Provisions) Regulations 2007, SI 2007/175 amended by SI 2012/1151 (and partly revoked by SI 2017/1050) fix the range within which local authorities may set fixed penalties under various statutory provisions including discounts for early payment. Provision is also made for destination of receipts to the benefit of authorities performing at the level of "excellent" or "good" or "4 stars", "3 stars" and "2 stars".

Local Government Act 1972
(1972 c 70)
PART I
LOCAL GOVERNMENT AREAS AND AUTHORITIES IN ENGLAND

7.7423   1.   Local government areas in England   With the exception of Greater London[1] and the Isles of Scilly, England is divided into local government areas to be known as counties and in those counties there shall be local government areas known as districts[2]. The counties are either metropolitan counties or non-metropolitan counties.

[Local Government Act 1972, s 1   summarised.]

----

[1]   There shall be a council for every London borough (Sch 2).
[2]   The districts in metropolitan counties are to be known as "metropolitan districts" (Sch 2). Districts in non-metropolitan countries are to be established under Sch 3; and "non-metropolitan district" means any district other than a metropolitan district (s 270(2)).

7.7424   2.   Councils   There shall be a council for each non-metropolitan county and district: the "County Council" and "District Council" respectively.

[Local Government Act 1972, s 2, amended by the Local Government Act 1985, Sch 16 and the Local Government Act 2000, Sch 3—summarised.]

PART II
LOCAL GOVERNMENT AREAS AND AUTHORITIES IN WALES

7.7425   20.   Local Government areas in Wales   With effect from 1st April 1996 Wales is divided into local government areas to be known as counties and county boroughs ("principal areas") and communities[1].

[Local Government Act 1972, s 20 as substituted by the Local Government (Wales) Act 1994, s 1—summarised.]

----

[1]   References in pre-existing legislation to councils or areas of a county or district are to be construed as references to the principal areas (Local Government (Wales) Act 1994, s 17. Other transitional provisions are made by Pt VI of the Act.)

7.7426   21.   Councils in Wales   There shall be a council for every county and county borough.

[Local Government Act 1972, s 21 amended by the Local Government (Wales) Act 1994, s 2 and the Local Government Act 2000, Sch 3—summarised.]

7.7427   27–35.   *Community Councils.*

PART V

7.7428   92.   Proceedings for disqualification   (1)   Proceedings against any person on the ground that he acted or claims to be entitled to act as a member of a local authority while disqualified[1] for so acting within the meaning of this section may be instituted by, and only by, any local government elector for the area concerned—

    (a)   in the High Court or a magistrates' court if that person so acted;

    (b)   in the High Court if that person claims to be entitled so to act;

but proceedings under paragraph (a) above shall not be instituted against any person after the expiration of more than six months from the date on which he so acted.

(2)   Where in proceedings instituted under this section it is proved that the defendant has acted as a member of a local authority while disqualified for so acting, then—

    (a)   if the proceedings are in the High Court, the High Court may—

        (i)   make a declaration to that effect and declare that the office in which the defendant has acted is vacant;

        (ii)   grant an injunction restraining the defendant from so acting;

        (iii)   order that the defendant shall forfeit to Her Majesty such sum as the court think fit, not exceeding £50 for each occasion on which he so acted while disqualified;

    (b)   if the proceedings are in a magistrates' court, the magistrates' court may, subject to the provisions of this section, convict the defendant and impose on him a fine not exceeding **level 3** on the standard scale for each occasion on which he so acted while disqualified.

(3)   Where proceedings under this section are instituted in a magistrates' court, then—

    (a)   if the court is satisfied that the matter would be more properly dealt with in the High Court, it shall by order discontinue the proceedings;

    (b)   if the High Court, on application made to it by the defendant within fourteen days after service of the summons, is satisfied that the matter would be more properly dealt with in the High Court, it may make an order, which shall not be subject to any appeal, requiring the magistrates' court by order to discontinue the proceedings.

(4)   Where in proceedings instituted under this section in the High Court it is proved that the defendant claims to act as a member of a local authority and is disqualified for so acting, the court may make a declaration to that effect and declare that the office in which the defendant claims to be entitled to act is vacant and grant an injunction restraining him from so acting.

(5)   No proceedings shall be instituted against a person otherwise than under this section on the ground that he has, while disqualified for acting as a member of a local authority, so acted or claimed to be entitled so to act.

(6)   For the purposes of this section a person shall be deemed to be disqualified for acting as a member of a local authority—

    (a)   if he is not qualified to be, or is disqualified for being, a member of the authority; or

    (b)   if by reason of failure to make and deliver the declaration of acceptance of office within the period required, or by reason of resignation or failure to attend meetings of the local authority, he has ceased to be a member of the authority.

(7)   In this section "local authority" includes a joint authority, an economic prosperity board and a combined authority; and in relation to a joint authority, an economic prosperity board and a combined authority the reference in subsection (1) above to a local government elector for the area concerned shall be construed as a reference to a local government elector for any local government area in the area for which the authority is established.

(7A)   *Repealed.*

(7B)   *Repealed.*

(8)   In relation to the Broads Authority, the reference in subsection (1) above to a local government elector for the area concerned shall be construed as a reference to a local government elector for the area of any of the local authorities mentioned in section 1(3)(a) of the Norfolk and Suffolk Broads Act 1988.

[Local Government Act 1972, s 92 as amended by the Criminal Justice Act 1982, ss 38 and 46, the Local Government Act 1985, Sch 14, the Norfolk and Suffolk Broads Act 1988, Sch 6. the Education Reform Act 1988, Sch 13, the Local Government and Public Involvement in Health Act 2007, Sch 13, the Local Democracy, Economic Development and Construction Act 2009, Sch 6 and the Deregulation Act 2015, Sch 13.]

---

[1] See ss 79 and 80 for provisions as to qualification and disqualification; and see *Bishop v Deakin* [1936] Ch 409, [1936] 1 All ER 255, 100 JP 201, as to time within which proceedings must be commenced.

7.7429   94.   Disability of members of authorities for voting on account of interest in contracts, etc   (1)   Subject to the provisions of section 97[1] below, if a member of a local authority has any pecuniary interest[2], direct or indirect, in any contract, proposed contract or other matter, and is present at a meeting of the local authority at which the contract or other matter is the subject of consideration, he shall at the meeting and as soon as practicable after its commencement disclose[3] the fact and shall not take part in the consideration or discussion of the contract or other matter or vote on any question with respect to it.

(2)   If any person fails to comply with the provisions of subsection (1) above he shall for each offence be liable on summary conviction to a fine not exceeding **level 4** on the standard scale unless he proves that he did not know that the contract, proposed contract or other matter in which he had

a pecuniary interest was the subject of consideration at that meeting.

(3)   A prosecution for an offence under this section shall not be instituted except by or on behalf of the Director of Public Prosecutions.

(4)   A local authority may by standing orders provide for the exclusion of a member of the authority from a meeting of the authority while any contract, proposed contract or other matter in which he has a pecuniary interest, direct or indirect, is under consideration.

(5)   The following, that is to say—

   (a)   the receipt by the chairman, vice-chairman or deputy chairman of a principal council of an allowance to meet the expenses of his office or his right to receive, or the possibility of his receiving, such an allowance;

   (b)   the receipt by a member of a local authority of an allowance or other payment under any provision of sections 173 to 176 below or under any scheme made by virtue of section 18 of the Local Government and Housing Act 1989 or paragraph 25 of Schedule 2 to the Police Act or his right to receive, or the possibility of his receiving, any such payment;

shall not be treated as a pecuniary interest for the purposes of this section. *

[Local Government Act 1972, s 94 as amended by the Criminal Justice Act 1982, ss 38 and 46, the Local Government and Housing Act 1989, Sch 11, the Police and Magistrates' Courts Act 1994, Sch 4, the Police Act 1996, Sch 7, the Police Act 1997, Sch 6 and the Criminal Justice and Police Act 2001, Sch 7.]

   * **Repealed by the Local Government Act 2000, Schs 5 and 6 from a date to be appointed.**
   [1] Section 97, which is not quoted in this work, contains provisions for the removal or exclusion of a disability.
   [2] See s 95, not quoted in this work, for provisions as to pecuniary interests. See also s 94(5): specified allowances not to be treated as a pecuniary interest. Where a pecuniary interest exists, the disability extends to a vote which is disadvantageous to that interest (*Brown v DPP* [1956] 2 QB 369, [1956] 2 All ER 189, 120 JP 303; *Rands v Oldroyd* [1959] 1 QB 204, [1958] 3 All ER 344, 123 JP 1). For the precise application of exemptions see *Readman v Payne* (1991) 155 JP 884, DC.
   [3] See s 96, not quoted in this work, containing provisions as to general notice of disclosure.

PART VA[1]

ACCESS TO MEETINGS AND DOCUMENTS OF CERTAIN AUTHORITIES, COMMITTEES AND SUB-COMMITTEES

7.7430   100A.   Admission to meetings of principal councils   (1)   A meeting of a principal council[2] shall be open to the public except to the extent that they are excluded (whether during the whole or part of the proceedings) under subsection (2) below or by resolution under subsection (4) below.

(2)   Public shall be excluded from a meeting of a principal council during an item of business whenever it is likely confidential information would be disclosed in breach of the obligation of confidence; and nothing in this Part shall be taken to authorise or require the disclosure of confidential information in breach of the obligation of confidence (*summarised*).

(3)–(8)   *Supplementary provisions as to admission of the public.*

[Local Government Act 1972, s 100A, as inserted by the Local Government (Access to Information) Act 1985, s 1 and amended by SI 2002/715.]

   [1] Part VA contains ss 100A–100K, and was inserted by the Local Government (Access to Information) Act 1985, s 1. Sections 100A to 100D, 100H, 100I et and Sch 12A to this Act are applied, with modifications, to a "joint committee", being a joint consultative committee appointed pursuant to an order under s 22 of the National Health Service Act 1977, or a sub-committee of such a committee, or a joint sub-committee of 2 or more such committees (Health Service Joint Consultative Committees (Access to Information) Act 1986, ss 1 and 2). Sections 100A to 100D are also applied, with modifications, to a Community Health Council, established under s 20 of the National Health Service Act 1977, and the Committees of those Councils (Community Health Councils (Access to Information) Act 1988, ss 1 and 2).
   [2] For meaning of "principal council", see ss 100J and 270(1), post.

7.7431   100B.   Access to agenda and connected reports   (1)   Copies of the agenda for a meeting of a principal council[1] and, subject to subsection (2) below, copies of any report for the meeting shall be open to inspection by members of the public at the offices of the council in accordance with subsection (3) below.

(2)   If the proper officer thinks fit, there may be excluded from the copies of reports provided in pursuance of subsection (1) above the whole of any report which, or any part which, relates only to items during which, in his opinion, the meeting is likely not to be open to the public.

(3)   Any document which is required by subsection (1) above to be open to inspection shall be so open at least five clear days before the meeting, except that—

   (a)   where the meeting is convened at shorter notice, the copies of the agenda and reports shall be open to inspection from the time the meeting is convened, and

   (b)   where an item is added to an agenda copies of which are open to inspection by the public, copies of the item (or of the revised agenda), and the copies of any report for the meeting relating to the item, shall be open to inspection from the time the item is added to the agenda;

but nothing in this subsection requires copies of any agenda, item or report to be open to inspection by the public until copies are available to members of the council.

(4)   An item of business may not be considered at a meeting of a principal council unless either—

(a)　　a copy of the agenda including the item (or a copy of the item) is open to inspection by members of the public in pursuance of subsection (1) above for at least five clear days before the meeting or, where the meeting is convened at shorter notice, from the time the meeting is convened; or

(b)　　by reason of special circumstances, which shall be specified in the minutes, the chairman of the meeting is of the opinion that the item should be considered at the meeting as a matter of urgency.

(5)　　Where by virtue of subsection (2) above the whole or any part of a report for a meeting is not open to inspection by the public under subsection (1) above—

(a)　　every copy of the report or of the part shall be marked "Not for publication"; and

(b)　　there shall be stated on every copy of the whole or any part of the report the description, in terms of Schedule 12A to this Act, of the exempt information by virtue of which the council are likely to exclude the public during the item to which the report relates.

(6)　　Where a meeting of a principal council is required by section 100A above to be open to the public during the proceedings or any part of them, there shall be made available for the use of members of the public present at the meeting a reasonable number of copies of the agenda and, subject to subsection (8) below, of the reports for the meeting.

(7)　　There shall, on request and on payment of postage or other necessary charge for transmission, be supplied for the benefit of any newspaper—

(a)　　a copy of the agenda for a meeting of a principal council and, subject to subsection (8) below, a copy of each of the reports for the meeting;

(b)　　such further statements or particulars, if any, as are necessary to indicate the nature of the items included in the agenda; and

(c)　　if the proper officer thinks fit in the case of any item, copies of any other documents supplied to members of the council in connection with the item.

(8)　　Subsection (2) above applies in relation to copies of reports provided in pursuance of subsection (6) or (7) above as it applies in relation to copies of reports provided in pursuance of subsection (1) above.

[Local Government Act 1972, s 100B as inserted by the Local Government (Access to Information) Act 1985, s 1 and amended by SI 2002/715.]

---

[1] For meaning of "principal council", see ss 100J and 270(1), post.

7.7432　100C.　Inspection of minutes and other documents after meetings　(1)　After a meeting of a principal council[1] the following documents shall be open to inspection by members of the public at the offices of the council until the expiration of the period of six years beginning with the date of the meeting, namely—

(a)　　the minutes, or a copy of the minutes, of the meeting, excluding so much of the minutes of proceedings during which the meeting was not open to the public as discloses exempt information;

(b)　　where applicable, a summary under subsection (2) below;

(c)　　a copy of the agenda for the meeting; and

(d)　　a copy of so much of any report for the meeting as relates to any item during which the meeting was open to the public.

(2)　　Where, in consequence of the exclusion of parts of the minutes which disclose exempt information, the document open to inspection under subsection (1)(a) above does not provide members of the public with a reasonably fair and coherent record of the whole or part of the proceedings, the proper officer shall make a written summary of the proceedings or the part, as the case may be, which provides such a record without disclosing the exempt information.

[Local Government Act 1972, s 100C as inserted by the Local Government (Access to Information) Act 1985, s 1.]

---

[1] For meaning of "principal council", see ss 100J and 270(1), post.

7.7433　100D.　Inspection of background papers　(1)　Subject, in the case of section 100C(1), to subsection (2) below, if and so long as copies of the whole or part of a report for a meeting of a principal council are required by section 100B(1) or 100C(1) above to be open to inspection by members of the public—

(a)　　those copies shall each include a copy of a list, compiled by the proper officer, of the background papers for the report or the part of the report, and

(b)　　at least one copy of each of the documents included in that list shall also be open to inspection at the offices of the council.

(2)　　Subsection (1) above does not require a copy of any document included in the list, to be open to inspection after the expiration of the period of four years beginning with the date of the meeting.

(3)　　Where a copy of any of the background papers for a report is required by subsection (1) above to be open to inspection by members of the public, the copy shall be taken for the purposes of this Part to be so open if arrangements exist for its production to members of the public as soon as is reasonably practicable after the making of a request to inspect the copy.

(4)　　Nothing in this section—

(a)　　requires any document which discloses exempt information to be included in the list referred to in subsection (1) above; or

    (b)   without prejudice to the generality of subsection (2) of section 100A above, requires or authorises the inclusion in the list of any document which, if open to inspection by the public, would disclose confidential information in breach of the obligation of confidence, within the meaning of that subsection.

(5)   For the purposes of this section the background papers for a report are those documents relating to the subject matter of the report which—

    (a)   disclose any facts or matters on which, in the opinion of the proper officer, the report or an important part of the report is based, and

    (b)   have, in his opinion, been relied on to a material extent in preparing the report,

but do not include any published works.

[Local Government Act 1972, s 100D as inserted by the Local Government (Access to Information) Act 1985, s 1 and amended by the Local Government Act 2000, s 97 and Sch 6.]

7.7434 100E. Application to committees and sub-committees (1) Sections 100A to 100D above shall apply in relation to a committee or sub-committee of a principal council as they apply in relation to a principal council.

(2)   In the application by virtue of this section of sections 100A to 100D above in relation to a committee or sub-committee—

    (a)   section 100A(6)(a) shall be taken to have been complied with if the notice is given by posting it at the time there mentioned at the offices of every constituent principal council and, if the meeting of the committee or sub-committee to which that section so applies is to be held at premises other than the offices of such a council, at those premises;

    (b)   for the purposes of section 100A(6)(c), premises belonging to a constituent principal council shall be treated as belonging to the committee or sub-committee; and

    (c)   for the purposes of sections 100B(1), 100C(1) and 100D(1), offices of any constituent principal council shall be treated as offices of the committee or sub-committee.

(3)   Any reference in this Part to a committee or sub-committee of a principal council is a reference to—

    (a)   a committee which is constituted under an enactment specified in section 101(9) below or which is appointed by one or more principal councils under section 102 below; or

    (b)   a joint committee not falling within paragraph (a) above which is appointed or established under any enactment by two or more principal councils and is not a body corporate; or

    (bba)   a committee in place by virtue of section 107D(3)(c)(ii) of the Local Democracy, Economic Development and Construction Act 2009;

    (bbb)   a joint committee in place by virtue of section 107E of that Act;

    (bb)   the Navigation Committee of the Broads Authority; or

    (c)   a sub-committee appointed or established under any enactment by one or more committees falling within paragraphs (a) to (bb) above.

(4)   Any reference in this Part to a constituent principal council, in relation to a committee or sub-committee, is a reference—

    (a)   in the case of a committee, to the principal council, or any of the principal councils, of which it is a committee; and

    (b)   in the case of a sub-committee, to any principal council which, by virtue of paragraph (a) above, is a constituent principal council in relation to the committee, or any of the committees, which established or appointed the sub-committee.

[Local Government Act 1972, s 100E as inserted by the Local Government (Access to Information) Act 1985, s 1 and amended by the Norfolk and Suffolk Broads Act 1988, Sch 6 and the Cities and Local Government Devolution Act 2016, Sch 5.]

7.7435 100EA. Inspection of records relating to functions exercisable by members

(1)   The Secretary of State may by regulations[1] make provision for written records of decisions made or action taken by a member of a local authority, in exercise of a function of the authority by virtue of arrangements made under section 236 of the Local Government and Public Involvement in Health Act 2007, to be made and provided to the authority by the member.

(2)   Any written record provided to the authority under regulations under subsection (1) shall be open to inspection by members of the public at the offices of the authority for the period of six years beginning with the date on which the decision was made or action was taken.

(3)   A statutory instrument containing regulations under subsection (1) shall be subject to annulment in pursuance of a resolution of either House of Parliament.

[Local Government Act 1972, s 100EA as inserted by the Local Government and Public Involvement in Health Act 2007, s 237.]

---

   [1] The Exercise of Functions by Local Councillors (Written Records) Regulations 2009, SI 2009/352 have been made.

7.7436 100F–100G.   *Additional rights[1] of access to documents for members of principal councils; principal councils to publish additional information.*

---

   [1] See also the Local Government (Inspection of Documents) (Summary of Rights) Order 1986, SI 1986/854, which specifies for these purposes additional enactments which confer rights to attend meetings and to inspect, copy and be furnished with documents.

7.7437   100H.   Supplemental provisions and offences   (1)   A document directed by any provision of this Part to be open to inspection shall be so open at all reasonable hours and—

    (a)   in the case of a document open to inspection by virtue of section 100D(1) above, upon payment of such reasonable fee as may be required for the facility; and

    (b)   in any other case, without payment.

    (2)   Where a document is open to inspection by a person under any provision of this Part, the person may, subject to subsection (3) below—

    (a)   make copies of or extracts from the document, or

    (b)   require the person having custody of the document to supply to him a photographic copy of or of extracts from the document,

upon payment of such reasonable fee as may be required for the facility.

    (3)   Subsection (2) above does not require or authorise the doing of any act which infringes the copyright in any work except that, where the owner of the copyright is a principal council, nothing done in pursuance of that subsection shall constitute an infringement of the copyright.

    (4)   If, without reasonable excuse, a person having the custody of a document which is required by section 100B(1), 100C(1) or 100EA(2) above to be open to inspection by the public—

    (a)   intentionally obstructs any person exercising a right conferred by this Part to inspect, or to make a copy of or extracts from the document, or

    (b)   refuses to furnish copies to any person entitled to obtain them under any provision of this Part,

he shall be liable on summary conviction to a fine not exceeding **level 1** on the standard scale.

    (5)   Where any accessible document for a meeting to which this subsection applies—

    (a)   is supplied to, or open to inspection by, a member of the public, or

    (b)   is supplied for the benefit of any newspaper, in pursuance of section 100B(7) above,

the publication thereby of any defamatory matter contained in the document shall be privileged unless the publication is proved to be made with malice.

    (6)   Subsection (5) above applies to any meeting of a principal council and any meeting of a committee or sub-committee of a principal council; and, for the purposes of that subsection, the "accessible documents" for a meeting are the following—

    (a)   any copy of the agenda or of any item included in the agenda for the meeting;

    (b)   any such further statements or particulars for the purpose of indicating the nature of any item included in the agenda as are mentioned in section 100B(7)(b) above;

    (c)   any copy of a document relating to such an item which is supplied for the benefit of a newspaper in pursuance of section 100B(7)(c) above;

    (d)   any copy of the whole or part of a report for the meeting;

    (e)   any copy of the whole or part of any background papers for a report for the meeting, within the meaning of section 100D above.

    (7)   The rights conferred by this Part to inspect, copy and be furnished with documents are in addition, and without prejudice, to any such rights conferred by or under any other enactment.

[Local Government Act 1972, s 100H as inserted by the Local Government (Access to Information) Act 1985, s 1 and amended by the Local Government and Public Involvement in Health Act 2007, s 237.]

7.7438   100I.   Exempt information and power to vary Schedule 12A   (1)   In relation to principal councils in England, the descriptions of information which are, for the purposes of this Part, exempt information are those for the time being specified in Part I of Schedule 12A to this Act, but subject to any qualifications contained in Part II of that Schedule; and Part III has effect for the interpretation of Parts 1 to 3 of that Schedule.

    (1A)   In relation to principal councils in Wales, the descriptions of information which are, for the purposes of this Part, exempt information are those for the time being specified in Part 4 of Schedule 12A to this Act, but subject to any qualifications contained in Part 5 of that Schedule; and Part 6 has effect for the interpretation of Parts 4 to 6 of that Schedule.

    (2)   The appropriate person may by order vary Schedule 12A to this Act by adding to it any description or other provision or by deleting from it or varying any description or other provision for the time being specified or contained in it.

    (3)   The appropriate person may exercise the power conferred by subsection (2) above by amending any Part of Schedule 12A to this Act, with or without amendment of any other Part.

    (3A)   In this section "the appropriate person" means—

    (a)   in relation to England, the Secretary of State;

    (b)   in relation to Wales, the National Assembly for Wales.

    (4)   Any statutory instrument containing an order under this section made by the Secretary of State shall be subject to annulment in pursuance of a resolution of either House of Parliament.

[Local Government Act 1972, s 100I as inserted by the Local Government (Access to Information) Act 1985, s 1 and amended by SI 2006/88.]

7.7439   100J.   Application to new authorities, Common Council, etc   (1)   Except in this section, any reference in this Part to a principal council[1] includes a reference to—

    (a)   repealed;

    (b)   a joint authority;

    (ba)   repealed;

    (bb)   the London Fire and Emergency Planning Authority;

(bc)   an economic prosperity board;

(bd)   a combined authority;

(be)   Transport for London;

(bf)   a sub-national transport body;

(c)   the Common Council;

(cc)   the Broads Authority;

(cd)   a National Park authority;

(d)   a joint board or joint committee falling within subsection (2) below;

(e)   *repealed*

(eza)   *repealed*

(ea)   *repealed*

(f)   a fire and rescue authority constituted by a scheme under section 2 of the Fire and Rescue Services Act 2004 or scheme to which section 4 of that Act applies.

(g)   the Homes and Communities Agency so far as it is exercising functions conferred on it in relation to a designated area by virtue of a designation order.

(h)   a Mayoral development corporation.

(2)   A joint board or joint committee falls within this subsection if—

(a)   it is constituted under any enactment as a body corporate; and

(b)   it discharges functions of two or more principal councils;

and for the purposes of this subsection any body falling within paragraph (a), (b), (bb), (bc), (bd) or (c) of subsection (1) above shall be treated as a principal council.

(2A)   In its application by virtue of subsection (1)(g) above in relation to the Homes and Communities Agency, a reference in this Part to the offices of the council (however expressed)—

(a)   is to be treated as a reference to such premises located within the designated area as the Homes and Communities Agency considers appropriate, and

(b)   in the application of section 100A(6)(a) above to a case where the meeting is to be held at premises other than those mentioned in paragraph (a) above, includes a reference to those other premises.

(2B)   In section 100A, subsections (5A), (7A) to (7F) and (9) do not apply to—

(a)   *repealed*

(b)   the Common Council other than in its capacity as a local authority or police authority;

(c)   a joint board or a joint committee falling within subsection (2) above;

(d)   the Homes and Communities Agency; or

(e)   a Mayoral development corporation.

(3)   In its application by virtue of subsection (1) above in relation to a body falling within paragraph (b), (bb), (be), (bf), (cc), (cd), (d), (f) or (h) of that subsection, section 100A(6)(a) above shall have effect with the insertion after the word "council" of the words "(and, if the meeting is to be held at premises other than those offices, at those premises)".

(3ZA)   In its application by virtue of subsection (1)(g) above in relation to the Homes and Communities Agency, section 100E above shall have effect as if—

(a)   in subsection (2), paragraph (c) was omitted, and

(b)   in subsection (3), for paragraphs (a) to (c) there were substituted—

"(a)   a committee established under paragraph 6(1) of Schedule 1 to the Housing and Regeneration Act 2008 for the purpose of exercising functions conferred on the Homes and Communities Agency in relation to a designated area by virtue of a designation order; or

(b)   a sub-committee of such a committee established under paragraph 6(2) of that Schedule to that Act for that purpose".

(3ZAA)   In its application by virtue of subsection (1)(h) above in relation to a Mayoral development corporation, section 100E(3) has effect as if for paragraphs (a) to (c) there were substituted—

"(a)   a committee which is established under Schedule 21 to the Localism Act 2011 by a principal council, or

(b)   a sub-committee established under that Schedule by a committee within paragraph (a).

(3ZB)   In its application by virtue of subsection (1)(g) above in relation to the Homes and Communities Agency, section 100G(1) above shall have effect as if paragraph (a) was omitted.]

(3A)   *Repealed.*

(4)   In its application by virtue of subsection (1) above, section 100G(1)(a) above shall have effect—

(a)   in relation to a joint authority, a sub-national transport body, an economic prosperity board or a combined authority, with the substitution for the words after "together with" of the words "the name or description of the body or other person that appointed him"; and

(aa)   in relation to the Broads Authority or its Navigation Committee or any National Park authority, with the substitution for the words after "together with" of the words "the name of the person who appointed him"; and (b)　　in relation to a Mayoral development corporation, or a joint board or joint committee falling within subsection (2) above, with the omission of the words after "for the time being"; and

(c)　　in relation to a fire and rescue authority falling within subsection (1)(*f*) above, with the substitution for the words ", in the case of a councillor, the ward or division" of the words "the constituent area".

(4A)　In its application by virtue of subsection (1)(*bb*) above in relation to the London Fire and Emergency Planning Authority, section 100G(1)(*a*) shall have effect with the substitution for the words "together with, in the case of a councillor, the ward or division which he represents" of the words "and whether he is an Assembly representative or a borough representative, and—

(i)　　if he is an Assembly representative, whether he is a London member or a constituency member and, if a constituency member, the Assembly constituency for which he is a member; or

(ii)　　if he is a borough representative, the council of which he is a member (whether a London borough council or the Common Council).

(4B)　In this section "designated area" and "designation order" have the same meanings as in Part 1 of the Housing and Regeneration Act 2008.

(5)　*Repealed.*

[Local Government Act 1972, s 100J as inserted by the Local Government (Access to Information) Act 1985, s 1 and amended by the Norfolk and Suffolk Broads Act 1988, Sch 6, the Education Reform Act 1988, Sch 13, the Police and Magistrates' Courts Act 1994, Sch 4, the Environment Act 1995, Sch 7, the Police Act 1996, Sch 7, the Police Act 1997, Sch 6, the Greater London Authority Act 1999, ss 313 and 331, the Criminal Justice and Police Act 2001, Schs 6 and 7, the Fire and Rescue Services Act 2004, Sch 1, the Local Government and Public Involvement in Health Act 2007, Sch 13, the Housing and Regeneration Act 2008, Sch 8, the Local Democracy, Economic Development and Construction Act 2009, Sch 6, the Police Reform and Social Responsibility Act 2011, Sch 16, the Localism Act 2011, Sch 22, SI 2014/2095, the Deregulation Act 2015, Sch 13 and the Cities and Local Government Devolution Act 2016, Sch 5.]

---

[1]　For meaning of "principal council", see also s 270(1), post.

7.7440　100K.　Interpretation and application of Part VA　(1)　In this Part—

"committee or sub-committee of a principal council" shall be construed in accordance with section 100E(3) above (and see section 100J(3ZA)(*b*) and (3ZAA) above);

"constituent principal council" shall be construed in accordance with section 100E(4) above;

"copy", in relation to any document, includes a copy made from a copy;

"exempt information" has the meaning given by section 100I above;

"information" includes an expression of opinion, any recommendations and any decision taken;

"newspaper" includes—

(a)　　a news agency which systematically carries on the business of selling and supplying reports or information to newspapers; and

(b)　　any organisation which is systematically engaged in collecting news—

(i)　　for sound or television broadcasts; or

(ii)　　for inclusion in programmes to be included in any programme service (within the meaning of the Broadcasting Act 1990) other than a sound or television broadcasting service;

"principal council" shall be construed in accordance with section 100J above.

(2)　Any reference in this Part to a meeting is a reference to a meeting held after 1st April 1986.

(3)　The Secretary of State may by order amend sections 100A(6)(*a*) and 100B(3) and (4)(*a*) above so as to substitute for each reference to three clear days such greater number of days as may be specified in the order.

(4)　Any statutory instrument containing an order under subsection (3) above shall be subject to annulment in pursuance of a resolution of either House of Parliament.

[Local Government Act 1972, s 100K as inserted by the Local Government (Access to Information) Act 1985, s 1 and amended by the Broadcasting Act 1990, Sch 20, the Local Government Act 2000, s 98(1), the Housing and Regeneration Act 2008, Sch 8 and the Localism Act 2011, Sch 22.]

PART VII

MISCELLANEOUS POWERS OF LOCAL AUTHORITIES

7.7441　117.　Disclosure by officers of interest in contracts　(1)　If it comes to the knowledge of an officer employed, whether under this Act or any other enactment, by a local authority that a contract in which he has any pecuniary interest, whether direct or indirect (not being a contract to which he is himself a party), has been, or is proposed to be, entered into by the authority or any committee thereof, he shall as soon as practicable give notice in writing to the authority of the fact that he is interested therein.

For the purposes of this section an officer shall be treated as having indirectly a pecuniary interest in a contract or proposed contract if he would have been so treated by virtue of section 95[1] above had he been a member of the authority.

(2)　An officer of a local authority shall not, under colour of his office or employment, accept any fee or reward whatsoever other than his proper remuneration.

(3)　Any person who contravenes the provisions of subsection (1) or (2) above shall be liable on summary conviction to a fine not exceeding **level 4** on the standard scale.

(4) References in this section to a local authority shall include references to a joint committee appointed under Part VI of this Act or any other enactment.

[Local Government Act 1972, s 117 as amended by the Criminal Justice Act 1982, ss 38 and 46.]

---

[1] Section 95 is not reproduced in this work.

PART X
JUDICIAL AND RELATED MATTERS
[See PART I: THE JUSTICES AND THE CLERK, ante.]

PART XI
GENERAL PROVISIONS AS TO LOCAL AUTHORITIES

Legal proceedings

7.7442 222. Power of local authorities to prosecute or defend legal proceedings

(1) Where a local authority consider[1] it expedient[2] for the promotion or protection of the interests of the inhabitants of their area—

(*a*)   they may prosecute or defend or appear in any legal proceedings and, in the case of civil proceedings, may institute them in their own name, and

(*b*)   they may, in their own name, make representations in the interests of the inhabitants at any public inquiry held by or on behalf of any Minister or public body under any enactment.

(2) In this section "local authority" includes the Common Council and the London Fire and Emergency Planning Authority.

[Local Government Act 1972, s 222 as amended by the Greater London Authority Act 1999, Sch 29.]

---

[1] In certain circumstances a local authority may institute proceedings in its own name seeking an injunction in the civil courts as a means of preventing a breach of the criminal law (*Stoke-on-Trent City Council v B & Q (Retail) Ltd* [1984] AC 754, [1984] 2 All ER 332, HL). This is subject to any legislation specifically designed to deal with the situation for which an injunction is sought such as in relation to anti-social behaviour under the Crime and Disorder Act 1998. An injunction to restrain anti-social behaviour would only be granted in an exceptional case. In such a case the criminal standard of proof applies except where the relief sought is not identical or almost identical to an ASBO where, subject to argument in a particular case, the civil standard might apply: *Birmingham City Council v Shafi* [2008] EWCA Civ 1186, [2009] 1 WLR 1961. See also *North Warwickshire Borough Council v Persons Unknown* [2018] EWHC 1603 (QB), [2019] RTR 5. A local authority can bring proceedings in public nuisance without having to show it has a special responsibility for enforcement of the criminal law eg against a person arrested for dealing in drugs for an injunction restraining him from entering a housing estate (*Nottingham City Council v Zain (a minor)* [2001] EWCA Civ 1248, [2002] 1 WLR 607). It is the duty of a local planning authority to protect the amenities of its area through a proper observance of planning control, and in order to perform that duty the authority is entitled in appropriate circumstances to seek a civil remedy under this section without first exhausting the processes of the criminal law (*Runnymede Borough Council v Ball* [1986] 1 All ER 629, [1986] 1 WLR 353). Where the conditions in sub-s (1) are met, a local authority is not precluded by s 4 of the Road Traffic Offenders Act 1988 from prosecuting an offence of using a motor vehicle without insurance contrary to s 143 of the Road Traffic Act 1988, (*Middlesborough Borough Council v Safeer* [2001] EWHC Admin 525, [2001] 4 All ER 630, [2002] 1 Cr App Rep 23, [2001] Crim LR 922, DC). See also: *Birmingham City Council v Sharif* [2020] EWCA Civ 1488, [2021] 1 WLR 685, [2021] RTR 15. There was no general principle that only in exceptional circumstances should a court grant an injunction where an alternative, specific statutory remedy was available or the court should not do so where breach could carry more severe sanctions than breach of a Public Spaces Protection Order, nor was there any basis for the argument that local authorities could not seek a remedy with more serious consequences in the event of a breach or that the court could not grant such a remedy if it considered it justified and proportionate so to do.

[2] In determining whether a local authority has considered whether it is expedient to prosecute, the maxim omnia praesumuntur rite esse acta applies. The burden of displacing this presumption is on the defendant by showing that the local authority made their decision on the basis of facts they should not have taken into account, or failed to take into account matters they should have taken into account (*R v Richards* [1999] Crim LR 598). The expediency must be for the promotion or protection of interests, and those interests must be of the in habitants of the local authority's area. To satisfy those elements the alleged criminality must have an actual or potential impact on those inhabitants, and if their interests are not engaged over and above their interests merely as ordinary citizens of the nation a decision to prosecute will not be within the ambit of s 222 and, because councils as creatures of statute have no common law power to prosecute, a prosecution cannot therefore be brought: *R v AB, CD and EF* [2017] EWCA Crim 534, [2017] 2 Cr App R 25.

The expediency must be for the promotion or protection of interests, and those interests must be of the inhabitants of the local authority's area. To satisfy those elements, the alleged criminality must have an actual or potential impact on those inhabitants, and if their interests are not engaged over and above their interests merely as ordinary citizens of the nation a decision to prosecute will not be within the ambit of s 222 and, because councils as creatures of statute have no common law power to prosecute, a prosecution cannot therefore be brought: *R v AB, CD and EF* [2017] EWCA Crim 534, [2017] 1 WLR 4071, [2017] 2 Cr App R 25, [2017] Crim L R 989.

The contention that it will invariably be in the interests of the inhabitants of its area for a local authority to prosecute offences of fraud committed by a trader located in its area, regardless of where the aggrieved customers are situated, is one which awaits an authoritative determination: *Qualter and others v Crown Court at Preston* [2019] EWHC 906 (Admin), [2019] ALL ER (D) 28 (May).

Section 222 is concerned with prosecutions or appearing in proceedings, and does not encompass an investigation or applications made for an investigatory purpose: *Qualter and others v Crown Court at Preston* [2019] EWHC 2563 (Admin), [2019] All ER (D) 30 (Oct). See *Birmingham City Council v Sharif* [2019] EWHC 1268 (QB), [2019] ALL ER (D) 09 (Jun) There was no general principle that only in exceptional circumstances should a court grant an injunction where an alternative, specific statutory remedy was available or the court should not do so where breach could carry more severe sanctions than breach of a Public Spaces Protection Order, nor was there any basis for the argument that local authorities could not seek a remedy with more serious consequences in the event of a breach or that the court could not grant such a remedy if it considered it justified and proportionate so to do.

7.7443   223.   Appearance of local authorities in legal proceedings   (1)   Any member or officer of a local authority who is authorised by that authority to prosecute or defend on their behalf, or to appear on their behalf in, proceedings before a magistrates' court shall be entitled to prosecute or defend or to appear in any such proceedings, and, to conduct any proceedings.

(2)   In this section "local authority" includes the Common Council, a joint authority, an economic prosperity board, a combined authority, the Greater London Authority, a police and crime commissioner and the Mayor's Office for Policing and Crime.

[Local Government Act 1972, s 223 as amended by the Local Government Act 1985, Sch 14, the Education Reform Act 1988, Sch 13, the Water Act 1989, Sch 25, the Police and Magistrates' Courts Act 1994, Sch 4, the Environment Act 1995, Sch 22, the Police Act 1996, Sch 7, the Police Act 1997, Sch 6, the Greater London Authority Act 1999, Sch 27, SI 2001/3719, the Criminal Justice and Police Act 2001, Sch 6, the Local Government and Public Involvement in Health Act 2007, Sch 13 the Legal Services Act 2007, Sch 21, the Local Democracy, Economic Development and Construction Act 2009, Sch 6, the Police Reform and Social Responsibility Act 2011, Sch 16 and the Deregulation Act 2015, Sch 13.]

Documents and Notices, etc

7.7444   225.   Deposit of documents with proper officer of authority, etc   (1)   In any case in which a document of any description is deposited[1] with the proper officer[2] of a local authority[3], or with the chairman of a parish or community council or with the chairman of a parish meeting, pursuant to the standing orders of either House of Parliament or to any enactment or instrument, the proper officer or chairman, as the case may be, shall receive and retain the document in the manner and for the purposes directed by the standing orders or enactment or instrument, and shall make such notes or endorsements on, and give such acknowledgments and receipts in respect of, the document as may be so directed.

(2)   All documents required by any enactment or instrument to be deposited with the proper officer[1] of a parish or community shall, in the case of a parish or community not having a separate parish or community council, be deposited in England with the chairman of the parish meeting or in Wales with the proper officer of the principal council.

(3)   In this section "local authority" includes a joint authority, an economic prosperity board and a combined authority.

[Local Government Act 1972, s 225 as amended by the Local Government Act 1985, Sch 14, the Education Reform Act 1988, Sch 13, the Local Government (Wales) Act 1994, Sch 15, the Local Government and Public Involvement in Health Act 2007, Sch 13, the Local Democracy, Economic Development and Construction Act 2009, Sch 6 and the Deregulation Act 2015, Sch 13.]

---

[1]   Claim forms submitted to a local authority pursuant to the Local Government (Allowances) Regulations 1974 are not documents deposited with a proper officer within the meaning of s 225(1) of this Act (*Brookman v Green* (1983) 147 JP 555).

[2]   Any reference in this Act to a proper officer shall, in relation to any purpose and any local authority or other body or any area, be construed as a reference to an officer appointed for that purpose by that body or for that area, as the case may be (s 270(3)).

[3]   "Local authority" means a county council, a district council, a London borough council or a parish and in relation to Wales, a county council, county borough or community council (s 270(1)).

7.7445   228.   Inspection of documents   (1)   The minutes of proceedings of a parish or community council shall be open to the inspection of any local government elector[1] for the area of the council and any such local government elector may make a copy of or extract from the minutes.

(2)   A local government elector[1] for the area of a local authority[2] may inspect and make a copy of or extract from an order for the payment of money made by the local authority.

(3)   The accounts of a local authority and of any proper officer of a local authority shall be open to the inspection of any member of the authority, and any such member may make a copy of or extract from the accounts.

(4)   *Repealed.*

(5)   Subject to any provisions to the contrary in any other enactment or instrument, a person interested in any document deposited as mentioned in section 225 above may, at all reasonable hours, inspect and make copies thereof or extracts therefrom on payment to the person having custody thereof of the sum of 10p for every such inspection, and of the further sum of 10p for every hour during which such inspection continues after the first hour.

(6)   A document directed by this section to be open to inspection shall be so open at all reasonable hours and, except where otherwise expressly provided, without payment.

(7)   If a person having the custody of any such document[3]—

    (a)   obstructs any person entitled to inspect the document or to make a copy thereof or extract therefrom in inspecting the document or making a copy or extract,

    (b)   refuses to give copies or extracts to any person entitled to obtain copies or extracts,[4]

he shall be liable on summary conviction to a fine not exceeding **level 1** on the standard scale.

(7A)   This section shall apply to the minutes of proceedings and the accounts of a joint authority, an economic prosperity board, or a combined authority as if that authority were a local authority and as if, references to a local government elector for the area of the authority were a reference to a local government elector for any local government area in the area for which the authority is established.

(7B)   *Repealed.*

(8)   This section shall apply to the minutes of proceedings and to the accounts of a parish meeting as if that meeting were a parish council.

(9)   In relation to the Broads Authority, the references in this section to a local government

elector for the area of the authority shall be construed as references to a local government elector for the area of any of the local authorities mentioned in section 1(3)(*a*) of the Norfolk and Suffolk Broads Act 1988.

[Local Government Act 1972, s 228 as amended by the Criminal Justice Act 1982, ss 38 and 46, the Local Government Finance Act 1982, Sch 6, the Local Government (Access to Information) Act 1985, Sch 2, the Local Government Act 1985, Sch 14, the Norfolk and Suffolk Broads Act 1988, Sch 6, the Education Reform Act 1988, Sch 13, the Police and Magistrates' Courts Act 1994, Sch 4, the Police Act 1996, Sch 7, the Police Act 1997, Sch 6, the Greater London Authority Act 1999, Sch 27, the Criminal Justice and Police Act 2001, Sch 6, the Local Government and Public Involvement in Health Act 2007, Sch 13, the Local Democracy, Economic Development and Construction Act 2009, Sch 6, the Police Reform and Social Responsibility Act 2011, Sch 16 and the Deregulation Act 2015, Sch 13.]

---

[1] "Local government elector" means a person registered as a local government elector in the register of electors in accordance with the provisions of the Representation of the People Acts (s 270(1)).

[2] For meaning of "local authority", see note 3 at para 7.7444, ante.

[3] Claim forms submitted to a local authority pursuant to the Local Government (Allowances) Regulations 1974 are not documents deposited with a proper officer within the meaning of s 225(1) of this Act (*Brookman v Green* (1983) 147 JP 555).

[4] There is no longer any obligation to give copies or extracts to any person entitled, since paragraph (*b*) related only to the circumstances in sub-s (4) which has now been repealed; see *Russell-Walker v Gimblett* (1985) 149 JP 448.

7.7446   229.   Photographic copies of documents   (1)   Subject to subsections (3) and (7) below, any requirement imposed by any enactment that a local authority or parish meeting shall keep a document of any description shall be satisfied by their keeping a photographic copy of the document.

(2)   Subject to subsection (7) below, any requirement imposed by any enactment that a document of any description in the custody or under the control of a local authority or parish meeting shall be made available for inspection shall be satisfied by their making available for inspection a photographic copy of the document.

(3)   Subsection (1) above shall not apply to any document deposited with a local authority under the Public Records Act 1958.

(4)   In legal proceedings a photographic copy of a document in the custody of a local authority or parish meeting, or of a document which has been destroyed while in the custody of a local authority or parish meeting, or of any part of any such document, shall, subject to subsection (6) below, be admissible in evidence to the like extent as the original.

(5)   A certificate purporting to be signed by the proper officer of the local authority, or the chairman of the parish meeting, concerned that a document is such a photographic copy as is mentioned in subsection (4) above, shall, subject to subsection (7) below, be evidence to that effect.

(6)   The court before which a photographic copy is tendered in evidence in pursuance of subsection (4) above may, if the original is in existence, require its production and thereupon that subsection shall not apply to the copy.

(7)   A photographic copy of a document in colour where the colours are relevant to the interpretation of the document shall not suffice for the purposes of this section unless it so distinguishes between the colours as to enable the document to be interpreted.

(8)   In this section "court" and "legal proceedings" have the same meanings as in the Civil Evidence Act 1968 and "local authority" includes a joint authority, an economic prosperity board, a combined authority, a police and crime commissioner and the Mayor's Office for Policing and Crime.

[Local Government Act 1972, s 229 as amended by the Local Government Act 1985, Sch 14, the Education Reform Act 1988, Sch 13, the Police and Magistrates' Courts Act 1994, Sch 4, the Police Act 1996, Sch 7, the Police Act 1997, Sch 6, the Greater London Authority Act 1999, Sch 27, the Criminal Justice and Police Act 2001, Sch 6, the Local Democracy, Economic Development and Construction Act 2009, Sch 6, the Police Reform and Social Responsibility Act 2011, Sch 16 and the Deregulation Act 2015, Sch 13.]

7.7447   231.   Service of notices on local authorities, etc   (1)   Subject to subsection (3) below, any notice, order or other document required or authorised by any enactment or any instrument made under an enactment to be given to or served on a local authority or the chairman or an officer of a local authority shall be given or served by addressing it to the local authority and leaving it at, or sending it by post to, the principal office of the authority or any other office of the authority specified by them as one at which they will accept documents of the same description as that document.

(2)   Any notice, order or other document so required or authorised to be given to or served on a parish meeting, or the chairman of the parish meeting, shall be given or served by addressing it to the chairman of the parish meeting and by delivering it to him, or by leaving it at his last known address, or by sending it by post to him at that address.

(3)   The foregoing provisions of this section do not apply to a document which is to be given or served in any proceedings in court, but except as aforesaid the method of giving or serving documents provided for by those provisions are in substitution for the methods provided for by any other enactment or any instrument made under an enactment so far as it relates to the giving or service of documents to or on a local authority, the chairman or an officer of a local authority or a parish meeting or the chairman of a parish meeting.

(4)   In this section "local authority" includes a joint authority, an economic prosperity board, a combined authority, a police and crime commissioner and the Mayor's Office for Policing and Crime.

[Local Government Act 1972, s 231 as amended by the Local Government Act 1985, Sch 14, the Education Reform Act 1988, Sch 13, the Police and Magistrates' Courts Act 1994, Sch 4, the Police Act 1996, Sch 7, the Police Act 1997, Sch 6, the Greater London Authority Act 1999, Sch 27, the Criminal Justice and Police Act 2001, Sch 7, the Local Government and Public Involvement in Health Act 2007, Sch 13, the Local Democracy, Economic Development and Construction Act 2009, Sch 6, the Police Reform and Social Responsibility Act 2011, Sch 16 and the Deregulation Act 2015, Sch 13.]

7.7448 233. Service of notices by local authorities (1) Subject to subsection (8) below, subsections (2) to (5) below shall have effect in relation to any notice, order or other document required or authorised by or under any enactment to be given to or served on any person by or on behalf of a local authority or by an officer of a local authority.

(2) Any such document may be given to or served on the person in question either by delivering it to him, or by leaving it at his proper address, or by sending it by post to him at that address.

(3) Any such document may—

(a) in the case of a body corporate, be given to or served on the secretary or clerk of that body;

(b) in the case of a partnership, be given to or served on a partner or a person having the control or management of the partnership business.

(4) For the purposes of this section and of section 26 of the Interpretation Act 1889 (service of documents by post) in its application to this section, the proper address of any person to or on whom a document is to be given or served shall be his last known address[1], except that—

(a) in the case of a body corporate or their secretary or clerk, it shall be the address of the registered or principal office of that body;

(b) in the case of a partnership or a person having the control or management of the partnership business, it shall be that of the principal office of the partnership;

and for the purposes of this subsection the principal office of a company registered outside the United Kingdom or of a partnership carrying on business outside the United Kingdom shall be their principal office within the United Kingdom.

(5) If the person to be given or served with any document mentioned in subsection (1) above has specified an address within the United Kingdom other than his proper address within the meaning of subsection (4) above as the one at which he or someone on his behalf will accept documents of the same description as that document, that address shall also be treated for the purposes of this section and section 26 of the Interpretation Act 1889 as his proper address.

(6) *Repealed.*

(7) If the name or address of any owner, lessee or occupier of land to or on whom any document mentioned in subsection (1) above is to be given or served cannot after reasonable inquiry be ascertained, the document may be given or served either by leaving it in the hands of a person who is or appears to be resident or employed on the land or by leaving it conspicuously affixed to some building or object on the land.

(8) This section shall apply to a document required or authorised by or under any enactment to be given to or served on any person by or on behalf of the chairman of a parish meeting as it applies to a document so required or authorised to be given to or served on any person by or on behalf of a local authority.

(9) The foregoing provisions of this section do not apply to a document which is to be given or served in any proceedings[2] in court.

(10) Except as aforesaid and subject to any provision of any enactment or instrument excluding the foregoing provisions of this section, the methods of giving or serving documents which are available under those provisions are in addition to the methods which are available under any other enactment or any instrument made under any enactment.

(11) In this section "local authority" includes a joint authority, an economic prosperity board, a combined authority, a police and crime commissioner and the Mayor's Office for Policing and Crime.

[Local Government Act 1972, s 233 as amended by the Local Government (Miscellaneous Provisions) Act 1976, Sch 2, the Local Government Act 1985, Sch 14, the Education Reform Act 1988, Sch 13, the Police and Magistrates' Courts Act 1994, Sch 4, the Police Act 1996, Sch 7, the Police Act 1997, Sch 6, the Greater London Authority Act 1999, Sch 27, the Criminal Justice and Police Act 2001, Sch 6, the Local Government and Public Involvement in Health Act 2007, Sch 13, the Local Democracy, Economic Development and Construction Act 2009, Sch 6, the Police Reform and Social Responsibility Act 2011, Sch 16 and the Deregulation Act 2015, Sch 13.]

---

[1] The word "known" in the phrases "last known address" (and in other legislation "last known place of abode") includes both actual knowledge and constructive knowledge: *R (Tull) v Camberwell Green Magistrates' Court* [2004] RA 31; *Collier v Williams* [2006] 1 WLR 1945. Thus a former address will only be the "last known" address if the server of the notice has taken reasonable steps to find out what the intended recipient's current address is. What he would have found out on making reasonable inquiries will be knowledge imputed to him. As a general rule, unless there is a statutory requirement to the contrary, in a case in which (i) a person wishes to serve notice relating to a particular property on the owner of that property, and (ii) title to that property is registered at HM Land Registry, that person's obligation to make reasonable inquiries goes no further than to search the proprietorship register to ascertain the address of the registered proprietor. It is the responsibility of the registered proprietor to keep his address up to date. If the person serving the notice has actually been given a more recent address than that shown in the proprietorship register as the address or place of abode of the intended recipient of the notice, then notice should be served at that address also. Where the function of serving notice is one that is given to a particular person eg in the case of an enforcement notice, the "the local planning authority" rather than to the council as a whole, the planning department, for example, cannot be expected to trawl through the records of the council as a whole to see whether the registered owners of property have another address in the borough for council tax purposes, by reason of having a market stall or other licence, because they receive some sort of welfare benefit or because their children are in local authority schools. Moreover, even if the planning authority did find

another address elsewhere in the Council it would not always be evident which would be the current address for the person on whom an enforcement notice is to be served: *Oldham Metropolitan Borough Council v Tanna* [2017] EWCA Civ 50, [2017] 1 WLR 1970.

[2] However, it would seem that these provisions may enable proof of the service of documents which took place before proceedings commenced or were in contemplation, otherwise they would have no purpose.

7.7449   234.   Authentication of documents   (1)   Any notice, order or other document which a local authority are authorised or required by or under any enactment (including any enactment in this Act) to give, make or issue may be signed[1] on behalf of the authority by the proper officer of the authority.

(2)   Any document purporting to bear the signature of the proper officer of the authority shall be deemed, until the contrary is proved, to have been duly given, made or issued by the authority of the local authority.

In this subsection the word "signature" includes a facsimile of a signature by whatever process reproduced.

(3)   Where any enactment or instrument made under an enactment makes, in relation to any document or class of documents, provision with respect to the matters dealt with by one of the two foregoing subsections, that subsection shall not apply in relation to that document or class of documents.

(4)   In this section "local authority" includes a joint authority, an economic prosperity board, a combined authority, a police and crime commissioner and the Mayor's Office for Policing and Crime.

[Local Government Act 1972, s 234 as amended by the Local Government Act 1985, Sch 14, the Education Reform Act 1988, Sch 13, the Police and Magistrates' Courts Act 1994, Sch 4, the Police Act 1996, Sch 7, the Police Act 1997, Sch 6, the Greater London Authority Act 1999, Sch 27, the Criminal Justice and Police Act 2001, Sch 6, the Local Government and Public Involvement in Health Act 2007, Sch 13, the Local Democracy, Economic Development and Construction Act 2009, Sch 6, the Police Reform and Social Responsibility Act 2011, Sch 16 and the Deregulation Act 2015, Sch 13.]

---

[1]   The requirement of a signature may be satisfied by a facsimile: see *Plymouth City Corpn v Hurrell* [1968] 1 QB 455, [1967] 3 All ER 354, 131 JP 479.

Bye-laws

7.7450   235.   Power of councils to make bye-laws for good rule and government and suppression of nuisances   (1)   The council of a district, the council of a principal area in Wales and the council of a London borough may make bye-laws[1] for the good rule and government of the whole or any part of the district, principal area or borough, as the case may be, and for the prevention and suppression of nuisances therein[2].

(2)   The confirming authority in relation to bye-laws made under this section shall be the Secretary of State.

(3)   Bye-laws shall not be made under this section for any purpose as respects any area if provision for that purpose as respects that area is made by, or is or may be made under, any other enactment.

[Local Government Act 1972, s 235 as amended by the Local Government (Wales) Act 1994, Sch 15.]

---

[1]   Justices are bound to decide on any objection to the validity of a bye-law, although it may have been regularly made and confirmed; and they will exceed their jurisdiction if they convict on the mere proof of facts bringing the case within the bye-law without also deciding the bye-law is good (*R v Rose* (1855) 19 JP 676). It was decided in that case that a power to make bye-laws for removal of dust, filth, etc, from streets by occupiers did not authorise the making a bye-law for removal of pure snow. Applied in *R v Crown Court at Reading, ex p Hutchinson* [1988] QB 384, [1988] 1 All ER 333, 152 JP 47, where it was held that it is neither necessary nor appropriate for proceedings before magistrates to be adjourned so that the validity of the byelaw can be determined in the High Court by way of judicial review. If byelaws are to be upheld as good in part notwithstanding that they are bad in part, they must be substantially severable. If textual severance is possible, the test of substantial severability will be satisfied when the valid text is unaffected by, and independent of, the invalid. But when the court must modify the text in order to achieve severance, the test of substantial severability will be satisfied only if the substance of what remains is essentially unchanged in its legislative purpose, operation and effect; see *DPP v Hutchinson* [1990] 2 AC 783, [1990] 2 All ER 836, 155 JP 71, HL. Where a properly constituted criminal court has ruled that byelaws on which a prosecution has been based are invalid, the authority responsible for promulgating those byelaws must have regard to that decision in its dealings with others who were not parties to those proceedings and if it fails to do so it may be acting *Wednesbury* unreasonably even if it is not bound by judicial precedent such as where the decision declaring the byelaw invalid is that of a magistrates' court or the Crown Court. If however there are serious doubts about the correctness of the Criminal court's decision as to the validity of the byelaws, and there are serious reasons of public safety or security which require the retention of the byelaws pending an appeal, a case might be made for retaining them, provided an appeal is pursued with expedition, or other means found urgently to establish their validity in a court. See the remarks of Carnwath J in *Secretary of State for Defence v Percy* [1999] 1 All ER 732, Ch D (a case concerning byelaws made under s 14 of the Military Lands Act 1892).

As to a nuisance caused by a failure to remove snow, see *Slater v Worthington's Cash Stores (1930) Ltd* [1941] 1 KB 488, [1941] 3 All ER 28. As to infraction of bye-laws against collecting a crowd by shouting, etc, see *Phillips v Canham* (1872) 36 JP 310. A bye-law made by the Worcester County Council under the repealed s 16 of the Local Government Act 1888, against using obscene language in a street or public place or on land adjacent thereto without words importing that the language must be used to cause annoyance was held to be invalid, and repugnant to the general law because it was not limited to the use of such language to the annoyance of the public or by any limitation to the like effect (*Strickland v Hayes* [1896] 1 QB 290, 60 JP 164). This case was commented on in a later case, and it was held that a bye-law, made under s 16 of the Local Government Act 1888, which provided that "No person shall in any house, building, garden, land, or other place abutting on or near to a street or public place, make use of any violent, abusive, profane, indecent, or obscene language, gesture, or conduct, to the annoyance of any person in such street or public place", was a valid bye-law, and justified a conviction for using such language in a private house abutting on a street to the annoyance of the persons in the street (*Mantle v Jordan* [1897] 1 QB 248, 61 JP 119). *Strickland v Hayes* seems to conflict with *Kruse v Johnson*, infra, as to reasonableness, and it may be doubted whether it is now good law. Further doubt was thrown in this case in *Gentel v*

Rapps [1902] 1 KB 160, 66 JP 117, where it was held that a tramway bye-law was not invalid because it omitted the words "to the annoyance of the passengers". See also *Brabham v Wookey* (1901) 18 TLR 99. A publican using indecent language in a public house to two constables who had entered the house on business does not infringe a bye-law prohibiting the use of indecent language in a "public place to the annoyance of passengers" (*Russon v Dutton (No 2)* (1911) 75 JP 207).

A bye-law relating to betting in a public place which did not make provision for a person charged defences for which the public Acts provided, was held to be repugnant to the general law and invalid (*Powell v May* [1946] KB 330, [1946] 1 All ER 444, 110 JP 157). A bye-law against selling any paper devoted wholly or mainly to giving information as to the probable result of races, steeplechases, or other competitions was held by the Divisional Court (ALVERSTONE LCJ and KENNEDY J, PHILLIMORE J, diss) to be invalid on the ground of its being uncertain and unreasonable (*Scott v Pilliner* [1904] 2 KB 855, 68 JP 518). RUSSELL LCJ, laid down a general rule with regard to the construction that should be put upon bye-laws, and said in his opinion the courts were bound to support as far as possible bye-laws issued by local authorities unless it could be shown the bye-law was made without jurisdiction or was obviously unreasonable. He said the court ought not willingly to "pick holes" in rules that dealt with local matters and local requirements, which the local authorities were often better able to judge than the courts (*Walker v Stretton* (1896) 60 JP 313). Great regard will be paid to findings of local justices upon a bye-law made by a body with knowledge of local conditions (*Everton v Walker* (1927) 91 JP 125). See also *Friend v Brehout* (1914) 79 JP 25.

A local bye-law at Cambridge rendered liable to a penalty any person making a violent noise or outcry in the street "to the annoyance of the inhabitants". A newsboy cried his papers outside the house of one of the inhabitants for some minutes to the annoyance of that inhabitant. The Queen's Bench Division held the bye-law was reasonable and the defendant was not the less liable to conviction because one particular inhabitant only was annoyed (*Innes v Newman* [1894] 2 QB 292, 58 JP 543; followed in *Raymond v Cook* [1958] 3 All ER 407, 123 JP 35). A bye-law provided that "every person who shall sound or play upon any musical instrument, or sing, or make any noise whatsoever in any street, or near any house within the borough, after having been required by any householder resident in such street or by any police constable to desist from making such sound or noise either on account of the illness of any inmate or from any other reasonable cause", shall be liable, etc. The defendant, a "Captain" in the Salvation Army, played on a concertina on a Sunday morning surrounded by a crowd in a square in Truro, and refused to desist at the request of the superintendent of police, who told him he had reasonable cause for the request by reason of the complaints of the inhabitants. The Queen's Bench Division held there was nothing unreasonable or void in such a bye-law, and it was for the justices to decide whether there was a reasonable cause for requiring the appellant to desist (*R v Powell, etc, Truro Justices* (1884) 48 JP 740). A bye-law at St Albans made liable to a penalty any person blowing a horn "or any other noisy instrument", to the annoyance of any of the inhabitants. The justices found that a concertina was a noisy instrument, and a conviction was upheld. The Queen's Bench Division held it was sufficient to prove the instrument was a nuisance or annoyance to some of the inhabitants (*Booth v Howell* (1889) 53 JP 678); if, indeed, it is found as a fact that the noise in question was calculated to be an annoyance, evidence that inhabitants were annoyed is unnecessary (*Raymond v Cook* [1958] 3 All ER 407, 123 JP 35). Similarly, in relation to the use of obscene language in a street, justices are entitled to infer annoyance in the absence of positive evidence that any person was annoyed (*Nicholson v Glasspool* (1959) 123 JP 229).

A bye-law made by the county council of Kent provided that "No person shall sound or play upon any musical or noisy instrument, or sing in any public place or highway within fifty yards of any dwelling-house, after being required by any constable, or by an inmate of such house personally, or by his or her servant to desist". Defendant was conducting an open-air religious service on a public highway, and persisted in singing within fifty yards of a dwelling-house, after having been requested by a police constable to desist. The case was considered of such great importance that it was heard by a specially constituted court of seven judges and the conviction was upheld. RUSSELL LCJ, made some important observations as to the principles to be applied by the court in deciding as to the validity of bye-laws and held that bye-laws made by local authorities ought to be benevolently interpreted, and credit ought to be given to those who have to administer them that they will be benevolently administered. This case must be looked upon as a leading case (*Kruse v Johnson* [1898] 2 QB 91, 62 JP 469. See also *Brownscombe v Johnson* (1898) 62 JP 326, which led to the case of *Kruse v Johnson*). A bye-law made by the Town Council of Southend under a local Act provided that "No organ or other musical instrument worked by steam or other mechanical means shall be used within the borough provided that this bye-law shall not apply to any locomotive or steam engine in use on any railway within the borough"; (other steam whistles, etc, then permitted by statute were also excluded). A travelling showman erected in a field within the borough a roundabout worked by steam, to which an organ was attached, also worked by steam. The organ was in the centre of a field 116 yards from a public road, and played from 7 a.m. until 9.30 p.m. The Queen's Bench Division held the bye-law was valid (*Southend Corpn v Davis* (1900) 16 TLR 167). A bye-law made by the Town Council of Croydon provided that "No person not being a member of Her Majesty's Army or Auxiliary Forces, under the orders of his commanding officer, shall sound or play upon any musical instrument in any of the streets in the borough on Sunday". The appellant, one of the Salvation Army, played a musical instrument on a Sunday and was fined. The Queen's Bench Division held that as the bye-law stated no qualification or exception in any circumstances, it was unreasonable and void (*Johnson v Croydon Corpn* (1886) 16 QBD 708, 50 JP 487, Treat 163). So also was a bye-law that every person who shall play a noisy instrument or sing or preach in any street without a previously written licence from the mayor shall be fined, etc, as it would enable a mayor to legalise a nuisance or prohibit a lawful act which was not a nuisance (*Munro v Watson* (1887) 51 JP 660). But a bye-law which prohibited the exposure for sale of any commodity, etc, or for hire of any chair, etc, on the sea beach, esplanade, etc, except by direction of the sanitary authority, or in such parts as they might by notice appoint, made under a local Act, which authorised bye-laws to be made for regulation of the esplanade, was upheld (*Gray v Sylvester* (1897) 61 JP 807). The court distinguished a bye-law for the good government of a town from bye-laws for the regulation of an esplanade. See also *Slee v Meadows* (1911) 75 JP 246. A bye-law that no person shall wilfully annoy passengers in the public streets was held to be invalid for uncertainty (*Nash v Finlay* (1901) 66 JP 183). So was a bye-law preventing any person hawking on beach or foreshore except in pursuance of agreement with corporation (*Parker v Bournemouth Corpn* (1902) 66 JP 440). This was followed in *Moorman v Tordoff* (1908) 72 JP 142. But see *Williams v Weston-super-Mare UDC (No 1)* (1907) 72 JP 54, where *Parker v Bournemouth Corpn, supra*, was distinguished; *Williams v Weston-super-Mare UDC (No 2)* (1910) 74 JP 370 and *Cassell v Jones* (1913) 77 JP 197. A bye-law made under s 69 (repealed by the Statute Law (Repeals) Act 1975) of the Town Police Clauses Act 1847, as to bathing, and providing that the prescribed charges should include charges for the use of towels and bathing costume, thus purporting to prohibit any extra charge being made therefore, was declared *ultra vires* (*Parker v Clegg* (1903) 2 LGR 608).

A bye-law at Luton provided that "no person shall to the annoyance or disturbance of residents or passengers keep or manage a shooting gallery, swing boat, roundabout, or other like thing in any street or public place or on land adjoining or near to such street or public place, provided that the bye-law shall not apply to any fair lawfully held". It was contended by the appellant that the bye-law was *ultra vires* on the ground that the town council had no authority to make a bye-law affecting private property, and because it created a new criminal offence. The Queen's Bench Division upheld the bye-law (*Teale v Harris* (1896) 60 JP 744). Where a bye-law prohibited touting for hackney carriages in any public thoroughfare, it was held that the respondent committed an offence though he stood at the time on a piece of land adjoining the street and belonging to private persons (*Dereham v Strickland* (1911) 75 JP 300; *McQuade v Barnes* [1949] 1 All ER 154, 113 JP 89).

A licence proposed to be granted by the Edinburgh magistrates under the provisions of an Act regulating the selling of ice-cream, and professing to limit the days and hours when premises should be kept open, was held by the House of Lords to be *ultra vires* (*Rossi v Edinburgh Corpn* [1905] AC 21). Football had been played many years on open ground crossed by footpaths. Appellants set up that the paths were not streets within the meaning of a bye-law, and claimed a right as sons of freemen to play on the open space. The Queen's Bench Division held that justices properly overruled the claim, as such a right could not possibly exist (*Pearson v Whitfield* (1888) 52 JP Jo 708). As to bye-laws regulating games on a public common, see *Harris v Harrison* (1914) 78 JP 398. A local authority has no power to sanction building plans not in accordance with bye-laws; they have no dispensing power, any purported approval of plans contravening bye-laws is inoperative (*Yabbicom v King* [1899] 1 QB 444, 63 JP 149).

    ² As to offences against bye-laws, and penalties, see s 237 and notes thereto, post.

7.7451   236.   Procedure etc, for bye-laws   (1)   Subject to subsection (2) below, the following provisions of this section shall apply to bye-laws¹ to be made by a local authority under this Act and to byelaws made by a local authority, the Greater London Authority, Transport for London or an Integrated Transport Authority for an integrated transport area in England under any other enactment and conferring on the authority, a power to make bye-laws and for which specific provision is not otherwise made.

    (2)   This section shall not apply to

      (a)   byelaws of a class prescribed by regulations under section 236A, or

      (b)   bye-laws made by the Civil Aviation Authority under section 29 of the Civil Aviation Act 1982 and the Local Government Act 1985, Sch 14.

    (3)–(11)   *Procedure for making and confirming bye-laws.*

[Local Government Act 1972, s 236 as amended by the Civil Aviation Act 1982, Sch 15, the Local Government Act 1985, Sch 14, the Education Reform Act 1988, Sch 12, the Water Act 1989, Sch 27, the Local Government (Wales) Act 1994, Sch 15, the Greater London Authority Act 1999, ss 76 and 166, SI 2001/3719, the Local Government and Public Involvement in Health Act 2007, s 129 and the Local Transport Act 2008, Sch 4.]

---

    ¹ Section 236 is modified by SI 1986/143 in relation to byelaws for marine nature reserves made under ss 36 and 37 of the Wildlife and Countryside Act 1981.

7.7452   236A.   Alternative procedure for certain byelaws   (1)   The Secretary of State may, in relation to England, by regulations¹—

      (a)   prescribe classes of byelaws to which section 236 does not apply, and

      (b)   make provision about the procedure for the making and coming into force of such byelaws.

    (2)   The regulations may prescribe a class of byelaws by reference, in particular, to one or more of the following—

      (a)   the enactment under which byelaws are made,

      (b)   the subject-matter of byelaws,

      (c)   the authority by whom byelaws are made,

      (d)   the authority or person by whom byelaws are confirmed.

    (3)   The regulations may, in particular, include provision about—

      (a)   consultation to be undertaken before a byelaw is made,

      (b)   publicising a byelaw after it is made.

    (4)   The regulations may make—

      (a)   such incidental, consequential, transitional or supplemental provision (including provision amending, repealing or revoking enactments) as the Secretary of State considers appropriate, and

      (b)   different provision for different areas, including different provision for different localities and for different authorities.

    (5)   Regulations may not be made under subsection (1) unless a draft of the instrument containing the regulations has been laid before, and approved by a resolution of, each House of Parliament.

[Local Government Act 1972, s 236A as inserted by the Local Government and Public Involvement in Health Act 2007, s 129.]

---

    ¹ The Byelaws (Alternative Procedure) (England) Regulations 2016, SI 2016/165 have been made. The Explanatory Note to the regulations outlines the policy background.

    "The policy aim is to specify a procedure for making and bringing into force certain byelaws without any central Government confirmation involvement, which decentralises this power to specified local authorities, who then assume complete responsibility for these byelaws and their lawfulness. The Regulations do not give authorities powers to create new categories of byelaws; authorities already have a wide range of byelaw-making powers. What is new is that following leave to proceed to make the byelaw by the Secretary of State, there is no requirement for subsequent confirmation by the Secretary of State – it will be a matter for the authority having taken account of any representations made about the proposed byelaw. The Secretary of State for Communities and Local Government is responsible for byelaws made by local authorities on Good Rule and Government. Under the alternative procedure authorities will undertake a two stage process for byelaw preparation and consultation before advertising and making a new byelaw. As such the resolving of any objections and the bringing into force of certain byelaws will be undertaken locally, instead of by the Secretary of State, as currently happens."

7.7453   236B.   Revocation of byelaws   (1)   This section applies to—

      (a)   a local authority;

      (b)   the Greater London Authority;

      (c)   Transport for London;

      (d)   an Integrated Transport Authority for an integrated transport area in England.

      (e)   a combined authority.

    (2)   Such an authority may make a byelaw under this section to revoke a byelaw made by the

authority.

(3)   The power under subsection (2) may be exercised only where the authority has no other power to revoke the byelaw.

(4)   The confirming authority in relation to a byelaw made under this section shall be—

(a)   in relation to a byelaw made by a local authority in Wales, the Welsh Ministers;

(b)   in relation to any other byelaw, the Secretary of State.

(5)   The Secretary of State may, in relation to England, by order revoke any byelaw which appears to him to have become spent, obsolete or unnecessary.

(6)   The Welsh Ministers may, in relation to Wales, by order revoke any byelaw which appears to them to have become spent, obsolete or unnecessary.

(7)   An order under this section may make—

(a)   such incidental, consequential, transitional or supplemental provision (including provision amending, repealing or revoking enactments) as the person making the order considers appropriate, and

(b)   different provision for different areas, including different provision for different localities and for different authorities.

(8)   A statutory instrument containing an order under this section which amends or repeals any provision of an Act may not be made by the Secretary of State unless a draft of the instrument containing the order has been laid before, and approved by a resolution of, each House of Parliament.

(9)   Otherwise, a statutory instrument containing an order made by the Secretary of State under this section shall be subject to annulment in pursuance of a resolution of either House of Parliament.

(10)   A statutory instrument containing an order under this section which amends or repeals any provision of an Act may not be made by the Welsh Ministers unless a draft of the instrument containing the order has been laid before, and approved by a resolution of, the National Assembly for Wales.

(11)   Otherwise, a statutory instrument containing an order made by the Welsh Ministers under this section shall be subject to annulment in pursuance of a resolution of the National Assembly for Wales.

[Local Government Act 1972, s 236B, as inserted by the Local Government and Public Involvement in Health Act 2007, s 134 and amended by the Local Transport Act 2008, Sch 4 and the Local Democracy, Economic Development and Construction Act 2009, Sch 6.]

7.7454   237.   Offences against bye-laws[1]   Bye-laws to which section 236 above applies and byelaws of a class prescribed by regulations under section 236A may provide that persons contravening the bye-laws shall be liable on summary conviction to a fine not exceeding such sum as may be fixed by the enactment conferring the power to make the bye-laws, or, if no sum is so fixed, the sum of **level 2** on the standard scale[1], and in the case of a continuing offence a further fine not exceeding such sum as may be fixed as aforesaid, or, if no sum is so fixed, the sum of £5[2] for each day during which the offence continues after conviction thereof.

[Local Government Act 1972, s 237 as amended by the Criminal Law Act 1977, s 31(3), the Criminal Justice Act 1982, s 46 and the Local Government and Public Involvement in Health Act 2007, s 129.]

---

[1] Notwithstanding its repeal, byelaws made under the Local Government Act 1933, are by virtue of s 272(2) of the Local Government Act 1972, preserved and remain in force (*DPP v Jackson* (1990) 154 JP 967).

[2] Justices always have jurisdiction to inquire into the validity of a byelaw (*R v Crown Court at Reading, ex p Hutchinson* [1988] QB 384, [1988] 1 All ER 333, 152 JP 47).

A bye-law made by virtue of the Public Health Act 1875, s 183 or the Local Government Act 1933, s 251, or the Local Government Act 1972, s 237, which was in force on 17 July 1978 and specified £20 as the maximum fine (including a bye-law which specified £5 and was increased to £20 by virtue of the Criminal Justice Act 1967 s 92(3) and Sch 3 Part II), had effect as if the bye-law specified a fine of £50 (Criminal Law Act 1977, s 31(2) and (3)). By virtue of s 46 of the Criminal Justice Act 1982 the reference to a maximum of £50 was converted to a reference to level 2 on the standard scale. However, if on 17 July 1978 such bye-law specified an amount less than £20 it remains unchanged (Criminal Law Act 1977, s 31(2) and (3)). In the case of a bye-law made by virtue of an enactment or instrument after 30 April 1984 and before the commencement of s 52 of the Criminal Justice Act 1988, the maximum fine on conviction of a summary offence specified in the bye-law shall be construed as the level in the first column of the standard scale corresponding to that amount (Criminal Justice Act 1988, s 52, when in force).

Byelaws of local authorities made under this section dealing with the burning of straw, stubble or other crop residues on agricultural land have been repealed by the Burning of Crop Residues (Repeal of Byelaws) Order 1992, SI 1992/693. Section 152 of the Environmental Protection Act 1990, title PUBLIC HEALTH, post, enables regulations to be made prohibiting or restricting the burning of crop residue on agricultural land. Where the byelaws were made under ss 36 or 37 of the Wildlife and Countryside Act 1981 for marine nature reserves, the penalty prescribed here by SI 1986/143 is £1,000.

7.7455   237ZA.   Section 235 byelaws: powers of seizure etc   A byelaw made under section 235 may include provision for or in connection with—

(a)   the seizure and retention of any property in connection with any contravention of the byelaw, and

(b)   the forfeiture of any such property on a person's conviction of an offence of contravention of the byelaw.*

[Local Government Act 1972, s 237ZA as inserted by the Police Reform and Social Responsibility Act 2011, s 150.]

---

* Section in force from 19 December 2011 (insofar as it relates to byelaws made by local authorities in England): see SI 2011/2834, art 2(k), and from a date to be appointed for remaining purposes.

7.7456   237A.   Fixed penalty notices   (1)   The Secretary of State may, in relation to England, by regulations prescribe classes of byelaws to which this section applies.

(2)   The regulations may prescribe a class of byelaws by reference, in particular, to one or more of the following—

    (a)   the enactment under which byelaws are made,

    (b)   the subject-matter of byelaws,

    (c)   the authority by whom byelaws are made,

    (d)   the authority or person by whom byelaws are confirmed.

(3)   Where—

    (a)   an authorised officer of an authority which has made a byelaw to which this section applies has reason to believe that a person has committed an offence against the byelaw, or

    (b)   an authorised officer of a parish council has reason to believe that a person has in its area committed an offence against a byelaw to which this section applies made by an authority other than the parish council,

the officer may give that person a notice offering him the opportunity of discharging any liability to conviction for the offence by payment of a fixed penalty.

(4)   A fixed penalty notice under this section is payable to the authority whose officer gave the notice.

(5)   Where a person is given a notice under this section in respect of an offence—

    (a)   no proceedings may be instituted for the offence before the end of the period of fourteen days following the date of the notice, and

    (b)   he may not be convicted of the offence if he pays the fixed penalty before the end of that period.

(6)   A notice under this section must give such particulars of the circumstances alleged to constitute the offence as are necessary for giving reasonable information about the offence.

(7)   A notice under this section must also state—

    (a)   the period during which, by virtue of subsection (5), proceedings will not be taken for the offence,

    (b)   the amount of the fixed penalty, and

    (c)   the person to whom and the address at which the fixed penalty may be paid.

(8)   Without prejudice to payment by any other method, payment of the fixed penalty may be made by pre-paying and posting a letter containing the amount of the penalty (in cash or otherwise) to the person mentioned in subsection (7)(c) at the address so mentioned.

(9)   Where a letter is sent in accordance with subsection (8) payment is to be regarded as having been made at the time at which that letter would be delivered in the ordinary course of post.

(10)   The form of a notice under this section may be specified in regulations under subsection (1).

(11)   In any proceedings a certificate which—

    (a)   purports to be signed on behalf of the chief finance officer of an authority, and

    (b)   states that payment of a fixed penalty was or was not received by a date specified in the certificate,

is evidence of the facts stated.

(12)   In this section—

"authorised officer", in relation to an authority, means—

    (a)   an employee of the authority who is authorised in writing by the authority for the purpose of giving notices under this section,

    (b)   any person who, in pursuance of arrangements made with the authority, has the function of giving such notices and is authorised in writing by the authority to perform the function, and

    (c)   any employee of such a person who is authorised in writing by the authority for the purpose of giving such notices,

"chief finance officer", in relation to an authority, means the person having responsibility for the financial affairs of the authority.

(13)   Regulations under subsection (1) may prescribe conditions to be satisfied by a person before a parish council may authorise him in writing for the purpose of giving notices under this section.

[Local Government Act 1972, s 237A as inserted by the Local Government and Public Involvement in Health Act 2007, s 130.]

7.7457   237B.   Amount of fixed penalty   (1)   The amount of a fixed penalty payable in pursuance of a notice under section 237A is—

    (a)   the amount specified by the authority which made the byelaw, or

    (b)   if no amount is so specified, £75.

(2)   An authority may specify different amounts in relation to different byelaws.

(3)   The Secretary of State may by regulations make provision in connection with the powers under subsections (1)(a) and (2).

(4)   Regulations under subsection (3) may, in particular—

(a)   require an amount specified under subsection (1)(a) to fall within a range prescribed in the regulations,

(b)   restrict the extent to which, and the circumstances in which, an authority can make provision under subsection (2).

(5)   The Secretary of State may by order substitute a different amount for the amount for the time being specified in subsection (1)(b).

[Local Government Act 1972, s 237B as inserted by the Local Government and Public Involvement in Health Act 2007, s 130.]

7.7458   237C.   Power to require name and address in connection with fixed penalty

(1)   If an authorised officer proposes to give a person a notice under section 237A, the officer may require the person to give him his name and address.

(2)   A person commits an offence if—

(a)   he fails to give his name and address when required to do so under subsection (1), or

(b)   he gives a false or inaccurate name or address in response to a requirement under that subsection.

(3)   A person guilty of an offence under subsection (2) is liable on summary conviction to a fine not exceeding level 3 on the standard scale.

(4)   In this section, "authorised officer" has the same meaning as in section 237A.

[Local Government Act 1972, s 237C as inserted by the Local Government and Public Involvement in Health Act 2007, s 130.]

7.7459   237D.   Use of fixed penalty receipts   (1)   "Fixed penalty receipts" means amounts paid to an authority in pursuance of notices under section 237A.

(2)   The authority shall have regard to the desirability of using its fixed penalty receipts for the purpose of combating any relevant nuisance.

(3)   A "relevant nuisance" is a nuisance in the authority's area for the prevention of which any byelaw to which section 237A applies was made.

[Local Government Act 1972, s 237D as inserted by the Local Government and Public Involvement in Health Act 2007, s 131.]

7.7460   237E.   Guidance relating to sections 236A and 237A to 237D   An authority which makes byelaws of a class prescribed by regulations under section 236A or 237A must have regard to any guidance issued by the Secretary of State about—

(a)   procedure for which provision is made by regulations under section 236A(1);

(b)   fixed penalties;

(c)   anything related to the matters mentioned in paragraph (a) or (b).

[Local Government Act 1972, s 237E as inserted by the Local Government and Public Involvement in Health Act 2007, s 132.]

7.7461   237F.   Further provision about regulations and orders under section 237A or 237B

(1)   Regulations under section 237A or 237B, and an order under section 237B, may make—

(a)   such incidental, consequential, transitional or supplemental provision (including provision amending, repealing or revoking enactments) as the Secretary of State considers appropriate, and

(b)   different provision for different areas, including different provision for different localities and for different authorities.

(2)   A statutory instrument containing—

(a)   regulations under section 237A or 237B which amend or repeal any provision of an Act, or

(b)   an order under section 237B which amends or repeals any provision of an Act,

may not be made unless a draft of the instrument containing the regulations or order has been laid before, and approved by a resolution of, each House of Parliament.

(3)   Otherwise, a statutory instrument containing regulations under section 237A or 237B, or an order under section 237B, shall be subject to annulment in pursuance of a resolution of either House of Parliament.

[Local Government Act 1972, s 237F as inserted by the Local Government and Public Involvement in Health Act 2007, s 130.]

7.7462   238.   Evidence of bye-laws   The production of a printed copy of a bye-law purporting to be made by a local authority, the Greater London Authority, an Integrated Transport Authority for an integrated transport area in England or a combined authority upon which is endorsed a certificate purporting to be signed by the proper officer of the authority stating—

(a)   that the bye-law was made by the authority;

(b)   that the copy is a true copy of the bye-law;

(c)   that on a specified date the bye-law was confirmed by the authority named in the certificate or, as the case may require, was sent to the Secretary of State and has not been disallowed[1];

(d)   the date, if any, fixed by the confirming authority for the coming into operation of the bye-law[1];

shall be prima facie evidence of the facts stated in the certificate and without proof of the handwriting or official position of any person purporting to sign the certificate.

[Local Government Act 1972, s 238 as amended by the Local Government Act 1985, Sch 14, the Education Reform Act 1988, Sch 12, SI 2001/3719, the Local Transport Act 2008, Sch 4 and the Local Democracy, Economic Development and Construction Act 2009, Sch 6.]

---

[1] Where the byelaws were made under s 37 of the Wildlife and Countryside Act 1981 for marine nature reserves, paras (c) and (d) are omitted by the operation of SI 1986/143.

7.7463 265–265A. *Application of Act to Isles of Scilly; application in relation to the Broads Authority.*

7.7464 270. General provisions as to interpretation (1) In the Act, except where the context otherwise requires, the following expressions have the following meanings respectively, that is to say—

"alternative arrangements" has the same meaning as in Part II of the Local Government Act 2000;

"the Broads" has the same meaning as in the Norfolk and Suffolk Broads Act 1988;

"combined authority" means a combined authority established under section 103 of the Local Democracy, Economic Development and Construction Act 2009;

"economic prosperity board" means an economic prosperity board established under section 88 of the Local Democracy, Economic Development and Construction Act 2009;

"joint authority" means an authority established by Part IV of the Local Government Act 1985;

"local authority" means a county council, a district council, a London borough council or a parish council, but in relation to Wales, means a county council, county borough or community council;

"principal area" means a county, Greater London, a district or a London borough;

"principal council" means a council elected for a principal area;

"sub-national transport body" means a sub-national transport body established under section 102E of the Local Transport Act 2008.[1]

(2) In this Act and in any other enactment, whether passed before, at the same time as, or after this Act, the expression "non-metropolitan county" means any county other than a metropolitan county, and the expression "non-metropolitan district" means any district other than a metropolitan district.

(3) Any reference in this Act to a proper officer and any reference which by virtue of this Act is to be construed as such a reference shall, in relation to any purpose and any local authority or other body or any area, be construed as a reference to an officer appointed for that purpose by that body or for that area, as the case may be.

(4) In any provision of this Act which applies to a London borough, except Schedule 2 to this Act,—

(a) any reference to the chairman of the council or of any class of councils comprising the council or to a member of a local authority shall be construed as or, as the case may be, as including a reference to the mayor of the borough;

(b) any reference to the vice-chairman of the council or any such class of councils shall be construed as a reference to the deputy mayor of the borough; and

(c) any reference to the proper officer of the council or any such class of councils shall be construed as a reference to the proper officer of the borough.

(4A) Where a London borough council are operating executive arrangements which involve a mayor and cabinet executive, subsection (4) above shall have effect with the omission of paragraphs (a) and (b).

(5) In this Act, except where the context otherwise requires, references to any enactment shall be construed as references to that enactment as amended, extended or applied by or under any other enactment, including any enactment contained in this Act.

[Local Government Act 1972, s 270 as amended by the Local Government Act 1985, Schs 14 and 17, the Norfolk and Suffolk Broads Act 1988, Sch 6, the Local Government (Wales) Act 1994, s 1(5), the Local Government Act 2000, s 46, SI 2001/2237, the Local Government and Public Involvement in Health Act 2007, Sch 13, the Local Democracy, Economic Development and Construction Act 2009, Sch 6, the Localism Act 2011, Sch 3, the Deregulation Act 2015, Sch 13 and the Cities and Local Government Devolution Act 2016, Sch 5.]

---

[1] Only the definitions relevant to the provisions reproduced in Stone are included.

SCHEDULE 12A
ACCESS TO INFORMATION: EXEMPT INFORMATION

(As substituted by SI 2006/88 and amended by SI 2007/2194 and the Charities Act 2011, Sch 7.)

PART 1
DESCRIPTIONS OF EXEMPT INFORMATION

7.7465 1. Information relating to any individual.

2. Information which is likely to reveal the identity of an individual.

3. Information relating to the financial or business affairs of any particular person (including the authority holding that information).

4. Information relating to any consultations or negotiations, or contemplated consultations or negotiations, in connection with any labour relations matter arising between the authority or a Minister of the Crown and employees of, or office holders under, the authority.

5. Information in respect of which a claim to legal professional privilege could be maintained in legal proceedings.

6.   Information which reveals that the authority proposes—
   (a)   to give under any enactment a notice under or by virtue of which requirements are imposed on a person; or
   (b)   to make an order or direction under any enactment.
7.   Information relating to any action taken or to be taken in connection with the prevention, investigation or prosecution of crime.

PART 2
QUALIFICATIONS: ENGLAND

8.   Information falling within paragraph 3 above is not exempt information by virtue of that paragraph if it is required to be registered under—
   (a)   the Companies Acts (as defined in section 2 of the Companies Act 2006);
   (b)   the Friendly Societies Act 1974;
   (c)   the Friendly Societies Act 1992;
   (d)   the Industrial and Provident Societies Acts 1965 to 1978;
   (e)   the Building Societies Act 1986; or
   (f)   the Charities Act 2011.
9.   Information is not exempt information if it relates to proposed development for which the local planning authority may grant itself planning permission pursuant to regulation 3 of the Town and Country Planning General Regulations 1992.
10.   Information which—
   (a)   falls within any of paragraphs 1 to 7 above; and
   (b)   is not prevented from being exempt by virtue of paragraph 8 or 9 above,
is exempt information if and so long, as in all the circumstances of the case, the public interest in maintaining the exemption outweighs the public interest in disclosing the information.

PART 3
INTERPRETATION: ENGLAND

11.   (1)   In Parts 1 and 2 and this Part of this Schedule—
"employee" means a person employed under a contract of service;
"financial or business affairs" includes contemplated, as well as past or current, activities;
"labour relations matter" means—
   (a)   any of the matters specified in paragraphs (a) to (g) of section 218(1) of the Trade Union and Labour Relations (Consolidation) Act 1992 (matters which may be the subject of a trade dispute, within the meaning of that Act); or
   (b)   any dispute about a matter falling within paragraph (a) above;
   and for the purposes of this definition the enactments mentioned in paragraph (a) above, with the necessary modifications, shall apply in relation to office-holders under the authority as they apply in relation to employees of the authority;
"office-holder", in relation to the authority, means the holder of any paid office appointments to which are or may be made or confirmed by the authority or by any joint board on which the authority is represented or by any person who holds any such office or is an employee of the authority;
"registered" in relation to information required to be registered under the Building Societies Act 1986, means recorded in the public file of any building society (within the meaning of that Act).
   (2)   Any reference in Parts 1 and 2 and this Part of this Schedule to "the authority" is a reference to the principal council or, as the case may be, the committee or sub-committee in relation to whose proceedings or documents the question whether information is exempt or not falls to be determined and includes a reference—
   (a)   in the case of a principal council, to any committee or sub-committee of the council; and
   (b)   in the case of a committee, to—
      (i)   any constituent principal council;
      (ii)   any other principal council by which appointments are made to the committee or whose functions the committee discharges; and
      (iii)   any other committee or sub-committee of a principal council falling within sub-paragraph (i) or (ii) above; and
   (c)   in the case of a sub-committee, to—
      (i)   the committee, or any of the committees, of which it is a sub-committee; and
      (ii)   any principal council which falls within paragraph (b) above in relation to that committee.

PART 4
DESCRIPTIONS OF EXEMPT INFORMATION: WALES

(As substituted by SI 2007/969.)
12.   Information relating to a particular individual.
13.   Information which is likely to reveal the identity of an individual.
14.   Information relating to the financial or business affairs of any particular person (including the authority holding that information).
15.   Information relating to any consultations or negotiations, or contemplated consultations or negotiations, in connection with any labour relations matter arising between the authority or a Minister of the Crown and employees of, or office holders under, the authority.
16.   Information in respect of which a claim to legal professional privilege could be maintained in legal proceedings.
17.   Information which reveals that the authority proposes—
   (a)   to give under any enactment a notice under or by virtue of which requirements are imposed on a person; or
   (b)   to make an order or direction under any enactment.
18.   Information relating to any action taken or to be taken in connection with the prevention, investigation or prosecution of crime.

PART 5
QUALIFICATIONS: WALES

(As substituted by SI 2007/969 and amended by SI 2007/2194 and the Charities Act 2011, Sch 7.)

19. Information falling within paragraph 14 above is not exempt information by virtue of that paragraph if it is required to be registered under—

    (a)   the Companies Acts (as defined in section 2 of the Companies Act 2006);

    (b)   the Friendly Societies Act 1974;

    (c)   the Friendly Societies Act 1992;

    (d)   the Industrial and Provident Societies Acts 1965 to 1978;

    (e)   the Building Societies Act 1986; or

    (f)   the Charities Act 2011.

20. Information is not exempt information if it relates to proposed development for which the local planning authority may grant itself planning permission pursuant to regulation 3 of the Town and Country Planning General Regulations 1992.

21. Information which—

    (a)   falls within any of paragraphs 12 to 15, 17 and 18 above; and

    (b)   is not prevented from being exempt by virtue of paragraph 19 or 20 above,

is exempt information if and so long, as in all the circumstances of the case, the public interest in maintaining the exemption outweighs the public interest in disclosing the information.

PART 6
INTERPRETATION: WALES

(As substituted by SI 2007/969.)

22.   (1)   In Parts 4 and 5 and this Part of this Schedule—

"employee" means a person employed under a contract of service;

"financial or business affairs" includes contemplated, as well as past or current, activities;

"labour relations matter" means—

    (a)   any of the matters specified in paragraphs (a) to (g) of section 218(1) of the Trade Union and Labour Relations (Consolidation) Act 1992 (matters which may be the subject of a trade dispute, within the meaning of that Act); or

    (b)   any dispute about a matter falling within paragraph (a) above;

and for the purposes of this definition the enactments mentioned in paragraph (a) above, with the necessary modifications, shall apply in relation to office-holders under the authority as they apply in relation to employees of the authority;

"office-holder", in relation to the authority, means the holder of any paid office appointments to which are or may be made or confirmed by the authority or by any joint board on which the authority is represented or by any person who holds any such office or is an employee of the authority;

"registered" in relation to information required to be registered under the Building Societies Act 1986, means recorded in the public file of any building society (within the meaning of that Act).

(2)   Any reference in Parts 4 and 5 and this Part of this Schedule to "the authority" is a reference to the principal council or, as the case may be, the committee or sub-committee in relation to whose proceedings or documents the question whether information is exempt or not falls to be determined and includes a reference—

    (a)   in the case of a principal council, to any committee or sub-committee of the council; and

    (b)   in the case of a committee, to—

        (i)   any constituent principal council;

        (ii)   any other principal council by which appointments are made to the committee or whose functions the committee discharges; and

        (iii)   any other committee or sub-committee of a principal council falling within sub-paragraph (i) or (ii) above; and

    (c)   in the case of a sub-committee, to—

        (i)   the committee, or any of the committees, of which it is a sub-committee; and

        (ii)   any principal council which falls within paragraph (b) above in relation to that committee.

Local Government (Miscellaneous Provisions) Act 1976
(1976 c 57)

PART I
GENERAL

Highways

7.7466   **7. Control of road-side sales**   (1)   If a highway authority considers that, for the purpose of avoiding danger on or facilitating the passage of traffic over a highway for which it is the highway authority, it is appropriate to make an order under this subsection in respect of the highway, the authority may make an order (hereafter in this section referred to as a "control order") specifying the highway and providing that, subject to subsection (5) of this section—

    (a)   no person shall sell anything on the highway or offer or expose anything for sale on the highway; and

    (b)   no person shall, for the purpose of selling anything or offering or exposing anything for sale on the highway or of attracting from users of the highway offers to buy anything, put, keep or use on the highway or on land within fifteen metres from any part of the highway any stall or similar structure or any container or vehicle.

(2)   The highway authority for a highway in respect of which a control order is in force may vary or revoke the order by a subsequent order.

(3)   Paragraphs 20 to 23, paragraph 24 (except so much of it as relates to appeals by district councils) and paragraph 25 of Schedule 9 to the Road Traffic Regulation Act 1984 (which relates to

the procedure for making orders under the provisions of that Act mentioned in paragraphs 20(1) and 24(*a*) and (*b*) of that Schedule) shall have effect as if subsections (1) and (2) of this section were included among those provisions[1].

(4)   If a person contravenes a control order which is in force for a highway, the highway authority for the highway may by a notice served on him require him not to contravene the order after a date specified in the notice (which must not be before the expiration of the period of 7 days beginning with the date of service of the notice); and—

(*a*)   if a person on whom a notice relating to a contravention of a control order is served in pursuance of this subsection contravenes the order after the expiration of that period, or causes, permits or procures another person to contravene it after the expiration of that period, he shall be guilty of an offence and liable on summary conviction to a fine not exceeding **level 3** on the standard scale;

(*b*)   if a contravention in respect of which a person is convicted of an offence in pursuance of the preceding paragraph is continued by him after the expiration of the period of 7 days beginning with the date of the conviction he shall, as respects each day on which the contravention is so continued, be guilty of a further offence and liable on summary conviction to a fine not exceeding £10.

(5)   A control order does not apply—

(*a*)   to anything done at premises used as a shop or petrol filling station either—

      (i)   in pursuance of planning permission granted or deemed to be granted under the Town and Country Planning Act 1990, or

      (ii)   in a case where the premises are, without such permission, lawfully used as a shop or petrol filling station;

(*b*)   to anything done at a market in respect of which tolls, stallages or rents are payable;

(*c*)   to the sale, offer or exposure for sale of things from or on a vehicle which is used only for the purposes of itinerant trading with the occupiers of premises or which is used only for that purpose and for purposes other than trading;

(*d*)   to such a vehicle as is mentioned in the preceding paragraph or to containers on the vehicle;

(*e*)   to, or to containers used in connection with, the sale, offer or exposure for sale, by or on behalf of the occupier of land used for agriculture and on that land, of agricultural produce produced on that land;

(*f*)   to the provision, in a lay-by situated on a highway, of facilities for the purchase of refreshments by persons travelling on the highway or on another highway near to the highway;

(*g*)   to anything as respects which the control order provides that the order is not to apply to it.

In paragraph (*e*) of this subsection "agriculture" and "agricultural" have the same meanings as in the Agriculture Act 1947.

(6)   References in the preceding provisions of this section to a control order are, in the case of a control order which has been varied in pursuance of subsection (2) of this section, references to the order as so varied.

[Local Government (Miscellaneous Provisions) Act 1976, s 7 as amended by the Criminal Justice Act 1982, ss 38 and 46, the Road Traffic Regulation Act 1984, Sch 13, the Planning (Consequential Provisions) Act 1990, Sch 2 and the Planning and Compensation Act 1991, Sch 7.]

---

[1]   The Control of Road-side Sales Orders (Procedure) Regulations 1978, SI 1978/932, have been made.

Heating etc

7.7467   11.   *Production and supply of heat etc by local authorities[1].*

---

[1]   Under this provision the Sale of Electricity by Local Authorities (England and Wales) Regulations 2010, SI 2010/1910 have been made.

7.7468   12.   Provisions supplementary to section 11   (1)   A local authority which supplies or proposes to supply heat, hot air, hot water or steam in pursuance of the preceding section may make byelaws—

(*a*)   with respect to the works and apparatus to be provided or used by persons other than the authority in connection with the supply;

(*b*)   for preventing waste and unauthorised use of the supply and unauthorised interference with works and apparatus used by the authority or any other person in connection with the supply;

(*c*)   providing for any specified contravention of the byelaws to be an offence punishable on summary conviction with a fine of such an amount, not exceeding **level 3** on the standard scale, as is specified in the byelaws.

[Local Government (Miscellaneous Provisions) Act 1976, s 12, as amended by the Criminal Justice Act 1982, ss 40 and 46 and the Building Act 1984, Sch 6.]

Land

7.7469 15. Power of local authorities to survey land which they propose to acquire compulsorily (1) A person authorised in writing in that behalf by a local authority may at any reasonable time—

    (a)   survey any land in connection with a proposal by the authority to acquire compulsorily an interest in the land or a right over the land which is not such an interest; and

    (b)   for the purpose of surveying any land in pursuance of the preceding paragraph, enter on the land and other land.

(2) The power to survey land conferred by the preceding subsection includes power to search and bore on and in the land for the purpose of ascertaining the nature of the subsoil or whether minerals are present in the subsoil, and the power to enter on land conferred by that subsection includes power to place and leave, on or in the land, apparatus for use in connection with the survey in question and power to remove the apparatus; and it is hereby declared that references to surveying in this section include surveying from the air.

(3) [1]A person authorised by a local authority to enter on land in pursuance of subsection (1) of this section—

    (a)   shall, if so required before or after entering on the land, produce evidence of his authority to enter;

    (b)   may take with him on to the land such other persons and such equipment as are necessary for the survey in question;

    (c)   shall not if the land is occupied demand admission to the land as of right unless notice of the intended entry has been served by the local authority on the occupier not less than fourteen days before the demand;

    (d)   shall, if the land is unoccupied when he enters or the occupier is then temporarily absent, leave the land as effectually secured against trespassers as he found it;

    (e)   shall not place or leave apparatus on or in the land or remove apparatus from the land—

        (i)   unless notice of his intention to do so has been served by the local authority on an owner of the land, and if the land is occupied on the occupier, not less than fourteen days before he does so, and

        (ii)   if the land is held by relevant undertakers who within that period serve on the local authority a notice stating that they object to the placing or leaving or removal of the apparatus on the ground that to do so would be seriously detrimental to the carrying on of their undertaking, unless the Secretary of State authorises him in writing to do so;

    (f)   shall not search or bore on or in the land which is the subject of the survey in question if the land is held by relevant undertakers—

        (i)   unless notice of his intention to do so has been served by the local authority on the undertakers not less than fourteen days before he does so, and

        (ii)   if within that period the undertakers serve on the local authority a notice stating that they object to the searching or boring on the ground that to do so would be seriously detrimental to the carrying on of their undertaking, unless the Secretary of State authorises him in writing to do so;

and in paragraphs (e) and (f) of this subsection "relevant undertakers" means any statutory undertakers, any person authorised to carry on a light railway undertaking, a ferry undertaking or an undertaking for supplying district heating, the Civil Aviation Authority and a person who holds a licence under Chapter I of Part I of the Transport Act 2000 (air traffic services).

(3A) For the purposes of subsection (3) of this section—

    (a)   a person who holds a licence under Chapter I of Part I of the Transport Act 2000 shall not be considered to be a relevant undertaker unless the person is carrying out activities authorised by the licence;

    (b)   the person's undertaking shall not be considered to be that of a relevant undertaker except to the extent that it is the person's undertaking as licence holder.

(4)–(6) *Survey in a street or controlled land within the meaning of the New Roads and Street Works Act 1991; compensation for damage arising from a survey.*

(7) If a person—

    (a)   wilfully obstructs another person in the exercise of a power conferred on the other person by subsection (1) or (3)(b) of this section; or

    (b)   while another person is on any land in pursuance of the said subsection (3)(b), wilfully obstructs him in doing things connected with the survey in question; or

    (c)   removes or otherwise interferes with apparatus left on or in land in pursuance of this section,

he shall be guilty of an offence and liable on summary conviction to a fine not exceeding **level 3** on the standard scale.

(8) If a person who has entered on any land in pursuance of this section discloses to another person information obtained by him there about a manufacturing process or trade secret, then, unless the disclosure is made in the course of performing his duty in connection with the purposes for which he was authorised to enter on the land, he shall be guilty of an offence and liable[2], on summary conviction, to a fine not exceeding **the statutory maximum** or, on conviction on

indictment, to imprisonment for a term not exceeding **two years** or a fine or both.

(9)   A local authority which has power by virtue of section 289(1) of the Highways Act 1980, section 324(6) of the Town and Country Planning Act 1990, section 88(5) of the Planning (Listed Buildings and Conservation Areas) Act 1990, or paragraph 20(1) of Schedule 4 to the Community Land Act 1975 to authorise a person to survey or enter on any land as mentioned in subsection (1) of this section shall not be entitled by virtue of that subsection to authorise a person to survey or enter on the land.

[Local Government (Miscellaneous Provisions) Act 1976, s 15 as amended by the Criminal Law Act 1977, s 28, the Highways Act 1980, Sch 24, the Criminal Justice Act 1982, ss 38 and 46, the Airports Act 1986, Sch 6, the Coal Industry Act 1987, Sch 1, the Planning (Consequential Provisions) Act 1990, Sch 2, the New Roads and Street Works Act 1991, Sch 8, the Coal Industry Act 1994, Sch 9, SI 2001/4050 and SI 2009/1307.]

---

[1]   For the purposes of s 15(3) of this Act, the holder of a licence under s 6(1) of the Electricity Act 1989 shall be deemed to be a statutory undertaker and his undertaking a statutory undertaking (Electricity Act 1989, Sch 16, para 1).

[2]   For procedure in respect of this offence which is triable either way, see the Magistrates' Courts Act 1980, ss 17A–21, in PART I: MAGISTRATES' COURTS, PROCEDURE, ante.

7.7470   16.   Power[1] of local authorities to obtain particulars of persons interested in land
(1)   Where, with a view to performing a function conferred on a local authority by any enactment, the authority considers that it ought to have information connected with any land, the authority may serve on one or more of the following persons, namely—

(*a*)   the occupier of the land; and

(*b*)   any person who has an interest in the land either as freeholder, mortgagee or lessee or who directly or indirectly receives rent for the land; and

(*c*)   any person who, in pursuance of an agreement between himself and a person interested in the land, is authorised to manage the land or to arrange for the letting of it,

a notice specifying the land and the function and the enactment which confers the function and requiring the recipient of the notice to furnish to the authority, within a period specified in the notice (which shall not be less than fourteen days beginning with the day on which the notice is served) the nature of his interest in the land and the name and address of each person whom the recipient of the notice believes is the occupier of the land and of each person whom he believes is, as respects the land, such a person as is mentioned in the provisions of paragraphs (*b*) and (*c*) of this subsection.

(2)   A person who—

(*a*)   fails to comply with the requirements of a notice served on him in pursuance of the preceding subsection; or

(*b*)   in furnishing any information in compliance with such a notice makes a statement which he knows to be false in a material particular or recklessly makes a statement which is false in a material particular,

shall be guilty of an offence and liable[2] on summary conviction to a fine not exceeding **level 5** on the standard scale.

[Local Government (Miscellaneous Provisions) Act 1976, s 16 as amended by the Criminal Justice Act 1982, ss 38 and 46.]

---

[1]   This power shall not be exercisable with a view to performing any function under Pt I of the Local Government Finance Act 1992 (council tax): Local Government Finance Act 1992, Sch 13.

[2]   For liability of director, etc, where offence is committed by a body corporate, see s 44(3), post.

Bathing and boating

7.7471   17.   Byelaws about bathing and boating   The power of a local authority to make byelaws under section 231 of the Public Health Act 1936 and section 76 of the Public Health Act 1961 may be exercised as respects any area of sea which is outside the area of the authority and within 1,000 metres to seaward of any place where the low water mark is within or on the boundary of the area of the authority; an offence against a byelaw made under the above provision may be dealt with as if committed within the area of the authority.

[Local Government (Miscellaneous Provisions) Act 1976, s 17—summarised.]

Places of entertainment

7.7472   19.   *Recreational facilities.*

7.7473   20.   Provision of sanitary appliances at places of entertainment   (1)   A local authority (other than a county council in England and the Greater London Council[1]) may, by a notice served on an owner or occupier of a relevant place[2] in the area of the authority, require him—

(*a*)   to provide, before the expiration of a period specified in the notice and in such positions at the place as are so specified, sanitary appliances[2] of such kinds and numbers as are so specified;

(*b*)   to maintain and keep clean the appliances to the reasonable satisfaction of the authority;

(*c*)   to provide and maintain a proper supply of such things for use in connection with the appliances as are so specified (which may be or include cold water or hot water or both); and

(*d*)   to make the appliances and things available for use by members of the public resorting to the place and, if the notice so requires, to make them so available free of charge.

(2)   A notice in pursuance of this section may require the provision of sanitary appliances on such occasions as are specified in the notice but if it does so it shall not also require the provision of sanitary appliances as respects which occasions are not so specified.

(3)   A notice in pursuance of this section—

   (a)   shall not require the provision, in connection with any building for which fixed sanitary appliances could be required by virtue of building regulations in force when the notice is served if the building were to be newly constructed then, of fixed sanitary appliances which are of a different kind from, or which as respects a particular kind are more numerous than, those which could be required as aforesaid;

   (b)   shall not require the provision of movable sanitary appliances at a betting office[2];

   (c)   shall, unless it is an occasional notice[2], specify as the period before the expiration of which sanitary appliances are to be provided in pursuance of the notice a period equal to or longer than that during which the recipient of the notice may appeal against it in pursuance of the following section.

(4)   It is hereby declared that a notice in pursuance of this section in respect of a relevant place may—

   (a)   be served on an owner or occupier of the place notwithstanding that he is for the time being required to comply with a previous notice served on him in pursuance of this section in respect of the place;

   (b)   require the provision at the place of appliances already provided there.

(5)   A person authorised in writing in that behalf by a local authority (other than a county council in England and the Greater London Council) may at any reasonable time, upon producing if so required evidence that he is so authorised, enter any relevant place for the purpose of determining whether the authority should serve a notice in pursuance of this section in respect of the place or of ascertaining whether the requirements of such a notice served on a person who is an owner or occupier of the place are being complied with; and a person who wilfully obstructs another person acting in the exercise of powers conferred on the other person by this subsection shall be guilty of an offence and liable on summary conviction to a fine not exceeding **level 3** on the standard scale.

(6)   Subject to subsections (7) and (8) of this section, a person who without reasonable excuse fails to comply with a notice in respect of a relevant place which was served on him in pursuance of this section when he was an owner or occupier of the place shall be guilty of an offence and liable[3] on summary conviction to a fine not exceeding **the prescribed sum** or, on conviction on indictment, to a fine; and if after the conviction of a person of such an offence the failure in question continues he shall, as respects each day on which it continues, be guilty of a further offence and liable on summary conviction to a fine not exceeding £50 or, on conviction on indictment, to a fine.

(7)   In proceedings for an offence under the preceding subsection of failing to comply with a notice it shall be a defence to prove that at the time of the failure the person on whom the notice was served was neither an owner nor an occupier of the relevant place in question and that he did not cease to be an owner or occupier of it by reason of anything done or omitted by him or any other person with a view to avoiding compliance with the notice.

(8)   In proceedings for an offence under subsection (6) of this section which is alleged to have been committed on a particular day it shall be a defence to prove that on that day the relevant place in question was closed to members of the public or was used neither as a betting office nor for any of the purposes mentioned in paragraph (a) of the definition of relevant place in the following subsection; and in proceedings for an offence under subsection (6) of this section of failing to comply with an occasional notice it shall be a defence to prove—

   (a)   that the alleged offence is in respect of a requirement of the notice which is unreasonable; or

   (b)   that it would have been fairer to serve the notice on a person, other than the defendant—

      (i)   who was an owner or occupier of the relevant place in question when the notice was served on the defendant, and

      (ii)   whose name and address were furnished by the defendant, to the local authority which served the notice, before the expiration of the period specified in the notice in pursuance of subsection (1)(a) of this section.

(9)   In this section and the following section—

"betting office" means premises, other than a track within the meaning of the Gambling Act 2005, in respect of which a betting premises licence under Part 8 of that Act has effect;

"occasional notice" means a notice in pursuance of this section requiring the provision of sanitary appliances on occasions specified in the notice;

"sanitary appliances" means water closets, other closets, urinals and wash basins;

"relevant place" means any of the following places—

   (a)   a place which is normally used or is proposed to be normally used for any of the following purposes, namely—

      (i)   the holding of any entertainment, exhibition or sporting event to which members of the public are admitted either as spectators or otherwise,

  (ii) the sale of food or drink to members of the public for consumption at the place[4];

 (b) a place which is used on some occasion or occasions or is proposed to be used on some occasion or occasions for any of the purposes aforesaid; and

 (c) a betting office.

(10) *Consequential amendment.*

(11) A notice under this section shall draw the attention of the person on whom it is served—

 (a) to sections 6(1) and 7 of the Chronically Sick and Disabled Persons Act 1970; and

 (b) to the Code of Practice for Access for the Disabled to Buildings.

(12) In subsection (11) of this section "the Code of Practice for Access for the Disabled to Buildings" means, subject to subsection (13) of this section, the British Standards Institution code of practice referred to as BS 5810: 1979.

(13) Section 28 of the Chronically Sick and Disabled Persons Act 1970 (power to define certain expressions for the purposes of provisions of that Act) shall have effect as if any reference in it to a provision of that Act included a reference to this section.

[Local Government (Miscellaneous Provisions) Act 1976, s 20 as amended by the Criminal Law Act 1977, s 28, the Disabled Persons Act 1981, s 4, the Criminal Justice Act 1982, ss 38 and 46 and the Gambling Act 2005, Sch 16.]

---

[1] The Greater London Council was abolished by the Local Government Act 1985, s 1.

[2] Defined in sub-s (9), post.

[3] For procedure in respect of this offence which is triable either way, see the Magistrates' Courts Act 1980, ss 17A–21, in PART I: MAGISTRATES' COURTS, PROCEDURE, ante. For liability of director, etc, where offence is committed by a body corporate, see s 44(3), post.

[4] "Normal use" is not the same as "predominant" use; it is "normal" use of premises for a customer to sit down and eat and drink at a seat provided in the premises for such use even though most customers take away their purchases and do not stay long. Where "advice and guidance" has been issued by a "primary authority" in accordance with s 27(1)(b) of the Regulatory Enforcement and Sanctions Act 2008, it must state the law correctly. Any construction of s 20 of the 1976 Act ultimately remains for the court. The discretionary functions under the 1976 Act remain with the authority for the area concerned. It must take the advice very seriously but, as decision-maker, it must satisfy itself that the advice and guidance is satisfactory: *R (Kingston upon Hull City Council) v Secretary of State for Business, Innovation and Skills* [2016] EWHC 1064 (Admin), 181 JP 20.

7.7474 **21.** *Appeal to county court against certain notices under s 20.*

Dangerous trees and excavations

7.7475 **23.** *Power of local authorities to deal with dangerous trees.*

7.7476 **24. Provisions supplementary to section 23** (1) A person authorised in writing in that behalf by such a council as is mentioned in subsection (1)[1] of the preceding section may enter on any land for the purpose of—

 (a) determining whether the council should take steps in pursuance of subsection (2) or (7)[2] or serve a notice in pursuance of subsection (3)[2] of that section in respect of a tree on the land; or

 (b) exercising on behalf of the council a power conferred on the council by subsection (2) or (7)[2] of that section in respect of a tree on the land.

(2) A person authorised to enter on any land in pursuance of the preceding subsection—

 (a) shall, if so required before or after entering on the land, produce evidence of his authority to enter;

 (b) may take with him on to the land such other persons and such equipment as are necessary for achieving the purpose for which he was authorised to enter on the land;

 (c) shall, if the land is unoccupied when he enters or the occupier is then temporarily absent, leave the land as effectually secured against trespassers as he found it.

(3) If a person—

 (a) wilfully obstructs another person in the exercise of a power conferred on the other person by subsection (1) or (2)(b) of this section; or

 (b) while another person is on land in pursuance of the said subsection (1) or (2)(b), wilfully obstructs the other person in doing things connected with the purpose for which the other person is authorised to be on the land,

he shall be guilty of an offence and liable on summary conviction to a fine not exceeding **level 3** on the standard scale.

(4) If a person interested in any land suffers damage by reason of—

 (a) the exercise of the power to enter on the land which is conferred by virtue of subsection (1)(a) of this section; or

 (b) the exercise on the land, in connection with the exercise of the power mentioned in the preceding paragraph, of the power conferred by subsection (2)(b) of this section; or

 (c) a failure to perform the duty imposed by subsection (2)(c) of this section in respect of the land,

he shall be entitled to recover compensation for the damage from the local authority which authorised the entry in question.

(5)–(6) *Compensation for damage; council to recover expenses with interest.*

[Local Government (Miscellaneous Provisions) Act 1976, s 24 amended by the Local Government, Planning and Land Act 1980, Sch 6, the Criminal Justice Act 1982, ss 38 and 46 and SI 2009/1307.]

[1] This means a district council, a London borough council or the Common Council (s 23(1)).

[2] Where a council receives from an owner or occupier of land a notice requesting that it makes safe a tree on other land which is not owned or occupied by that person, and the council considers that the tree is likely to cause damage, and does not know the name and address of the owner or occupier of the other land, it may take steps on the land, by felling or otherwise, to make the tree safe (s 23(2)—*SUMMARISED*). Where a council receives such a request to make a tree safe, and considers the tree is likely to cause damage, and knows the name and address of the owner or occupier of the land, the council may serve on such person a notice requiring him within a specified time to make the tree safe (s 23(3)—*SUMMARISED*). If a person fails to comply with a notice under s 23(3), the council may take the steps specified in the notice and recover from that person the expenses reasonably incurred (s 23(7)—*SUMMARISED*).

7.7477   25.   *Power of certain councils with respect to dangerous excavations.*

7.7478   26.   Provisions supplementary to s 25[1]   (1)   A person authorised in writing in that behalf by such a council as is mentioned in subsection (1)[2] of the preceding section may enter on any land in the area of the council for the purpose of—

    (*a*)   ascertaining whether the land is suitable as the site of works which the council may carry out or for which the council may serve a notice in pursuance of that section[3]; or

    (*b*)   carrying out, maintaining, repairing or removing in pursuance of that section[3] any works on behalf of the council; or

    (*c*)   ascertaining whether any works carried out by the council in pursuance of that section[3] should be or have been maintained, repaired or removed.

(2)   A person authorised by a council to enter on land in pursuance of the preceding subsection—

    (*a*)   shall, if so required before or after entering on the land, produce evidence of his authority to enter;

    (*b*)   may take with him on to the land such other persons and such equipment as are necessary for achieving the purpose for which he was authorised to enter on the land;

    (*c*)   shall, if the land is unoccupied when he enters or the occupier is then temporarily absent, leave the land as effectually secured against trespassers as he found it.

(3)–(4)   *Compensation for damage.*

(5)   If a person—

    (*a*)   wilfully obstructs another person in the exercise of a power conferred on the other person by subsection (1) or (2)(*b*) of this section; or

    (*b*)   while another person is on land in pursuance of the said subsection (2)(*b*) wilfully obstructs him in doing things connected with the works in question; or

    (*c*)   without the agreement of the council by which works have been carried out in pursuance of the preceding section, removes or otherwise interferes with the works,

he shall be guilty of an offence and liable on summary conviction to a fine not exceeding **level 3** on the standard scale.

(6)   Nothing in the preceding section or the preceding provisions of this section applies to an excavation—

    (*a*)   on operational land of statutory undertakers; or

    (*b*)   on land of the Coal Authority of such a description as the Secretary of State may specify by regulations made by statutory instrument;

and the definition of "operational land" in section 263 of the Town and Country Planning Act 1990 shall apply for the purposes of paragraph (*a*) of this subsection as if in that section "statutory undertakers" had the same meaning as in that paragraph and "undertaking" had a corresponding meaning.

[Local Government (Miscellaneous Provisions) Act 1976, s 26, as amended by the Criminal Justice Act 1982, ss 38 and 46, the Coal Industry Act 1987, Sch 1, the Planning (Consequential Provisions) Act 1990, Sch 2 and the Coal Industry Act 1994, Sch 9.]

[1] For the purposes of s 26 of this Act, the holder of a licence under s 6(1) of the Electricity Act 1989 shall be deemed to be a statutory undertaker and his undertaking a statutory undertaking (Electricity Act 1989, Sch 16, para 1).

[2] This means a district council, a London borough council or the Common Council (s 25(1)).

[3] Where a council considers that an excavation on land is accessible to the public from a highway or a place of public resort and, by reason of its being unenclosed or inadequately enclosed, is a danger to the public, and the council does not know the name and address of the owner or occupier of the land on which works to remove the danger should be carried out, the council may carry out on that land works for the purpose of removing the danger (s 25(1)—*SUMMARISED*). Where a council considers that an excavation is as mentioned in s 25(1), and knows the name and address of the owner or occupier of the land on which works to remove the danger should be carried out, the council may serve on the owner or occupier of the land a notice specifying the excavation and stating that the council proposes to carry out works specified in the notice (s 25(2)—*SUMMARISED*).

Miscellaneous

7.7479   35.   Removal of obstructions from private sewers   (1)   If a private sewer is obstructed at a point within the area of a local authority (other than a county council in England), the authority may serve on each of the persons who is an owner or occupier of premises served by the sewer, or on each of such of those persons as the authority thinks fit, a notice requiring the recipients of notices in pursuance of this subsection in respect of the obstruction to remove it before a time specified in the notice; and that time shall not be earlier than forty-eight hours after the service of the notice or, if different notices in respect of the same obstruction are served in pursuance of this subsection at different times, shall not be earlier than forty-eight hours after the latest of those times.

(2)   If an obstruction in respect of which notices have been served by an authority in pursuance of the preceding subsection is not removed within the period specified in the notices, the authority may remove it.

(3)–(6)   *Recovery of expenses incurred in pursuance of subsection* (2).

(7)   Expressions used in this section and in Part II of the Public Health Act 1936 have the same meanings in this section as in that Part; and sections 287 and 288 of that Act[1] (which confer power to enter premises and penalise obstruction) shall have effect as if references to that Act included references to this section.

[Local Government (Miscellaneous Provisions) Act 1976, s 35 as amended by the Local Government Act 1985, Sch 17 and SI 1996/3071.]

---

[1] See title PUBLIC HEALTH, post.

7.7480   36.   *Power of local authorities to appoint times and charges for markets.*

7.7481   41.   Evidence[1] of resolutions and minutes of proceedings etc   (1)   A document which—

(*a*)   purports to be a copy of—

(i)   a resolution, order or report of a local authority or a precursor of a local authority, or

(ii)   the minutes of the proceedings at a meeting of a local authority or a precursor of a local authority; and

(*b*)   bears a certificate purporting to be signed by the proper officer of the authority or a person authorised in that behalf by him or the authority and stating that the resolution was passed or the order or report was made by the authority or precursor on a date specified in the certificate or, as the case may be, that the minutes were signed in accordance with paragraph 41 of Schedule 12 to the Local Government Act 1972 or the corresponding provision specified in the certificate of the enactments relating to local government which were in force when the minutes were signed,

shall be evidence in any proceedings of the matters stated in the certificate and of the terms of the resolution, order, report or minutes in question.

(2)   In the preceding subsection references to a local authority, except the first and second references in paragraph (*b*), include references to a committee of a local authority and a sub-committee of such a committee and references to a precursor of a local authority include references to a committee of such a precursor and a sub-committee of such a committee.

(2A)   In the case of a local authority which are operating executive arrangements, a document which—

(*a*)   purports to be a copy of a record of any decision made by the executive of that authority or a member of that executive, or any person acting on behalf of that executive, where that record is required to be kept or produced by section 22 of the Local Government Act 2000 or any regulations made under that section; and

(*b*)   bears a certificate purporting to be signed by the proper officer of the authority or by a person authorised in that behalf by him or any other person who, by virtue of regulations made under section 22 of the Local Government Act 2000, is authorised or required to produce such a record, stating that the decision was made on the date specified in the certificate by that executive, or as the case may be, by the member of that executive or by the person acting on behalf of that executive,

shall be evidence in any proceedings of the matters stated in the certificate and of the terms of the decision in question.

(2B)   Subsection (2C) applies to a record if—

(*a*)   it records a decision made or action taken by a member of a local authority or of a precursor of a local authority in exercise of a function of the authority or precursor by virtue of arrangements made under section 236 of the Local Government and Public Involvement in Health Act 2007, and

(*b*)   it is required to be made by regulations under section 100EA of the Local Government Act 1972.

(2C)   If a document which purports to be a copy of a record to which this subsection applies bears a certificate—

(*a*)   purporting to be signed by—

(i)   the proper officer of the local authority, or

(ii)   a person authorised in that behalf by that officer or by the local authority, and

(*b*)   stating that the decision was made or the action was taken by the member of the local authority on the date specified in the certificate,

the document shall be evidence in any proceedings of the matters stated in the certificate and of the terms of the decision, or nature of the action, in question.

(3)   A document which—

(*a*)   purports to be a copy of an instrument by which the proper officer of a local authority appointed a person to be an officer of the authority or authorised a person to perform functions specified in the instrument; and

(b)   bears a certificate purporting to be signed as mentioned in subsection (1)(b) of this section and stating that the document is a copy of the instrument in question,

shall be evidence in any proceedings of the fact that the instrument was made by the said proper officer and of the terms of the instrument.

(4)   In the preceding provisions of this section "precursor", in relation to a local authority, means any authority which has ceased to exist but which when it existed was constituted, in pursuance of the enactments relating to local government which were then in force, for an area any part of which is included in the area of the local authority.

[Local Government (Miscellaneous Provisions) Act 1976, s 41 as amended by SI 2001/2237 and the Local Government and Public Involvement in Health Act 2007, s 237.]

---

[1] Note the requirement for strict compliance with s 41(1) when prosecuting an alleged breach of the system of licensing sex establishments (*Smakowski v Westminster City Council* (1989) 154 JP 345).

Supplemental

7.7482   44.   Interpretation etc of Part I   (1)   In this Part of this Act, except where the contrary intention appears—

"apparatus" includes any structure constructed in order that apparatus may be lodged in it;

"the Common Council" means the Common Council of the City of London;

"executive" and "executive arrangements" have the same meaning as in Part II of the Local Government Act 2000;

"functions" includes powers and duties;

"highway" has the same meaning as in the Highways Act 1980[1];

"local Act" includes a provisional order confirmed by an Act;

"local authority" means a county council, a county borough council, a district council, a London borough council, the Common Council, the Council of the Isles of Scilly and—

(a)   in sections 13 to 16, 29, 30, 38, 39 and 41 of this Act, a police and crime commissioner, the Mayor's Office for Policing and Crime, a joint authority established by Part IV of the Local Government Act 1985 an economic prosperity board established under section 88 of the Local Democracy, Economic Development and Construction Act 2009, a combined authority established under section 103 of that Act and the London Fire and Emergency Planning Authority;

(b)   in sections 1, 16, 19, 30, 36, 39 and 41 of this Act, a parish council and a community council;

(c)   in section 40 of this Act, a joint authority established by Part IV of the Local Government Act 1985, an authority established under section 10 of that Act (waste regulation and disposal authorities), an economic prosperity board established under section 88 of the Local Democracy, Economic Development and Construction Act 2009, a combined authority established under section 103 of that Act, the London Fire and Emergency Planning Authority and the South Yorkshire Pensions Authority;

"notice" means notice in writing;

"owner", in relation to any land, place or premises, means a person who, either on his own account or as agent or trustee for another person, is receiving the rackrent of the land, place or premises or would be entitled to receive it if the land, place or premises were let at a rackrent, and "owned" shall be construed accordingly;

"statutory undertakers"[2] means any of the following bodies, namely, any statutory undertakers within the meaning of the Highways Act 1980; and, a universal service provider in connection with the provision of a universal postal service; and

"traffic sign" has the same meaning as in the Road Traffic Regulation Act 1984;

"universal service provider" has the same meaning as in the Postal Services Act 2000; and references to the provision of a universal postal service shall be construed in accordance with that Act.

(1ZA)   The undertaking of a universal service provider so far as relating to the provision of a universal postal service shall be taken to be his statutory undertaking for the purposes of this Part; and references in this Part to his undertaking shall be construed accordingly.

(1A)   Sections 13, 15, 16, 29, 30, 32, 38, 39 and 41 of this Act shall have effect as if the Broads Authority were a local authority and the Broads (as defined in the Norfolk and Suffolk Broads Act 1988) were its local government area.

(1B)   Section 16 of this Act shall have effect as if the Environment Agency were a local authority.

(2)   Section 32[2] of the Highways Act 1980 (which relates to the service of documents) shall apply to the service of any document by or on the Secretary of State in pursuance of section 7 of this Act as if that section were a provision of that Act.

(3)   When an offence under this Part of this Act (including an offence under byelaws made by virtue of section 12 of this Act) which has been committed by a body corporate is proved to have been committed with the consent or connivance of, or to be attributable to any neglect on the part of, any director, manager, secretary or other similar officer of the body corporate or any person who was purporting to act in any such capacity, he as well as the body corporate shall be guilty of that

offence and be liable to be proceeded against and punished accordingly.

Where the affairs of a body corporate are managed by its members the preceding provisions of this subsection shall apply in relation to the acts and defaults of a member in connection with his functions of management as if he were a director of the body corporate.

(4)   Except so far as this Part of this Act expressly provides otherwise and subject to the provisions of section 33 of the Interpretation Act 1889[3] (which relates to offences under two or more laws), nothing in this Part of this Act—

    (a)   confers a right of action in any civil proceedings (other than proceedings for the recovery of a fine) in respect of any contravention of this Part of this Act or an instrument made in pursuance of this Part of this Act;

    (b)   affects any restriction imposed by or under any other enactment, whether public, local or private; or

    (c)   derogates from any right of action or other remedy (whether civil or criminal) in proceedings instituted otherwise than under this Part of this Act.

(5)   Nothing in paragraph (a) of the preceding subsection applies to the failure of a person to perform a duty imposed on him by section 1(4), 2(5), 25(6) or (7)(b) of this Act or section 61(2)(c) of the Road Traffic Regulation Act 1984.

(6)   References in this Part of this Act to any enactment are references to it as amended by or under any other enactment.

[Local Government (Miscellaneous Provisions) Act 1976, s 44 as amended by the Highways Act 1980, Schs 24 and 25, the British Telecommunications Act 1981, Sch 3, the Road Traffic Regulation Act 1984, Sch 13, the Local Government Act 1985, Schs 14 and 17, the Telecommunications Act 1984, Sch 7, the Norfolk and Suffolk Broads Act 1988, Sch 6, the Education Reform Act 1988, Sch 13, the Water Act 1989, Sch 27, SI 1990/1765, the Police and Magistrates' Courts Act 1994, Sch 4, the Environment Act 1995, Sch 22, the Police Act 1996, Sch 7, the Police Act 1997, Sch 6, the Greater London Authority Act 1999, Schs 27, 29 and 34, SI 2001/1149, the Criminal Justice and Police Act 2001, Sch 6, SI 2002/808, the Local Government and Public Involvement in Health Act 2007, Sch 13, the Local Democracy, Economic Development and Construction Act 2009, Sch 6, the Police Reform and Social Responsibility Act 2011, Sch 16 and the Deregulation Act 2015, Sch 13.]

---

[1]   See s 328 of the Highways Act 1980, PART VI: TRANSPORT, title HIGHWAYS.

[2]   The National Rivers Authority, every water undertaker and every sewerage undertaker is deemed to be a statutory undertaker for the purposes of this Act (Water Act 1989, Sch 25, para 1).

[3]   Now s 18 of the Interpretation Act 1978.

PART II[1]
HACKNEY CARRIAGES AND PRIVATE HIRE VEHICLES

7.7483   **45. Application of Part II**   (1)   The provisions of this Part of this Act, except this section, shall come into force in accordance with the following provisions of this section.

(2)   If the Act of 1847[2] is in force in the area of a district council, the council may resolve that the provisions of this Part of this Act, other than this section, are to apply to the relevant area; and if the council do so resolve those provisions shall come into force in the relevant area on the day specified in that behalf in the resolution (which must not be before the expiration of the period of one month beginning with the day on which the resolution is passed).

In this subsection "the relevant area", in relation to a council, means—

    (a)   if the Act of 1847 is in force throughout the area of the council, that area; and

    (b)   if the Act of 1847 is in force for part only of the area of the council, that part of that area.

(3)   A council shall not pass a resolution in pursuance of the foregoing subsection unless they have—

    (a)   published in two consecutive weeks, in a local newspaper circulating in their area, notice of their intention to pass the resolution; and

    (b)   served a copy of the notice, not later than the date on which it is first published in pursuance of the foregoing paragraph, on the council of each parish or community which would be affected by the resolution or, in the case of such a parish which has no parish council, on the chairman of the parish meeting.

(4)   If after a council has passed a resolution in pursuance of subsection (2) of this section the Act of 1847 comes into force for any part of the area of the council for which it was not in force when the council passed the resolution, the council may pass a resolution in accordance with the foregoing provisions of this section in respect of that part as if that part were included in the relevant area for the purposes of subsection (2) of this section.

[Local Government (Miscellaneous Provisions) Act 1976, s 45.]

---

[1]   Part II of this Act amended and extended the controls over hackney carriages under the Town Police Clauses Act 1847, and introduced new powers to control private hire vehicles and their drivers, proprietors and operators. Part II does not apply to London. Sections 1, 2, and 42 of the Public Passenger Vehicles Act 1981, post, provide certain exemptions from the PSV licensing system; it shall however continue to be treated as such for the purposes of a local act or Pt II of this Act (Public Passenger Vehicles Act 1981, s 79, post).

Part II of this Act, to the extent to which it is part of the taxi code, subject to modifications and exceptions, shall apply to a licensed taxi which is being used to provide a local service under a special licence under s 12 of the Transport Act 1985 (Local Services (Operation by Taxis) Regulations 1986, SI 1986/567).

Sections 47, 65(5), 66 and 67 of the Act are modified or disapplied in relation to the hiring of taxis at separate fares under ss 10 and 11 of the Transport Act 1985 (Licensed Taxis (Hiring at Separate Fares) Order 1986, SI 1986/1386).

[2]   "The Act of 1847" means the provisions of the Town Police Clauses Act 1847 with respect to hackney carriages (s 80(1), post). For that Act, see title TOWNS IMPROVEMENTS: TOWN POLICE, post.

7.7484　46.　Vehicle, drivers' and operators' licences　(1)　Except as authorised by this Part of this Act—

> (a)　no person being the proprietor[1] of any vehicle, not being a hackney carriage[1] or London cab in respect of which a vehicle licence[1] is in force, shall use or permit the same to be used in a controlled district[1] as a private hire vehicle[1] without having for such a vehicle a current licence under section 48 of this Act[2];
>
> (b)　no person shall in a controlled district act as driver[3] of any private hire vehicle without having a current licence under section 51 of this Act[4];
>
> (c)　no person being the proprietor of a private hire vehicle licensed under this Part of this Act shall employ as the driver[3] thereof for the purpose of any hiring any person who does not have a current licence under the said section 51;
>
> (d)　no person shall in a controlled district operate[1] any vehicle as a private hire vehicle without having a current licence under section 55 of this Act[5];
>
> (e)　no person licensed under the said section 55 shall in a controlled district operate[1] any vehicle as a private hire vehicle—
>
>> (i)　if for the vehicle a current licence under the said section 48 is not in force; or
>>
>> (ii)　if the driver does not have a current licence under the said section 51[6].

(2)　If any person knowingly contravenes the provisions of this section, he shall be guilty of an offence[7].

[Local Government (Miscellaneous Provisions) Act 1976, s 46 as amended by the Transport Act 1985, Sch 7.]

---

[1]　For meaning of "proprietor", "hackney carriage", "vehicle licence", "controlled district", "operate" and "private hire vehicle", see s 80(1), post. The fact that a vehicle is licensed as a hackney carriage by one local authority does not preclude its being a private hire vehicle in the area of another local authority (*Kingston upon Hull City Council v Wilson* (1995) Times, 25 July). For the purposes of s 46(1)(d) and (e), the meaning of "operate" is that provided in s 80(1), post (*Adur District Council v Fry* [1997] RTR 257). See also *Brentwood Borough Council v Gladen* [2004] EWHC 2500 (Admin), [2005] RTR 12; and *R (on the application of Newcastle City Council) v Berwick-Upon-Tweed Borough Council* [2008] EWHC 2369 (Admin), [2009] RTR 34.)

For the purposes of s 46(1)(d) and (e), the meaning of "operate" is that provided in s 80(1), post (*Adur District Council v Fry* [1997] RTR 257).

It was held in *Stockton-on-Tees Borough Council v Fidler* [2010] EWHC 2430 (Admin), 175 JP 49 that "hackney carriage" in s 80(1) of the 1976 Act, meant a hackney carriage wherever it had been licensed as such. A hackney carriage was always a hackney carriage, no matter what it was doing, or where, and its use, for whatever purpose, could never make it a private hire vehicle in the statutory sense. There were entirely separate and distinct regimes for the licensing of hackney carriages and private hire vehicles, and the regime that regulated private hire vehicles had no application to a vehicle registered as a hackney carriage. The purpose of the 1976 Act was to impose a scheme of licensing on otherwise unlicensed vehicles and their drivers; it was not to impose further regulation on already-regulated hackney carriages. To "operate" within the meaning of the 1976 Act, including for the purposes of ss 46(1)(d) and 46(1)(e) of that Act, was, as the definition of "operate" in s 80(1) made clear, an activity that could have been carried out only in relation to a private hire vehicle as defined by s 80(1) and that definition explicitly excluded a hackney carriage; it was not an activity carried out, or capable of being carried out, in relation to a hackney carriage, however or wherever it was being used. The provision of a hackney carriage for hire together with the services of the driver pursuant to an advance booking was not a licensable activity. It had always been an activity unregulated under any statute.

[2]　Where a hackney carriage, in respect of which a vehicle licence was in force, was used to collect a passenger in a controlled district outside the area of the local authority that had issued the vehicle licence, it was held no offence had been committed (*Britain v ABC Cabs (Camberley) Ltd* [1981] RTR 395).

[3]　A short-staffed licensed operator whose wife drove pre-arranged bookings for no cost was "operating" for the purposes of this section and s 80(1) post and thus liable as his wife was not a licensed driver: (*St Albans District Council v Taylor* [1991] RTR 400, DC).

[4]　Section 46(1)(b) applies to all driving in a controlled district of a vehicle characterised under s 80(1), post, as a private hire vehicle, whatever the specific activity in connection with which the vehicle is in fact being driven. Accordingly, it is no defence in a prosecution under s 46(1)(b) that the vehicle was not actually being used for private hire (*Benson v Boyce* [1997] RTR 226). Section 46(2) requires the prosecution, if it is to establish guilt in relation to s 46(1)(b), to prove that the defendant knew that: (i) he was driving in a controlled district; (ii) the vehicle he was driving was a private hire vehicle; and (iii) at the time, he was not the holder of a driver's licence to drive such a vehicle. Providing knowledge of those three factors is proved, it matters not that the defendant did not appreciate that he was committing an offence (*Reading Borough Council v Ahmad* (1998) 163 JP 451).

[5]　The collection of a passenger within a controlled district in pursuance of a contract for hire made outside the controlled district is not "operating" for the purposes of s 46(1)(d) (*Britain v ABC Cabs (Camberley) Ltd* [1981] RTR 395; followed in *Stockton-on-Tees Borough Council v Fidler*, supra.).

[6]　Section 46(1)(e) must be read subject to the provisions of s 80(2), post, so as to require private hire operators licensed under s 55, post, to make use only of vehicles and drivers licensed by the council of the district by which the operators are licensed when operating in that controlled district (*Dittah v Birmingham City Council* (1993) 157 JP 1110, [1993] RTR 356, [1993] Crim LR 610).

[7]　For penalty, see s 76, post, and note possible defences under s 75, post.

7.7485　47.　Licensing of hackney carriages　(1)　A district council may attach to the grant of a licence of a hackney carriage under the Act of 1847[1] such conditions[2] as the district council may consider reasonably necessary.

(2)　Without prejudice to the generality of the foregoing subsection, a district council may require any hackney carriage licensed by them under the Act of 1847 to be of such design or appearance or bear such distinguishing marks as shall clearly identify it as a hackney carriage.

(3)　Any person aggrieved by any conditions attached to such a licence may appeal[3] to a magistrates' court.

[Local Government (Miscellaneous Provisions) Act 1976, s 47.]

---

[1]　See note 2 to para 7.7483, ante.

[2]　A condition requiring adaptation of vehicles and applying only to new licences is valid (*R v Manchester City Justices,*

ex p McHugh [1989] RTR 285—disabled facilities). Conditions cannot be imposed to restrict new licences to certain parts of the District Council's area; such an approach would create a two-tier system that flew in the face of the legislative approach to remove restraints and to allow market forces to take effect (*R (on the application of Maud) v Castle Point Borough Council* [2002] EWCA Civ 1526, [2002] JPN 782, [2003] RTR 122). However, the wide manner in which s 47 is framed empowers a local authority to attach to a hackney carriage licence any condition it considers to be reasonably necessary to further the objectives of the licensing regime provided for in conjunction with the Town Police Clauses Act 1847; it is desirable in principle that licensing authorities are able to restrict the issue of licences to proprietors and drivers intending to ply for hire in its area and to refuse to license those who do not intend to ply for hire in its area to a material extent; therefore, a condition that the licence holder must ensure that full and contemporaneous records are kept of all uses of the vehicle either as a hackney carriage or as a private hire vehicle, such records would be considered by the local authority when determining annual licence renewal applications, is workable, rational and lawful: *R (Shanks and others (trading as Blue Line Taxis)) v Northumberland County Council* [2012] EWHC 1539 (Admin), (2013) PTSR 154.

    [3] The procedure shall be in accordance with ss 300–302 of the Public Health Act 1936, title PUBLIC HEALTH, post (s 77, post). See also Magistrates' Court's Rules 1981, r 34, in PART I: MAGISTRATES' COURTS Procedure, ante.

7.7486 48. Licensing of private hire vehicles (1) Subject to the provisions of this Part of this Act, a district council may on the receipt of an application from the proprietor[1] of any vehicle for the grant in respect of such vehicle of a licence to use the vehicle as a private hire vehicle[1], grant in respect thereof a vehicle licence:

Provided that a district council shall not grant such a licence unless they are satisfied—
   (*a*)   that the vehicle is—
         (i)   suitable[2] in type, size and design for use as a private hire vehicle;
         (ii)   not of such design and appearance as to lead any person to believe that the vehicle is a hackney carriage;
         (iii)   in a suitable mechanical condition;
         (iv)   safe; and
         (v)   comfortable;
   (*b*)   that there is in force in relation to the use of the vehicle a policy of insurance or such security as complies with the requirements of Part VI of the Road Traffic Act 1988,

and shall not refuse such a licence for the purpose of limiting the number of vehicles in respect of which such licences are granted by the council.

    (2) A district council may attach to the grant of a licence under this section such conditions as they may consider reasonably necessary[3] including, without prejudice to the generality of the foregoing provisions of this subsection, conditions requiring or prohibiting the display of signs on or from the vehicle to which the licence relates.

    (3) In every vehicle licence granted under this section there shall be specified—
   (*a*)   The name and address of—
         (i)   the applicant; and
         (ii)   every other person who is a proprietor of the private hire vehicle in respect of which the licence is granted, or who is concerned, either solely or in partnership with any other person, in the keeping, employing or letting on hire of the private hire vehicle;
   (*b*)   the number of the licence which shall correspond with the number to be painted or marked on the plate or disc to be exhibited on the private hire vehicle in accordance with subsection (6) of this section;
   (*c*)   the conditions attached to the grant of the licence; and
   (*d*)   such other particulars as the district council consider reasonably necessary.

    (4) Every licence granted under this section shall—
   (*a*)   be signed by an authorised officer[4] of the council which granted it;
   (*b*)   relate to not more than one private hire vehicle; and
   (*c*)   remain in force for such period not being longer than one year as the district council may specify in the licence.

    (5) Where a district council grant under this section a vehicle licence in respect of a private hire vehicle they shall issue a plate or disc identifying that vehicle as a private hire vehicle in respect of which a vehicle licence has been granted.

    (6)
   (*a*)   Subject to the provisions of this Part of this Act, no person shall use or permit to be used in a controlled district as a private hire vehicle a vehicle in respect of which a licence has been granted under this section unless the plate or disc issued in accordance with subsection (5) of this section is exhibited on the vehicle in such manner as the district council shall prescribe by condition attached to the grant of the licence.
   (*b*)   If any person without reasonable excuse contravenes the provisions of this subsection he shall be guilty of an offence[5].

    (7) Any person aggrieved[6] by the refusal of a district council to grant a vehicle licence under this section, or by any conditions specified in such a licence, may appeal[7] to a magistrates' court.

    [Local Government (Miscellaneous Provisions) Act 1976, s 48 as amended by the Road Traffic (Consequential Provisions) Act 1988, Sch 3.]

_____

    [1] See note 1 to para 7.7484, ante.
    [2] Safety of the vehicle for use as a private hire vehicle is part of the suitability for such proposed use. "Safe" in para (iv) might refer to whether the vehicle, suitable in other respects, is safe in the sense, for example, that its components are not defective (*Chauffeur Bikes v Leeds City Council* [2005] EWHC 2369 (Admin), 170 JP 24).
    [3] A condition which prohibited a private hire vehicle to stand in any public place other than in connection with a

pre-arranged booking was held to be beyond the purpose envisaged by the statute and to be unenforceable, or alternatively, not "reasonably necessary" (*R v Blackpool Borough Council, ex p Red Cab Taxis Ltd* (1994) 158 JP 1069).

[4] For meaning of "authorised officer", see s 80(1), post.

[5] For penalty, see s 76, post.

[6] A hackney carriage licence holder may be a 'person aggrieved' by a condition imposed on private hire vehicles (*R v Swansea City and County, ex p Davies* [2001] RTR 54, (2000) Times, 7 July, DC).

[7] The procedure shall be in accordance with ss 300–302 of the Public Health Act 1936, title Public Health, post (s 77, post). See also Magistrates' Courts Rules 1981, r 34, in Part I: Magistrates' Courts Procedure, ante. The size and design of a licence disc or plate cannot be the subject of an appeal, the only exemptions from display are contained in s 75, post, the nature of the appellant's business is irrelevant to the appeal (*Solihull Metropolitan Borough Council v Silverline Cars* (1988) 153 JP 209, [1989] RTR 142 DC).

7.7487 49. Transfer of hackney carriages and private hire vehicles (1) If the proprietor[1] of a hackney carriage[1] or of a private hire vehicle[1] in respect of which a vehicle licence has been granted by a district council transfers his interest in the hackney carriage or private hire vehicle to a person other than the proprietor whose name is specified in the licence, he shall within fourteen days after such transfer give notice in writing thereof to the district council specifying the name and address of the person to whom the hackney carriage or private hire vehicle has been transferred.

(2) If a proprietor without reasonable excuse fails to give notice to a district council as provided by subsection (1) of this section he shall be guilty of an offence[2].

[Local Government (Miscellaneous Provisions) Act 1976, s 49.]

[1] For meaning of "proprietor", "hackney carriage" and "private hire vehicle", see s 80(1), post.

[2] For penalty, see s 76 post.

7.7488 50. Provisions as to proprietors (1) Without prejudice to the provisions of section 68 of this Act, the proprietor[1] of any hackney carriage[1] or of any private hire vehicle[1] licensed by a district council shall present such hackney carriage or private hire vehicle for inspection and testing by or on behalf of the council within such period and at such place within the area of the council as they may by notice reasonably require:

Provided that a district council shall not under the provisions of this subsection require a proprietor to present the same hackney carriage or private hire vehicle for inspection and testing on more than three separate occasions during any one period of twelve months.

(2) The proprietor of any hackney carriage or private hire vehicle—

(a) licensed by a district council under the Act of 1847[2] or under this Part of this Act; or

(b) in respect of which an application for a licence has been made to a district council under the Act of 1847 or under this Part of this Act;

shall, within such period as the district council may by notice reasonably require, state in writing the address of every place where such hackney carriage or private hire vehicle is kept when not in use, and shall if the district council so require afford to them such facilities as may be reasonably necessary to enable them to cause such hackney carriage or private hire vehicle to be inspected and tested there.

(3) Without prejudice to the provisions of section 170 of the Road Traffic Act 1988, the proprietor of a hackney carriage or of a private hire vehicle licensed by a district council shall report to them as soon as reasonably practicable, and in any case within seventy-two hours of the occurrence thereof, any accident to such hackney carriage or private hire vehicle causing damage materially affecting the safety, performance or appearance of the hackney carriage or private hire vehicle or the comfort or convenience of persons carried therein.

(4) The proprietor of any hackney carriage or of any private hire vehicle licensed by a district council shall at the request of any authorised officer[3] of the council produce for inspection the vehicle, licence for such hackney carriage or private hire vehicle and the certificate of the policy of insurance or security required by Part VI of the Road Traffic Act 1988 in respect of such hackney carriage or private hire vehicle.

(5) If any person without reasonable excuse contravenes the provisions of this section, he shall be guilty of an offence[4].

[Local Government (Miscellaneous Provisions) Act 1976, s 50 amended by the Road Traffic (Consequential Provisions) Act 1988, Sch 3.]

[1] For meaning of "proprietor", "hackney carriage" and "private hire vehicle", see s 80(1), post.

[2] "The Act of 1847" means the provisions of the Town Police Clauses Act 1847 with respect to hackney carriages (s 80(1), post). For that Act, see title Towns Improvements: Town Police, post.

[3] For meaning of "authorised officer", see s 80(1), post.

[4] See note 4 to para 7.7486, ante.

7.7489 51. Licensing of drivers of private hire vehicles (1) Subject to the provisions of this Part of this Act, a district council shall, on the receipt of an application from any person for the grant to that person of a licence to drive private hire vehicles, grant to that person a driver's licence:

Provided that a district council shall not grant a licence—

(a) unless they are satisfied—

(i) that the applicant is a fit and proper person to hold a driver's licence; and

(ii) that the applicant is not disqualified by reason of the applicant's immigration status from driving a private hire vehicle; or

(b) to any person who has not for at least twelve months[1] been authorised to drive a motor car, or is not at the date of the application for a driver's licence so authorised.

(1)   For the purposes of subsection (1) of this section a person is authorised to drive a motor car if—

(a)   he holds a licence granted under Part III of the Road Traffic Act 1988 (not being a provisional licence) authorising him to drive a motor car, or

(b)   he is authorised by virtue of section 99A(1) or section 109(1) of that Act to drive in Great Britain a motor car.*

(1ZA)   In determining for the purposes of subsection (1) whether an applicant is disqualified by reason of the applicant's immigration status from driving a private hire vehicle, a district council must have regard to any guidance issued by the Secretary of State.

(2)   A district council may attach to the grant of a licence under this section such conditions as they may consider reasonably necessary[2].

(3)   It shall be the duty of a council by which licences are granted in pursuance of this section to enter, in a register maintained by the council for the purpose, the following particulars of each such licence, namely—

(a)   the name of the person to whom it is granted;

(b)   the date on which and the period for which it is granted; and

(c)   if the licence has a serial number, that number,

and to keep the register available at its principal offices for inspection by members of the public during office hours free of charge.

[Local Government (Miscellaneous Provisions) Act 1976, s 51 amended by the Road Traffic (Consequential Provisions) Act 1988, Sch 3, the Road Traffic Act 1991, s 47, SI 1996/1974, the Police Act 1997, Sch 9, SI 1998/1946 and the Immigration Act 2016, Sch 5.]

---

* **It would appear that this subsection has been numbered incorrectly by the amending SI 1996/1974.**
[1] A person who has held a licence for 12 months in the past, and does in fact hold a licence at the date of the application, is entitled to qualify, notwithstanding that there is no continuity between the two periods (*Crawley Borough Council v Crabb* [1996] RTR 201).
[2] See note 2 to s 48(2) in para 7.7486.

7.7490   52.   Appeals in respect of drivers' licences   Any person aggrieved[1] by—

(1)   the refusal of the district council to grant a driver's licence under section 51 of this Act; or

(2)   any conditions attached to the grant of a driver's licence;

may appeal[2] to a magistrates' court.

[Local Government (Miscellaneous Provisions) Act 1976, s 52.]

---

[1] A person is not a "person aggrieved" and cannot bring an appeal under this section unless he has applied for a licence and his application has been refused or granted with conditions and he is aggrieved by that refusal or with those conditions: *Peddubrivny v Cambridge City Council* [2001] EWHC Admin 200, [2001] RTR 461.
[2] See note 2 to para 7.7501, post. Where the holder of a driver's licence in this application for renewal of the licence failed to give details of his conviction, it was held, on an appeal against the refusal of the district council to renew the licence, that the justices in determining whether the appellant was a fit and proper person had to consider whether the false statement was made knowingly or recklessly, in such circumstances, it was not permissible for the justices to review the question of whether or not the convictions recorded in earlier criminal proceedings were incorrectly arrived at (*Nottingham City Council v Farooq* (1998) Times, 28 October). In determining whether a person is "fit and proper" justices are entitled to rely on any evidential material which might reasonably and properly influence the making of a responsible judgment in good faith. Some evidence such as gossip, speculation and hearsay, might by its source, nature and inherent probability carry a greater degree of credibility. The civil standard of proof applies and in seeking to rebut the applicant's contention that he is a fit and proper person the onus on the local authority is to do this on the civil standard of proof even if the substance of what they seek to prove amounts to a criminal offence. (*McCool v Rushcliffe Borough Council* (1998) 163 JP 46, DC).

7.7491   53.   Drivers' licences for hackney carriages and private hire vehicles   (1)

(a)   Subject to section 53A, every licence granted by a district council under the provisions of this Part of this Act to any person to drive a private hire vehicle[1] shall remain in force for three years from the date of such licence or for such lesser period, specified in the licence, as the district council think appropriate in the circumstances of the case.

(b)   Notwithstanding the provisions of the Public Health Act 1875 and the Town Police Clauses Act 1889, but subject to section 53A, every licence granted by a district council under the provisions of the Act of 1847[2] to any person to drive a hackney carriage[1] shall remain in force for three years from the date of such licence or for such lesser period, specified in the licence, as the district council think appropriate in the circumstances of the case.

(2)   Notwithstanding the provisions of the Act of 1847, a district council may demand and recover for the grant to any person of a licence to drive a hackney carriage, or a private hire vehicle, as the case may be, such a fee as they consider reasonable with a view to recovering the costs of issue and administration[3] and may remit the whole or part of the fee in respect of a private hire vehicle in any case in which they think it appropriate to do so.

(3)   The driver of any hackney carriage or of any private hire vehicle licensed by a district council shall at the request of any authorised officer[1] of the council or of any constable produce for inspection his driver's licence either forthwith or—

(a)   in the case of a request by an authorised officer, at the principal offices of the council before the expiration of the period of five days beginning with the day following that on which the request is made;

(b)   in the case of a request by a constable, before the expiration of the period aforesaid at any police station which is within the area of the council and is nominated by the driver when the request is made.

(4)   If any person without reasonable excuse contravenes the provisions of this section, he shall be guilty of an offence[4].

[Local Government (Miscellaneous Provisions) Act, 1976, s 53 as amended by the Deregulation Act 2015, s 10 and the Immigration Act 2016, Sch 5.]

---

[1]   For meaning of "private hire vehicle", "hackney carriage", and "authorised officer", see s 80(1), post.
[2]   See note 2 to para 7.7488, ante.
[3]   The fee to be charged for the licensing of private hire vehicles cannot include an element for monitoring and undertaking enforcement action against drivers, but may be recovered under s 52(2) of the Local Government (Miscellaneous Provisions) Act 1976 as part of 'the costs of issue and administration': *Regina (Rehman) v City of Wakefield Council (Local Government Association intervening)* [2019] EWCA Civ 2166.
[3]   For penalty, see s 76, post.

---

[4]   The fee to be charged for the licensing of private hire vehicles cannot include an element for monitoring and undertaking enforcement action against drivers, but may be recovered under s 52(2) of the Local Government (Miscellaneous Provisions) Act 1976 as part of 'the costs of issue and administration': *Regina (Rehman) v City of Wakefield Council (Local Government Association intervening)* [2019] EWCA Civ 2166.

7.7492   53A.   Drivers'   licences   for   persons   subject   to   immigration   control
(1)   Subsection (2) applies if—
    (a)   a licence within section 53(1)(a) or (b) is to be granted to a person who has been granted leave to enter or remain in the United Kingdom for a limited period ("the leave period");
    (b)   the person's leave has not been extended by virtue of section 3C of the Immigration Act 1971 (continuation of leave pending variation decision); and
    (c)   apart from subsection (2), the period for which the licence would have been in force would have ended after the end of the leave period.
(2)   The district council which grants the licence must specify a period in the licence as the period for which it remains in force; and that period must end at or before the end of the leave period.
(3)   Subsection (4) applies if—
    (a)   a licence within section 53(1)(a) or (b) is to be granted to a person who has been granted leave to enter or remain in the United Kingdom for a limited period; and
    (b)   the person's leave has been extended by virtue of section 3C of the Immigration Act 1971 (continuation of leave pending variation decision).
(4)   The district council which grants the licence must specify a period in the licence as the period for which it remains in force; and that period must not exceed six months.
(5)   A licence within section 53(1)(a) ceases to be in force if the person to whom it was granted becomes disqualified by reason of the person's immigration status from driving a private hire vehicle.
(6)   A licence within section 53(1)(b) ceases to be in force if the person to whom it was granted becomes disqualified by reason of the person's immigration status from driving a hackney carriage.
(7)   If a licence granted in accordance with subsection (2) or (4) expires, the person to whom it was granted must, within the period of 7 days beginning with the day after that on which it expired, return the licence and the person's driver's badge to the district council which granted the licence.
(8)   If subsection (5) or (6) applies to a licence, the person to whom it was granted must, within the period of 7 days beginning with the day after the day on which the person first became disqualified, return the licence and the person's driver's badge to the district council which granted the licence.
(9)   A person who, without reasonable excuse, contravenes subsection (7) or (8) is guilty of an offence and liable on summary conviction—
    (a)   to a fine not exceeding level 3 on the standard scale; and
    (b)   in the case of a continuing offence, to a fine not exceeding ten pounds for each day during which an offence continues after conviction.
(10)   The Secretary of State may by regulations made by statutory instrument amend the amount for the time being specified in subsection (9)(b).
(11)   Regulations under subsection (10) may make transitional, transitory or saving provision.
(12)   A statutory instrument containing regulations under subsection (10) may not be made unless a draft of the instrument has been laid before, and approved by a resolution of, each House of Parliament.

[Local Government (Miscellaneous Provisions) Act, 1976, s 53A as inserted by the Immigration Act 2016, Sch 5.]

7.7493   54.   Issue of drivers' badges   (1)   When granting a driver's licence under section 51 of this Act a district council shall issue a driver's badge in such a form as may from time to time be prescribed by them.
(2)
    (a)   A driver shall at all times when acting in accordance with the driver's licence granted to him wear such badge in such position and manner as to be plainly and distinctly visible.
    (b)   If any person without reasonable excuse contravenes the provisions of this subsection, he shall be guilty of an offence[1].

[Local Government (Miscellaneous Provisions) Act 1976, s 54.]

---

[1] For penalty, see s 76, post.

7.7494   55. Licensing of operators of private hire vehicles   (1)   Subject to the provisions of this Part of this Act, a district council shall, on receipt of an application from any person for the grant to that person of a licence to operate private hire vehicles grant to that person an operator's licence:

Provided that a district council shall not grant a licence unless they are satisfied—

(a)   that the applicant is a fit and proper person to hold an operator's licence;

(b)   if the applicant is an individual, that the applicant is not disqualified by reason of the applicant's immigration status from operating a private hire vehicle.

(1A)   In determining for the purposes of subsection (1) whether an applicant is disqualified by reason of the applicant's immigration status from operating a private hire vehicle, a district council must have regard to any guidance issued by the Secretary of State.

(2)   Subject to section 55ZA, every licence granted under this section shall remain in force for five years or for such lesser period, specified in the licence, as the district council think appropriate in the circumstances of the case.

(3)   A district council may attach to the grant of a licence under this section such conditions as they may consider reasonably necessary[1].

(4)   Any applicant aggrieved by the refusal of a district council to grant an operator's licence under this section, or by any conditions attached to the grant of such a licence, may appeal[2] to a magistrates' court.

[Local Government (Miscellaneous Provisions) Act 1976, s 55 as amended by the Deregulation Act 2015, s 10.]

---

[1] See note 2 to s 48(2) at para 7.7486, ante.
[2] See note 5 to para 7.7486, ante.

7.7495   55ZA. Operators' licences for persons subject to immigration control
(1)   Subsection (2) applies if—

(a)   a licence under section 55 is to be granted to a person who has been granted leave to enter or remain in the United Kingdom for a limited period ("the leave period");

(b)   the person's leave has not been extended by virtue of section 3C of the Immigration Act 1971 (continuation of leave pending variation decision); and

(c)   apart from subsection (2), the period for which the licence would have been in force would have ended after the end of the leave period.

(2)   The district council which grants the licence must specify a period in the licence as the period for which it remains in force; and that period must end at or before the end of the leave period.

(3)   Subsection (4) applies if—

(a)   a licence under section 55 is to be granted to a person who has been granted leave to enter or remain in the United Kingdom for a limited period; and

(b)   the person's leave has been extended by virtue of section 3C of the Immigration Act 1971 (continuation of leave pending variation decision).

(4)   The district council which grants the licence must specify a period in the licence as the period for which it remains in force; and that period must not exceed six months.

(5)   A licence under section 55 ceases to be in force if the person to whom it was granted becomes disqualified by reason of the person's immigration status from operating a private hire vehicle.

(6)   If a licence granted in accordance with subsection (2) or (4) expires, the person to whom it was granted must, within the period of 7 days beginning with the day after that on which it expired, return the licence to the district council which granted the licence.

(7)   If subsection (5) applies to a licence, the person to whom it was granted must, within the period of 7 days beginning with the day after the day on which the person first became disqualified, return it to the district council which granted the licence.

(8)   A person who, without reasonable excuse, contravenes subsection (6) or (7) is guilty of an offence and liable on summary conviction—

(a)   to a fine not exceeding level 3 on the standard scale; and

(b)   in the case of a continuing offence, to a fine not exceeding ten pounds for each day during which an offence continues after conviction.

(9)   The Secretary of State may by regulations made by statutory instrument amend the amount for the time being specified in subsection (8)(b).

(10)   Regulations under subsection (9) may make transitional, transitory or saving provision.

(11)   A statutory instrument containing regulations under subsection (9) may not be made unless a draft of the instrument has been laid before, and approved by a resolution of, each House of Parliament.

[Local Government (Miscellaneous Provisions) Act 1976, s 55ZA as inserted by the Immigration Act 2016, Sch 5.]

7.7496   55A. Sub-contracting by operators   (1)   A person licensed under section 55 who has in a controlled district accepted a booking for a private hire vehicle may arrange for another person to provide a vehicle to carry out the booking if—

(a)   the other person is licensed under section 55 in respect of the same controlled district and the sub-contracted booking is accepted in that district;

(b)   the other person is licensed under section 55 in respect of another controlled district and the sub-contracted booking is accepted in that district[1];

(c)   the other person is a London PHV operator and the sub-contracted booking is accepted at an operating centre in London; or

(d)   the other person accepts the sub-contracted booking in Scotland.

(2)   It is immaterial for the purposes of subsection (1) whether or not sub-contracting is permitted by the contract between the person licensed under section 55 who accepted the booking and the person who made the booking.

(3)   Where a person licensed under section 55 in respect of a controlled district is also licensed under that section in respect of another controlled district, subsection (1) (so far as relating to paragraph (b) of that subsection) and section 55B(1) and (2) apply as if each licence were held by a separate person.

(4)   Where a person licensed under section 55 in respect of a controlled district is also a London PHV operator, subsection (1) (so far as relating to paragraph (c) of that subsection) and section 55B(1) and (2) apply as if the person holding the licence under section 55 and the London PHV operator were separate persons.

(5)   Where a person licensed under section 55 in respect of a controlled district also makes provision in the course of a business for the invitation or acceptance of bookings for a private hire car or taxi in Scotland, subsection (1) (so far as relating to paragraph (d) of that subsection) and section 55B(1) and (2) apply as if the person holding the licence under section 55 and the person making the provision in Scotland were separate persons.

In this subsection, "private hire car" and "taxi" have the same meaning as in sections 10 to 22 of the Civic Government (Scotland) Act 1982.

(6)   In this section, "London PHV operator" and "operating centre" have the same meaning as in the Private Hire Vehicles (London) Act 1998.

[Local Government (Miscellaneous Provisions) Act 1976, s 55A as inserted by the Deregulation Act 2015, s 11.]

---

[1] *In Milton Keynes Council v Skyline Taxis and Private Hire Ltd* [2017] EWHC 2794 (Admin), [2018] LL7 73 a private hire operator (R1) and its director (R2) held licences in neighbouring licensing authorities, operating in one in the name Skyline SNC and in the other as Skyline MK. The two entities shared the same unitary computer system. The prosecution was brought in consequence of Skyline MK taking a booking and allocating it to Skyline SNC, ie to a driver and vehicle not licensed by the appellant local authority but to a neighbouring one. The issue was whether or not this fell within s 55A, in which case there was no offence. At first instance the charges were dismissed on the ground that the prosecutor had failed to prove that the booking had not been "subcontracted".

The decision was upheld in the subsequent appeal by way of case stated. The prosecutor had contended that s 55A required that the two operators had separate controlling minds and that there had to be a positive decision by the sub-contractor to accept the booking. The Administrative Court disagreed. Section 55A(3) required the matter to be approached on the basis that the operator's licences were held by separate persons. The scheme R1 and R2 had adopted fulfilled the obvious purpose of s 55A. The provisions clearly contemplated a single operator having multiple licences in different areas. Section 55A(1)(b) was focused on the district in which the sub-contracted booking was accepted. It mattered not that the initial acceptance happened in a different area. The integrity of the scheme required that the second operator accepted the booking as one made in the district in which that operator held its licence, so that the booking would be subject to that licence.'

7.7497   55B.   Sub-contracting by operators: criminal liability   (1)   In this section—

"the first operator" means a person licensed under section 55 who has in a controlled district accepted a booking for a private hire vehicle and then made arrangements for another person to provide a vehicle to carry out the booking in accordance with section 55A(1);

"the second operator" means the person with whom the first operator made the arrangements (and, accordingly, the person who accepted the sub-contracted booking).

(2)   The first operator is not to be treated for the purposes of section 46(1)(e) as operating a private hire vehicle by virtue of having invited or accepted the booking.

(3)   The first operator is guilty of an offence if—

(a)   the second operator is a person mentioned in section 55A(1)(a) or (b),

(b)   the second operator contravenes section 46(1)(e) in respect of the sub-contracted booking, and

(c)   the first operator knew that the second operator would contravene section 46(1)(e) in respect of the booking.

[Local Government (Miscellaneous Provisions) Act 1976, s 55B as inserted by the Deregulation Act 2015, s 11.]

7.7498   56.   Operators of private hire vehicles   (1)   For the purposes of this Part of this Act every contract for the hire of a private hire vehicle licensed under this Part of this Act shall be deemed to be made with the operator who accepted the booking for that vehicle whether or not he himself provided the vehicle.

(2)   Every person to whom a licence in force under section 55 of this Act has been granted by a district council shall keep a record in such form as the council may, by condition attached to the grant of the licence, prescribe and shall enter therein, before the commencement of each journey, such particulars of every booking of a private hire vehicle invited or accepted by him, whether by accepting the same from the hirer or by undertaking it at the request of another operator, as the district council may by condition prescribe and shall produce such record on request to any

authorised officer[1] of the council or to any constable for inspection.

(3)   Every person to whom a licence in force under section 55 of this Act has been granted by a district council shall keep such records as the council may, by conditions attached to the grant of the licence, prescribe of the particulars of any private hire vehicle operated by him and shall produce the same on request to any authorised officer of the council or to any constable for inspection.

(4)   A person to whom a licence in force under section 55 of this Act has been granted by a district council shall produce the licence on request to any authorised officer of the council or any constable for inspection.

(5)   If any person without reasonable excuse contravenes the provisions of this section, he shall be guilty of an offence[2].

[Local Government (Miscellaneous Provisions) Act 1976, s 56.]

---

[1]   For meaning of "authorised officer", see s 80(1), post.
[2]   For penalty, see s 76, post.

7.7499 57.   Power to require applicants to submit information   (1)   A district council may require any applicant for a licence under the Act of 1847[1] or under this Part of this Act to submit to them such information as they may reasonably consider necessary to enable them to determine whether the licence should be granted and whether conditions should be attached to any such licence.

(2)   Without prejudice to the generality of the foregoing subsection—

(a)   a district council may require an applicant for a driver's licence[2] in respect of a hackney carriage[2] or a private hire vehicle[2]—

(i)   to produce a certificate signed by a registered medical practitioner to the effect that he is physically fit to be the driver of a hackney carriage or a private hire vehicle; and

(ii)   whether or not such a certificate has been produced, to submit to examination by a registered medical practitioner selected by the district council as to his physical fitness to be the driver of a hackney carriage or a private hire vehicle;

(b)   a district council may require an applicant for an operator's licence to submit to them such information as to—

(i)   the name and address of the applicant;

(ii)   the address or addresses whether within the area of the council or not from which he intends to carry on business in connection with private hire vehicles licensed under this Part of this Act;

(iii)   any trade or business activities he has carried on before making the application;

(iv)   any previous application he has made for an operator's licence;

(v)   the revocation or suspension of any operator's licence previously held by him;

(vi)   any convictions recorded against the applicant;

as they may reasonably consider necessary to enable them to determine whether to grant such licence;

(c)   in addition to the information specified in paragraph (b) of this subsection, a district council may require an applicant for an operator's licence[3] to submit to them—

(i)   if the applicant is or has been a director or secretary of a company, information as to any convictions recorded against that company at any relevant time; any trade or business activities carried on by that company; any previous application made by that company for an operator's licence; and any revocation or suspension of an operator's licence previously held by that company;

(ii)   if the applicant is a company, information as to any convictions recorded against a director or secretary of that company; any trade or business activities carried on by any such director or secretary; any previous application made by any such director or secretary for an operator's licence; and any revocation or suspension of an operator's licence previously held by such director or secretary;

(iii)   if the applicant proposes to operate the vehicle in partnership with any other person, information as to any convictions recorded against that person; any trade or business activities carried on by that person; any previous application made by that person for an operator's licence; and any revocation or suspension of an operator's licence previously held by him.

(3)   If any person knowingly or recklessly makes a false statement or omits any material particular in giving information under this section, he shall be guilty of an offence[4].

[Local Government (Miscellaneous Provisions) Act 1976, s 57.]

---

[1]   "The Act of 1847" means the provisions of the Town Police Clauses Act 1847 with respect to hackney carriages (s 80(1), post). For that Act, see title TOWNS IMPROVEMENTS: TOWN POLICE, post.
[2]   For meaning of "driver's licence", "hackney carriage" and "private hire vehicle", see s 80(1), post.
[3]   "Operator's licence" means a licence under s 55 of this Act (s 80(1), post).
[4]   For penalty, see s 76, post.

7.7500 58.   Return of identification plate or disc on revocation or expiry of licence etc
(1)   On—

    (a)   the revocation or expiry of a vehicle licence[1] in relation to a hackney carriage[1] or private hire vehicle[1]; or

    (b)   the suspension of a licence under section 68 of this Act;

a district council may by notice require the proprietor of that hackney carriage or private hire vehicle licensed by them to return to them within seven days after the service on him of the notice the plate or disc which—

    (a)   in the case of a hackney carriage, is required to be affixed to the carriage as mentioned in section 38 of the Act of 1847; and

    (b)   in the case of a private hire vehicle, was issued for the vehicle under section 48(5) of this Act.

(2)   If any proprietor[1] fails without reasonable excuse to comply with the terms of a notice under subsection (1) of this section—

    (a)   he shall be guilty of an offence and liable on summary conviction to a fine not exceeding **level 3** on the standard scale and to a daily fine[1] not exceeding **£10**; and

    (b)   any authorised officer[1] of the council or constable shall be entitled to remove and retain the said plate or disc from the said hackney carriage or private hire vehicle.

[Local Government (Miscellaneous Provisions) Act 1976, s 58, as amended by the Criminal Justice Act 1982, ss 38 and 46.]

---

[1] For meaning of "vehicle licence", "hackney carriage", "private hire vehicle", "proprietor", "daily fine" and "authorised officer", see s 80(1), post.

7.7501   59.   Qualifications for drivers of hackney carriages   (1) Notwithstanding anything in the Act of 1847[1], a district council shall not grant a licence to drive a hackney carriage—

    (a)   unless they are satisfied—

        (i)   that the applicant is a fit and proper person[2] to hold a driver's licence; and

        (ii)   that the applicant is not disqualified by reason of the applicant's immigration status from driving a hackney carriage; or

    (b)   to any person who has not for at least twelve months been authorised to drive a motor car, or is not at the date of the application for a driver's licence so authorised.

(1ZA)   In determining for the purposes of subsection (1) whether an applicant is disqualified by reason of the applicant's immigration status from driving a hackney carriage, a district council must have regard to any guidance issued by the Secretary of State.

(1A)   For the purposes of subsection (1) of this section a person is authorised to drive a motor car if—

    (a)   he holds a licence granted under Part III of the Road Traffic Act 1988 (not being a provisional licence) authorising him to drive a motor car, or

    (b)   he is authorised by virtue of section 99A(1) or section 109(1) of that Act to drive in Great Britain a motor car.

(2)   Any applicant aggrieved by the refusal of a district council to grant a driver's licence on the ground that he is not a fit and proper person to hold such licence may appeal[3] to a magistrates' court.

[Local Government (Miscellaneous Provisions) Act 1976, s 59 amended by the Road Traffic (Consequential Provisions) Act 1988, Sch 3, the Road Traffic Act 1991, s 47, SI 1996/1974, the Police Act 1997, Sch 9, SI 1998/1946 and the Immigration Act 2016, Sch 5.]

---

[1] See note 1 to para 7.7499, ante.

[2] A local authority is entitled in considering whether a person is a fit and proper person to hold a licence to have regard to that person's standard of driving, and to adopt, following proper consultation, a policy to apply in the generality of cases that it will not to regard as fit and proper somebody who has not passed the Driving Standards Agency taxi driver test: *Darlington Borough Council v Kaye* [2004] EWHC (Admin) 2836, [2005] RTR 14.

    When deciding, exceptionally, to admit spent convictions under s 7(3) of the Rehabilitation of Offenders Act 1974 (in PART III: SENTENCING, ante) the local authority or justices hearing an appeal should first identify the issue before them to which those convictions must relate. The party furnishing the spent convictions should consider objectively whether any are relevant to that issue, and give a broad indication of the nature, age and seriousness of the offence. The justices will then consider whether to admit some or all of the convictions in the light of the issue before them. Once some or all of the convictions have been admitted, the applicant is entitled to be heard and make representations to persuade the local authority or the justices of the irrelevancy of those convictions to the issue before them (*Adamson v Waveney District Council* [1997] 2 All ER 898, 161 JP 787, DC).

[3] The procedure shall be in accordance with ss 300–302 of the Public Health Act 1936, title PUBLIC HEALTH, post (s 77, post). See also Magistrates' Courts Rules 1981, r 34, in PART I, ante. The appeal is by way of a complete rehearing (*Darlington Borough Council v Wakefield* (1989) 153 JP 481). However, the justices must have regard to the policy of the local authority and should not lightly reverse the authority's decision: *Cherwell District Council v Anwar* [2011] EWHC 2943 (Admin), [2012] RTR 15. The personal circumstances of the appellant are irrelevant, save, perhaps, in very rare cases to explain or excuse some conduct of the driver: *Leeds City Council v Hussain* [2002] EWHC 1145 (Admin), [2003] RTR 199. However, the justices must have regard to the policy of the local authority and should not lightly reverse the authority's decision: *Cherwell District Council v Anwar* [2011] EWHC 2943 (Admin), [2012] RTR 15. The personal circumstances of the appellant are irrelevant, save, perhaps, in very rare cases to explain or excuse some conduct of the driver: *Leeds City Council v Hussain* [2002] EWHC 1145 (Admin), [2003] RTR 199.

7.7502   60.   Suspension and revocation of vehicle licences   (1) Notwithstanding anything in the Act of 1847[1] or in this Part of this Act, a district council may suspend or revoke, or (on application therefor under section 40 of the Act of 1847 or section 48 of this Act, as the case may be) refuse to renew a vehicle licence[2] on any of the following grounds—

(a)   that the hackney carriage[2] or private hire vehicle[2] is unfit for use as a hackney carriage or private hire vehicle;

(b)   any offence under, or non-compliance with, the provisions of the Act of 1847 or of this Part of this Act by the operator or driver; or

(c)   any other reasonable cause[3].

(2)   Where a district council suspend, revoke or refuse to renew any licence under this section they shall give to the proprietor of the vehicle notice of the grounds on which the licence has been suspended or revoked or on which they have refused to renew the licence within fourteen days of such suspension, revocation or refusal.

(3)   Any proprietor aggrieved by a decision of a district council under this section may appeal[4] to a magistrates' court.

[Local Government (Miscellaneous Provisions) Act 1976, s 60.]

---

[1] See note 1 to para 7.7499, ante.

[2] For meaning of "vehicle licence", "hackney carriage", "private hire vehicle", and see s 80(1), post.

[3] "Any other reasonable cause" confers a wide discretion on a council; where there is a pending prosecution there is no need for a conclusion to be reached as to the chance of the licence holder being convicted, there is no requirement before deciding to suspend the licence to hear evidence from witnesses to the alleged offence and hearsay evidence is admissible (*Leeds City Council v Hussain* [2002] EWHC 1145 (Admin), [2003] RTR 199). The impact of a suspension on the driver and the absence of compensation if he is ultimately acquitted of the offence are not relevant considerations; personal circumstances are irrelevant save perhaps in very rare cases to explain or to excuse the conduct of the driver (*Leeds City Council v Hussain*, supra).

[4] The procedure shall be in accordance with ss 300–302 of the Public Health Act 1936, title Public Health, post (s 77, post). See also Magistrates' Courts Rules 1981, r 34, in Part I: Magistrates' Courts, Procedure, ante.

7.7503   61.   Suspension and revocation of drivers' licences   (1)   Notwithstanding any thing in the Act of 1847[1] or in this Part of this Act, a district council may suspend or revoke or (on application therefor under section 46 of the Act of 1847 or section 51 of this Act, as the case may be) refuse to renew the licence of a driver of a hackney carriage or a private hire vehicle on any of the following grounds—

(a)   that he has since the grant of the licence—
   (i)   been convicted of an offence involving dishonesty, indecency or violence; or
   (ii)   been convicted of an offence under or has failed to comply with the provisions of the Act of 1847 or of this Part of this Act;

(aa)   that he has since the grant of the licence been convicted of an immigration offence or required to pay an immigration penalty; or

(b)   any other reasonable cause[2].

(1A)   Subsection (1)(aa) does not apply if—

(a)   in a case where the driver has been convicted of an immigration offence, the conviction is a spent conviction within the meaning of the Rehabilitation of Offenders Act 1974, or

(b)   in a case where the driver has been required to pay an immigration penalty—
   (i)   more than three years have elapsed since the date on which the penalty was imposed, and
   (ii)   the amount of the penalty has been paid in full.

(2)

(a)   Where a district council suspend, revoke or refuse to renew any licence under this section they shall give to the driver notice of the grounds on which the licence has been suspended or revoked or on which they have refused to renew such licence within fourteen days of such suspension, revocation or refusal and the driver shall on demand return to the district council the driver's badge issued to him in accordance with section 54 of this Act.

(b)   If any person without reasonable excuse contravenes the provisions of this section he shall be guilty of an offence and liable on summary conviction to a fine not exceeding **level 1** on the standard scale.

(2ZA)   The requirement in subsection (2)(a) to return a driver's badge does not apply in a case where section 62A applies (but see subsection (2) of that section).

(2A)   Subject to subsection (2B) of this section, a suspension or revocation of the licence of a driver under this section takes effect at the end of the period of 21 days beginning with the day on which notice is given to the driver under subsection (2)(a) of this section.

(2B)   If it appears that the interests of public safety require the suspension or revocation of the licence to have immediate effect, and the notice given to the driver under subsection (2)(a) of this section includes a statement that that is so and an explanation why, the suspension or revocation takes effect when the notice is given to the driver.

(3)   Any driver aggrieved by a decision of a district council under subsection (1) of this section may appeal[3] to a magistrates' court.

[Local Government (Miscellaneous Provisions) Act 1976, s 61 as amended by the Criminal Justice Act 1982, ss 38 and 46, the Road Safety Act 2006, s 52 and the Immigration Act 2016, Sch 5.]

---

[1] See note 1 to para 7.7499, ante.

[2] See note to s 60(1)(c), ante.

[3] See note 2 to para 7.7501, ante. On the hearing of an appeal under this section justices should make findings of fact and record reasons for their decision and the appellant is entitled to be so informed (*R v Burton-upon-Trent Justices, ex p Hussain* (1996) 160 JP 808).

7.7504   **62. Suspension and revocation of operators' licences**   (1) Notwithstanding anything in this Part of this Act a district council may suspend or revoke, or (on application therefor under section 55 of this Act) refuse to renew an operator's licence[1] on any of the following grounds—

     (*a*)   any offence under, or non-compliance with, the provisions of this Part of this Act;

     (*b*)   any conduct on the part of the operator which appears to the district council to render him unfit to hold an operator's licence;

     (*c*)   any material change since the licence was granted in any of the circumstances of the operator on the basis of which the licence was granted;

     (*ca*)   that the operator has since the grant of the licence been convicted of an immigration offence or required to pay an immigration penalty; or

     (*d*)   any other reasonable cause.

   (1A)   Subsection (1)(ca) does not apply if—

     (a)   in a case where the operator has been convicted of an immigration offence, the conviction is a spent conviction within the meaning of the Rehabilitation of Offenders Act 1974, or

     (b)   in a case where the operator has been required to pay an immigration penalty—

         (i)   more than three years have elapsed since the date on which the penalty was imposed, and

         (ii)   the amount of the penalty has been paid in full.

   (2)   Where a district council suspend, revoke or refuse to renew any licence under this section they shall give to the operator notice of the grounds on which the licence has been suspended or revoked or on which they have refused to renew such licence within fourteen days of such suspension, revocation or refusal.

   (3)   Any operator aggrieved by a decision of a district council under this section may appeal[2] to a magistrates' court.

[Local Government (Miscellaneous Provisions) Act 1976, s 62 as amended by the Immigration Act 2016, Sch 5.]

---

   [1]   "Operator's licence" means a licence under s 55 of this Act (s 80(1), post).
   [2]   See note 2 to para 7.7501, ante. On the hearing of an appeal under this section justices should make findings of fact and record reasons for their decision and the appellant is entitled to be so informed (*R v Burton-upon-Trent Justices, ex p Hussain* (1996) 160 JP 808).

7.7505   **62A. Return of licences suspended or revoked on immigration grounds**
   (1)   Subsection (2) applies if—

     (a)   under section 61 a district council suspend, revoke or refuse to renew the licence of a driver of a hackney carriage or a private hire vehicle on the ground mentioned in subsection (1)(aa) of that section, or

     (b)   under section 62 a district council suspend, revoke or refuse to renew an operator's licence on the ground mentioned in subsection (1)(ca) of that section.

   (2)   The person to whom the licence was granted must, within the period of 7 days beginning with the relevant day, return to the district council—

     (a)   the licence, and

     (b)   in the case of a licence of a driver of a hackney carriage or a private hire vehicle, the person's driver's badge.

   (3)   In subsection (2) "the relevant day" means—

     (a)   where the licence is suspended or revoked, the day on which the suspension or revocation takes effect;

     (b)   where the district council refuse to renew the licence, the day on which the licence expires as a result of the failure to renew it.

   (4)   A person who, without reasonable excuse, contravenes subsection (2) is guilty of an offence and liable on summary conviction—

     (a)   to a fine not exceeding level 3 on the standard scale, and

     (b)   in the case of a continuing offence, to a fine not exceeding ten pounds for each day during which an offence continues after conviction.

   (5)   The Secretary of State may by regulations made by statutory instrument amend the amount for the time being specified in subsection (4)(b).

   (6)   Regulations under subsection (5) may make transitional, transitory or saving provision.

   (7)   A statutory instrument containing regulations under subsection (5) may not be made unless a draft of the instrument has been laid before, and approved by a resolution of, each House of Parliament.

[Local Government (Miscellaneous Provisions) Act 1976, s 62A as inserted by the Immigration Act 2016, Sch 5.]

7.7506   **63. Stands for hackney carriages**   (1)   For the purposes of their functions under the Act of 1847[1], a district council may from time to time appoint stands for hackney carriages[2] for the whole or any part of a day in any highway in the district which is maintainable at the public expense and, with the consent[3] of the owner, on any land in the district which does not form part of a highway so maintainable and may from time to time vary the number of hackney carriages permitted to be at each stand.

   (2)   Before appointing any stand for hackney carriages or varying the number of hackney carriages to be at each stand in exercise of the powers of this section, a district council shall give

notice to the chief officer of police for the police area in which the stand is situated and shall also give public notice of the proposal by advertisement in at least one local newspaper circulating in the district and shall take into consideration any objections or representations in respect of such proposal which may be made to them in writing within twenty-eight days of the first publication of such notice.

(3)   Nothing in this section shall empower a district council to appoint any such stand—

    (*a*)   so as unreasonably to prevent access to any premises;

    (*b*)   so as to impede the use of any points authorised to be used in connection with a local service within the meaning of the Transport Act 1985 or PSV operator's licence granted under the Public Passenger Vehicles Act 1981, as points for the taking up or setting down of passengers, or in such a position as to interfere unreasonably with access to any station or depot of any passenger road transport operators, except with the consent of those operators;

    (*c*)   on any highway except with the consent of the highway authority;

and in deciding the position of stands a district council shall have regard to the position of any bus stops for the time being in use.

(4)   Any hackney carriage byelaws[4] for fixing stands for hackney carriages which were made by a district council before the date when this section comes into force in the area of the council and are in force immediately before that date shall cease to have effect, but any stands fixed by such byelaws shall be deemed to have been appointed under this section.

(5)   The power to appoint stands for hackney carriages under subsection (1) of this section shall include power to revoke such appointment and to alter any stand so appointed and the expressions "appointing" and "appoint" in subsections (2) and (3) of this section shall be construed accordingly.

[Local Government (Miscellaneous Provisions) Act 1976, s 63, as amended by the Transport Act 1980, Sch 5, the Transport Act 1985, Sch 1 and the Public Passenger Vehicles Act 1981, Sch 7.]

---

  [1]   "The Act of 1847" means the provisions of the Town Police Clauses Act 1847 with respect to hackney carriages (s 80(1), post). For that Act, see title Towns Improvements: Town Police, post.
  [2]   For meaning of "hackney carriage", see s 80(1), post.
  [3]   The landowner is entitled to withhold consent, or to give subject to conditions, for example, of the payment of charges: *Jones v First Greater Western Ltd* [2014] EWCA Civ 301, [2015] RTR 3.
  [4]   For meaning of "hackney carriage byelaws", see s 80(1), post.

7.7507   64.   Prohibition of other vehicles on hackney carriage stands   (1)   No person shall cause or permit any vehicle other than a hackney carriage to wait on any stand for hackney carriages during any period for which that stand has been appointed, or is deemed to have been appointed, by a district council under the provisions of section 63 of this Act.

(2)   Notice of the prohibition in this section shall be indicated by such traffic signs as may be prescribed or authorised for the purpose by the Secretary of State in pursuance of his powers under section 64 of the Road Traffic Regulation Act 1984[1].

(3)   If any person without reasonable excuse contravenes the provisions of this section, he shall be guilty of an offence[2].

(4)   In any proceedings under this section against the driver of a public service vehicle it shall be a defence to show that, by reason of obstruction to traffic or for other compelling reason, he caused his vehicle to wait on a stand or part thereof and that he caused or permitted his vehicle so to wait only for so long as was reasonably necessary for the taking up or setting down of passengers.

[Local Government (Miscellaneous Provisions) Act 1976, s 64 as amended by the Road Traffic Regulation Act 1984, Sch 13.]

---

  [1]   See Part VI: Transport, title Road Traffic.
  [2]   For penalty, see s 76, post.

7.7508   65.   *Fixing of fares for hackney carriages.*

7.7509   66.   Fares for long journeys   (1)   No person, being the driver of a hackney carriage[1] licensed by a district council, and undertaking for any hirer a journey ending outside the district[1] and in respect of which no fare and no rate of fare was agreed before the hiring was effected, shall require for such journey a fare greater than that indicated on the taximeter[1] with which the hackney carriage is equipped or, if it is not equipped with a taximeter, greater than that which, if the current byelaws fixing rates or fares and in force in the district in pursuance of section 68 of the Act of 1847[2] or, as the case may be, the current table of fares in force within the district in pursuance of section 65 of this Act had applied to the journey, would have been authorised for the journey by the byelaws or table.

(2)   If any person knowingly contravenes the provisions of this section, he shall be guilty of an offence[3].

[Local Government (Miscellaneous Provisions) Act 1976, s 66.]

---

  [1]   For meaning of "hackney carriage", "district" and "taximeter", see s 80(1), post.
  [2]   See note 1 to para 7.7506, ante.
  [3]   For penalty, see s 76, post.

7.7510   67.   Hackney carriages used for private hire   (1)   No hackney carriage[1] shall be used in the district[1] under a contract or purported contract for private hire except at a rate of fares or charges not greater than that fixed by the byelaws or table mentioned in section 66 of this Act, and, when any such hackney carriage is so used, the fare or charge shall be calculated from the point in the district at which the hirer commences his journey.

(2)   Any person who knowingly contravenes this section shall be guilty of an offence[2].

(3)   In subsection (1) of this section "contract" means—

(a)   a contract made otherwise than while the relevant hackney carriage is plying for hire in the district or waiting at a place in the district which, when the contract is made, is a stand for hackney carriages appointed by the district council under section 63 of this Act; and

(b)   a contract made, otherwise than with or through the driver of the relevant hackney carriage, while it is so plying or waiting.

[Local Government (Miscellaneous Provisions) Act 1976, s 67.]

---

[1] For meaning of "hackney carriage", and "district" see s 80(1), post.

[2] For penalty, see s 76, post. It is permissible for a hackney carriage to undertake a journey at a fixed price, but it is an offence under s 67(1) to do so at a price in excess of the metered fare; a licensed hackney driver could safely be assumed, unless the contrary was shown, to have sufficiently good knowledge of both his area and the metered fares within it to know that it was unlawful to charge £32 when the metered fare would have been £21.10: *Stratford-on-Avon District Council v Dyde* [2009] EWHC 3011 (Admin), [2010] RTR 13.

7.7511   68.   Fitness of hackney carriages and private hire vehicles   Any authorised officer[1] of the council in question or any constable shall have power at all reasonable times to inspect and test, for the purpose of ascertaining its fitness, any hackney carriage[1] or private hire vehicle[1] licensed by a district council, or any taximeter[1] affixed to such a vehicle, and if he is not satisfied as to the fitness of the hackney carriage or private hire vehicle or as to the accuracy of its taximeter he may by notice in writing require the proprietor[1] of the hackney carriage or private hire vehicle to make it or its taximeter available for further inspection and testing at such reasonable time and place as may be specified in the notice and suspend the vehicle licence[1] until such time as such authorised officer or constable is so satisfied:

Provided that, if the authorised officer or constable is not so satisfied before the expiration of a period of two months, the said licence shall, by virtue of this section, be deemed to have been revoked and subsections (2) and (3) of section 60[2] of this Act shall apply with any necessary modifications.

[Local Government (Miscellaneous Provisions) Act 1976, s 68.]

---

[1] For meaning of "authorised officer", "hackney carriage", "private hire vehicle", "proprietor", "taximeter", and "vehicle licence", see s 80(1), post.

[2] Ante.

7.7512   69.   Prolongation of journeys   (1)   No person being the driver of a hackney carriage[1] or of a private hire vehicle[1] licensed by a district council shall without reasonable cause unnecessarily prolong, in distance or in time, the journey for which the hackney carriage or private hire vehicle has been hired.

(2)   If any person contravenes the provisions of this section, he shall be guilty of an offence[2].

[Local Government (Miscellaneous Provisions) Act 1976, s 69.]

---

[1] For meaning of "hackney carriage", and "private hire vehicle", see s 80(1), post.

[2] For penalty, see s 76, post.

7.7513   70.   Fees[1] for vehicle and operators' licences.

---

[1] A local authority is entitled to charge fees for inspections at the time they are carried out and whether or not the vehicle passed the inspection. Furthermore it is lawful for there to be a graduated scale of fees where further tests were required and an additional fee on grant of the licence (*Kelly v Liverpool City Council* [2003] EWCA Civ 197, [2003] 2 All ER 772, [2003] RTR 236).

7.7514   71.   Taximeters   (1)   Nothing in this Act shall require any private hire vehicle[1] to be equipped with any form of taximeter[1] but no private hire vehicle so equipped shall be used for hire in a controlled district[1] unless such taximeter has been tested and approved by or on behalf of the district council for the district or any other district council by which a vehicle licence[1] in force for the vehicle was issued.

(2)   Any person who—

(a)   tampers with any seal on any taximeter without lawful excuse; or

(b)   alters any taximeter with intent to mislead; or

(c)   knowingly causes or permits a vehicle of which he is the proprietor to be used in contravention of subsection (1) of this section,

shall be guilty of an offence[2].

[Local Government (Miscellaneous Provisions) Act 1976, s 71.]

---

[1] For meaning of "controlled district", "private hire vehicle", "taximeter", and "vehicle licence", see s 80(1), post.

[2] For penalty, see s 76, post.

7.7515   72.   Offences due to fault of other person etc   (1)   Where an offence by any person under this Part of this Act is due to the act or default of another person, then, whether proceedings are taken against the first-mentioned person or not, that other person may be charged with and convicted of that offence, and shall be liable on conviction to the same punishment as might have been imposed on the first-mentioned person if he had been convicted of the offence.

(2)   Section 44(3)[1] of this Act shall apply to an offence under this Part of the Act as it applies to an offence under Part I of this Act.

[Local Government (Miscellaneous Provisions) Act 1976, s 72.]

---

[1] Ante.

7.7516   73.   Obstruction of authorised officer   (1)   Any person who—

(a)   wilfully obstructs an authorised officer[1] or constable acting in pursuance of this Part of this Act or the Act of 1847[2]; or

(b)   without reasonable excuse fails to comply with any requirement properly made to him by such officer or constable under this Part of this Act; or

(c)   without reasonable cause fails to give such an officer or constable so acting any other assistance or information which he may reasonably require of such person for the purpose of the performance of his functions under this Part of this Act or the Act of 1847;

shall be guilty of an offence[3].

(2)   If any person, in giving any such information as is mentioned in the preceding subsection, makes any statement which he knows to be false, he shall be guilty of an offence[3].

[Local Government (Miscellaneous Provisions) Act 1976, s 73.]

---

[1] For meaning of "authorised officer", see s 80(1), post.
[2] "The Act of 1847" means the provisions of the Town Police Clauses Act 1847 with respect to hackney carriages (s 80(1), post). For that Act, see title TOWNS IMPROVEMENTS: TOWN POLICE, post.
[3] For penalty, see s 76, post.

7.7517   74.   *Saving for certain businesses.*

7.7518   75.   Saving for certain vehicles etc   (1)   Nothing in this Part of this Act shall—

(a)   apply to a vehicle used for bringing passengers or goods within a controlled district[1] in pursuance of a contract for the hire of the vehicle made outside the district if the vehicle is not made available for hire within the district;

(b)   *repealed*

(c)   apply to a vehicle while it is being used in connection with a funeral or a vehicle used wholly or mainly, by a person carrying on the business of a funeral director, for the purpose of funerals;

(cc)   apply to a vehicle while it is being used in connection with a wedding;

(d)   require the display of any plate, disc or notice in or on any private hire vehicle licensed by a council under this Part of this Act during such period that such vehicle is used for carrying passengers for hire or reward—

     (i)   *repealed*

     (ii)   under a contract for the hire of the vehicle for a period of not less than 24 hours.

(2)   Paragraphs (a), (b) and (c) of section 46(1) of this Act shall not apply to the use or driving of a vehicle or to the employment of a driver of a vehicle while the vehicle is used as a private hire vehicle in a controlled district if a licence issued under section 48 of this Act by the council whose area consists of or includes another controlled district is then in force for the vehicle and a driver's licence issued by such a council is then in force for the driver of the vehicle.

(2A)   Where a vehicle is being used as a taxi or private hire car, paragraphs (a), (b) and (c) of section 46(1) of this Act shall not apply to the use or driving of the vehicle or the employment of a person to drive it if—

(a)   a licence issued under section 10 of the Civic Government (Scotland) Act 1982 for its use as a taxi or, as the case may be, private hire car is then in force, and

(b)   the driver holds a licence issued under section 13 of that Act for the driving of taxis or, as the case may be, private hire cars.

In this subsection "private hire car" and "taxi" have the same meaning as in sections 10 to 22 of the Civic Government (Scotland) Act 1982.

(2B)   Paragraphs (a), (b) and (c) of section 46(1) of this Act shall not apply to the use or driving of a vehicle, or to the employment of a driver of a vehicle, if—

(a)   a London PHV licence issued under section 7 of the Private Hire Vehicles (London) Act 1998 is in force in relation to that vehicle; and

(b)   the driver of the vehicle holds a London PHV driver's licence issued under section 13 of that Act.]

(3)   Where a licence under section 48 of this Act is in force for a vehicle, the council which issued the licence may, by a notice in writing given to the proprietor of the vehicle, provide that paragraph (a) of subsection (6) of that section shall not apply to the vehicle on any occasion specified in the notice or shall not so apply while the notice is carried in the vehicle; and on any occasion on which by virtue of this subsection that paragraph does not apply to a vehicle section 54(2)(a) of this Act shall not apply to the driver of the vehicle.

[Local Government (Miscellaneous Provisions) Act 1976, s 75 as amended by the Civic Government (Scotland) Act 1982, s 16, the Transport Act 1985, Sch 7, the Private Hire Vehicles (London) Act 1998, Sch 1 and the Road Safety Act 2006, Sch 7.]

---

[1] For meaning of "controlled district", see s 80(1), post. Section 75(1)(*a*) is concerned with the vehicle which brings passengers into a controlled district; it is not concerned with a vehicle which makes an initial journey within the controlled district; see *Braintree District Council v Howard* [1993] RTR 193.

7.7519   76.   Penalties   Any person who commits an offence against any of the provisions of this Part of this Act in respect of which no penalty is expressly provided shall be liable on summary conviction to a fine not exceeding **level 3** on the standard scale.

[Local Government (Miscellaneous Provisions) Act 1976, s 76 as amended by the Criminal Justice Act 1982, ss 38 and 46.]

7.7520   77.   Appeals   (1)   Sections 300 to 302 of the Act of 1936[1], which relate to appeals, shall have effect as if this Part of this Act were part of that Act.

(2)   If any requirement, refusal or other decision of a district council against which a right of appeal is conferred by this Act—

> (*a*)   involves the execution of any work or the taking of any action; or
>
> (*b*)   makes it unlawful for any person to carry on a business which he was lawfully carrying on up to the time of the requirement, refusal or decision;

then, until the time for appealing has expired, or, when an appeal is lodged, until the appeal is disposed of or withdrawn or fails for want of prosecution—

> (i)   no proceedings shall be taken in respect of any failure to execute the work, or take the action; and
>
> (ii)   that person may carry on that business.

(3)   Subsection (2) of this section does not apply in relation to a decision under subsection (1) of section 61 of this Act which has immediate effect in accordance with subsection (2B) of that section.

(4)   On an appeal under this Part of this Act or an appeal under section 302 of the Act of 1936 as applied by this section, the court is not entitled to entertain any question as to whether—

> (a)   a person should be, or should have been, granted leave to enter or remain in the United Kingdom; or
>
> (b)   a person has, after the date of the decision being appealed against, been granted leave to enter or remain in the United Kingdom.

[Local Government (Miscellaneous Provisions) Act 1976, s 77 as amended by the Road Safety Act 2006, s 52 and the Immigration Act 2016, Sch 5.]

---

[1] See title PUBLIC HEALTH, post.

7.7521   78.   Application of provisions of Act of 1936   Subsection (1) of section 283[1] and section 304[2] of the Act of 1936 shall have effect as if references therein to that Act included a reference to this Part of this Act.

[Local Government (Miscellaneous Provisions) Act 1976, s 78.]

---

[1] Section 283(1) of the Public Health Act 1936 provides that all notices, etc shall be in writing.
[2] Section 304 of the Public Health Act 1936 provides that judges and justices shall not be disqualified by liability to pay rates.

7.7522   79.   Authentication of licences   Notwithstanding anything in section 43 of the Act of 1847, any vehicle licence or driver's licence granted by a district council under that Act, or any licence granted by a district council under this Part of this Act, shall not be required to be under the common seal of the district council, but if not so sealed shall be signed by an authorised officer of the council.

[Local Government (Miscellaneous Provisions) Act 1976, s 79.]

7.7523   79A.   Persons disqualified by reason of immigration status   (1)   For the purposes of this Part of this Act a person is disqualified by reason of the person's immigration status from carrying on a licensable activity if the person is subject to immigration control and—

> (a)   the person has not been granted leave to enter or remain in the United Kingdom; or
>
> (b)   the person's leave to enter or remain in the United Kingdom—
>
> > (i)   is invalid;
> >
> > (ii)   has ceased to have effect (whether by reason of curtailment, revocation, cancellation, passage of time or otherwise); or
> >
> > (iii)   is subject to a condition preventing the person from carrying on the licensable activity.

(2)   Where a person is on immigration bail within the meaning of Part 1 of Schedule 10 to the Immigration Act 2016—

> (a)   the person is to be treated for the purposes of this Part of this Act as if the person had been granted leave to enter the United Kingdom; but
>
> (b)   any condition as to the person's work in the United Kingdom to which the person's immigration bail is subject is to be treated for those purposes as a condition of leave.

(3)   For the purposes of this section a person is subject to immigration control if under the Immigration Act 1971 the person requires leave to enter or remain in the United Kingdom.

(4)   For the purposes of this section a person carries on a licensable activity if the person—

> (a)   drives a private hire vehicle;

(b)   operates a private hire vehicle; or

(c)   drives a hackney carriage.

[Local Government (Miscellaneous Provisions) Act 1976, s 79A as inserted by the Immigration Act 2016, Sch 5.]

7.7524   79B.   Immigration offences and immigration penalties   (1)   In this Part of this Act "immigration offence" means—

(a)   an offence under any of the Immigration Acts;

(b)   an offence under section 1 of the Criminal Attempts Act 1981 of attempting to commit an offence within paragraph (a); or

(c)   an offence under section 1 of the Criminal Law Act 1977 of conspiracy to commit an offence within paragraph (a).

(2)   In this Part of this Act "immigration penalty" means a penalty under—

(a)   section 15 of the Immigration, Asylum and Nationality Act 2006 ("the 2006 Act"); or

(b)   section 23 of the Immigration Act 2014 ("the 2014 Act").

(3)   For the purposes of this Part of this Act a person to whom a penalty notice under section 15 of the 2006 Act has been given is not to be treated as having been required to pay an immigration penalty if—

(a)   the person is excused payment by virtue of section 15(3) of that Act; or

(b)   the penalty is cancelled by virtue of section 16 or 17 of that Act.

(4)   For the purposes of this Part of this Act a person to whom a penalty notice under section 15 of the 2006 Act has been given is not to be treated as having been required to pay an immigration penalty until such time as—

(a)   the period for giving a notice of objection under section 16 of that Act has expired and the Secretary of State has considered any notice given within that period; and

(b)   if a notice of objection was given within that period, the period for appealing under section 17 of that Act has expired and any appeal brought within that period has been finally determined, abandoned or withdrawn.

(5)   For the purposes of this Part of this Act a person to whom a penalty notice under section 23 of the 2014 Act has been given is not to be treated as having been required to pay an immigration penalty if—

(a)   the person is excused payment by virtue of section 24 of that Act; or

(b)   the penalty is cancelled by virtue of section 29 or 30 of that Act.

(6)   For the purposes of this Part of this Act a person to whom a penalty notice under section 23 of the 2014 Act has been given is not to be treated as having been required to pay an immigration penalty until such time as—

(a)   the period for giving a notice of objection under section 29 of that Act has expired and the Secretary of State has considered any notice given within that period; and

(b)   if a notice of objection was given within that period, the period for appealing under section 30 of that Act has expired and any appeal brought within that period has been finally determined, abandoned or withdrawn.

[Local Government (Miscellaneous Provisions) Act 1976, s 79B as inserted by the Immigration Act 2016, Sch 5.]

7.7525   80.   Interpretation of Part II   (1)   In this Part of this Act, unless the subject or context otherwise requires—

"the Act of 1847" means the provisions of the Town Police Clauses Act 1847 with respect to hackney carriages;

"the Act of 1936" means the Public Health Act 1936;

"authorised officer" means any officer of a district council authorised in writing by the council for the purposes of this Part of this Act;

"contravene" includes fail to comply;

"controlled district" means any area for which this Part of this Act is in force by virtue of—

(*a*)   a resolution passed by a district council under section 45 of this Act; or

(*b*)   section 255(4) of the Greater London Authority Act 1999;

"daily fine" means a fine for each day during which an offence continues after conviction thereof;

"the district", in relation to a district council in whose area the provisions of this Part of this Act are in force, means—

(*a*)   if those provisions are in force throughout the area of the council, that area; and

(*b*)   if those provisions are in force for part only of the area of the council, that part of that area;

"driver's badge" means, in relation to the driver of a hackney carriage, any badge issued by a district council under byelaws made under section 68 of the Act of 1847 and, in relation to the driver of a private hire vehicle, any badge issued by a district council under section 54 of this Act;

"driver's licence" means, in relation to the driver of a hackney carriage, a licence under section 46 of the Act of 1847 and, in relation to the driver of a private hire vehicle, a licence under section 51 of this Act;

"hackney carriage" has the same meaning as in the Act of 1847;

"hackney carriage byelaws" means the byelaws for the time being in force in the controlled district in question relating to hackney carriages;

"London cab" means a vehicle which is a hackney carriage within the meaning of the Metropolitan Public Carriage Act 1869;

"operate" means in the course of business to make provision for the invitation[1] or acceptance of bookings for a private hire vehicle[2];

"operator's licence" means a licence under section 55 of this Act;

"private hire vehicle" means a motor vehicle constructed or adapted to seat fewer than nine passengers, other than a hackney carriage or public service vehicle or a London cab or tramcar, which is provided for hire[3] with the services of a driver for the purpose of carrying passengers;

"proprietor" includes a part-proprietor and, in relation to a vehicle which is the subject of a hiring agreement or hire-purchase agreement, means the person in possession of the vehicle under that agreement;

"public service vehicle" has the same meaning as in the Public Passenger Vehicles Act 1981;

"taximeter" means any device for calculating the fare to be charged in respect of any journey in a hackney carriage or private hire vehicle by reference to the distance travelled or time elapsed since the start of the journey, or a combination of both; and

"vehicle licence" means in relation to a hackney carriage a licence under sections 37 to 45 of the Act of 1847 in relation to a London cab in a licence under section 6 of the Metropolitan Public Carriage Act 1869 and in relation to a private hire vehicle means a licence under section 48 of this Act.

(2)   In this Part of this Act references to a licence, in connection with a controlled district, are references to a licence issued by the council whose area consists of or includes that district, and "licensed" shall be construed accordingly.

(3)   Except where the context otherwise requires, any reference in this Part of this Act to any enactment shall be construed as a reference to that enactment as applied, extended, amended or varied by, or by virtue of, any subsequent enactment including this Act.

(4)   In this Part of this Act, except where the context otherwise requires, references to a district council shall, in relation to Wales, be construed as references to a county council or county borough council.

[Local Government (Miscellaneous Provisions) Act 1976, s 80 as amended by the Transport Act 1980, Sch 5, Part II, the Public Passenger Vehicles Act 1981, Sch 7, the Transport Act 1985, Sch 7, the Road Traffic (Consequential Provisions) Act 1988, Sch 1, the Transport and Works Act 1992, s 62, SI 1996/3071 and SI 2000/412.]

---

[1] The determining factor is not whether any individual booking was accepted, let alone where it was accepted, but whether the defendant had in the area in question made provision for the invitation or acceptance of bookings in general (*Windsor and Maidenhead Royal Borough Council v Khan*) [1994] RTR 87).

[2] It would seem that activity taking place outside an operator's premises may come within the definition of "operate"; see *Adur District Council v Fry* [1997] RTR 257.

[3] The words "provided for hire" relate to the nature of the vehicle rather than to the nature of the activity (*Benson v Boyce* [1997] RTR 226).

Local Government, Planning and Land Act 1980
(1980 c 65)
Part XVI[1]
Urban Development

Highways

7.7526   157B.   Traffic regulation orders for private streets   (1)   Where

(a)   an urban development corporation[2] submits to the Secretary of State that an order under this section should be made in relation to any road in the urban development area[2] which is a private street; and

(b)   it appears to the Secretary of State that the traffic authority do not intend to make an order under section 1 or, as the case may be, section 6 of the Road Traffic Regulation Act 1984 (orders concerning traffic regulation) in relation to the road,

the Secretary of State may by order under this section make in relation to the road any such provision as he might have made by order under that section if he had been the traffic authority.

(2)   The Road Traffic Regulation Act 1984 applies to an order under this section as it applies to an order made by the Secretary of State under section 1 or, as the case may be, section 6 of that Act in relation to a road for which he is the traffic authority.

(3)   In this section—

"private street" has the same meaning as in Part XI of the Highways Act 1980;

"road" and "traffic authority" have the same meanings as in the Road Traffic Regulation Act 1984.

(4)   This section does not extend to Scotland.

[Local Government, Planning and Land Act 1980, s 157B as inserted by the Leasehold Reform, Housing and Urban Development Act 1993, s 178.]

---

[1] Part XVI contains ss 134–172. For the purposes of Pt XVI of this Act, the holder of a licence under s 6(1) of the Electricity Act 1989 shall be deemed to be a statutory undertaker and his undertaking a statutory undertaking (Electricity Act 1989, Sch 16, para 1).

[2] For the meaning of "urban development area" and "urban development corporation", see ss 134 and 135 respectively.

Miscellaneous

7.7527 167. Power to survey land etc (1) A person to whom this subsection applies may at any reasonable time—

    (*a*)   survey any land, or estimate its value, in connection with a proposal by an urban development corporation[1] to acquire the land compulsorily;

    (*b*)   for the purpose of surveying, or estimating the value of, any land in pursuance of paragraph (*a*) above, enter on the land and other land.

    (2)   Subsection (1) above applies—

    (*a*)   to a person authorised in writing by the urban development corporation; and

    (*b*)   to an officer of the Valuation Office.

    (3)   The power to survey land conferred by subsection (1) above includes power for a person to whom that subsection applies by virtue of subsection (2)(*a*) above to search and bore on and in the land for the purpose of ascertaining the nature of the subsoil or whether minerals are present in the subsoil, and the power to enter on land conferred by that subsection includes power for such a person to place and leave, on or in the land, apparatus for use in connection with the survey in question and to remove the apparatus.

    (4)   A person authorised by an urban development corporation to enter on land in pursuance of subsection (1) above—

    (*a*)   shall, if so required before or after entering on the land, produce evidence of his authority to enter;

    (*b*)   may take with him on to the land such other persons and such equipment as are necessary for the survey in question;

    (*c*)   shall not (if the land is occupied) demand admission to the land as of right unless notice of the intended entry has been served by the corporation on the occupier not less than 28 days before the demand;

    (*d*)   shall (if the land is unoccupied when he enters or the occupier is then temporarily absent) leave the land as effectually secured against trespassers as he found it;

    (*e*)   shall not place or leave apparatus on or in the land or remove apparatus from the land—

        (i)   unless notice of his intention to do so has been served by the corporation on an owner of the land, and if the land is occupied on the occupier, not less than 28 days before he does so, and

        (ii)   if the land is held by a local authority or statutory undertakers[2] who within that period serve on the corporation a notice stating that they object to the placing or leaving or removal of the apparatus on the ground that to do so would be seriously detrimental to the performance of any of their functions or, as the case may be, the carrying on of their undertakings unless he has a written Ministerial authorisation to do so;

    (*f*)   shall not search or bore on or in the land which is the subject of the survey in question if the land is held by a local authority or statutory undertakers—

        (i)   unless notice of his intention to do so has been served by the corporation on the authority or undertakers not less than 28 days before he does so, and

        (ii)   if within that period the authority or undertakers serve on the corporation a notice stating that they object to the searching or boring on the ground that to do so would be seriously detrimental to the performance of any of their functions or, as the case may be, the carrying on of their undertaking, unless he has a written Ministerial authorisation to do so.

    (5)   In subsection (4) above "Ministerial authorisation" means—

    (*a*)   in relation to land held by a local authority, the authorisation of the Secretary of State; and

    (*b*)   in relation to land held by statutory undertakers, the authorisation of the Secretary of State and the appropriate Minister.

    (6)   In exercising the powers of this section to survey land held by a local authority or statutory undertakers a person to whom subsection (1) above applies shall comply with all reasonable conditions imposed by the authority or undertakers with regard to the entry on, surveying of, searching or boring on or in the land, or placing or leaving on, or removal of apparatus from the land.

    (7)   Where it is proposed to search or bore in pursuance of this section in a street within the meaning of Part III of the New Roads and Street Works Act 1991 or, in Scotland, a road within the meaning of Part IV of that Act—

    (*a*)   section 55 or 114 of that Act (notice of starting date of works), so far as it requires notice to be given to a person having apparatus in the street or road which is likely to be affected by the works,

    (*b*)   section 69 or 128 of that Act (requirements to be complied with where works likely to affect another person's apparatus in the street or road), and

    (*c*)   section 82 or 141 of that Act (liability for damage or loss caused),

have effect in relation to the searching or boring as if they were street works within the meaning of the said Part III or (*Scotland*).

(8)   If, in connection with such a proposal of a corporation as is mentioned in subsection (1)(*a*) above, a person interested in any land suffers damage in consequence of the exercise of a power conferred by subsection (1) or (4)(*b*) above or a failure to perform the duty imposed by subsection (4)(*d*) above in respect of the land, he shall be entitled to recover compensation for the damage from the corporation.

(9)   Any dispute as to a person's entitlement to compensation in pursuance of subsection (8) above or as to the amount of the compensation shall be determined by the Upper Tribunal, and section 4 of the Land Compensation Act 1961 (which relates to costs) shall with the necessary modifications apply in relation to the determination by the Tribunal of such a dispute.

(10)   If a person—

    (*a*)   wilfully obstructs another person in the exercise of a power conferred on the other person by subsection (1) or (4)(*b*) above; or

    (*b*)   while another person is on any land in pursuance of the said subsection (4)(*b*), wilfully obstructs him in doing things connected with the survey in question; or

    (*c*)   removes or otherwise interferes with apparatus left on or in land in pursuance of this section,

he shall be guilty of an offence and liable on summary conviction to a fine not exceeding **level 3** on the standard scale.

(11)   If a person who has entered on any land in pursuance of this section discloses to another person information obtained by him there about a manufacturing process or trade secret, then, unless the disclosure is made in the course of performing his duty in connection with the purposes for which he was authorised to enter on the land, he shall be guilty of an offence and liable[3], on summary conviction, to a **fine** not exceeding the statutory maximum or, on conviction on indictment, to imprisonment for a term not exceeding **2 years** or a **fine** or both.

(12)   It is hereby declared that references to surveying in this section include references to surveying from the air.

(13)   *Scotland*.

(14)   In this section—

"the Valuation Office" means the Valuation Office of the Inland Revenue Department.

(15)   *Repealed*.

[Local Government, Planning and Land Act 1980, s 167 as amended by the Criminal Justice Act 1982, s 46, the New Roads and Street Works Act 1991, Sch 8, the Statute Law (Repeals) Act 1993, Sch 1 and SI 2009/1307.]

---

[1]   For meaning of "urban development corporation", see s 135.

[2]   For meaning of "statutory undertakers", see s 170, post.

[3]   For procedure in respect of this offence which is triable either way, see the Magistrates' Courts Act 1980, ss 17A–21, in PART I: MAGISTRATES' COURTS, PROCEDURE, ante.

7.7528   168.   Service of notices   (1)   This section has effect in relation to any notice required or authorised by this Part of this Act to be served on any person by an urban development corporation.

(2)   Any such notice may be served on the person in question either by delivering it to him, or by leaving it at his proper address, or by sending it by post to him at that address.

(3)   Any such notice may—

    (*a*)   in the case of a body corporate, be given to or served on the secretary or clerk of that body;

    (*b*)   in the case of a partnership, be given to or served on a partner or a person having the control or management of the partnership business.

(4)   For the purposes of this section and of section 7 of the Interpretation Act 1978 (service of documents by post) in its application to this section, the proper address of any person to or on whom a notice is to be given or served shall be his last known address, except that—

    (*a*)   in the case of a body corporate or its secretary or clerk, it shall be the address of the registered or principal office of that body;

    (*b*)   in the case of a partnership or a person having the control or management of the partnership business, it shall be that of the principal office of the partnership;

and for the purposes of this subsection the principal office of a company registered outside the United Kingdom or of a partnership carrying on business outside the United Kingdom shall be its principal office within the United Kingdom.

(5)   If the person to be given or served with any notice mentioned in subsection (1) above has specified an address within the United Kingdom other than his proper address within the meaning of subsection (4) above as the one at which he or someone on his behalf will accept documents of the same description as that notice, that address shall also be treated for the purposes of this section and section 7 of the Interpretation Act 1978 as his proper address.

(6)   If the name or address of any owner, lessee or occupier of land to or on whom any notice mentioned in subsection (1) above is to be served cannot after reasonable inquiry be ascertained, the document may be served either by leaving it in the hands of a person who is or appears to be resident or employed on the land or by leaving it conspicuously affixed to some building or object on the land.

[Local Government, Planning and Land Act 1980, s 168.]

7.7529   170.   Interpretation; statutory undertakers etc   (1)   In this Part of this Act, unless the context otherwise requires, "statutory undertakers"[1] means—

    (a)   persons authorised by any enactment to carry on any railway, light railway, tramway, road transport, water transport, canal, inland navigation, dock, harbour, pier or lighthouse undertaking, or any undertaking for the supply of hydraulic power,

    (b)   the Civil Aviation Authority, a universal service provider in connection with the provision of a universal postal service and any other authority, body or undertakers which by virtue of any enactment are to be treated as statutory undertakers for any of the purposes of the 1990 Act or of the 1997 Act,

    (c)   any other authority, body or undertakers specified in an order made by the Secretary of State under this paragraph, and

    (d)   any wholly-owned subsidiary within the meaning assigned by section 1159 of the Companies Act 2006) of any person, authority, body or undertakers mentioned in paragraphs (a) and (b) above or specified in an order made under paragraph (c) above,

and "statutory undertaking" shall be construed accordingly.

  (2)   In section 141 above "statutory undertakers" also includes British Shipbuilders, and any wholly-owned subsidiary as defined by section 1159 of the Companies Act 2006) of any of them.

  (2A)   The undertaking of a universal service provider so far as relating to the provision of a universal postal service shall be taken to be his statutory undertaking for the purposes of this Part of this Act; and references in this Part of this Act to his undertaking shall be construed accordingly.

  (2B)   In subsection (1) and (2A) above "universal service provider" has the same meaning as in the Postal Services Act 2000; and references to the provision of a universal postal service shall be construed in accordance with that Act.

  (3)   In this Part of this Act the expression "the appropriate Minister", and any reference to the Secretary of State and the appropriate Minister—

    (a)   in relation to any statutory undertakers who are also statutory undertakers for the purposes of any provision of Part XI of the 1990 Act or Part X of the 1997 Act, shall have the same meanings as in the said Part XI, and

    (b)   in relation to any other statutory undertakers, shall have the meanings given by an order made by the Secretary of State under this subsection.

  (4)   If, in relation to anything required or authorised to be done under this Part of this Act, any question arises as to which Minister is the appropriate Minister in relation to any statutory undertakers; that question shall be determined by the Treasury.

  (5)   An order made under this section shall be made by statutory instrument subject to annulment in pursuance of a resolution of either House of Parliament.

[Local Government, Planning and Land Act 1980, s 170 as amended by the Companies Consolidation (Consequential Provisions) Act 1985, Sch 2, the Airports Act 1986, Sch 6, the Gas Act 1986 Sch 9, the Coal Industry Act 1987, Sch 1, the British Steel Act 1988, Sch 2, the Water Act 1989, Sch 25, the Companies Act 1989, Sch 18, the Electricity Act 1989, Sch 18, the Planning (Consequential Provisions) Act 1990, Sch 2, the British Technology Group Act 1991, Sch 2, the Coal Industry Act 1994, Schs 9 and 11, SI 2001/1149 and SI 2009/1941.]

---

[1] The Environment Agency, every water undertaker and every sewerage undertaker is deemed to be a statutory undertaker for the purposes of Part XVI of this Act (Water Act 1989, Sch 25, para 1).

7.7530   171.   Interpretation: general   In this Part of this Act, except in so far as the context otherwise requires—

"ecclesiastical property" means land belonging to an ecclesiastical benefice of the Church of England, or being or forming part of a church subject to the jurisdiction of a bishop, of any diocese of the Church of England or the site of such a church, or being or forming part of a burial ground subject to such jurisdiction;

"the 1981 Act" means the Acquisition of Land Act 1981;

"the 1947 Act" means the Acquisition of Land (Authorisation Procedure) (Scotland) Act 1947;

"the 1990 Act" means the Town and Country Planning Act 1990;

"the 1997 Act" means the Town and Country Planning (Scotland) Act 1997;

"urban development area" means so much of an area designated by an order under subsection (1) of section 134 above as is not excluded from it by an order under subsection (3A) of that section;

"urban development corporation" means a corporation established by an order under section 135 above.

[Local Government, Planning and Land Act 1980, s 171 as amended by the Acquisition of Land Act 1981, Sch 4, the Planning (Consequential Provisions) Act 1990, Sch 2, the Leasehold Reform, Housing and Urban Development Act 1993, s 179 and the Church of England (Miscellaneous Provisions) Measure 2006, s 16.]

PART XIX[1]
MISCELLANEOUS AND SUPPLEMENTARY

Pleasure Boats

7.7531   185.   Pleasure boats bye laws   (1)   Subject to the provisions of this section, any of the following authorities, namely—

    (i)   a district council;

    (ii)   a London borough council;

(iii)   the Common Council of the City of London;

(iv)   the council of a Welsh county or county borough,

may make byelaws—

(a)   for regulating the numbering and naming of pleasure boats and vessels which are let for hire to the public and the mooring places for such boats and vessels; and

(b)   for fixing the qualifications of the boatmen or other persons in charge of such boats or vessels; and

(c)   for securing their good and orderly conduct while in charge.

(2)   No authority mentioned in subsection (1) above shall have power to make byelaws under that subsection in relation to pleasure boats or vessels operating—

(a)   on any water owned or managed by the British Waterways Board;

(b)   on any inland waters (within the meaning of the Water Resources Act 1991) in respect of which the Environment Agency may make byelaws by virtue of paragraph 1 of Schedule 25 to that Act;

(c)   subject to subsection (3) below, on any canal or other inland navigation which a navigation authority, as defined in section 135(1) of the Water Resources Act 1963², are required or empowered to manage or maintain under any enactment; or

(d)   on any harbour maintained or managed by a harbour authority, as defined in section 57(1) of the Harbours Act 1964.

(3)   Subsection 2(c) above does not preclude a local authority making byelaws under subsection (1) above in relation to pleasure boats or vessels operating on any canal or inland navigation which they themselves are required or empowered to manage or maintain.

[Local Government, Planning and Land Act 1980, s 18, as amended by the Water Act 1989, Sch 25, the Water Consolidation (Consequential Provisions) Act 1991, Sch 1, the Local Government (Wales) 1994 Act, Sch 16 and SI 1996/593.]

---

¹ Part XIX contains ss 180–197.

² This reference continues to have effect despite the repeal and re-enactment of those provisions: see the Water Consolidation (Consequential Provisions) Act 1991, Sch 1, para 35.

Local Government (Miscellaneous Provisions) Act 1982

(1982 c 30)

PART II¹
CONTROL OF SEX ESTABLISHMENTS

7.7532   2.   Control of sex establishments   (1)   A local authority may resolve that Schedule 3 to this Act is to apply to their area; and if a local authority do so resolve, that Schedule shall come into force in their area on the day specified in that behalf in the resolution (which must not be before the expiration of the period of one month beginning with the day on which the resolution is passed).

(2)   A local authority shall publish notice that they have passed a resolution under this section in two consecutive weeks in a local newspaper circulating in their area.

(3)   The first publication shall not be later than 28 days before the day specified in the resolution for the coming into force of Schedule 3 to this Act in the local authority's area.

(4)   The notice shall state the general effect of that Schedule.

(5)   In this Part of this Act "local authority" means—

(a)   the council of a district;

(b)   the council of a London borough; and

(c)   the Common Council of the City of London.

[Local Government (Miscellaneous Provisions) Act 1982, s 2.]

---

¹ Part II contains s 2.

PART III¹
STREET TRADING

7.7533   3.   Power of district council to adopt Schedule 4   A district council may resolve that Schedule 4 to this Act shall apply to their district and, if a council so resolve, that Schedule shall come into force in their district on such day as may be specified in the resolution.

[Local Government (Miscellaneous Provisions) Act 1982, s 3.]

---

¹ Part III contains s 3.

PART VII¹
BYELAWS

7.7534   12.   General provisions relating to byelaws   (1)   Notwithstanding anything in section 298 of the Public Health Act 1936 or section 253 of the Public Health Act 1875 or any other enactment, a constable may take proceedings in respect of an offence against a byelaw made by a relevant local authority under any enactment without the consent of the Attorney General.

(2)   In subsection (1) above "relevant local authority" means—

(a)   a local authority, as defined in section 270 of the Local Government Act 1972; and

(b)   any body that was the predecessor of a local authority as so defined.

(3)   It is immaterial for the purposes of this section that a byelaw was made after the passing of this Act.

[Local Government (Miscellaneous Provisions) Act 1982, s 12.]

---

¹ Part VII contains s 12.

PART VIII¹
ACUPUNCTURE, TATTOOING, EAR-PIERCING AND ELECTROLYSIS

7.7535   13.   Application of Part VIII   (1)   The provisions of this Part of this Act, except this section, shall come into force in accordance with the following provisions of this section.

(2)   A local authority may resolve that the provisions of this Part of this Act which are mentioned in paragraph (a), (b) or (c) of subsection (3) below are to apply to their area; and if a local authority do so resolve, the provisions specified in the resolution shall come into force in their area on the day specified in that behalf in the resolution (which must not be before the expiration of the period of one month beginning with the day on which the resolution is passed).

(3)   The provisions that may be specified in a resolution under subsection (2) above are—
   (a)   sections 14, 16 and 17 below; or
   (b)   sections 15 to 17 below; or
   (c)   sections 14 to 17 below.

(4)   A resolution which provides that section 15 below is to apply to the area of a local authority need not provide that it shall apply to all the descriptions of persons specified in subsection (1) of that section; and if such a resolution does not provide that section 15 below is to apply to persons of all of those descriptions, the reference in subsection (2) above to the coming into force of provisions specified in the resolution shall be construed, in its application to section 15 below, and to section 16 below so far as it has effect for the purposes of section 15 below, as a reference to the coming into force of those sections only in relation to persons of the description or descriptions specified in the resolution.

(5)   If a resolution provides for the coming into force of section 15 below in relation to persons of more than one of the descriptions specified in subsection (1) of that section, it may provide that that section, and section 16 below so far as it has effect for the purposes of that section, shall come into force on different days in relation to persons of each of the descriptions specified in the resolution.

(6)   A local authority shall publish notice that they have passed a resolution under this section in two consecutive weeks in a local newspaper circulating in their area.

(7)   The first publication shall not be later than 28 days before the day specified in the resolution for the coming into force of the provisions specified in it in the local authority's area.

(8)   The notice shall state which provisions are to come into force in that area.

(9)   The notice shall also—
   (a)   if the resolution provides for the coming into force of section 14 below, explain that that section applies to persons carrying on the practice of acupuncture; and
   (b)   if it provides for the coming into force of section 15 below, specify the descriptions of persons in relation to whom that section is to come into force.

(10)   Any such notice shall state the general effect, in relation to persons to whom the provisions specified in the resolution will apply, of the coming into force of those provisions.

(11)   In this Part of the Act "local authority" means—
   (a)   the council of a district;
   (b)   the council of a London borough; and
   (c)   the Common Council of the City of London.

[Local Government (Miscellaneous Provisions) Act 1982, s 13.]

---

¹ Part VIII contains ss 13–17.

7.7536   14.   Acupuncture   (1)   A person shall not in any area in which this section is in force carry on the practice of acupuncture unless he is registered by the local authority for the area under this section.

(2)   A person shall only carry on the practice of acupuncture in any area in which this section is in force in premises registered by the local authority for the area under this section; but a person who is registered under this section does not contravene this subsection merely because he sometimes visits people to give them treatment at their request.

(3)   Subject to section 16(8)(b) below, on application for registration under this section a local authority shall register the applicant and the premises where he desires to practise and shall issue to the applicant a certificate of registration.

(4)   An application for registration under this section shall be accompanied by such particulars as the local authority may reasonably require.

(5)   The particulars that the local authority may require include, without prejudice to the generality of subsection (4) above,—
   (a)   particulars as to the premises where the applicant desires to practise; and
   (b)   particulars of any conviction of the applicant under section 16 below,

but do not include information about individual people to whom the applicant has given treatment.

(6) A local authority may charge such reasonable fees as they may determine for registration under this section.

(7) A local authority may make byelaws for the purpose of securing—

(a) the cleanliness of premises registered under this section and fittings in such premises;

(b) the cleanliness of persons so registered and persons assisting persons so registered in their practice;

(c) the cleansing and, so far as is appropriate, the sterilisation of instruments, materials and equipment used in connection with the practice of acupuncture.

(8) Nothing in this section shall extend to the practice of acupuncture by or under the supervision of a person who is registered as a medical practitioner or a dentist or to premises on which the practice of acupuncture is carried on by or under the supervision of such a person.

[Local Government (Miscellaneous Provisions) Act 1982, s 14.]

7.7537 15. Tattooing, semi-permanent skin-colouring, cosmetic piercing and electrolysis

(1) A person shall not in any area in which this section is in force carry on the business—

(a) of tattooing;

(aa) of semi-permanent skin-colouring;

(b) of cosmetic piercing; or

(c) of electrolysis,

unless he is registered by the local authority for the area under this section.

(2) A person shall only carry on a business mentioned in subsection (1) above in any area in which this section is in force in premises registered under this section for the carrying on of that business; but a person who carries on the business of tattooing, semi-permanent skin-colouring, cosmetic piercing or electrolysis and is registered under this section as carrying on that business does not contravene this subsection merely because he sometimes visits people at their request to tattoo them or, as the case may be, to carry out semi-permanent skin-colouring on them, pierce their bodies or give them electrolysis.

(3) Subject to section 16(8)(b) below, on application for registration under this section a local authority shall register the applicant and the premises where he desires to carry on his business and shall issue to the applicant a certificate of registration.

(4) An application for registration under this section shall be accompanied by such particulars as the local authority may reasonably require.

(5) The particulars that the local authority may require include, without prejudice to the generality of subsection (4) above,—

(a) particulars as to the premises where the applicant desires to carry on his business; and

(b) particulars of any conviction of the applicant under section 16 below,

but do not include information about individual people whom the applicant has tattooed or given electrolysis, whose bodies he has pierced or on whom he has carried out semi-permanent skin-colouring.

(6) A local authority may charge such reasonable fees as they may determine for registration under this section.

(7) A local authority may make byelaws for the purposes of securing—

(a) the cleanliness of premises registered under this section and fittings in such premises;

(b) the cleanliness of persons so registered and persons assisting persons so registered in the business in respect of which they are registered;

(c) the cleansing and, so far as is appropriate, the sterilisation of instruments, materials and equipment used in connection with a business in respect of which a person is registered under this section.

(8) Nothing in this section shall extend to the carrying on of a business such as is mentioned in subsection (1) above by or under the supervision of a person who is registered as a medical practitioner or to premises on which any such business is carried on by or under the supervision of such a person.

(9) In this section "semi-permanent skin-colouring" means the insertion of semi-permanent colouring into a person's skin.

[Local Government (Miscellaneous Provisions) Act 1982, s 15 as amended by the Local Government Act 2003, s 120.]

7.7538 16. Provisions supplementary to ss 14 and 15 (1) Any person who contravenes—

(a) section 14(1) or (2) above; or

(b) section 15(1) or (2) above,

shall be guilty of an offence and liable on summary conviction to a fine not exceeding **level 3** on the standard scale.

(2) Any person who contravenes a byelaw made—

(a) under section 14(7) above; or

(b) under section 15(7) above,

shall be guilty of an offence and liable on summary conviction to a fine not exceeding **level 3** on the standard scale.

(3) If a person registered under section 14 above is found guilty of an offence under subsection (2)(a) above, the court, instead of or in addition to imposing a fine under subsection (2) above, may

order the suspension or cancellation of his registration.

(4)   If a person registered under section 15 above is found guilty of an offence under subsection (2)(*b*) above, the court, instead of or in addition to imposing a fine under subsection (2) above, may order the suspension or cancellation of his registration.

(5)   A court which orders the suspension or cancellation of a registration by virtue of subsection (3) or (4) above may also order the suspension or cancellation of any registration under section 14 or, as the case may be, 15 above of the premises in which the offence was committed, if they are occupied by the person found guilty of the offence.

(6)   Subject to subsection (7) below, a court ordering the suspension or cancellation of registration by virtue of subsection (3) or (4) above may suspend the operation of the order until the expiration of the period prescribed by Criminal Procedure Rules for giving notice of appeal to the Crown Court.

(7)   If notice of appeal is given within the period so prescribed, an order under subsection (3) or (4) above shall be suspended until the appeal is finally determined or abandoned.

(8)   Where the registration of any person under section 14 or 15 above is cancelled by order of the court under this section—

(a)   he shall within 7 days deliver up to the local authority the cancelled certificate of registration, and, if he fails to do so, he shall be guilty of an offence and liable on summary conviction to a fine not exceeding **level 2** on the standard scale and thereafter to a daily fine not exceeding £5; and

(b)   he shall not again be registered by the local authority under section 14 or, as the case may be, 15 above except with the consent of the magistrates' court which convicted him.

(9)   A person registered under this Part of this Act shall keep a copy—

(a)   of any certificate of registration issued to him under this Part of this Act; and

(b)   of any byelaws under this Part of this Act relating to the practice or business in respect of which he is so registered,

prominently displayed at the place where he carries on that practice or business.

(10)   A person who contravenes subsection (9) above shall be guilty of an offence and liable on summary conviction to a fine not exceeding **level 2** on the standard scale.

(11)   It shall be a defence for a person charged with an offence under subsection (1), (2), (8) or (10) above to prove that he took all reasonable precautions and exercised all due diligence to avoid commission of the offence.

(12)   Nothing in this Part of this Act applies to anything done to an animal.

[Local Government (Miscellaneous Provisions) Act 1982, s 16 as amended by the Criminal Justice Act 1982, s 46 and SI 2004/2035.]

7.7539   **17.   Power to enter premises (acupuncture etc)**   (1)   Subject to subsection (2) below, an authorised officer of a local authority may enter any premises in the authority's area if he has reason to suspect that an offence under section 16 above is being committed there.

(2)   The power conferred by this section may be exercised by an authorised officer of a local authority only if he has been granted a warrant by a justice of the peace.

(3)   A justice may grant a warrant under this section only if he is satisfied—

(a)   that admission to any premises has been refused, or that refusal is apprehended, or that the case is one of urgency, or that an application for admission would defeat the object of the entry; and

(b)   that there is reasonable ground for entry under this section.

(4)   A warrant shall not be granted unless the justice is satisfied either that notice of the intention to apply for a warrant has been given to the occupier, or that the case is one of urgency, or that the giving of such notice would defeat the object of the entry.

(5)   A warrant shall continue in force—

(a)   for seven days; or

(b)   until the power conferred by this section has been exercised in accordance with the warrant,

whichever period is the shorter.

(6)   Where an authorised officer of a local authority exercises the power conferred by this section, he shall produce his authority if required to do so by the occupier of the premises.

(7)   Any person who without reasonable excuse refuses to permit an authorised officer of a local authority to exercise the power conferred by this section shall be guilty of an offence and shall for every such refusal be liable on summary conviction to a fine not exceeding **level 3** on the standard scale.

[Local Government (Miscellaneous Provisions) Act 1982, s 17, as amended by the Criminal Justice Act 1982, s 46.]

PART XII[1]
MISCELLANEOUS

7.7540   **33.   Enforceability by local authorities of certain covenants relating to land**
(1)   The provisions of this section shall apply if a principal council (in the exercise of their powers under section 111 of the Local Government Act 1972 or otherwise) and any other person are parties to an instrument under seal which—

(a)   is executed for the purpose of securing the carrying out of works on land in the council's area in which the other person has an interest; or

(b)   is executed for the purpose of regulating the use of or otherwise connected with land in or outside the council's area in which the other person has an interest,

and which is neither executed for the purpose of facilitating nor connected with the development of the land in question.

(2)   If, in a case where this section applies,—

(a)   the instrument contains a covenant on the part of any person having an interest in land, being a covenant to carry out any works or do any other thing on or in relation to that land, and

(b)   the instrument defines the land to which the covenant relates, being land in which that person has an interest at the time the instrument is executed, and

(c)   the covenant is expressed to be one to which this section or section 126 of the Housing Act 1974 (which is superseded by this section) applies,

the covenant shall be enforceable (without any limit of time) against any person deriving title from the original covenantor in respect of his interest in any of the land defined as mentioned in paragraph (b) above and any person deriving title under him in respect of any lesser interest in that land as if that person had also been an original covenanting party in respect of the interest for the time being held by him.

(3)   Without prejudice to any other method of enforcement of a covenant falling within subsection (2) above, if there is a breach of the covenant in relation to any of the land to which the covenant relates, then, subject to subsection (4) below, the principal council who are a party to the instrument in which the covenant is contained may—

(a)   enter on the land concerned and carry out the works or do anything which the covenant requires to be carried out or done or remedy anything which has been done and which the covenant required not to be done; and

(b)   recover from any person against whom the covenant is enforceable (whether by virtue of subsection (2) above or otherwise) any expenses incurred by the council in exercise of their powers under this subsection.

(4)   Before a principal council exercise their powers under subsection (3)(a) above they shall give not less than 21 days notice of their intention to do so to any person—

(a)   who has for the time being an interest in the land on or in relation to which the works are to be carried out or other thing is to be done; and

(b)   against whom the covenant is enforceable (whether by virtue of subsection (2) above or otherwise).

(5)   If a person against whom a covenant is enforceable by virtue of subsection (2) above requests the principal council to supply him with a copy of the covenant, it shall be their duty to do so free of charge.

(6)   The Public Health Act 1936 shall have effect as if any reference to that Act in —

(a)   section 283[2] of that Act (notices to be in writing; forms of notices, etc),

(b)   section 288[2] of that Act (penalty for obstructing execution of Act), and

(c)   section 291 of that Act (certain expenses recoverable from owners to be a charge on the premises; power to order payment by instalments),

included a reference to subsections (1) to (4) above and as if any reference in those sections of that Act—

(i)   to a local authority were a reference to a principal council; and

(ii)   to the owner of the premises were a reference to the holder of an interest in land.

(7)   Section 16[3] of the Local Government (Miscellaneous Provisions) Act 1976 shall have effect as if references to a local authority and to functions conferred on a local authority by any enactment included respectively references to such a board as is mentioned in subsection (9) below and to functions of such a board under this section.

(8)   In its application to a notice or other document authorised to be given or served under subsection (4) above or by virtue of any provision of the Public Health Act 1936 specified in subsection (6) above, section 233 of the Local Government Act 1972 (service of notices by local authorities) shall have effect as if any reference in that section to a local authority included a reference to the Common Council of the City of London and such a board as is mentioned in the following subsection.

(9)   In this section—

(a)   "principal council" means the council of a county, district or London borough, the Broads Authority, a board constituted in pursuance of section 2 of the Town and Country Planning Act 1990, the Common Council of the City of London, the London Residuary Body, the London Fire and Emergency Planning Authority, a police authority established under section 3 of the Police Act 1996, the Metropolitan Police Authority, the Residuary Body for Wales (Corff Gweddilliol Cymru), a joint authority established by Part 4 of the Local Government Act 1985, an economic prosperity board established under section 88 of the Local Democracy, Economic Development and Construction Act 2009, or a combined authority established under section 103 of that Act; and

(b)   "area" in relation to such a board means the district for which the board is constituted in relation to the London Residuary Body means Greater London, in relation to the Residuary Body for Wales (Corff Gweddilliol Cymru) means Wales and in relation to such a joint authority, economic prosperity board or combined authority means the area for which the authority was established.

(10)   Section 126 of the Housing Act 1974 (which is superseded by this section) shall cease to have effect; but in relation to a covenant falling within subsection (2) of that section, section 1(1)(d) of the Local Land Charges Act 1975 shall continue to have effect as if the reference to the commencement of that Act had been a reference to the coming into operation of the said section 126.

[Local Government (Miscellaneous Provisions) Act 1982, s 33 as amended by the Local Government Act 1985, Schs 14 and 17, the Education Reform Act 1988, Sch 13, the Norfolk and Suffolk Broads Act 1988, Sch 6, the Planning (Consequential Provisions) Act 1990, Sch 2, the Planning and Compensation Act 1991, Sch 7, the Police and Magistrates' Courts Act 1994, Sch 4, the Environment Act 1995, Sch 24, the Police Act 1996, Sch 7, the Police Act 1997, Sch 6, the Greater London Authority Act 1999, Schs 27 and 29, the Criminal Justice and Police Act 2001, Sch 6, the Local Government and Public Involvement in Health 2007, Sch 13, the Local Democracy, Economic Development and Construction Act 2009, Sch 6 and the Deregulation Act 2015, Sch 13.]

---

[1]   Part XII contains ss 33–46.
[2]   See title, PUBLIC HEALTH, post.
[3]   Ante.

7.7541   37.   Temporary markets   (1)   The council of a district or a London borough may resolve that the following provisions of this section shall apply to their district or borough; and if a council so resolve and within 14 days of the passing of the resolution give notice of the resolution by advertising in a local newspaper circulating in their area, those provisions shall come into force in their district or borough on the day specified in the resolution.

(2)   Subject to subsection (3) below, any person intending to hold a temporary market in a district or London borough where the provisions of this section have come into force, and any occupier of land in such a district or borough who intends to permit the land to be used as the site of a temporary market or for purposes of that market, shall give the council of the district or the borough not less than one month before the date on which it is proposed to hold the market notice of his intention to hold it or to permit the land to be so used, as the case may be.

(3)   No notice is required under subsection (2) above if the proceeds of the temporary market are to be applied solely or principally for charitable, social, sporting or political purposes.

(4)   Any notice given under subsection (2) above shall state—

     (a)   the full name and address of the person intending to hold the market;

     (b)   the day or days on which it is proposed that the market shall be held and its proposed opening and closing times;

     (c)   the site on which it is proposed that it shall be held;

     (d)   the full name and address of the occupier of that site, if he is not the person intending to hold the market.

(5)   A person who without giving the notice required by subsection (2) above holds a temporary market or permits land occupied by him to be used as the site of a temporary market shall be guilty of an offence and liable on summary conviction to a fine not exceeding **level 4** on the standard scale.

(6)   In this section "temporary market" means a concourse of buyers and sellers of articles held otherwise than in a building or on a highway, and comprising not less than five stalls, stands, vehicles (whether movable or not) or pitches from which articles are sold, but does not include—

     (a)   a market or fair the right to hold which was acquired by virtue of a grant (including a presumed grant) or acquired or established by virtue of an enactment or order; or

     (b)   a sale by auction of farm livestock or deadstock.

(7)   A person holds a temporary market for the purposes of this section if—

     (a)   he is entitled to payment for any space or pitch hired or let on the site of the market to persons wishing to trade in the market; or

     (b)   he is entitled, as a person promoting the market, or as the agent, licensee or assignee of a person promoting the market, to payment for goods sold or services rendered to persons attending the market.

(8)   This section does not apply to a market held on any land in accordance with planning permission granted on an application made under Part III of the Town and Country Planning Act 1990.

[Local Government (Miscellaneous Provisions) Act 1982, s 37, as amended by the Criminal Justice Act 1982, s 46 and the Planning (Consequential Provisions) Act 1990, Sch 2.]

PART XIII[1]
SUPPLEMENTARY

7.7542   48.   Consequential repeal or amendment of local statutory provisions   (1)   The Secretary of State may by order—

     (a)   repeal any provision of a local Act passed before or in the same Session as this Act or of an order or other instrument made under or confirmed by any Act so passed if it appears to him that the provision is inconsistent with or has become unnecessary in consequence of any provision of this Act; and

    (b)   amend any provision of such a local Act, order or instrument if it appears to him that the provision requires amendment in consequence of any provision contained in this Act or any repeal made by virtue of paragraph (a) above.

(2)   An order under subsection (1) above may contain such incidental or transitional provisions as the Secretary of State considers appropriate in connection with the order.

(3)   It shall be the duty of the Secretary of State, before he makes an order under subsection (1) above repealing or amending any provision of a local Act, to consult each local authority which he considers would be affected by the repeal or amendment of that provision.

(4)   A statutory instrument containing an order under subsection (1) above shall be subject to annulment in pursuance of a resolution of either House of Parliament.

[Local Government (Miscellaneous Provisions) Act 1982, s 48.]

---

¹ Part XIII contains ss 47–49.

7.7543 49. Citation and extent (1)   This Act may be cited as the Local Government (Miscellaneous Provisions) Act 1982.

(2)   Subject to sections 38(3) and 47(4) above, and to paragraph 8(2) of Schedule 6 to this Act, this Act extends to England and Wales only.

[Local Government (Miscellaneous Provisions) Act 1982, s 49 as amended by the Statute Law (Repeals) Act 2004.]

SCHEDULES

SCHEDULE 3
CONTROL OF SEX ESTABLISHMENTS
Section 2

(As amended by the Criminal Justice Act 1982, s 46, SI 1984 No 447, the Cinemas Act 1985, Sch 2, the London Local Authorities Act 1990, s 18, SI 2005/886, the Licensing Act 2005, Sch 6, SI 2005/1541, the Serious Organised Crime and Police Act 2005, Sch 7, SI 2006/484, SI 2009/2999, the Policing and Crime Act 2009, s 27, SI 2010/723, SI 2015/664, SI 2019/742.)

Saving for existing law

7.7544 1.   Nothing in this Schedule—
    (a)   shall afford a defence to a charge in respect of any offence at common law or under an enactment other than this Schedule; or
    (b)   shall be taken into account in any way—
        (i)   at a trial for such an offence; or
        (ii)   in proceedings for forfeiture under section 3 of the Obscene Publications Act 1959 or section 5* of the Protection of Children Act 1978; or
        (iii)   in proceedings for condemnation under Schedule 3 to the Customs and Excise Management Act 1979 of goods which section 42 of the Customs Consolidation Act 1876 prohibits to be imported or brought into the United Kingdom as being indecent or obscene; or
    (c)   shall in any way limit the other powers exercisable under any of those Acts.

---

* **Words substituted by the Police and Justice Act 2006, Sch 14 from a date to be appointed.**

Meaning of "sex establishment"

2.   In this Schedule "sex establishment" means a sexual entertainment venue, sex cinema, a hostess bar or a sex shop.

Meaning of "sexual entertainment venue"

2A.   (1)   In this Schedule "sexual entertainment venue" means any premises at which relevant entertainment is provided before a live audience for the financial gain of the organiser or the entertainer.

(2)   In this paragraph "relevant entertainment" means—
    (a)   any live performance; or
    (b)   any live display of nudity;
which is of such a nature that, ignoring financial gain, it must reasonably be assumed to be provided solely or principally for the purpose of sexually stimulating any member of the audience (whether by verbal or other means).

(3)   The following are not sexual entertainment venues for the purposes of this Schedule—
    (a)   sex cinemas and sex shops;
    (b)   premises at which the provision of relevant entertainment as mentioned in sub-paragraph (1) is such that, at the time in question and including any relevant entertainment which is being so provided at that time—
        (i)   there have not been more than eleven occasions on which relevant entertainment has been so provided which fall (wholly or partly) within the period of 12 months ending with that time;
        (ii)   no such occasion has lasted for more than 24 hours; and
        (iii)   no such occasion has begun within the period of one month beginning with the end of any previous occasion on which relevant entertainment has been so provided (whether or not that previous occasion falls within the 12 month period mentioned in sub-paragraph (i));
    (c)   premises specified or described in an order made by the relevant national authority.

(4)   The relevant national authority may by order amend or repeal sub-paragraph (3)(b).

(5)   But no order under sub-paragraph (4) may—
    (a)   increase the number or length of occasions in any period on which sub-paragraph (3)(b) as originally enacted would permit relevant entertainment to be provided; or
    (b)   provide for shorter intervals between such occasions.

(6)   The relevant national authority may by order provide for descriptions of performances, or of displays of nudity, which are not to be treated as relevant entertainment for the purposes of this Schedule.

(7)   Any power of the relevant national authority to make an order under this paragraph—

    (a)   is exercisable by statutory instrument;

    (b)   may be exercised so as to make different provision for different cases or descriptions of case or for different purposes; and

    (c)   includes power to make supplementary, incidental, consequential, transitional, transitory or saving provision.

(8)   A statutory instrument containing an order under sub-paragraph (4) may not be made by the Secretary of State unless a draft of the instrument has been laid before, and approved by a resolution of, each House of Parliament.

(9)   A statutory instrument containing an order made under sub-paragraph (3)(c) or (6) by the Secretary of State is subject to annulment in pursuance of a resolution of either House of Parliament.

(10)   A statutory instrument containing an order under sub-paragraph (4) may not be made by the Welsh Ministers unless a draft of the instrument has been laid before, and approved by a resolution of, the National Assembly for Wales.

(11)   A statutory instrument containing an order made under sub-paragraph (3)(c) or (6) by the Welsh Ministers is subject to annulment in pursuance of a resolution of the National Assembly for Wales.

(12)   For the purposes of this paragraph relevant entertainment is provided if, and only if, it is provided, or permitted to be provided, by or on behalf of the organiser.

(13)   For the purposes of this Schedule references to the use of any premises as a sexual entertainment venue are to be read as references to their use by the organiser.

(14)   In this paragraph—

"audience" includes an audience of one;

"display of nudity" means—

    (a)   in the case of a woman, exposure of her nipples, pubic area, genitals or anus; and

    (b)   in the case of a man, exposure of his pubic area, genitals or anus;

"the organiser", in relation to the provision of relevant entertainment at premises, means any person who is responsible for the organisation or management of—

    (a)   the relevant entertainment; or

    (b)   the premises;

"premises" includes any vessel, vehicle or stall but does not include any private dwelling to which the public is not admitted;

"relevant national authority" means—

    (a)   in relation to England, the Secretary of State; and

    (b)   in relation to Wales, the Welsh Ministers;

and for the purposes of sub-paragraphs (1) and (2) it does not matter whether the financial gain arises directly or indirectly from the performance or display of nudity.

Meaning of "sex cinema"

3. (1) In this Schedule, "sex cinema" means any premises, vehicle, vessel or stall used to a significant degree for the exhibition of moving pictures, by whatever means produced, which—

    (a)   are concerned primarily with the portrayal of, or primarily deal with or relate to, or are intended to stimulate or encourage—

        (i)   sexual activity; or

        (ii) acts of force or restraint which are associated with sexual activity; or

    (b)   are concerned primarily with the portrayal of, or primarily deal with or relate to, genital organs or urinary or excretory functions,

but does not include a dwelling-house to which the public is not admitted.

(2)   No premises shall be treated as a sex cinema by reason only—

    (a)   if they may be used for an exhibition of a film (within the meaning of paragraph 15 of Schedule 1 to the Licensing Act 2003) by virtue of an authorisation (within the meaning of section 136 of that Act), of their use in accordance with that authorisation; or

    (b)   of their use for an exhibition to which section 6 of that Act (certain non-commercial exhibitions) applies given by an exempted organisation within the meaning of section 6(6) of the Cinemas Act 1985.

3A. *Repealed.**

---

* **New para 3B inserted in relation to the City of Westminster and certain London boroughs by the London Local Authorities Act 2007, s 33. In force for remaining purposes for a date to be appointed.**

Meaning of "sex shop" and "sex article"

4. (1) In this Schedule[1] "sex shop" means any premises, vehicle, vessel or stall used for a business which consists to a significant[2] degree of selling, hiring, exchanging, lending, displaying or demonstrating—

    (a)   sex articles; or

    (b)   other things intended for use in connection with, or for the purpose of stimulating or encouraging—

        (i)   sexual activity; or

        (ii) acts of force or restraint which are associated with sexual activity.

(2)   No premises shall be treated as a sex shop by reason only of their use for the exhibition of moving pictures by whatever means produced.

(3)   In this Schedule "sex article" means—

    (a)   anything made for use in connection with, or for the purpose of stimulating or encouraging—

        (i)   sexual activity; or

        (ii) acts of force or restraint which are associated with sexual activity; and

    (b)   anything to which sub-paragraph (4) below applies.

(4)   This sub-paragraph applies—

    (a)   to any article containing or embodying matter to be read or looked at or anything intended to be used, either alone or as one of a set, for the reproduction or manufacture of any such article; and

    (b)   to any recording of vision or sound, which—

        (i)   is concerned primarily with the portrayal of, or primarily deals with or relates to, or is intended to stimulate or encourage, sexual activity or acts of force or restraint which are associated with sexual activity; or

(ii)   is concerned primarily with the portrayal of, or primarily deals with or relates to, genital organs, or urinary or excretory functions.

---

[1] This Schedule is additionally amended by the Greater London Council (General Powers) Act 1986, s 12 where a borough council so resolves. This is to enable there to be regulation of sex encounter establishments. See also *McMonagle v Westminster City Council* [1990] 2 AC 716, [1990] 1 All ER 993, 154 JP 854, HL.

[2] "Significant" means more than "more than trifling"; in deciding whether an establishment is a "sex shop", the ratio between the sexual and other aspects of the business will always be material, so also will be the absolute quantity of sales, and the character of the remainder of the business. The court must decide which considerations are material to the individual case and what weight is to be attached to them (*Lambeth London Borough Council v Grewal* (1985) 150 JP 138, [1986] Crim LR 260).

Miscellaneous definitions

5. (1)   In this Schedule—
"the appropriate authority" means, in relation to any area for which a resolution has been passed under section 2 above, the local authority who passed it;
"the chief officer of police", in relation to any locality, means the chief officer of police for the police area in which the locality is situated; and
"vessel" includes any ship, boat, raft or other apparatus constructed or adapted for floating on water.
    (2)   This Schedule applies to hovercraft as it applies to vessels.

Requirement for licences for sex establishments

6. (1)   Subject to the provisions of this Schedule, no person shall in any area in which this Schedule is in force use any premises, vehicle, vessel or stall as a sex establishment except under and in accordance with the terms of a licence granted under this Schedule by the appropriate authority.
    (2)   Sub-paragraph (1) above does not apply to the sale, supply or demonstration of articles which—
    (a)   are manufactured for use primarily for the purposes of birth control; or
    (b)   primarily relate to birth control.
7. (1)   Any person who—
    (a)   uses any premises, vehicle, vessel or stall as a sex establishment; or
    (b)   proposes to do so,
may apply to the appropriate authority for them to waive the requirement of a licence.
    (2)   An application under this paragraph may be made either as part of an application for a licence under this Schedule or without any such application.
    (3)   An application under this paragraph shall be made in writing and shall contain the particulars specified in paragraph 10(2) to (5) below and such particulars as the appropriate authority may reasonably require in addition.
    (4)   The appropriate authority may waive the requirement of a licence in any case where they consider that to require a licence would be unreasonable or inappropriate.
    (5)   A waiver may be for such period as the appropriate authority think fit.
    (6)   Where the appropriate authority grant an application for a waiver, they shall give the applicant for the waiver notice that they have granted his application.
    (7)   The appropriate authority may at any time give a person who would acquire a licence but for a waiver notice that the waiver is to terminate on such date not less than 28 days from the date on which they give the notice as may be specified in the notice.

Grant, renewal and transfer of licences for sex establishments

8. (1)   Subject to sub-paragraph (2) and paragraph 12(1) below, the appropriate authority may grant to any applicant, and from time to time renew, a licence under this Schedule for the use of any premises, vehicle, vessel or stall specified in it for a sex establishment on such terms and conditions and subject to such restrictions as may be so specified.
    (2)   No term, condition or restriction may be specified under sub-paragraph (1) above in so far as it relates to any matter in relation to which requirements or prohibitions are or could be imposed by or under the Regulatory Reform (Fire Safety) Order 2005 in respect of the premises, vehicle, vessel or stall.
9. (1)   Subject to paragraphs 11 and 27 below, any licence under this Schedule shall, unless previously cancelled under paragraph 16 or 27A below or revoked under paragraph 17(1) below, remain in force for one year or for such shorter period specified in the licence as the appropriate authority may think fit.
    (2)   Where a licence under this Schedule has been granted to any person, the appropriate authority may, if they think fit, transfer that licence to any other person on the application of that other person.
10. (1)   An application for the grant, renewal or transfer of a licence under this Schedule shall be made in writing to the appropriate authority.
    (2)   An application made otherwise than by or on behalf of a body corporate or an unincorporated body shall state—
    (a)   the full name of the applicant;
    (b)   his permanent address; and
    (c)   his age.
    (3)   An application made by a body corporate or an unincorporated body shall state—
    (a)   the full name of the body;
    (b)   the address of its registered or principal office; and
    (c)   the full names and private addresses of the directors or other persons responsible for its management.
    (4)   An application relating to premises shall state the full address of the premises.
    (5)   An application relating to a vehicle, vessel or stall shall state where it is to be used as a sex establishment.
    (6)   Every application shall contain such particulars as the appropriate authority may reasonably require in addition to any particulars required under sub-paragraphs (2) to (5) above.
    (7)   An applicant for the grant, renewal or transfer of a licence under this Schedule shall give public notice of the application.
    (8)   Notice shall in all cases be given by publishing an advertisement in a local newspaper circulating in the appropriate authority's area.

(9)   The publication shall not be later than 7 days after the date of the application.

(10)   Where the application is in respect of premises, notice of it shall in addition be displayed for 21 days beginning with the date of the application on or near the premises and in a place where the notice can conveniently be read by the public.

(11)   Every notice under this paragraph which relates to premises shall identify the premises.

(12)   Every such notice which relates to a vehicle, vessel or stall shall specify where it is to be used as a sex establishment.

(13)   Subject to sub-paragraphs (11) and (12) above, a notice under this paragraph shall be in such form as the appropriate authority may prescribe.

(14)   A copy of an application for the grant, renewal or transfer of a licence under this Schedule shall be sent to the chief officer of police—

    (*a*)   in a case where the application is made by means of a relevant electronic facility, by the appropriate authority not later than 7 days after the date the application is received by the authority;

    (*b*)   in any other case, by the applicant not later than 7 days after the date of the application.

(14A)   In sub-paragraph (14) above "relevant electronic facility" means—

    (*a*)   the electronic assistance facility referred to in regulation 38 of the Provision of Services Regulations 2009, or

    (*b*)   any facility established and maintained by the appropriate authority for the purpose of receiving applications under this Schedule electronically.

(15)   Any person objecting to an application for the grant, renewal or transfer of a licence under this Schedule shall give notice in writing of his objection to the appropriate authority, stating in general terms the grounds of the objection, not later than 28 days after the date of the application.

(16)   Where the appropriate authority receive notice of any objection under sub-paragraph (15) above, the authority shall, before considering the application, give notice in writing of the general terms of the objection to the applicant.

(17)   The appropriate authority shall not without the consent of the person making the objection reveal his name or address to the applicant.

(18)   In considering any application for the grant, renewal or transfer of a licence the appropriate authority shall have regard to any observations submitted to them by the chief officer of police and any objections of which notice has been sent to them under subparagraph (15) above.

(19)   The appropriate authority shall give an opportunity of appearing before and of being heard by a committee or sub-committee of the authority—

    (*a*)   before refusing to grant a licence, to the applicant;

    (*b*)   before refusing to renew a licence, to the holder; and

    (*c*)   before refusing to transfer a licence, to the holder and the person to whom he desires that it shall be transferred.

(20)   Where the appropriate authority refuse to grant, renew or transfer a licence, they shall give him a statement in writing of the reasons for their decision.

11.   (1)   Where, before the date of expiry of a licence, an application has been made for its renewal, it shall be deemed to remain in force notwithstanding that the date has passed until the withdrawal of the application or its determination by the appropriate authority.

(2)   Where, before the date of expiry of a licence, an application has been made for its transfer, it shall be deemed to remain in force with any necessary modifications until the withdrawal of the application or its determination, notwithstanding that the date has passed or that the person to whom the licence is to be transferred if the application is granted is carrying on the business of the sex establishment.

Refusal of licences

12.   (1)   A licence under this Schedule shall not be granted—

    (*a*)   to a person under the age of 18; or

    (*b*)   to a person who is for the time being disqualified under paragraph 17(3) below; or

    (*c*)   to a person, other than a body corporate, who is not resident in the United Kingdom or an EEA state or was not so resident throughout the period of six months immediately preceding the date when the application was made; or

    (*d*)   to a body corporate which is not incorporated in the United Kingdom or an EEA state; or

    (*e*)   to a person who has, within a period of 12 months immediately preceding the date when the application was made, been refused the grant or renewal of a licence for the premises, vehicle, vessel or stall in respect of which the application is made, unless the refusal has been reversed on appeal.

(2)   Subject to paragraph 27 below, the appropriate authority may refuse—

    (*a*)   an application for the grant or renewal of a licence on one or more of the grounds specified in sub-paragraph (3) below;

    (*b*)   an application for the transfer of a licence on either or both of the grounds specified in paragraphs (*a*) and (*b*) of that sub-paragraph.

(3)   The grounds mentioned in sub-paragraph (2) above are—

    (*a*)   that the applicant is unsuitable to hold the licence by reason of having been convicted of an offence or for any other reason;

    (*b*)   that if the licence were to be granted, renewed or transferred the business to which it relates would be managed by or carried on for the benefit of a person, other than the applicant, who would be refused the grant, renewal or transfer of such a licence if he made the application himself;

    (*c*)   that the number of sex establishments, or of sex establishments of a particular kind, in the relevant locality at the time the application is determined is equal to or exceeds the number which the authority consider is appropriate for that locality; (*d*) that the grant or renewal[1] of the licence would be inappropriate, having regard—

      (i)   to the character of the relevant locality; or

      (ii)   to the use to which any premises in the vicinity are put; or

      (iii)   to the layout, character or condition of the premises, vehicle, vessel or stall in respect of which the application is made.

(4)   Nil may be an appropriate number for the purposes of sub-paragraph (3)(*c*) above.

(5)   In this paragraph "the relevant locality" means—

    (*a*)   in relation to premises, the locality where they are situated; and

(b)   in relation to a vehicle, vessel or stall, any locality where it is desired to use it as a sex establishment.

---

[1] The licensing authority is entitled to refuse to renew an existing licence on the grounds specified in para 12(3)(d), despite the fact that there has not been any change of circumstances, provided it gives due weight to the fact that the licence has previously been granted and gives rational reasons for its refusal (*R v Birmingham City Council, ex p Sheptonhurst Ltd* [1990] 1 All ER 1026, 87 LGR 830, CA). The Sch 3 regime gives a wide discretion to licensing authorities, in particular in forming value judgements as to whether the grant or renewal of a licence would be appropriate having regard to the character of the locality. On an application to renew an SEV licence it is not necessary for an objector to demonstrate that something has changed since the decision granting the licence. But whilst it is open to the local authority to depart from the decision of its predecessor, it has to have due regard to the fact that a licence was previously granted. It is under a duty to take account of the earlier decision, to grasp the nettle of any disagreement with the earlier decision and to state its reasons for coming to a different conclusion: *R (on the application of Thompson) v Oxford City Council (Spearmint Rhino Ventures (UK) Ltd intervening)* [2014] EWCA Civ 94, [2014] 1 WLR 1811.

Power to prescribe standard conditions

13.   (1)   Subject to the provisions of this Schedule, the appropriate authority may make regulations prescribing standard conditions applicable to licences for sex establishments, that is to say, terms, conditions and restrictions on or subject to which licences under this Schedule are in general to be granted, renewed or transferred by them.

(1A)   No standard condition may be prescribed by regulation under sub-paragraph (1) above in so far as it relates to any matter in relation to which requirements or prohibitions are or could be imposed by or under the Regulatory Reform (Fire Safety) Order 2005.

(2)   Regulations under sub-paragraph (1) above may make different provision—

(a)   for sexual entertainment venues, sex cinemas, hostess bars and sex shops; and

(b)   for different kinds of sexual entertainment venues, sex cinemas, hostess bars and sex shops.

(3)   Without prejudice to the generality of sub-paragraphs (1) and (2) above, regulations under this paragraph may prescribe conditions regulating—

(a)   the hours of opening and closing of sex establishments;

(b)   displays or advertisements on or in such establishments;

(c)   the visibility of the interior of sex establishments to passers-by, and

(d)   any change from one kind of sex establishment mentioned in sub-paragraph (2)(a) above to another kind of sex establishment so mentioned.

(4)   Where the appropriate authority have made regulations under sub-paragraph (1) above, every such licence granted, renewed or transferred by them shall be presumed to have been so granted, renewed or transferred subject to any standard conditions applicable to it unless they have been expressly excluded or varied.

(5)   Where the appropriate authority have made regulations under sub-paragraph (1) above, they shall, if so requested by any person, supply him with a copy of the regulations on payment of such reasonable fee as the authority may determine.

(6)   In any legal proceedings the production of a copy of any regulations made by the appropriate authority under sub-paragraph (1) above purporting to be certified as a true copy by an officer of the authority authorised to give a certificate for the purposes of this paragraph shall be prima facie evidence of such regulations, and no proof shall be required of the handwriting or official position or authority of any person giving such certificate.

Copies of licences and standard conditions

14.   (1)   The holder of a licence under this Schedule shall keep exhibited in a suitable place to be specified in the licence a copy of the licence and any regulations made under paragraph 13(1) above which prescribe standard conditions subject to which the licence is held.

(2)   The appropriate authority shall send a copy of any licence granted under this Schedule to the chief officer of police for the area where the sex establishment is situated.

Transmission and cancellation of licences

15.   In the event of the death of the holder of a licence granted under this Schedule, that licence shall be deemed to have been granted to his personal representatives and shall, unless previously revoked, remain in force until the end of the period of 3 months beginning with the death and shall then expire; but the appropriate authority may from time to time, on the application of those representatives, extend or further extend the period of three months if the authority are satisfied that the extension is necessary for the purpose of winding up the deceased's estate and that no other circumstances make it undesirable.

16.   The appropriate authority may, at the written request of the holder of a licence, cancel the licence.

Revocation of licences

17.   (1)   The appropriate authority may, after giving the holder of a licence under this Schedule an opportunity of appearing before and being heard by them, at any time revoke the licence—

(a)   on any ground specified in sub-paragraph (1) of paragraph 12 above; or

(b)   on either of the grounds specified in sub-paragraph (3)(a) and (b) of that paragraph.

(2)   Where a licence is revoked, the appropriate authority shall, if required to do so by the person who held it, give him a statement in writing of the reasons for their decision within 7 days of his requiring them to do so.

(3)   Where a licence is revoked, its holder shall be disqualified from holding or obtaining a licence in the area of the appropriate authority for a period of 12 months beginning with the date of revocation.

Variation of licences

18.   (1)   The holder of a licence under this Schedule may at any time apply to the appropriate authority for any such variation of the terms, conditions or restrictions on or subject to which the licence is held as may be specified in the application.

(2)   Subject to sub-paragraph (4) below, the appropriate authority—

(a)   may make the variation specified in the application; or

(b)   may make such variations as they think fit; or

(c)   may refuse the application.

(3)   The variations that an authority may make by virtue of sub-paragraph (2)(b) above include, without prejudice to the generality of that sub-paragraph, variations involving the imposition of terms, conditions or

restrictions other than those specified in the application.

(4)   No variation is to be made under this paragraph in so far as it relates to any matter in relation to which requirements or prohibitions are or could be imposed by or under the Regulatory Reform (Fire Safety) Order 2005.

Fees

19.   An applicant for the grant, variation, renewal or transfer of a licence under this Schedule shall pay a reasonable fee determined by the appropriate authority[1].

---

[1] A licensing authority is permitted by this provision to require an applicant for the grant or renewal of a licence to pay a reasonable fee to cover the running and enforcement costs of a licensing scheme, and to make this fee payable as and when the licence is actually granted, pursuant to the application. But the authority is not entitled to charge such a fee on a refundable basis if the application is refused, at the time when the application is lodged see *R (Hemming (trading as Simply Pleasure Ltd) and others) v Westminster City Council (Architects Registration Board and others intervening) (Case C-316/15)* [2017] 3 WLR 317, ECJ; *Hemming (trading as Simply Pleasure Ltd) and others v Westminster City Council (Architects Registration Board and others intervening) (No 2)* [2017] UKSC 50, [2017] 3 WLR 342.

Enforcement

20.   (1)   A person who—
- (a)   knowingly[1] uses, or knowingly causes or permits the use of, any premises, vehicle, vessel or stall contrary to paragraph 6 above[2]; or
- (b)   being the holder of a licence for a sex establishment, employs in the business of the establishment any person known to him to be disqualified from holding such a licence; or
- (c)   being the holder of a licence under this Schedule, without reasonable excuse knowingly contravenes, or without reasonable excuse knowingly permits the contravention of, a term, condition or restriction specified in the licence; or
- (d)   being the servant or agent of the holder of a licence under this Schedule, without reasonable excuse knowingly contravenes, or without reasonable excuse knowingly permits the contravention of, a term, condition or restriction specified in the licence,

shall be guilty of an offence.

21.   Any person who, in connection with an application for the grant, renewal or transfer of a licence under this Schedule, makes a false statement which he knows to be false in any material respect or which he does not believe to be true, shall be guilty of an offence.

22.   (1)   A person guilty of an offence under paragraph 20 or 21 above shall be liable on summary conviction to a fine.

(2)   A person who, being the holder of a licence under this Schedule, fails without reasonable excuse to comply with paragraph 14(1) above shall be guilty of an offence and liable on summary conviction to a fine not exceeding **level 3** on the standard scale.

---

[1] The prosecution must establish not only that the person knew that the premises were used as a sex establishment but also that he knew that they were being so used without a licence. Such knowledge may be proved either by proving actual knowledge or by showing that the defendant had deliberately shut his eyes to the obvious or refrained from inquiry because he suspected the truth but did not want to have his suspicions confirmed (*Westminster City Council v Croyalgrange Ltd* [1986] 2 All ER 353, [1986] 1 WLR 674, HL).

[2] On such a prosecution, the court cannot investigate and determine the validity of a licensing authority's refusal to grant a licence (*Quietlynn Ltd v Plymouth City Council* [1988] QB 114, [1987] 2 All ER 1040, 151 JP 810, DC).

Offences relating to persons under 18

23.   (1)   A person who, being the holder of a licence for a sex establishment—
- (a)   without reasonable excuse knowingly permits a person under 18 years of age to enter the establishment; or
- (b)   employs a person known to him to be under 18 years of age in the business of the establishment,

shall be guilty of an offence.

(2)   A person guilty of an offence under this paragraph shall be liable on summary conviction to a fine.

Powers of constables and local authority officers

24.   Repealed.

25.   (1)   A constable may, at any reasonable time, enter and inspect any sex establishment in respect of which a licence under this Schedule is for the time being in force, with a view to seeing—
- (i)   whether the terms, conditions or restrictions on or subject to which the licence is held are complied with;
- (ii)   whether any person employed in the business of the establishment is disqualified from holding a licence under this Schedule;
- (iii)   whether any person under 18 years of age is in the establishment; and
- (iv)   whether any person under that age is employed in the business of the establishment.

(2)   Subject to sub-paragraph (4) below, a constable may enter and inspect a sex establishment if he has reason to suspect that an offence under paragraph 20, 21 or 23 above has been, is being, or is about to be committed in relation to it.

(3)   An authorised officer of a local authority may exercise the powers conferred by sub-paragraphs (1) and (2) above in relation to a sex establishment in the local authority's area.

(4)   No power conferred by sub-paragraph (2) above may be exercised by a constable or an authorised officer of a local authority unless he has been authorised to exercise it by a warrant granted by a justice of the peace.

(5)   Where an authorised officer of a local authority exercises any such power, he shall produce his authority if required to do so by the occupier of the premises or the person in charge of the vehicle, vessel or stall in relation to which the power is exercised.

(6)   Any person who without reasonable excuse refuses to permit a constable or an authorised officer of a local authority to exercise any such power shall be guilty of an offence and shall for every such refusal be liable on summary conviction to a fine not exceeding **level 5** on the standard scale.

25A.   (1)   A person acting under the authority of a warrant under paragraph 25(4) may seize and remove anything found on the premises concerned that the person reasonably believes could be forfeited under sub-paragraph (4).

(2)   The person who, immediately before the seizure, had custody or control of anything seized under sub-paragraph (1) may request any authorised officer of a local authority who seized it to provide a record of what was seized.

(3)   The authorised officer must provide the record within a reasonable time of the request being made.

(4)   The court by or before which a person is convicted of an offence under paragraph 20 or 23 of this Schedule may order anything—

(a)   produced to the court; and

(b)   shown to the satisfaction of the court to relate to the offence;

to be forfeited and dealt with in such manner as the court may order.

(5)   But the court may not order the forfeiture of anything under sub-paragraph (4) if it (whether alone or taken together with other things being forfeited which appear to the court to have been in the custody or control of the same person) is worth more than the amount of the maximum fine specified in paragraph 22(1).

(6)   Sub-paragraph (7) applies if a person claiming to be the owner of, or otherwise interested in, anything that may be forfeited applies to be heard by the court.

(7)   The court may not order the forfeiture unless the person has had an opportunity to show why the order should not be made.

Offences by bodies corporate

26.   (1)   Where an offence under this Schedule committed by a body corporate is proved to have been committed with the consent or connivance of, or to be attributable to any neglect on the part of, any director, manager, secretary or other similar officer of the body corporate, or any person who was purporting to act in any such capacity, he, as well as the body corporate, shall be guilty of the offence.

(2)   Where the affairs of a body corporate are managed by its members sub-paragraph (1) above shall apply to the acts and defaults of a member in connection with his function of management as if he were a director of the body corporate.

Appeals

27.   (1)   Subject to sub-paragraphs (2) and (3) below, any of the following persons, that is to say—

(a)   an applicant for the grant, renewal or transfer of a licence under this Schedule whose application is refused;

(b)   an applicant for the variation of the terms, conditions or restrictions on or subject to which any such licence is held whose application is refused;

(c)   a holder of any such licence who is aggrieved by any term, condition or restriction on or subject to which the licence is held; or

(d)   a holder of any such licence whose licence is revoked,

may at any time before the expiration of the period of 21 days beginning with the relevant date appeal to a magistrates' court

(2)   An applicant whose application for the grant or renewal of a licence is refused, or whose licence is revoked, on any ground specified in paragraph 12(1) above shall not have a right to appeal under this paragraph unless the applicant seeks to show that the ground did not apply to him.

(3)   An applicant whose application for the grant or renewal of a licence is refused on either ground specified in paragraph 12(3)(c) or (d) above shall not have the right to appeal under this paragraph.

(4)   In this paragraph—

"the relevant date" means the date on which the person in question is notified of the refusal of his application, the imposition of the term, condition or restriction by which he is aggrieved or the revocation of his licence, as the case may be.

(5)   An appeal against the decision of a magistrates' court under this paragraph may be brought to the Crown Court.

(6)   Where an appeal is brought to the Crown Court under sub-paragraph (5) above, the decision of the Crown Court shall be final.

(7)   On an appeal to the magistrates' court or the Crown Court under this paragraph the court may make such order as it thinks fit.

(8)   Subject to sub-paragraphs (9) to (12) below, it shall be the duty of the appropriate authority to give effect to an order of the magistrates' court or the Crown Court.

(9)   The appropriate authority need not give effect to the order of the magistrates' court until the time for bringing an appeal under sub-paragraph (5) above has expired and, if such an appeal is duly brought, until the determination or abandonment of the appeal.

(10)   Where a licence is revoked or an application for the renewal of a licence is refused, the licence shall be deemed to remain in force—

(a)   until the time for bringing an appeal under this paragraph has expired and, if such an appeal is duly brought, until the determination or abandonment of the appeal; and

(b)   where an appeal relating to the refusal of an application for such a renewal is successful and no further appeal is available, until the licence is renewed by the appropriate authority.

(10A)   Sub-paragraph (10) does not apply if the grounds for refusing an application for the renewal of a licence are those set out in paragraph 12(3)(c) or (d) of this Schedule.

(11)   Where—

(a)   the holder of a licence makes an application under paragraph 18 above; and

(b)   the appropriate authority impose any term, condition or restriction other than one specified in the application,

the licence shall be deemed to be free of it until the time for bringing an appeal under this paragraph has expired.

(12)   Where an appeal is brought under this paragraph against the imposition of any such term, condition or restriction, the licence shall be deemed to be free of it until the determination or abandonment of the appeal.

Premises which are deemed sexual entertainment venues

27A.   (1)   This paragraph applies if—

(a)   premises are subject to a licence for a sexual entertainment venue; and

(b)   their use would be use as such a venue but for the operation of paragraph 2A(3)(b).

(2)   This Schedule applies as if—

(a)   the premises were a sexual entertainment venue; and

(b)   the use or business of the premises was use as, or the business of, such a venue.

(3)   But the appropriate authority must cancel the licence if the holder of the licence asks them in writing to do so.

(4)   In this paragraph "premises" has the same meaning as in paragraph 2A.

Provisions relating to existing premises

28.   (1)   Without prejudice to any other enactment it shall be lawful for any person who—

(a)   was using any premises, vehicle, vessel or stall as a sex establishment immediately before the date of the first publication under subsection (2) of section 2 above of a notice of the passing of a resolution under that section by the local authority for the area; and

(b)   had before the appointed day duly applied to the appropriate authority for a licence for the establishment,

to continue to use the premises, vehicle, vessel or stall as a sex establishment until the determination of his application.

(2)   In this paragraph and paragraph 29 below "the appointed day", in relation to any area, means the day specified in the resolution passed under section 2 above as the date upon which this Schedule is to come into force in that area.

29.   (1)   This paragraph applies to an application for the grant of a licence under this Schedule made before the appointed day.

(2)   A local authority shall not consider any application to which this paragraph applies before the appointed day.

(3)   A local authority shall not grant any application to which this paragraph applies until they have considered all such applications.

(4)   In considering which of several applications to which this paragraph applies should be granted a local authority shall give preference over other applicants to any applicant who satisfies them—

(a)   that he is using the premises, vehicle, vessel or stall to which the application relates as a sex establishment; and

(b)   that some person was using the premises, vehicle, vessel or stall as a sex establishment on 22nd December 1981; and

(c)   that—

(i)   he is that person; or

(ii)   he is a successor of that person in the business or activity which was being carried on there on that date.

Commencement of Schedule

30.   (1)   So far as it relates to sex cinemas, this Schedule shall come into force on such day as the Secretary of State may by order[1] made by statutory instrument appoint.

(2)   Subject to sub-paragraph (1) above, this Schedule shall come into force on the day on which this Act is passed.

(3)   Where, in relation to any area, the day appointed under sub-paragraph (1) above falls after the day specified in a resolution passed under section 2 above as the day upon which this Schedule is to come into force in that area, the day so appointed shall, for the purposes of paragraphs 28 and 29 above, be the appointed day in relation to sex cinemas in the area.

---

[1]   The Local Government (Miscellaneous Provisions) Act 1982 (Commencement No 1) Order 1982, SI 1982/1119, brought into force on 13 October 1982, Sch 3 so far as it relates to sex cinemas.

SCHEDULE 4
STREET TRADING

Section 3

(As amended by the Criminal Justice Act 1982, s 46, the Food Act 1984, Sch 10, the Government of Wales Act 1998, Sch 15 and Sch 18, the Housing and Regeneration Act 2008, Sch 8 and the Localism Act 2011, Schs 19 and 22.)

Interpretation

7.7545   1.   (1)   In this Schedule—

"consent street" means a street in which street trading is prohibited without the consent of the district council;

"licence street" means a street in which street trading is prohibited without a licence granted by the district council;

"principal terms", in relation to a street trading licence, has the meaning assigned to it by paragraph 4(3) below;

"prohibited street" means a street in which street trading is prohibited;

"street" includes—

(a)   any road, footway, beach or other area to which the public have access without payment; and

(b)   a service area as defined in section 329 of the Highways Act 1980,

and also includes any part of a street;

"street trading" means, subject to sub-paragraph (2) below, the selling or exposing or offering for sale of any article (including a living thing) in a street; and

"subsidiary terms", in relation to a street trading licence, has the meaning assigned to it by paragraph 4(4) below.

(2)   The following are not street trading for the purposes of this Schedule—

(a)   trading by a person acting as a pedlar[1] under the authority of a pedlar's certificate granted under the Pedlars Act 1871;

(b)   anything done in a market[2] or fair the right to hold which was acquired by virtue of a grant (including a presumed grant) or acquired or established by virtue of an enactment or order.

(c)   trading in a trunk road picnic area provided by the Secretary of State under section 112 of the Highways Act 1980;

(d)   trading as a news vendor;

(e)   trading which—

      (i)   is carried on at premises used as a petrol filling station; or

      (ii)   is carried on at premises used as a shop or in a street adjoining premises so used and as part of the business of the shop;

(f)   selling things, or offering or exposing them for sale, as a roundsman[3];

(g)   the use for trading under Part VIIA of the Highways Act 1980 of an object or structure placed on, in or over a highway;

(h)   the operation of facilities for recreation or refreshment under Part VIIA of the Highways Act 1980;

(j)   the doing of anything authorised by regulations made under section 5 of the Police, Factories, etc (Miscellaneous Provisions) Act 1916.[*]

(3)   The reference to trading as a news vendor in sub-paragraph (2)(d) is a reference to trading where—

    (a)   the only articles sold or exposed or offered for sale are newspapers or periodicals; and

    (b)   they are sold or exposed or offered for sale without a stall or receptacle for them or with a stall or receptacle for them which does not—

       (i)   exceed one metre in length or width or two metres in height;

       (ii)   occupy a ground area exceeding 0·25 square metres; or

       (iii)   stand on the carriageway of a street.

---

[*] **Para 1(2)(j) substituted by the Charities Act 1992, Sch 6 from a date to be appointed. Further substituted by the Charities Act 2006, Sch 8 from a date to be appointed.**

[1]   See the definition of "pedlar" in s 3 of the 1871 Act in this PART, post. The burden of proving that the defendant was trading as a pedlar with a certificate is on the defendant: *Jones v Bath and North East Somerset Council* [2012] EWHC 1361 (Admin), (2012) 176 JP 530.

[2]   In the first instance, it is for the defendant to prove that the place where he was trading was a market. The holder of a market right may, however, restrict the holding of the market to an area smaller than that over which his right subsists, see *Jones v Lewis* (1989) Times, 14 June, DC.

[3]   "Roundsman" means "one who goes the round of his customers for orders and the delivery of goods" and "denotes a person who follows a set route to attend on specific/identifiable customers for the purpose of either taking orders or for the delivery of goods"; the Act clearly envisages that "intermediate sales" may be made, but that is ancillary to the "round": *Kempin (t/a British Bulldog) v Brighton and Hove Council* [2001] EWHC Admin 140, [2001] All ER (D) 125 (Feb)).

Designation of streets

2.   (1)   A district council may by resolution designate any street in their district as—

    (a)   a prohibited street;

    (b)   a licence street; or

    (c)   a consent street.

(2)   If a district council pass such a resolution as is mentioned in sub-paragraph (1) above, the designation of the street shall take effect on the day specified in that behalf in the resolution (which must not be before the expiration of the period of one month beginning with the day on which the resolution is passed).

(3)   A council shall not pass such a resolution unless—

    (a)   they have published notice of their intention to pass such a resolution in a local newspaper circulating in their area;

    (b)   they have served a copy of the notice—

       (i)   on the chief officer of police for the area in which the street to be designated by the resolution is situated; and

       (ii)   on any highway authority responsible for that street; and

    (c)   where sub-paragraph (4) below applies, they have obtained the necessary consent.

(4)   This sub-paragraph applies—

    (a)   where the resolution relates to a street which is owned or maintainable by a relevant corporation; and

    (b)   where the resolution designates as a licence street any street maintained by a highway authority;

and in sub-paragraph (3) above "necessary consent" means—

    (i)   in the case mentioned in paragraph (a) above, the consent of the relevant corporation; and

    (ii)   in the case mentioned in paragraph (b) above, the consent of the highway authority.

(5)   The following are relevant corporations for the purposes of this paragraph—

    (a)   the British Railways Board;

    (b)   new towns residuary body;

    (ba)   a Mayoral development corporation;

    (c)   a development corporation for a new town; and

    (d)   an urban development corporation established under the Local Government, Planning and Land Act 1980.

    (e)   *repealed.*

(5A)   In sub-paragraph (5)(b) above "new towns residuary body" means—

    (a)   in relation to England, the Homes and Communities Agency so far as exercising functions in relation to anything transferred (or to be transferred) to it as mentioned in section 52(1)(a) to (d) of the Housing and Regeneration Act 2008 or the Greater London Authority so far as exercising its new towns and urban development functions; and

    (b)   in relation to Wales, the Welsh Ministers so far as exercising functions in relation to anything transferred (or to be transferred) to them as mentioned in section 36(1)(a)(i) to (iii) of the New Towns Act 1981.

(6)   The notice referred to in sub-paragraph (3) above—

    (a)   shall contain a draft of the resolution; and

    (b)   shall state that representations relating to it may be made in writing to the council within such period, not less than 28 days after publication of the notice, as may be specified in the notice.

(7)   As soon as practicable after the expiry of the period specified under sub-paragraph (6) above, the council shall consider any representations relating to the proposed resolution which they have received before the expiry of that period.

(8)   After the council have considered those representations, they may, if they think fit, pass such a resolution relating to the street as is mentioned in sub-paragraph (1) above.

(9)   The council shall publish notice that they have passed such a resolution in two consecutive weeks in a

local newspaper circulating in their area.

(10) The first publication shall not be later than 28 days before the day specified in the resolution for the coming into force of the designation.

(11) Where a street is designated as a licence street, the council may resolve—

(*a*) in the resolution which so designates the street; or

(*b*) subject to sub-paragraph (12) below, by a separate resolution at any time,

that a street trading licence is not to be granted to any person who proposes to trade in the street for a number of days in every week less than a number specified in the resolution.

(12) Sub-paragraphs (3)(*a*) and (6) to (10) above shall apply in relation to a resolution under sub-paragraph (11)(*b*) above as they apply in relation to a resolution under sub-paragraph (1) above.

(13) Any resolution passed under this paragraph may be varied or rescinded by a subsequent resolution so passed.

Street trading licences

3. (1) An application for a street trading licence or the renewal of such a licence shall be made in writing to the district council.

(2) The applicant shall state—

(*a*) his full name and address;

(*b*) the street in which, days on which and times between which he desires to trade;

(*c*) the description of articles in which he desires to trade and the description of any stall or container which he desires to use in connection with his trade in those articles; and

(*d*) such other particulars as the council may reasonably require.

(3) If the council so require, the applicant shall submit two photographs of himself with his application.

(4) A street trading licence shall not be granted—

(*a*) to a person under the age of 17 years; or

(*b*) for any trading in a highway in relation to which a control order under section 7 of the Local Government (Miscellaneous Provisions) Act 1976 (road-side sales) is in force, other than trading to which the control order does not apply.

(5) Subject to sub-paragraph (4) above, it shall be the duty of the council to grant an application for a street trading licence or the renewal of such a licence unless they consider that the application ought to be refused on one or more of the grounds specified in sub-paragraph (6) below.

(6) Subject to sub-paragraph (8) below, the council may refuse an application on any of the following grounds—

(*a*) that there is not enough space in the street for the applicant to engage in the trading in which he desires to engage without causing undue interference or inconvenience to persons using the street;

(*b*) that there are already enough traders trading in the street from shops or otherwise in the goods in which the applicant desires to trade;

(*c*) that the applicant desires to trade on fewer days than the minimum number specified in a resolution under paragraph 2(11) above;

(*d*) that the applicant is unsuitable to hold the licence by reason of having been convicted of an offence or for any other reason;

(*e*) that the applicant has at any time been granted a street trading licence by the council and has persistently refused or neglected to pay fees due to them for it or charges due to them under paragraph 9(6) below for services rendered by them to him in his capacity as licence-holder;

(*f*) that the applicant has at any time been granted a street trading consent by the council and has persistently refused or neglected to pay fees due to them for it;

(*g*) that the applicant has without reasonable excuse failed to avail himself to a reasonable extent of a previous street trading licence.

(7) If the council consider that grounds for refusal exist under sub-paragraph (6)(*a*), (*b*) or (*g*) above, they may grant the applicant a licence which permits him—

(*a*) to trade on fewer days or during a shorter period in each day than specified in the application; or

(*b*) to trade only in one or more of the descriptions of goods specified in the application.

(8) If—

(*a*) a person is licensed or otherwise authorised to trade in a street under the provisions of any local Act; and

(*b*) the street becomes a licence street; and

(*c*) he was trading from a fixed position in the street immediately before it became a licence street; and

(*d*) he applied for a street trading licence to trade in the street, his application shall not be refused on any of the grounds mentioned in sub-paragraph (6)(*a*) to (*c*) above.

4. (1) A street trading licence shall specify—

(*a*) the street in which, days on which and times between which the licence-holder is permitted to trade; and

(*b*) the description of articles in which he is permitted to trade.

(2) If the district council determine that a licence-holder is to confine his trading to a particular place in the street, his street trading licence shall specify that place.

(3) Matters that fall to be specified in a street trading licence by virtue of sub-paragraph (1) or (2) above are referred to in this Schedule as the "principal terms" of the licence.

(4) When granting or renewing a street trading licence, the council may attach such further conditions (in this Schedule referred to as the "subsidiary terms" of the licence) as appear to them to be reasonable.

(5) Without prejudice to the generality of sub-paragraph (4) above, the subsidiary terms of a licence may include conditions—

(*a*) specifying the size and type of any stall or container which the licence-holder may use for trading;

(*b*) requiring that any stall or container so used shall carry the name of the licence-holder or the number of his licence or both; and

(*c*) prohibiting the leaving of refuse by the licence-holder or restricting the amount of refuse which he may leave or the places in which he may leave it.

(6) A street trading licence shall, unless previously revoked or surrendered, remain valid for a period of

12 months from the date on which it is granted or, if a shorter period is specified in the licence, for that period.

(7)   If a district council resolve that the whole or part of a licence street shall be designated a prohibited street, then, on the designation taking effect, any street trading licence issued for trading in that street shall cease to be valid so far as it relates to the prohibited street.

5.   (1)   A district council may at any time revoke a street trading licence if they consider—
- (a)   that, owing to circumstances which have arisen since the grant or renewal of the licence, there is not enough space in the street for the licence-holder to engage in the trading permitted by the licence without causing undue interference or inconvenience to persons using the street;
- (b)   that the licence-holder is unsuitable to hold the licence by reason of having been convicted of an offence or for any other reason;
- (c)   that, since the grant or renewal of the licence, the licence-holder has persistently refused or neglected to pay fees due to the council for it or charges due to them under paragraph 9(6) below for services rendered by them to him in his capacity as licence-holder; or
- (d)   that, since the grant or renewal of the licence, the licence-holder has without reasonable excuse failed to avail himself of the licence to a reasonable extent.

(2)   If the council consider that they have ground for revoking a licence by virtue of sub-paragraph (1)(a) or (d) above, they may, instead of revoking it, vary its principal terms—
- (a)   by reducing the number of days or the period in any one day during which the licence-holder is permitted to trade; or
- (b)   by restricting the descriptions of goods in which he is permitted to trade.

(3)   A licence-holder may at any time surrender his licence to the council and it shall then cease to be valid.

6.   (1)   When a district council receive an application for the grant or renewal of a street trading licence, they shall within a reasonable time—
- (a)   grant a licence in the terms applied for; or
- (b)   serve notice on the applicant under sub-paragraph (2) below.

(2)   If the council propose—
- (a)   to refuse an application for the grant or renewal of a licence; or
- (b)   to grant a licence on principal terms different from those specified in the application; or
- (c)   to grant a licence confining the applicant's trading to a particular place in a street; or
- (d)   to vary the principal terms of a licence; or
- (e)   to revoke a licence,

they shall first serve a notice on the applicant or, as the case may be, the licence-holder—
- (i)   specifying the ground or grounds on which their decision would be based; and
- (ii)   stating that within 7 days of receiving the notice he may in writing require them to give him an opportunity to make representations to them concerning it.

(3)   Where a notice has been served under sub-paragraph (2) above, the council shall not determine the matter until either—
- (a)   the person on whom it was served has made representations to them concerning their decision; or
- (b)   the period during which he could have required them to give him an opportunity to make representations has elapsed without his requiring them to give him such an opportunity; or
- (c)   the conditions specified in sub-paragraph (4) below are satisfied.

(4)   The conditions mentioned in sub-paragraph (3)(c) above are—
- (a)   that the person on whom the notice under sub-paragraph (2) above was served has required the council to give him an opportunity to make representations to them concerning it, as provided by sub-paragraph (2)(ii) above;
- (b)   that the council have allowed him a reasonable period for making his representations; and
- (c)   that he has failed to make them within that period.

(5)   A person aggrieved—
- (a)   by the refusal of a council to grant or renew a licence, where—
  - (i)   they specified in their notice under sub-paragraph (2) above one of the grounds mentioned in paragraph 3(6)(d) to (g) above as the only ground on which their decision would be based; or
  - (ii)   they specified more than one ground in that notice but all the specified grounds were grounds mentioned in those paragraphs; or
- (b)   by a decision of a council to grant him a licence with principal terms different from those of a licence which he previously held, where they specified in their notice under sub-paragraph (2) above the ground mentioned in paragraph 3(6)(g) above as the only ground on which their decision would be based; or
- (c)   by a decision of a council—
  - (i)   to vary the principal terms of a licence; or
  - (ii)   to revoke a licence,

  in a case where they specified in their notice under sub-paragraph (2) above one of the grounds mentioned in paragraph 5(1)(b) to (d) above as the only ground on which their decision would be based or they specified more than one ground in that notice but all the specified grounds were grounds mentioned in those paragraphs,

may, at any time before the expiration of the period of 21 days beginning with the date upon which he is notified of the refusal or decision, appeal to the magistrates' court acting for the petty sessions area in which the street is situated.

(6)   An appeal[1] against the decision of a magistrates' court under this paragraph may be brought to the Crown Court.

(7)   On an appeal to the magistrates' court or the Crown Court under this paragraph the court may make such order as it thinks fit.

(8)   Subject to sub-paragraphs (9) to (11) below, it shall be the duty of the council to give effect to an order of the magistrates' court or the Crown Court.

(9)   The council need not give effect to the order of the magistrates' court until the time for bringing an appeal under sub-paragraph (6) above has expired and, if such an appeal is duly brought, until the determination or abandonment of the appeal.

(10)   If a licence-holder applies for renewal of his licence before the date of its expiry, it shall remain valid—
- (a)   until the grant by the council of a new licence with the same principal terms; or
- (b)   if—

    (i)   the council refuse renewal of the licence or decide to grant a licence with principal terms different from those of the existing licence, and

    (ii)   he has a right of appeal under this paragraph,

    until the time for bringing an appeal has expired or, where an appeal is duly brought, until the determination or abandonment of the appeal; or

  (c)   if he has no right of appeal under this paragraph, until the council either grant him a new licence with principal terms different from those of the existing licence or notify him of their decision to refuse his application.

(11)   Where—

  (a)   a council decide—

    (i)   to vary the principal terms of a licence; or

    (ii)   to revoke a licence; and

  (b)   a right of appeal is available to the licence-holder under this paragraph,

the variation or revocation shall not take effect until the time for bringing an appeal has expired or, where an appeal is duly brought, until the determination or abandonment of the appeal.

---

[1] The position in London is governed by the London County Council (General Powers) Act 1947 and is somewhat different: see *R v Crown Court at Southwark, ex p Watts* (1989) 153 JP 666, 88 LGR 86, DC.

Street trading consents

7.   (1)   An application for a street trading consent or the renewal of such a consent shall be made in writing to the district council.

  (2)   Subject to sub-paragraph (3) below, the council may grant a consent if they think fit.

  (3)   A street trading consent shall not be granted—

  (a)   to a person under the age of 17 years; or

  (b)   for any trading in a highway to which a control order under section 7 of the Local Government (Miscellaneous Provisions) Act 1976 is in force, other than trading to which the control order does not apply.

  (4)   When granting or renewing a street trading consent the council may attach such conditions to it as they consider reasonably necessary.

  (5)   Without prejudice to the generality of sub-paragraph (4) above, the conditions that may be attached to a street trading consent by virtue of that sub-paragraph include conditions to prevent—

  (a)   obstruction of the street or danger to persons using it; or

  (b)   nuisance or annoyance (whether to persons using the street or otherwise).

  (6)   The council may at any time vary the conditions of a street trading consent.

  (7)   Subject to sub-paragraph (8) below, the holder of a street trading consent shall not trade in a consent street from a van or other vehicle or from a stall, barrow or cart.

  (8)   The council may include in a street trading consent permission for its holder to trade in a consent street—

  (a)   from a stationary van, cart, barrow or other vehicle; or

  (b)   from a portable stall.

  (9)   If they include such a permission, they may make the consent subject to conditions—

  (a)   as to where the holder of the street trading consent may trade by virtue of the permission; and

  (b)   as to the times between which or periods for which he may so trade.

(10)   A street trading consent may be granted for any period not exceeding 12 months but may be revoked at any time.

(11)   The holder of a street trading consent may at anytime surrender his consent to the council and it shall then cease to be valid.

General

8.   The holder of a street trading licence or a street trading consent may employ any other person to assist him in his trading without a further licence or consent being required.

9.   (1)   A district council may charge such fees as they consider reasonable for the grant or renewal of a street trading licence or a street trading consent.

  (2)   A council may determine different fees for different types of licence or consent and, in particular, but without prejudice to the generality of this sub-paragraph, may determine fees differing according—

  (a)   to the duration of the licence or consent;

  (b)   to the street in which it authorises trading; and

  (c)   to the descriptions of articles in which the holder is authorised to trade.

  (3)   A council may require that applications for the grant or renewal of licences or consents shall be accompanied by so much of the fee as the council may require, by way of a deposit to be repaid by the council to the applicant if the application is refused.

  (4)   A council may determine that fees may be paid by instalments.

  (5)   Where a consent is surrendered or revoked, the council shall remit or refund, as they consider appropriate, the whole or a part of any fee paid for the grant or renewal of the consent.

  (6)   A council may recover from a licence-holder such reasonable charges as they may determine for the collection of refuse, the cleansing of streets and other services rendered by them to him in his capacity as licence-holder.

  (7)   Where a licence—

  (a)   is surrendered or revoked; or

  (b)   ceases to be valid by virtue of paragraph 4(7) above,

the council may remit or refund, as they consider appropriate, the whole or a part—

    (i)   of any fee paid for the grant or renewal of the licence; or

    (ii)   of any charges recoverable under sub-paragraph (6) above.

  (8)   The council may determine—

  (a)   that charges under sub-paragraph (6) above shall be included in a fee payable under sub-paragraph (1) above; or

(b)   that they shall be separately recoverable.

(9)   Before determining charges to be made under sub-paragraph (6) above or varying the amount of such charges the council—

(a)   shall give notice of the proposed charges to licence-holders; and

(b)   shall publish notice of the proposed charges in a local newspaper circulating in their area.

(10)   A notice under sub-paragraph (9) above shall specify a reasonable period within which representations concerning the proposed charges may be made to the council.

(11)   It shall be the duty of a council to consider any such representations which are made to them within the period specified in the notice.

Offences

10.   (1)   A person who—

(a)   engages in street trading in a prohibited street; or

(b)   engages in street trading in a licence street or a consent street without being authorised[1] to do so under this Schedule; or

(c)   contravenes any of the principal terms of a street trading licence; or

(d)   being authorised by a street trading consent to trade in a consent street, trades in that street—

(i)   from a stationary van, cart, barrow or other vehicle; or

(ii)   from a portable stall,

without first having been granted permission to do so under paragraph 7(8) above; or

(e)   contravenes a condition imposed under paragraph 7(9) above,

shall be guilty of an offence[2].

(2)   It shall be a defence for a person charged with an offence under sub-paragraph (1) above to prove that he took all reasonable precautions and exercised all due diligence to avoid commission of the offence.

(3)   Any person who, in connection with an application for a street trading licence or for a street trading consent, makes a false statement which he knows to be false in any material respect, or which he does not believe to be true, shall be guilty of an offence.

(4)   A person guilty of an offence under this paragraph shall be liable on summary conviction to a fine not exceeding **level 3** on the standard scale.

---

[1] The burden of establishing the statutory exception is on the defendant: *Jones v Bath and North East Somerset Council* [2012] EWHC 1361 (Admin), 176 JP 530.

[2] In *Caradon District Council v Cheeseman* [2000] Crim LR 190, it was held that a trader had common law rights, including the right to be treated fairly and that justices rightly held that a public law challenge was available as a defence to a criminal charge for an offence under this Schedule.

Savings

11.   Nothing in this Schedule shall affect—

(a)   section 13 of the Markets and Fairs Clauses Act 1847 (prohibition of sales elsewhere than in market or in shops etc) as applied by any other Act;

(b)   section 56 of the Food Act 1984 (prohibition of certain sales during market hours).

Local Government Act 1986

(1986 c 10)

PART II[1]

LOCAL AUTHORITY PUBLICITY

7.7546 2.   Prohibition of political publicity   (1)   A local authority shall not publish, or arrange for the publication of, any material which, in whole or in part, appears to be designed to affect public support for a political party.

(2)   In determining whether material falls within the prohibition regard shall be had to content and style of the material, the time and other circumstances of publication and the likely effect on those to whom it is directed and, in particular, to the following matters—

(a)   whether material refers to a political party or to persons identified with a political party or promotes or opposes a point of view on a question of political controversy which is identifiable as the view of one political party and not of another;

(b)   where the material is part of a campaign, the effect which the campaign appears to be designed to achieve.

(3)   A local authority shall not give financial or other assistance to a person for the publication of material which the authority are prohibited by this section from publishing themselves.

[Local Government Act 1986, s 2 as amended by the Local Government Act 1988, s 27 and the Communications Act 2003, s 349.]

---

[1] Part II contains ss 2–6.

7.7547 4.   Codes of recommended practice as regards publicity   *Secretary of State may issue codes of recommended practice as regards the content, style, distribution and cost of local authority publicity.*

7.7548 5.   Separate account of expenditure on publicity   (1)   A local authority shall keep a separate account of their expenditure on publicity.

(2)   Any person interested may at any reasonable time and without payment inspect the account and make copies of it or any part of it.

(3)   A person having custody of the account who intentionally obstructs a person in the exercise of the rights conferred by subsection (2) commits an offence and is liable on summary conviction to a fine not exceeding **level 3** on the standard scale.

(4)   The regulation making power conferred by section 32(1)(e) of the Local Audit and

Accountability Act 2014, section 39(1)(e) of the Public Audit (Wales) Act 2004 or section 105(1)(d) of the Local Government (Scotland) Act 1973 (power to make provision as to exercise of right of inspection and as to informing persons of those rights) applies to the right of inspection conferred by subsection (2).

(5) The Secretary of State may by order[2] provide that subsection (1) does not apply to publicity or expenditure of a prescribed description.

(6) Before making an order the Secretary of State shall consult such associations of local authorities as appear to him to be concerned and any local authority with whom consultation appears to him to be desirable.

(7) An order shall be made by statutory instrument which shall be subject to annulment in pursuance of a resolution of either House of Parliament.

[Local Government Act 1986, s 5 as amended by the Public Audit (Wales) Act 2004, Sch 2 and the Local Audit and Accountability Act 2014, Sch 12.]

---

[1] See this title, post.
[2] The Local Authorities (Publicity Account) (Exemption) Order 1987, SI 1987/2004 has been made.

7.7549 6. Interpretation and application of Part II (1) References in this Part to local authorities and to publicity, and related expressions, shall be construed in accordance with the following provisions.

(2) "Local authority" means—

(a) in England and Wales—
a county, district or London borough council,
the Common Council of the City of London,
the Broads Authority (except in section 3),
a police and crime commissioner,
the Mayor's Office for Policing and Crime,
a joint authority established by Part IV of the Local Government Act 1985,
an economic prosperity board established under section 88 of the Local Democracy, Economic Development and Construction Act 2009,
a combined authority established under section 103 of that Act,
the London Fire and Emergency Planning Authority
the Council of the Isles of Scilly, or
a parish or community council;

(b) Scotland;

and includes any authority, board or committee which discharges functions which would otherwise fall to be discharged by two or more such authorities.

(3) This Part applies to the Common Council of the City of London as local authority, police authority or port health authority.

(4) "Publicity", "publish" and "publication" refer to any communication, in whatever form, addressed to the public at large or to a section of the public.

(5) This Part applies to any such publicity expressly or impliedly authorised by any statutory provision, including—

section 111 of the Local Government Act 1972 or section 69 of the Local Government (Scotland) Act 1973 (general subsidiary powers of local authorities),

section 141 of the Local Government Act 1972 or section 87 of the Local Government (Scotland) Act 1973 (research and collection of information), and

section 145(1)(a) of the Local Government Act 1972 or section 16(1)(a) of the Local Government and Planning (Scotland) Act 1982 (provision of entertainments, etc).

(6) Nothing in this Part shall be construed as applying to anything done by a local authority in the discharge of their duties under Part VA of the Local Government Act 1972 or Part IIIA of the Local Government (Scotland) Act 1973 (duty to afford public access to meetings and certain documents).

(7) Nothing in this Part shall be construed as applying to anything done by a person in the discharge of any duties under regulations made under section 22 of the Local Government Act 2000 (access to information etc).

[Local Government Act 1986, s 6 as amended by the Norfolk and Suffolk Broads Act 1988, Sch 6, the Education Reform Act 1988, Sch 13, the Police and Magistrates' Courts Act 1994, Sch 4, the Police Act 1996, Sch 7, the Police Act 1997, Sch 6, the Greater London Authority Act 1999, Sch 27, SI 2001/2237, the Criminal Justice and Police Act 2001, Sch 7, the Local Democracy, Economic Development and Construction Act 2009, Sch 6 and the Police Reform and Social Responsibility Act 2011, Sch 16.]

Local Government Finance Act 1988
(1988 c 41)

Non-domestic rate

7.7550 Part III of the 1988 Act and Regulations make provision for the payment of rates for non-domestic hereditaments; see in particular the Non-Domestic Rating (Collection and Enforcement) (Local Lists) Regulations 1989 ("the Regulations"), post. Under reg 12(5) of the Regulations a magistrates' court to whom a charging authority has applied shall make a liability order if satisfied that the sum has become payable and has not been paid, to include costs.

Section 43 deals with liability for occupied hereditaments and s 45 for unoccupied hereditaments. Exemptions are covered by Sch 5, valuation by Sch 6 and administration by Sch 9.

At the liability order hearing, the magistrates' court will need satisfying on the following matters:

(1) The local authority officer conducting proceedings is duly authorised under s 233 of the Local Government Act 1972 (ante).
(2) An entry appears in the local rating list and the sums have been calculated, demanded or notified in accordance with statutory provision.
(3) Full payment has not been made by the due date.
(4) A second notice or reminder has been issued, and the sum not having been paid within 7 days of the service thereof thus making the full sum due.
(5) A summons has been served for the remaining year's rates and the full sum claimed has not been paid.

The following defences may be raised:

(1) The property in respect of which the amount is claimed did not appear for the relevant period in the local rating list.
(2) The amount due has not been demanded or notified in accordance with statutory provisions.
(3) The amount has not been paid.
(4) The amount has not been calculated correctly.
(5) Joint and several liability has been alleged and the defendant's relationship with the defaulting ratepayer was not such at the time the debt was incurred.
(6) The defendant is not in occupation of the hereditament[1].

Once the liability order has been made, enforcement is under the Regulations alone; reg 14 provides for distress (now warrant of control) (with appeal to a magistrates' courts by a person aggrieved, under reg 15); thereafter imprisonment (see comments on this above in relation to community charge). The authority may consider insolvency (reg 18).

PART III[1]
NON-DOMESTIC RATING

---

[1] For an example of a case where a purported lease from one company to another was held to a sham and, thus, not an effective transfer of rateable occupation, see *Broxfield Ltd v Sheffield City Council* [2019] EWHC 1946 (admin), [2019] ALL ER (D) 151 (Jul).

Local rating

7.7551   41.   *Local rating lists.*

---

[1] Part III contains ss 41–67. Part III is extensively amended by the Local Government and Housing Act 1989, Sch 5. Provision for the exchange of information between rating officials is made by the Non-Domestic Rating (Information) Act 1996.

7.7552   41A.   *Local non-domestic rating lists for Welsh billing authorities.*

7.7553   42.   *Contents of local lists[1].*

---

[1] Section 42 is supplemented by SI 1989/1060. The Non-Domestic Rating (Alteration of Lists and Appeals) (England) Regulations 2009, SI 2009/2268 have also been made.

7.7554   42A–B.   *Rural settlement list.*

7.7555   43.   Occupied hereditaments: liability   (1) A person (the ratepayer) shall as regards a hereditament be subject to a non-domestic rate in respect of a chargeable financial year if the following conditions are fulfilled in respect of any day in the year—

(a)   on the day the ratepayer is in occupation[1] of all or part of the hereditament, and
(b)   the hereditament is shown for the day in a local non-domestic rating list in force for the year[2].

(2)   In such a case the ratepayer shall be liable to pay an amount calculated by—

(a)   finding the chargeable amount for each chargeable day, and
(b)   aggregating the amounts found under paragraph (a) above.

(3)   A chargeable day is one which falls within the financial year and in respect of which the conditions mentioned in subsection (1) above are fulfilled.

(4)   Subject to subsections (4A), (4E), (5) and (6A) below, the chargeable amount for a chargeable day shall be calculated in accordance with the formula—

$$\frac{A \times B}{C}$$

(4A)   Where subsection (4B) below applies, the chargeable amount for a chargeable day shall be calculated—

(a)   in relation to England, in accordance with the formula—

$$(A \times D)/(C \times E)$$

(b)   in relation to Wales, in accordance with the formula—

$$(A \times B)/(C \times E)$$

(4B)   This subsection applies—

    (a)   in relation to England, where—

        (i)   *repealed*

        (ii)   on the day concerned any conditions prescribed by the Secretary of State by order[2] are satisfied, and

        (iii) *repealed*

    (b)   in relation to Wales, where—

        (i)   the rateable value of the hereditament shown in the local non-domestic rating list for the first day of the chargeable financial year is not more than any amount prescribed by the National Assembly for Wales by order[3], and

        (ii)   on the day concerned any conditions prescribed by the National Assembly for Wales by order[4] are satisfied.

(4C)   *Repealed.*

(4D)   If the ratepayer makes an application in order to satisfy a condition prescribed under subsection (4B)(a)(ii) above and—

    (a)   makes a statement in the application which he knows to be false in a material particular, or

    (b)   recklessly makes a statement in the application which is false in a material particular,

he shall be liable on summary conviction to imprisonment for a term not exceeding 3 months or to a fine not exceeding level 3 on the standard scale or to both.

(4E)   Where subsection (4F) below applies, the chargeable amount for a chargeable day shall be calculated in accordance with the formula—

(A x B x F) / C

(4F)   This subsection applies where—

    (a)   on the day concerned, the hereditament is wholly or mainly used for the purposes of facilitating the transmission of communications by any means involving the use of electrical or electromagnetic energy,

    (b)   the day concerned falls before 1 April 2022, and

    (c)   any conditions prescribed by the appropriate national authority by regulations are satisfied on the day concerned.

(4G)   The appropriate national authority may by regulations amend paragraph (b) of subsection (4F) above so as to substitute a later date for the date for the time being specified in that paragraph.

(4H)   For the purposes of subsections (4F) and (4G) above the "appropriate national authority" is—

    (a)   in relation to England, the Secretary of State;

    (b)   in relation to Wales, the Welsh Ministers.

(5)   Where subsection (6) below applies the chargeable amount for a chargeable day shall be calculated in accordance with the formula—

$$\frac{A \times B}{C \times 5}$$

(6)   This subsection applies where on the day concerned—

    (a)   the ratepayer is a charity or trustees for a charity and the hereditament is wholly or mainly used for charitable purposes (whether of that charity or of that and other charities), or

    (b)   the ratepayer is a registered club for the purposes of Schedule 18 to the Finance Act 2002 (community amateur sports clubs) and the hereditament is wholly or mainly used—

        (i)   for the purposes of that club, or

        (ii)   for the purposes of that club and of other such registered clubs.[5]

(6A)   Where subsection (6B) below applies, or, subject to subsection (6I) below, subsection (6F) below applies, the chargeable amount for a chargeable day shall be calculated in accordance with the formula—

$$\frac{A \times B}{C \times 2}$$

(6B)   This subsection applies where—

    (aa)   the hereditament is situated in England,

    (a)   on the day concerned the hereditament is within a settlement identified in the billing authority's rural settlement list for the chargeable financial year,

    (b)   the rateable value of the hereditament shown in the local non-domestic rating list at the beginning of that year is not more than any amount prescribed by the Secretary of State by order[6], and

    (c)   on the day concerned—

        (i)   the whole or part of the hereditament is used as a qualifying general store, a qualifying food store or qualifying post office, or

        (ii)   any conditions prescribed by the Secretary of State by order[7] are satisfied;

and subsections (6C) to (6E) below apply for the purposes of this subsection.

(6C)   A hereditament, or part of a hereditament, is used as a qualifying general store on any day in a chargeable financial year if—

(a)   a trade or business consisting wholly or mainly of the sale by retail of both food for human consumption (excluding confectionery) and general household goods is carried on there, and

(b)   such a trade or business is not carried on in any other hereditament, or part of a hereditament, in the settlement concerned.

(6CA)   A hereditament, or part of a hereditament, is used as a qualifying food store on any day in a chargeable financial year if a trade or business consisting wholly or mainly of the sale by retail of food for human consumption (excluding confectionery and excluding the supply of food in the course of catering) is carried on there.

(6CB)   In subsection (6CA) above the supply of food in the course of catering includes—

(a)   any supply of food for consumption on the premises on which it is supplied; and

(b)   any supply of hot food for consumption off those premises;

and for the purposes of paragraph (b) above "hot food" means food which, or any part of which—

(i)   has been heated for the purposes of enabling it to be consumed at a temperature above the ambient air temperature; and

(ii)   is at the time of supply above that temperature.

(6D)   A hereditament, or part of a hereditament, is used as a qualifying post office on any day in a chargeable financial year if—

(a)   it is used for the purposes of a universal service provider (within the meaning of the Postal Services Act 2000) and in connection with the provision of a universal postal service (within the meaning of that Act), and

(b)   no other hereditament, or part of a hereditament, in the settlement concerned is so used.

(6E)   Where a hereditament or part is used as a qualifying general store or qualifying post office on any day in a chargeable financial year, it is not to be treated as ceasing to be so used on any subsequent day in that year merely because the condition in subsection (6C)(b) or (6D)(b) above ceases to be satisfied.

(6F)   This subsection applies where—

(a)   on the day concerned the condition mentioned in subsection (6G) below is fulfilled in respect of the hereditament; and

(b)   the rateable value of the hereditament shown in the local non-domestic rating list at the beginning of the chargeable financial year is not more than any amount prescribed by the Secretary of State by order[8].

(6G)   The condition is that the hereditament—

(a)   consists wholly or mainly of land or buildings which were, on at least 183 days during the period of one year ending immediately before this subsection comes into effect, agricultural land or agricultural buildings for the purposes of the exemption under paragraph 1 of Schedule 5 to this Act; and

(b)   includes land or a building which is not agricultural for the purposes of that exemption but was agricultural for those purposes on at least 183 days during the period mentioned in paragraph (a) above.

(6H)   For the purposes of subsection (6G) above—

(a)   in relation to any hereditament which includes property which is domestic within the meaning of section 66 below, paragraph (a) has effect as if that part of the hereditament which does not consist of such property were the entire hereditament; and

(b)   a building which has replaced a building which was an agricultural building for the purposes of the exemption mentioned in that subsection ("the original building") is to be treated as if it were the original building.

(6I)   Subsection (6A) above shall not have effect, in relation to a hereditament to which subsection (6F) above applies, on a chargeable day on which paragraph 2A of Schedule 6 to this Act applies in relation to the hereditament.

(6J)   Subject to subsection (6K) below, subsections (6F) to (6I) above shall cease to have effect at the end of the period of five years beginning with the day on which those subsections come into effect.

(6K)   The Secretary of State may by order extend or further extend the period mentioned in subsection (6J).

(6L)   If the period is so extended or further extended—

(a)   subsection (6F) above cannot apply to a hereditament after the end of the period of five years beginning with the day on which it first applies; and

(b)   where a hereditament to which subsection (6F) above applies ("the original hereditament") includes land or a building which is subsequently included in a different hereditament, that subsection cannot apply to the different hereditament after the end of the period of five years beginning with the day on which it first applies to the original hereditament.

(7)   The amount the ratepayer is liable to pay under this section shall be paid to the billing

authority in whose local non-domestic rating list the hereditament is shown.

(8)   The liability to pay any such amount shall be discharged by making a payment or payments in accordance with regulations under Schedule 9 below.

(8A)   In relation to any hereditament in respect of which both subsections (4A) and (6A) above (but not subsection (5) above) have effect on the day concerned, the chargeable amount—

(a)   in relation to England, shall be calculated in accordance with subsection (6A) above,

(b)   in relation to Wales, shall be calculated in accordance with whichever of subsections (4A) and (6A) above produces the smaller amount.

(8B)   In relation to any hereditament in respect of which—

(a)   subsections (4A), (5) and (6A) above each have effect on the day concerned,

(b)   subsections (4A) and (5) above both have effect on that day, or

(c)   subsections (5) and (6A) above both have effect on that day,

the chargeable amount shall be calculated in accordance with subsection (5) above.

(8C)   In relation to any hereditament in respect of which the subsections of this section mentioned in the first column of the table below each have effect on the day concerned, the chargeable amount shall be calculated in accordance with the corresponding subsection in the second column of the table—

Subsections having effect in respect of hereditament	Subsection to be used for calculating chargeable amount
Subsections (4A) and (4E)	Subsection (4A)
Subsections (4E) and (5)	Subsection (5)
Subsections (4E) and (6A)	Subsection (6A)
Subsections (4A), (4E) and (5)	Subsection (5)
Subsections (4A), (4E) and (6A)	Subsection (6A)
Subsections (4E), (5) and (6A)	Subsection (5)
Subsections (4A), (4E), (5) and (6A)	Subsection (5)

[Local Government Finance Act 1988, s 43 as amended by the Local Government Finance Act 1992, Sch 13, the Local Government and Finance Act 1997, Sch 1, the Rating (Former Agricultural Premises and Rural Shops) Act 2001, ss 1(1), 3(1), the Local Government Act 2003, s 61 and 63, the Localism Act 2011, s 70 and Sch 25 and the Telecommunications Infrastructure (Relief from Non-Domestic Rates) Act 2018, s 1.]

[1] The actions of a receiver and manager in running a company's business do not, without more, amount to rateable occupation of the company's premises by him, since his occupation amounts to occupation by the company; if the company subsequently goes into liquidation (which terminates the receiver's agency by virtue of s 44(1)(a) of the Insolvency Act 1986), but the receiver continues to run the company as before, the company remains in rateable occupation and the receiver does not become liable for the rates (*Rees v Boston Borough Council* [2001] EWCA Civ 1934, [2002] 1 WLR 1304).

[2] A local authority has the power to retrospectively alter the ratings list under the authority given by the Non-Domestic Rating (Alteration of Lists and Appeals) (England) Regulations 2009, SI 2009/2268: see *R (on the application of Andy Mann Ltd) v York Magistrates' Court* [2020] EWHC 2540 where the occupier of a property was unsuccessful in challenging a liability order made in circumstances where the property in question had been retrospectively placed on the local non-domestic rating list after he had entered into occupation of it.

[3] The Non-Domestic Rating (Reliefs, Thresholds and Amendment) (England) Order 2017, SI 2017/102 has been made.

[4] The Non-Domestic Rating (Small Business Relief) (Wales) Order 2017, SI 2017/1229 has been made.

[5] In liability order proceedings the occupier has the burden of proving that the properties had been used wholly or mainly for charitable purposes, and that the purposes for which the properties had been used were wholly or mainly charitable, including that the purposes had been wholly or mainly charitable. The mere description of the purposes as charitable was insufficient to discharge that burden (*R (on the application of Preservation and Promotion of the Arts Ltd) v Greater Manchester Magistrates' Court; Preservation and Promotion of the Arts Ltd v Birmingham City Council* [2020] EWHC 2435 (Admin)). In order to qualify for the exemption the charity must make extensive use of the premises for charitable purpose, rather than leaving them mainly unused: *Public Safety Charitable Trust v Milton Keynes Council; Public Safety Charitable Trust v South Cambridgeshire District Council; Cheshire West and Chester Borough Council v Public Safety Charitable Trust* ([2013] EWHC 1237 (Admin). "Extensive" has the sense of "substantially and in real terms for the public benefit" (*Preservation and Promotion of the Arts Ltd v Birmingham City Council* [2020] EWHC 2435 (Admin)). An institution which was established for charitable purposes and for other purposes was not a charity, even if, in practice, the institution pursued only its charitable purposes. *Derby Teaching Hospitals NHS Foundation Trust and others v Derby City Council and others* ([2019] EWHC 3436 (Ch)).

[6] See the Non-Domestic Rating (Rural Settlements) (England) Order 1997, SI 1997/2792, the Non-Domestic Rating (Rural Settlements) (Wales) Order 1998, SI 1998/2963 and the Non-domestic Rating (Rural Rate Relief) (Wales) Order 2002, SI 2002/331.

[7] The Non-domestic Rating Contributions (Public Houses and Petrol Filling Stations) (England) Order 2001, SI 2001/1345 has been made.

[8] The Non-domestic Rating (Former Agricultural Premises) (England) Order 2004, SI 2004/3152 has been made.

7.7556   44. Occupied hereditaments: supplementary   (1)   This section applies for the purposes of section 43 above.

(2)   A is the rateable value shown for the day under section 42(4) above as regards the hereditament.

(3)   *Repealed.*

(4)   Subject to subsection (5) below, B is the non-domestic rating multiplier for the financial year.

(5)   Where the billing authority is a special authority, B is the authority's non-domestic rating

multiplier for the financial year.

(6)   C is the number of days in the financial year.

(7)   Subject to subsection (8) below, D is the small business non-domestic rating multiplier for the financial year.

(8)   Where the billing authority is a special authority, D is the authority's small business non-domestic rating multiplier for the financial year.

(9)   E is such amount as may be prescribed—

(*a*)   in relation to England, by the Secretary of State by order[1],

(*b*)   in relation to Wales, by the National Assembly for Wales by order[2].

(10)   F is an amount prescribed, or calculated in accordance with provision prescribed—

(a)   in relation to England, by the Secretary of State by regulations;

(b)   in relation to Wales, by the Welsh Ministers by regulations.

(11)   Regulations under subsection (10) may, in particular—

(a)   impose duties or confer powers on the valuation officer for a billing authority (whether as regards determinations, certificates or otherwise) in relation to the ascertainment of rateable values;

(b)   make provision as to appeals relating to things done or not done by valuation officers.

[Local Government Finance Act 1988, s 44, as amended by the Local Government and Housing Act 1989, Schs 5 and 12, the Local Government Finance Act 1992, Sch 13, the Local Government Act 2003, s 61 and the Telecommunications Infrastructure (Relief from Non-Domestic Rates) Act 2018, s 1.]

___

[1]   The Non-domestic Rating (Small Business Rate Relief) (England) Order 2012, SI 2012/148 has been made.
[2]   The Non-Domestic Rating (Small Business Relief) (Wales) Order 2008, SI 2008/2770 has been made.

7.7557   44A.   Partly occupied hereditaments   (1)   Where a hereditament is shown in a billing authority's local non-domestic rating list and it appears to the authority that part of the hereditament is unoccupied but will remain so for a short time only the authority may require the valuation officer for the authority to apportion the rateable value of the hereditament between the occupied and unoccupied parts of the hereditament and to certify the apportionment to the authority.

(2)   The reference in subsection (1) above to the rateable value of the hereditament is a reference to the rateable value shown under section 42(4) above as regards the hereditament for the day on which the authority makes its requirement.

(3)   For the purposes of this section an apportionment under subsection (1) above shall be treated as applicable for any day which—

(a)   falls within the operative period in relation to the apportionment, and

(b)   is a day for which the rateable value shown under section 42(4) above as regards the hereditament to which the apportionment relates is the same as that so shown for the day on which the authority requires the apportionment.

(4)   References in this section to the operative period in relation to an apportionment are references to the period beginning—

(a)   where requiring the apportionment does not have the effect of bringing to an end the operative period in relation to a previous apportionment under subsection (1) above, with the day on which the hereditament to which the apportionment relates became partly unoccupied, and

(b)   where requiring the apportionment does have the effect of bringing to an end the operative period in relation to a previous apportionment under subsection (1) above, with the day immediately following the end of that period,

and ending with the first day on which one or more of the events listed below occurs.

(5)   The events are—

(a)   the occupation of any of the unoccupied part of the hereditament to which the apportionment relates;

(b)   the ending of the rate period in which the authority requires the apportionment;

(c)   the requiring of a further apportionment under subsection (1) above in relation to the hereditament to which the apportionment relates;

(d)   the hereditament to which the apportionment relates becoming completely unoccupied.

(6)   Subsection (7) below applies where—

(a)   a billing authority requires an apportionment under subsection (1) above, and

(b)   the hereditament to which the apportionment relates—

(i)   does not fall within a class prescribed under section 45(1)(*d*), or

(ii)   would (if unoccupied) be zero-rated under section 45A.

(7)   In relation to any day for which the apportionment is applicable, section 43 above shall have effect as regards the hereditament as if the following subsections were substituted for section 44(2)—

"(2)   A is such part of the rateable value shown for the day under section 42(4) above as regards the hereditament as is assigned by the relevant apportionments to the occupied part of the hereditament.

(2A)   In subsection (2) above "the relevant apportionment" means the apportionment under section 44A(1) below which relates to the hereditament and is treated for the purposes of section 44A below as applicable for the day."

(8)   Subsection (9) below applies where—

    (*a*)   a billing authority requires an apportionment under subsection (1) above, and

    (*b*)   the hereditament to which the apportionment relates—

        (i)   falls within a class prescribed under section 45(1)(*d*), and

        (ii)   would (if unoccupied) not be zero-rated under section 45A, and

    (*c*)   an order under section 45(4A) is in force and has effect in relation to the hereditament.

(9)   In relation to any day for which the apportionment is applicable, section 43 above shall have effect as regards the hereditament as if the following subsections were substituted for section 44(2)—

"(2)   A is the sum of—

    (*b*)   such part of that rateable value as is assigned by the relevant apportionment to the unoccupied part of the hereditament, divided by the number prescribed by the order under section 45(4A) as it has effect in relation to the hereditament.

    (*b*)   one half of such part of that rateable value as is assigned by the relevant apportionment to the unoccupied part of the hereditament.

(2A)   In subsection (2) above "the relevant apportionment" means the apportionment under section 44A(1) below which relates to the hereditament and is treated for the purposes of section 44A below as applicable for the day.".

(9A)   In relation to a day to which neither subsection (7) nor subsection (9) applies, an apportionment under subsection (1) does not have any effect in relation to the chargeable amount.

(10)   References in subsections (1) to (5) above to the hereditament, in relation to a hereditament which is partly domestic property or partly exempt from local non-domestic rating, shall, except where the reference is to the rateable value of the hereditament, be construed as references to such part of the hereditament as is neither domestic property nor exempt from local non-domestic rating.

[Local Government Finance Act 1988, s 44A, as inserted with retrospective effect by the Local Government and Housing Act 1989, s 139, Sch 5, paras 22, 79(3) and amended by the Local Government and Housing Act 1989, Schs 5 and 12, the Local Government Finance Act 1992, Sch 13 and the Rating (Empty Properties) Act 2007, Sch 1.]

7.7558   45.   Unoccupied hereditaments: liability   (1)   A person (the ratepayer) shall as regards a hereditament be subject to a non-domestic rate in respect of a chargeable financial year if the following conditions are fulfilled in respect of any day in the year—

    (*a*)   on the day none of the hereditament is occupied,

    (*b*)   on the day the ratepayer is the owner[1] of the whole of the hereditament,

    (*c*)   the hereditament is shown for the day in a local non-domestic rating list in force for the year, and

    (*d*)   on the day the hereditament falls within a class prescribed by the Secretary of State by regulations[2].

(2)   In such a case the ratepayer shall be liable to pay an amount calculated by—

    (*a*)   finding the chargeable amount for each chargeable day, and

    (*b*)   aggregating the amounts found under paragraph (*a*) above.

(3)   A chargeable day is one which falls within the financial year and in respect of which the conditions mentioned in subsection (1) are fulfilled.

(4)   Subject to subsections (4A) and (4D) and to section 45A below, the chargeable amount for a chargeable day shall be calculated in accordance with the formula—

$$(A \times B) / C$$

where A, B and C have the meanings given by section 46.

(4A)   An order may provide that subsection (4) shall have effect as if the following formula were substituted—

$$(A \times B) / (C \times N)$$

where N is such number (greater than one but not greater than two) as may be prescribed.

(4B)   An order under subsection (4A) may be made—

    (*a*)   in relation to England, by the Secretary of State;

    (*b*)   in relation to Wales, by the Welsh Ministers.

(4C)   Subsection (4D) applies where—

    (a)   on a chargeable day, the hereditament is wholly or mainly used for the purposes of facilitating the transmission of communications by any means involving the use of electrical or electromagnetic energy,

    (b)   the chargeable day falls before 1 April 2022, and

    (c)   any conditions prescribed by the appropriate national authority by regulations are satisfied on the chargeable day.

(4D)   The chargeable amount for the chargeable day shall be calculated in accordance with the formula—

$$(A \times B \times T) / C$$

where T is an amount prescribed, or calculated in accordance with provision prescribed, by regulations made by the appropriate national authority.

(4E)   Regulations under subsection (4D) may, in particular—

(a)   impose duties or confer powers on the valuation officer for a billing authority (whether as regards determinations, certificates or otherwise) in relation to the ascertainment of rateable values;

(b)   make provision as to appeals relating to things done or not done by valuation officers.

(4F)   The appropriate national authority may by regulations amend paragraph (b) of subsection (4C) so as to substitute a later date for the date for the time being specified in that paragraph.

(4G)   For the purposes of subsections (4C) to (4F) the "appropriate national authority" is—

(a)   in relation to England, the Secretary of State;

(b)   in relation to Wales, the Welsh Ministers.

(5)   *Repealed.*

(6)   *Repealed.*

(7)   The amount the ratepayer is liable to pay under this section shall be paid to the billing authority in whose local non-domestic rating list the hereditament is shown.

(8)   The liability to pay any such amount shall be discharged by making a payment or payments in accordance with regulations under Schedule 9 below.

(9)   For the purposes of subsection (1)(*d*) above a class may be prescribed by reference to such factors as the Secretary of State sees fit.

(10)   Without prejudice to the generality of subsection (9) above a class may be prescribed by reference to one or more of the following factors—

(*a*)   the physical characteristics of the hereditaments;

(*b*)   the fact that hereditaments have been unoccupied at any time preceding the day mentioned in subsection (1) above;

(*c*)   the fact that the owners of hereditaments fall within prescribed descriptions.

[Local Government Finance Act 1988, s 45, as amended by the Local Government and Housing Act 1989, Sch 5 and the Local Government Finance Act 1992, Sch 13, the Rating (Empty Properties) Act 2007, s 1, Sch 2 and the Telecommunications Infrastructure (Relief from Non-Domestic Rates) Act 2018, s 2.]

---

[1] Where a landlord brings a claim for forfeiture of a lease and the tenant accepts that repudiation of the lease and vacates the premises, it is the landlord who is responsible for the non-domestic rate in respect of the unoccupied premises (*Royal Borough of Kingston upon Thames v Marlow* (1995) 160 JP 502, DC.)

[2] The Non-Domestic Rating (Unoccupied Property) (England) Regulations 2008, post, have been made. Provision for Wales is made by the Non-Domestic Rating (Unoccupied Property) (Wales) Regulations 2008, SI 2008/2499.

7.7559 45A. Unoccupied hereditaments: zero-rating[1] (1) Where section 45 applies in relation to a hereditament, the chargeable amount for a chargeable day is zero in the following cases.

(2)   The first case is where—

(*a*)   the ratepayer is a charity or trustees for a charity, and

(*b*)   it appears that when next in use the hereditament will be wholly or mainly used for charitable purposes (whether of that charity or of that and other charities).

(3)   The second case is where—

(*a*)   the ratepayer is a registered club for the purposes of Schedule 18 to the Finance Act 2002 (community amateur sports clubs), and

(*b*)   it appears that when the hereditament is next in use—

(i)   it will be wholly or mainly used for the purposes of that club and that club will be such a registered club, or

(ii)   it will be wholly or mainly used for the purposes of two or more clubs including that club, and each of those clubs will be such a registered club.

[Local Government Finance Act 1988, s 45A as inserted by the Rating (Empty Properties) Act 2007, s 1.]

---

[1] For the meaning of "charity" and "wholly or mainly used for charitable purposes" see the footnote to s 43(6) above.

7.7560 46. Unoccupied hereditaments: supplementary (1) This section applies for the purposes of section 45 above.

(2)   A is the rateable value shown for the day under section 42(4) above as regards the hereditament.

(3)   Subject to subsection (4) below, B is the non-domestic rating multiplier for the financial year.

(4)   Where the billing authority is a special authority, B is the authority's non-domestic rating multiplier for the financial year.

(5)   C is the number of days in the financial year.

[Local Government Finance Act 1988, s 46 as amended by the Local Government and Housing Act 1989, Sch 5 and the Local Government Finance Act 1992, Sch 13.]

7.7561 46A. Unoccupied hereditaments: new buildings (1) Schedule 4A below (which makes provision with respect to the determination of a day as the completion day in relation to a new building) shall have effect.

(2)   Where—

(*a*)   a completion notice is served under Schedule 4A below, and

(*b*)   the building to which the notice relates is not completed on or before the relevant day,

then for the purposes of section 42 above and Schedule 6 below the building shall be deemed to be completed on that day.

   (3)   For the purposes of subsection (2) above the relevant day in relation to a completion notice is—

     (a)   where an appeal against the notice is brought under paragraph 4 of Schedule 4A below, the day stated in the notice, and

     (b)   where no appeal against the notice is brought under that paragraph, the day determined under that Schedule as the completion day in relation to the building to which the notice relates.

   (4)   Where—

     (a)   a day is determined under Schedule 4A below as the completion day in relation to a new building, and

     (b)   the building is not occupied on that day,

it shall be deemed for the purposes of section 45 above to become unoccupied on that day.

   (5)   Where—

     (a)   a day is determined under Schedule 4A below as the completion day in relation to a new building, and

     (b)   the building is one produced by the structural alteration of an existing building,

the hereditament which comprised the existing building shall be deemed for the purposes of section 45 above to have ceased to exist, and to have been omitted from the list, on that day.

   (6)   In this section—

     (a)   "building" includes part of a building, and

     (b)   references to a new building include references to a building produced by the structural alteration of an existing building where the existing building is comprised in a hereditament which, by virtue of the alteration, becomes, or becomes part of, a different hereditament or different hereditaments.

[Local Government Finance Act 1988, s 46A inserted with retrospective effect by the Local Government and Housing Act 1989, s 139, Sch 5.]

7.7562 47. Discretionary relief (1) Where the condition mentioned in subsection (3) below is fulfilled for a day which is a chargeable day within the meaning of section 43 or 45 above (as the case may be)—

     (a)   the chargeable amount for the day shall be such as is determined by, or found in accordance with rules determined by, the billing authority concerned, and

     (b)   sections 43(4) to (6B) and 44 above, sections 45(4) to (4D) and 46 above, regulations under section 57A or 58 below or any provision of or made under Schedule 7A below (as the case may be) shall not apply as regards the day.

   (2)   *Repealed.*

   (3)   The condition is that, during a period which consists of or includes the chargeable day, a decision of the billing authority concerned operates to the effect that this section applies as regards the hereditament concerned.

   (3A)–(3D)   *Repealed.*

   (4)   A determination under subsection (1)(a) above—

     (a)   must be such that the chargeable amount for the day is less than the amount it would be apart from this section;

     (b)   may be such that the chargeable amount for the day is 0;

     (c)   may be varied by a further determination of the authority under subsection (1)(a) above.

   (5)   In deciding what the chargeable amount for the day would be apart from this section the effect of any regulations under section 57A or 58 below or any provision of or made under Schedule 7A below shall be taken into account but anything which has been done or could be done under section 49 below shall be ignored.

   (5A)   So far as a decision under subsection (3) above would have effect where none of section 43(6) above, section 43(6B) above and subsection (5B) below applies, the billing authority may make the decision only if it is satisfied that it would be reasonable for it to do so, having regard to the interests of persons liable to pay council tax set by it.

   (5B)   This subsection applies on the chargeable day if—

     (a)   all or part of the hereditament is occupied for the purposes of one or more institutions or other organisations—

         (i)   none of which is established or conducted for profit, and

         (ii)   each of whose main objects are charitable or are otherwise philanthropic or religious or concerned with education, social welfare, science, literature or the fine arts, or

     (b)   the hereditament—

         (i)   is wholly or mainly used for purposes of recreation, and

         (ii)   all or part of it is occupied for the purposes of a club, society or other organisation not established or conducted for profit.

   (5C)   A billing authority in England, when making a decision under subsection (3) above, must have regard to any relevant guidance issued by the Secretary of State.

   (5D)   A billing authority in Wales, when making a decision under subsection (3) above, must have regard to any relevant guidance issued by the Welsh Ministers.

(6)   A decision under subsection (3) above may be revoked by a further decision of the authority.

(7)   A decision under subsection (3) above is invalid as regards a day if made more than six months after the end of the financial year in which the day falls.

(8)   *Regulations.*[1]

(8A)   This section does not apply where the hereditament is an excepted hereditament.

(9)   A hereditament is an excepted hereditament if all or part of it is occupied (otherwise than as trustee) by—

(a)   a billing authority; or

(b)   a precepting authority, other than the Receiver for the Metropolitan Police District or* charter trustees; or

(c)   a functional body, within the meaning of the Greater London Authority Act 1999, s 138.

(10)   This section does not apply where the hereditament is zero-rated under section 45A.

[Local Government Finance Act 1988, s 47, as amended by the Local Government and Housing Act 1989, Sch 5, the Local Government Finance Act 1992, Sch 13, the Local Government and Rating Act 1997, Schs 1 and 3, the Greater London Authority Act 1999, s 138, the Rating (Former Agricultural Premises and Rural Shops) Act 2001, s 2(1), the Local Government Act 2003, s 63 and Sch 7, the Rating (Empty Properties) Act 2007, Sch 1, the Localism Act 2011, s 69 and Sch 25 and the Telecommunications Infrastructure (Relief from Non-Domestic Rates) Act 2018, Schedule.]

---

* Repealed by the Greater London Authority Act 1999, Sch 34, as from a day to be appointed.
[1] The Non-Domestic Rating (Discretionary Relief) Regulations 1989, SI 1989/1059 have been made. See also the Non Domestic Rating Contributions (England) Regulations 1992, SI 1992/3082; and the Non-Domestic Rating Contributions (Wales) Regulations 1992, SI 1992/3238.

7.7563   48.   Discretionary relief: supplementary   (1)   This section applies for the purposes of section 47 above.

(2)   *Repealed.*

(3)   A hereditament not in use shall be treated as wholly or mainly used for purposes of recreation if it appears that when next in use it will be wholly or mainly used for purposes of recreation.

(4)   A hereditament which is wholly unoccupied shall be treated as an excepted hereditament if it appears that when any of it is next occupied the hereditament will be an excepted hereditament.

(5)   If a hereditament is wholly unoccupied but it appears that it or any part of it when next occupied will be occupied for particular purposes, the hereditament or part concerned (as the case may be) shall be treated as occupied for those purposes.

[Local Government Finance Act 1988, s 48 as amended by the Local Government and Rating Act 1997, Sch 1, the Rating (Empty Properties) Act 2007, Sch 2 and the Localism Act 2011, Sch 25.]

7.7564   48A.   Discretionary relief: functions of Mayoral development corporations   (1)   The Mayor of London may require a billing authority to provide the Mayor with information to assist the Mayor with making decisions under section 214 of the Localism Act 2011 (Mayor's power to decide that a Mayoral development corporation should have functions under section 47 above).

(2)   A Mayoral development corporation which has, or expects to have, functions under section 47 above may require a billing authority to provide the corporation with information to assist the corporation to exercise functions under that section.

(3)   A billing authority must comply with a requirement imposed on it under subsection (1) or (2) above so far as the requirement relates to information available to the billing authority.

(4)   A person to whom information is provided in response to a requirement imposed under subsection (1) or (2) above may use the information only for the purposes for which it was sought.

(5)   The Secretary of State may by regulations make transitional provision in connection with, or in anticipation of, a Mayoral development corporation—

(a)   beginning to exercise functions under section 47 above, or

(b)   ceasing to exercise functions under that section.

(6)   The Secretary of State may by regulations make provision about payment by a Mayoral development corporation to a billing authority of amounts—

(a)   as regards the operation of section 47 above in cases where the corporation has exercised functions under that section;

(b)   as regards costs of collection and recovery in such cases.

[Local Government Finance Act 1988, s 48A as inserted by the Localism Act 2011, Sch 22.]

7.7565   49.   Reduction or remission of liability   (1)   A billing authority may—

(a)   reduce any amount a person is liable to pay to it under section 43 or 45 above, or

(b)   remit payment of the whole of any amount a person would otherwise be liable to pay to it under section 43 or 45 above.

(2)   But an authority may not act under this section unless it is satisfied that—

(a)   the ratepayer would sustain hardship if the authority did not do so, and

(b)   it is reasonable for the authority to do so, having regard to the interests of persons liable to pay council tax set by it.

(3)   The amount as regards which a reduction or remittance may be made under subsection (1) above is the amount the person would be liable to pay (apart from this section) taking account of anything done under section 47 above, the effect of any regulations under section 57A or 58 below,

and the effect of any provision of or made under Schedule 7A below.

(4)   Where an authority acts under this section, section 43 or 45 above shall be construed accordingly as regards the case concerned.

[Local Government Finance Act 1988, s 49 as amended by the Local Government and Housing Act 1989, Sch 5, the Local Government Finance Act 1992, Sch 13 and the Local Government Act 2003, Sch 7.]

7.7566   49A.   Cancellation of backdated liabilities for days in years 2005 to 2010   (1)   The Secretary of State may by regulations[1] provide that, in a prescribed case, the chargeable amount under section 43 or 45 for a hereditament in England for a chargeable day is zero.

(2)   The regulations may give that relief in relation to a hereditament and a chargeable day only if—

   (a)   the hereditament is shown for the day in a local non-domestic rating list compiled on 1 April 2005, and

   (b)   it is shown for that day as it is shown as the result of an alteration of the list made after the list was compiled.

(3)   The regulations may give that relief in relation to a hereditament and a chargeable day subject to the fulfilment of prescribed conditions.

(4)   A prescribed condition may be—

   (a)   a condition to be fulfilled in relation to the hereditament,

   (b)   a condition to be fulfilled in relation to some other hereditament, or

   (c)   some other condition.

(5)   The conditions that may be prescribed include, in particular

   (a)   conditions relating to the circumstances in which an alteration of a local non-domestic rating list was made;

   (b)   conditions relating to the consequences of the alteration;

   (c)   conditions relating to the length of the period beginning with the first day from which an alteration had effect and ending with the day on which the alteration was made;

   (d)   conditions relating to a person's liability or otherwise to non-domestic rates at any time.

[Local Government Finance Act 1988, s 49A as inserted by the Localism Act 2011, s 71.]

---

[1] The Non-Domestic Rating (Cancellation of Backdated Liabilities) Regulations 2012, SI 2012/537 have been made.

7.7567   50.   Joint owners or occupiers   (1)   The Secretary of State may make such regulations[1] as he sees fit to deal with any case where (apart from the regulations) there would be more than one owner or occupier of a hereditament or part or of land at a particular time.

(2)   Nothing in the following provisions of this section shall prejudice the generality of subsection (1) above.

(3)   The regulations may provide for the owner or occupier at the time concerned to be taken to be such one of the owners or occupiers as is identified in accordance with prescribed rules.

(4)   The regulations may provide that—

   (a)   as regards any time when there is only one owner or occupier, section 43 or 45 above (as the case may be) shall apply;

   (b)   as regards any time when there is more than one owner or occupier, the owners or occupiers shall be jointly and severally liable to pay a prescribed amount by way of non-domestic rate.

(5)   The regulations may include provision that prescribed provisions shall apply instead of prescribed provisions of this Part, or that prescribed provisions of this Part shall not apply or shall apply subject to prescribed amendments or adaptations.

[Local Government Finance Act 1988, s 50.]

---

[1] See Part II of the Non-Domestic Rating (Collection and Enforcement) (Miscellaneous Provisions) Regulations 1990, SI 1990/145. The occupier of part of a hereditament is not liable under these Regulations to a liability order being made against him for the whole of the hereditament since it is not the intention of the Regulations themselves to impose such a liability (*Ford v Burnley Borough Council* (1995) 160 JP 541, [1995] RA 205).

7.7568   51.   Exemption   Schedule 5 below shall have effect to determine the extent (if any) to which a hereditament is for the purposes of this Part exempt from local non-domestic rating.

[Local Government Finance Act 1988, s 51.]

Central rating

7.7569   52.   Central rating lists   (1)   In accordance with this Part the central valuation officer shall compile, and then maintain, lists (to be called central non-domestic rating lists).

(2)   A list must be compiled on 1st April 1990 and on 1st April in every fifth year afterwards.

(3)   A list shall come into force on the day on which it is compiled and shall remain in force until the next one is compiled five years later.

(4)   Before a list is compiled the central valuation officer must take such steps as are reasonably practicable to ensure that it is accurately compiled on 1st April concerned.

(5)   Not later than 30th September preceding a day on which a list is to be compiled the central valuation officer shall send to the Secretary of State a copy of the list he proposes (on the information then before him) to compile.

(6)   As soon as is reasonably practicable after receiving the copy the Secretary of State shall

deposit it at his principal office.

(6A)   As soon as is reasonably practicable after compiling a list the central valuation officer shall send a copy of it to the Secretary of State.

(6B)   As soon as is reasonably practicable after receiving the copy the Secretary of State shall deposit it at his principal office.

(7)   A list must be maintained for so long as is necessary for the purposes of this Part, so that the expiry of the five year period for which it is in force does not detract from the duty to maintain it.

[Local Government Finance Act 1988, s 52 as amended by the Local Government and Housing Act 1989, Sch 5 and the Local Government Act 2003, s 60.]

7.7570   53.   Contents of central lists   (1)   With a view to securing the central rating en bloc of certain hereditaments, the Secretary of State may by regulations[1] designate a person and prescribe in relation to him one or more descriptions of relevant non-domestic hereditament.

(2)   Where the regulations so require, a central non-domestic rating list must show, for each day in each chargeable financial year for which it is in force, the name of the designated person and, against it, each hereditament (wherever situated) which on the day concerned—

     (*a*)   is occupied or (if unoccupied) owned by him, and

     (*b*)   falls within any description prescribed in relation to him.

(3)   For each such day the list must also show against the name of the designated person the rateable value (as a whole) of the hereditaments so shown.

(4)   Where regulations are for the time being in force under this section prescribing a description of non-domestic hereditament in relation to a person designated in the regulations ("the previously designated person"), amending regulations altering the designated person in relation to whom that description of hereditament is prescribed may have effect from a date earlier than that on which the amending regulations are made.

(4A)   Where, by virtue of subsection (4) above, the designated person in relation to any description of non-domestic hereditament is changed from a date earlier than the making of the regulation,—

     (*a*)   any necessary alteration shall be made with effect from that date to a central non-domestic rating list on which any hereditament concerned is shown; and

     (*b*)   an order making the provision referred to in paragraph 3(2) of Schedule 6 below and specifying a description of hereditament by reference to the previously designated person shall be treated, with effect from that date, as referring to the person designated by the amending regulations.[*]

(5)   A central non-domestic rating list must also contain such information about hereditaments shown in it as may be prescribed by the Secretary of State by regulations[2].

[Local Government Finance Act 1988, s 53 as amended by the Local Government and Housing Act 1989, Sch 5.]

---

[*]   **Repealed by the Local Government Act 2003, Sch 8 from a date to be appointed.**
[1]   The Central Rating List (Wales) Regulations 2005, SI 2005/422 and the Central Rating List (England) Regulations 2005, SI 2005/551 have been made.
[2]   The Non-Domestic Rating (Alteration of Lists and Appeals) (England) Regulations 2009, SI 2009/2268 have been made.

7.7571   54.   Central rating: liability   (1)   A person (the ratepayer) shall be subject to a non-domestic rate in respect of a chargeable financial year if for any day in the year his name is shown in a central non-domestic rating list in force for the year.

(2)   In such a case the ratepayer shall be liable to pay an amount calculated by—

     (*a*)   finding the chargeable amount for each chargeable day, and

     (*b*)   aggregating the amounts found under paragraph (*a*) above.

(3)   A chargeable day is one which falls within the financial year and for which the ratepayer's name is shown in the list.

(4)   Subject to section 54ZA below, the chargeable amount for a chargeable day shall be calculated in accordance with the formula—

$$\frac{A \times B}{C}$$

(5)   A is the rateable value shown for the day in the list against the ratepayer's name.

(6)   B is the non-domestic rating multiplier for the financial year.

(7)   C is the number of days in the financial year.

(8)   The amount the ratepayer is liable to pay under this section shall be paid to the Secretary of State.

(9)   The liability to pay any such amount shall be discharged by making a payment or payments in accordance with regulations under Schedule 9 below.

[Local Government Finance Act 1988, s 54 as amended by the Telecommunications Infrastructure (Relief from Non-Domestic Rates) Act 2018, s 3.]

7.7572   54ZA.   Relief for telecommunications infrastructure   (1)   This section applies where—

     (*a*)   for any day in a chargeable financial year a person's name is shown in a central non-domestic rating list in force for the year,

     (*b*)   on that day ("the chargeable day"), the condition in subsection (2) is met in relation to any description of hereditament shown against the person's name in the list,

(c)   the chargeable day falls before 1st April 2022, and

(d)   any conditions prescribed by the appropriate national authority by regulations are satisfied on the chargeable day.

(2)   The condition in this subsection is met in relation to a description of hereditament if—

(a)   in a case where there is only one hereditament falling within the description, the hereditament is wholly or mainly used for the purposes of facilitating the transmission of communications by any means involving the use of electrical or electromagnetic energy, or

(b)   in a case where there is more than one hereditament falling within the description, those hereditaments are, taken together, wholly or mainly so used.

(3)   The chargeable amount for the chargeable day in respect of that description of hereditament shall be calculated in accordance with the formula—

$(A \times B \times T) / C$

where—

       A, B and C have the same meaning as they have for the purposes of section 54(4), and

       T is an amount prescribed, or calculated in accordance with provision prescribed, by the appropriate national authority by regulations.

(4)   Regulations under subsection (3) may, in particular—

(a)   impose duties or confer powers on the central valuation officer (whether as regards determinations, certificates or otherwise) in relation to the ascertainment of rateable values;

(b)   make provision as to appeals relating to things done or not done by the central valuation officer.

(5)   The appropriate national authority may by regulations amend paragraph (c) of subsection (1) so as to substitute a later date for the date for the time being specified in that paragraph.

(6)   In this section the "appropriate national authority" is—

(a)   in relation to England, the Secretary of State;

(b)   in relation to Wales, the Welsh Ministers.

[Local Government Finance Act 1988, s 54ZA as inserted by the Telecommunications Infrastructure (Relief from Non-Domestic Rates) Act 2018, s 3.]

General

7.7573   55.   *Alteration of lists.*

7.7574   62. Administration   Schedule 9 below (which contains provisions about administration, including collection and recovery) shall have effect.

[Local Government Finance Act 1988, s 62.]

7.7575   62A. Recovery by taking control of goods   Where a liability order has been made against a person under regulations under Schedule 9, the billing authority may use the procedure in Schedule 12 to the Tribunals, Courts and Enforcement Act 2007 (taking control of goods) to recover the amount in respect of which the order was made, to the extent that it remains unpaid.

[Local Government Finance Act 1988, s 62A as inserted by the Tribunals, Courts and Enforcement Act 2007, Sch 13.]

7.7576   63.   *Death.*

Interpretation

7.7577   64. Hereditaments   (1)   A hereditament is anything which, by virtue of the definition of hereditament in section 115(1) of the 1967 Act, would have been a hereditament for the purposes of that Act had this Act not been passed.

(2)   In addition, a right is a hereditament if it is a right to use any land for the purpose of exhibiting advertisements and—

(*a*)   the right is let out or reserved to any person other than the occupier[1] of the land, or

(*b*)   where the land is not occupied for any other purpose, the right is let out or reserved to any person other than the owner of the land.

(2A)   In addition, a right is a hereditament if—

(*a*)   it is a right to use any land for the purpose of operating a meter to measure a supply of gas or electricity or such other service as—

       (i)   the Secretary of State in relation to England, or

       (ii)   the National Assembly for Wales in relation to Wales,

       may by order specify, and

(*b*)   the meter is owned by a person other than the consumer of the service.

(3)   The Secretary of State may make regulations[2] providing that in prescribed cases—

(*a*)   anything which would (apart from the regulations) be one hereditament shall be treated as more than one hereditament;

(*b*)   anything which would (apart from the regulations) be more than one hereditament shall be treated as one hereditament[3].

(3A)   The Secretary of State may make regulations providing that where on any land there are two or more moorings which—

    (*a*)   are owned by the same person,

    (*b*)   are not domestic property, and

    (*c*)   are separately occupied, or available for separate occupation, by persons other than that person,

a valuation officer may determine that, for the purposes of the compilation or alteration of a local non-domestic rating list, all or any of the moorings, or all or any of them together with any adjacent moorings or land owned and occupied by that person, shall be treated as one hereditament.

   (3B)   Regulations under subsection (3A) above may provide that—

    (*a*)   where a valuation officer makes a determination as mentioned in that subsection, he shall, if prescribed conditions are fulfilled, supply prescribed persons with prescribed information;

    (*b*)   while such a determination is in force—

        (i)   the person who on any day is the owner of the moorings (or the moorings and land) which constitute the hereditament shall be treated for the purposes of sections 43, 44A and 45 above as being in occupation of all of the hereditament on that day; and

        (ii)   no other person shall be treated for those purposes as being in occupation of all or any part of the hereditament on that day.

   (4)   A hereditament is a relevant hereditament if it consists of property of any of the following descriptions—

    (*a*)   lands;

    (*b*)   coal mines;

    (*c*)   mines of any other description, other than a mine of which the royalty or dues are for the time being wholly reserved in kind;

    (*d*)   *repealed;*

    (*e*)   any right which is a hereditament by virtue of subsection (2) or (2A) above.

   (5)–(7D)   *Repealed.*

   (8)   A hereditament is non-domestic if either—

    (*a*)   it consists entirely of property which is not domestic, or

    (*b*)   it is a composite hereditament.

   (9)   A hereditament is composite if part only of it consists of domestic property.

   (10)   A hereditament shall be treated as wholly or mainly used for charitable purposes at any time if at the time it is wholly or mainly used for the sale of goods donated to a charity and the proceeds of sale of the goods (after any deduction of expenses) are applied for the purposes of a charity.

   (11)   In subsection (2) above "land" includes a wall or other part of a building and a sign, hoarding, frame, post or other structure erected or to be erected on land.

   (11A)   The Secretary of State in relation to England, and the National Assembly in relation to Wales, may by regulations make provision as to what is to be regarded as being a meter for the purposes of subsection (2A) above.

   (11B)   In subsection (2A) above "land" includes a wall or other part of a building.

   (12)   In subsections (3A) and (3B) above "owner", in relation to a mooring, means the person who (if the mooring is let) is entitled to receive rent, whether on his own account or as agent or trustee for any other person, or (if the mooring is not let) would be so entitled if the mooring were let, and "owned" shall be construed accordingly.

[Local Government Finance Act 1988, s 64 as amended by the Local Government and Housing Act 1989, Sch 5, the Local Government Finance Act 1992, Sch 10, the Local Government and Rating Act 1997, s 2 and Sch 3 and the Local Government Act 2003, s 66]

---

[1] Where a person has been granted the right to use a flank wall of a building for advertising and place structures thereon, it is the wall on which a fixture is placed that is the "land" and not the fixture so that a hereditament in the advertising structure is created within the terms of s 64(2)(*a*) as the beneficiary of the right is a person other than the occupier of the land (*O'Brien v Secker* [1996] RA 409, CA).

[2] See the Non-Domestic Rating (Miscellaneous Provisions) Regulations 1989, SI 1989/1060, the Non-Domestic Rating (Caravan Sites) Regulations 1990, SI 1990/673, the Non-Domestic Rating (Electricity Generators) Regulations 1991, SI 1991/475, the Non-Domestic Rating (Police Authorities) Order 1995, SI 1995/1679, the Non-Domestic Rating (Communications and Light Railways) (England) Regulations 2005, SI 2005/549, the Central Rating List (Wales) Regulations 2005, SI 2005/422 and the Central Rating List (England) Regulations 2005, SI 2005/551, the Non-Domestic Rating (Waterways) (Wales) Regulations 2015, SI 2015/539 and the Non-Domestic Rating (Miscellaneous Provisions) (Wales) Regulations 2017, SI 2017/327.

[3] Cross-boundary property is dealt with by SI 1989/1060.

7.7578   65.   Owners and occupiers   (1)   The owner of a hereditament or land is the person entitled to possession of it[1].

   (2)   Whether a hereditament or land is occupied, and who is the occupier, shall be determined by reference to the rules which would have applied for the purposes of the 1967 Act had this Act not been passed (ignoring any express statutory rules such as those in sections 24 and 46A of that Act).

   (3)   Subsections (1) and (2) above shall have effect subject to the following provisions of this section.

   (4)   Regulations under section 64(3) above may include rules for ascertaining—

       whether the different hereditaments or the one hereditament (as the case may be) shall   treated as occupied or unoccupied;

(b)   who shall be treated as the owner or occupier of the different hereditaments or the one hereditament (as the case may be).

(5) A hereditament which is not in use shall be treated as unoccupied if (apart from this subsection) it would be treated as occupied by reason only of there being kept in or on the hereditament plant, machinery or equipment—

(a)   which was used in or on the hereditament when it was last in use, or

(b)   which is intended for use in or on the hereditament.

(6) A hereditament shall be treated as unoccupied if (apart from this subsection) it would be treated as occupied by reason only of—

(a)   the use of it for the holding of public meetings in furtherance of a person's candidature at a parliamentary or local government election, or

(b)   if it is a house, the use of a room in it by a returning officer for the purpose of taking the poll in a parliamentary or local government election.

(7) In subsection (6) above "returning officer" shall be construed in accordance with section 24 or 35 of the Representation of the People Act 1983 (as the case may be).

(8) A right which is a hereditament by virtue of section 64(2) above shall be treated as occupied by the person for the time being entitled to the right.

(8A) In a case where—

(a)   land consisting of a hereditament is used (permanently or temporarily) for the exhibition of advertisements or for the erection of a structure used for the exhibition of advertisements,

(b)   section 64(2) above does not apply, and

(c)   apart from this subsection, the hereditament is not occupied,

the hereditament shall be treated as occupied by the person permitting it to be so used or, if that person cannot be ascertained, its owner.

(9) *Repealed.*

[Local Government Finance Act 1988, s 65 as amended by the Local Government and Housing Act 1989, Sch 5 and the Local Government and Rating Act 1997, s 2.]

---

[1] If a landlord claims forfeiture of a lease, it is open to the tenant to accept it and thereby terminate all future rights and liabilities under the lease including his right to possession as well as his liability for rent (*Royal Borough of Kingston upon Thames v Marlow* (1995) 160 JP 502, DC). Receivers who were appointed as agents under the terms of the debentures to take possession of the charged properties were held not to be entitled, by reason only of that appointment, to possession of the premises and thus were not "owners" for the purposes of s 65(1) of the Act; accordingly, the receivers were not personally liable for the non-domestic unoccupied property rates (*Brown v City of London Corpn* [1996] 1 WLR 1070).

7.7579 65A. Crown Property (1) This Part applies to the Crown as it applies to other persons.

(2) Accordingly, liability to a non-domestic rate in respect of a hereditament is not affected by the fact that—

(a)   the hereditament is occupied by the Crown or by a person acting on behalf of the Crown or is used for Crown purposes, or

(b)   the Crown or a person acting on behalf of the Crown is the owner of the hereditament.

(3) If (apart from this subsection) any property would consist of two or more Crown hereditaments, the property is to be treated for the purposes of this Part as if it were a single hereditament occupied by such one of the occupiers as appears to the billing authority to occupy the largest part of the property.

(4) In this section, "Crown hereditament" means a hereditament which—

(a)   is occupied by a Minister of the Crown or Government department or by any officer or body exercising functions on behalf of the Crown, but

(b)   is not provided or maintained by a local authority or by a police and crime commissioner.

(5) In this section—

(a)   references to this Part include any subordinate legislation (within the meaning of the Interpretation Act 1978) made under it, and

(b)   "local authority" has the same meaning as in the Local Government Act 1972, and includes the Common Council of the City of London.

(6) The Secretary of State may by order amend subsection (4)(b) above so as to alter the persons for the time being referred to there.

(7) Subsection (3) above does not affect the power conferred by section 64(3) above.

[Local Government Finance Act 1988, s 65A as inserted by the Local Government and Rating Act 1997, s 3 and amended by the Criminal Justice and Police Act 2001, Sch 6 and the Police Reform and Social Responsibility Act 2011, Sch 16.]

7.7580 66. Domestic property (1) Subject to subsections (2), (2B) and (2E) below, property is domestic if—

(a)   it is used wholly for the purposes of living accommodation,

(b)   it is a yard, garden, outhouse or other appurtenance belonging to or enjoyed with property falling within paragraph (a) above,

(c)   it is a private garage which either has a floor area of 25 square metres or less or is used wholly or mainly for the accommodation of a private motor vehicle, or (*d*)   it is private storage premises used wholly or mainly for the storage of articles of domestic use.

    (2)   Property is not domestic property if it is wholly or mainly used in the course of a business for the provision of short-stay accommodation, that is to say accommodation—

    (*a*)   Which is provided for short periods to individuals whose sole or main residence is elsewhere, and

    (*b*)   which is not self-contained self-catering accommodation provided commercially.

    (2A)   Subsection (2) above does not apply if—

    (*a*)   it is intended that within the year beginning with the end of the day in relation to which the question is being considered, short-stay accommodation will not be provided within the hereditament for more than six persons simultaneously; and

    (*b*)   the person intending to provide such accommodation intends to have his sole or main residence within that hereditament throughout any period when such accommodation is to be provided, and that any use of living accommodation within the hereditament which would, apart from this subsection, cause any part of it to be treated as non-domestic, will be subsidiary to the use of the hereditament for, or in connection with, his sole or main residence.

    (2B)   A building or self-contained part of a building is not domestic property if—

    (*a*)   the relevant person intends that, in the year beginning with the end of the day in relation to which the question is being considered, the whole of the building or self-contained part will be available for letting commercially, as self-catering accommodation, for short periods totalling 140 days or more,

    (*b*)   on that day his interest in the building or part is such as to enable him to let it for such periods.

    (*c*)   the whole of the building or self-contained part of the building was available for letting commercially, as self-catering accommodation, for short periods totalling 140 days or more in the year prior to the year beginning with the end of the day in relation to which the question referred to in paragraph (a) is being considered, and

    (*d*)   the short periods for which it was so let amounted in total to at least 70 days

    (2C)   For the purposes of subsection (2B) the relevant person is—

    (*a*)   where the property in question is a building and is not subject as a whole to a relevant leasehold interest, the person having the freehold interest in the whole of the building; and

    (*b*)   in any other case, any person having a relevant leasehold interest in the building or self-contained part which is not subject (as a whole) to a single relevant leasehold interest inferior to his interest.

    (2D)   Subsection (2B) above does not apply where the building or self-contained part is used as the sole or main residence of any person.

    (2E)   Property is not domestic property if it is timeshare accommodation within the meaning of the Timeshare Act 1992.

    (3)   Subsection (1) above does not apply in the case of a pitch occupied by a caravan, but if in such a case the caravan is the sole or main residence of an individual, the pitch and the caravan, together with any garden, yard, outhouse or other appurtenance belonging to or enjoyed with them, are domestic property'.

    (4)   Subsection (1) above does not apply in the case of a mooring occupied by a boat, but if in such a case the boat is the sole or main residence of an individual, the mooring and the boat, together with any garden, yard, outhouse or other appurtenance belonging to or enjoyed with them, are domestic property.

    (4A)   Subsection (3) or (4) above does not have effect in the case of a pitch occupied by a caravan, or a mooring occupied by a boat, which is an appurtenance enjoyed with other property to which subsection (1)(*a*) above applies¹.

    (5)   Property not in use is domestic if it appears that when next in use it will be domestic.

    (6)   *Repealed.*

    (7)   Whether anything is a caravan shall be construed in accordance with Part I of the Caravan Sites and Control of Development Act 1960.

    (8)   *Repealed.*

    (8A)   In this section—

"business" includes—

    (*a*)   any activity carried on by a body of persons, whether corporate or unincorporate, and

    (*b*)   any activity carried on by a charity;

"commercially" means on a commercial basis, and with a view to the realisation of profits; and "relevant leasehold interest" means an interest under a lease or underlease which was granted for a term of 6 months or more and conferred the right to exclusive possession throughout the term.

    (9)   The Secretary of State may by order² amend, or substitute another definition for, any definition of domestic property for the time being effective for the purposes of this Part.

[Local Government Finance Act 1988, s 66 amended by SI 1990/162, the Caravans (Standard Community Charge and Rating) Act 1991, s 1, SI 1991/474, the Local Government Finance Act 1992, Sch 13, SI 1993/542, the Rating (Caravan and Boats) Act 1996, s 1 and SI 2022/217.]

<hr>

¹ The Rating (Caravan and Boats) Act 1996, s 1(4) and (5) provides that sub-ss (3) and (4) of the 1988 Act as substituted by the 1996 Act are to be treated as having had effect on and after 1 April 1990 and any additional sums payable thereby in respect of non-domestic rates may accordingly be recovered. Exception is made in respect of a hereditament where:

    (a)   a proposal for the alteration of a local non-domestic rating list in respect of the hereditament has been made, and not withdrawn, before 30 January 1995 in accordance with regulations under s 55 of the Local Government Finance Act 1988;

    (b)   the ground for the proposal was that the list was inaccurate because the hereditament ought not to be shown in the list or, in the case of a composite hereditament, the rateable value shown in the list was too high; and

    (c)   the reason or one of the reasons given in the proposal, or on an appeal (in accordance with those regulations) to a tribunal against a refusal to make the proposed alteration, for the list being inaccurate was that any pitch occupied by a caravan or (as the case may be) mooring occupied by a boat was domestic property by virtue of s 66(1)(*a*) or (*b*) of that Act.

It is further provided by subsection (6) that—

Local non-domestic rating lists compiled on 1 April 1990, 1 April 1995 or 1 April 1996 must be altered so far as required in consequence of this section: and the alterations are to be treated as having had effect from 1 April 1990 or, in the case of lists compiled on 1 April 1995 or 1 April 1996, from 1 April 1995 or from such other date as may be applicable in accordance with regulations under s 2.

² The Non-Domestic Rating (Definition of Domestic Property) (Wales) Order 2010, SI 2010/682 and the Non-Domestic Rating and Council Tax (Definition of Domestic Property and Dwelling) (England) Order 2013, SI 2013/468 have been made.

7.7581 66A. Unoccupied hereditaments: change of state of property to be disregarded

(1)   Regulations may provide that, for the purposes of this Part as it applies in relation to an unoccupied hereditament, the state of any property comprising or included in the hereditament shall be deemed not to have changed—

    (*a*)   since before any event of a prescribed description, or

    (*b*)   by reason of any act done by or on behalf of a prescribed person.

(2)   The regulations may make provision as to the circumstances in which, and period for which, that is deemed to be the case.

(3)   The regulations may provide for the making of such assumptions or apportionments as may be prescribed in determining whether, or to what extent, the state of any property has changed in comparison with an earlier point in time.

(4)   The regulations may—

    (*a*)   provide that an act is to be treated as done on behalf of a prescribed person if it is done by any person connected with that person, and

    (*b*)   define in what circumstances persons are to be treated for that purpose as connected.

(5)   The regulations may provide that they have effect (with any necessary adaptations) in relation to omissions as well as to acts.

(6)   Regulations under this section may be made—

    (*a*)   in relation to England, by the Secretary of State;

    (*b*)   in relation to Wales, by the Welsh Ministers.

[Local Government Finance Act 1988, s 66A as inserted by the Rating (Empty Properties) Act 2007, Sch 1.]

7.7582 67. Interpretation: other provisions

(1)   Unless the context otherwise requires, references to lists are to local and central non-domestic rating lists.

(2)   Unless the context otherwise requires, references to valuation officers are to valuation officers for billing authorities and the central valuation officer.

(3)   A right or other property is a hereditament on a particular day if (and only if) it is a hereditament immediately before the day ends.

(4)   A hereditament is relevant, non-domestic, composite, unoccupied or wholly or partly occupied on a particular day if (and only if) it is relevant, non-domestic, composite, unoccupied or wholly or partly occupied (as the case may be) immediately before the day ends.

(5)   For the purpose of deciding the extent (if any) to which a hereditament consists of domestic property on a particular day, or is exempt from local non-domestic rating on a particular day, the state of affairs existing immediately before the day ends shall be treated as having existed throughout the day.

(5A)   In subsection (5) above "Crown hereditament" has the same meaning as in section 65A above.

(6)   A person is the owner, or in occupation of all or part, of a hereditament on a particular day if (and only if) he is its owner or in such occupation (as the case may be) immediately before the day ends.

(7)   A relevant provision applies on a particular day if (and only if) it applies immediately before the day ends; and for this purpose relevant provisions are sections 43(4F) and (6), 45(4D), 45A(2) and (3) and 54ZA above.

(8)   For the purpose of deciding what is shown in a list for a particular day the state of the list as it has effect immediately before the day ends shall be treated as having been its state throughout the day; and "effect" here includes any effect which is retrospective by virtue of an alteration of the list.

(9)   A hereditament shall be treated as shown in a central non-domestic rating list for a day if on the day it falls within a class of hereditament shown for the day in the list; and for this purpose a hereditament falls within a class on a particular day if (and only if) it falls within the class immediately before the day ends.

(9A)   In subsection (9) above "class" means a class expressed by reference to whether hereditaments—

    (a)   are occupied or owned by a person designated under section 53(1) above, and

    (b)   fall within any description prescribed in relation to him under section 53(1).

(10)   A charity is an institution or other organisation established for charitable purposes only or any persons administering a trust established for charitable purposes only.

(10A)   The times at which a club is a registered club for the purposes of Schedule 18 to the Finance Act 2002 (community amateur sports clubs)—

    (a)   shall, where it is registered with retrospective effect, be taken to have included those within the period beginning with the date with effect from which it is registered and ending with its registration; but

    (b)   shall, where its registration is terminated with retrospective effect, be taken not to have included those within the period beginning with the date with effect from which its registration is terminated and ending with the termination of its registration.

(11)   The 1967 Act is the General Rate Act 1967.

(12)   Nothing in a private or local Act passed before this Act shall have the effect that a hereditament is exempt as regards non-domestic rating, or prevent a person being subject to a non-domestic rate, or prevent a person being designated or a description of hereditament being prescribed under section 53 above.

(13)   This section and sections 64 to 66 above apply for the purposes of this Part.

[Local Government Finance Act 1988, s 67 as amended by the Local Government Finance Act 1992, Sch 13 and the Local Government and Rating Act 1997, Sch 3, the Local Government Act 2003, s 64, the Rating (Empty Properties) Act 2007, Sch 1 and the Telecommunications Infrastructure (Relief from Non-Domestic Rates) Act 2018, Schedule.]

Part XI[1]
Miscellaneous and General

General

7.7583   138.   Judicial review   (1)   The matters mentioned in subsection (2) below shall not be questioned except by an application for judicial review.

(2)   The matters are—

    (a)–(d) *repealed,*

    (e)   a levy issued under regulations under section 74 above,

    (f)   a special levy issued under regulations under section 75 above,

    (g)   *repealed,*

    (h)   the specification of a non-domestic rating multiplier under paragraph 2 of Schedule 7 below,

    (i)   the specification of a non-domestic rating multiplier under paragraph 7 of Schedule 7 below, and

    (j)   the setting by a special authority of a non-domestic rating multiplier or small business non-domestic rating multiplier under Schedule 7 below, whether originally or by way of substitute.

(3)   If on an application for judicial review the court decides to grant relief in respect of the matters mentioned in subsection (2)(e) or (f) or (h) to (j) above, it shall quash the levy, special levy, specification or setting (as the case may be).

[Local Government Finance Act 1988, s 138 as amended by the Local Government Finance Act 1992, Sch 13 and the Local Government Act 2003, Sch 7.]

---

[1]   Part XI contains ss 130–152.

SCHEDULES

SCHEDULE 5
Non-Domestic Rating: Exemption   Section 51

(As amended by the Water Act 1989, Sch 25, the Local Government and Housing Act 1989, Sch 5, the Water Consolidation (Consequential Provisions) Act 1991, Sch 1, the Local Government Finance Act 1992, Sch 10, the Merchant Shipping Act 1995 Sch 13, the Local Government and Rating Act 1997, ss 2 and 4 and Sch 3, the Transport Act 2000, s 200, the National Health Service (Consequential Provisions) Act 2006, Sch 1 and SI 2015/914.)

Agricultural premises

7.7584   1.   A hereditament is exempt to the extent that it consists of any of the following—

    (a)   agricultural land;

    (b)   agricultural buildings.

2.   (1)   Agricultural land is—

    (a)   land used as arable, meadow or pasture ground only,

    (b)   land used for a plantation or a wood or for the growth of saleable underwood.

    (c)   land exceeding 0.10 hectare and used for the purposes of poultry farming,

    (d)   anything which consists of a market garden, nursery ground, orchard or allotment (which here includes an allotment garden within the meaning of the Allotments Act 1922), or

    (e)   land occupied with, and used solely in connection with the use of, a building which (or buildings each of which) is an agricultural building by virtue of paragraph 4, 5, 6 or 7 below.

    (2)   But agricultural land does not include—

    (a)   land occupied together with a house as a park,

    (b)   gardens (other than market gardens),

    (c)   pleasure grounds,

    (d)   land used mainly or exclusively for purposes of sport or recreation, or

    (e)   land used as a racecourse.

3.   A building is an agricultural building if it is not a dwelling and—

    (a)   it is occupied together with agricultural land and is used solely in connection with agricultural operations on the land, or

    (b)   it is or forms part of a market garden and is used solely in connection with agricultural operations at the market garden.

4.   (1)   A building is an agricultural building if it is used solely in connection with agricultural operations carried on on agricultural land and sub-paragraph (2) or (3) below applies.

    (2)   This sub-paragraph applies if the building is occupied by the occupiers of all the land concerned.

    (3)   This sub-paragraph applies if the building is occupied by individuals each of whom is appointed by the occupiers of the land concerned to manage the use of the building and is—

    (a)   an occupier of some of the land concerned, or

    (b)   a member of the board of directors or other governing body of a person who is both a body corporate and an occupier of the land concerned.

    (4)   This paragraph does not apply unless the number of occupiers of the land concerned is less than 25.

5.   (1)   A building is an agricultural building if—

    (a)   it is used for the keeping or breeding of livestock, or

    (b)   it is not a dwelling, it is occupied together with a building or buildings falling within paragraph (a) above, and it is used in connection with the operations carried on in that building or those buildings.

    (2)   Sub-paragraph (1)(a) above does not apply unless—

    (a)   the building is solely used as there mentioned, or

    (b)   the building is occupied together with agricultural land and used also in connection with agricultural operations on that land, and that other use together with the use mentioned in sub-paragraph (1)(a) is its sole use.

    (3)   Sub-paragraph (1)(b) above does not apply unless—

    (a)   the building is solely used as there mentioned, or

    (b)   the building is occupied also together with agricultural land and used also in connection with agricultural operations on that land, and that other use together with the use mentioned in sub-paragraph (1)(b) is its sole use.

    (4)   A building (the building in question) is not an agricultural building by virtue of this paragraph unless it is surrounded by or contiguous to an area of agricultural land which amounts to not less than 2 hectares.

    (5)   In deciding for the purposes of sub-paragraph (4) above whether an area is agricultural land and what is its size, the following shall be disregarded—

    (a)   any road, watercourse or railway (which here includes the former site of a railway from which railway lines have been removed);

    (b)   any agricultural building other than the building in question;

    (c)   any building occupied together with the building in question.

6.   (1)   A building is an agricultural building if it is not a dwelling, is occupied by a person keeping bees, and is used solely in connection with the keeping of those bees.

    (2)   Sub-paragraphs (4) and (5) of paragraph 5 above apply for the purposes of this paragraph as for those of that.

7.   (1)   A building is an agricultural building if it is not a dwelling and—

    (a)   it is used in connection with agricultural operations carried on on agricultural land, and

    (b)   it is occupied by a body corporate any of whose members are or are together with the body the occupiers of the land, and

    (c)   the members who are occupiers of the land together have control of the body.

    (2)   A building is also an agricultural building if it is not a dwelling and—

    (a)   it is used in connection with the operations carried on in a building which, or buildings each of which, is used for the keeping or breeding of livestock and is an agricultural building by virtue of paragraph 5 above, and

    (b)   sub-paragraph (3), (4) or (5) below applies as regards the building first mentioned in this sub-paragraph (the building in question).

    (3)   This sub-paragraph applies if—

    (a)   the building in question is occupied by a body corporate any of whose members are, or are together with the body, the occupiers of the building or buildings mentioned in sub-paragraph (2)(a) above, and

    (b)   the members who are occupiers of the land together have control of the body.

    (4)   This sub-paragraph applies if the building in question, and the building or buildings mentioned in sub-paragraph (2)(a) above, are occupied by the same persons.

    (5)   This sub-paragraph applies if the building in question is occupied by individuals each of whom is appointed by the occupiers of the building or buildings mentioned in sub-paragraph (2)(a) above to manage the use of the building in question and is—

    (a)   an occupier of part of the building, or of part of one of the buildings, mentioned in sub-paragraph (2)(a) above, or

    (b)   a member of the board of directors or other governing body of a person who is both a body corporate and an occupier of the building or buildings mentioned in sub-paragraph (2)(a) above.

    (6)   Sub-paragraph (1) above does not apply unless the use there mentioned, or that use together with the use mentioned in sub-paragraph (2) above, is its sole use.

    (7)   Sub-paragraph (2) above does not apply unless the use there mentioned, or that use together with the use mentioned in sub-paragraph (1) above, is its sole use.

    (8)   Sub-paragraph (4) or (5) above does not apply unless the number of occupiers of the building or buildings mentioned in sub-paragraph (2)(a) above is less than 25.

    (9)   In this paragraph "control" shall be construed in accordance with section 416(2) to (6) of the Income and Corporation Taxes Act 1988.

8.   (1)   In paragraphs 1 and 3 to 7 above "agricultural land" shall be construed in accordance with paragraph 2 above.

    (2)   In paragraphs 1 and 5(5)(b) above "agricultural building" shall be construed in accordance with

paragraphs 3 to 7 above.

(3)   In determining for the purposes of paragraphs 3 to 7 above whether a building used in any way is solely so used, no account shall be taken of any time during which it is used in any other way, if that time does not amount to a substantial part of the time during which the building is used.

(4)   In paragraphs 2 to 7 above and sub-paragraph (2) above "building" includes a separate part of a building.

(5)   In paragraphs 5 and 7 above "livestock" includes any mammal or bird kept for the production of food or wool or for the purpose of its use in the farming of land.

Fish farms

9.   (1)   A hereditament is exempt to the extent that it consists of any of the following—
    (a)   land used solely for or in connection with fish farming;
    (b)   buildings (other than dwellings) so used.

(2)   In determining whether land or a building used for or in connection with fish farming is solely so used, no account shall be taken of any time during which it is used in any other way, if that time does not amount to a substantial part of the time during which the land or building is used.

(3)   "Building" includes a separate part of a building.

(4)   "Fish farming" means the breeding or rearing of fish, or the cultivation of shellfish, for the purpose of (or for purposes which include) transferring them to other waters or producing food for human consumption.

(4A)   But an activity does not constitute fish farming if the fish or shellfish are or include fish or shellfish which—
    (a)   are purely ornamental, or
    (b)   are bred, reared or cultivated for exhibition.

(5)   "Shellfish" includes crustaceans and molluscs of any description.

10.   *Repealed.*

Places of religious worship etc

11.   (1)   A hereditament is exempt to the extent that it consists of any of the following—
    (a)   a place of public religious worship which belongs to the Church of England or the Church in Wales (within the meaning of the Welsh Church Act 1914) or is for the time being certified as required by law as a place of religious worship;*
    (b)   a church hall, chapel hall or similar building used in connection with a place falling within paragraph (a) above for the purposes of the organisation responsible for the conduct of public religious worship in that place.

(2)   A hereditament is exempt to the extent that it is occupied by an organisation responsible for the conduct of public religious worship in a place falling within sub-paragraph (1)(a) above, and—
    (a)   is used for carrying out administrative or other activities relating to the organisation of the conduct of public religious worship in such a place;
    (b)   is used as an office or for office purposes, or for purposes ancillary to its use as an office or for office purposes.

(3)   In this paragraph "office purposes" include administration, clerical work and handling money; and "clerical work" includes writing, book-keeping, sorting papers or information, filing, typing, duplicating, calculating (by whatever means), drawing and the editorial preparation of matter for publication.

---

* **Substituted by the Local Government Act 2003, s 68 from a date to be appointed.**

Certain property of Trinity House

12.   (1)   A hereditament is exempt to the extent that it belongs to or is occupied by the Trinity House and consists of any of the following—
    (a)   a lighthouse;
    (b)   a buoy;
    (c)   a beacon;
    (d)   property within the same curtilage as, and occupied for the purposes of, a lighthouse.

(2)   No other hereditament (or part of a hereditament) belonging to or occupied by the Trinity House is exempt, notwithstanding anything in section 221 (1) of the Merchant Shipping Act 1995.

Sewers

13.   (1)   A hereditament is exempt to the extent that it consists of any of the following—
    (a)   a sewer;
    (b)   an accessory belonging to a sewer.

(2)   "Sewer" has the meaning given by section 343 of the Public Health Act 1936.

(3)   "Accessory" means a manhole, ventilating shaft, pumping station, pump or other accessory.

(4)   The Secretary of State may by order repeal sub-paragraphs (1) to (3) above.

Property of drainage authorities

14.   (1)   A hereditament is exempt to the extent that it consists of any of the following—
    (a)   land which is occupied by a drainage authority and which forms part of a main river or of a watercourse maintained by the authority;
    (b)   a structure maintained by a drainage authority for the purpose of controlling or regulating the flow of water in, into or out of a watercourse which forms part of a main river or is maintained by the authority;
    (c)   an appliance so maintained for that purpose.

(2)   "Drainage authority", means the Environment Agency or any internal drainage board and "main river" and "watercourse" have the same meanings, respectively as they have in the Water Resources Act 1991 and the Land Drainage Act 1991.

(3)   *Repealed.*

Parks

15.   (1)   A hereditament is exempt to the extent that it consists of a park which—

    (*a*)   has been provided by, or is under the management of, a relevant authority or two or more relevant authorities acting in combination, and

    (*b*)   is available for free and unrestricted use by members of the public.

    (2)   The reference to a park includes a reference to a recreation or pleasure ground, a public walk, an open space within the meaning of the Open Spaces Act 1906, and a playing field provided under the Physical Training and Recreation Act 1937.

    (3)   Each of the following is a relevant authority—

    (*aa*)   a Minister of the Crown or Government department or any officer or body exercising functions on behalf of the Crown,

    (*a*)   a county council,

    (*aa*)   a county borough council;

    (*b*)   a district council,

    (*c*)   a London borough council,

    (*d*)   the Common Council,

    (*e*)   the Council of the Isles of Scilly,

    (*f*)   a parish or community council, and

    (*g*)   the chairman of a parish meeting.

    (4)   In construing sub-paragraph (1)(*b*) above any temporary close (at night or otherwise) shall be ignored.

Property used for the disabled

16.   (1)   A hereditament is exempt to the extent that it consists of property used wholly for any of the following purposes—

    (*a*)   the provision of facilities for training, or keeping suitably occupied, persons who are disabled or who are or have been suffering from illness;

    (*b*)   the provision of welfare services for disabled persons;

    (*c*)   the provision of facilities under section 15 of the Disabled Persons (Employment) Act 1944;

    (*d*)   the provision of a workshop or of other facilities under section 3(1) of the Disabled Persons (Employment) Act 1958.

    (1A)   For the purposes of this paragraph in its application to hereditaments in England, a person is disabled if he has a disability within the meaning given by section 6 of the Equality Act 2010.

    (2)   For the purposes of this paragraph in its application to hereditaments in Wales, a person is disabled if he is blind, deaf or dumb or suffers from mental disorder of any description or is substantially and permanently handicapped by illness, injury, congenital deformity or any other disability for the time being prescribed for the purposes of section 29(1) of the National Assistance Act 1948.

    (3)   "Illness" has the meaning given by section 275 of the National Health Service Act 2006.

    (4)   "Welfare services for disabled persons" means services or facilities (by whomsoever provided) of a kind which a local authority has power to provide under section 29 of the National Assistance Act 1948 or, in the case of a local authority in England, had power to provide under that section immediately before it ceased to apply to local authorities in England.

Air-raid protection works

17.   A hereditament is exempt to the extent that it consists of property which—

    (*a*)   is intended to be occupied or used solely for the purpose of affording protection in the event of hostile attack from the air, and

    (*b*)   is not occupied or used for any other purpose.

Swinging moorings

18.   A hereditament is exempt to the extent that it consists of a mooring which is used or intended to be used by a boat or ship and which is equipped only with a buoy attached to an anchor, weight or other device—

    (*a*)   which rests on or in the bed of the sea or any river or other waters when in use, and

    (*b*)   which is designed to be raised from that bed from time to time.

Road crossings over watercourses etc

18A.   (1)   A hereditament which is occupied (as mentioned in section 65 of this Act) is exempt to the extent that it consists of, or of any of the appurtenances of, a fixed road crossing over an estuary, river or other watercourse.

    (2)   For the purposes of this paragraph, a fixed road crossing means a bridge, viaduct, tunnel or other construction providing a means for road vehicles or pedestrians or both to cross the estuary, river or other watercourse concerned.

    (3)   For the purposes of sub-paragraph (2) above—

    (*a*)   a bridge may be a fixed road crossing notwithstanding that it is designed so that part of it can be swung, raised or otherwise moved in order to facilitate passage across, above or below it; but

    (*b*)   the expression "bridge" does not include a floating bridge, that is to say, a ferry operating between fixed chains.

    (4)   The reference in sub-paragraph (1) above to the appurtenances of a fixed road crossing is a reference to—

    (*a*)   the carriageway and any footway thereof;

    (*b*)   any building, other than office buildings, used in connection with the crossing; and

    (*c*)   any machinery, apparatus or works used in connection with the crossing or with any of the items mentioned in paragraphs (*a*) and (*b*) above.

Property used for road user charging schemes

18B.   (1)   A hereditament which is occupied (as mentioned in section 65 of this Act) is exempt to the extent that—

    (*a*)   it consists of a road in respect of which charges are imposed by a charging scheme under Schedule 23 to the Greater London Authority Act 1999 or Part III of the Transport Act 2000, or

    (*b*)   it is used solely for or in connection with the operation of such a scheme.

    (2)   But office buildings are not exempt under sub-paragraph (1)(*b*) above.

Property in enterprise zones

19. (1)	A hereditament is exempt to the extent that it is situated in an enterprise zone.

(2)	An enterprise zone is an area for the time being designated as an enterprise zone under Schedule 32 to the Local Government, Planning and Land Act 1980.

Visiting Forces etc.

19A. (1)	A hereditament is exempt to the extent that it consists of property which is occupied for the purposes of a visiting force, or a headquarters, in pursuance of arrangements made in that behalf with any Government department.

(2)	In this paragraph—

"headquarters" means an international headquarters or defence organisation designated by an Order in Council under section 1 of the International Headquarters and Defence Organisations Act 1964; and

"visiting force" means any such body, contingent or detachment of the forces of any country as is a visiting force for the purposes of any provision of the Visiting Forces Act 1952.

Power to confer exemption

20. (1)	The Secretary of State may make regulations providing that prescribed hereditaments or hereditaments falling within any prescribed description are exempt to such extent (whether as to the whole or some lesser extent) as may be prescribed.

(2)	But the power under sub-paragraph (1) above may not be exercised so as to confer exemption which in his opinion goes beyond such exemption or privilege (if any) as fulfils the first and second conditions.

(3)	The first condition is that the exemption or privilege operated or was enjoyed in practice, immediately before the passing of this Act, in respect of a general rate in its application to the hereditaments prescribed or falling within the prescribed description.

(4)	The second condition is that the exemption or privilege—

(a)	was conferred by a local Act or order passed or made on or after 22 December 1925, or

(b)	was conferred by a local Act or order passed or made before 22 December 1925 and was saved by section 117(5)(b) of the 1967 Act.

(5)	Regulations under sub-paragraph (1) above in their application to a particular financial year (including regulations amending or revoking others) shall not be effective unless they come into force before 1 January in the preceding financial year.

Interpretation

21. (1)	This paragraph applies for the purposes of this Schedule.

(2)	"Exempt" means exempt from local non-domestic rating.

(3)	Any land, building or property not in use shall be treated as used in a particular way if it appears that when next in use it will be used in that way.

(4)	Any land or building which is not occupied shall be treated as occupied in a particular way if it appears that when next occupied it will be occupied in that way.

(5)	A person shall be treated as an occupier of any land or building which is not occupied if it appears that when it is next occupied he will be an occupier of it.

SCHEDULE 6

NON-DOMESTIC RATING: VALUATION[1]					Section 56

7.7585

(Amended by the Local Government and Housing Act 1989, Schs 5 and 12, the Local Government Finance Act 1992, Sch 10, SI 1993/544, the Local Government and Rating Act 1997, s 2 and the Rating (Valuation) Act 1999, s 1.)

[1]	See the Non-Domestic Rating (Miscellaneous Provisions) Regulations 1989, SI 1989/1060, the Non-Domestic Rating (Miscellaneous Provisions) (No 2) Regulations 1989, SI 1989/2303; Non-Domestic Rating (Material Day for List Alterations) Regulations 1992, SI 1992/556; the Water Undertakers (Rateable Values) (Wales) Order 2000, SI 2000/299, the BG plc (Rateable Value) (Wales) Order 2000;, the Railtrack plc (Rateable Value) (Wales) Order 2000, SI 2003/555, the Valuation for Rating (Plant and Machinery) (England) Regulations 2000, SI 2000/540, the Valuation for Rating (Plant and Machinery) (Wales) Regulations 2000, SI 2000/1097; Non-domestic Rating (Stud Farms) (England) Order 2004, SI 2004/3151; Non-Domestic Rating (Communications Hereditaments) (Valuation, Alteration of Lists and Appeals and Material Day) (England) Regulations 2008, SI 2008/2333; Non-Domestic Rating (Communications Hereditaments) (Valuation, Alteration of Lists and Appeals and Material Day) (Wales) Regulations 2008, SI 2008/2671; Non-Domestic Rating (Stud Farms) (England) Order 2009, SI 2009/3177; Rating Lists (Valuation Date) (England) Order 2014, SI 2014/2841 and Rating Lists (Valuation Date) (Wales) Order 2014, SI 2014/2917.

SCHEDULE 9

NON-DOMESTIC RATING: ADMINISTRATION					Section 62

(As amended by the Local Government and Housing Act 1989, Sch 5 and 12, the Local Government Finance Act 1992, Sch 13, the Local Government Act 2003, s 72, the Local Government (Wales) Act 1994, Sch 16, the Local Government and Public Involvement in Health Act 2007, Sch 16, the Tribunals, Courts and Enforcement Act 2007, Sch 13 and SI 2015/982.)

Collection and recovery

7.7586 1.	The Secretary of State may make regulations containing such provision as he sees fit in relation to the collection and the recovery, otherwise than under Schedule 12 to the Tribunals, Courts and Enforcement Act 2007 (taking control of goods), of amounts persons are liable to pay under sections 43, 45 and 54 above.

2–4A.	*Regulations*[1].

[1]	See the Non-Domestic Rating (Collection and Enforcement) (Local Lists) Regulations 1989, post, the Non-Domestic Rating (Collection and Enforcement) (Central Lists) Regulations 1989, SI 1989/2260, the Council Tax and Non-domestic Rating (Demand Notices) (England) Regulations 2003, SI 2003/2613; Non-Domestic Rating (Deferred Payments) (England) Regulations 2009, SI 2009/1597; Non-Domestic Rating (Deferred Payments) (Wales) Regulations 2009, SI 2009/2154; Non-Domestic Rating (Deferred Payments) (Wales) Regulations 2012, SI 2012/466 and SI 2017/113; Non-Domestic Rating (Deferred Payments) (England) Regulations 2012, SI 2012/994; Non-Domestic Rating

(Demand Notices) (Wales) Regulations 2017, SI 2017/113 have been made.

Information

5. (1) A valuation officer may serve a notice on a person who is an owner or occupier of a hereditament requesting him to supply to the officer information—

    (a)   which is specified in the notice, and

    (b)   which the officer reasonably believes will assist him in carrying out functions conferred or imposed on him by or under this Part.

(1A) A notice under this paragraph must state that the officer believes the information requested will assist him in carrying out functions conferred or imposed on him by or under this Part.

(2) A person on whom a notice is served under this paragraph shall supply the information requested in such form and manner as is specified in the notice.

(3) *Repealed.*

(4) If a notice has been served on a person under this paragraph, and in supplying information in purported compliance with sub-paragraph (2) above he makes a statement which he knows to be false in a material particular or recklessly makes a statement which is false in a material particular, he shall be liable on summary conviction to imprisonment for a term not exceeding **3 months** or to a fine not exceeding **level 3** on the standard scale or to both.

5A. (1) If a person on whom a notice is served under paragraph 5 above fails to comply with paragraph 5(2) within the period of 56 days beginning with the day on which the notice is served, he shall be liable to a penalty of £100.

(2) Where a person becomes liable to a penalty under sub-paragraph (1) above, the valuation officer shall serve on him a notice (a "penalty notice") stating—

    (a)   that he has failed to comply with paragraph 5(2) above within the period mentioned in sub-paragraph (1) above,

    (b)   that he is liable to a penalty of £100,

    (c)   the effect of sub-paragraphs (3) and (4) below, and

    (d)   that he has a right of appeal under paragraph 5C below.

(3) If the person on whom a penalty notice is served fails to comply with paragraph 5(2) within the period of 21 days beginning with the day on which the notice is served, he shall be liable—

    (a)   to a further penalty of £100, and

    (b)   subject to sub-paragraph (4) below, to a further penalty of £20 for each day in respect of which the failure continues after the end of that period.

(4) The amount to which a person shall be liable under this paragraph in respect of a failure to comply with a notice served under paragraph 5 above shall not exceed the greater of—

    (a)   the rateable value of the hereditament concerned for the day on which the penalty notice is served, and

    (b)   £500.

(5) For the purposes of sub-paragraph (4)(a) above—

    (a)   the hereditament concerned is the hereditament in respect of which the notice under paragraph 5 above was served, and

    (b)   a list compiled under this Part shall be used to find the rateable value of the hereditament for the day concerned.

5B. A valuation officer may mitigate or remit any penalty imposed under paragraph 5A above.

5C. (1) A person may appeal to a valuation tribunal if he is aggrieved by the imposition on him of a penalty under paragraph 5A above.

(2) An appeal under this paragraph must be made before the end of the period of 28 days beginning with the day on which the penalty notice is served.

(3) An appeal under this paragraph shall not prevent liability to any further penalty or penalties arising under paragraph 5A(3) above.

(4) An appeal under this paragraph shall be treated as an appeal against the penalty imposed under paragraph 5A(1) above and any further penalty which may be imposed under paragraph 5A(3) above.

(5) On an appeal under this paragraph the valuation tribunal may mitigate or remit any penalty under paragraph 5A above if it is satisfied on either or both of the grounds specified in sub-paragraph (6) below.

(6) Those grounds are—

    (a)   that the appellant had a reasonable excuse for not complying with paragraph 5(2) above, or

    (b)   that the information requested is not in the possession or control of the appellant.

(7) In this paragraph "valuation tribunal" means—

    (a)   in relation to England: the Valuation Tribunal for England;

    (b)   in relation to Wales: a valuation tribunal established under paragraph 1 of Schedule 11.

5D. (1) Subject to sub-paragraph (2) below, any penalty imposed under paragraph 5A above may be recovered by the valuation officer concerned as a civil debt due to him.

(2) No claim to recover any such penalty may be made—

    (a)   before the end of the period mentioned in paragraph 5C(2) above, or

    (b)   if an appeal is made under paragraph 5C above, before the appeal is finally disposed of.

5E. Any sums received by a valuation officer by way of penalty under paragraph 5A above must be paid into the Consolidated Fund.

5F. (1) The Secretary of State in relation to England, and the National Assembly of Wales in relation to Wales, may by regulations make provision in relation to notices served under paragraphs 5 and 5A above.

(2) The provision that may be made by regulations under this paragraph includes—

    (a)   provision enabling a valuation officer to request or obtain information for the purpose of identifying the owner or occupier of a hereditament;

    (b)   provision enabling a notice to be served on a person either by name or by such description as may be prescribed.

5G. The Secretary of State in relation to England, and the National Assembly in relation to Wales, may by order amend paragraph 5A above to increase or decrease the amount of any penalty under that paragraph.

5H. Where a valuation officer requires the name or address of a person on whom a notice under paragraph 5 or 5A above is to be served, he may serve a notice on a billing authority which he reasonably believes may have that information requesting the authority to supply him with that information.

6. (1)   If in the course of the exercise of its functions any information comes to the notice of a billing authority which leads it to suppose that a list requires alteration it shall be the authority's duty to inform the valuation officer who has the duty to maintain the list.

(1A)   *Regulations*[1].

---

[1] The Non-Domestic Rating (Alteration of Lists and Appeals) (England) Regulations 2009, SI 2009/2268 have been made.

6A.   *Regulations may require information to be supplied to the billing authority.*

Power of entry

6B. (1)   If a valuation officer needs to value a hereditament in England for the purpose of carrying out functions conferred or imposed on the officer by or under this Part, the officer and any person authorised by the officer in writing may enter on, survey and value the hereditament if sub-paragraphs (2) and (4) are fulfilled and (where it applies) subparagraph (5) is fulfilled.

(2)   The valuation officer must obtain the approval of the tribunal before the officer or a person authorised by the officer exercises the power under sub-paragraph (1).

(3)   The tribunal must not give its approval unless it is satisfied that the valuation officer needs to value the hereditament.

(4)   After the tribunal has given its approval, at least 3 days' notice in writing must be given of the proposed exercise of the power.

(5)   In a case where a person authorised by the valuation officer proposes to exercise the power, the person must if required produce the authorisation.

(6)   A person who wilfully delays or obstructs a person in the exercise of a power under this paragraph is liable on summary conviction to a fine not exceeding level 1 on the standard scale.

(7)   For the purpose of the requirement under sub-paragraph (4), the following days are to be disregarded—

(a)   a Saturday, a Sunday, Christmas Day or Good Friday;

(b)   a day which is a bank holiday under the Banking and Financial Dealings Act 1971 in England and Wales.

(8)   The tribunal may—

(a)   determine any application brought under this paragraph and any question arising from that application;

(b)   specify the arrangements by which any entry approved by it must be conducted, including whether the entry may occur on more than one day.

(9)   In this paragraph "the tribunal" means the First-tier Tribunal.

7. (1)   If a valuation officer needs to value a hereditament in Wales for the purpose of carrying out functions conferred or imposed on him by or under this Part, he and any person authorised by him in writing may enter on, survey and value the hereditament if sub-paragraph (2) below is fulfilled and (where it applies) sub-paragraph (3) below is fulfilled.

(2)   At least 24 hours' notice in writing of the proposed exercise of the power must be given.

(3)   In a case where a person authorised by the valuation officer proposes to exercise the power, the person must if required produce his authority.

(4)   If a person wilfully delays or obstructs a person in the exercise of a power under this paragraph, he shall be liable on summary conviction to a fine not exceeding **level 1** on the standard scale.

Inspection

8. (1)   A person may require a valuation officer to give him access to such information as will enable him to establish what is the state of a list, or has been its state at any time since it came into force, if—

(a)   the officer is maintaining the list, and

(b)   the list is in force or has been in force at any time in the preceding 5 years.

(2)   A person may require a billing authority to give him access to such information as will enable him to establish what is the state of a copy of a list, or has been its state at any time since it was deposited, if—

(a)   the authority has deposited the copy under section 41(6B) or 41A(10) above, and

(b)   the list is in force or has been in force at any time in the preceding 5 years.

(3)   A person may require the Secretary of State to give him access to such information as will enable him to establish what is the state of a copy of a list, or has been its state at any time since it was deposited, if—

(a)   the Secretary of State has deposited the copy under section 52(6B) above, and

(b)   the list is in force or has been in force at any time in the preceding 5 years.

(4)   A person may require a billing authority to give him access to such information as will enable him to establish what is the state of a copy of a proposed list if—

(a)   the authority has deposited the copy under section 41(6) above, and

(b)   the list itself is not yet in force.

(5)   A person may require the Secretary of State to give him access to such information as will enable him to establish what is the state of a copy of a proposed list if—

(a)   the Secretary of State has deposited the copy under section 52(6) above, and

(b)   the list itself is not yet in force.

(6)   A requirement under any of the preceding provisions of this paragraph must be complied with at a reasonable time and place and without payment being sought; but the information may be in documentary or other form, as the person or authority of whom the requirement is made thinks fit.

(7)   Where access is given under this paragraph to information in documentary form the person to whom access is given may—

(a)   make copies of (or of extracts from) the document;

(b)   require a person having custody of the document to supply to him a photographic copy of (or of extracts from) the document.

(8)   Where access is given under this paragraph to information in a form which is not documentary the person to whom access is given may—

(a)   make transcripts of (or of extracts from) the information;

(b)   require a person having control of access to the information to supply to him a copy in documentary form of (or of extracts from) the information.

(9)   If a reasonable charge is required for a facility under sub-paragraph (7) or (8) above, the sub-paragraph

concerned shall not apply unless the person seeking to avail himself of the facility pays the charge.

(10) If without reasonable excuse a person having custody of a document containing, or having control of access to, information access to which is sought under this paragraph—

(a) intentionally obstructs a person in exercising a right under sub-paragraph (1), (2), (3), (4), (5), (7)(a) or (8)(a) above, or

(b) refuses to comply with a requirement under sub-paragraph (7)(b) or 8(b) above,

he shall be liable on summary conviction to a fine not exceeding **level 1** on the standard scale.

9. (1) A person may, at a reasonable time and without making payment, inspect any proposal made or notice of appeal given under regulations made under section 55 above, if made or given as regards a list which is in force when inspection is sought or has been in force at any time in the preceding years.

(2) A person may—

(a) make copies of (or of extracts from) a document mentioned in sub-paragraph (1) above, or

(b) require a person having custody of such a document to supply him a photographic copy of (or of extracts from) the document.

(3) If a reasonable charge is required for a facility under sub-paragraph (2) above, the sub-paragraph shall not apply unless the person seeking to avail himself of the facility pays the charge.

(4) If without reasonable excuse a person having custody of a document mentioned in sub-paragraph (1) above—

(a) intentionally obstructs a person in exercising a right under sub-paragraph (1) or (2)(a) above, or

(b) refuses to supply a copy to a person entitled to it under sub-paragraph (2)(b) above,

he shall be liable on summary conviction to a fine not exceeding **level 1** on the standard scale.

Local Government Finance Act 1992
(1992 c 14)

Introduction: council tax

7.7587 The Local Government Finance Act 1992 ("the Act") and regulations made thereunder establish a system of council tax replacing the community charge ("poll tax") and thus reverting to a property-based liability.

Part I (ss 1–69) is divided into six Chapters. Chapter I gives the main provisions of the council tax, Chapter II sets out provisions relating to valuation lists; intentional delay or obstruction exercising a power of entry following three clear days' notice (excluding Saturday, Sunday, Christmas Day, Good Friday, bank holidays) is punishable by a level 2 fine (s 26); failing to comply with notice requiring information about property is punishable by a level 2 fine (s **27(4)** and knowingly or recklessly making a statement false in a material particular is punishable by 3 months' imprisonment and/or a level 3 fine (s **27(5)**). Chapter III is concerned with the setting of the council tax and Chapter IV with precepts. Limitation of council tax and precepts by the Secretary of State is dealt with in Chapter V and Chapter VI (ss 65–69) covers miscellaneous and supplemental matters including Part I interpretation. Part III (ss 100–102) provides for transition from community charges. Schedule 4 is the most relevant part for magistrates' courts, in providing for the Secretary of State to make regulations relating to enforcement.

PART I
COUNCIL TAX: ENGLAND AND WALES

CHAPTER I
MAIN PROVISIONS

Preliminary

7.7588 **1. Council tax in respect of dwellings** (1) As regards the financial year beginning in 1993 and subsequent financial years, each billing authority shall, in accordance with this Part, levy and collect a tax, to be called council tax, which shall be payable in respect of dwellings situated in its area.

(2) In this Part "billing authority" means—

(a) in relation to England, a district council or London borough council, the Common Council or the Council of the Isles of Scilly, and

(b) in relation to Wales, a county council or county borough council.

(3) For the purposes of this Part the Secretary of State may make regulations[1] containing rules for treating a dwelling as situated in a billing authority's area if part only of the dwelling falls within the area.

[Local Government Finance Act 1992, s 1 as amended by the Local Government (Wales) Act 1994, s 35(5).]

---

[1] See Pt II of the Council Tax (Situation and Valuation of Dwellings) Regulations 1992, SI 1992/550.

7.7589 **2. Liability to tax determined on a daily basis** (1) Liability to pay council tax shall be determined on a daily basis.

(2) For the purposes of determining for any day—

(a) whether any property is a chargeable dwelling;

(b) which valuation band is shown in the billing authority's valuation list as applicable to any chargeable dwelling;

(c) the person liable to pay council tax in respect of any such dwelling; or

(d) whether any amount of council tax is subject to a discount and (if so) the amount of the discount, it shall be assumed that any state of affairs subsisting at the end of the day had subsisted throughout the day.

[Local Government Finance Act 1992, s 2.]

Chargeable dwellings

7.7590   3.   Meaning of "dwelling"   (1)   This section has effect for determining what is a dwelling for the purposes of this Part.

(2)   Subject to the following provisions of this section, a dwelling is any property which—

    (a)   by virtue of the definition of hereditament in section 115(1) of the General Rate Act 1967, would have been a hereditament for the purposes of that Act if that Act remained in force; and

    (b)   is not for the time being shown or required to be shown in a local or a central non-domestic rating list in force at that time; and

    (c)   is not for the time being exempt from local non-domestic rating for the purposes of Part III of the Local Government Finance Act 1988 ("the 1988 Act");

and in applying paragraphs (b) and (c) above no account shall be taken of any rules as to Crown exemption.

(3)   A hereditament which—

    (a)   is a composite hereditament for the purposes of Part III of the 1988 Act; and

    (b)   would still be such a hereditament if paragraphs (b) to (d) of section 66(1) of that Act (domestic property) were omitted,

is also, subject to subsection (6) below, a dwelling for the purposes of this Part.

(4)   Subject to subsection (6) below, none of the following property, namely—

    (a)   a yard, garden, outhouse or other appurtenance belonging to or enjoyed with property used wholly for the purposes of living accommodation; or

    (b)   a private garage which either has a floor area of not more than 25 square metres or is used wholly or mainly for the accommodation of a private motor vehicle; or

    (c)   private storage premises used wholly or mainly for the storage of articles of domestic use,

is a dwelling except in so far as it forms part of a larger property which is itself a dwelling by virtue of subsection (2) above.

(5)   The Secretary of State may by order[1] provide that in such cases as may be prescribed by or determined under the order—

    (a)   anything which would (apart from the order) be one dwelling shall be treated as two or more dwellings; and

    (b)   anything which would (apart from the order) be two or more dwellings shall be treated as one dwelling.

(6)   The Secretary of State may by order amend any definition of "dwelling" which is for the time being effective for the purposes of this Part.

[Local Government Finance Act 1992, s 3.]

---

[1]   The Council Tax (Chargeable Dwellings) Order 1992, SI 1992/549 has been made.

7.7591   4.   Dwellings chargeable to council tax   (1)   Council tax shall be payable in respect of any dwelling which is not an exempt dwelling.

(2)   In this Chapter—

"chargeable dwelling" means any dwelling in respect of which council tax is payable;

"exempt dwelling" means any dwelling of a class prescribed[1] by an order made by the Secretary of State.

(3)   For the purposes of subsection (2) above, a class of dwellings may be prescribed by reference to such factors as the Secretary of State sees fit.

(4)   Without prejudice to the generality of subsection (3) above, a class of dwellings may be prescribed by reference to one or more of the following factors—

    (a)   the physical characteristics of dwellings;

    (b)   the fact that dwellings are unoccupied or are occupied for prescribed purposes or are occupied or owned by persons of prescribed descriptions.

[Local Government Finance Act 1992, s 4.]

---

[1]   The Council Tax (Exempt Dwellings) Order 1992, SI 1992/558.

7.7592   5.   Different amounts for dwellings in different valuation bands   (1)   The amounts of council tax payable in respect of dwellings situated in the same billing authority's area (or the same part of such an area) and listed in different valuation bands shall be in the proportion—

6: 7: 8: 9: 11: 13: 15: 18

where 6 is for dwellings listed in valuation band A, 7 is for dwellings listed in valuation band B, and so on.

(1A)   For the purposes of the application of subsection (1) to dwellings situated in Wales, for the purposes of financial years beginning on or after 1st April 2005, for the proportion specified in that subsection there is substituted the following proportion:

6: 7: 8: 9: 11: 13: 15: 18: 21

(2)   The valuation bands for dwellings in England are set out in the following Table—

Range of values	Valuation band
Values not exceeding £40,000	A
Values exceeding £40,000 but not exceeding £52,000	B
Values exceeding £52,000 but not exceeding £68,000	C
Values exceeding £68,000 but not exceeding £88,000	D
Values exceeding £88,000 but not exceeding £120,000	E
Values exceeding £120,000 but not exceeding £160,000	F
Values exceeding £160,000 but not exceeding £320,000	G
Values exceeding £320,000	H

(3)   The valuation bands for dwellings in Wales are set out in the following Table—

Range of values	Valuation band
Values not exceeding £44,000	A
Values exceeding £44,000 but not exceeding £65,000	B
Values exceeding £65,000 but not exceeding £91,000	C
Values exceeding £91,000 but not exceeding £123,000	D
Values exceeding £123,000 but not exceeding £162,000	E
Values exceeding £162,000 but not exceeding £223,000	F
Values exceeding £223,000 but not exceeding £324,000	G
Values exceeding £324,000 but not exceeding £424,000	H
Values exceeding £424,000	I

(4)   The Secretary of State may by order[1], as regards financial years beginning on or after such date as is specified in the order—

    (a)   substitute another proportion for that which is for the time being effective for the purposes of subsection (1) above;

    (b)   substitute other valuation bands for those which are for the time being effective for the purposes of subsection (2) or (3) above.

(4A)   The power under subsection (4)(b) above includes power to make provision for a different number of valuation bands from those which are for the time being effective for the purposes of subsection (2) or (3) above.

(5)   No order under subsection (4) above shall be made unless a draft of the order has been laid before and approved by resolution of the House of Commons.

(6)   Any reference in this Part to dwellings listed in a particular valuation band shall be construed as a reference to dwellings to which that valuation band is shown as applicable in the billing authority's valuation list.

[Local Government Finance Act 1992, s 5 as amended by SI 2003/3046 and the Local Government Act 2003, s 78.]

---

[1] The Council Tax (Valuation Bands) (Wales) Order 2003, SI 2003/3046 has been made.

Liability to tax

7.7593   6.   Persons liable to pay council tax   (1)   The person who is liable to pay council tax in respect of any chargeable dwelling and any day is the person who falls within the first paragraph of subsection (2) below to apply, taking paragraph (a) of that subsection first, paragraph (b) next, and so on.

(2)   A person falls within this subsection in relation to any chargeable dwelling and any day if, on that day—

    (a)   he is a resident of the dwelling and has a freehold interest in the whole or any part of it;

    (b)   he is such a resident and has a leasehold interest in the whole or any part of the dwelling which is not inferior to another such interest held by another such resident;

    (c)   he is both such a resident and a statutory, secure or introductory tenant of the whole or any part of the dwelling;

    (d)   he is such a resident and has a contractual licence to occupy the whole or any part of the dwelling;

    (e)   he is such a resident; or

    (f)   he is the owner of the dwelling.

(3)   Where, in relation to any chargeable dwelling and any day, two or more persons fall within the first paragraph of subsection (2) above to apply, they shall each be jointly and severally liable to

pay the council tax in respect of the dwelling and that day.

(4)   Subsection (3) above shall not apply as respects any day on which one or more of the persons there mentioned fall to be disregarded for the purposes of discount by virtue of paragraph 2 of Schedule 1 to this Act (the severely mentally impaired) and one or more of them do not; and liability to pay the council tax in respect of the dwelling and that day shall be determined as follows—

(a)   if only one of those persons does not fall to be so disregarded, he shall be solely liable;

(b)   if two or more of those persons do not fall to be so disregarded, they shall each be jointly and severally liable.

(5)   In this Part, unless the context otherwise requires—

"owner", in relation to any dwelling, means the person as regards whom the following conditions are fulfilled—

(a)   he has a material interest in the whole or any part of the dwelling; and

(b)   at least part of the dwelling or, as the case may be, of the part concerned is not subject to a material interest inferior to his interest;

"resident", in relation to any dwelling, means an individual who has attained the age of 18 years and has his sole or main residence[1] in the dwelling.

(6)   In this section—

"introductory tenant" means a tenant under an introductory tenancy within the meaning of Chapter I of Part V of the Housing Act 1996;

"material interest" means a freehold interest or a leasehold interest which was granted for a term of six months or more;

"secure tenant" means a tenant under a secure tenancy within the meaning of Part IV of the Housing Act 1985;

"statutory tenant" means a statutory tenant within the meaning of the Rent Act 1977 or the Rent (Agriculture) Act 1976.

[Local Government Finance Act 1992, s 6 as amended by SI 1997/74.]

---

[1]   The words "sole or main residence" in s 6(5) of the 1992 Act refer to premises in which a taxpayer actually resided, and the qualification "sole or main" addresses the fact that a person could reside in more than one place: *Williams v Horsham District Council* [2004] EWCA Civ 39, [2004] 3 All ER 30.

7.7594   7.   Liability in respect of caravans and boats   (1)   Subsections (2) to (4) below shall have effect in substitution for section 6 above in relation to any chargeable dwelling which consists of a pitch occupied by a caravan, or a mooring occupied by a boat.

(2)   Where on any day the owner of the caravan or boat is not, but some other person is, a resident of the dwelling, that other person shall be liable to pay the council tax in respect of the dwelling and that day.

(3)   Where on any day subsection (2) above does not apply, the owner of the caravan or boat shall be liable to pay the council tax in respect of the dwelling and that day.

(4)   Where on any day two or more persons fall within subsection (2) or (3) above, they shall each be jointly and severally liable to pay the council tax in respect of the dwelling and that day.

(5)   Subsection (4) of section 6 above shall apply for the purposes of subsection (4) above as it applies for the purposes of subsection (3) of that section.

(6)   In this section "caravan" shall be construed in accordance with Part I of the Caravan Sites and Control of Development Act 1960.

(7)   Any reference in this section to the owner of a caravan or boat shall be construed—

(a)   in relation to a caravan or boat which is subject to an agreement for hire-purchase or conditional sale, as a reference to the person in possession under the agreement;

(b)   in relation to a caravan or boat which is subject to a bill of sale or mortgage, as a reference to the person entitled to the property in it apart from the bill or mortgage.

[Local Government Finance Act 1992, s 7.]

7.7595   8.   Liability in prescribed cases   (1)   Subsections (3) and (4) below shall have effect in substitution for section 6 or (as the case may be) section 7 above in relation to any chargeable dwelling of a class prescribed[1] for the purposes of this subsection.

(2)   Subsections (3) and (4) below shall have effect in substitution for section 6 or (as the case may be) section 7 above in relation to any chargeable dwelling of a class prescribed for the purposes of this subsection, if the billing authority so determines in relation to all dwellings of that class which are situated in its area.

(3)   Where on any day this subsection has effect in relation to a dwelling, the owner of the dwelling shall be liable to pay the council tax in respect of the dwelling and that day.

(4)   Where on any day two or more persons fall within subsection (3) above, they shall each be jointly and severally liable to pay the council tax in respect of the dwelling and that day.

(5)   Subsection (4) of section 6 above shall apply for the purposes of subsection (4) above as it applies for the purposes of subsection (3) of that section.

(6)   Regulations prescribing a class of chargeable dwellings for the purposes of subsection (1) or (2) above may provide that, in relation to any dwelling of that class, subsection (3) above shall have effect as if for the reference to the owner of the dwelling there were substituted a reference to the

person falling within such description as may be prescribed[1].

(7)   Subsections (3) and (4) of section 4 above shall apply for the purposes of subsections (1) and (2) above as they apply for the purposes of subsection (2) of that section.

[Local Government Finance Act 1992, s 8.]

---

[1] The Council Tax (Liability for Owners) Regulations 1992, SI 1992/551 have been made.

7.7596 9.   Liability of spouses   (1)   Where—

(*a*)   a person who is liable to pay council tax in respect of any chargeable dwelling of which he is a resident and any day is married, or is the civil partner of, to another person; and*

(*b*)   that other person is also a resident of the dwelling on that day but would not, apart from this section, be so liable,

those persons shall each be jointly and severally liable to pay the council tax in respect of the dwelling and that day.

(2)   Subsection (1) above shall not apply as respects any day on which the other person there mentioned falls to be disregarded for the purposes of discount by virtue of paragraph 2 of Schedule 1 to this Act (the severely mentally impaired).

(3)   For the purposes of this section, two persons are to be treated as married to, or civil partners of, each other if they are living together as if they were a married couple or civil partners.

(4)   For the purposes of this section two persons are civil partners of each other if they are of the same sex and either—

(*a*)   they are civil partners of each other; or

(*b*)   They are not civil partners of each other but are living together as if they were civil partners.

[Local Government Finance Act 1992, s 9 as amended by the Civil Partnership Act 2004, Sch 27 and SI 2019/1458.]

Amounts of tax payable

7.7597 10.   Basic amounts payable   (1)   Subject to sections 11 to 13 below, a person who is liable to pay council tax in respect of any chargeable dwelling and any day shall, as respects the dwelling and the day, pay to the billing authority for the area in which the dwelling is situated an amount calculated in accordance with the formula—

$$\frac{A}{B}$$

where—

A is the amount which, for the financial year in which the day falls and for dwellings in the valuation band listed for the dwelling, has been set by the authority for its area or (as the case may be) the part of its area in which the dwelling is situated;

D is the number of days in the financial year.

(2)   For the purposes of this Part the Secretary of State may make regulations containing rules for ascertaining in what part of a billing authority's area a dwelling is situated (whether situated in the area in fact or by virtue of regulations[1] made under section 1(3) above).

[Local Government Finance Act 1992, s 10.]

---

[1] See Pt III of the Council Tax (Situation and Valuation of Dwellings) Regulations 1992, SI 1992/550.

7.7598 11.   Discounts   (1)   The amount of council tax payable in respect of any chargeable dwelling and any day shall be subject to a discount equal to the appropriate percentage of that amount if on that day—

(*a*)   there is only one resident of the dwelling and he does not fall to be disregarded for the purposes of discount; or

(*b*)   there are two or more residents of the dwelling and each of them except one falls to be disregarded for those purposes.

(2)   Subject to sections 11A and 12 below, the amount of council tax payable in respect of any chargeable dwelling and any day shall be subject to a discount equal to twice the appropriate percentage of that amount if on that day—

(*a*)   there is no resident of the dwelling; or

(*b*)   there are one or more residents of the dwelling and each of them falls to be disregarded for the purposes of discount.

(3)   In this section "the appropriate percentage" means 25 per cent or, if the Secretary of State by order so provides in relation to the financial year in which the day falls, such other percentage as is specified in the order.

(4)   No order under subsection (3) above shall be made unless a draft of the order has been laid before and approved by resolution of the House of Commons.

(5)   Schedule 1 to this Act shall have effect for determining who shall be disregarded for the purposes of discount.

[Local Government Finance Act 1992, s 11 as amended by the Local Government Act 2003, Schs 7 and 8.]

7.7599 11A.   Discounts: special provision for England   (1)   The Secretary of State may for any financial year by regulations[1] prescribe one or more classes of dwelling in England for the purposes of subsection (3) or (4) below.

(2)   A class of dwellings may be prescribed under subsection (1) above by reference to such factors as the Secretary of State sees fit and may, in particular, be prescribed by reference to—

(a)   the physical characteristics of dwellings, or

(b)   the fact that dwellings are unoccupied.

(3)   For any financial year for which a class of dwellings is prescribed for the purposes of this subsection, a billing authority in England may by determination provide in relation to all dwellings of that class in its area, or in such part of its area as it may specify in the determination, that the discount under section 11(2)(a) shall be such lesser percentage of at least 10 as it may so specify.

(4)   For any financial year for which a class of dwellings is prescribed for the purposes of this subsection, a billing authority in England may by determination provide in relation to all dwellings of that class in its area, or in such part of its area as it may specify in the determination—

(a)   that the discount under section 11(2)(a) above shall not apply, or

(b)   that the discount under that provision shall be such lesser percentage as it may so specify.

(5)   A billing authority may make a determination varying or revoking a determination under subsection (3) or (4) for a financial year, but only before the beginning of the year.

(6)   A billing authority which makes a determination under this section shall publish a notice of it in at least one newspaper circulating in its area and do so before the end of the period of 21 days beginning with the date of the determination.

(7)   Failure to comply with subsection (6) above shall not affect the validity of a determination.

[Local Government Finance Act 1992, s 11A as inserted by the Local Government Act 2003, s 75(1).]

---

[1] The Council Tax (Prescribed Classes of Dwellings) (England) Regulations 2003, SI 2003/3011 have been made.

11B.   Higher amount for long-term empty dwellings: England

7.7600   12.   Discounts: special provision for Wales   (1)   Where any class of dwellings in Wales is prescribed[1] for the purposes of this section for any financial year, a Welsh billing authority may determine that for the year subsection (2) or (3) below shall have effect in substitution for section 11(2)(a) above in relation to all dwellings of that class which are situated in its area.

(2)   Where this subsection has effect for any year in relation to any class of dwellings, the amount of council tax payable in respect of—

(a)   any chargeable dwelling of that class; and

(b)   any day in the year on which there is no resident of the dwelling,

shall be subject to a discount equal to the appropriate percentage of that amount.

(3)   Where this subsection has effect for any year in relation to any class of dwellings, the amount of council tax payable in respect of—

(a)   any chargeable dwelling of that class; and

(b)   any day in the year on which there is no resident of the dwelling,

shall not be subject to a discount.

(4)   A determination under subsection (1) above for a financial year may be varied or revoked at any time before the year begins.

(5)   Subsections (3) and (4) of section 4 above shall apply for the purposes of subsection (1) above as they apply for the purposes of subsection (2) of that section.

(6)   A billing authority which has made a determination under subsection (1) above shall, before the end of the period of 21 days beginning with the day of doing so, publish a notice of the determination in at least one newspaper circulating in the authority's area.

(7)   Failure to comply with subsection (6) above does not make the making of the determination invalid.

[Local Government Finance Act 1992, s 12.]

---

[1] The Council Tax (Prescribed Class of Dwellings) (Wales) Regulations 1992, SI 1992/3023 have been made.

7.7601   13.   Reduced amounts   (1)   The Secretary of State may make regulations[1] as regards any case where—

(a)   a person is liable to pay an amount to a billing authority in respect of council tax for any financial year which is prescribed; and

(b)   prescribed conditions are fulfilled.

(2)   The regulations may provide that the amount he is liable to pay shall be an amount which—

(a)   is less than the amount it would be apart from the regulations; and

(b)   is determined in accordance with prescribed rules.

(3)   This section applies whether the amount mentioned in subsection (1) above is determined under section 10 above or under that section read with section 11, 11A or 12 above.

(4)   The conditions mentioned in subsection (1) above may be prescribed by reference to such factors as the Secretary of State thinks fit; and in particular such factors may include the making of an application by the person concerned and all or any of—

(a)   the factors mentioned in subsection (5) below; or

(b)   the factors mentioned in subsection (6) below.

(5)   The factors referred to in subsection (4)(a) above are—

(a)   community charges for a period before 1st April 1993;

(b)   the circumstances of, or other matters relating to, the person concerned;

(c)   an amount relating to the authority concerned and specified, or to be specified, for the purposes of the regulations in a report laid, or to be laid, before the House of Commons;

(d)   such other amounts as may be prescribed or arrived at in a prescribed manner.

(6)   The factors referred to in subsection (4)(b) above are—

(a)   a disabled person having his sole or main residence in the dwelling concerned;

(b)   the circumstances of or other matters relating to, that person;

(c)   the physical characteristics of, or other matters relating to, that dwelling.

(7)   The rules mentioned in subsection (2) above may be prescribed by reference to such factors as the Secretary of State thinks fit; and in particular such factors may include all or any of the factors mentioned in subsection (5) or subsection (6)(b) or (c) above.

(8)   Without prejudice to the generality of section 113(2) below, regulations under this section may include—

(a)   provision requiring the Secretary of State to specify in a report, for the purposes of the regulations, an amount in relation to each billing authority;

(b)   provision requiring him to lay the report before the House of Commons;

(c)   provision for the review of any prescribed decision of a billing authority relating to the application or operation of the regulations;

(d)   provision that no appeal may be made to a valuation tribunal in respect of such a decision, notwithstanding section 16(1) below.

(9)   To the extent that he would not have power to do so apart from this subsection, the Secretary of State may—

(a)   include in regulations under this section such amendments of any social security instrument as he thinks expedient in consequence of the regulations under this section;

(b)   include in any social security instrument such provision as he thinks expedient in consequence of regulations under this section.

(10)   In subsection (9) above "social security instrument" means an order or regulations made, or falling to be made, by the Secretary of State under the Social Security Acts, that is to say, the Social Security Contributions and Benefits Act 1992 and the Social Security Administration Act 1992.

[Local Government Finance Act 1992, s 13 as amended by the Local Government Act 2003, Sch 7.]

---

[1] The Council Tax (Reductions for Disabilities) Regulations 1992, SI 1992/554, the Local Government Reorganisation (Wales) (Council Tax Reduction Scheme) Regulations 1996, SI 1996/309, the Local Government Reorganisation (Wales) (Council Tax Reduction Scheme) Regulations 1997, SI 1997/261 and the Council Tax Reduction Scheme (Wales) Regulations 1998, SI 1998/266, the Council Tax Reduction Scheme (Wales) Regulations 1999, SI 1999/347 and the Council Tax (Reduction Scheme) and (Demand Notices Transitional Provisions) (Wales) Regulations 2000, SI 2000/501 have been made. Transitional relief for the year 1993/4 is afforded by the Council Tax (Transitional Reduction Scheme) (England) Regulations 1993, SI 1993/175 amended by SI 1993/253 and 401 for the year 1995/6 by SI 1995/209 and for the year 1996/7 by SI 1996/176 (the 1996 Regulations) amended by SI 1996/333 and SI 1997/215.

The 1996 Regulations are modified by the Local Government Changes for England (Council Tax) (Transitional Reduction) Regulations 1997, SI 1997/215 and 1998, SI 1998/214 and are revoked with savings by the Local Government Changes for England (Council Tax) (Transitional Reduction) Regulations 1999, SI 1999/259 which have effect for the financial year 1999/2000.

The Council Tax (Reductions for Annexes) (England) Regulations 2013, SI 2013/2977 have been made.

7.7602 13A. Billing authority's power to reduce amount of tax payable (1) Where a person is liable to pay council tax in respect of any chargeable dwelling and any day, the billing authority for the area in which the dwelling is situated may reduce the amount which he is liable to pay as respects the dwelling and the day to such extent as it thinks fit.

(2)   The power under subsection (1) above includes power to reduce an amount to nil.

(3)   The power under subsection (1) may be exercised in relation to particular cases or by determining a class of case in which liability is to be reduced to an extent provided by the determination[1].

[Local Government Finance Act 1992, s 13A inserted by the Local Government Act 2003, s 76.]

---

[1] Regulations have been made under powers in Sch 1B, post.

7.7603 13B. Transitional arrangements[1]

---

[1] The Council Tax Reduction Schemes (Transitional Provisions) (Wales) Regulations 2013, SI 2013/111 have been made.

Administration and appeals

7.7604 14. Administration, penalties and enforcement (1) Schedule 2 to this Act (which contains provisions about administration, including collection) shall have effect.

(2)   Schedule 3 to this Act (which contains provisions about civil penalties) shall have effect.

(3)   Schedule 4 to this Act (which contains provisions about the recovery of sums due, including sums due as penalties) shall have effect.

(4)   Where a liability order has been made against a person under regulations under Schedule 4, the billing authority concerned may use the procedure in Schedule 12 to the Tribunals, Courts and

Enforcement Act 2007 (taking control of goods) to recover the amount in respect of which the order was made, to the extent that it remains unpaid.

[Local Government Finance Act 1992, s 14 as amended by the Tribunals, Courts and Enforcement Act 2007, Sch 13.]

7.7605   14A.   Regulations[1] about powers to require information

[1] The Council Tax Reduction Schemes (Detection of Fraud and Enforcement) (England) Regulations 2013, SI 2013/501 have been made.

7.7606   14B.   Regulations about offences

7.7607   14C.   Regulations about penalties

7.7608   14D.   Sections 14A to 14C: supplementary

7.7609   15.   Valuation tribunals   (1)   Valuation and community charge tribunals established under Schedule 11 to the 1988 Act shall be known as valuation tribunals.

(2)   Such tribunals shall exercise, in addition to the jurisdiction conferred on them by or under the 1988 Act, the jurisdiction conferred on them by—

   (a)   section 16 below;

   (b)   regulations made under section 24 below; and

   (c)   paragraph 3 of Schedule 3 to this Act.

[Local Government Finance Act 1992, s 15.]

7.7610   16.   Appeals: general   (1)   A person may appeal to a valuation tribunal if he is aggrieved by—

   (a)   any decision of a billing authority that a dwelling is a chargeable dwelling, or that he is liable to pay council tax in respect of such a dwelling; or

   (b)   any calculation made by such an authority of an amount which he is liable to pay to the authority in respect of council tax.

(2)   In subsection (1) above the reference to any calculation of an amount includes a reference to any estimate of the amount.

(3)   Subsection (1) above shall not apply where the grounds on which the person concerned is aggrieved fall within such category or categories as may be prescribed[1].

(4)   No appeal may be made under subsection (1) above unless—

   (a)   the aggrieved person serves a written notice under this subsection; and

   (b)   one of the conditions mentioned in subsection (7) below is fulfilled.

(5)   A notice under subsection (4) above must be served on the billing authority concerned.

(6)   A notice under subsection (4) above must state the matter by which and the grounds on which the person is aggrieved.

(7)   The conditions are that—

   (a)   the aggrieved person is notified in writing, by the authority on which he served the notice, that the authority believes the grievance is not well founded, but the person is still aggrieved;

   (b)   the aggrieved person is notified in writing, by the authority on which he served the notice, that steps have been taken to deal with the grievance, but the person is still aggrieved;

   (c)   the period of two months, beginning with the date of service of the aggrieved person's notice, has ended without his being notified under paragraph (a) or (b) above.

(8)   Where a notice under subsection (4) above is served on an authority, the authority shall—

   (a)   consider the matter to which the notice relates;

   (b)   include in any notification under subsection (7)(a) above the reasons for the belief concerned;

   (c)   include in any notification under subsection (7)(b) above a statement of the steps taken.

[Local Government Finance Act 1992, s 16.]

[1] See reg 30 of the Council Tax (Administration and Enforcement) Regulations 1992, in this PART, post.

Miscellaneous

7.7611   17.   Completion of new dwellings   (1)   Subject to the provisions of this section, Schedule 4A to the 1988 Act (which makes provision with respect to the determination of a day as the completion day in relation to a new building) shall, with the exception of paragraph 6, apply for the purposes of this Part as it applies for the purposes of Part III of that Act.

(2)   Any reference in this section to the Schedule is a reference to Schedule 4A to the 1988 Act as it applies for the purposes of this Part.

(3)   Where—

   (a)   a completion notice is served under the Schedule; and

   (b)   the building to which the notice relates is not completed on or before the relevant day,

any dwelling in which the building or any part of it will be comprised shall be deemed for the purposes of this Part to have come into existence on that day.

(4)   For the purposes of subsection (3) above the relevant day in relation to a completion notice is—

   (*a*)   where no appeal against the notice is brought under paragraph 4 of the Schedule, the day stated in the notice; and

   (*b*)   where an appeal against the notice is brought under that paragraph, the day determined under the Schedule as the completion day in relation to the building to which the notice relates.

(5)   Where—

   (*a*)   a day is determined under the Schedule as the completion day in relation to a new building; and

   (*b*)   the building is one produced by the structural alteration of a building which is comprised in one or more existing dwellings,

the existing dwelling or dwellings shall be deemed for the purposes of this Part to have ceased to exist on that day.

(6)   Any reference in this section or the Schedule to a new building includes a reference to a building produced by the structural alteration of an existing building where—

   (*a*)   the existing building or any part of it is comprised in a dwelling which, by virtue of the alteration, becomes, or becomes part of a different dwelling or different dwellings; or

   (*b*)   neither the existing building nor any part of it is, except by virtue of the alteration, comprised in any dwelling.

(7)   Any reference in this section to a building includes a reference to a part of a building; and any reference in the Schedule to the valuation officer shall be construed as a reference to the listing officer.

[Local Government Finance Act 1992, s 17 as amended by the Local Government Act 2003, Sch 7.]

7.7612   18.   Death of persons liable   *Secretary of State may make regulations*[1]

[Local Government Finance Act 1992, s 18—summarised.]

---

[1] See reg 58 of the Council Tax (Administration and Enforcement) Regulations in this PART post.

7.7613   19.   *Exclusion of Crown exemption in certain cases.*

SCHEDULES

SCHEDULE 1
PERSONS DISREGARDED FOR PURPOSES OF DISCOUNT   Sections 11(5) and 79(5)

(As amended by the Powers of Criminal Courts (Sentencing) Act 2000, Sch 9, the Care Standards Act 2000, Schs 3 and 4, SSI 2005/465, the National Health Service (Consequential Provisions) Act 2006, Sch 1, the Armed Forces Act 2006, Schs 16 and 17 and SI 2015/914.)

SCHEDULE 1A
COUNCIL TAX REDUCTION SCHEMES: ENGLAND[1]

---

[1] The Council Tax Reduction Schemes (Transitional Provision) (England) Regulations 2013, SI 2013/215 have been made.

SCHEDULE 1B
COUNCIL TAX REDUCTION SCHEMES: WALES[1]

---

[1] The Council Tax Reduction Schemes and Prescribed Requirements (Wales) Regulations 2013, SI 2013/3029 and the Council Tax Reduction Schemes (Default Scheme) (Wales) Regulations 2013, SI 2013/3035 have been made.

SCHEDULE 2
ADMINISTRATION[1]   Sections 14(1) and 97(3)

---

[1] This Schedule empowers the Secretary of State to make regulations covering specific matters such as collection, discounts, reduction for lump sum payments, exempt dwellings, supply of information and its use. See Pts I to IV of the Council Tax (Administration and Enforcement) Regulations 1992. Under this provision the following regulations have been made: Council Tax (Demand Notices) (England) Regulations 2011, SI 2011/3038 and the Council Tax Reduction Schemes (Prescribed Requirements) (England) Regulations 2012, SI 2012/2885 have been made. The Council Tax (Demand Notices) (Wales) Regulations 1993, SI 1993/255.

SCHEDULE 3
PENALTIES[1]   Sections 14(2) and 97(4)

---

[1] This Schedule enables a billing authority or levying authority to impose penalties for failure to supply information. Appeal lies to a valuation tribunal. The same conduct shall not lead both to a conviction and a penalty. As to the collection of penalties see reg 29 of the Council Tax (Administration and Enforcement) Regulations 1992 in this PART post.

SCHEDULE 4
Enforcement: England and Wales[1]   Section 14(3)

Regulations for recovery of sums payable

1.   (1)   The Secretary of State may make regulations[2] in relation to the recovery[, otherwise than under Schedule 12 to the Tribunals, Courts and Enforcement Act 2007 (taking control of goods),] of any sum which has become payable to a billing authority under any provision included in regulations under—

   (a)   paragraph 2, 3 or 6(2) or (3) of Schedule 2 to this Act; or

(b)   paragraph 6 of Schedule 3 to this Act,

and has not been paid.

(2)   The Secretary of State may also make regulations in relation to the recovery[, otherwise than under Schedule 12 to the Tribunals, Courts and Enforcement Act 2007 (taking control of goods),] of any sum which has become payable (by way of repayment) to a person other than a billing authority under any provision included in regulations under paragraph 2, 3 or 6(2) or (3) of Schedule 2 to this Act and has not been paid.

(3)   References in sub-paragraphs (1) and (2) above to a sum which has become payable and has not been paid include references to a sum forming part of a larger sum which has become payable and the other part of which has been paid.

Provision which may be made

2.   (1)   Regulations under sub-paragraph (1) of paragraph 1 above may make, in relation to the recovery of any sum falling within that sub-paragraph which a person is solely liable to pay, any such provision as is authorised by the following paragraphs of this Schedule.

(2)   Regulations under that sub-paragraph may make, in relation to any sum falling within that sub-paragraph which persons are jointly and severally liable to pay, provision equivalent to any so authorised subject to any modifications the Secretary of State thinks fit.

(3)   Regulations under sub-paragraph (2) of that paragraph may provide that any sum falling within that sub-paragraph shall be recoverable in a court of competent jurisdiction.

Liability orders

3.   (1)   Regulations under paragraph 1(1) above may provide that—
   (a)   the authority concerned may apply to a magistrates' court for an order (a "liability order") against the person by whom the sum is payable;
   (b)   the magistrates' court shall make the order if it is satisfied that the sum has become payable by the person concerned and has not been paid.

(2)   The regulations may include provision that the order shall be made in respect of an amount equal to the aggregate of—
   (a)   the sum payable; and
   (b)   a sum (of a prescribed amount or an amount determined in accordance with prescribed rules) in respect of the costs incurred in obtaining the order.

(3)   The regulations may include provision that, where the sum payable is paid after the order has been applied for but before it is made, the magistrates' court shall nonetheless make the order in respect of a sum (of a prescribed amount or an amount determined in accordance with prescribed rules) in respect of the costs incurred in applying for it.

(4)   The regulations may include
   (a)   provision prescribing steps to be taken before an application may be made;
   (b)   provision that no application may be made after a prescribed period has expired;
   (c)   provision prescribing the procedure to be followed for the initiation of an application (which may include provision as to form);
   (d)   provision prescribing the procedure to be followed in dealing with an application;
   (e)   provision prescribing the form and contents of an order.

Information

4.   (1)   Regulations under paragraph 1(1) above may provide that where a magistrates' court has made a liability order against a person ("the debtor") he shall, during such time as the amount in respect of which the order was made remains wholly or partly unpaid, be under a duty to supply relevant information to the authority concerned.

(2)   For the purposes of this paragraph relevant information is such information as fulfils the following conditions—
   (a)   it is in the debtor's possession or control;
   (b)   the authority requests him to supply it; and
   (c)   it falls within a prescribed description of information.

(3)   The regulations may include provision that the information is to be supplied in a prescribed form and within a prescribed period of the request being made.

Attachment of earnings etc

5.   (1)   Regulations under paragraph 1(1) above may provide that where a magistrates' court has made a liability order against a person ("the debtor") and the debtor is an individual—
   (a)   the authority concerned may make an order (an "attachment of earnings order") to secure the payment of [the appropriate amount];
   (b)   such an order shall be expressed to be directed to a person who has the debtor in his employment, and shall operate as an instruction to such a person to make deductions from the debtor's earnings and to pay the amounts deducted to the authority;
   (c)   the authority may serve a copy of the order on a person who appears to the authority to have the debtor in his employment; and
   (d)   a person who has the debtor in his employment shall comply with the order if a copy of it is served on him.

[(1A)   For the purposes of this paragraph the appropriate amount is the aggregate of—
   (a)   any outstanding sum which is or forms part of the amount in respect of which the liability order was made [(unless paragraph (b) applies);]
   (b)

     [where a person authorised to act under the power conferred by section 14(4) (power to use the procedure in Schedule 12 to the Tribunals, Courts and Enforcement Act 2007) has reported to the authority concerned that he was unable (for whatever reason) to find sufficient goods of the debtor to pay the amount outstanding—
     (i)   the amount outstanding at the time when the attachment of earnings order is made, and]
     (ii)   if the authority has applied for the issue of a warrant committing the debtor to prison under provision included by virtue of paragraph 8 below, a sum (of a prescribed amount or an amount

determined in accordance with prescribed rules) in respect of the costs of the application.]

(2)   The regulations may include—

(a)   provision allowing an attachment of earnings order to be varied;

(b)   provision requiring a person who has the debtor in his employment to comply with the order as varied if a copy of the order as varied is served on him;

(c)   provision requiring an order to be in a prescribed form;

(d)   provision requiring an order to specify the sum to which the order relates, the rate at which the debtor's earnings are to be applied to meet the sum, and such other particulars as may be prescribed;

(e)   rules about the rate which may be so specified;

(f)   provision allowing the person who deducts and pays amounts under the order to deduct from the debtor's earnings prescribed sums, or sums determined in accordance with prescribed rules, towards his administrative costs;

(g)   provision requiring the person who deducts and pays amounts under the order to notify the debtor, in a prescribed manner and at any prescribed time, of the total amount of sums (including sums towards administrative costs) deducted up to the time of the notification or of the total amount of sums (including sums towards such costs) that will fall to be deducted after that time;

(h)   provision requiring any person on whom a copy of the order is served to notify the authority in a prescribed manner and within a prescribed period if he does not have, or subsequently ceases to have, the debtor in his employment;

(i)   provision that, where the whole amount to which the order relates has been paid, the authority shall give notice of that fact to any person who appears to it to have the debtor in his employment and who has been served with a copy of the order;

(j)   provision allowing or requiring an order to be discharged.

(3)   The regulations may include provision that while an attachment of earnings order is in force—

(a)   the debtor shall from time to time notify the authority concerned, in a prescribed manner and within a prescribed period, of each occasion when he leaves any employment or becomes employed or re-employed, and shall include in such a notification a statement of his earnings and expected earnings from the employment concerned and of such other matters as may be prescribed;

(b)   any person who becomes the debtor's employer and knows that the order is in force and by what authority it was made shall notify the authority concerned, in a prescribed manner and within a prescribed period, that he is the debtor's employer, and shall include in such a notification a statement of the debtor's earnings and expected earnings from the employment concerned and of such other matters as may be prescribed.

(4)   The regulations may include provision with respect to the priority to be accorded as between—

(a)   two or more orders made under the regulations;

(b)   orders made under the regulations and orders made under the Attachment of Earnings Act 1971 or the Child Support Act 1991.

(5)   The regulations may include provision that a person may appeal to a magistrates' court if he is aggrieved by the making or the terms of an attachment of earnings order, or there is a dispute whether payments constitute earnings or as to any other prescribed matter relating to the order.

(6)   The regulations may include—

(a)   provision prescribing the procedure to be followed for initiating an appeal;

(b)   provision prescribing the procedure to be followed in dealing with an appeal;

(c)   provision as to the powers of the court (which may include provision as to the quashing of an attachment of earnings order or the variation of the terms of such an order).

(7)   The provisions of this paragraph (except sub-paragraphs (3) and (4)(b) above) shall apply to elected members of billing authorities or relevant precepting authorities as they apply to persons in employment; and for the purposes of the application of those provisions in relation to any such members—

(a)   any reference to a person having the debtor in his employment shall be construed as a reference to such an authority having the debtor as an elected member; and

(b)   any reference to the debtor's earnings shall be construed as a reference to allowances payable to the debtor by such an authority.

(8)   For the purposes of sub-paragraph (7) above—

(a)   a relevant precepting authority is a major precepting authority *other than the Receiver for the Metropolitan Police District*; and

(b)   a person is an elected member of a relevant precepting authority other than a county council if he is appointed to the authority by a constituent council of which he is an elected member.

[(9)   In this paragraph "the amount outstanding" has the meaning given by paragraph 50(3) of Schedule 12 to the Tribunals, Courts and Enforcement Act 2007.]

Deductions from income support

6.   (1)   Regulations under paragraph 1(1) above may provide that where a magistrates' court has made a liability order against a person ("the debtor") and the debtor is entitled to [universal credit] *income support*[, a jobseeker's allowance[, state pension credit or an employment and support allowance]] . . .—

(a)   the authority concerned may apply to the Secretary of State asking him to deduct sums from any amounts payable to the debtor by way of [that benefit], in order to secure the payment of any outstanding sum which is or forms part of the amount in respect of which the liability order was made; and

(b)   the Secretary of State may deduct such sums and pay them to the authority towards satisfaction of any such outstanding sum.

(2)   The regulations may include—

(a)   provision allowing or requiring adjudication as regards an application, and provision as to *appeals and reviews* [appeals to appeal tribunals constituted under Chapter I of Part I of the Social Security Act 1998 and decisions under section 9 or 10 of that Act];

(b)   a scheme containing provision as to the circumstances and manner in which and times at which sums are to be deducted and paid, provision about the calculation of such sums (which may include provision to secure that amounts payable to the debtor by way of [universal credit] *income support*[, a jobseeker's allowance[, state pension credit or an employment and support allowance]] do not fall below prescribed figures), and provision as to the circumstances in which the Secretary of State is to cease making deductions;

    (c)   provision requiring the Secretary of State to notify the debtor, in a prescribed manner and at any prescribed time, of the total amount of sums deducted up to the time of the notification;

    (d)   provision that, where the whole amount to which the application relates has been paid, the authority shall give notice of that fact to the Secretary of State.

. . .

7. . . .

Commitment to prison

8.   (1)   Regulations under paragraph 1(1) above may provide[, in relation to the recovery of any sum which has become payable to a billing authority in England,] that—

    (a)   where . . ., the debtor is an individual who has attained the age of 18 years, and [there are insufficient goods to satisfy an amount under section 14(4)], the authority may apply to a magistrates' court for the issue of a warrant committing the debtor to prison;

    (b)   on such application being made the court shall (in the debtor's presence) inquire as to his means and inquire whether the failure to pay which has led to the application is due to his wilful refusal or culpable neglect;

    (c)   if (and only if) the court is of opinion that his failure is due to his wilful refusal or culpable neglect it may if it thinks fit issue a warrant of commitment against the debtor, or fix a term of imprisonment and postpone the issue of the warrant until such time and on such conditions (if any) as the court thinks just;

    (d)   the warrant shall be made in respect of the relevant amount (within the meaning given by sub-paragraph (2) below);

    (e)   the warrant shall state that amount;

    (f)   the order in the warrant shall be that the debtor be imprisoned for a time specified in the warrant (which shall not exceed three months), unless the amount stated in the warrant is sooner paid;

    (g)   the period of imprisonment shall be reduced by a prescribed amount in respect of part payment in prescribed circumstances;

    (h)   a warrant may be directed to the authority concerned and to such other persons (if any) as the court issuing it thinks fit,

    (i)   a warrant may be executed anywhere in England and Wales by any person to whom it is directed.

[(1A)   In sub paragraph (1) the reference to insufficient goods to satisfy an amount under section 14(4) is a reference to circumstances where a person authorised to act under the power conferred by section 14(4) (power to use the procedure in Schedule 12 to the Tribunals, Courts and Enforcement Act 2007) has reported to the authority concerned that he was unable (for whatever reason) to find sufficient goods of the debtor to pay the amount outstanding.]

   (2)   For the purposes of sub-paragraph (1) above the relevant amount is the aggregate of—

    [(a)   the amount outstanding at the time when the warrant of commitment is issued; and]

    (b)   a sum (of a prescribed amount or an amount determined in accordance with prescribed rules) in respect of the costs of commitment.

   (3)   The regulations may include—

    (a)   provision that a single warrant shall not be issued, under any provision included under this paragraph, against more than one person;

    (b)   provision as to the form of a warrant;

    (c)   provision allowing remission of payment where no warrant is issued or term of imprisonment fixed;

    (d)   provision allowing an application to be renewed where no warrant is issued or term of imprisonment fixed;

    (e)   provision that a statement in writing to the effect that wages of any amount have been paid to the debtor during any period, purporting to be signed by or on behalf of his employer, shall be evidence of the facts there stated;

    (f)   provision that, for the purpose of enabling inquiry to be made as to the debtor's conduct and means, a justice of the peace may issue a summons to him to appear before a magistrates' court and (if he does not obey the summons) may issue a warrant for his arrest;

    (g)   provision that, for the purpose of enabling such inquiry, a justice of the peace may issue a warrant for the debtor's arrest without issuing a summons;

    (h)   provision as to the execution of a warrant for arrest (which may include provision allowing it to be executed anywhere in England and Wales).

[(4)   In this paragraph "the amount outstanding" has the meaning given by paragraph 50(3) of Schedule 12 to the Tribunals, Courts and Enforcement Act 2007.]

Bankruptcy

9.   (1)   Regulations under paragraph 1(1) above may provide that where a magistrates' court has made a liability order against a person ("the debtor") and the debtor is an individual, the amount due shall be deemed to be a debt for the purposes of section 267 of the Insolvency Act 1986 (grounds of creditor's petition).

   (2)   The amount due is an amount equal to any outstanding sum which is or forms part of the amount in respect of which the liability order was made.

Winding up

10.   (1)   Regulations under paragraph 1(1) above may provide that where a magistrates' court has made a liability order against a person ("the debtor") and the debtor is a company, the amount due shall be deemed to be a debt for the purposes of section 122(1)(f) of the Insolvency Act 1986 (winding up of companies by the court) or, as the case may be, section 221(5)(b) of that Act (winding up of unregistered companies).

   (2)   The amount due is an amount equal to any outstanding sum which is or forms part of the amount in respect of which the liability order was made.

Charging orders

11. (1) Regulations under paragraph 1(1)(a) above may provide that where a magistrates' court has made a liability order against a person ("the debtor") and prescribed conditions are fulfilled—

(a) the authority concerned may apply to a court for an order (a "charging order") imposing, on any interest held by the debtor beneficially in the relevant dwelling, a charge for securing the due amount; and

(b) a charge imposed by a charging order shall have the like effect and shall be enforceable in the same courts and in the same manner as an equitable charge created by the debtor by writing under his hand.

(2) For the purposes of sub-paragraph (1) above the relevant dwelling is the dwelling in respect of which, at the time the application for the liability order was made, the debtor was liable to pay the sum falling within paragraph 1(1)(a) above.

(3) For the purposes of sub-paragraph (1) above the due amount is the aggregate of—

(a) an amount equal to any outstanding sum which is or forms part of the amount in respect of which the liability order was made; and

(b) a sum (of a prescribed amount or an amount determined in accordance with prescribed rules) in respect of costs connected with the charging order.

(4) The regulations may include provision—

(a) as to the court to which an application may be made (which may be the High Court or [the county court]);

(b) as to the factors to be considered by the court in deciding whether to make a charging order;

(c) requiring an order to specify the dwelling and interest concerned, and such other matters as may be prescribed;

(d) requiring an order to be in a prescribed form;

(e) allowing an order to be made absolutely or subject to conditions;

(f) as to the discharge or variation of an order.

[**11A.** Regulations under paragraph 1(1)(a) above may provide that two or more liability orders against the same person shall be treated as a single liability order for the purposes of provision included by virtue of paragraph 11 above if an application under such provision could be made in respect of each of them in relation to the same dwelling.]

Relationship between remedies

12. (1) As regards a case where a magistrates' court has made a liability order, regulations under paragraph 1(1) above may include provision that—

(a) attachment of earnings may be resorted to more than once;

[(aa) deductions from universal credit may be resorted to more than once;]

(b) *deductions from income support [jobseeker's allowance payable to any person whose claim to the allowance is based on meeting condition B in section 1A of the Jobseekers Act 1995] may be resorted to more than once;*

[(bb) deductions from state pension credit may be resorted to more than once;]

[(bc) deductions from an employment and support allowance may be resorted to more than once;]

(c) . . .

(d) attachment of earnings [deductions from universal credit], *deductions from income support* [jobseeker's allowance payable as mentioned in paragraph (b)] [, deductions from state pension credit][, deductions from an employment and support allowance] and [the power conferred by section 14(4)] (or any two of them) may be resorted to in any order or alternately (or both);

(e) steps by way of attachment, deduction, [exercise of the power conferred by section 14(4)], commitment, bankruptcy, winding up or charging may not be taken while steps by way of another of those methods are being taken;

(f) where a warrant of commitment is issued against (or a term of imprisonment is fixed in the case of) the person concerned no steps, or no further steps, by way of attachment, deduction, [exercise of the power conferred by section 14(4)], bankruptcy or charging may be taken.

(2) Any reference in this paragraph to attachment of earnings includes a reference to attachment of allowances.

[Quashing of liability orders

12A. Regulations under paragraph 1(1) above may provide—

(a) that, where on an application by the authority concerned a magistrates' court is satisfied that a liability order should not have been made, it shall quash the order;

(b) that, where on an application to a magistrates' court for the quashing of a liability order, the court is satisfied that, had the original application been for a liability order in respect of a lesser sum payable, such an order could properly have been made, it shall substitute a liability order in respect of the aggregate of—

(i) that lesser sum, and

(ii) any sum included in the quashed order in respect of the costs incurred in obtaining it.]

Magistrates and justices

13. Regulations under paragraph 1(1) above may include—

(a) provision for determining what justices and magistrates' courts are to have jurisdiction in cases provided for by the regulations;

(b) provision as to the composition of magistrates' courts in cases provided for by the regulations.

Admissibility of evidence

14. (1) Regulations under paragraph 1(1) above may include provision that, in any proceedings before a magistrates' court under any provision included by virtue of the preceding provisions of this Schedule—

(a) a statement contained in a document of record shall be admissible as evidence of any fact stated in it of which direct oral evidence would be admissible; and

(b) a certificate which is made with respect to a document of record produced by a computer and purports to be signed by a responsible person shall be admissible as evidence of anything which is stated in it to the best of his information and belief.

(2) In this paragraph—

"document of record" means a document constituting or forming part of a record compiled by the authority concerned;

"responsible person" means a person occupying a responsible position in relation to the operation of the computer;

"statement" includes any representation of fact, whether made in words or otherwise.

Exclusion of certain matters

15. Regulations under paragraph 1(1) above may provide that any matter which could be the subject of an appeal under section 16 of this Act, or regulations under section 24 of this Act, may not be raised in proceedings under the regulations.

Costs

16. Regulations under paragraph 1(1) above may provide that where an authority has received in proceedings under the regulations an amount by way of costs it shall pay a prescribed amount, or an amount determined in accordance with prescribed rules, to a prescribed person for the benefit of such court as is identified in accordance with prescribed rules.

Termination of proceedings

17. (1) Regulations under paragraph 1(1) above may provide that in a case where—

(a) proceedings under the regulations have been taken as regards the recovery of any sum mentioned in paragraph 1(1) above; and

(b) the outstanding amount is paid or tendered to the authority to which it is payable;

the authority shall accept the amount, no further steps shall be taken as regards its recovery, and any person committed to prison in pursuance of the proceedings shall be released.

(2) The outstanding amount is an amount equal to the sum concerned or to so much of it as remains outstanding (as the case may be).

(3) In a case where costs and charges are relevant the outstanding amount shall be treated as augmented by a sum (of a prescribed amount or an amount determined in accordance with prescribed rules) in respect of costs and charges incurred in the proceedings up to the time of payment or tender.

Offences

18. (1) Regulations under paragraph 1(1) above may provide that a person shall be guilty of an offence if he is required by any provision included by virtue of paragraph 4 above to supply information and—

(a) he fails without reasonable excuse to supply the information in accordance with the provision; or

(b) in supplying information in purported compliance with the provision he makes a statement which he knows to be false in a material particular or recklessly makes a statement which is false in a material particular.

(2) Regulations under paragraph 1(1) above may provide that—

(a) a person shall be guilty of an offence if he is required by any provision included by virtue of paragraph 5(1)(d) or (2)(b) above to comply with an attachment of earnings order and fails to do so;

(b) it shall be a defence for a person charged with such an offence to prove that he took all reasonable steps to comply with the order.

(3) Regulations under paragraph 1(1) above may provide that a person shall be guilty of an offence if he is required by any provision included by virtue of paragraph 5(2)(g) or (h) or (3)(a) or (b) above to notify another person and—

(a) he fails without reasonable excuse to notify the other person in accordance with the provision; or

(b) in notifying the other person in purported compliance with the provision he makes a statement which he knows to be false in a material particular or recklessly makes a statement which is false in a material particular.

(4) Regulations under paragraph 1(1) above may provide that a person guilty of an offence under any provision included by virtue of sub-paragraphs (1) to (3) above shall be liable on summary conviction to a fine not exceeding—

(a) level 2 on the standard scale (where the provision is included by virtue of sub-paragraph (1)(a) or (3)(a) above); or

(b) level 3 on the standard scale (where the provision is included by virtue of sub-paragraph (1)(b), (2) or (3)(b) above).

Other enactments

19. (1) Regulations under paragraph 1(1) above may apply any provision contained in or made under a relevant enactment, or may apply any such provision subject to prescribed modifications, or may contain provision equivalent to any such provision (whether or not subject to prescribed modifications).

(2) For the purposes of sub-paragraph (1) above relevant enactments are the Attachment of Earnings Act 1971, the Charging Orders Act 1979, Part II of the Social Security Administration Act 1992, and any enactment applied by any of those enactments.

(3) . . .

[Interpretation

20. In this Schedule, except [paragraphs 5(1A)(b)(ii), 6 and 8], "prescribed" means prescribed by regulations made—

(a) in relation to England, by the Secretary of State, and

(b) in relation to Wales, by the National Assembly for Wales.]

[As amended by the Jobseekers Act 1995, the Social Security Act 1998, the State Pension Credit Act 2002, the Local Government Act 2003, the Tribunals, Courts and Enforcement Act 2007, the Tribunals, Courts and Enforcement Act 2007, the Welfare Reform Act 2007, the Welfare Reform Act 2012.]

---

[1] There is no evidence of systemic unfairness in the operation of the scheme for the enforcement of council tax, despite examples of a very small proportion of magistrates and their legal advisers failing to comply with the requirements of the scheme *Regina (Woolcock) v Secretary of State for Communities and Local Government and others* [2018] 4 WLR 49.
[2] See Council Tax (Administration and Enforcement) Regulations 1992 in this PART post.

LICENSING OF ALCOHOL, ENTERTAINMENT AND LATE NIGHT REFRESHMENT

7.7616 Introduction The Licensing Act 2003 (LA 2003) has introduced a new regime for the licensing of alcohol (both in premises open to the general public and to qualifying clubs), and has amalgamated it with the licensing of regulated entertainment (previously called "public entertainment" under the provisions of the Local Government (Miscellaneous Provisions) Act 1982, or licensed separately under legislation dealing with theatres and cinemas), and, for the first time, "late night refreshment".

The LA 2003 was intended to provide a "more efficient"; "more responsive" and "flexible" system of licensing which did not interfere unnecessarily. It aimed to give business greater freedom and flexibility to meet the expectations of customers and to provide greater choice for consumers whilst protecting local residents from disturbance and anti-social behaviour. The LA 2003 expects licensable activities to be restricted only where that is necessary to promote the four licensing objectives set out in s 4(2)[1].

---

[1] See the review of the law by Black J in *R (Daniel Thwaites plc) v Wirral Borough Magistrates' Court* [2008] EWCH 838 (Admin), 172 JP 301.

7.7617 *Transfer of responsibilities* The Act removes the responsibility for licensing such activities from the licensing justices (who were previously responsible for the licensing of alcohol) and hands the responsibilities to "licensing authorities". These are defined in the LA 2003, s 3, and include district councils, unitary authorities and London boroughs. The role of magistrates' courts is to act as an appellate court against the myriad of decisions that can be appealed; to deal with the raft of criminal offences under the Act; and to consider closure orders made by the police under Part 8 of the Act. Because primary responsibility for such matters has been removed from licensing justices, what follows is a short commentary by way of an overview of the LA 2003, and a more detailed commentary on those parts of the Act that magistrates' courts retain jurisdiction over.

7.7618 Licensable activities and qualifying club activities These are defined as the sale by retail[1] of alcohol[2]; the supply of alcohol by or on behalf of a club to, or to the order of, a member of the club; the provision of regulated entertainment; and the provision of late night refreshment[3]. Regulated entertainment is defined fully in Sch 1, and includes both entertainment and entertainment facilities that are provided for the public or a section of the public, and to entertainment provided exclusively for members of a qualifying club. The previous public entertainment regime did not require entertainment provided for club members to be licensed because it was not "public". Entertainment includes those activities listed in Sch 1, para 2. Certain activities listed in Sch 1, Part 2 are exempt from the definition. The provision of late night refreshment is defined in Sch 2. It involves the provision of hot food or hot drink to members of the public between 11pm and 5am on or from any premises, whether for consumption on or off the premises[4]. Certain supplies, such as to residents in hotels, are exempt[5]. If a licensable activity is taking place, it must be licensed either by virtue of a premises licence issued under Part 3 of the Act or by virtue of it being a "permitted temporary activity" under Part 5[6]. A qualifying club activity can only take place by virtue of a club premises certificate issued under Part 4[7].

---

[1] Defined in the LA 2003, s 192.
[2] Defined in the LA 2003, s 191.
[3] LA 2003, s 1(1). Qualifying club activities are further defined in ss 1(2) and (3). Activities that are carried on in certain locations are not licensable activities: LA 2003, s 173. However, licensable activities or qualifying club activities that take place on vessels, vehicles or other moveable structures do require a premises licence: LA 2003, s 189. Premises licences that purport to licence roadside service areas or premises used primarily as a garage for the sale or supply of alcohol are invalid: LA 2003, s 176.
[4] LA 2003, Sch 2, para 1(1).
[5] For a full list, see the LA 2003, Sch 2, paras 3, 4 and 5.
[6] LA 2003, s 2(1).
[7] LA 2003, s 2(2).

7.7619 Certain entertainments fall outside the definition of "regulated entertainment" such as performances of plays, indoor sport and the exhibition of dance in all locations to audiences of up to 500 people (1000 indoor sport). Other entertainments are exempted from the requirement for licensing including: religious services, places of worship, entertainment at Garden fêtes and Morris dancing. Particular provision is made for activities organised by, or on behalf of, Local Authorities (including parish councils), hospitals and schools on their own premises; activities organised by, or on behalf of hospitals and schools (including sixth form colleges on their own premises) and for live and recorded music at activities held on community premises (such as church halls, village halls and community halls etc)[1]. Various exemptions are provided in respect of live and recorded music at licensed venues. In particular, performances of live music and the playing of recorded music on licensed premises is exempt where the specified conditions are satisfied which include the condition that the maximum number of persons in the audience is 500[2]. Provision is made for the suspension of any licence condition which relates to live music and also applies to licence conditions which relate to recorded music or to both live and recorded music[3].

[1] Licensing Act 2003, Sch 1, in this title, post.
[2] LA 2003, Sch 1, para 12A, in this title, post.
[3] LA 2003, s 177A, in this title, post.

7.7620 Functions of licensing authorities and licensing objectives A licensing authority must carry out its functions under the Act with a view to promoting the four licensing objectives of prevention of crime and disorder; public safety; prevention[1] of public nuisance; and the protection of children from harm[2]. In addition, those licensing authorities that are local authorities within the meaning of s 270(1) of the Local Government Act 1972, must have regard to the need to do all that they reasonably can to prevent crime and disorder in their areas[3]. Magistrates' courts dealing with appeals must also have regard to the need to promote the licensing objectives and, because they stand in the feet of licensing authorities when carrying out their appellate functions, it is submitted that they must also have regard to the duty imposed on licensing authorities by the Crime and Disorder Act 1998. Licensing authorities (and magistrates' courts dealing with appeals) must also have regard to the Statement of Licensing Policy issued under s 5 of the Act; and the Secretary of State's guidance issued under s 182 of the Act[4]. A licensing authority must establish a licensing committee of between 10 and 15 members of the authority[5], and most matters are delegated to that committee[6] (or sub-committees consisting of three members[7]) to deal with. Matters can be further delegated to local government officers to determine if they are uncontested[8]. A licensing authority is required to keep a register containing prescribed information[9].

[1]. This duty is prospective. It is concerned with prevention and not with whether a crime has been committed, let alone prosecuted: *East Lindsey DC v Hanif (T/A Zaraf Restaurant and Takeaway)* [2016] EWHC 1265 (Admin), [2016] CTLC 81 (where, in any event, crimes had been committed; a chef working at the restaurant was an illegal immigrant and had been paid cash in hand at less than the minimum wage, with "tax" deducted but not forwarded to HMRC).
[2] LA 2003, s 4.
[3] Crime and Disorder Act 1998, s 17(1).
[4] See the Guidance issued under s 182 of the LA 2003 issued by the DCMS in July 2004.
[5] LA 2003, s 6(1).
[6] LA 2003, s 7.
[7] LA 2003, s 9.
[8] LA 2003, s 10.
[9] LA 2003, s 8 and Sch 3.

7.7621 Late night levy A licensing authority may, having considered the costs of policing and other arrangements for the reduction or prevention of crime and disorder, decide that the late night levy requirement is to apply in the whole of its area in connection with the supply of alcohol between midnight and 6 am[1]. The levy may apply to a premises licence or club premises certificate which authorises the supply of alcohol at a time or times during the late night supply period on one or more days in the related payment year. The late night supply period is decided by the authority and must begin at or after midnight, and end at or before 6 am. The amount and enforcement of the late night levy is prescribed by regulations[2], and ss 55A and 92A of the LA 2003 (suspension of premises licence or club premises certificate for failure to pay annual fee) apply. The licensing authority must pay a specified proportion being not less that 70 per cent of that amount to the relevant local policing body, and apply the remainder of that amount in accordance with regulations[2].

[1] See the Police Reform and Social Responsibility Act 2011, Part 2 Chapter 2 (ss 125–139).
[2] See the Late Night Levy (Expenses, Exemptions and Reductions) Regulations 2012, SI 2012/2550.

7.7622 Early morning alcohol restriction order If a licensing authority considers it appropriate for the promotion of the licensing objectives, it may make an order providing that premises licences and club premises certificates, and temporary event notices do not have effect to the extent that they authorise the sale or supply of alcohol during the period specified in the order which must begin no earlier than midnight, and end no later than 6 am[1]. It is immaterial whether a premises licence or club premises certificate is granted, or a temporary event notice is given, before or after the order is made. The proposed order must be advertised in a manner prescribed by regulations[2], and the authority must hold a hearing to consider any relevant representations, unless the authority and each person who has made such representations agree that a hearing is unnecessary. An early morning alcohol restriction order may be revoked or varied by the authority and is subject to an order under s 172 (relaxation of opening hours for special occasions).

[1] See the LA 2003, s 172A–172E, in this title, post.
[2] See the Licensing Act 2003 (Early Morning Alcohol Restriction Orders) Regulations 2012, SI 2012/2551.

7.7623 Premises licences A person listed in s 16 of the Act may apply to a licensing authority for a premises licence which authorises premises to be used for one or more licensable activities[1]. The application must be in the prescribed manner and must be properly advertised[2]. The application must be accompanied by an "operating schedule", which must be in the prescribed form and must summarise, amongst other things, the licensable activities (and the times during which they will take place); details about the "premises supervisor" (if one of the licensable activities is the supply of alcohol); and the steps that the applicant intends to take to promote the licensing objectives[3]. A licensing authority receiving a valid application must grant the licence (subject only to such conditions as are consistent with the operating schedule submitted and any mandatory conditions[4]) unless "relevant representations"[5] have been received. Relevant representations can only be made by an "interested party"[6] or a "responsible authority"[7]. If relevant representations are received, the authority must hold a hearing to consider them (unless all parties to the application agree that a hearing is unnecessary)[8] and, having regard to the representations, must take such of the prescribed steps[9] (if any) as it considers necessary for the promotion of the licensing objectives[10]. Once granted, a premises licence has effect until it is revoked, unless the licence has been granted for a limited period or it has been suspended[11]. Application can be made to vary a premises licence[12], and an interested party or responsible authority may make relevant representations about such an application. An application can also be made to transfer a premises licence into the name of any person who could, by virtue of s 16, apply for a licence in his own right. An applicant can apply for such an application to have interim effect[13], and only the chief officer of police can object to a transfer application[14].

More than one party may simultaneously hold licences in respect of particular premises and the licences need not be in identical or near identical terms; if there are sound policy reasons to take issue with any differences between the terms of a shadow application and the primary application these can be considered at the hearing before the licensing committee[15].

---

[1] LA 2003, s 11. Applications can also be made for provisional statements under s 29 in respect of premises that are being, or are about to be constructed, extended or otherwise altered. There are only limited powers to make relevant representations in respect of an application for a premises licence where the premises already enjoys the benefit of a provisional statement: LA 2003, s 32.

[2] LA 2003, s 17(2) and the Licensing Act 2003 (Premises licences and club premises certificates) Regulations 2005, SI 2005/42 (for amending instruments, see the note to s 13, post).

[3] LA 2003, s 17(4).

[4] LA 2003, s 18(2). Mandatory conditions are those listed in the LA 2003, ss 19–21.

[5] Defined in s 18(6) as those which are about the likely effect of the grant of the premises licence on the promotion of the licensing objectives, and which are, in all other requirements, valid.

[6] Defined in the LA 2003, s 13(3).

[7] Defined in the LA 2003, s 13(4).

[8] LA 2003, s 18(3)(*a*).

[9] The prescribed steps are listed in the LA 2003, s 18(4). The licensing authority has a wide discretion, including modifying or adding to proposed conditions, excluding certain licensable activities, refusing to specify a person as the premises supervisor, and rejecting the application outright.

[10] LA 2003, s 18(3)(*b*).

[11] LA 2003, s 26. A premises licence will also lapse in any of the circumstances listed in s 27, and it can be surrendered under s 28. If it has lapsed, s 47 provides for a person with a prescribed interest in the premises or a person connected to the premises licence holder to give an "interim authority notice" to the licensing authority. This has the effect of reinstating the premises licence in the name of the person giving the notice for a maximum period of seven days, during which time an application for transfer must be made. The chief officer of police may object to an interim authority notice, in which case the licensing authority must hold a hearing to consider his representations: LA 2003, s 48. Even if no interim authority notice is given, any person who could apply for a licence by virtue of s 16 of the LA 2003 can apply within 7 days of the lapse or surrender of the licence for a transfer of the premises licence to him: LA 2003, s 50. Where such an application is made, the premises licence is reinstated from the date of receipt of the application by the licensing authority.

[12] LA 2003, s 34. There is a separate provision in s 37 to apply to vary a premises licence so as to change the name of the premises supervisor. Such an application can have interim effect if requested: LA 2003, s 38. Only the Chief Officer of Police can object to such an application, and only if he is satisfied that the exceptional circumstances of the case are such that granting the application would undermine the crime prevention licensing objective: LA 2003, s 37(5).

[13] LA 2003, s 43.

[14] LA 2003, s 42(6).

[15] *Extreme Oyster and Star Oyster Ltd v Guildford Borough Council* [2013] EWHC 2174 (Admin), 177 JP 481.

7.7624   *Reviews of premises licences*   An interested party or responsible authority may apply to the licensing authority for a review of a premises licence at any time[1]. Unless the grounds for the application are irrelevant to the licensing objectives, frivolous, vexatious or repetitious, the licensing authority must hold a hearing to consider the application[2], and must, having regard to the application and the relevant representations, take such of a number of steps[3] (if any) as it considers necessary to promote the licensing objectives.

---

[1] LA 2003, s 51(1). Repeated applications based on the same grounds are prohibited by s 51(4)(*b*)(ii).

[2] LA 2003, s 52(2).

[3] The steps are listed at the LA 2003, s 52(4).

7.7625   **Club premises certificates**   A qualifying club[1] may apply to a licensing authority for a club premises certificate in respect of any premises which are occupied by, and habitually used for the purposes of, the club[2]. A club does not need to specify a premises supervisor, and it is not subject to the same powers of the police to close it[3], but in all other respects the regime for the licensing of clubs is very similar to that of other premises. An application for a club premises certificate must be in a prescribed form and must be advertised correctly[4]. The application must be accompanied by a "club operating schedule"[5] listing, amongst other things, the qualifying club activities (and the times during which they are proposed to take place), whether alcohol is to be supplied for consumption on or off the premises (if applicable), and the steps which the club proposes to take to promote the licensing objectives. A licensing authority receiving a valid application must grant the licence (subject only to such conditions as are consistent with the club operating schedule submitted and any mandatory conditions[6]) unless "relevant representations"[7] have been received. Relevant representations can only be made by an "interested party"[8] or a "responsible authority"[9]. If relevant representations are received, the authority must hold a hearing to consider them (unless all parties to the application agree that a hearing is unnecessary)[10] and, having regard to the representations, must take such of the prescribed steps[11] (if any) as it considers necessary for the promotion of the licensing objectives[12]. The licensing authority may not impose conditions restricting the right of a club to sell alcohol to an associate member[13] or their guest[14]; nor may it impose a condition restricting the nature of plays that may be performed at a club premises that is licensed for that form of regulated entertainment[15]. Once granted a club premises certificate has effect until such time as it is withdrawn (following a review or the club ceasing to be a qualifying club[16]) or it is surrendered[17]. Where a justice of the peace is satisfied, on information on oath, that there are reasonable grounds for believing that a club which holds a club premises certificate does not satisfy the conditions for being a qualifying club in relation to a qualifying club activity to which the certificate relates, and that evidence of that fact is to be obtained at the premises to which the certificate relates, he may issue a warrant authorising a constable to enter the premises, if necessary by force, at any time within one month from the time of issue of the warrant, and to seize and retain any documents relating to the business of the club[18]. Application can be made to vary a club premises certificate[19], and there is power for an interested party or responsible authority to make relevant representations about such an application. An interested party, a responsible authority or a member of the club can apply for a review of the certificate at any time[20]. Unless the grounds for the application are irrelevant to the licensing objectives, frivolous, vexatious or repetitious, the licensing authority must hold a hearing to consider the application[21], and must, having regard to the application and the relevant representations, take such of a number of steps[22] (if any) as it considers necessary to promote the licensing objectives.

---

[1] Section 61 of the LA 2003 defines what is a qualifying club. General conditions (listed in the LA 2003, s 62) must be satisfied as must additional conditions (listed in the LA 2003, s 64) if the club wants to be licensed for the supply of alcohol.

[2] LA 2003, s 71(1).

[3] LA 2003, Part 8. Those powers only exist in relation to premises which have the benefit of a premises licence or a TEN.

[4] LA 2003, s 71.

[5] LA 2003, s 71(5).

[6] LA 2003, s 72(2). Mandatory conditions are those listed in the LA 2003, ss 73(2)–(5) and 74.

[7] Defined in the LA 2003, s 72(7) as those which are about the likely effect of the grant of the premises licence on the promotion of the licensing objectives, and which are, in all other requirements, valid.

[8] Defined in the LA 2003, s 69(3).

[9] Defined in the LA 2003, s 69(4).

[10] LA 2003, s 72(3)(a).

[11] The prescribed steps are listed in s 72(4). The licensing authority has a wide discretion, including modifying or adding to proposed conditions, excluding certain licenceable activities, and rejecting the application outright.

[12] LA 2003, s 72(3)(b).

[13] "Associate member" is defined in the LA 2003, s 67.

[14] LA 2003, s 75.

[15] LA 2003, s 76.

[16] LA 2003, s 90. If the licensing authority is of the opinion that this is the case in relation to one or more of its qualifying club activities, it must give a notice to the club withdrawing the certificate so far as it relates to that activity or those activities.

[17] LA 2003, s 90(1).

[18] LA 2003, s 90(5) and (6).

[19] LA 2003, s 84.

[20] LA 2003, s 87(1).

[21] LA 2003, s 88(2).

[22] The steps are listed at the LA 2003, s 88(4).

7.7626 *Mandatory licensing conditions*   The Secretary of State has prescribed mandatory conditions applicable to premises licences and club premises certificates which authorise the supply of alcohol[1].

---

[1] See the Licensing Act 2003 (Mandatory Licensing Conditions) Order 2010, in this title, post.

7.7627 Permitted temporary activities   Aside from applying for a premises licence, the only other way to receive permission to carry on a licensable activity is for a premises user to apply for a "Temporary Event Notice" ("TEN"). A licensable activity carried out in accordance with a permission given using the TENs procedure is a permitted temporary activity[1]. There are limitations on when the TENs procedure can be used. An activity cannot last more than 96 hours[2]. The maximum number of persons permitted at the event at any one time cannot exceed 499[3]. A TEN is void if the period specified in it starts or ends within 24 hours of another notice given in respect of the same premises by the premises user, or an associate or business colleague of that premises user[4]. A licensing authority must give a "counter notice" (effectively refusing the application for a TEN) if the premises user has already given 50 such notices in the last calendar year (if the premises user is a personal licence holder[5]); or 5 such notices (in the case of anybody else[6]); or if 12 such notices have been given in the last calendar year in respect of the same premises[7]; or if there have been 15 days worth of such events at the premises in the last calendar year[8]. To apply for a permitted temporary activity, the premises user gives a TEN to the licensing authority. The TEN must be in the prescribed form and must contain the prescribed information[9]. A copy of the notice must be served in duplicate on the licensing authority no later than 10 working days before the day on which the event period begins[10], and a copy must be served on the chief officer of police[11]. The chief officer of police must object within 48 hours if he is satisfied that the use of the premises in accordance with the notice would undermine the crime prevention objective[12]. If objection is made the licensing authority must hold a hearing to consider the objection notice[13] and, having regard to the objection notice, must give the premises user a counter notice if it considers it necessary for the promotion of the crime prevention licensing objective[14]. The decision to give or not to give a counter notice under this section can be appealed to the magistrates' court[15], but a decision to give a counter notice because a premises user has exceeded the permitted limits under the TENs procedure cannot.

¹ LA 2003, s 98.
² LA 2003, s 100(1).
³ LA 2003, s 100(5)(*d*).
⁴ LA 2003, s 101.
⁵ LA 2003, s 107(2).
⁶ LA 2003, s 107(3).
⁷ LA 2003, s 107(4).
⁸ LA 2003, s 107(5).
⁹ LA 2003, s 100(5).
¹⁰ LA 2003, s 100(7)(*a*).
¹¹ LA 2003, s 104(1).
¹² LA 2003, s 104(2) and (3). However, there is provision in s 106 for the premises user and the Police to negotiate away any objections by making modifications to the TEN. If this happens the objection notice is treated as withdrawn: LA 2003, s 106(3).
¹³ LA 2003, s 105(2)(*a*).
¹⁴ LA 2003, s 105(2)(*b*).
¹⁵ LA 2003, Sch 5, para 16.

7.7628   Personal licences   A personal licence is granted by a licensing authority[1] to an individual and authorises that person to supply (whether by retail or by or on behalf of a club to, or to the order of a member of the club) alcohol, or authorise the supply of alcohol, in accordance with a premises licence[2]. Once granted, it has effect for a period of ten years[3] unless it is surrendered[4], revoked, forfeited or suspended. It must be renewed every ten years.

An application must be made in the prescribed form and must be granted if it appears to the licensing authority that the four prescribed conditions are met[5]. If it appears to the licensing authority that any of the first three prescribed conditions are not met, it must reject the application[6]. If it appears to the authority that the fourth condition is not met (because the applicant has been convicted of a "relevant offence[7]" or "foreign offence[8]") it must give notice to that effect to the chief officer of police. If the chief officer of police is satisfied that, because of those convictions, the grant of a personal licence would undermine the crime prevention objective, he must give the licensing authority an objection notice[9], and the authority must hold a hearing to consider the notice[10]. It must refuse the application if it considers it necessary to promote the crime prevention licensing objective[11].

Similar provisions apply on an application for renewal if the applicant has been convicted of a relevant or foreign offence since the grant of the licence[12]. If the licensing authority becomes aware of a conviction of a personal licence holder for a relevant or foreign offence since that individual was granted a personal licence (whether on first application or renewal), it must give a notice to that effect to the chief officer of police. A process akin to that referred to above (on an application for a grant or renewal of a personal licence) then begins, and the licence must be revoked by a licensing authority after a hearing if it considers this necessary to promote the crime prevention licensing objective[13].

¹ Application must be made to the licensing authority for the area in which the applicant is ordinarily resident.
² LA 2003, s 111(1).
³ LA 2003, s 115(1).
⁴ LA 2003, s 116.
⁵ The prescribed conditions are listed in the LA 2003, s 120(2).
⁶ LA 2003, s 120(3).
⁷ Relevant offences are listed in Sch 4 of the Act. Offences which are spent within the meaning of the Rehabilitation of Offenders Act 1974 must be disregarded: LA 2003, s 114.
⁸ Defined in the LA 2003, s 113(3). Offences which are spent within the meaning of the Rehabilitation of Offenders Act 1974 must be disregarded: LA 2003, s 114.
⁹ LA 2003, s 120(5).
¹⁰ LA 2003, s 120(7)(*a*).
¹¹ LA 2003, s 120(7)(*b*)(i),
¹² LA 2003, s 121.
¹³ LA 2003, s 124.

7.7629   *Personal licence holders appearing before a magistrates' court*   Where a personal licence holder is charged with a relevant offence he must, no later than the time he makes his first appearance in a magistrates' court in connection with that offence, produce his personal licence to the court or, if that is not practicable, notify the court of its existence[1].

A similar obligation is placed on a person who is granted a personal licence after a first court appearance but before the matter is dealt with[2]. A personal licence holder in such a situation must also keep the court notified of any changes in the status of his personal licence[3]. Where a personal licence holder is convicted of a relevant offence, the convicting court may order the forfeiture or suspension for up to 6 months of the personal licence[4]. The convicting court may suspend the operation of any such order pending an appeal[5], as may the court to which an appeal is made[6]. A convicting court must also notify the licensing authority that granted the personal licence of the outcome of the prosecution and the sentence imposed[7].

¹ LA 2003, s 128(1).
² LA 2003, s 128(2) and (3).
³ LA 2003, s 128(4) and (5).
⁴ LA 2003, s 129.
⁵ LA 2003, s 129(4).

[6] LA 2003, s 130.
[7] LA 2003, s 130(2).

7.7630   Appeals   The powers of applicants, interested parties and responsible authorities to appeal against decisions of a licensing authority are wide and varied. Essentially, any party to an original decision of the licensing authority following a hearing may appeal against the decision to grant, vary, impose conditions or refuse an application[1]. Magistrates' courts will sit as a final court of appeal, from which appeals will only be permitted on a point of law[2]. Magistrates' courts hearing an appeal are empowered to dismiss the appeal, substitute the decision of the licensing authority with its own decision, or remit the case to the licensing authority to dispose of in accordance with its direction; and can make such order as to costs as it thinks fit[3]. Appeals must be commenced by notice of appeal given to the designated officer of the magistrates' court within the period of 21 days beginning with the day on which the appellant was notified of the decision appealed against[4].

Magistrates must have regard to the licensing objectives, take account of the changed approach to licensing introduced by the LA 2003, the Secretary of State's Guidance and in deciding what regulation was required, look for real evidence that it was required in the circumstances of the case and not give excessive weight to their own views[5].

---

[1] This right does not extend to certain decisions that can be made by a licensing authority without the need for a hearing. Such decisions would have to be challenged by way of an application for judicial review. Examples include a decision of the licensing authority that a representation is irrelevant, frivolous, vexatious or repetitious; and a decision of a licensing authority to serve a counter notice to a TEN where the permitted limits have been exceeded: LA 2003, s 107. Some appeals may only be brought by the holder of a licence. In such cases where an appeal is brought by a person intending to appeal but having no standing to do so, the court cannot amend the complaint to refer to the holder of the licence as that would be substituting one legal entity for another and is not merely a misnaming of the appellant. Such an amendment is outside the scope of the Magistrates' Courts Act 1980, s 123. The issue for the magistrates' court considering an application to amend the complaint will be whether the matter is one of identity or misdescription. For the approach to deciding this issue, see *R (Essence Bars Ltd) v Wimbledon Magistrates' Court* [2016] EWCA Civ 63, [2016] 1 WLR 3265, 181 JP 297 and the Magistrates' Courts Act 1980, s 123 and notes thereto in Part I: Magistrates' Courts, Procedure, ante and also para 1.191 **Objection to the information or charge**.
[2] There is an exception to this rule in the case of closure orders: LA 2003, s 166.
[3] LA 2003, s 181(2). For a more detailed commentary on the award of costs see para 7.7637.
[4] LA 2003, Sch 5, paras 9(2), 15(2), 16(5), 17(7) and 18(5). The Licensing Act (Hearings) Regulations 2005, SI 2005/44 require a notice of determination to be given in writing: reg 34.
[5] See the comments by Black J in *R (Daniel Thwaites plc) v Wirral Borough Magistrates' Court* [2008] EWHC 838 (Admin), [2009] 1 All ER 239, 172 JP 301.

7.7631   *Appeals in respect of premises licences*   Where a licensing authority rejects an application for a premises licence under s 18; rejects an application (in whole or part) to vary a premises licence under s 35; rejects an application under s 35 to vary a premises licence so as to specify a new premises supervisor; or rejects an application to transfer a premises licence under s 44, the applicant may appeal to the magistrates' court[1]. Where a licensing authority grant a premises licence, the applicant may appeal against any decision to impose conditions under s 18(2)(*a*) or (3)(*b*), or to exclude specific licensable activities (s 18(4)(*b*)), or to refuse to specify an individual as the premises supervisor (s 18(4)(*c*))[2]; whilst a person who made relevant representations may appeal on the grounds that the licence ought not to have been granted or that, on granting the licence, different or additional conditions should have been imposed or a decision should have been taken to exclude certain licensable activities or refuse to specify a person as the premises supervisor[3]. Similar rights of appeal exist in relation to the issuing of a provisional statement under s 31[4]; the grant (in whole or part) of an application to vary a premises licence[5]; and a decision on a review of the premises licence under s 52[6]. In addition a chief officer of police may appeal against a decision to vary a premises licence under s 39(2) so as to specify a new premises supervisor[7] or a decision to transfer a licence under s 44[8], so long as, in both cases, he gave a notice objecting to the application in the first place which was not withdrawn. Where an interim authority notice is given under s 47 and a chief officer of police gives a notice under s 48(2), the person given the notice can appeal against a decision to cancel the interim authority and the chief officer of police can appeal against a decision not to cancel it[9]. Where such an appeal is brought, the magistrates' court hearing the appeal may, on such terms as it thinks fit, order the reinstatement of the interim authority notice pending the disposal of the appeal or the expiry of the interim authority period (two months after the notice was given[10]), whichever occurs first[11].

---

[1] LA 2003, Sch 5, para 1.
[2] LA 2003, Sch 5, para 2(2).
[3] LA 2003, Sch 5, para 2(3).
[4] LA 2003, Sch 5, para 3.
[5] LA 2003, Sch 5, para 4.
[6] LA 2003, Sch 5, para 8.
[7] LA 2003, Sch 5, para 5(2).
[8] LA 2003, Sch 5, para 6(2).
[9] LA 2003, Sch 5, para 7.
[10] LA 2003, s 47(10).
[11] LA 2003, Sch 5, para 7(4).

7.7632   *Appeals in respect of club premises certificates*   Where a licensing authority rejects an application for a club premises certificate or rejects (in whole or part) an application to vary a club premises certificate, the club that made the application may appeal against the decision[1]. Where a licensing authority grants a club premises certificate, the club may appeal against any decision to impose conditions under s 72(2) or (3)(*b*), or to exclude specific qualifying club activities (s 72(4)(*b*)); whilst a person who made relevant representations may appeal on the grounds that the certificate ought not to have been granted or that, on granting the certificate, different or additional conditions should have been imposed or a decision should have been taken to exclude certain qualifying club activities[2]. Similar rights of appeal exist in relation to the grant (in whole or part) of an application to vary a certificate[3]; and a decision on a review of the certificate under s 88[4]. A club may also appeal against a decision of a licensing authority to give a notice under s 90 withdrawing the club premises certificate[5].

---

[1] LA2003, Sch 5, para 10.
[2] LA 2003, Sch 5, para 11.
[3] LA 2003, Sch 5, para 12.
[4] LA 2003, Sch 5, para 13.
[5] LA 2003, Sch 5, para 14.

7.7633 *Appeals in respect of permitted temporary activities*   A premises user may appeal against a decision of a licensing authority to give a counter notice[1], and a chief officer of police may appeal against a decision of a licensing authority not to give one[2]. No appeal in respect of a permitted temporary activity may be brought later than five working days before the day on which the event period specified in the TEN begins[3].

---

[1] LA 2003, Sch 5, para 16(2).
[2] LA 2003, Sch 5, para 16(3).
[3] LA 2003, Sch 5, para 16(6).

7.7634 *Appeals in respect of personal licences*   An applicant may appeal against a decision to reject an application for a personal licence[1], or a decision to revoke a licence[2]. A chief officer of police may appeal against a decision to grant an application for a personal licence where he has served an objection notice to the application[3], and a decision not to revoke a personal licence[4].

---

[1] Whether that decision was made on a first application or on an application for renewal: LA 2003, Sch 5, para 17(1).
[2] LA 2003, Sch 5, para 17(4).
[3] Whether that decision was made on a first application or on an application for renewal: LA 2003, Sch 5, para 17(2) and (3).
[4] LA 2003, Sch 5, para 17(5).

7.7635 *Appeals in respect of closure orders*   The licence holder or any person who made representations in respect of a review of a premises licence under s 167 may appeal against the licensing authority's decision[1].

---

[1] LA 2003, Sch 5, para 18.

7.7636 *Procedure on appeals*   Appeals to the magistrates' court are to be by way of a rehearing[1] on both the merits and the law, and the magistrates' court is not limited to considering only those grounds of complaint that were raised in the notice application or the representations which were made to the licensing authority; the parties are free to adduce such evidence as they think fit, subject to the control of the court[2]. Although it is a rehearing, justices must pay proper regard to the decision of the local authority and should not exercise their discretion uninfluenced by the local authorities' opinion[3]. This principle is not limited to decisions which can be classified as "policy based". In *R (on the application of Hope and Glory Public House Ltd) v City of Westminster Magistrates' Court (The Lord Mayor and the Citizens of the City of Westminster Intervening)*[4] it was held that the magistrates' court should approach its task in accordance with the following guidance and principles:

"39. Since (counsel for the appellant) accepted (in our view rightly) that the decision of the licensing authority was a relevant matter for the District Judge to take into consideration, whether or not the decision is classified as 'policy based', the issues are quite narrow. They are:

(1) How much weight was the District Judge entitled to give to the decision of the licensing authority?

(2) More particularly, was he right to hold that he should only allow the appeal if satisfied that the decision of the licensing authority was wrong?

(3) (Compliance with art 6)

40. We do not consider that it is possible to give a formulaic answer to the first question because it may depend on a variety of factors — the nature of the issue, the nature and quality of the reasons given by the licensing authority and the nature and quality of the evidence on the appeal.

41. As (was) rightly submitted, the licensing function of a licensing authority is an administrative function. By contrast, the function of the District Judge is a judicial function. The licensing authority has a duty, in accordance with the rule of law, to behave fairly in the decision-making procedure, but the decision itself is not a judicial or quasi-judicial act. It is the exercise of a power delegated by the people as a whole to decide what the public interest requires...

42. Licensing decisions often involve weighing a variety of competing considerations: the demand for licensed establishments, the economic benefit to the proprietor and to the locality by drawing in visitors and stimulating the demand, the effect on law and order, the impact on the lives of those who live and work in the vicinity, and so on. Sometimes a licensing decision may involve narrower questions, such as whether noise, noxious smells or litter coming from premises amount to a public nuisance. Although such questions are in a sense questions of fact, they are not questions of the 'heads or tails'; variety. They involve an evaluation of what is to be regarded as reasonably acceptable in the particular location. In any case, deciding what (if any) conditions

should be attached to a licence as necessary and proportionate to the promotion of the statutory licensing objectives is essentially a matter of judgment rather than a matter of pure fact.

43. The statutory duty of the licensing authority to give reasons for its decision serves a number of purposes. It informs the public, who can make their views known to their elected representatives if they do not like the licensing sub-committee's approach. It enables a party aggrieved by the decision to know why it has lost and to consider the prospects of a successful appeal. If an appeal is brought, it enables the magistrates' court to know the reasons which led to the decision. The fuller and clearer the reasons, the more force they are likely to carry.

44. The evidence called on the appeal may, or may not, throw a very different light on matters. Someone whose representations were accepted by the licensing authority may be totally discredited as a result of cross-examination. By contrast, in the present case the District Judge heard a mass of evidence over four days, as a result of which he reached essentially the same factual conclusions as the licensing authority had reached after five hours.

45. Given all the variables, the proper conclusion to the first question can only be stated in very general terms. It is right in all cases that the magistrates' court should pay careful attention to the reasons given by the licensing authority for arriving at the decision under appeal, bearing in mind that Parliament has chosen to place responsibility for making such decisions on local authorities. The weight which the magistrates should ultimately attach to those reasons must be a matter for their judgment in all the circumstances, taking into account the fullness and clarity of the reasons, the nature of the issues and the evidence given on the appeal.

46. As to the second question, we agree with the way in which Burton J dealt with the matter in paras 43–45 of his judgment:

'("43.... What the appellate court will have to do is to be satisfied that the judgment below "is wrong", that is to reach its conclusion on the basis of the evidence put before it and then to conclude that the judgment below is wrong, even if it was not wrong at the time. That is what this District Judge was prepared to do by allowing fresh evidence in, on both sides.

44. The onus still remains on the claimant, hence the correct decision that the claimant should start, one that cannot be challenged as I have indicated.

45. At the end of the day, the decision before the District Judge is whether the decision of the licensing committee is wrong. (Counsel for the appellant) has submitted that the word "wrong" is difficult to understand, or, at any rate, insufficiently clarified. What does it mean? It is plainly not "Wednesbury unreasonable" because this is not a question of judicial review. It means that the task of the District Judge — having heard the evidence which is now before him, and specifically addressing the decision of the court below — is to give a decision whether, because he disagrees with the decision below in the light of the evidence before him, it is therefore wrong.')

47. We do not accept (the) submission that the statement of Lord Goddard in *Stepney BC v Joffe*, applied by Edmund Davies LJ in *Sagnata Investments Ltd v Norwich Corporation* is applicable only in a case where the original decision was based on 'policy considerations'. We doubt whether such a distinction would be practicable, because it involves the unreal assumption that all decisions can be put in one of two boxes, one marked policy and the other not.....

48. It is normal for an appellant to have the responsibility of persuading the court that it should reverse the order under appeal, and the Magistrates' Courts Rules envisage that this is so in the case of statutory appeals to magistrates' courts from decisions of local authorities. We see no indication that Parliament intended to create an exception in the case of appeals under the Licensing Act.

49. We are also impressed by (the) point that in a case such as this, where the licensing sub-committee has exercised what amounts to a statutory discretion to attach conditions to the licence, it makes good sense that the licensee should have to persuade the magistrates' court that the sub-committee should not have exercised its discretion in the way that it did rather than that the magistrates' court should be required to exercise the discretion afresh on the hearing of the appeal."

Justices will need to be familiar with the scheme of the 2003 Act, the licensing objectives, the DCMS Guidance and the statement of policy of the licensing authority whose decision is being appealed. The court must carry out its appellate function with a view to promoting the licensing objectives[5]. Licensing and planning objectives plainly overlap and, except in relation to the protection of children from harm, each of the licensing objectives is also a land use planning objective. However, the framework and substance of the LA 2003, and its underlying rationale, point strongly to operational matters being regulated primarily in the former jurisdiction, though each case must be considered on its own facts; justices should not in involve themselves in planning matters, and in a licensing appeal it is not for them to examine whether a particular variation requires planning consent or to speculate whether, if it does, this will be forthcoming because these are matters exclusively within the competence of the planning authority[6]. The licensing authority will be a respondent to every appeal, with additional named respondents being specified depending on the decision being appealed against[7]. No express right is granted to either an interested party or a responsible authority to appear as a respondent to an appeal, although either may appear in specified circumstances as an appellant. Nevertheless, magistrates may permit an interested party or responsible authority to appear where, balancing the need to protect the appellant from any undue burden, they consider that to do so would further a fair and just resolution of the appeal in accordance with the licensing objectives[8]. No guidance has yet been given to magistrates' courts about the giving of directions, but it would seem to be good practice to issue standardised directions covering disclosure, exchange of evidence (lay and expert) and lodging of appeal bundles. If not resolved between the parties, these should be discussed at a pre-trial review. In considering the appeal, the court will be exercising an administrative function. Accordingly, strict rules of evidence do not apply, hearsay evidence is admissible[9] and there is no burden of proof. Although the LA 2003 does not specify the procedure by which an appeal is brought (referring throughout Sch 5 to "notices of appeal"), r 14 of the Magistrates' Court Rules 1981[10] states that the complainant should present his case first. This may not always be the most appropriate order, since in complex cases it will mean the justices will hear why the decision was allegedly wrong before it hears what the decision was and why it was reached. It is open to a court to vary the order (with the consent of all parties) so that the licensing authority presents its case first. If there is a second respondent then it would be sensible for their case to follow the licensing authority, so that the appellant goes last. Justices are advised to give comprehensive reasons for the decision that they reach[11].

Where a court is considering imposing conditions it will almost always be good practice for the conditions under consideration to be outlined for debate by the parties. Errors of drafting can then be identified, as can improvements and consideration of the underlying propositions behind the conditions themselves[12].

---

[1] Because of this, fresh evidence may be adduced that was not available at the original hearing (*Rushmoor Borough Council v Richards* (1996) 160 LG Rev 460).

[2] *Khan v Coventry Magistrates' Court, Coventry City Council (Interested Party)* [2011] EWCA Civ 751, 175 JP 429.

[3] *Sagnata Investments v Norwich Corpn* [1971] 2 All ER 1441. The Court of Appeal expressly approved the approach outlined in *Stepney Borough Council v Joffe* [1949] 1 All ER 256, that the appellate court ought "to pay great attention to the fact that the duly constituted and elected local authority have come to an opinion on the matter and ought not lightly to reverse their opinion . . . the function of a court of appeal is to exercise its powers when it is satisfied that the judgment below is wrong, not merely because it is not satisfied that the judgment was right".

[4] [2011] EWCA Civ 31, [2011] 3 All ER 579, 175 JP 77.

[5] And, it is submitted, must also have regard to the duty imposed on a licensing authority under s 17 of the Crime and Disorder Act 1998: see para 7.7618.

[6] *R (on the application of Blackwood) v Birmingham Magistrates and Birmingham City Council, Mitchells and Butler Leisure Retail Ltd (Interested Party)* [2006] EWHC 1800 (Admin), 170 JP 613.

[7] LA 2003, Sch 5, paras 9(4), 15(3), 16(7), 17(8) and 18(6).

[8] *R (Chief Constable of Nottinghamshire Police) v Nottingham Magistrates' Court* [2009] EWHC 3182 (Admin), [2010] 2 All ER 342, 174 JP 1.

[9] *Kavanagh v Chief Constable of Devon & Cornwall* [1974] 1QB 624; *Westminster City Council v Zestfair Ltd* (1989) 88 LGR 288.

[10] SI 1981/552 as amended: see para 1.2362.

[11] However, see *R (on the application of Blackwood) v Birmingham Magistrates and Birmingham City Council, Mitchells and Butler Leisure Retail Ltd (Interested Party)*, supra, where the reasons, though "somewhat sparse", were held to be adequate to bring home to anyone familiar with the licensing regime that the proposed variation in respect of opening hours was reasonable in the light of the licensing objectives, particularly those concerning public nuisance.

[12] *R (Westminster City Council) v Metropolitan Stipendiary Magistrate* [2008] EWHC 1202 (Admin), 172 JP 462.

7.7637 *The role of the DCMS Guidance and the licensing authority's statement of policy in appeal hearings*
Chapter 10 of the DCMS Guidance advises that magistrates' courts must have regard to the Guidance and the licensing authority's statement of licensing policy when hearing an appeal[1]. The Guidance says that the court may depart from either document if it considers that it is justified in doing so because of the individual circumstances of the case; or because it finds any part of either document to be ultra vires[2]. It is submitted that, in this last respect, the Guidance is wrong in law and that a proper method of challenging the validity of a statement of licensing policy is by way of an application for judicial review[3].

The court must give reasons where it departs from the guidance. When considering an appeal involving the use of premises for criminal purposes, furtherance of the licensing objectives includes the prevention of crime. In this regard deterrence is an appropriate consideration so that the court must address the guidance on this point[4].

---

[1] Guidance issued under s 182 of the LA 2003, July 2004, para 10.8.

[2] Guidance issued under s 182 of the LA 2003, July 2004, para 10.8. This would appear to run contrary to the decision of the High Court in *R (Westminster City Council) v Middlesex Crown Court & Chorion plc* [2002] LLR 538.

[3] For an example of a challenge by way of judicial review to a licensing authority's statement of licensing policy, see *R (on the application of British Beer and Pub Association) v Canterbury City Council* [2005] EWHC 1318 (Admin), 6169 JP 521.

[4] *R (Bassetlaw District Council v Worksop Magistrates' Court)* [2008] EWHC 3530 (Admin), 173 JP 599.

7.7638 *Costs on appeal* A magistrates' court hearing an appeal may make such order as to costs as it thinks fit[1]. This power is in wider terms than that where the costs of an appeal are ordered under other powers[2]. In licensing cases the permutations of result may be frequently more complex than simple success or failure. The court has an unfettered power in relation to costs subject to the requirement that in making such order as is just it must take into account all relevant matters and not take into account irrelevant matters. The court is not limited to ordering costs to follow the event so that where an appellant had succeeded on her appeal but it was hardly a resounding victory, the court was upheld in ordering the appellant to pay the respondent licensing authority's (substantial) costs[3]. As regards ordering a licensing authority to pay costs, existing principles in other areas of administrative law dealt with by magistrates' courts as an appellate body are that costs should not be routinely awarded against an authority that acted honestly, reasonably and properly on sound grounds[4]. Financial prejudice to the successful private party can potentially justify departure from the normal position of no costs against the local authority, but this requires evidence that the private party will suffer exceptional or substantial financial hardship[5]. In relation to the power to order costs under s 181(2) of the LA 2003 whilst there has been emphasis on the very wide nature of the justices' discretion[6], it has been held that although the power to award costs was not confined to cases where the local authority acted unreasonably or in bad faith, the fact that the local authority had acted reasonably and in good faith was plainly a most important factor[7].

---

[1] Licensing Act 2003, s 181(2).
[2] Ie under s 64 of the Magistrates' Courts Act 1980 where costs may only be claimed by a successful party, see further para 1.377, in PART I: MAGISTRATES' COURTS, PROCEDURE, ante.
[3] *Prasannan v Royal Borough of Kensington and Chelsea* [2010] EWHC 319 (Admin), 174 JP 418.
[4] *Bradford Metropolitan District Council v Booth* (2000) 164 JP 485 (a case concerning the licensing of a private hire operator).
[5] *R (on the application of Newham London Borough Council) v Stratford Magistrates' Court* [2012] All ER (D) 184 (Jan).
[6] *Prasannan*, supra, also *Crawley Borough Council v Attenborough* [2006] EWHC 1278 (Admin), (2006) 170 JP 593.
[7] *R (on the application of Cambridge City Council) v Alex Nesting Ltd* [2006] EWHC 1374 (Admin), 170 JP 539.

7.7639 Closure of premises A police officer of the rank of Superintendent or above may apply to a magistrates' court for an order to close premises licensed under a premises licence or TEN[1] for up to 24 hours if there is or is expected to be disorder in the area and the premises concerned are situated at or near the place of disorder or expected disorder[2]. A magistrates' court may make such an order only if it is satisfied that it is necessary to prevent disorder[3]. Once an order has been made a constable may use such force as may be necessary to close premises which have been ordered to close[4]. Additionally, a police officer of the rank of Inspector or above may make a "closure order" in relation to premises licensed under a premises licence or TEN if he reasonably believes that there is, or is likely imminently to be, disorder on, or in the vicinity of and related to, the premises and their closure is necessary in the interests of public safety; or that a public nuisance is being caused by noise coming from the premises and the closure of the premises is necessary to prevent that nuisance[5]. The effect of the closure order is to require the premises to be closed for a period not exceeding 24 hours from the moment that notice of the order is given to an appropriate person[6] who is connected with any of the activities to which the disorder or nuisance relates[7]. It is an offence to permit premises to be open in contravention of an order[8]. As soon as reasonably practicable after a closure order has come into force, the police officer that decided to make the order must apply to a magistrates' court for it to consider the order and any extension of it[9]. If the police officer reasonably believes that a magistrates' court will not have determined whether to exercise its powers under s 165(2) by the end of the initial 24 hour closure period he may, before that initial period expires, extend it by a further period of up to 24 hours if certain conditions are satisfied[10]. Equally, the police officer must cancel the order if he does not reasonably believe that the conditions for it remain.

---

[1] But not a premises that has the benefit of a club premises certificate.
[2] Licensing Act 2003, s 160(1).
[3] LA 2003, s 160(3).
[4] LA 2003, s 160(7).
[5] LA 2003, s 161(1).
[6] Defined in the LA 2003, s 171(5).
[7] LA 2003, s 161(2) and (5).
[8] LA 2003, s 161(6).
[9] LA 2003, s 164(1).
[10] LA 2003, s 162.

7.7640 *Consideration of closure order by magistrates' court* As soon as reasonably practicable after receipt of an application under s 164(1) a magistrates' court must hold a hearing to consider whether it is appropriate to exercise any of its powers in relation to the order[1]. The powers are listed in s 164(2) and are wide ranging. In coming to a determination the court must consider, in particular, whether continued closure is necessary for the same reasons as the order was made in the first place[2]. Offences are committed if, without reasonable excuse, a person permits premises to be open in contravention of the magistrates' order. There is a right of appeal to the Crown Court against the decision of a magistrates' court[3]. Once a decision has been made by a magistrates' court in relation to a premises with the benefit of a premises licence, it must notify the licensing authority of that decision[4]. The licensing authority must then review the premises licence[5].

---

[1] LA 2003, s 165(1). The court does not need to exercise its powers if the premises have ceased to be licensed (for example, because the premises had the benefit of a TEN that has subsequently expired). The hearing is to be by way of a complaint for an order: LA 2003, s 165(9).
[2] LA 2003, s 165(3).
[3] LA 2003, s 166(1).
[4] LA 2003, s 165(4).
[5] LA 2003, s 167(2).

7.7641 Offences – introduction All offences in the LA 2003 are summary only, but the time limit for instituting proceedings is raised to 12 months[1]. Proceedings for offences may be instituted by a licensing authority, the DPP, or (in the case of offences under ss 146 and 147 by a local weights and measures authority[2]). Offences may be committed by bodies corporate, partnerships and unincorporated associations and by individuals in those organisations if the requirements of s 187 are satisfied.

---

[1] LA 2003, s 186(3).
[2] LA 2003, s 186(2).

7.7642 *"Documentary" offences* Part 7 outlines the substantive offences contained in the Act. However, there are a raft of documentary offences throughout the Act, dealing with such matters as failing to notify a licensing authority of a change in the name or address of a premises licence holder or premises supervisor[1]; a change in the name, rules[2] or address[3] of a club; a conviction of a personal licence holder for a relevant or foreign offence[4]; and the name or address of a personal licence holder[5]. Offences are also committed if a summary of a premises licence or club premises certificate, or a copy of a temporary event notice is not displayed at the premises to which they relate[6]. Furthermore, offences are committed if a premises licence, club premises certificate or personal licence is not provided to the licensing authority to be updated when requested[7]. There are also offences relating to the obstruction of an authorised person who is carrying out his duties in relation to personal licences, club premises certificates or permitted temporary activities[8]; and offences of failing to produce a premises licence, club premises certificate, temporary event notice or personal licence to an authorised officer or police constable[9].

---

[1] LA 2003, s 33(6).
[2] LA 2003, s 82(6).
[3] LA 2003, s 83(6).
[4] Either during the application period for a licence: LA 2003, s 123(2); or after a licence has been granted: LA 2003, s 132(4).
[5] LA 2003, s 127(1).
[6] See, for example, LA 2003, ss 57(4), 94(5), 94(6) and 109(4).
[7] See, for example, LA 2003, ss 41(5), 56(3), 93(3) and 134(5).
[8] See, for example, LA 2003, ss 59(5), 96(5) and 108(3). The offence does not apply to obstruction of a police officer because that is already an offence: Police Act 1996, s 89(2).
[9] See, for example, LA 2003, ss 57(7), 94(9), 109(8) and 135(4).

7.7643 *Offences – unauthorised licensable activities* A person commits an offence if he carries on, attempts to carry on or knowingly allows to be carried on a licensable activity on or from any premises otherwise than under and in accordance with a premises licence, club premises certificate or valid temporary event notice[1]. This provision is directed at persons who *as a matter of fact* actually carry on etc a licensable activity on or from the premises. It is not directed at holders of premises licences as such who do not automatically incur liability by the mere fact of holding a licence[2]. It is also an offence to expose alcohol for sale by retail[3] in circumstances where the sale would be an unauthorised licensable activity[4]; and to keep alcohol in one's possession or under one's control with the intention of selling it by retail or supplying it in circumstances where the sale or supply would be an unauthorised licensable activity[5]. A due diligence defence[6] is available for all of these offences except for one committed under s 136(1)(*b*).

---

[1] LA 2003, s 136(1). No offence is committed solely by reason of the person being a performer in an unlicensed performance of regulated entertainment: LA 2003, 136(2). Conviction carries a maximum penalty of six months' imprisonment and/or a £20,000 fine.
[2] *Hall & Woodhouse Ltd v Borough and County of the Town of Poole* [2009] EWHC 1587 (Admin), [2010] 1 All ER 425, 173 JP 433.
[3] "Sale by retail" is defined in the LA 2003, s 192.
[4] LA 2003, s 137(1). Conviction carries a maximum penalty of six months' imprisonment and/or a £20,000 fine. A convicting court may order forfeiture of the alcohol in question: LA 2003, s 137(4).
[5] LA 2003, s 138(1). Conviction carries a maximum of a level 2 fine on the standard scale. A convicting court may order forfeiture of the alcohol in question: LA 2003, s 138(5).
[6] LA 2003, s 139.

7.7644 *Offences – drunkenness and disorderly conduct* A large number of people can commit an offence of knowingly[1] allowing disorderly conduct[2] on relevant premises[3]. Those people include any person who works at the premises in a capacity, paid or unpaid, which authorises him to prevent the conduct; the holder of a premises licence; a premises supervisor; any member or officer of a club who is present at the club when the disorder takes place in a capacity which enables him to prevent it; and the premises user in relation to a permitted temporary activity[4]. The same group of people may commit an offence of knowingly[5] selling, attempting to sell or allowing to be sold alcohol to a person who is drunk[6]. It is an offence for a person, on relevant premises[7], to knowingly obtain or attempt to obtain alcohol for consumption on those premises by a person who is drunk[8]; and it is an offence for a drunk or disorderly person, without reasonable excuse, to fail to leave relevant premises[9] when requested to do so by a constable or a person to whom s 143(2) applies[10], or to enter or attempt to enter such premises after that person has requested him not to do so[11].

---

[1] See the case of *R v Winson* [1968] 1 All ER 197. The doctrine of delegation applies to the concept of "knowingly", so that a defendant can be guilty of an offence committed by another if he has delegated responsibility for compliance with the law to that other person who did knowingly allow the offence to occur. See also *Howker v Robinson* [1972] 2 All ER 786.
[2] "Disorderly conduct" is not defined.
[3] LA 2003, s 140(1). The offence carries a maximum of a level 3 fine on the standard scale. "Relevant premises" are defined in s 159 and include premises covered by a premises licence, club premises certificate or temporary event notice.
[4] LA 2003, s 140(2).
[5] See note 1, above.
[6] LA 2003, 141(1). The offence carries a maximum of a level 3 fine on the standard scale. "Drunk" is not defined, but in the case of *Neale v E (a minor)* (1983) 80 Cr App Rep 20, (a case on the meaning of "drunk" under the offence of

drunkenness in a public place, contrary to s 91 of the Criminal Justice Act 1967), it was held that it referred to a person who has taken intoxicating liquor to excess so that he has lost the power of self-control.

[7] See note 3, above, for definition of "relevant premises".

[8] LA 2003, s 142(1). The offence carries a maximum of a level 3 fine on the standard scale. See note 6, above, for guidance on the meaning of "drunk".

[9] See note 3, ante, for definition of "relevant premises".

[10] LA 2003, s 143(1)(a). The offence carries a maximum of a level 1 fine on the standard scale.

[11] Licensing Act 2003, s 143(1)(b). The offence carries a maximum of a level 1 fine on the standard scale.

7.7645 *Offences – smuggled goods* The same group of people who can commit an offence under s 140(1)[1], can also commit an offence of knowingly[2] keeping or allowing to be kept, on any relevant premises[3], any goods which have been imported without payment of duty or which have otherwise been unlawfully imported[4].

[1] See para 7.7644, ante.

[2] See note 1 to para 7.7644, ante, for discussion of "knowingly". The defendant need only know that the goods are on the premises, not that they are smuggled.

[3] See note 3, to para 7.7644, ante, for meaning of "relevant premises".

[4] LA 2003, s 144(1). The offence carries a maximum of a level 3 fine on the standard scale. A convicting court may order forfeiture of the goods in question: LA 2003, s 144(4).

7.7646 *Offences – children and alcohol – unaccompanied children on certain premises* It is an offence[1] for a person listed in s 145(3) to allow an unaccompanied child under 16 to be on premises that he knows are exclusively or primarily used for the supply of alcohol for consumption there[2] at a time when they are open for that purpose[3]; or to allow an unaccompanied[4] child under 16 to be on those premises between midnight and 5am when the premises[5] are open for the purposes of being used for the supply of alcohol for consumption there[6]. No offence is committed if the child is on the premises solely for the purpose of passing to or from some other place and there is no other convenient means of getting to or from that place[7]. If a person is charged with the offence by reason of his own conduct, it is a defence[8] that the person believed the child to be 16 or over or the accompanying person (if there was one) to be 18 or over, and he had either taken all reasonable steps[9] to establish the individual's age, or nobody could reasonably have suspected from the individual's appearance that he was aged under 16 or under 18, as the case may be. A person charged because of the act or default of another has a defence if he exercised all due diligence to avoid committing it[10].

[1] The offences carry a maximum of a level 3 fine on the standard scale: LA 2003, s 145(9).

[2] The premises can be licensed by virtue of a premises licence, club premises certificate or temporary event notice: LA 2003, s 145(4) and (10).

[3] LA 2003, s 145(1)(a).

[4] "Unaccompanied" means not accompanied by an individual aged 18 or over: LA 2003, s 145(2)(b).

[5] See note 1 ante for definition of premises.

[6] LA 2003, s 145(1)(b).

[7] LA 2003, s 145(5),

[8] Ms 2003, s 145(6).

[9] A person is deemed to have taken all reasonable steps if he asked the individual for evidence of age and the evidence would have convinced a reasonable person: LA 2003, s 145(7).

[10] LA 2003, s 145(8).

7.7647 *Offences – children and alcohol – sale or supply of alcohol to children* There are numerous offences involving the sale of alcohol to children. A person commits an offence if he sells alcohol to a child under 18[1]. A club commits an offence[2] if alcohol is supplied by it or on its behalf to, or to the order of, a member of the club who is under 18[3]. A person charged with an offence by reason of his own conduct has the same defence as is available in respect of a s 145 charge[4]; and a person charged because of the act or default of another has a due diligence defence available[5]. It is also an offence to knowingly[6] allow the sale of alcohol, on relevant premises[7], to a child under 18[8]. Further, there are offences in relation to the sale or supply liqueur confectionery[9] to children under 16[10].

[1] LA 2003, s 149(1)(a). The offence can be committed anywhere, even on unlicensed premises. A similar offence is created if an under 18 member of a club is supplied with, or attempts to be supplied with, alcohol: LA 2003, s 149(1)(b).

[2] LA 2003, s 149(2).

[3] LA 2003, s 149(3)(a). A similar offence is committed if the person is a member of a club: LA 2003, s 149(3)(b). Both offences carry a defence that the person charged had no reason to suspect that the individual was under 18: LA 2003, s 149(6).

[4] LA 2003, s 149(4)(a). A similar offence is committed if the person is a member of a club: LA 2003, s 149(4)(b). "Relevant premises" are defined in s 159. Both offences carry a defence that the person charged had no reason to suspect that the individual was under 18: LA 2003, s 149(6).

[5] "The table meal exemption": LA 2003, s 149(5).

[6] So the offence would not be committed if the child unwittingly consumed a spiked drink.

[7] LA 2003, s 150(1). No offence is committed if the "table meal exemption" applies: LA 2003, s 150(4). "Relevant premises" are defined in LA 2003, s 159.

[8] Licensing Act 2003, s 150(2). No offence is committed if the "table meal exemption" applies: LA 2003, s 150(4). "Relevant premises" are defined in s 159.

[9] "Relevant premises" are defined in s 159.

[10] LA 2003, s 151(1).

7.7648 *Offences – children and alcohol – purchase and consumption of alcohol by children* A child under 18 commits an offence if he buys or attempts to buy alcohol[1], unless that act is committed in the course of him being used for a test purchase operation[2]. A person who acts as an agent for a child under 18 by buying or attempting to buy alcohol on behalf of the child also commits an offence[3], as does a person who acts as agent for a child under 18 and buys or attempts to buy alcohol for him for consumption on relevant premises[4]. However, this last offence does not apply if the person purchasing or attempting to purchase the alcohol is over 18; the child is 16 or 17; the alcohol is beer, wine or cider; the purchase is for consumption at a table meal; and the child is accompanied by an adult[5]. A child also commits an offence if he knowingly[6] consumes alcohol on relevant premises[7], and a person to whom s 150(3) applies commits an offence if he knowingly allows the consumption of alcohol by a child under 18 on relevant premises[8].

---

[1] LA 2003, s 149(1)(*a*). The offence can be committed anywhere, even on unlicensed premises. A similar offence is created if an under 18 member of a club is supplied with, or attempts to be supplied with, alcohol: LA 2003, s 149(1)(*b*).
[2] LA 2003, s 149(2).
[3] LA 2003, s 149(3)(*a*). A similar offence is committed if the person is a member of a club: LA 2003, s 149(3)(*b*). Both offences carry a defence that the person charged had no reason to suspect that the individual was under 18: LA 2003, 149(6).
[4] LA 2003, s 149(4)(*a*). A similar offence is committed if the person is a member of a club: LA 2003, s 149(4)(*b*). "Relevant premises" are defined in s 159. Both offences carry a defence that the person charged had no reason to suspect that the individual was under 18: LA 2003, 149(6).
[5] "The table meal exemption": LA 2003, s 149(5).
[6] So the offence would not be committed if the child unwittingly consumed a spiked drink.
[7] LA 2003, s 150(1). No offence is committed if the "table meal exemption" applies: LA 2003, s 150(4). "Relevant premises" are defined in LA 2003, s 159.
[8] LA 2003, s 150(2). No offence is committed if the "table meal exemption" applies: LA 2003, s 150(4). "Relevant premises" are defined in s 159.

7.7649   *Offences – children and alcohol – delivering alcohol to children and sending children to obtain alcohol*
A person who works on relevant premises[1] in any capacity commits an offence if he knowingly delivers to a child under 18 alcohol sold on the premises, or supplied on the premises (in the case of a club)[2]. Similar offences are committed by a person who knowingly allows anybody else to deliver the alcohol[3]. The offences are not committed if the alcohol is delivered to a place where the buyer or person supplied lives or works[4]; if the child under 18 is himself working on relevant premises in a capacity that involves the delivery of alcohol; or if the alcohol is sold or supplied for consumption on relevant premises[5]. It is also an offence to knowingly send a child under 18 to obtain alcohol sold or supplied on relevant premises for consumption off those premises[6].

---

[1] "Relevant premises" are defined in the LA 2003, s 159.
[2] LA 2003, s 151(1).
[3] LA2003, s 151(2) and (4). The person must work in a capacity which authorises him to prevent the delivery: LA 2003, s 151(3) and (5).
[4] This would seem to mean that a child can take delivery of the alcohol on behalf of a parent or employer and no offence is committed.
[5] LA 2003, s 151(6).
[6] LA 2003, s 152(1). An example would be a parent sending a child to collect alcohol which had already been paid for from an off licence, although it is immaterial where the alcohol is actually collected from: LA 2003, s 152(2). Exceptions are provided in the case of test purchase operations (LA 2003, s 152(4)) and where the child works on the relevant premises in a capacity that involves the delivery of alcohol (LA 2003, s 152(3)).

7.7650   *Offences – children and alcohol – unsupervised sales by children*   It is an offence for a responsible person[1] on relevant premises[2] to knowingly allow a child under 18 to make a sale or supply of alcohol on the premises unless the sale or supply has been specifically approved by that or another responsible person[3]. However, no offence is committed if the child serves or supplies alcohol to a person for consumption with a table meal in an area set aside for that purpose[4].

---

[1] "Responsible person" is defined in the LA 2003, s 153(4).
[2] "Relevant premises" are defined in the LA 2003, s 159.
[3] LA 2003, s 153(1).
[4] LA 2003, s 153(2).

7.7651   *Offences – vehicles and trains*   A person commits an offence if he sells by retail[1] alcohol on or from a vehicle[2] at a time when the vehicle is not permanently or temporarily parked[3]. A magistrates' court, if it is satisfied that it is necessary to prevent disorder, may, on the application of a police officer of the rank of Inspector or above, make an order prohibiting the sale of alcohol during a specified period on any railway vehicle that is at a station or stations in the petty sessional area of the court, or on any railway vehicle that is travelling between such stations, one of which must be in that petty sessional area[4]. It is an offence to knowingly sell, attempt to sell or allow the sale of alcohol in contravention of such an order[5].

---

[1] "Sale by retail" is defined in the LA 2003, s 192.
[2] "Vehicle" is defined in the LA 2003, s 193 as "a vehicle intended or adapted for use on roads".
[3] LA 2003, s 156(1). The offence carries a maximum penalty of three months' imprisonment and/or a £20,000 fine. A due diligence defence is available: LA 2003, s 156(3).
[4] LA 2003, s 157(1)–(3). The order must be served by the police officer on the train operator(s) affected by the order. It would seem that this power is designed to compliment the power in the LA 2003, s 160 for magistrates to order the closure of premises in an area of ongoing or expected disorder: see para 7.7639, ante.
[5] LA 2003, s 157(5). The offence carries a maximum penalty of three months' imprisonment and/or a £20,000 fine: LA 2003, s 157(6).

7.7652   *Offences – false statements*   It is an offence for a person to knowingly or recklessly make a false statement[1] in or in connection with any of numerous applications under the Act[2].

---

[1] A person is treated as making a false statement if he produces, furnishes, signs or otherwise makes use of a document that contains a false statement: LA 2003, s 158(2).

² LA 2003, s 158(1). The offence carries a maximum of a level 5 fine on the standard scale.

Licensing Act 2003[1]
(2003 c 17)
PART 1[2]
LICENSABLE ACTIVITIES

7.7653   **1.**   **Licensable activities and qualifying club activities**   (1)   For the purposes of this Act the following are licensable activities[3]—

(a)   the sale by retail[4] of alcohol[5],

(b)   the supply of alcohol by or on behalf of a club to, or to the order of, a member of the club,

(c)   the provision of regulated entertainment, and

(d)   the provision of late night refreshment.

(2)   For those purposes the following licensable activities are also qualifying club activities—

(a)   the supply of alcohol by or on behalf of a club to, or to the order of, a member of the club,

(b)   the sale by retail of alcohol by or on behalf of a club to a guest of a member of the club for consumption on the premises where the sale takes place, and

(c)   the provision of regulated entertainment where that provision is by or on behalf of a club for members of the club or members of the club and their guests.

(3)   In this Act references to the supply of alcohol by or on behalf of a club to, or to the order of, a member of the club do not include a reference to any supply which is a sale by retail of alcohol.

(4)   Schedule 1 makes provision about what constitutes the provision of regulated entertainment for the purposes of this Act.

(5)   Schedule 2 makes provision about what constitutes the provision of late night refreshment for those purposes (including provision that certain activities carried on in relation to certain clubs or hotels etc, or certain employees, do not constitute provision of late night refreshment and are, accordingly, not licensable activities).

(6)   For the purposes of this Act premises are "used" for a licensable activity if that activity is carried on or from the premises.

(7)   This section is subject to sections 173 to 175 (which exclude activities from the definition of licensable activity in certain circumstances).

[Licensing Act 2003, s 1.]

---

¹ This Act is to be brought into force in accordance with orders made under s 201. At the date of going to press the following commencement orders have been made:(Commencement) Order 2003, SI 2003/1911, (Commencement No 2) Order 2003, SI 2003/2100; (Commencement No 3) Order 2003, SI 2003/3222; (Commencement No 4) Order 2004, SI 2004/1738; (Commencement No 5) Order 2004, SI 2004/2360; (Commencement No 6) Order 2005, SI 2005/2090; and (Commencement No 7 and Transitional Provisions) Order 2005, SI 2005/3056.

² Part 1 comprises ss 1–2 and Schs 1 and 2.

³ For activities in certain locations which are not licensable, see s 173, post and for exemptions for raffles and tombola, etc., see s 175, post.

⁴ For meaning of "sale by retail", see s 192, post.

⁵ For meaning of "alcohol", see s 191, post.

7.7654   **2.**   **Authorisation for licensable activities and qualifying club activities**   (1)   A licensable activity may be carried on—

(a)   under and in accordance with a premises licence (see Part 3), or

(b)   in circumstances where the activity is a permitted temporary activity by virtue of Part 5

(2)   A qualifying club activity may be carried on under and in accordance with a club premises certificate (see Part 4).

(3)   Nothing in this Act prevents two or more authorisations having effect concurrently in respect of the whole or a part of the same premises or in respect of the same person.

(4)   For the purposes of subsection (3) "authorisation" means—

(a)   a premises licence;

(b)   a club premises certificate;

(c)   a temporary event notice.*

[Licensing Act 2003, s 2.]

---

* **Amended by the Deregulation Act 2015, s 67 from a date to be appointed.**

PART 2[1]
LICENSING AUTHORITIES

The authorities

7.7655   **3.**   **Licensing authorities**   (1)   In this Act "licensing authority" means—

(a)   the council of a district in England,

(b)   the council of a county in England in which there are no district councils,

(c)   the council of a county or county borough in Wales,

(d)   the council of a London borough,

(e)   the Common Council of the City of London,

(f)   the Sub-Treasurer of the Inner Temple,

(g)   the Under-Treasurer of the Middle Temple, or

(h)   the Council of the Isles of Scilly.

(2)   For the purposes of this Act, a licensing authority's area is the area for which the authority acts.

[Licensing Act 2003, s 3.]

---

[1] Part 2 comprises ss 3–10 and Sch 3.

Functions of licensing authorities etc

7.7656   4.   General duties of licensing authorities   (1)   A licensing authority must carry out its functions under this Act ("licensing functions") with a view to promoting the licensing objectives.

(2)   The licensing objectives are—

(a)   the prevention of crime and disorder[1];

(b)   public safety;

(c)   the prevention of public nuisance; and

(d)   the protection of children from harm.

(3)   In carrying out its licensing functions, a licensing authority must also have regard to—

(a)   its licensing statement published under section 5, and

(b)   any guidance issued by the Secretary of State under section 182[2].

[Licensing Act 2003, s 4.]

---

[1] The council (or magistrates' court on appeal) may take into account issues relating to crime and disorder away from the proposed premises and beyond the direct control of the licensee: *Brooke Leisure Ltd v Luminar Leisure Ltd* [2008] EWHC 1002 (Admin), 172 JP 345.

The terms "crime" and "disorder" are to be regarded disjunctively; thus, evidence of smoking in licensed premises, which is an offence under s 8 of the Health Act 2006, is relevant to the licensing objective of preventing crime even though it does not involve "disorder" and even though the offence did not exist when the Licensing Act 2003 was passed, because the words of a statute can apply to future events: *Blackpool Council v Howitt (Secretary of State for the Culture Media and Sport Intervening)* [2008] EWHC 3300 (Admin), 173 JP 101.

[2] The guidance is not to be construed as if it were a statute: *Blackpool Council v Howitt (Secretary of State for the Culture, Media and Sport Intervening)*, supra.

7.7657   5.   Statement of licensing policy   *Every licensing authority, in accordance with any regulations published, is required to make in consultation with interested parties, publish and keep under review a Statement of licensing policy in respect of each 5 year period[1].*

---

[1] The Licensing Act 2003 (Licensing statement period) Order 2004, SI 2004/2362 made under s 5(2) appoints 7 January 2005 as the day the first period of three years begins.

7.7658   5A.   Cumulative impact assessments   *A licensing authority may publish a document ("a cumulative impact assessment") stating that the licensing authority considers that the number of relevant authorisations in respect of premises in one or more parts of its area described in the assessment is such that it is likely that it would be inconsistent with the authority's duty under s 4(1) to grant any further relevant authorisations in respect of premises in that part or those parts.*

7.7659   6, 7.   *Licensing authority must establish a licensing committee; certain functions may be delegated and exercised at various levels of the authority.*

7.7660   8.   Requirement to keep a register   *Licensing authority must keep a register containing specified information and such other information as may be prescribed by the Secretary of State[1].*

---

[1] The Licensing Act 2003 (Licensing Authority's Register) (Other Information) Regulations 2005, SI 2005/43 have been made.

Licensing committees

7.7661   9.   *Power of licensing committee to establish sub-committees and to regulate its own procedure. Power of Secretary of State to make Regulations regarding the proceedings of licensing committees and sub-committees. The Licensing Act 2003 (Hearings) Regulations 2005, SI 2005/44 amended by SI 2005/78, SI 2007/2502 and SI 2014/2341 and the Gambling Act 2005 (Proceedings of Licensing Committees and Sub-committees) (Premises Licences and Provisional Statements) (England and Wales) Regulations 2007, SI 2007/173 amended by SI 2010/2440 have been made.*

PART 3[1]

PREMISES LICENCES

Introductory

7.7662   11.   Premises licence   In this Act "premises licence" means a licence granted under this Part, in respect of any premises, which authorises the premises[2] to be used for one or more licensable activities.

[Licensing Act 2003, s 11.]

---

[1] Part 3 comprises ss 11–59.
[2] For meaning of "premises", see s 193, post.

7.7663   12.   The relevant licensing authority   *Determination of relevant licensing authority for a premises is dependent upon the location of the whole, or greater part of the premises.*

7.7664   13.   Authorised persons and responsible authorities   (1)   In this Part in relation to any premises each of the following expressions has the meaning given to it by this section—
   "authorised person",
   "responsible authority".
   (2)   "Authorised person" means any of the following—
   (a)   an officer of a licensing authority in whose area the premises are situated who is authorised by that authority for the purposes of this Act,
   (b)   an inspector appointed by the fire and rescue authority for the area in which the premises are situated,
   (c)   an inspector appointed under section 19 of the Health and Safety at Work etc Act 1974 (c 37),
   (d)   an officer of a local authority, in whose area the premises are situated, who is authorised by that authority for the purposes of exercising one or more of its statutory functions in relation to minimising or preventing the risk of pollution of the environment or of harm to human health,
   (e)   in relation to a vessel, an inspector, or a surveyor of ships, appointed under section 256 of the Merchant Shipping Act 1995 (c 21),
   (f)   a person prescribed for the purposes of this subsection.
   (3)   *Repealed.*
   (4)   "Responsible authority" means any of the following—
   (za)   the relevant licensing authority and any other licensing authority in whose area part of the premises is situated,
   (a)   the chief officer of police for any police area in which the premises are situated,
   (b)   the fire and rescue authority for any area in which the premises are situated,
   (ba)   the Primary Care Trust or Local Health Board for any area in which the premises are situated,
   (c)   the enforcing authority within the meaning given by section 18 of the Health and Safety at Work etc Act 1974 for any area in which the premises are situated,
   (d)   the local planning authority within the meaning given by the Town and Country Planning Act 1990 (c 8) for any area in which the premises are situated,
   (e)   the local authority by which statutory functions are exercisable in any area in which the premises are situated in relation to minimising or preventing the risk of pollution of the environment or of harm to human health,
   (f)   a body which—
      (i)   represents those who, in relation to any such area, are responsible for, or interested in, matters relating to the protection of children from harm, and
      (ii)   is recognised by the licensing authority for that area for the purposes of this section as being competent to advise it on such matters,
   (g)   *repealed*
   (h)   in relation to a vessel—
      (i)   a navigation authority (within the meaning of section 221(1) of the Water Resources Act 1991 (c 57) having functions in relation to the waters where the vessel is usually moored or berthed or any waters where it is, or is proposed to be, navigated at a time when it is used for licensable activities,
      (ii)   the Environment Agency,
      (iii)   the British Waterways Board, or
      (iv)   the Secretary of State,
   (ha)   where the premises (not being a vessel) are being, or are proposed to be, used for a licensable activity within section 1(1)(a) or (d), the Secretary of State,
   (i)   a person prescribed[1] for the purposes of this subsection.
   (5)   For the purposes of this section, "statutory function" means a function conferred by or under any enactment.
   [Licensing Act 2003, s 13 as amended by the Fire and Rescue Services Act 2004, Sch 1, SI 2005/1541, the Policing and Crime Act 2009, s 33, the Police Reform and Social Responsibility Act 2011, ss 103–105 and the Immigration Act 2016, Sch 4.]

---

[1]   See the Licensing Act 2003 (Premises Licences and Club Premises Certificates) Regulations 2005, SI 2005/42.

7.7665   14.   Meaning of "supply of alcohol"   For the purposes of this Part the "supply of alcohol" means—
   (a)   the sale by retail of alcohol, or
   (b)   the supply of alcohol by or on behalf of a club to, or to the order of, a member of the club.

[Licensing Act 2003, s 14.]

7.7666   15.   Meaning of "designated premises supervisor"   (1)   In this Act references to the "designated premises supervisor", in relation to a premises licence, are to the individual for the time being specified in that licence as the premises supervisor.

(2)   Nothing in this Act prevents an individual who holds a premises licence from also being specified in the licence as the premises supervisor.

[Licensing Act 2003, s 15.]

Grant of premises licence

7.7667   16.   Applicant for premises licence   _Prescribes persons or bodies who can apply for a premises licence. Residual power to Secretary of State to prescribe persons of other descriptions who can also apply (as amended by the Immigration Act 2016, Sch 4)_

7.7668   17.   Application for premises licence   _Application to be in the prescribed form and accompanied by an Operating Schedule; application to be advertised in accordance with regulations._ [1]

---

[1]   See the Licensing Act 2003 (Premises Licences and Club Premises Certificates) Regulations 2005, SI 2005/42 (for amending instruments, see note to s 13, ante) and the Welsh Language (Gambling and Licensing Forms) Regulations 2010, SI 2010/2440 have been made. Where it is alleged that there has been non-compliance with the procedural requirements in the LA 2003 or the 2005 Regulations, the general modern approach to the consequences of such non-compliance is a purposive one as in _R v Immigration Appeal Tribunal, ex p Jeyeanthan; Ravichandran v Secretary of State for the Home Department_ [1999] 3 All ER 231, [2000] 1 WLR 354, [1999] All ER (D) 519, CA. This requires analysis of the statutory intent of the legislation taken as a whole. The questions to be posed and answered are: (1) whether there has been substantial compliance with the requirements, although not strict compliance; (2) whether non-compliance is capable of being waived, and if so, whether it is; (3) if non-compliance is not capable of being waived or is not been waived what are the consequences of non-compliance: _R (on the application of Akin) v Stratford Magistrates Court_ [2014] EWHC 4633 (Admin), [2015] 1 WLR 4829 (The advertised notice set out the fact that there was to be a review by the licensing sub-committee; the grounds of review could be read and the period for which representations could be made, the licensing objectives on which representations had to be based, and the penal notice. Review not invalidated where the advertised notice stated the grounds could be read and the court held that there was substantial compliance, that the failure to comply strictly had not and could not be waived, but that the failure did not invalidate the sub-committee's decision because the purpose of the legislation was to give local people an opportunity to know what is going on and to be heard if they wished.)

7.7669   18.   Determination of application for premises licence[1]   (1)   This section applies where the relevant licensing authority—

(_a_)   receives an application for a premises licence made in accordance with section 17, and

(_b_)   is satisfied that the applicant has complied with any requirement imposed on him under subsection (5) of that section.

(2)   Subject to subsection (3), the authority must grant the licence in accordance with the application subject only to—

(_a_)   such conditions[2] as are consistent with the operating schedule accompanying the application, and

(_b_)   any conditions which must under section 19, 20 or 21 be included in the licence.

(3)   Where relevant representations are made, the authority must—

(_a_)   hold a hearing to consider them, unless the authority, the applicant and each person who has made such representations agree that a hearing is unnecessary, and

(_b_)   having regard to the representations, take such of the steps mentioned in subsection (4) (if any) as it considers appropriate for the promotion of the licensing objectives.

(4)   The steps are—

(_a_)   to grant the licence subject to—

(i)   the conditions mentioned in subsection (2)(_a_) modified to such extent as the authority considers appropriate for the promotion of the licensing objectives, and

(ii)   any condition which must under section 19, 20 or 21 be included in the licence;

(_b_)   to exclude from the scope of the licence any of the licensable activities to which the application relates;

(_c_)   to refuse to specify a person in the licence as the premises supervisor;

(_d_)   to reject the application.

(5)   For the purposes of subsection (4)(_a_)(i) the conditions mentioned in subsection (2)(_a_) are modified if any of them is altered or omitted or any new condition is added.

(6)   For the purposes of this section, "relevant representations" means representations which—

(_a_)   are about the likely effect of the grant of the premises licence on the promotion of the licensing objectives,

(_b_)   meet the requirements of subsection (7),

(_c_)   if they relate to the identity of the person named in the application as the proposed premises supervisor, meet the requirements of subsection (9), and

(_d_)   are not excluded representations by virtue of section 32 (restriction on making representations following issue of provisional statement).

(7)   The requirements of this subsection are—

(_a_)   that the representations were made by a responsible authority or other person within the period prescribed under section 17(5)(_c_),

(_b_)   that they have not been withdrawn, and

(c)   in the case of representations made by a person who is not a responsible authority, that they are not, in the opinion of the relevant licensing authority, frivolous or vexatious.

(8)   Where the authority determines for the purposes of subsection (7)(c) that any representations are frivolous or vexatious, it must notify the person who made them of the reasons for its determination.

(9)   The requirements of this subsection are that the representations—

(a)   were made by a chief officer of police for a police area in which the premises are situated, and

(b)   include a statement that, due to the exceptional circumstances of the case, he is satisfied that the designation of the person concerned as the premises supervisor under the premises licence would undermine the crime prevention objective.

(10) In discharging its duty under subsection (2) or (3)(b), a licensing authority may grant a licence under this section subject to different conditions in respect of—

(a)   different parts of the premises concerned;

(b)   different licensable activities.

[Licensing Act 2003, s 18 as amended by the Police Reform and Social Responsibility Act 2011, ss 105, 109.]

---

[1] For appeal to a magistrates' court against a decision of a licensing authority under this section, see s 181 and Sch 5, post.

[2] Where a court is considering imposing conditions it will almost always be good practice for the conditions under consideration to be outlined for debate by the parties. Errors of drafting can then be identified, as can improvements and consideration of the underlying propositions behind the conditions themselves: *R (Westminster City Council) v Metropolitan Stipendiary Magistrate* [2008] EWHC 1202 (Admin), 172 JP 462.

7.7670   19.   Mandatory conditions where licence authorises supply of alcohol   (1)   Where a premises licence authorises the supply of alcohol, the licence must include the following conditions.

(2)   The first condition is that no supply of alcohol may be made under the premises licence—

(a)   at a time when there is no designated premises supervisor in respect of the premises licence, or

(b)   at a time when the designated premises supervisor does not hold a personal licence or his personal licence is suspended.

(3)   The second condition is that every supply of alcohol under the premises licence must be made or authorised by a person who holds a personal licence.

(4)   The other conditions are any conditions specified in an order under section 19A and applicable to the premises licence.

[Licensing Act 2003, s 19 as amended by the Policing and Crime Act 2009, Sch 4.]

7.7671   19A.   Power of Secretary of State to impose section 19(4) mandatory conditions

(1)   The Secretary of State may by order[1] specify conditions relating to the supply of alcohol and applicable to all relevant premises licences or relevant premises licences of a particular description if the Secretary of State considers it appropriate to do so for the promotion of the licensing objectives.

(2)   The number of conditions in force by virtue of subsection (1) in relation to all relevant premises licences and the number of conditions in force by virtue of that subsection in relation to relevant premises licences of particular descriptions must not (when added together) exceed at any time nine.

(3)   An order under subsection (1) may

(a)   relate to existing or future relevant premises licences,

(b)   specify conditions which involve, or consist of, the exercise of a discretion by any person.

(4)   Any conditions specified by an order under subsection (1) in relation to existing relevant premises licences are to be treated as—

(a)   included in those licences from the coming into force of the order, and

(b)   overriding any conditions already included in those licences ("the existing conditions") so far as they are—

(i)   identical to the existing conditions, or

(ii)   inconsistent with, and more onerous than, the existing conditions.

(5)   Any conditions included, or treated as included, in relevant premises licences by virtue of section 19(4) and this section cease to have effect so far as they cease to be specified under this section in relation to those licences.

(6)   Any conditions treated as mentioned in subsection (4)(b) cease to be so treated so far as they cease to be specified under this section in relation to the relevant premises licences concerned.

(7)   So far as conditions cease to be treated as mentioned in subsection (4)(b), the existing conditions revive.

(8)   Subsections (5) to (7) are subject to any alternative transitional or saving provision made by the order revoking the specification.

(9)   In this section—

"existing relevant premises licence", in relation to an order, means a relevant premises licence granted before the coming into force of the order and in effect, or capable of having effect, on its coming into force, "future relevant premises licence", in relation to an order, means a relevant premises licence granted on or after the coming into force of the order,

"relevant premises licence" means a premises licence authorising the supply of alcohol.

[Licensing Act 2003, s 19A as inserted by the Policing and Crime Act 2009, Sch 4.]

---

[1] The Licensing Act 2003 (Mandatory Licensing Conditions) Orders 2010, SI 2010/860 and 2014/1252 have been made, in this title, post.

7.7672 20. Mandatory condition: exhibition of films (1) Where a premises licence authorises the exhibition of films, the licence must include a condition requiring the admission of children to the exhibition of any film to be restricted in accordance with this section.

(2) Where the film classification body is specified in the licence, unless subsection (3)(b) applies, admission of children must be restricted in accordance with any recommendation made by that body.

(3) Where—
   (a) the film classification body is not specified in the licence, or
   (b) the relevant licensing authority has notified the holder of the licence that this subsection applies to the film in question,

admission of children must be restricted in accordance with any recommendation made by that licensing authority.

(4) In this section—
"children" means persons aged under 18; and
"film classification body" means the person or persons designated as the authority under section 4 of the Video Recordings Act 1984 (c 39) (authority to determine suitability of video works for classification).

[Licensing Act 2003, s 20.]

7.7673 21. Mandatory condition: door supervision (1) Where a premises licence includes a condition that at specified times one or more individuals must be at the premises to carry out a security activity, the licence must include a condition that each such individual must—
   (a) be authorised to carry out that activity by a licence granted under the Private Security Industry Act 2001; or
   (b) be entitled to carry out that activity by virtue of section 4 of that Act.

(2) But nothing in subsection (1) requires such a condition to be imposed—
   (a) in respect of premises within paragraph 8(3)(a) of Schedule 2 to the Private Security Industry Act 2001 (c 12)[1] (premises with premises licences authorising plays or films), or
   (b) in respect of premises in relation to—
      (i) any occasion mentioned in paragraph 8(3)(b) or (c) of that Schedule (premises being used exclusively by club with club premises certificate, under a temporary event notice authorising plays or films or under a gaming licence), or
      (ii) any occasion within paragraph 8(3)(d) of that Schedule (occasions prescribed by regulations under that Act).

(3) For the purposes of this section—
   (a) "security activity" means an activity to which paragraph 2(1)(a) of that Schedule applies and which is licensable conduct for the purposes of that Act (see section 3(2) of that Act), and
   (b) paragraph 8(5) of that Schedule (interpretation of references to an occasion) applies as it applies in relation to paragraph 8 of that Schedule.

[Licensing Act 2003, s 21 as amended by the Violent Crime Reduction Act 2006, s 25.]

---

[1] In this PART, title, INDUSTRY AND COMMERCE, post.

7.7674 22. Prohibited conditions: plays (1) In relation to a premises licence which authorises the performance of plays, no condition may be attached to the licence as to the nature of the plays which may be performed, or the manner of performing plays, under the licence.

(2) But subsection (1) does not prevent a licensing authority imposing, in accordance with section 18(2)(a) or (3)(b), 35(3)(b) or 52(3), any condition which it considers appropriate on the grounds of public safety.

[Licensing Act 2003, s 22 as amended by the Police Reform and Social Responsibility Act 2011, s 109.]

7.7675 23. Grant or rejection of application (1) Where an application is granted under section 18, the relevant licensing authority must forthwith—
   (a) give a notice to that effect to—
      (i) the applicant,
      (ii) any person who made relevant representations in respect of the application, and
      (iii) the chief officer of police for the police area (or each police area) in which the premises are situated, and
   (b) issue the applicant with the licence and a summary of it.

(2) Where relevant representations were made in respect of the application, the notice under subsection (1)(a) must state the authority's reasons for its decision as to the steps (if any) to take

under section 18(3)(*b*).

(3)   Where an application is rejected under section 18, the relevant licensing authority must forthwith give a notice to that effect, stating its reasons for the decision, to—

(*a*)   the applicant,

(*b*)   any person who made relevant representations in respect of the application, and

(*c*)   the chief officer of police for the police area (or each police area) in which the premises are situated.

(4)   In this section "relevant representations" has the meaning given in section 18(6).

[Licensing Act 2003, s 23.]

7.7676   24.   Form of licence and summary   *Licence and summary of it to be in prescribed form[1].*

---

[1] See the Licensing Act 2003 (Premises Licences and Club Premises Certificates) Regulations 2005, SI 2005/42 (for amending instruments, see note to s 13, ante) and the Welsh Language (Gambling and Licensing Forms) Regulations 2010, SI 2010/2440 have been made.

7.7677   25.   Theft, loss, etc of premises licence or summary   *Power to apply for duplicate licence or summary on payment of fee.*

7.7678   25A.   Grant of premises licence: supply of alcohol from community premises

(1)   Where a management committee of community premises makes an application under section 17 for a premises licence authorising the supply of alcohol, the application may include an application for the alternative licence condition to be included in the licence instead of the conditions in section 19(2) and (3).

(2)   In this section "the alternative licence condition" is the condition that every supply of alcohol under the premises licence must be made or authorised by the management committee.

(3)   In a case where an application under section 17 includes an application under subsection (1), sections 17 to 19 are modified as follows.

(4)   Section 17 has effect as if subsections (3)(*c*) and (4)(*e*) were omitted.

(5)   Section 18 has effect as if—

(*a*)   subsection (4)(*c*) were omitted;

(*b*)   in subsection (6)(*c*), the reference to the identity of the person named in the application as the proposed premises supervisor were to the inclusion of the alternative licence condition;

(*c*)   in subsection (9)(*b*), the reference to the designation of the person concerned as the premises supervisor under the premises licence were to the inclusion of the alternative licence condition.

(6)   Section 19 has effect as if at the end there were inserted—

"(5)   But where—

(*a*)   the relevant licensing authority is satisfied that the arrangements for the management of the premises by the applicant are sufficient to ensure adequate supervision of the supply of alcohol on the premises, and

(*b*)   if any representations are made pursuant to section 18(6)(*c*), the authority does not consider the inclusion of the conditions in subsections (2) and (3) to be appropriate to promote the crime prevention objective,

the licence must not include the conditions in subsections (2) and (3) but must include the alternative licence condition referred to in section 25A(2) instead."

[Licensing Act 2003, s 25A as inserted by SI 2009/1724 and amended by the Policing and Crime Act 2009, Sch 7 and the Police Reform and Social Responsibility Act 2011, s 109.]

Duration of licence

7.7679   26.   Period of validity of premises licence   *Premises licence to have effect until revoked, lapses, is surrendered, or is for a limited period and comes to an end. Licence of no effect if suspended following a review under s 52.*

7.7680   27.   Death, incapacity, insolvency etc of licence holder   (1)   A premises licence lapses if the holder of the licence—

(*a*)   dies,

(*b*)   becomes a person who lacks capacity (within the meaning of the Mental Capacity Act 2005) to hold the licence,

(*c*)   becomes insolvent,

(*d*)   is dissolved, or

(*e*)   if it is a club, ceases to be a recognised club.

(1A)   A premises licence that authorises premises to be used for a licensable activity within section 1(1)(a) or (d) also lapses if the holder of the licence ceases to be entitled to work in the United Kingdom at a time when the holder of the licence is resident in the United Kingdom (or becomes so resident without being entitled to work in the United Kingdom).

(2)   This section is subject to sections 47 and 50 (which make provision for the reinstatement of the licence in certain circumstances).

(3)   For the purposes of this section, an individual becomes insolvent on—

(*a*)   the approval of a voluntary arrangement proposed by him,

(b)   being adjudged bankrupt or having his estate sequestrated, or

(c)   entering into a trust deed for his creditors.

(4)   For the purposes of this section, a company becomes insolvent on—

(a)   the approval of a voluntary arrangement proposed by its directors,

(b)   the appointment of an administrator in respect of the company,

(c)   the appointment of an administrative receiver in respect of the company, or

(d)   going into liquidation.

(5)   An expression used in this section and in the Insolvency Act 1986 (c 45) has the same meaning in this section as in that Act.

[Licensing Act 2003, s 27 as amended by the Mental Capacity Act 2005, Sch 6, the Deregulation Act 2015, Sch 6 and the Immigration Act 2016, Sch 4.]

7.7681   28.   Surrender of premises licence   *Premises licence holder may surrender licence by giving notice to licensing authority. Licence lapses on receipt of notice.*

Provisional statement

7.7682   29, 30.   *Application for provisional statement to be in the prescribed form and accompanied by a Schedule of Works[1].*

---

[1] The Licensing Act 2003 (Premises Licences and Club Premises Certificates) Regulations 2005, SI 2005/42 (for amending instruments, see note to s 13, ante) and the Welsh Language (Gambling and Licensing Forms) Regulations 2010, SI 2010/2440 have been made. Application to be advertised in accordance with Regulations.

7.7683   31.   Determination of application for provisional statement[1]   (1) This section applies where the relevant licensing authority—

(a)   receives a provisional statement application, and

(b)   is satisfied that the applicant has complied with any requirement imposed on him by virtue of section 30.

(2)   Where no relevant representations are made, the authority must issue the applicant with a statement to that effect.

(3)   Where relevant representations are made, the authority must—

(a)   hold a hearing to consider them, unless the authority, the applicant and each person who has made such representations agree that a hearing is unnecessary,

(b)   determine whether, on the basis of those representations and the provisional statement application, it would consider it appropriate to take any steps under section 18(3)(b) if, on the work being satisfactorily completed, it had to decide whether to grant a premises licence in the form described in the provisional statement application, and

(c)   issue the applicant with a statement which—

(i)   gives details of that determination, and

(ii)   states the authority's reasons for its decision as to the steps (if any) that it would be appropriate to take under section 18(3)(b).

(4)   The licensing authority must give a copy of the provisional statement to—

(a)   each person who made relevant representations, and

(b)   the chief officer of police for each police area in which the premises are situated.

(5)   In this section "relevant representations" means representations—

(a)   which are about the likely effect on the licensing objectives of the grant of a premises licence in the form described in the provisional statement application, if the work at the premises was satisfactorily completed, and

(b)   which meet the requirements of subsection (6).

(6)   The requirements are—

(a)   that the representations are made by a responsible authority or other person within the period prescribed under section 17(5)(c) by virtue of section 30,

(b)   that the representations have not been withdrawn, and

(c)   in the case of representations made by a person who is not a responsible authority, that they are not, in the opinion of the relevant licensing authority, frivolous or vexatious.

(7)   Where the authority determines for the purposes of subsection (6)(c) that any representations are frivolous or vexatious, it must notify the person who made them of the reasons for its determination.

(8)   In this section "provisional statement application" means an application made in accordance with section 29.

[Licensing Act 2003, s 31 as amended by the Police Reform and Social Responsibility Act 2011, ss 105, 109.]

---

[1] For appeal to a magistrates' court against a decision of a licensing authority under this section, see s 181 and Sch 5, post.

7.7684   32.   Restriction on representations following provisional statement   (1) This section applies where a provisional statement has been issued in respect of any premises ("the relevant premises") and a person subsequently applies for a premises licence in respect of—

(a)   the relevant premises or a part of them, or

(b)   premises that are substantially the same as the relevant premises or a part of them.

(2)   Where—

(a)   the application for the premises licence is an application for a licence in the same form as the licence described in the application for the provisional statement, and

(b)   the work described in the schedule of works accompanying the application for that statement has been satisfactorily completed,

representations made by a person ("the relevant person") in respect of the application for the premises licence are excluded representations for the purposes of section 18(6)(d) if subsection (3) applies.

(3)   This subsection applies if—

(a)   given the information provided in the application for the provisional statement, the relevant person could have made the same, or substantially the same, representations about that application but failed to do so, without reasonable excuse, and

(b)   there has been no material change in circumstances relating either to the relevant premises or to the area in the vicinity of those premises since the provisional statement was made.

[Licensing Act 2003, s 32.]

Duty to notify certain changes

7.7685   33.   Notification of change of name or address   (1)   The holder of a premises licence must, as soon as is reasonably practicable, notify the relevant licensing authority of any change in—

(a)   his name or address,

(b)   unless the designated premises supervisor has already notified the authority under subsection (4), the name or address of that supervisor.

(2)   Subsection (1) is subject to regulations under section 55(1) (fee to accompany application).

(3)   A notice under subsection (1) must also be accompanied by the premises licence (or the appropriate part of the licence) or, if that is not practicable, by a statement of the reasons for the failure to produce the licence (or part).

(4)   Where the designated premises supervisor under a premises licence is not the holder of the licence, he may notify the relevant licensing authority under this subsection of any change in his name or address.

(5)   Where the designated premises supervisor gives a notice under subsection (4), he must, as soon as is reasonably practicable, give the holder of the premises licence a copy of that notice.

(6)   A person commits an offence if he fails, without reasonable excuse, to comply with this section.

(7)   A person guilty of an offence under subsection (6) is liable on summary conviction to a fine not exceeding level 2 on the standard scale.

[Licensing Act 2003, s 33.]

Variation of licences

7.7686   34.   Application to vary premises licence   *Application for variation of premises licence to be in the prescribed form and advertised in accordance with regulations[1].*

---

[1] See the Licensing Act 2003 (Premises Licences and Club Premises Certificates) Regulations 2005, SI 2005/42 (for amending instruments, see note to s 13, ante) and the Welsh Language (Gambling and Licensing Forms) Regulations 2010, SI 2010/2440.

7.7687   35.   Determination of application under section 34[1]   (1)   This section applies where the relevant licensing authority—

(a)   receives an application, made in accordance with section 34, to vary a premises licence, and

(b)   is satisfied that the applicant has complied with any requirement imposed on him by virtue of subsection (5) of that section.

(2)   Subject to subsection (3) and section 36(6), the authority must grant the application.

(3)   Where relevant representations are made, the authority must—

(a)   hold a hearing to consider them, unless the authority, the applicant and each person who has made such representations agree that a hearing is unnecessary, and

(b)   having regard to the representations, take such of the steps mentioned in subsection (4) (if any) as it considers appropriate for the promotion of the licensing objectives.

(4)   The steps are—

(a)   to modify the conditions of the licence;

(b)   to reject the whole or part of the application;

and for this purpose the conditions of the licence are modified if any of them is altered or omitted or any new condition is added.

(5)   In this section "relevant representations" means representations which—

(a)   are about the likely effect of the grant of the application on the promotion of the licensing objectives, and

(b)   meet the requirements of subsection (6).

(6)   The requirements are—

(a)   that the representations are made by a responsible authority or other person within the period prescribed under section 17(5)(c) by virtue of section 34(5),

(b)   that they have not been withdrawn, and

    (c)   in the case of representations made by a person who is not a responsible authority, that
           they are not, in the opinion of the relevant licensing authority, frivolous or vexatious.
    (7)   Subsections (2) and (3) are subject to sections 19 to 21 (which require certain conditions to
be included in premises licences).[2]

[Licensing Act 2003, s 35 as amended by the Policing and Crime Act 2009, Sch 7 and the Police Reform and Social
Responsibility Act 2011, ss 105, 109.]

---

   [1] For appeal to a magistrates' court against a decision of a licensing authority under this section, see s 181 and Sch 5,
post.
   [2] There is no mechanism for amending an application. If representations are made, that triggers the decision-making
process of the licensing authority. The authority exercises an administrative function within restrictions imposed by the
legislation: an application to vary never triggers a general review of the licence. Where a licensee wishes to modify his
application in the light of representations received, whilst not amounting to a formal amendment of the application, the
authority is bound to take account of the views of the licensee in exercising its discretion and it is not required to consult
local residents and other interested parties in the form of re-advertisement: *Taylor v Manchester City Council* [2012]
EWHC 3467 (Admin), [2013] 2 All ER 490, 177 JP 1.

7.7688   36. Supplementary provision about determinations under section 35   (1)   Where
an application (or any part of an application) is granted under section 35, the relevant licensing
authority must forthwith give a notice to that effect to—
    (a)   the applicant,
    (b)   any person who made relevant representations in respect of the application, and
    (c)   the chief officer of police for the police area (or each police area) in which the premises
           are situated.
    (2)   Where relevant representations were made in respect of the application, the notice under
subsection (1) must state the authority's reasons for its decision as to the steps (if any) to take under
section 35(3)(b).
    (3)   The notice under subsection (1) must specify the time when the variation in question takes
effect.
That time is the time specified in the application or, if that time is before the applicant is given that
notice, such later time as the relevant licensing authority specifies in the notice.
    (4)   Where an application (or any part of an application) is rejected under section 35, the
relevant licensing authority must forthwith give a notice to that effect stating its reasons for rejecting
the application to—
    (a)   the applicant,
    (b)   any person who made relevant representations in respect of the application, and
    (c)   the chief officer of police for the police area (or each police area) in which the premises
           are situated.
    (5)   Where the relevant licensing authority determines for the purposes of section 35(6)(c) that
any representations are frivolous or vexatious, it must notify the person who made them of the
reasons for that determination.
    (6)   A licence may not be varied under section 35 so as—
    (a)   to extend the period for which the licence has effect, or
    (b)   to vary substantially the premises to which it relates.
    (7)   In discharging its duty under subsection (2) or (3)(b) of that section, a licensing authority
may vary a premises licence so that it has effect subject to different conditions in respect of—
    (a)   different parts of the premises concerned;
    (b)   different licensable activities.
    (8)   In this section "relevant representations" has the meaning given in section 35(5).
[Licensing Act 2003, s 36.]

7.7689   37. Application to vary licence to specify individual as premises supervisor
    (1)–(4B)   *Application for variation of premises licence to specify individual as premises supervisor to be
in the prescribed form and in accordance with regulations*[1].
    (5)   Where a chief officer of police notified under subsection (4) is satisfied that the exceptional
circumstances of the case are such that granting the application would undermine the crime
prevention objective, he must give the relevant licensing authority a notice stating the reasons why
he is so satisfied.
    (6)   The chief officer of police must give that notice within the period of 14 days beginning with
the day on which he is notified of the application under subsection (4).
[Licensing Act 2003, s 37 as amended by SI 2009/2999.]

---

   [1] See the Licensing Act 2003 (Premises Licences and Club Premises Certificates) Regulations 2005, SI 2005/42 (for
amending instruments, see note to s 13, ante) and the Welsh Language (Gambling and Licensing Forms) Regulations
2010, SI 2010/2440.

7.7690   38. Circumstances in which section 37 application given interim effect   *Section 37
application to have interim effect if requested.*

7.7691   39. Determination of section 37 application[1]   (1)   This section applies where an
application is made, in accordance with section 37, to vary a premises licence so as to specify a new
premises supervisor ("the proposed individual").
    (2)   Subject to subsection (3), the relevant licensing authority must grant the application.
    (3)   Where a notice is given under section 37(5) (and not withdrawn), the authority must—

(a)   hold a hearing to consider it, unless the authority, the applicant and the chief officer of police who gave the notice agree that a hearing is unnecessary, and

(b)   having regard to the notice, reject the application if it considers it appropriate for the promotion of the crime prevention objective to do so.

(4)   Where an application under section 37 is granted or rejected, the relevant licensing authority must give a notice to that effect to—

(a)   the applicant,

(b)   the proposed individual, and

(c)   the chief officer of police for the police area (or each police area) in which the premises are situated.

(5)   Where a chief officer of police gave a notice under subsection (5) of that section (and it was not withdrawn), the notice under subsection (4) of this section must state the authority's reasons for granting or rejecting the application.

(6)   Where the application is granted, the notice under subsection (4) must specify the time when the variation takes effect.

That time is the time specified in the application or, if that time is before the applicant is given that notice, such later time as the relevant licensing authority specifies in the notice.

[Licensing Act 2003, s 39 as amended by the Police Reform and Social Responsibility Act 2011, s 109.]

---

[1] For appeal to a magistrates' court against a decision of a licensing authority under this section, see s 181 and Sch 5, post.

7.7692 40. Duty of applicant following determination under section 39 (1) Where the holder of a premises licence is notified under section 39(4), he must forthwith—

(a)   if his application has been granted, notify the person (if any) who has been replaced as the designated premises supervisor of the variation, and

(b)   if his application has been rejected, give the designated premises supervisor (if any) notice to that effect.

(2)   A person commits an offence if he fails, without reasonable excuse, to comply with subsection (1).

(3)   A person guilty of an offence under subsection (2) is liable on summary conviction to a fine not exceeding level 3 on the standard scale.

[Licensing Act 2003, s 40.]

7.7693 41. Request to be removed as designated premises supervisor (1) Where an individual wishes to cease being the designated premises supervisor in respect of a premises licence, he may give the relevant licensing authority a notice to that effect.

(2)   Subsection (1) is subject to regulations under section 54 (form etc of notices etc).

(3)   Where the individual is the holder of the premises licence, the notice under subsection (1) must also be accompanied by the premises licence (or the appropriate part of the licence) or, if that is not practicable, by a statement of the reasons for the failure to provide the licence (or part).

(4)   In any other case, the individual must no later than 48 hours after giving the notice under subsection (1) give the holder of the premises licence—

(a)   a copy of that notice, and

(b)   a notice directing the holder to send to the relevant licensing authority within 14 days of receiving the notice

(i)   the premises licence (or the appropriate part of the licence), or

(ii)   if that is not practicable, a statement of the reasons for the failure to provide the licence (or part).

(5)   A person commits an offence if he fails, without reasonable excuse, to comply with a direction given to him under subsection (4)(b).

(6)   A person guilty of an offence under subsection (5) is liable on summary conviction to a fine not exceeding level 3 on the standard scale.

(7)   Where an individual—

(a)   gives the relevant licensing authority a notice in accordance with this section, and

(b)   satisfies the requirements of subsection (3) or (4),

he is to be treated for the purposes of this Act as if, from the relevant time, he were not the designated premises supervisor.

(8)   For this purpose "the relevant time" means—

(a)   the time the notice under subsection (1) is received by the relevant licensing authority, or

(b)   if later, the time specified in the notice.

[Licensing Act 2003, s 41.]

Variation of licences: minor variations

7.7694 41A. Application for minor variation of premises licence] (1) Subject to subsection (3), the holder of a premises licence may apply under this section (instead of under section 34) to the relevant licensing authority for variation of the licence.

(2)   Subsection (1) is subject to regulations under—

(a)   section 54 (form etc of applications etc);

(*b*)   section 55 (fees to accompany applications etc).

(3)   An application may not be made under this section to vary a premises licence so as to—

(*a*)   extend the period for which it has effect,

(*b*)   vary substantially the premises to which it relates,

(*c*)   specify an individual as the premises supervisor,

(*d*)   add the supply of alcohol as an activity authorised by the licence,

(*e*)   authorise—

(i)   the supply of alcohol at any time between 11pm and 7am, or

(ii)   an increase in the amount of time on any day during which alcohol may be sold by retail or supplied, or

(*f*)   include the alternative licence condition referred to in section 41D(3).

(4)   The duty to make regulations imposed on the Secretary of State by subsection (5)(*a*) of section 17 (advertisement etc of application) applies in relation to applications under this section as it applies in relation to applications under that section.

[Licensing Act 2003, s 41A as inserted by SI 2009/1772.]

7.7695   41B.   Determination of application under section 41A   (1)   This section applies where the relevant licensing authority receives an application made under section 41A.

(2)   In determining the application the authority must—

(*a*)   consult such of the responsible authorities as it considers appropriate, and

(*b*)   take into account any relevant representations—

(i)   made by those authorities, or

(ii)   made by any other person and received by the authority within ten working days beginning on the initial day.

(3)   If the authority considers that—

(*a*)   the variation proposed in the application could not have an adverse effect on the promotion of any of the licensing objectives, or

(*b*)   if more than one variation is proposed, none of them, whether considered separately or together could have such an effect,

it must grant the application.

(4)   In any other case the authority must reject the application.

(5)   A determination under this section must be made within the period of fifteen working days beginning on the initial day.

(6)   If at the expiry of the period referred to in subsection (5) the authority has not determined the application—

(*a*)   the application is rejected, and

(*b*)   the authority must forthwith return the fee that accompanied the application.

(7)   But nothing in subsection (6) prevents the authority, with the agreement of the applicant, from treating—

(*a*)   an application rejected by virtue of that subsection ("the first application") as a new application made under section 41A,

(*b*)   the prescribed fee that accompanied the first application as the prescribed fee accompanying a new application, or

(*c*)   both.

(8)   A new application of the kind referred to in subsection (7)(*a*) is to be treated as having been made on the date of the agreement referred to in that provision, or on such other date as is specified in the agreement.

(9)   Any fee owed to an applicant under subsection (6) may be recovered as a debt due to the applicant.

(10)   For the purposes of this section—

"initial day" in relation to an application means the first working day after the day on which the authority receives the application;

"relevant representations" in relation to an application means representations which are about the likely effect of the grant of the application on the promotion of the licensing objectives.

[Licensing Act 2003, s 41B as inserted by SI 2009/1772 and amended by the Police Reform and Social Responsibility Act 2011, s 105.]

7.7696   41C.   Supplementary provision about determinations under section 41B

(1)   Where an application is granted under section 41B, the relevant licensing authority must forthwith give a notice to that effect to the applicant.

(2)   The notice under subsection (1) must specify—

(*a*)   any variation of the premises licence which is to have effect as a result of the grant of the application, and

(*b*)   the time at which that variation takes effect.

(3)   The time referred to in subsection (2)(*b*) is the time specified in the application or, if that time is before the applicant is given the notice referred to in subsection (2), such later time as the authority specifies in the notice.

(4)   Where an application is rejected under section 41B, the relevant licensing authority must

forthwith give a notice to that effect to the applicant.

(5)   The notice under subsection (4) must include a statement by the authority of the reasons for its decision.

[Licensing Act 2003, s 41C as inserted by SI 2009/1772.]

7.7697   41D.   Variation of premises licence: supply of alcohol from community premises

(1)   Where a management committee which holds a premises licence in respect of community premises makes an application under section 34 for variation of the licence so as to authorise the supply of alcohol, the application may include an application for the alternative licence condition to be included in the licence instead of the conditions in section 19(2) and (3).

(2)   A management committee which holds a premises licence in respect of community premises which includes the conditions in section 19(2) and (3) may make an application under section 34 for (or which includes an application for) variation of the licence to include the alternative licence condition instead of those conditions.

(3)   In this section "the alternative licence condition" is the condition that every supply of alcohol under the premises licence must be made or authorised by the management committee.

(4)   In a case where an application under section 34 includes an application under subsection (1), or is made pursuant to subsection (2), section 19 (as it applies by virtue of section 35(7)) and section 35 are modified as follows.

(5)   Section 19 has effect as if at the end there were inserted—

"(5)   But where—

(a)   the relevant licensing authority is satisfied that the arrangements for the management of the premises by the applicant are sufficient to ensure adequate supervision of the supply of alcohol on the premises, and

(b)   if any representations are made pursuant to section 35(5)(aa), the authority does not consider the inclusion of the conditions in subsections (2) and (3) to be appropriate to promote the crime prevention objective,

the licence must not include the conditions in subsections (2) and (3) but must include the alternative licence condition referred to in section 41D(3) instead.".

(6)   Section 35 has effect as if—

(a)   after subsection (5)(a) there were inserted—

"(aa)   if they relate to the inclusion of the alternative licence condition referred to in section 41D(3)—

(i)   were made by the chief officer of police for a police area in which the premises are situated, and

(ii)   include a statement that, due to the exceptional circumstances of the case, he is satisfied that including the alternative licence condition instead of the conditions in section 19(2) and (3) would undermine the crime prevention objective, and",

and

(b)   subsection (6)(c) were omitted.

[Licensing Act 2003, s 41D as inserted by SI 2009/1724 and amended by the Policing and Crime Act 2009. Sch 7 and the Police Reform and Social Responsibility Act 2011, ss 105, 109.]

Transfer of premises licence

7.7698   42.   Application for transfer of premises licence   (1)–(4)   *Application for transfer of premises licence to be in prescribed form and in accordance with regulations*[1].

(5)   The relevant person must give notice of the application to the chief officer of police for the police area (or each police area) in which the premises are situated.

(5ZA)   Where the premises licence authorises premises to be used for a licensable activity within section 1(1)(a) or (d), the relevant person must also give notice of the application to the Secretary of State.

(5A)   In subsections (5) and (5ZA), "relevant person" means—

(a)   the relevant licensing authority, in a case where the applicant submitted the application to the relevant licensing authority by means of a relevant electronic facility;

(b)   the applicant, in any other case.

(6)   Where a chief officer of police notified under subsection (5) is satisfied that the exceptional circumstances of the case are such that granting the application would undermine the crime prevention objective, he must give the relevant licensing authority a notice stating the reasons why he is so satisfied.

(7)   The chief officer of police must give that notice within the period of 14 days beginning with the day on which he is notified of the application under subsection (5).

(8)   Where the Secretary of State is given notice under subsection (5ZA) and is satisfied that the exceptional circumstances of the case are such that granting the application would be prejudicial to the prevention of illegal working in licensed premises, the Secretary of State must give the relevant licensing authority a notice stating the reasons for being so satisfied.

(9)   The Secretary of State must give that notice within the period of 14 days beginning with the day on which the Secretary of State is notified of the application under subsection (5ZA).

[Licensing Act 2003, s 42 as amended by SI 2009/2999 and the Immigration Act 2016, Sch 4.]

¹ See the Licensing Act 2003 (Premises Licences and Club Premises Certificates) Regulations 2005, SI 2005/42 (for amending instruments, see note to s 13, ante) and the Welsh Language (Gambling and Licensing Forms) Regulations 2010, SI 2010/2440.

7.7699 43. Circumstances in which transfer application given interim effect *Transfer application given interim effect if requested and with consent of existing premises licence holder (unless exempted from that requirement by licensing authority).*

7.7700 44. Determination of transfer application¹ (1) This section applies where an application for the transfer of a licence is made in accordance with section 42.

(2) Subject to subsections (3) and (5), the authority must transfer the licence in accordance with the application.

(3) The authority must reject the application if none of the conditions in subsection (4) applies.

(4) The conditions are—

  (a)   that section 43(1) (applications given interim effect) applies to the application,

  (b)   that the holder of the premises licence consents to the transfer,

  (c)   that the applicant is exempted under subsection (6) from the requirement to obtain the holder's consent to the transfer.

(5) Where a notice is given under section 42(6) or (8) (and not withdrawn), and subsection (3) above does not apply, the authority must—

  (a)   hold a hearing to consider it, unless the authority, the applicant and the person who gave the notice agree that a hearing is unnecessary, and

  (b)   having regard to the notice—

    (i)   where the notice is given under section 42(6), reject the application if it considers it appropriate for the promotion of the crime prevention objective to do so, or

    (ii)   where the notice is given under section 42(8), reject the application if it considers it appropriate for the prevention of illegal working in licensed premises to do so.

(6) The relevant licensing authority must exempt the applicant from the requirement to obtain the holder's consent if the applicant shows to the authority's satisfaction—

  (a)   that he has taken all reasonable steps to obtain that consent, and

  (b)   that, if the application were granted, he would be in a position to use the premises for the licensable activity or activities authorised by the premises licence.

(7) Where the relevant licensing authority refuses to exempt an applicant under subsection (6), it must notify the applicant of its reasons for that decision.

[Licensing Act 2003, s 44 as amended by the Police Reform and Social Responsibility Act 2011, s 109 and the Immigration Act 2016, Sch 4.]

¹ For appeal to a magistrates' court against a decision of a licensing authority under this section, see s 181 and Sch 5, post.

7.7701 45. Notification of determination under section 44 (1) Where an application under section 42 is granted or rejected, the relevant licensing authority must give a notice to that effect to—

  (a)   the applicant, and

  (b)   the chief officer of police for the police area (or each police area) in which the premises are situated.

(2) Where a chief officer of police gave a notice under subsection (6) of that section or the Secretary of State gave a notice under subsection (8) of that section (which, in either case, was not withdrawn), the notice under subsection (1) of this section must state the licensing authority's reasons for granting or rejecting the application.

(2A) Where the Secretary of State gave a notice under subsection (8) of section 42 (which was not withdrawn), the notice under subsection (1) of this section must also be given to the Secretary of State.

(3) Where the application is granted, the notice under subsection (1) must specify the time when the transfer takes effect.
That time is the time specified in the application or, if that time is before the applicant is given that notice, such later time as the relevant licensing authority specifies in the notice.

(4) The relevant licensing authority must also give a copy of the notice given under subsection (1)—

  (a)   where the application is granted—

    (i)   to the holder of the licence immediately before the application was granted, or

    (ii)   if the application was one to which section 43(1) applied, to the holder of the licence immediately before the application was made (if any),

  (b)   where the application is rejected, to the holder of the premises licence (if any).

[Licensing Act 2003, s 45 as amended by the Immigration Act 2016, Sch 4.]

7.7702 46. Duty to notify designated premises supervisor of transfer (1) This section applies where—

(a)   an application is made in accordance with section 42 to transfer a premises licence in respect of which there is a designated premises supervisor, and

(b)   the applicant and that supervisor are not the same person.

(2)   Where section 43(1) applies in relation to the application, the applicant must forthwith notify the designated premises supervisor of the application.

(3)   If the application is granted, the applicant must forthwith notify the designated premises supervisor of the transfer.

(4)   A person commits an offence if he fails, without reasonable excuse, to comply with this section.

(5)   A person guilty of an offence under subsection (4) is liable on summary conviction to a fine not exceeding level 3 on the standard scale.

[Licensing Act 2003, s 46.]

Interim authority notices

7.7703   47.   Interim authority notice following death etc of licence holder   *(As amended by the Immigration Act 2016, Sch 4)* Power for a person with a prescribed interest to serve an interim authority notice on licensing authority within 7 days of a licence having lapsed because of death, incapacity or insolvency of licence holder. Application to be in prescribed form and in accordance with regulations[1].

---

[1]   See the Licensing Act 2003 (Premises Licences and Club Premises Certificates) Regulations 2005, SI 2005/42 (for amending instruments, see note to s 13, ante) and the Welsh Language (Gambling and Licensing Forms) Regulations 2010, SI 2010/2440.

7.7704   48.   Cancellation   of   interim   authority   notice   following   objections[1]

(1)   Subsection (2) applies where—

(a)   an interim authority notice by a person ("the relevant person") is given in accordance with section 47,

(b)   the chief officer of police for the police area (or each police area) in which the premises are situated is given a copy of the interim authority notice before the end of the initial 28 day period (within the meaning of that section), and

(c)   that chief officer (or any of those chief officers) is satisfied that the exceptional circumstances of the case are such that a failure to cancel the interim authority notice would undermine the crime prevention objective.

(2)   The chief officer of police must before the end of the second working day following the day on which he receives the copy of the interim authority notice give the relevant licensing authority a notice stating why he is so satisfied.

(2A)   Subsection (2B) applies where—

(a)   an interim authority notice by a person ("the relevant person") is given in accordance with section 47,

(b)   the Secretary of State is given a copy of the interim authority notice before the end of the initial 28 day period (within the meaning of that section), and

(c)   the Secretary of State is satisfied that the exceptional circumstances of the case are such that a failure to cancel the interim authority notice would be prejudicial to the prevention of illegal working in licensed premises.

(2B)   The Secretary of State must before the end of the second working day following receipt of the copy of the interim authority notice give the relevant licensing authority a notice stating why the Secretary of State is so satisfied.

(3)   Where a notice is given under subsection (2) or (2B) (and not withdrawn), the authority must—

(a)   hold a hearing to consider it, unless the authority, the relevant person and the person who gave the notice agree that a hearing is unnecessary, and

(b)   having regard to the notice—

(i)   where the notice is given under subsection (2), cancel the interim authority notice if it considers it appropriate for the promotion of the crime prevention objective to do so, or

(ii)   where the notice is given under subsection (2B), cancel the interim authority notice if it considers it appropriate for the prevention of illegal working in licensed premises to do so.

(4)   An interim authority notice is cancelled under subsection (3)(b) by the licensing authority giving the relevant person a notice stating that it is cancelled and the authority's reasons for its decision.

(5)   The licensing authority must give a copy of a notice under subsection (4) to the chief officer of police for the police area (or each police area) in which the premises are situated.

(5A)   Where an interim authority notice is cancelled under subsection (3)(b)(ii), the licensing authority must also give a copy of the notice under subsection (4) to the Secretary of State.

(6)   The premises licence lapses if, and when, a notice is given under subsection (4). This is subject to paragraph 7(5) of Schedule 5 (reinstatement of premises licence where appeal

made against cancellation of interim authority notice).

(7)   The relevant licensing authority must not cancel an interim authority notice after a relevant transfer application (within the meaning of section 47) is made in respect of the premises licence.

[Licensing Act 2003, s 48 as amended by SI 2010/2452, the Police Reform and Social Responsibility Act 2011, s 109 and the Immigration Act 2016, Sch 4.]

---

[1] For appeal to a magistrates' court against a decision of a licensing authority under this section, see s 181 and Sch 5, post.

7.7705 49. Supplementary provision about interim authority notices   (1)   On receipt of an interim authority notice, the relevant licensing authority must issue to the person who gave the notice a copy of the licence and a copy of the summary (in each case certified by the authority to be a true copy).

(2)   The copies issued under this section must be copies of the premises licence and summary in the form in which they existed immediately before the licence lapsed under section 27, except that they must specify the person who gave the interim authority notice as the person who is the holder.

(3)   This Act applies in relation to a copy issued under this section as it applies in relation to an original licence or summary.

(4)   Where a person becomes the holder of a premises licence by virtue of section 47, he must (unless he is the designated premises supervisor under the licence) forthwith notify the supervisor (if any) of the interim authority notice.

(5)   A person commits an offence if he fails, without reasonable excuse, to comply with subsection (4).

(6)   A person guilty of an offence under subsection (5) is liable on summary conviction to a fine not exceeding level 3 on the standard scale.

[Licensing Act 2003, s 49.]

Transfer following death etc of licence holder

7.7706 50. Reinstatement of licence on transfer following death etc of holder   *(As amended by the Immigration Act 2016, Sch 4) Power to any person who could apply for a premises licence under s 16(1) to apply for reinstatement of lapsed licence on transfer under s 42.*

Review of licences

7.7707 51. Application for review of premises licence   (1)   Where a premises licence has effect, a responsible authority or any other person may apply to the relevant licensing authority for a review of the licence.

(2)   Subsection (1) is subject to regulations[1] under section 54 (form etc of applications etc).

(3)   The Secretary of State must by regulations under this section—

    (a)   require the applicant to give a notice containing details of the application to the holder of the premises licence and each responsible authority within such period as may be prescribed;

    (b)   require the authority to advertise the application and invite representations about it to be made to the authority by responsible authorities and other persons;

    (c)   prescribe the period during which representations may be made by the holder of the premises licence, any other person;

    (d)   require any notice under paragraph (a) or advertisement under paragraph (b) to specify that period.

(4)   The relevant licensing authority may, at any time, reject any ground for review specified in an application under this section if it is satisfied—

    (a)   that the ground is not relevant to one or more of the licensing objectives, or

    (b)   in the case of an application made by a person other than a responsible authority, that—

        (i)   the ground is frivolous or vexatious, or

        (ii)   the ground is a repetition.

(5)   For this purpose a ground for review is a repetition if—

    (a)   it is identical or substantially similar to—

        (i)   a ground for review specified in an earlier application for review made in respect of the same premises licence and determined under section 52, or

        (ii)   representations considered by the relevant licensing authority in accordance with section 18, before it determined the application for the premises licence under that section, or

        (iii)   representations which would have been so considered but for the fact that they were excluded representations by virtue of section 32, and

    (b)   a reasonable interval has not elapsed since that earlier application for review or the grant of the licence (as the case may be).

(6)   Where the authority rejects a ground for review under subsection (4)(b), it must notify the applicant of its decision and, if the ground was rejected because it was frivolous or vexatious, the authority must notify him of its reasons for making that decision.

(7)   The application is to be treated as rejected to the extent that any of the grounds for review

are rejected under subsection (4).

Accordingly the requirements imposed under subsection (3)(*a*) and (*b*) and by section 52 (so far as not already met) apply only to so much (if any) of the application as has not been rejected.

[Licensing Act 2003, s 51 as amended by the Police Reform and Social Responsibility Act 2011, s 106.]

---

¹ See the Licensing Act 2003 (Premises Licences and Club Premises Certificates) Regulations 2005, SI 2005/42 (for amending instruments, see note to s 13, ante) and the Welsh Language (Gambling and Licensing Forms) Regulations 2010, SI 2010/2440. For effect of any failure to comply with procedural requirements, see note to s 17, ante.

7.7708   52.   Determination of application for review¹   (1)   This section applies where—

   (*a*)   the relevant licensing authority receives an application made in accordance with section 51,

   (*b*)   the applicant has complied with any requirement imposed on him under subsection (3)(*a*) or (*d*) of that section, and

   (*c*)   the authority has complied with any requirement imposed on it under subsection (3)(*b*) or (*d*) of that section.

   (2)   Before determining the application, the authority must hold a hearing to consider it and any relevant representations.

   (3)   The authority must, having regard to the application and any relevant representations, take such of the steps mentioned in subsection (4) (if any) as it considers appropriate for the promotion of the licensing objectives.

   (4)   The steps are—

   (*a*)   to modify the conditions of the licence;

   (*b*)   to exclude a licensable activity from the scope of the licence;

   (*c*)   to remove the designated premises supervisor;

   (*d*)   to suspend the licence for a period not exceeding three months;

   (*e*)   to revoke the licence;

and for this purpose the conditions of the licence are modified if any of them is altered or omitted or any new condition is added.

   (5)   Subsection (3) is subject to sections 19 to 21 (requirement to include certain conditions in premises licences).

   (6)   Where the authority takes a step mentioned in subsection (4)(*a*) or (*b*), it may provide that the modification or exclusion is to have effect for only such period (not exceeding three months) as it may specify.

   (7)   In this section "relevant representations" means representations which—

   (*a*)   are relevant to one or more of the licensing objectives, and

   (*b*)   meet the requirements of subsection (8).

   (8)   The requirements are—

   (*a*)   that the representations are made

      (i)   by the holder of the premises licence, a responsible authority or any other person, and

      (ii)   within the period prescribed under section 51(3)(*c*),

   (*b*)   that they have not been withdrawn, and

   (*c*)   if they are made by a person who is not a responsible authority, that they are not, in the opinion of the relevant licensing authority, frivolous or vexatious.

   (9)   Where the relevant licensing authority determines that any representations are frivolous or vexatious, it must notify the person who made them of the reasons for that determination.

   (10)   Where a licensing authority determines an application for review under this section it must notify the determination and its reasons for making it to—

   (*a*)   the holder of the licence,

   (*b*)   the applicant,

   (*c*)   any person who made relevant representations, and

   (*d*)   the chief officer of police for the police area (or each police area) in which the premises are situated.

   (11)   A determination under this section does not have effect—

   (*a*)   until the end of the period given for appealing against the decision, or

   (*b*)   if the decision is appealed against, until the appeal is disposed of.

[Licensing Act 2003, s 52 as amended by the Policing and Crime Act 2009, Sch 7 and the Police Reform and Social Responsibility Act 2011, ss 105, 109.]

---

¹ For appeal to a magistrates' court against a decision of a licensing authority under this section, see s 181 and Sch 5, post.

7.7709   52A.   Review: supply of alcohol from community premises   (1)   In a case where an application is made under section 51 for review of a premises licence which—

   (*a*)   is held by a management committee in respect of community premises, and

   (*b*)   includes the alternative licence condition,

section 52 is modified as follows.

   (2)   Subsection (4) has effect as if paragraph (*c*) were omitted.

   (3)   Subsection (5) has effect as if for that subsection there were substituted—

"(5)   Subsection (3) is subject—

     (*a*)   to the requirement that the licence must include—

          (i)   the conditions in section 19(2) and (3), or

          (i)   the alternative licence condition referred to in section 52A(4)

(but not both), and

     (*b*)   to sections 19(4) and 19A to 21 (requirement to include certain conditions in premises licences)".

(4)   In this section "the alternative licence condition" is the condition that every supply of alcohol under the premises licence must be made or authorised by the management committee.

[Licensing Act 2003, s 52A as inserted by SI 2009/1724 and amended by the Policing and Crime Act 2009, Sch 7.]

7.7710   53.   Supplementary provision about review   *Licensing authority able to determine review which has been applied for by itself in its separate capacity as a responsible authority under s 13(4).*

Summary reviews in serious cases of crime or disorder

7.7711   53A.   Summary reviews on application of senior police officer   (1)   The chief officer of police of a police force for a police area may apply under this section to the relevant licensing authority for a review of the premises licence for any premises wholly or partly in that area if—

     (*a*)   the premises are licensed premises in relation to the sale of alcohol by retail; and

     (*b*)   a senior member of that force has given a certificate that it is his opinion that the premises are associated with[1] serious crime or serious disorder or both;

and that certificate must accompany the application.

(2)   On receipt of such an application, the relevant licensing authority must—

     (*a*)   within 48 hours of the time of its receipt, consider under section 53B whether it is necessary to take interim steps pending the determination of a review of the premises licence; and

     (*b*)   within 28 days after the day of its receipt, review that licence in accordance with section 53C and reach a determination on that review.

(3)   The Secretary of State must by regulations[2]—

     (*a*)   require a relevant licensing authority to whom an application for a review under this section has been made to give notice of the review to the holder of the premises licence and to every responsible authority;

     (*b*)   prescribe the period after the making of the application within which the notice under paragraph (*a*) must be given;

     (*c*)   require a relevant licensing authority to advertise the review, inviting representations about it to be made to the authority by the responsible authorities and other persons;

     (*d*)   prescribe the period after the making of the application within which the advertisement must be published;

     (*e*)   prescribe the period after the publication of the advertisement during which representations may be made by the holder of the premises licence, any responsible authority or any other person; and

     (*f*)   require a notice or advertisement under paragraph (*a*) or (*c*) to specify the period prescribed under paragraph (*e*).

(4)   In this section—

"senior member", in relation to a police force, means a police officer who is a member of that force and of or above the rank of superintendent; and

"serious crime" has the same meaning as in the Regulation of Investigatory Powers Act 2000 (c 23) (see section 81(2) and (3) of that Act).

(5)   In computing the period of 48 hours mentioned in subsection (2)(*a*) time that is not on a working day is to be disregarded.

[Licensing Act 2003, s 53A as inserted by the Violent Crime Reduction Act 2006, s 21 and amended by the Police Reform and Social Responsibility Act 2011, s 106.]

---

[1] There must be a connection or link between the premises and serious crime or serious disorder, and this may require more than the fact that serious crime or serious disorder occurred in, or close to, the premises. It is unnecessary, however, to show a pattern of such behaviour; a single incident can suffice. The licensing authority must carry out a review even if it considers that the information available to the senior police officer when he gave the certificate does not establish the required association: *Lalli v Metropolitan Police Commissioner and another* [2015] EWHC 14 (Admin), [2015] All ER (D) 48 (Jan).

[2] See the Licensing Act 2003 (Premises Licences and Club Premises Certificates) Regulations 2005, SI 2005/42 (for amending instruments, see note to s 13, ante).

7.7712   53B.   Interim steps pending review   (1)   This section applies to the consideration by a relevant licensing authority on an application under section 53A whether it is necessary to take interim steps pending the determination of the review applied for.

(2)   The consideration may take place without the holder of the premises licence having been given an opportunity to make representations to the relevant licensing authority.

(3)   The interim steps the relevant licensing authority must consider taking are—

     (*a*)   the modification of the conditions of the premises licence;

     (*b*)   the exclusion of the sale of alcohol by retail from the scope of the licence;

    (c)   the removal of the designated premises supervisor from the licence;

    (d)   the suspension of the licence.

  (4)   For the purposes of subsection (3)(a) the conditions of a premises licence are modified if any of them is altered or omitted or any new condition is added.

  (5)   Where on its consideration of whether to take interim steps the relevant licensing authority does take one or more such steps—

    (a)   its decision takes effect immediately or as soon after that as that authority directs; but

    (b)   it must give immediate notice of its decision and of its reasons for making it to—

        (i)   the holder of the premises licence; and

        (ii)   the chief officer of police for the police area in which the premises are situated (or for each police area in which they are partly situated).

  (6)   Subject to subsection (9A), if the holder of the premises licence makes, and does not withdraw, representations against any interim steps taken by the relevant licensing authority, the authority must, within 48 hours of the time of its receipt of the representations, hold a hearing to consider those representations.

  (7)   The relevant licensing authority must give advance notice of the hearing to—

    (a)   the holder of the premises licence;

    (b)   the chief officer of police for the police area in which the premises are situated (or for each police area in which they are partly situated).

  (8)   At the hearing, the relevant licensing authority must—

    (a)   consider whether the interim steps are appropriate for the promotion of the licensing objectives; and

    (b)   determine whether to withdraw or modify the steps taken.

  (9)   In considering those matters the relevant licensing authority must have regard to—

    (a)   the certificate that accompanied the application;

    (b)   any representations made by the chief officer of police for the police area in which the premises are situated (or for each police area in which they are partly situated); and

    (c)   any representations made by the holder of the premises licence.

  (9A) Where the relevant licensing authority has determined under subsection (8) whether to withdraw or modify the interim steps taken, the holder of the premises licence may only make further representations under subsection (6) if there has been a material change in circumstances since the authority made its determination.

  (10) In computing the period of 48 hours mentioned in subsection (6) time that is not on a working day is to be disregarded.

[Licensing Act 2003, s 53B as inserted by the Violent Crime Reduction Act 2006, s 21 and amended by the Police Reform and Social Responsibility Act 2011, s 109 and the Policing and Crime Act 2017, s 136]

7.7713   53C. Review of premises licence following review notice   (1)   This section applies to a review of a premises licence which a relevant licensing authority has to conduct on an application under section 53A.

  (2)   The relevant licensing authority must—

    (a)   hold a hearing to consider the application for the review and any relevant representations; and

    (b)   take such steps mentioned in subsection (3) (if any) as it considers appropriate for the promotion of the licensing objectives.

    (c)   *repealed.*

  (3)   Those steps are—

    (a)   the modification of the conditions of the premises licence,

    (b)   the exclusion of a licensable activity from the scope of the licence,

    (c)   the removal of the designated premises supervisor from the licence,

    (d)   the suspension of the licence for a period not exceeding three months, or

    (e)   the revocation of the licence.

  (4)   For the purposes of subsection (3)(a) the conditions of a premises licence are modified if any of them is altered or omitted or any new condition is added.

  (5)   Subsection (2)(b) is subject to sections 19 to 21 (requirement to include certain conditions in premises licences).

  (6)   Where the authority takes a step within subsection (3)(a) or (b), it may provide that the modification or exclusion is to have effect only for a specified period (not exceeding three months).

  (7)   In this section "relevant representations" means representations which—

    (a)   are relevant to one or more of the licensing objectives, and

    (b)   meet the requirements of subsection (8).

  (8)   The requirements are—

    (a)   that the representations are made by the holder of the premises licence, a responsible authority or any other person within the period prescribed under subsection 53A(3)(e),

    (b)   that they have not been withdrawn, and

    (c)   if they are made by a person who is not a responsible authority, that they are not, in the opinion of the relevant licensing authority, frivolous or vexatious.

  (9)   Where the relevant licensing authority determines that any representations are frivolous or

vexatious, it must notify the person who made them of the reasons for that determination.

(10)   Where a relevant licensing authority determines a review under this section it must notify the determination and its reasons for making it to—

(a)   the holder of the premises licence,

(b)   any person who made relevant representations, and

(c)   the chief officer of police for the police area in which the premises are situated (or for each police area in which they are partly situated).

(11)   A decision under this section does not have effect until—

(a)   the end of the period given for appealing against the decision, or

(b)   if the decision is appealed against, the time the appeal is disposed of.

(12)   Section 53D makes provision about the application and review of any interim steps that have been taken under section 53B in relation to a premises licence before a decision under this section comes into effect in relation to the licence.

[Licensing Act 2003, s 53C as inserted by the Violent Crime Reduction Act 2006, s 21 and amended by the Policing and Crime Act 2009, Sch 7, the Police Reform and Social Responsibility Act 2011, ss 106, 109 and the Policing and Crime Act 2017, s 137.]

7.7714   53D.   Interim steps pending section 53C decision coming into effect   (1)   At the hearing to consider an application for a review under section 53A, the relevant licensing authority must review any interim steps that have been taken by the relevant licensing authority under section 53B that have effect on the date of the hearing.

(2)   In conducting the review under this section, the relevant licensing authority must—

(a)   consider whether the interim steps are appropriate for the promotion of the licensing objectives;

(b)   consider any relevant representations; and

(c)   determine whether to withdraw or modify the interim steps taken.

(3)   The power of the relevant licensing authority on a review under this section includes a power to take any of the following interim steps—

(a)   the modification of the conditions of the premises licence;

(b)   the exclusion of the sale of alcohol by retail from the scope of the licence;

(c)   the removal of the designated premises supervisor from the licence;

(d)   the suspension of the licence;

and for this purpose the conditions of the licence are modified if any of them is altered or omitted or any new condition is added.

(4)   Any interim steps taken under subsection (3) apply until—

(a)   the end of the period given for appealing against a decision made under section 53C,

(b)   if the decision under section 53C is appealed against, the time the appeal is disposed of, or

(c)   the end of a period determined by the relevant licensing authority (which may not be longer than the period of time for which such interim steps could apply under paragraph (a) or (b)).

(5)   Any interim steps taken under section 53B in relation to a premises licence cease to have effect when the decision made under section 53C comes into effect.

(6)   In subsection (2) "relevant representations" means representations which—

(a)   are relevant to one or more of the licensing objectives, and

(b)   meet the requirements of subsection (7).

(7)   The requirements are—

(a)   that the representations are made by the holder of the premises licence, a responsible authority or any other person within the period prescribed under subsection 53A(3)(e),

(b)   that they have not been withdrawn, and

(c)   if they are made by a person who is not a responsible authority, that they are not, in the opinion of the relevant licensing authority, frivolous or vexatious.

(8)   Where the relevant licensing authority determines that any representations are frivolous or vexatious, it must notify the person who made them of the reasons for that determination.

(9)   A decision under this section may be appealed (see paragraph 8B of Part 1 of Schedule 5 (appeals: premises licences)).

[Licensing Act 2003, s 53D as inserted by the Policing and Crime Act 2017, s 137.]

7.7715   55A.   Suspension of premises licence for failing to pay annual fee   *Licensing authority must suspend a club premises certificate if the holder of the certificate has failed to pay an annual fee.*

Production of licence, rights of entry, etc

7.7716   56.   Licensing authority's duty to update licence document   (1)   Where—

(a)   the relevant licensing authority, in relation to a premises licence, makes a determination or receives a notice under this Part,

(b)   a premises licence lapses under this Part, or

(c)   an appeal against a decision under this Part is disposed of,

the relevant licensing authority must make the appropriate amendments (if any) to the licence and, if necessary, issue a new summary of the licence.

(2) Where a licensing authority is not in possession of the licence (or the appropriate part of the licence) it may, for the purposes of discharging its obligations under subsection (1), require the holder of a premises licence to produce the licence (or the appropriate part) to the authority within 14 days from the date on which he is notified of the requirement.

(3) A person commits an offence if he fails, without reasonable excuse, to comply with a requirement under subsection (2).

(4) A person guilty of an offence under subsection (3) is liable on summary conviction to a fine not exceeding level 2 on the standard scale.

[Licensing Act 2003, s 56.]

7.7717 57. Duty to keep and produce licence etc (1) This section applies whenever premises in respect of which a premises licence has effect are being used for one or more licensable activities authorised by the licence.

(2) The holder of the premises licence must secure that the licence or a certified copy of it and a list of any relevant mandatory conditions applicable to the licence are kept at the premises in the custody or under the control of—

(a) the holder of the licence, or

(b) a person who works at the premises and whom the holder of the licence has nominated in writing for the purposes of this subsection.

(3) The holder of the premises licence must secure that—

(a) the summary of the licence or a certified copy of that summary, and

(b) a notice specifying the position held at the premises by any person nominated for the purposes of subsection (2),

are prominently displayed at the premises.

(4) The holder of a premises licence commits an offence if he fails, without reasonable excuse, to comply with subsection (2) or (3).

(5) A constable or an authorised person may require the person who, by virtue of arrangements made for the purposes of subsection (2), is required to have the premises licence (or a certified copy of it) or a list of relevant mandatory conditions in his custody or under his control to produce the licence (or such a copy) or the list for examination.

(6) An authorised person exercising the power conferred by subsection (5) must, if so requested, produce evidence of his authority to exercise the power.

(7) A person commits an offence if he fails, without reasonable excuse, to produce a premises licence or certified copy of a premises licence or a list of relevant mandatory conditions in accordance with a requirement under subsection (5).

(8) A person guilty of an offence under this section is liable on summary conviction to a fine not exceeding level 2 on the standard scale.

(9) In subsection (3) the reference to the summary of the licence is a reference to the summary issued under section 23 or, where one or more summaries have subsequently been issued under section 56, the most recent summary to have been so issued.

(10) Section 58 makes provision about certified copies of documents for the purposes of this section.

(11) In this section "relevant mandatory conditions", in relation to a premises licence, means conditions applicable to the licence by virtue of section 19(4) or 19A.

[Licensing Act 2003, s 57 as amended by the Policing and Crime Act 2009, Sch 7.]

7.7718 58. Provision supplementary to section 57 (1) Any reference in section 57 to a certified copy of any document is a reference to a copy of that document which is certified to be a true copy by—

(a) the relevant licensing authority,

(b) a solicitor or notary, or

(c) a person of a prescribed[1] description.

(2) Any certified copy produced in accordance with a requirement under section 57(5) must be a copy of the document in the form in which it exists at the time.

(3) A document which purports to be a certified copy of a document is to be taken to be such a copy, and to comply with the requirements of subsection (2), unless the contrary is shown.

(4) In this section "notary" means a person (other than a solicitor) who, for the purposes of the Legal Services Act 2007, is an authorised person in relation to any activity which constitutes a notarial activity (within the meaning of that Act).

[Licensing Act 2003, s 58 as amended by the Legal Services Act 2007, Sch 21.]

---

[1] I.e. prescribed by regulations, see s 193, post. At the date of going to press no such regulations had been made.

7.7719 59. Inspection of premises before grant of licence etc (1) In this section "relevant application" means an application under—

(a) section 17 (grant of licence),

(b) section 29 (provisional statement),

(c) section 34 (variation of licence), or

(d)   section 51 (review of licence).

(2)   A constable or an authorised person may, at any reasonable time before the determination of a relevant application, enter the premises to which the application relates to assess—

(a)   in a case within subsection (1)(a), (b) or (c), the likely effect of the grant of the application on the promotion of the licensing objectives, and

(b)   in a case within subsection (1)(d), the effect of the activities authorised by the premises licence on the promotion of those objectives.

(3)   An authorised person exercising the power conferred by this section must, if so requested, produce evidence of his authority to exercise the power.

(4)   A constable or an authorised person exercising the power conferred by this section in relation to an application within subsection (1)(d) may, if necessary, use reasonable force.

(5)   A person commits an offence if he intentionally obstructs an authorised person exercising a power conferred by this section.

(6)   A person guilty of an offence under this section is liable on summary conviction to a fine not exceeding level 2 on the standard scale.

[Licensing Act 2003, s 59.]

PART 4[1]
CLUBS

Introductory

7.7720   60.   Club premises certificate   (1)   In this Act "club premises certificate" means a certificate granted under this Part—

(a)   in respect of premises[2] occupied by, and habitually used for the purposes of, a club,

(b)   by the relevant licensing authority, and

(c)   certifying the matters specified in subsection (2).

(2)   Those matters are—

(a)   that the premises may be used by the club for one or more qualifying club activities[3] specified in the certificate, and

(b)   that the club is a qualifying club in relation to each of those activities (see section 61).

[Licensing Act 2003, s 60.]

---

[1]   Part 4 comprises ss 60–97.
[2]   For meaning of "premises", see s 193, post.
[3]   For meaning of "qualifying club activities", see s 1(2), ante.

Qualifying clubs

7.7721   61.   Qualifying clubs   (1)   This section applies for determining for the purposes of this Part whether a club is a qualifying club in relation to a qualifying club activity.

(2)   A club is a qualifying club in relation to the supply of alcohol to members or guests[1] if it satisfies both—

(a)   the general conditions in section 62, and

(b)   the additional conditions in section 64.

(3)   A club is a qualifying club in relation to the provision of regulated entertainment[2] if it satisfies the general conditions in section 62.

[Licensing Act 2003, s 61.]

---

[1]   For meaning of "supply of alcohol to members or guests", see s 70, post.
[2]   For meaning of "regulated entertainment, see Sch 1, post.

7.7722   62.   The general conditions   (1)   The general conditions which a club must satisfy if it is to be a qualifying club in relation to a qualifying club activity are the following.

(2)   Condition 1 is that under the rules of the club persons may not—

(a)   be admitted to membership, or

(b)   be admitted, as candidates for membership, to any of the privileges of membership,

without an interval of at least two days between their nomination or application for membership and their admission.

(3)   Condition 2 is that under the rules of the club persons becoming members without prior nomination or application may not be admitted to the privileges of membership without an interval of at least two days between their becoming members and their admission.

(4)   Condition 3 is that the club is established and conducted in good faith as a club (see section 63).

(5)   Condition 4 is that the club has at least 25 members.

(6)   Condition 5 is that alcohol is not supplied, or intended to be supplied, to members on the premises otherwise than by or on behalf of the club.

[Licensing Act 2003, s 62.]

7.7723   63.   Determining whether a club is established and conducted in good faith
(1)   In determining for the purposes of condition 3 in subsection (4) of section 62 whether a club is established and conducted in good faith as a club, the matters to be taken into account are

those specified in subsection (2).

(2) Those matters are—

(a)   any arrangements restricting the club's freedom of purchase of alcohol;

(b)   any provision in the rules, or arrangements, under which—

(i)   money or property of the club, or

(ii)   any gain arising from the carrying on of the club,

is or may be applied otherwise than for the benefit of the club as a whole or for charitable, benevolent or political purposes;

(c)   the arrangements for giving members information about the finances of the club;

(d)   the books of account and other records kept to ensure the accuracy of that information;

(e)   the nature of the premises[1] occupied by the club.

(3) If a licensing authority decides for any purpose of this Act that a club does not satisfy condition 3 in subsection (4) of section 62, the authority must give the club notice of the decision and of the reasons for it.

[Licensing Act 2003, s 63.]

---

[1] For meaning of "premises", see s 193, post.

7.7724 64. The additional conditions for the supply of alcohol (1) The additional conditions which a club must satisfy if it is to be a qualifying club in relation to the supply of alcohol to members or guests[1] are the following.

(2) Additional condition 1 is that (so far as not managed by the club in general meeting or otherwise by the general body of members) the purchase of alcohol for the club, and the supply of alcohol by the club, are managed by a committee whose members—

(a)   are members of the club;

(b)   have attained the age of 18 years; and

(c)   are elected by the members of the club.

This subsection is subject to section 65 (which makes special provision for industrial and provident societies, friendly societies etc).

(3) Additional condition 2 is that no arrangements are, or are intended to be, made for any person to receive at the expense of the club any commission, percentage or similar payment on, or with reference to, purchases of alcohol by the club.

(4) Additional condition 3 is that no arrangements are, or are intended to be, made for any person directly or indirectly to derive any pecuniary benefit from the supply of alcohol by or on behalf of the club to members or guests, apart from—

(a)   any benefit accruing to the club as a whole, or

(b)   any benefit which a person derives indirectly by reason of the supply giving rise or contributing to a general gain from the carrying on of the club.

[Licensing Act 2003, s 64.]

---

[1] For meaning of "supply of alcohol to members or guests", see s 70, post.

7.7725 65. Industrial and provident societies, friendly societies etc (1) Subsection (2) applies in relation to any club which is—

(a)   a registered society, within the meaning of the Industrial and Provident Societies Act 1965 (c 12)(see section 74(1) of that Act),

(b)   a registered society, within the meaning of the Friendly Societies Act 1974 (c 46) (see section 111(1) of that Act), or

(c)   a registered friendly society, within the meaning of the Friendly Societies Act 1992 (c 40) (see section 116 of that Act).

(2) Any such club is to be taken for the purposes of this Act to satisfy additional condition 1 in subsection (2) of section 64 if and to the extent that—

(a)   the purchase of alcohol for the club, and

(b)   the supply of alcohol by the club,

are under the control of the members or of a committee appointed by the members.

(3) References in this Act, other than this section, to—

(a)   subsection (2) of section 64, or

(b)   additional condition 1 in that subsection,

are references to it as read with subsection (1) of this section.

(4) Subject to subsection (5), this Act applies in relation to an incorporated friendly society as it applies in relation to a club, and accordingly—

(a)   the premises[1] of the society are to be treated as the premises of a club,

(b)   the members of the society are to be treated as the members of the club, and

(c)   anything done by or on behalf of the society is to be treated as done by or on behalf of the club.

(5) In determining for the purposes of section 61 whether an incorporated friendly society is a qualifying club in relation to a qualifying club activity[2], the society is to be taken to satisfy the following conditions—

(a)   condition 3 in subsection (4) of section 62,

(b)   condition 5 in subsection (6) of that section,

(c)   the additional conditions in section 64.

(6)   In this section "incorporated friendly society" has the same meaning as in the Friendly Societies Act 1992 (see section 116 of that Act).

[Licensing Act 2003, s 65.]

---

[1] For meaning of "premises", see s 193, post.
[2] For "qualifying club activities", see s 1(2), ante.

7.7726 66. Miners' welfare institutes (1) Subject to subsection (2), this Act applies to a relevant miners' welfare institute as it applies to a club, and accordingly—

(a)   the premises of the institute are to be treated as the premises of a club,

(b)   the persons enrolled as members of the institute are to be treated as the members of the club, and

(c)   anything done by or on behalf of the trustees or managers in carrying on the institute is to be treated as done by or on behalf of the club.

(2)   In determining for the purposes of section 61 whether a relevant miners' welfare institute is a qualifying club in relation to a qualifying club activity, the institute is to be taken to satisfy the following conditions—

(a)   condition 3 in subsection (4) of section 62,

(b)   condition 4 in subsection (5) of that section,

(c)   condition 5 in subsection (6) of that section,

(d)   the additional conditions in section 64.

(3)   For the purposes of this section—

(a)   "miners' welfare institute" means an association organised for the social well-being and recreation of persons employed in or about coal mines (or of such persons in particular), and

(b)   a miners' welfare institute is "relevant" if it satisfies one of the following conditions.

(4)   The first condition is that—

(a)   the institute is managed by a committee or board, and

(b)   at least two thirds of the committee or board consists—

      (i)   partly of persons appointed or nominated, or appointed or elected from among persons nominated, by one or more licensed operators within the meaning of the Coal Industry Act 1994 (c 21), and

      (ii)   partly of persons appointed or nominated, or appointed or elected from among persons nominated, by one or more organisations representing persons employed in or about coal mines.

(5)   The second condition is that—

(a)   the institute is managed by a committee or board, but

(b)   the making of—

      (i)   an appointment or nomination falling within subsection (4)(b)(i), or

      (ii)   an appointment or nomination falling within subsection (4)(b)(ii),

      is not practicable or would not be appropriate, and

(c)   at least two thirds of the committee or board consists—

      (i)   partly of persons employed, or formerly employed, in or about coal mines, and

      (ii)   partly of persons appointed by the Coal Industry Social Welfare Organisation or a body or person to which the functions of that Organisation have been transferred under section 12(3) of the Miners' Welfare Act 1952 (c 23).

(6)   The third condition is that the premises of the institute are held on trusts to which section 2 of the Recreational Charities Act 1958 (c 17) applies.

[Licensing Act 2003, s 66.]

Interpretation

7.7727 67. Associate members and their guests (1) Any reference in this Act (other than this section) to a guest of a member of a club includes a reference to—

(a)   an associate member of the club, and

(b)   a guest of an associate member of the club.

(2)   For the purposes of this Act a person is an "associate member" of a club if—

(a)   in accordance with the rules of the club, he is admitted to its premises as being a member of another club, and

(b)   that other club is a recognised club (see section 193).

[Licensing Act 2003, s 67.]

7.7728 68. The relevant licensing authority *Determination of relevant licensing authority for a club dependent on location of whole, or greater part of club premises.*

7.7729 69. Authorised persons, interested parties and responsible authorities *Authorised persons, interested parties and responsible authorities are the same for club premises as they are for premises licences[1].*

7.7730   70.   Other definitions relating to clubs   In this Part—
"secretary", in relation to a club, includes any person (whether or not an officer of the club) performing the duties of a secretary;
"supply of alcohol to members or guests" means, in the case of any club,—

(a)   the supply of alcohol by or on behalf of the club to, or to the order of, a member of the club, or

(b)   the sale by retail of alcohol by or on behalf of the club to a guest of a member of the club for consumption on the premises where the sale takes place,

and related expressions are to be construed accordingly.

[Licensing Act 2003, s 70.]

Grant of club premises certificate

7.7731   71.   Application for club premises certificate   *Application to be in the prescribed form and accompanied by a Club Operating Schedule; application to be advertised in accordance with regulations¹.*

¹ See the Licensing Act 2003 (Premises Licences and Club Premises Certificates) Regulations 2005, SI 2005/42 (for amending instruments, see note to s 13, ante) and the Welsh Language (Gambling and Licensing Forms) Regulations 2010, SI 2010/2440.

7.7732   72.   Determination of application for club premises certificate   (1)   This section applies where the relevant licensing authority—

(a)   receives an application for a club premises certificate made in accordance with section 71, and

(b)   is satisfied that the applicant has complied with any requirement imposed on the applicant under subsection (6) of that section.

(2)   Subject to subsection (3), the authority must grant the certificate in accordance with the application subject only to—

(a)   such conditions as are consistent with the club operating schedule accompanying the application, and

(b)   any conditions which must under section 73(2) to (5), 73A or 74 be included in the certificate.

(3)   Where relevant representations are made, the authority must—

(a)   hold a hearing to consider them, unless the authority, the applicant and each person who has made such representations agree that a hearing is unnecessary, and

(b)   having regard to the representations, take such of the steps mentioned in subsection (4) (if any) as it considers appropriate for the promotion of the licensing objectives.

(4)   The steps are—

(a)   to grant the certificate subject to—

(i)   the conditions mentioned in subsection (2)(a) modified to such extent as the authority considers appropriate for the promotion of the licensing objectives, and

(ii)   any conditions which must under section 73(2) to (5) or 74 be included in the certificate;

(b)   to exclude from the scope of the certificate any of the qualifying club activities to which the application relates;

(c)   to reject the application.

(5)   Subsections (2) and (3)(b) are subject to section 73(1) (certificate may authorise off-supplies only if it authorises on-supplies).

(6)   For the purposes of subsection (4)(a)(1)(a) the conditions mentioned in subsection (2)(a) are modified if any of them is altered or omitted or any new condition is added.

(7)   For the purposes of this section, "relevant representations" means representations which—

(a)   are about the likely effect of the grant of the certificate on the promotion of the licensing objectives, and

(b)   meet the requirements of subsection (8).

(8)   The requirements are—

(a)   that the representations were made by a responsible authority or other person within the period prescribed under section 71(6)(c),

(b)   that they have not been withdrawn, and

(c)   in the case of representations made by a person who is not a responsible authority, that they are not, in the opinion of the relevant licensing authority, frivolous or vexatious.

(9)   Where the authority determines for the purposes of subsection (8)(c) that any representations are frivolous or vexatious, it must notify the person who made them of the reasons for its determination.

(10)   In discharging its duty under subsection (2) or (3)(b) a licensing authority may grant a club premises certificate subject to different conditions in respect of—

(a)   different parts of the premises concerned;

(b)   different qualifying club activities.

[Licensing Act 2003, s 72 as amended by the Policing and Crime Act 2009, Sch 7 and the Police Reform and Social Responsibility Act 2011, ss 107, 110.]

7.7733 73. Certificate authorising supply of alcohol for consumption off the premises
(1)   A club premises certificate may not authorise the supply of alcohol for consumption off the premises unless it also authorises the supply of alcohol to a member of the club for consumption on those premises.

(2)   A club premises certificate which authorises the supply of alcohol for consumption off the premises must include the following conditions.

(3)   The first condition is that the supply must be made at a time when the premises are open for the purposes of supplying alcohol, in accordance with the club premises certificate, to members of the club for consumption on the premises.

(4)   The second condition is that any alcohol supplied for consumption off the premises must be in a sealed container.

(5)   The third condition is that any supply of alcohol for consumption off the premises must be made to a member of the club in person.

[Licensing Act 2003, s 73.]

7.7734 73A. Mandatory conditions relating to the supply of alcohol to members or guests
Where a club premises certificate authorises the supply of alcohol to members or guests, the certificate must include any conditions specified in an order under section 73B and applicable to the certificate.

[Licensing Act 2003, s 73A as inserted by the Policing and Crime Act 2009, Sch 4.]

7.7735 73B. Power of Secretary of State to impose section 73A mandatory conditions
(1)   The Secretary of State may by order[1] specify conditions relating to the supply of alcohol to members or guests and applicable to all relevant club premises certificates or relevant club premises certificates of a particular description if the Secretary of State considers it appropriate to do so for the promotion of the licensing objectives.

(2)   The number of conditions in force by virtue of subsection (1) in relation to all relevant club premises certificates and the number of conditions in force by virtue of that subsection in relation to relevant club premises certificates of particular descriptions must not (when added together) exceed at any time nine.

(3)   An order under subsection (1) may—
    (a)   relate to existing or future relevant club premises certificates,
    (b)   specify conditions which involve, or consist of, the exercise of a discretion by any person.

(4)   Any conditions specified by an order under subsection (1) in relation to existing relevant club premises certificates are to be treated as—
    (a)   included in those certificates from the coming into force of the order, and
    (b)   overriding any conditions already included in those certificates ("the existing conditions") so far as they are—
        (i)   identical to the existing conditions, or
        (ii)   inconsistent with, and more onerous than, the existing conditions.

(5)   Any conditions included, or treated as included, in relevant club premises certificates by virtue of section 73A and this section cease to have effect so far as they cease to be specified under this section in relation to those certificates.

(6)   Any conditions treated as mentioned in subsection (4)(b) cease to be so treated so far as they cease to be specified under this section in relation to the relevant club premises certificates concerned.

(7)   So far as conditions cease to be treated as mentioned in subsection (4)(b), the existing conditions revive.

(8)   Subsections (5) to (7) are subject to any alternative transitional or saving provision made by the order revoking the specification.

(9)   In this section—
    "existing relevant club premises certificate", in relation to an order, means a relevant club premises certificate granted before the coming into force of the order and in effect, or capable of having effect, on its coming into force,
    "future relevant club premises certificate", in relation to an order, means a relevant club premises certificate granted on or after the coming into force of the order,
    "relevant club premises certificate" means a club premises certificate authorising the supply of alcohol to members or guests.

[Licensing Act 2003, s 73B as inserted by the Policing and Crime Act 2009, Sch 4.]

---

[1] The Licensing Act 2003 (Mandatory Licensing Conditions) Orders 2010, SI 2010/860 and 2014/1252 have been made, in this title, post.

7.7736 74. Mandatory condition: exhibition of films (1)   Where a club premises certificate authorises the exhibition of films, the certificate must include a condition requiring the admission of children to the exhibition of any film to be restricted in accordance with this section.

(2)   Where the film classification body is specified in the certificate, unless subsection (3)(b) applies, admission of children must be restricted in accordance with any recommendation made by

that body.

(3) Where—

    (a)   the film classification body is not specified in the certificate, or

    (b)   the relevant licensing authority has notified the club which holds the certificate that this subsection applies to the film in question,

admission of children must be restricted in accordance with any recommendation made by that licensing authority.

(4) In this section—

"children" means persons aged under 18; and

"film classification body" means the person or persons designated as the authority under section 4 of the Video Recordings Act 1984 (c 39) (authority to determine suitability of video works for classification).

[Licensing Act 2003, s 74.]

7.7737   75. Prohibited conditions: associate members and their guests (1) Where the rules of a club provide for the sale by retail of alcohol on any premises by or on behalf of the club to, or to a guest of, an associate member[1] of the club, no condition may be attached to a club premises certificate in respect of the sale by retail of alcohol on those premises by or on behalf of the club so as to prevent the sale by retail of alcohol to any such associate member or guest.

(2) Where the rules of a club provide for the provision of any regulated entertainment on any premises by or on behalf of the club to, or to a guest of, an associate member of the club, no condition may be attached to a club premises certificate in respect of the provision of any such regulated entertainment on those premises by or on behalf of the club so as to prevent its provision to any such associate member or guest.

[Licensing Act 2003, s 75.]

---

[1] For "associate members" and "guests", see s 67, ante.

7.7738   76. Prohibited conditions: plays (1) In relation to a club premises certificate which authorises the performance of plays, no condition may be attached to the certificate as to the nature of the plays which may be performed, or the manner of performing plays, under the certificate.

(2) But subsection (1) does not prevent a licensing authority imposing, in accordance with section 72(2) or (3)(b), 85(3)(b) or 88(3), any condition which it considers appropriate on the grounds of public safety.*

[Licensing Act 2003, s 76 as amended by the Police Reform and Social Responsibility Act 2011, s 110.]

7.7739   77. Grant or rejection of application for club premises certificate (1) Where an application is granted under section 72, the relevant licensing authority must forthwith—

    (a)   give a notice to that effect to—

        (i)   the applicant,

        (ii)   any person who made relevant representations in respect of the application, and

        (iii)   the chief officer of police for the police area (or each police area) in which the premises are situated, and

    (b)   issue the club with the club premises certificate and a summary of it.

(2) Where relevant representations were made in respect of the application, the notice under subsection (1)(a) must specify the authority's reasons for its decision as to the steps (if any) to take under section 72(3)(b).

(3) Where an application is rejected under section 72, the relevant licensing authority must forthwith give a notice to that effect, stating its reasons for that decision, to—

    (a)   the applicant,

    (b)   any person who made relevant representations in respect of the application, and

    (c)   the chief officer of police for the police area (or each police area) in which the premises are situated.

(4) In this section "relevant representations" has the meaning given in section 72(6).

[Licensing Act 2003, s 77.]

7.7740   78. Form of certificate and summary *Licence and summary to be in form prescribed[1].*

---

[1] See the Licensing Act 2003 (Premises Licences and Club Premises Certificates) Regulations 2005, SI 2005/42 (for amending instruments, see note to s 13, ante) and the Welsh Language (Gambling and Licensing Forms) Regulations 2010, SI 2010/2440.

7.7741   79. Theft, loss, etc of certificate or summary *Power to apply for duplicate licence or summary on payment of fee.*

Duration of certificate

7.7742   80. Period of validity of club premises certificate *Club premises certificate to have effect until withdrawn under ss 88 or 90 or until lapses. Certificate of no effect if suspended following a review under s 88.*

7.7743   81. Surrender of club premises certificate *Club may surrender certificate by giving notice to licensing authority. Certificate lapses on receipt of notice.*

Duty to notify certain changes

7.7744 82. Notification of change of name or alteration of rules of club (1) Where a club—

   (a)   holds a club premises certificate, or

   (b)   has made an application for a club premises certificate which has not been determined by the relevant licensing authority,

the secretary[1] of the club must give the relevant licensing authority notice of any change in the name, or alteration made to the rules, of the club.

(2) Subsection (1) is subject to regulations under section 92(1) (power to prescribe fee to accompany application).

(3) A notice under subsection (1) by a club which holds a club premises certificate must be accompanied by the certificate or, if that is not practicable, by a statement of the reasons for the failure to produce the certificate.

(4) An authority notified under this section of a change in the name, or alteration to the rules, of a club must amend the club premises certificate accordingly.

(5) But nothing in subsection (4) requires or authorises the making of any amendment to a club premises certificate so as to change the premises to which the certificate relates (and no amendment made under that subsection to a club premises certificate has effect so as to change those premises).

(6) If a notice required by this section is not given within the 28 days following the day on which the change of name or alteration to the rules is made, the secretary of the club commits an offence.

(7) A person guilty of an offence under subsection (6) is liable on summary conviction to a fine not exceeding level 2 on the standard scale.

[Licensing Act 2003, s 82.]

---

[1] For the secretary of a club, see s 70, ante.

7.7745 83. Change of relevant registered address of club (1) A club which holds a club premises certificate may give the relevant licensing authority notice of any change desired to be made in the address which is to be the club's relevant registered address.

(2) If a club which holds a club premises certificate ceases to have any authority to make use of the address which is its relevant registered address, it must as soon as reasonably practicable give to the relevant licensing authority notice of the change to be made in the address which is to be the club's relevant registered address.

(3) Subsections (1) and (2) are subject to regulations under section 92(1) (power to prescribe fee to accompany application).

(4) A notice under subsection (1) or (2) must also be accompanied by the club premises certificate or, if that is not practicable, by a statement of the reasons for the failure to produce the certificate.

(5) An authority notified under subsection (1) or (2) of a change to be made in the relevant registered address of a club must amend the club premises certificate accordingly.

(6) If a club fails, without reasonable excuse, to comply with subsection (2) the secretary commits an offence.

(7) A person guilty of an offence under subsection (6) is liable on summary conviction to a fine not exceeding level 2 on the standard scale.

(8) In this section "relevant registered address" has the meaning given in section 184(7).

[Licensing Act 2003, s 83.]

Variation of certificates

7.7746 84. Application to vary club premises certificate *Application for variation of club premises certificate to be in the prescribed form and advertised in accordance with Regulations. The Licensing Act 2003 (Premises Licences and Club Premises Certificates) Regulations 2005, SI 2005/42 (for amending instruments, see note to s 13, ante) and the Welsh Language (Gambling and Licensing Forms) Regulations 2010, SI 2010/2440 have been made.*

7.7747 85. Determination of application under section 84 (1) This section applies where the relevant licensing authority—

   (a)   receives an application, made in accordance with section 84, to vary a club premises certificate, and

   (b)   is satisfied that the applicant has complied with any requirement imposed by virtue of subsection (4) of that section.

(2) Subject to subsection (3) and section 86(6), the authority must grant the application.

(3) Where relevant representations are made, the authority must—

   (a)   hold a hearing to consider them, unless the authority, the applicant and each person who has made such representations agree that a hearing is unnecessary, and

   (b)   having regard to the representations, take such of the steps mentioned in subsection (4) (if any) as it considers appropriate for the promotion of the licensing objectives.

(4) The steps are—

   (a)   to modify the conditions of the certificate;

   (b)   to reject the whole or part of the application;

and for this purpose the conditions of the certificate are modified if any of them is altered or omitted or any new condition is added.

    (5)   In this section "relevant representations" means representations which—

        (a)   are about the likely effect of the grant of the application on the promotion of the licensing objectives, and

        (b)   meet the requirements of subsection (6).

    (6)   The requirements are—

        (a)   that the representations are made by a responsible authority or other person within the period prescribed under section 71(6)(c) by virtue of section 84(4),

        (b)   that they have not been withdrawn, and

        (c)   in the case of representations made by a person who is not a responsible authority, that they are not, in the opinion of the relevant licensing authority, frivolous or vexatious.

    (7)   Subsections (2) and (3) are subject to sections 73 to 74 (mandatory conditions relating to alcohol and to exhibition of films).

[Licensing Act 2003, s 85 as amended by the Policing and Crime Act 2009, Sch 7 and the Police Reform and Social Responsibility Act 2011, ss 107, 110.]

7.7748   **86.**   **Supplementary provision about applications under section 84**   (1)   Where an application (or any part of an application) is granted under section 85, the relevant licensing authority must forthwith give a notice to that effect to—

        (a)   the applicant,

        (b)   any person who made relevant representations in respect of the application, and

        (c)   the chief officer of police for the police area (or each police area) in which the premises are situated.

    (2)   Where relevant representations were made in respect of the application, the notice under subsection (1) must specify the authority's reasons for its decision as to the steps (if any) to take under section 85(3)(b).

    (3)   The notice under subsection (1) must specify the time when the variation in question takes effect.

That time is the time specified in the application or, if that time is before the applicant is given the notice, such later time as the relevant licensing authority specifies in the notice.

    (4)   Where an application (or any part of an application) is rejected under section 85, the relevant licensing authority must forthwith give a notice to that effect stating its reasons for rejecting the application to—

        (a)   the applicant,

        (b)   any person who made relevant representations, and

        (c)   the chief officer of police for the police area (or each police area) in which the premises are situated.

    (5)   Where the relevant licensing authority determines for the purposes of section 85(6)(c) that any representations are frivolous or vexatious, it must give the person who made them its reasons for that determination.

    (6)   A club premises certificate may not be varied under section 85 so as to vary substantially the premises to which it relates.

    (7)   In discharging its duty under subsection (2) or (3)(b) of that section, a licensing authority may vary a club premises certificate so that it has effect subject to different conditions in respect of—

        (a)   different parts of the premises concerned;

        (b)   different qualifying club activities.

    (8)   In this section "relevant representations" has the meaning given in section 85(5).

[Licensing Act 2003, s 86.]

7.7749   **86A.**   **Application for minor variation of club premises certificate**   (1)   Subject to subsection (3), a club which holds a club premises certificate may apply under this section (instead of under section 84) to the relevant licensing authority for variation of the certificate.

    (2)   Subsection (1) is subject to regulations under—

        (a)   section 91 (form etc of applications etc);

        (b)   section 92 (fees to accompany applications etc).

    (3)   An application may not be made under this section to vary a club premises certificate so as to—

        (a)   vary substantially the premises to which it relates,

        (b)   add the supply of alcohol to members or guests as an activity authorised by the certificate, or

        (c)   authorise—

            (i)   the supply of alcohol to members or guests at any time between 11pm and 7am, or

            (ii)   an increase in the amount of time on any day during which alcohol may be supplied to members or guests.

    (4)   The duty to make regulations imposed on the Secretary of State by subsection (6)(a) of section 71 (advertisement etc of application) applies in relation to applications under this section as it applies in relation to applications under that section.

[Licensing Act 2003, s 86A as inserted by SI 2009/1772.]

7.7750   86B.   Determination of application under section 86A   (1)   This section applies where the relevant licensing authority receives an application made under section 86A.

(2)   In determining the application the authority must—

(*a*)   consult such of the responsible authorities as it considers appropriate, and

(*b*)   take into account any relevant representations—

(i)   made by those authorities, or

(ii)   made by any other person and received by the authority within ten working days beginning on the initial day.

(3)   If the authority considers that—

(*a*)   the variation proposed in the application could not have an adverse effect on the promotion of any of the licensing objectives, or

(*b*)   if more than one variation is proposed, none of them, whether considered separately or together could have such an effect,

it must grant the application.

(4)   In any other case the authority must reject the application.

(5)   A determination under this section must be made within the period of fifteen working days beginning on the initial day.

(6)   If at the expiry of the period referred to in subsection (5) the authority has not determined the application—

(*a*)   the application is rejected, and

(*b*)   the authority must forthwith return the fee that accompanied the application.

(7)   But nothing in subsection (6) prevents the authority, with the agreement of the applicant, from treating—

(*a*)   an application rejected by virtue of that subsection ("the first application") as a new application made under section 86A,

(*b*)   the prescribed fee that accompanied the first application as the prescribed fee accompanying a new application, or

(*c*)   both.

(8)   A new application of the kind referred to in subsection (7)(*a*) is to be treated as having been made on the date of the agreement referred to in that provision, or on such other date as is specified in the agreement.

(9)   Any fee owed to an applicant under subsection (6) may be recovered as a debt due to the applicant.

(10)   For the purposes of this section—

"initial day" in relation to an application means the first working day after the day on which the authority receives the application;

"relevant representations" in relation to an application means representations which are about the likely effect of the grant of the application on the promotion of the licensing objectives.

[Licensing Act 2003, s 86B as inserted by SI 2009/1772 and the Police Reform and Social Responsibility Act 2011, s 107.]

7.7751   86C.   Supplementary provision about determinations under section 86B   (1)   Where an application is granted under section 86B, the relevant licensing authority must forthwith give a notice to that effect to the applicant.

(2)   The notice under subsection (1) must specify—

(*a*)   any variation of the club premises certificate which is to have effect as a result of the grant of the application, and

(*b*)   the time at which that variation takes effect.

(3)   The time referred to in subsection (2)(*b*) is the time specified in the application or, if that time is before the applicant is given the notice referred to in subsection (2), such later time as the authority specifies in the notice.

(4)   Where an application is rejected under section 86B, the relevant licensing authority must forthwith give a notice to that effect to the applicant.

(5)   The notice under subsection (4) must include a statement by the authority of the reasons for its decision.

[Licensing Act 2003, s 86C as inserted by SI 2009/1772.]

Review of certificates

7.7752   87.   Application for review of club premises certificate   (1)   Where a club holds a club premises certificate, a responsible authority or any other person may apply to the relevant licensing authority for a review of the certificate.

(2)   Subsection (1) is subject to regulations under section 91 (form etc of applications).

(3)   The Secretary of State must by regulations[1] under this section—

(*a*)   require the applicant to give a notice containing details of the application to the club and each responsible authority within such period as may be prescribed;

(*b*)   require the authority to advertise the application and invite representations relating to it to be made to the authority by the club, responsible authorities and other persons;

(*c*)   prescribe the period during which representations may be made by the club, any responsible authority and any other person;

    (*d*)   require any notice under paragraph (*a*) or advertisement under paragraph (*b*) to specify that period.

  (4)   The relevant licensing authority may, at any time, reject any ground for review specified in an application under this section if it is satisfied—

    (*a*)   that the ground is not relevant to one or more of the licensing objectives, or

    (*b*)   in the case of an application made by a person other than a responsible authority, that—

        (i)   the ground is frivolous or vexatious, or

        (ii)   the ground is a repetition.

  (5)   For this purpose a ground for review is a repetition if—

    (*a*)   it is identical or substantially similar to—

        (i)   a ground for review specified in an earlier application for review made in respect of the same club premises certificate and determined under section 88, or

        (ii)   representations considered by the relevant licensing authority in accordance with section 72, before it determined the application for the club premises certificate under that section, and

    (*b*)   a reasonable interval has not elapsed since that earlier application or that grant.

  (6)   Where the authority rejects a ground for review under subsection (4)(*b*), it must notify the applicant of its decision and, if the ground was rejected because it was frivolous or vexatious, the authority must notify him of its reasons for making that decision.

  (7)   The application is to be treated as rejected to the extent that any of the grounds for review are rejected under subsection (4).

Accordingly, the requirements imposed under subsection (3)(*a*) and (*b*) and by section 88 (so far as not already met) apply only to so much (if any) of the application as has not been rejected.

[Licensing Act 2003, s 87 as amended by the Police Reform and Social Responsibility Act 2011, s 108.]

---

  [1] See the Licensing Act 2003 (Premises Licences and Club Premises Certificates) Regulations 2005, SI 2005/42 (for amending instruments, see note to s 13, ante) and the Welsh Language (Gambling and Licensing Forms) Regulations 2010, SI 2010/2440.

7.7753 88. Determination of application for review (1) This section applies where—

    (*a*)   the relevant licensing authority receives an application made in accordance with section 87,

    (*b*)   the applicant has complied with any requirement imposed by virtue of subsection (3)(*a*) or (*d*) of that section, and

    (*c*)   the authority has complied with any requirement imposed on it under subsection (3)(*b*) or (*d*) of that section.

  (2)   Before determining the application, the authority must hold a hearing to consider it and any relevant representations.

  (3)   The authority must, having regard to the application and any relevant representations, take such of the steps mentioned in subsection (4) (if any) as it considers appropriate for the promotion of the licensing objectives.

  (4)   The steps are—

    (*a*)   to modify the conditions of the certificate;

    (*b*)   to exclude a qualifying club activity from the scope of the certificate;

    (*c*)   to suspend the certificate for a period not exceeding three months;

    (*d*)   to withdraw the certificate;

and for this purpose the conditions of the certificate are modified if any of them is altered or omitted or any new condition is added.

  (5)   Subsection (3) is subject to sections 73 to 74 (mandatory conditions relating to alcohol and to exhibition of films).

  (6)   Where the authority takes a step within subsection (4)(*a*) or (*b*), it may provide that the modification or exclusion is to have effect for only such period (not exceeding three months) as it may specify.

  (7)   In this section "relevant representations" means representations which—

    (*a*)   are relevant to one or more of the licensing objectives, and

    (*b*)   meet the requirements of subsection (8).

  (8)   The requirements are—

    (*a*)   that the representations are made by the club, a responsible authority or any other person within the period prescribed under section 87(3)(*c*),

    (*b*)   that they have not been withdrawn, and

    (*c*)   if they are made by a person who is not a responsible authority, that they are not, in the opinion of the relevant licensing authority, frivolous or vexatious.

  (9)   Where the relevant licensing authority determines that any representations are frivolous or vexatious, it must give the person who made them its reasons for that determination.

  (10)   Where a licensing authority determines an application for review under this section it must notify the determination and its reasons for making it to—

    (*a*)   the club,

    (*b*)   the applicant,

    (*c*)   any person who made relevant representations, and

    (d)   the chief officer of police for the police area (or each police area) in which the premises are situated.

(11)   A determination under this section does not have effect—

    (a)   until the end of the period given for appealing against the decision, or

    (b)   if the decision is appealed against, until the appeal is disposed of.

[Licensing Act 2003, s 88 as amended by the Policing and Crime Act 2009, Sch 7 and the Police Reform and Social Responsibility Act 2011, ss 108, 110.]

7.7754 89. Supplementary provision about review *Licensing authority able to determine review which has been applied for by itself in its separate capacity as a responsible authority.*

Withdrawal of certificates

7.7755 90. Club ceasing to be a qualifying club (1) Where—

    (a)   a club holds a club premises certificate, and

    (b)   it appears to the relevant licensing authority that the club does not satisfy the conditions for being a qualifying club in relation to a qualifying club activity to which the certificate relates (see section 61),

the authority must give a notice to the club withdrawing the certificate, so far as relating to that activity.

(2)   Where the only reason that the club does not satisfy the conditions for being a qualifying club in relation to the activity in question is that the club has fewer than the required number of members, the notice withdrawing the certificate must state that the withdrawal—

    (a)   does not take effect until immediately after the end of the period of three months following the date of the notice, and

    (b)   will not take effect if, at the end of that period, the club again has at least the required number of members.

(3)   The references in subsection (2) to the required number of members are references to the minimum number of members required by condition 4 in section 62(5) (25 at the passing of this Act).

(4)   Nothing in subsection (2) prevents the giving of a further notice of withdrawal under this section at any time.

(5)   Where a justice of the peace is satisfied, on information on oath, that there are reasonable grounds for believing—

    (a)   that a club which holds a club premises certificate does not satisfy the conditions for being a qualifying club in relation to a qualifying club activity to which the certificate relates, and

    (b)   that evidence of that fact is to be obtained at the premises to which the certificate relates,

he may issue a warrant authorising a constable to enter the premises, if necessary by force, at any time within one month from the time of the issue of the warrant, and search them.

(6)   A person who enters premises under the authority of a warrant under subsection (5) may seize and remove any documents relating to the business of the club in question.

[Licensing Act 2003, s 90.]

General provision

7.7756 91. Form etc of applications and notices under Part 4 *Applications and notices to be in the form prescribed by regulations[1].*

---

[1] See the Licensing Act 2003 (Premises Licences and Club Premises Certificates) Regulations 2005, SI 2005/42 (for amending instruments, see note to s 13, ante) and the Welsh Language (Gambling and Licensing Forms) Regulations 2010, SI 2010/2440.

7.7757 92A. Suspension of premises licence for failing to pay annual fee *Licensing authority must suspend a club premises certificate if the holder of the certificate has failed to pay an annual fee.*

Production of certificate, rights of entry, etc

7.7758 93. Licensing authority's duty to update club premises certificate (1) Where—

    (a)   the relevant licensing authority, in relation to a club premises certificate, makes a determination or receives a notice under this Part, or

    (b)   an appeal against a decision under this Part is disposed of,

the relevant licensing authority must make the appropriate amendments (if any) to the certificate and, if necessary, issue a new summary of the certificate.

(2)   Where a licensing authority is not in possession of the club premises certificate, it may, for the purpose of discharging its obligations under subsection (1), require the secretary of the club to produce the certificate to the authority within 14 days from the date on which the club is notified of the requirement.

(3)   A person commits an offence if he fails, without reasonable excuse, to comply with a requirement under subsection (2).

(4)   A person guilty of an offence under subsection (3) is liable on summary conviction to a fine not exceeding level 2 on the standard scale.

[Licensing Act 2003, s 93.]

7.7759   94.   Duty to keep and produce certificate etc   (1)   This section applies whenever premises in respect of which a club premises certificate has effect are being used for one or more qualifying club activities authorised by the certificate.

(2)   The secretary[1] of the club must secure that the certificate, or a certified copy of it, and a list of any relevant mandatory conditions applicable to the certificate are kept at the premises in the custody or under the control of a person (the "nominated person") who—

    (a)   falls within subsection (3),

    (b)   has been nominated for the purpose by the secretary in writing, and

    (c)   has been identified to the relevant licensing authority in a notice given by the secretary.

(3)   The persons who fall within this subsection are—

    (a)   the secretary of the club,

    (b)   any member of the club,

    (c)   any person who works at the premises for the purposes of the club.

(4)   The nominated person must secure that—

    (a)   the summary of the certificate or a certified copy of that summary, and

    (b)   a notice specifying the position which he holds at the premises,

are prominently displayed at the premises.

(5)   The secretary commits an offence if he fails, without reasonable excuse, to comply with subsection (2).

(6)   The nominated person commits an offence if he fails, without reasonable excuse, to comply with subsection (4).

(7)   A constable or an authorised person may require the nominated person to produce the club premises certificate (or certified copy) or any list of relevant mandatory conditions for examination.

(8)   An authorised person exercising the power conferred by subsection (7) must, if so requested, produce evidence of his authority to exercise the power.

(9)   A person commits an offence if he fails, without reasonable excuse, to produce a club premises certificate or any list of relevant mandatory conditions or certified copy of a club premises certificate in accordance with a requirement under subsection (7).

(10)   A person guilty of an offence under this section is liable on summary conviction to a fine not exceeding level 2 on the standard scale.

(11)   In subsection (4) the reference to the summary of the certificate is a reference to the summary issued under section 77 or, where one or more summaries have subsequently been issued under section 93, the most recent summary to be so issued.

(12)   Section 95 makes provision about certified copies of club premises certificates and of summaries of club premises certificates for the purposes of this section.

(13)   In this section "relevant mandatory conditions", in relation to a club premises certificate, means conditions applicable to the certificate by virtue of section 73A or 73B.

[Licensing Act 2003, s 94 as amended by the Policing and Crime Act 2009, Sch 7.]

---

[1]   For the secretary of a club, see s 70, ante.

7.7760   95.   Provision supplementary to section 94   (1)   Any reference in section 94 to a certified copy of a document is a reference to a copy of the document which is certified to be a true copy by—

    (a)   the relevant licensing authority,

    (b)   a solicitor or notary, or

    (c)   a person of a prescribed description.

(2)   Any certified copy produced in accordance with a requirement under subsection 94(7) must be a copy of the document in the form in which it exists at the time.

(3)   A document which purports to be a certified copy of a document is to be taken to be such a copy, and to comply with the requirements of subsection (2), unless the contrary is shown.

(4)   In this section "notary" means a person (other than a solicitor) who, for the purposes of the Legal Services Act 2007, is an authorised person in relation to any activity which constitutes a notarial activity (within the meaning of that Act).

[Licensing Act 2003, s 95 as amended by the Legal Services Act 2007, Sch 21.]

7.7761   96.   Inspection of premises before grant of certificate etc   (1)   Subsection (2) applies where—

    (a)   a club applies for a club premises certificate in respect of any premises,

    (b)   a club applies under section 84 for the variation of a club premises certificate held by it, or

    (c)   an application is made under section 87 for review of a club premises certificate.

(2)   On production of his authority—

    (a)   an authorised person, or

    (b)   a constable authorised by the chief officer of police,

may enter and inspect the premises.

(3)   Any entry and inspection under this section must take place at a reasonable time on a day—

    (a)   which is not more than 14 days after the making of the application in question, and (*b*)   which is specified in the notice required by subsection (4).

    (4)   Before an authorised person or constable enters and inspects any premises under this section, at least 48 hours' notice must be given to the club.

    (5)   Any person obstructing an authorised person in the exercise of the power conferred by this section commits an offence.

    (6)   A person guilty of an offence under subsection (5) is liable on summary conviction to a fine not exceeding level 2 on the standard scale.

    (7)   The relevant licensing authority may, on the application of a responsible authority, extend by not more than 7 days the time allowed for carrying out an entry and inspection under this section.

    (8)   The relevant licensing authority may allow such an extension of time only if it appears to the authority that—

    (*a*)   reasonable steps had been taken for an authorised person or constable authorised by the applicant to inspect the premises in good time, but

    (*b*)   it was not possible for the inspection to take place within the time allowed.

    [Licensing Act 2003, s 96.]

7.7762   97.   Other powers of entry and search   (1)   Where a club premises certificate has effect in respect of any premises, a constable may enter and search the premises if he has reasonable cause to believe—

    (*a*)   that an offence under section 4(3)(*a*), (*b*) or (*c*) of the Misuse of Drugs Act 1971 (c 38) (supplying or offering to supply, or being concerned in supplying or making an offer to supply, a controlled drug) has been, is being, or is about to be, committed there,

    (*aa*)   that an offence under section 5(1) or (2) of the Psychoactive Substances Act 2016 (supplying, or offering to supply, a psychoactive substance) has been, is being, or is about to be, committed there, or

    (*b*)   that there is likely to be a breach of the peace there.

    (2)   A constable exercising any power conferred by this section may, if necessary, use reasonable force.

    [Licensing Act 2003, s 97 as amended by the Psychoactive Substances Act 2015, Sch 5.]

PART 5[1]

PERMITTED TEMPORARY ACTIVITIES

Introductory

7.7763   98.   Meaning of "permitted temporary activity"   (1)   A licensable activity[2] is a permitted temporary activity by virtue of this Part if—

    (*a*)   it is carried on in accordance with—

        (i)   a notice given in accordance with section 100, and

        (ii)   any conditions imposed under section 106A, and

    (*b*)   the following conditions are satisfied.

    (2)   The first condition is that the requirements of section 102 (acknowledgement of notice) are met in relation to the notice.

    (3)   The second condition is that the notice has not been withdrawn under this Part.

    (4)   The third condition is that no counter notice has been given under this Part in respect of the notice.

    [Licensing Act 2003, s 98 as amended by the Police Reform and Social Responsibility Act 2011, ss 113, 114.]

---

    [1]   Part 5 comprises ss 98–110.
    [2]   For meaning of "licensable activity", see s 1(1), ante.

7.7764   99.   The relevant licensing authority   In this Part references to the "relevant licensing authority", in relation to any premises, are references to—

    (*a*)   the licensing authority in whose area the premises are situated, or

    (*b*)   where the premises are situated in the areas of two or more licensing authorities, each of those authorities.

    [Licensing Act 2003, s 99.]

7.7765   99A.   Meaning of "relevant person"   In this Part references to a "relevant person", in relation to any premises, are references to the following—

    (*a*)   the chief officer of police for any police area in which the premises are situated,

    (*b*)   the local authority by which statutory functions are exercisable in any area in which the premises are situated in relation to minimising or preventing the risk of pollution of the environment or of harm to human health.

    [Licensing Act 2003, s 99A as inserted by the Police Reform and Social Responsibility Act 2011, s 112.]

Temporary event notices

7.7766   100.   Temporary event notice   (1)   Where it is proposed to use premises[1] for one or more licensable activities during a period not exceeding 168 hours, an individual may give to the relevant licensing authority notice of that proposal (a "temporary event notice").

    (2)   In this Act, the "premises user", in relation to a temporary event notice, is the individual who gave the notice.

(3)   An individual may not give a temporary event notice unless he is aged 18 or over.

(4)   A temporary event notice must be in the prescribed form and contain—

    (*a*)   a statement of the matters mentioned in subsection (5),

    (*b*)   where subsection (6) applies, a statement of the condition mentioned in that subsection, and

    (*c*)   such other information as may be prescribed[2].

(5)   Those matters are—

    (*a*)   the licensable activities to which the proposal mentioned in subsection (1) relates ("the relevant licensable activities"),

    (*b*)   the period (not exceeding 168 hours) during which it is proposed to use the premises for those activities ("the event period"),

    (*c*)   the times during the event period when the premises user proposes that those licensable activities shall take place,

    (*d*)   the maximum number of persons (being a number less than 500) which the premises user proposes should, during those times, be allowed on the premises at the same time,

    (*e*)   where the relevant licensable activities include the supply of alcohol, whether supplies are proposed to be for consumption on the premises or off the premises, or both, and

    (*f*)   such other matters as may be prescribed[2].

(6)   Where the relevant licensable activities include the supply of alcohol, the notice must make it a condition of using the premises for such supplies that all such supplies are made by or under the authority of the premises user.

(7)   The temporary event notice—

    (*a*)   must be given in accordance with section 100A, and

    (*b*)   must be accompanied by the prescribed[3] fee when it is given by the premises user to the relevant licensing authority.

(8)   The Secretary of State may, by order—

    (*a*)   amend subsections (1) and (5)(*b*) so as to substitute any period for the period for the time being specified there;

    (*b*)   amend subsection (5)(*d*) so as to substitute any number for the number for the time being specified there.

(9)   In this section "supply of alcohol" means—

    (*a*)   the sale by retail of alcohol, or

    (*b*)   the supply of alcohol by or on behalf of a club to, or to the order of, a member of the club.★

[Licensing Act 2003, s 100 as amended by SI 2009/2999 and the Police Reform and Social Responsibility Act 2011, ss 114, 115.]

---

[1]   For meaning of "premises", see s 193, post.

[2]   The Licensing Act 2003 (Permitted Temporary Activities) (Notices) Regulations 2005, SI 2005/2918 and the Welsh Language (Gambling and Licensing Forms) Regulations 2010, SI 2010/2440 have been made.

[3]   The Licensing Act 2003 (Fees) Regulations 2005, SI 2005/79 have been made.

7.7767   100A. Standard and late temporary event notices   (1) For the purposes of section 100(7)(*a*), a temporary event notice must be given in accordance with—

    (*a*)   subsection (2), in which case the notice is a "standard temporary event notice", or

    (*b*)   subsection (3), in which case the notice is a "late temporary event notice".

(2)   A temporary event notice is given in accordance with this subsection if, no later than ten working days before the day on which the event period begins,—

    (*a*)   it is given to the relevant licensing authority by means of a relevant electronic facility, or

    (*b*)   it is given to the relevant licensing authority (otherwise than by means of a relevant electronic facility) and to each relevant person.

(3)   A temporary event notice is given in accordance with this subsection if—

    (*a*)   it is given to the relevant licensing authority by means of a relevant electronic facility no later than five working days, but no earlier than nine working days, before the day the event period begins, or

    (*b*)   both of the following are satisfied—

        (i)   it is given to the relevant licensing authority (otherwise than by means of a relevant electronic facility) and to each relevant person no later than five working days before the day on which the event period begins;

        (ii)   it is given to at least one of those persons no earlier than nine working days before the day on which that event period begins.

(4)   Where a temporary event notice (the "original notice") is given by the premises user to the relevant licensing authority by means of a relevant electronic facility as referred to in subsection (2)(*a*) or (3)(*a*)—

    (*a*)   the licensing authority must give a copy of the original notice to each relevant person no later than the end of the first working day after the day on which the original notice was given to the authority, and

(b)   for the purposes of this Act, the copy is to be treated as if it were the original notice.
(5)   In this section "event period" in relation to a temporary event notice means the event period specified in the notice.

[Licensing Act 2003, s 100A as inserted by the Police Reform and Social Responsibility Act 2011, s 114.]

7.7768   101.   Minimum of 24 hours between event periods   *Temporary Event Notice void if period specified in it starts or ends within 24 hours of another notice given in respect of the same premises by the premises user, or an associate or business colleague of that premises user.*

7.7769   102.   Acknowledgement of notice   *Licensing authority obliged to acknowledge receipt of Temporary Event Notice within one working day of receipt, unless counter notice served under s 107 because permitted limits have been exceeded.*

7.7770   103.   Withdrawal of notice   (1)   A temporary event notice may be withdrawn by the premises user giving the relevant licensing authority a notice to that effect no later than 24 hours before the beginning of the event period specified in the temporary event notice.
(2)   Nothing in section 102 or sections 104 to 107 applies in relation to a notice withdrawn in accordance with this section.

[Licensing Act 2003, s 103.]

Police objections

7.7771   104.   Objection to notice by the police   *Copy of Temporary Event Notice to be served on Chief Officer of Police no later than 10 working days before event begins. Police must give objection notice no later than 48 hours after the chief officer of police is given a copy of the temporary event notice if satisfied that use of premises in accordance with the Temporary Event Notice would undermine the crime prevention licensing objective.*

7.7772   104A.   Counter notice following objection to late notice   *Where an objection notice is given in respect of a late temporary event notice, the licensing authority must give the premises user a counter notice.*

[Licensing Act 2003, s 104A as inserted by the Police Reform and Social Responsibility Act 2011, s 114.]

7.7773   105.   Counter notice following objection to standard temporary event notice
(1)   This section applies where an objection notice is given under section 104(2) in respect of a standard temporary event notice.
(2)   The relevant licensing authority must—
    (a)   hold a hearing to consider the objection notice, unless the premises user, the relevant person who gave the objection notice and the authority agree that a hearing is unnecessary, and
    (b)   having regard to the objection notice, give the premises user a counter notice under this section if it considers it appropriate for the promotion of a licensing objective to do so.
(3)   The relevant licensing authority must—
    (a)   in a case where it decides not to give a counter notice under this section, give the premises user and each relevant person notice of the decision, and
    (b)   in any other case—
        (i)   give the premises user the counter notice and a notice stating the reasons for its decision, and
        (ii)   give each relevant person a copy of both of those notices.
(4)   A decision must be made under subsection (2)(b), and the requirements of subsection (3) must be met, at least 24 hours before the beginning of the event period specified in the temporary event notice.
(5)   Where the premises are situated in the area of more than one licensing authority, the functions conferred on the relevant licensing authority by this section must be exercised by those authorities jointly.
(6)   This section does not apply—
    (a)   if the objection notice has been withdrawn (whether by virtue of section 106 or otherwise), or
    (b)   if the premises user has been given a counter notice under section 107.
(7)   *Repealed.*

[Licensing Act 2003, s 105 as amended by the Police Reform and Social Responsibility Act 2011, ss 111, 112, 114.]

7.7774   106.   Modification of standard temporary event notice following objection   *Power of relevant person, where an objection notice has been given, to modify the temporary event notice with the agreement of the premises user and each other relevant person.*

7.7775   106A.   Conditions on standard temporary event notice following objection   *Licensing authority may impose one or more conditions on the standard temporary event notice if it considers it appropriate for the promotion of the licensing objectives to do so.*

[Licensing Act 2003, s 106A as inserted by the Police Reform and Social Responsibility Act 2011, s 113.]

Limits on temporary event notices

7.7776   107.   Counter notice where permitted limits exceeded   *Duty of licensing authority to give counter notice if permitted limits exceeded. The giving of a counter notice under this section cannot be appealed to the magistrates' court.*

Rights of entry, production of notice, etc

7.7777 108. Right of entry where temporary event notice given (1) A constable or an authorised officer may, at any reasonable time, enter the premises to which a temporary event notice relates to assess the likely effect of the notice on the promotion of the crime prevention objective.

(2) An authorised officer exercising the power conferred by this section must, if so requested, produce evidence of his authority to exercise the power.

(3) A person commits an offence if he intentionally obstructs an authorised officer exercising a power conferred by this section.

(4) A person guilty of an offence under this section is liable on summary conviction to a fine not exceeding level 2 on the standard scale.

(5) In this section "authorised officer" means—

(a) an officer of the licensing authority in whose area the premises are situated, or

(b) if the premises are situated in the area of more than one licensing authority, an officer of any of those authorities,

authorised for the purposes of this Act.

[Licensing Act 2003, s 108.]

7.7778 109. Duty to keep and produce temporary event notice and statement of conditions (1) This section applies whenever premises are being used for one or more licensable activities which are or are purported to be permitted temporary activities by virtue of this Part.

(2) The premises user must either—

(a) secure that a copy of the temporary event notice, together with a copy of any statement of conditions given under section 106A(3) in respect of the notice is prominently displayed at the premises, or

(b) meet the requirements of subsection (3).

(3) The requirements of this subsection are that the premises user must—

(a) secure that the temporary event notice, together with a copy of any statement of conditions given under section 106A(3) in respect of the notice is kept at the premises in—

(i) his custody, or

(ii) in the custody of a person who is present and working at the premises and whom he has nominated for the purposes of this section, and

(b) where the temporary event notice and any statement of conditions are in the custody of a person so nominated, secure that a notice specifying that fact and the position held at the premises by that person is prominently displayed at the premises.

(4) The premises user commits an offence if he fails, without reasonable excuse, to comply with subsection (2).

(5) Where—

(a) the temporary event notice or any statement of conditions is not displayed as mentioned in subsection (2)(a), and

(b) no notice is displayed as mentioned in subsection (3)(b),

a constable or authorised officer may require the premises user to produce the temporary event notice or statement of conditions for examination.

(6) Where a notice is displayed as mentioned in subsection (3)(b), a constable or authorised officer may require the person specified in that notice to produce the temporary event notice or statement of conditions for examination.

(7) An authorised officer exercising the power conferred by subsection (5) or (6) must, if so requested, produce evidence of his authority to exercise the power.

(8) A person commits an offence if he fails, without reasonable excuse, to produce a temporary event notice or statement of conditions in accordance with a requirement under subsection (5) or (6).

(9) A person guilty of an offence under this section is liable on summary conviction to a fine not exceeding level 2 on the standard scale.

(10) In this section "authorised officer" has the meaning given in section 108(5).

[Licensing Act 2003, s 109 as amended by the Police Reform and Social Responsibility Act 2011, s 113.]

Miscellaneous

7.7779 110. Theft, loss, etc of temporary event notice or statement of conditions *Power to apply for a duplicate temporary event notice or statement of conditions on payment of a fee.*

PART 5A

SALE OF ALCOHOL AT COMMUNITY EVENTS ETC AND ANCILLARY BUSINESS SALE OF ALCOHOL

Conditions for permitted sales

7.7780 110A. General conditions (1) A sale by retail of alcohol is a permitted sale by virtue of this Part if—

    (*a*)   the community event conditions (set out in section 110B or in regulations made under that section) or the ancillary business sales conditions (set out in section 110C or in regulations made under that section) are satisfied in relation to it, and

    (*b*)   the conditions set out in subsections (2) to (5) below are satisfied in relation to it.

(2)   The sale must take place on premises specified in a notice that complies with section 110D (a "Part 5A notice").

(3)   No counter notice under section 110J must have been given in relation to the Part 5A notice.

(4)   The sale must take place during the period of 36 months beginning with the date when the Part 5A notice takes effect.

(5)   The sale must take place between 07.00 am and 11.00 pm

[Licensing Act 2003, s 110A as inserted by the Deregulation Act 2015, Sch 17 from a date to be appointed.]

7.7781 110B. Community event conditions (1) The community event conditions, in relation to a sale by retail of alcohol, are the conditions set out in subsections (2) to (6) and any additional conditions set out in regulations under subsection (7).

(2)   The sale must be made by or on behalf of a body that—

    (*a*)   is of a prescribed description,

    (*b*)   does not trade for profit, and

    (*c*)   meets any prescribed criteria.

(3)   The sale must be ancillary to an event that—

    (*a*)   is taking place on the premises,

    (*b*)   is organised by the body by or on whose behalf the sale is made,

    (*c*)   has been advertised in advance, and

    (*d*)   meets any prescribed criteria.

(4)   The sale must take place on the premises during the course of the event.

(5)   The alcohol must be sold for consumption on the premises during the course of the event.

(6)   The number of persons present on the premises at the time of the sale must not exceed 300.

(7)   Regulations may provide for additional conditions prescribed in the regulations to be community event conditions.

[Licensing Act 2003, s 110B as inserted by the Deregulation Act 2015, Sch 17 from a date to be appointed.]

7.7782 110C. Ancillary business sales conditions (1) The ancillary business sales conditions, in relation to a sale by retail of alcohol, are the conditions set out in subsections (2) to (5) and any additional conditions set out in regulations under subsection (6).

(2)   The sale must be made by or on behalf of a body that—

    (*a*)   is of a prescribed description, and

    (*b*)   meets any prescribed criteria.

(3)   The sale must take place on premises that—

    (*a*)   are managed by the body by or on whose behalf the sale is made,

    (*b*)   are of a prescribed description, and

    (*c*)   meet any prescribed criteria.

(4)   The sale must be ancillary to the provision of goods or services to a person on the premises where the sale takes place.

(5)   Except in prescribed circumstances, the alcohol must be sold for consumption on those premises.

(6)   Regulations may provide for additional conditions prescribed in the regulations to be ancillary business sales conditions.

[Licensing Act 2003, s 110C as inserted by the Deregulation Act 2015, Sch 17 from a date to be appointed.]

Part 5A notices

7.7783 110D. Conditions for validity of notices (1) A notice complies with this section if the conditions set out in subsections (2) to (10) are satisfied in relation to the notice.

(2)   The notice must specify whether—

    (*a*)   the community event conditions (set out in section 110B or in regulations under that section), or

    (*b*)   the ancillary business sales conditions (set out in section 110C or in regulations under that section),

will be satisfied in relation to sales of alcohol on the premises in question.

(3)   The notice must specify (for the purposes of section 110A(2))—

    (*a*)   in the case of a notice that specifies the ancillary business sales conditions, the set of premises to which it relates;

    (*b*)   in the case of a notice that specifies the community event conditions, no more than three sets of community premises, each of which must be wholly or partly in the area of the same licensing authority.

(4)   The notice must be given, on behalf of the body by or on whose behalf the sale of alcohol on the premises would take place, by a person who is aged 18 or over and is concerned in the management of the body.

(5)   The notice must be given to the relevant licensing authority, accompanied by the prescribed

fee.

(6)   Unless the notice is given to the relevant licensing authority by means of a relevant electronic facility, a copy of the notice must be given to each relevant person.

(7)   The notice must be in the prescribed form.

(8)   The notice must specify the date when it takes effect.

(9)   The specified date must be at least 10 working days, but no more than 3 months, after the day on which the notice is given.

Where subsection (6) applies, the notice is treated as given only when that subsection is complied with.

(10)   The notice must contain any other information that regulations require it to contain.

(11)   In this Part, "relevant person", in relation to any premises, means—

    (a)   the chief officer of police for any police area in which the premises are situated;

    (b)   the local authority by which statutory functions are exercisable in any area in which the premises are situated in relation to minimising or preventing the risk of pollution of the environment or of harm to human health.

[Licensing Act 2003, s 110D as inserted by the Deregulation Act 2015, Sch 17 from a date to be appointed.]

7.7784   110E.   Special restriction on giving of notices   (1)   This section applies where—

    (a)   a Part 5A notice is given on behalf of a body, and

    (b)   a counter notice under section 110J is given in relation to the Part 5A notice.

(2)   No further Part 5A notice may be given in respect of any premises specified in the notice, whether on behalf of that body or on behalf of another body that is an associate of it, before the end of the period of 12 months beginning with the day on which the counter notice is given.

(3)   However, the restriction in subsection (2) ceases to apply if the counter notice is revoked under section 110K or quashed by a court.

(4)   For the purposes of this section, a body is an associate of another body if it would be an associate of the other body for the purposes of the Estate Agents Act 1979 (see section 32(4) to (6) of that Act).

[Licensing Act 2003, s 110E as inserted by the Deregulation Act 2015, Sch 17 from a date to be appointed.]

7.7785   110F.   Date when Part 5A notice takes effect   (1)   A Part 5A notice takes effect on the date specified under section 110D(8).

(2)   Subsection (1) does not apply if a counter notice is given under section 110J in relation to the notice.

(For the case where a counter notice is revoked or quashed by a court, see section 110K(2).)

[Licensing Act 2003, s 110F as inserted by the Deregulation Act 2015, Sch 17 from a date to be appointed.]

7.7786   110G.   Acknowledgement of notice etc   (1)   This section applies where a relevant licensing authority receives a notice that is, or purports to be, a Part 5A notice.

(2)   The authority must give written acknowledgement of the receipt of the notice to the person who gave it.

(3)   The acknowledgment must be given—

    (a)   before the end of the first working day following the day on which it was received, or

    (b)   if the day on which it was received was not a working day, before the end of the second working day following that day.

(4)   If the licensing authority is of the opinion that the notice does not comply with section 110D, the authority must as soon as possible give to the person who gave the notice written notification of the reasons for its opinion.

(5)   Subsection (2) does not apply where, before the time by which acknowledgement of the receipt of the notice must be given in accordance with subsection (3), the person who gave the notice has been given a counter notice under section 110J.

[Licensing Act 2003, s 110G as inserted by the Deregulation Act 2015, Sch 17 from a date to be appointed.]

7.7787   110H.   Theft, loss etc of Part 5A notice   (1)   Where a Part 5A notice is lost, stolen, damaged or destroyed, the person who gave the notice may apply to the relevant licensing authority for a copy of the notice.

(2)   The application must be accompanied by the prescribed fee.

(3)   Where an application is made in accordance with this section, the licensing authority must issue the applicant with a copy of the notice (certified by the authority to be a true copy) if it is satisfied that the notice has been lost, stolen, damaged or destroyed.

(4)   This Act applies in relation to a copy issued under this section as it applies in relation to an original notice.

[Licensing Act 2003, s 110H as inserted by the Deregulation Act 2015, Sch 17 from a date to be appointed.]

Objections and counter notices

7.7788   110I.   Objection to Part 5A notice by a relevant person   (1)   Where a relevant person who is given a Part 5A notice is satisfied that allowing alcohol to be sold on the premises (or any of the premises) to which the notice relates would undermine a licensing objective, the relevant person must give a notice stating the reasons for being so satisfied (an "objection notice")—

    (a)   to the relevant licensing authority,

    (b)   to the person who gave the Part 5A notice, and

(c)   to every other relevant person.

(2)   Subsection (1) does not apply at any time after the relevant person has received a copy of a counter notice under section 110J in relation to the Part 5A notice.

(3)   An objection notice may be given only during the period beginning with the day on which the relevant person is given the Part 5A notice and ending with the third working day following that day ("the three-day period").

(4)   The restriction in subsection (3) does not apply to an objection notice based on—

(a)   things occurring after the end of the three-day period, or

(b)   information that the relevant person was unaware of, and could not with reasonable diligence have discovered, until after the end of that period.

[Licensing Act 2003, s 110I as inserted by the Deregulation Act 2015, Sch 17 from a date to be appointed.]

7.7789 110J.   Counter notices   (1)   Where a relevant licensing authority receives a Part 5A notice, the relevant licensing authority may—

(a)   give the person who gave the Part 5A notice a counter notice under this section;

(b)   give a copy of the counter notice to each relevant person.

(2)   Where the relevant licensing authority receives an objection notice given in compliance with the requirement imposed by section 110I(3), the relevant licensing authority must decide whether to give a counter notice (and, if it does so decide, give that notice) no later than whichever of the following is the earlier—

(a)   the day before the date when the Part 5A notice would take effect (see section 110D(8));

(b)   the expiry of the period of 28 days beginning with the day on which the objection notice is received by the relevant licensing authority.

(3)   The power conferred by subsection (1) may not be exercised at any time after the Part 5A notice takes effect unless an objection notice under section 110I has been given, by virtue of subsection (4) of that section, in relation to the notice.

(4)   The counter notice must—

(a)   be in the prescribed form, and

(b)   be given in the prescribed manner.

[Licensing Act 2003, s 110J as inserted by the Deregulation Act 2015, Sch 17 from a date to be appointed.]

7.7790 110K.   Counter notices: revocation etc   (1)   A relevant licensing authority must revoke a counter notice given under section 110J if—

(a)   the counter notice was given in consequence of one or more objection notices under section 110I, and

(b)   the objection notice or (as the case may be) each of them is withdrawn by the person who gave it or is quashed by a court.

(2)   Where a counter notice is revoked or is quashed by a court—

(a)   the counter notice is disregarded for the purposes of section 110A(3), except in relation to any time before the day on which it is revoked or quashed,

(b)   the Part 5A notice takes effect on that day, and

(c)   the relevant licensing authority must as soon as possible notify the person who gave the Part 5A notice of the date on which it takes effect.

[Licensing Act 2003, s 110K as inserted by the Deregulation Act 2015, Sch 17 from a date to be appointed.]

Rights of entry, production of notice, etc

7.7791 110L.   Right of entry where Part 5A notice given   (1)   A constable or an authorised officer may, at any reasonable time, enter premises to which a Part 5A notice relates to assess the likely effect of the notice on the promotion of the crime prevention objective.

(2)   An authorised officer exercising the power conferred by this section must, if so requested, produce evidence of the officer's authority to exercise the power.

(3)   It is an offence intentionally to obstruct an authorised officer exercising a power conferred by this section.

(4)   A person guilty of an offence under this section is liable on summary conviction to a fine not exceeding level 2 on the standard scale.

(5)   In this section "authorised officer" means—

(a)   an officer of the licensing authority in whose area the premises are situated, or

(b)   if the premises are situated in the area of more than one licensing authority, an officer of any of those authorities,

authorised for the purposes of this Act.

[Licensing Act 2003, s 110L as inserted by the Deregulation Act 2015, Sch 17 from a date to be appointed.]

7.7792 110M.   Duty to keep and produce Part 5A notice   (1)   This section applies whenever premises are being used for sales of alcohol which are, or are purported to be, permitted sales by virtue of this Part.

(2)   The person who gave the Part 5A notice must secure that a copy of the notice is either—

(a)   prominently displayed at the premises, or

(b)   kept at the premises in the custody of that person or of someone who is present and working at the premises and whom that person has nominated for the purposes of this section (a "nominated person").

(3)   Where a copy of the Part 5A notice is kept in the custody of a nominated person (and not prominently displayed at the premises) the person who gave the Part 5A notice must secure that a notice—

    (*a*)   stating that a copy of the Part 5A notice is in the nominated person's custody, and

    (*b*)   specifying the position held at the premises by the nominated person,

is prominently displayed at the premises.

(4)   It is an offence for the person who gave the Part 5A notice to fail, without reasonable excuse, to comply with subsection (2) or (where it applies) subsection (3).

(5)   Where—

    (*a*)   a copy of the Part 5A notice is not prominently displayed at the premises, and

    (*b*)   no notice is displayed as mentioned in subsection (3),

a constable or authorised officer may require the person who gave the Part 5A notice to produce a copy of it for examination.

(6)   Where a notice is displayed as mentioned in subsection (3), a constable or authorised officer may require the nominated person to produce a copy of the Part 5A notice for examination.

(7)   An authorised officer exercising the power conferred by subsection (5) or (6) must, if so requested, produce evidence of the officer's authority to exercise the power.

(8)   It is an offence for a person to fail, without reasonable excuse, to produce a copy of a Part 5A notice in accordance with a requirement under subsection (5) or (6).

(9)   A person guilty of an offence under this section is liable on summary conviction to a fine not exceeding level 2 on the standard scale.

(10)   In this section "authorised officer" has the meaning given in section 110L(5).

[Licensing Act 2003, s 110M as inserted by the Deregulation Act 2015, Sch 17 from a date to be appointed.]

Supplementary

7.7793   110N.   The relevant licensing authority   (1)   For the purposes of this Part, the "relevant licensing authority", in relation to any premises, is determined in accordance with this section.

(2)   In the case of a Part 5A notice that specifies the ancillary business sales conditions or in the case of a Part 5A notice that specifies the community event conditions in relation to only one set of premises, the relevant licensing authority is, subject to subsection (3), the authority in whose area the premises are situated.

(3)   Where the premises are situated in the areas of two or more licensing authorities, the relevant licensing authority is—

    (*a*)   the licensing authority in whose area the greater or greatest part of the premises is situated, or

    (*b*)   if there is no authority to which paragraph (a) applies, such one of the authorities as the person giving the Part 5A notice may choose.

(4)   In the case of a Part 5A notice that specifies the community event conditions in relation to more than one set of premises, the relevant licensing authority is—

    (*a*)   if there is only one licensing authority in whose area each set of premises is wholly or partly situated, that licensing authority;

    (*b*)   if each set of premises falls partly in the area of one authority and also partly in the area of another, such one of them as the person giving the Part 5A notice may choose.

[Licensing Act 2003, s 110N as inserted by the Deregulation Act 2015, Sch 17 from a date to be appointed.]

PART 6[1]
PERSONAL LICENCES

Introductory

7.7794   111.   Personal licence   (1)   In this Act "personal licence" means a licence which—

    (*a*)   is granted by a licensing authority to an individual, and

    (*b*)   authorises that individual to supply alcohol, or authorise the supply of alcohol, in accordance with a premises licence.

(2)   In subsection (1)(*b*) the reference to an individual supplying alcohol is to him—

    (*a*)   selling alcohol by retail, or

    (*b*)   supplying alcohol by or on behalf of a club to, or to the order of, a member of the club.

[Licensing Act 2003, s 111.]

---

[1]   Part 6 comprises ss 111–135 and Sch 4.

7.7795   112.   The relevant licensing authority   For the purposes of this Part the "relevant licensing authority", in relation to a personal licence, is the licensing authority which granted the licence.

[Licensing Act 2003, s 112.]

7.7796   113.   Meaning of "relevant offence", "immigration offence", "foreign offence" and "immigration penalty"   (1)   In this Part "relevant offence" means an offence listed in Schedule 4.

(2)   The Secretary of State may by order amend that list so as to add, modify or omit any entry.

(2A)   In this Part "immigration offence" means—

(a)   an offence referred to in paragraph 7A of Schedule 4, or

(b)   an offence listed in paragraph 24 or 25 of Schedule 4 that is committed in relation to an offence referred to in paragraph 7A of that Schedule.

(3)   In this Part "foreign offence" means an offence (other than a relevant offence) under the law of any place outside England and Wales.

(4)   In this Part "immigration penalty" means a penalty under—

(a)   section 15 of the Immigration, Asylum and Nationality Act 2006 ("the 2006 Act"), or

(b)   section 23 of the Immigration Act 2014 ("the 2014 Act").

(5)   For the purposes of this Part a person to whom a penalty notice under section 15 of the 2006 Act has been given is not to be treated as having been required to pay an immigration penalty if—

(a)   the person is excused payment by virtue of section 15(3) of that Act, or

(b)   the penalty is cancelled by virtue of section 16 or 17 of that Act.

(6)   For the purposes of this Part a person to whom a penalty notice under section 15 of the 2006 Act has been given is not to be treated as having been required to pay an immigration penalty until such time as—

(a)   the period for giving a notice of objection under section 16 of that Act has expired and the Secretary of State has considered any notice given within that period, and

(b)   if a notice of objection was given within that period, the period for appealing under section 17 of that Act has expired and any appeal brought within that period has been finally determined, abandoned or withdrawn.

(7)   For the purposes of this Part a person to whom a penalty notice under section 23 of the 2014 Act has been given is not to be treated as having been required to pay an immigration penalty if—

(a)   the person is excused payment by virtue of section 24 of that Act, or

(b)   the penalty is cancelled by virtue of section 29 or 30 of that Act.

(8)   For the purposes of this Part a person to whom a penalty notice under section 23 of the 2014 Act has been given is not to be treated as having been required to pay an immigration penalty until such time as—

(a)   the period for giving a notice of objection under section 29 of that Act has expired and the Secretary of State has considered any notice given within that period, and

(b)   if a notice of objection was given within that period, the period for appealing under section 30 of that Act has expired and any appeal brought within that period has been finally determined, abandoned or withdrawn.

[Licensing Act 2003, s 113 as amended by the Immigration Act 2016, Sch 4.]

7.7797   114.   Spent convictions   For the purposes of this Part a conviction for a relevant offence or a foreign offence must be disregarded if it is spent for the purposes of the Rehabilitation of Offenders Act 1974 (c 53)[1].

[Licensing Act 2003, s 114.]

---

[1]   In PART III: SENTENCING, ante.

7.7798   115.   Period of validity of personal licence   *(As amended by the Immigration Act 2016, Sch 4) Personal licence to have effect indefinitely. Personal licence ceases to have effect if surrendered under s 116, revoked under s 119, or forfeited under s 129. Also of no effect during period of any suspension under s 129.*

7.7799   116.   Surrender of personal licence   *Personal licence may be surrendered by giving of notice to licensing authority. Licence lapses on receipt of notice.*

Grant of licences

7.7800   117.   Application for grant of personal licence   *An application by an individual for the grant of a personal licence must, if the applicant is ordinarily resident in the area of a licensing authority, be made to that authority, and may, in any other case, be made to any licensing authority.*

7.7801   118.   *Individual permitted to hold one personal licence only.*

7.7802   120.   Determination of application for grant   (1)   This section applies where an application for the grant of a personal licence is made to a licensing authority in accordance with section 117.

(2)   The authority must grant the licence if it appears to it that—

(a)   the applicant is aged 18 or over,

(aa)   he is entitled to work in the United Kingdom,

(b)   he possesses a licensing qualification or is a person of a prescribed[1] description,

(c)   no personal licence held by him has been forfeited in the period of five years ending with the day the application was made, and

(d)   he has not been convicted of any relevant offence[2] or any foreign offence or required to pay an immigration penalty.

(3)   The authority must reject the application if it appears to it that the applicant fails to meet the

condition in any of paragraphs (a) to (c) of subsection (2).

(4)   If it appears to the authority that the applicant meets the conditions in paragraphs (*a*) to (*c*) of that subsection but fails to meet the condition in paragraph (*d*) of that subsection, the authority must give the chief officer of police for its area a notice to that effect.

(5)   Where, having regard to—

(*a*)   any conviction of the applicant for a relevant offence,

(*b*)   any conviction of his for a foreign offence which the chief officer of police considers to be comparable to a relevant offence, and

(*c*)   the applicant having been required to pay any immigration penalty,

the chief officer of police is satisfied that granting the licence would undermine the crime prevention objective, he must, within the period of 14 days beginning with the day he received the notice under subsection (4), give the authority a notice stating the reasons why he is so satisfied (an "objection notice").

(5A)   If it appears to the authority that the applicant meets the conditions in paragraphs (a) to (c) of subsection (2) but fails to meet the condition in paragraph (d) of that subsection by virtue of having been—

(a)   convicted of an immigration offence,

(b)   convicted of a foreign offence that the authority considers to be comparable to an immigration offence, or

(c)   required to pay an immigration penalty,

the authority must give the Secretary of State a notice to that effect.

(5B)   Where, having regard to—

(a)   any conviction of the applicant for an immigration offence,

(b)   any conviction of the applicant for a foreign offence which the Secretary of State considers to be comparable to an immigration offence, and

(c)   the applicant having been required to pay any immigration penalty,

the Secretary of State is satisfied that granting the licence would be prejudicial to the prevention of illegal working in licensed premises, the Secretary of State must, within the period of 14 days beginning with the day the Secretary of State received the notice under subsection (5A), give the authority a notice stating the reasons for being so satisfied (an "immigration objection notice").

(6)   Where no objection notice or immigration objection notice is given within the period of 14 days referred to in subsection (5) or (5B) (as the case may be), or any such notice given is withdrawn, the authority must grant the application.

(7)   Where an objection notice or an immigration objection notice is given within the period of 14 days referred to in subsection (5) or (5B) (as the case may be), and not withdrawn, the authority—

(*a*)   must hold a hearing to consider the notice, unless the applicant, the person who gave the notice and the authority agree that it is unnecessary, and

(*b*)   having regard to the notice, must—

(i)   where the notice is an objection notice, reject the application if it considers it appropriate for the promotion of the crime prevention objective to do so, or

(ii)   where the notice is an immigration objection notice, reject the application if it considers it appropriate for the prevention of illegal working in licensed premises to do so.

(7A)   An application that is not rejected by the authority under subsection (7)(b) must be granted by it.

(8)   In this section "licensing qualification" means—

(*a*)   a qualification—

(i)   accredited at the time of its award, and

(ii)   awarded by a body accredited at that time,

(*b*)   a qualification awarded before the coming into force of this section which the Secretary of State certifies is to be treated for the purposes of this section as if it were a qualification within paragraph (*a*), or

(*c*)   a qualification obtained in Scotland or Northern Ireland or in an EEA State which is equivalent to a qualification within paragraph (*a*) or (*b*).

(9)   For this purpose—

"accredited" means accredited by the Secretary of State; and

"EEA State" means a state which is a contracting party to the Agreement on the European Economic Area signed at Oporto on 2nd May 1992, as adjusted by the Protocol signed at Brussels on 17th March 1993.

[Licensing Act 2003, s 120 as amended by the Police Reform and Social Responsibility Act 2011, s 111, the Immigration Act 2016, Sch 4 and SI 2019/742.]

---

[1] See the Licensing Act 2003 (Personal Licences) Regulations 2005, SI 2005/41 and the Welsh Language (Gambling and Licensing Forms) Regulations 2010, SI 2010/2440.
[2] For meaning of "relevant offence", see Sch 4, post.

7.7803   122. Notification of determinations   (1)   Where a licensing authority grants an application—

(a)   it must give the applicant and the chief officer of police for its area a notice to that effect, and

(b)   if the chief officer of police gave an objection notice or the Secretary of State gave an immigration objection notice (which, in either case) was not withdrawn), the notice under paragraph (a) must contain a statement of the licensing authority's reasons for granting the application.

(2)   A licensing authority which rejects an application must give the applicant and the chief officer of police for its area a notice to that effect containing a statement of the authority's reasons for rejecting the application.

(2A)   Where the Secretary of State gave an immigration objection notice (which was not withdrawn) the notice under subsection (1)(a) or (2), as the case may be, must also be given to the Secretary of State.

(3)   In this section—

"application" means an application for the grant of a personal licence; and

"objection notice" and "immigration objection notice" have the meaning given in section 120.

[Licensing Act 2003, s 122 as amended by the Deregulation Act 2015, Sch 18 and the Immigration Act 2016, Sch 4.]

7.7804 123.   Duty   to   notify   licensing   authority   of   convictions   etc   during application period   (1)   Where an applicant for the grant of a personal licence is convicted of a relevant offence or a foreign offence during the application period, he must as soon as reasonably practicable notify the conviction or the requirement to pay (as the case may be) to the authority to which the application is made.

(2)   A person commits an offence if he fails, without reasonable excuse, to comply with subsection (1).

(3)   A person guilty of an offence under this section is liable on summary conviction to a fine not exceeding level 4 on the standard scale.

(4)   In this section "the application period", or is required to pay an immigration penalty during that period means the period that—

(a)   begins when the application for grant is made, and

(b)   ends when the application is determined or withdrawn.

[Licensing Act 2003, s 123 as amended by the Deregulation Act 2015, Sch 18 and the Immigration Act 2016, Sch 4.]

7.7805 124.   Convictions coming to light after grant   (1)   This section applies where, after a licensing authority has granted a personal licence, it becomes aware (whether by virtue of section 123(1), 131 or 132 or otherwise) that the holder of a personal licence ("the licence holder") was convicted during the application period of any relevant offence or foreign offence or was required during that period to pay an immigration penalty.

(2)   The licensing authority must give a notice to that effect to the chief officer of police for its area.

(3)   Where, having regard to—

(a)   any conviction of the licence holder for a relevant offence which occurred before the end of the application period,

(b)   any conviction of his for a foreign offence which the chief officer of police considers to be comparable to a relevant offence and which occurred before the end of the application period, and

(c)   the licence holder having been required before the end of the application period to pay any immigration penalty,

the chief officer of police is satisfied that continuation of the licence would undermine the crime prevention objective, he must, within the period of 14 days beginning with the day he received the notice under subsection (2), give the authority a notice stating the reasons why he is so satisfied (an "objection notice").

(3A)   Where the licence holder was (during the application period)—

(a)   convicted of an immigration offence,

(b)   convicted of a foreign offence that the licensing authority considers to be comparable to an immigration offence, or

(c)   required to pay an immigration penalty,

the authority must give the Secretary of State a notice to that effect.

(3B)   Where, having regard to—

(a)   any conviction of the licence holder for an immigration offence which occurred before the end of the application period,

(b)   any conviction of the licence holder for a foreign offence which the Secretary of State considers to be comparable to an immigration offence and which occurred before the end of the application period, and

(c)   the licence holder having been required before the end of the application period to pay any immigration penalty,

the Secretary of State is satisfied that continuation of the licence would be prejudicial to the prevention of illegal working in licensed premises, the Secretary of State must, within the period of 14 days beginning with the day the Secretary of State received the notice under subsection (3A), give the authority a notice stating the reasons for being so satisfied (an "immigration objection notice").

(4)   Where an objection notice or an immigration objection notice is given within the period of 14 days referred to in subsection (3) or (3B), as the case may be, (and not withdrawn), the authority—

(a)   must hold a hearing to consider the notice, unless the licence holder, the person who gave the notice and the authority agree it is unnecessary, and

(b)   having regard to the notice, must—

(i)   where the notice is an objection notice, revoke the licence if it considers it appropriate for the promotion of the crime prevention objective to do so, or

(ii)   where the notice is an immigration objection notice, revoke the licence if it considers it appropriate for the prevention of illegal working in licensed premises to do so.

(5)   Where the authority revokes or decides not to revoke a licence under subsection (4) it must notify the offender and the chief officer of police of the decision and its reasons for making it.

(5A)   Where the authority revokes or decides not to revoke a licence under subsection (4)(b)(ii) it must also notify the Secretary of State of the decision and its reasons for making it.

(6)   A decision under this section does not have effect—

(a)   until the end of the period given for appealing against the decision, or

(b)   if the decision is appealed against, until the appeal is disposed of.

(7)   In this section "application period", in relation to the grant of a personal licence, means the period that—

(a)   begins when the application for the grant is made, and

(b)   ends at the time of the grant.

[Licensing Act 2003, s 124 as amended by the Police Reform and Social Responsibility Act 2011, s 111, the Deregulation Act 2015, Sch 18 and the Immigration Act 2016, Sch 4.]

7.7806   125.   Form of personal licence   (*as amended by the Immigration Act 2016, Sch 4) Form of personal licence prescribed by regulations[1].*

---

[1]   The Licensing Act 2003 (Personal Licences) Regulations 2005, SI 2005/41 (for amending instruments, see note to s 120, ante) and the Welsh Language (Gambling and Licensing Forms) Regulations 2010, SI 2010/2440 have been made.

7.7807   126.   Theft, loss, etc of personal licence   *Power to apply for duplicate personal licence on payment of fee.*

Duty to notify certain changes

7.7808   127.   Duty to notify change of name or address   (1)   The holder of a personal licence must, as soon as reasonably practicable, notify the relevant licensing authority of any change in his name or address as stated in the personal licence.

(2)   Subsection (1) is subject to regulations under section 133(2) (power to prescribe fee to accompany notice).

(3)   A notice under subsection (1) must also be accompanied by the personal licence or, if that is not practicable, by a statement of the reasons for the failure to provide the licence.

(4)   A person commits an offence if he fails, without reasonable excuse, to comply with this section.

(5)   A person guilty of an offence under subsection (4) is liable on summary conviction to a fine not exceeding level 2 on the standard scale.

[Licensing Act 2003, s 127.]

Conviction of licence holder for relevant offence

7.7809   128.   Duty to notify court of personal licence   (1)   Where the holder of a personal licence is charged with a relevant offence[1], he must, no later than the time he makes his first appearance in a magistrates' court in connection with that offence—

(a)   produce to the court the personal licence, or

(b)   if that is not practicable, notify the court of the existence of the personal licence and the identity of the relevant licensing authority and of the reasons why he cannot produce the licence.

(2)   Subsection (3) applies where a person charged with a relevant offence is granted a personal licence—

(a)   after his first appearance in a magistrates' court in connection with that offence, but

(b)   before—

(i)   his conviction, and sentencing for the offence, or his acquittal, or,

(ii)   where an appeal is brought against his conviction, sentence or acquittal, the disposal of that appeal.

(3)   At his next appearance in court in connection with that offence, that person must—

(a)   produce to the court the personal licence, or

(b)   if that is not practicable, notify the court of the existence of the personal licence and the identity of the relevant licensing authority and of the reasons why he cannot produce the licence.

(4)   Where—

(a)   a person charged with a relevant offence has produced his licence to, or notified, a court under subsection (1) or (3), and

(b)   before he is convicted of and sentenced for, or acquitted of, that offence, a notifiable event occurs in respect of the licence,

he must, at his next appearance in court in connection with that offence, notify the court of that event.

(5)   For this purpose a "notifiable event" in relation to a personal licence means any of the following—

(a)   *repealed*

(b)   the surrender of the licence under section 116;

(c)   *repealed*

(d)   the revocation of the licence under section 124.

(6)   A person commits an offence if he fails, without reasonable excuse, to comply with this section.

(7)   A person guilty of an offence under subsection (6) is liable on summary conviction to a fine not exceeding level 2 on the standard scale.

[Licensing Act 2003, s 128 as amended by the Deregulation Act 2015, Sch 18.]

---

[1]   For meaning of "relevant offence", see Sch 4, post.

7.7810   129. Forfeiture or suspension of licence on conviction for relevant offence
(1)   This section applies where the holder of a personal licence is convicted of a relevant offence[1] by or before a court in England and Wales.

(2)   The court may—

(a)   order the forfeiture of the licence, or

(b)   order its suspension for a period not exceeding six months.

(3)   In determining whether to make an order under subsection (2), the court may take account of any previous conviction of the holder for a relevant offence.

(4)   Where a court makes an order under this section it may suspend the order pending an appeal against it.

(5)   Subject to subsection (4) and section 130, an order under this section takes effect immediately after it is made.

[Licensing Act 2003, s 129.]

---

[1]   For meaning of "relevant offence", see Sch 4, post.

7.7811   131. Court's duty to notify licensing authority of convictions   (1)   This section applies where a person who holds a personal licence ("the relevant person") is convicted, by or before a court in England and Wales, of a relevant offence in a case where—

(a)   the relevant person has given notice under section 128 (notification of personal licence), or

(b)   the court is, for any other reason, aware of the existence of that personal licence.

(2)   The appropriate officer of the court must (as soon as reasonably practicable)—

(a)   send to the relevant licensing authority a notice specifying—

(i)   the name and address of the relevant person,

(ii)   the nature and date of the conviction, and

(iii)   any sentence passed in respect of it, including any order made under section 129, and

(b)   send a copy of the notice to the relevant person.

(3)   Where, on an appeal against the relevant person's conviction for the relevant offence or against the sentence imposed on him for that offence, his conviction is quashed or a new sentence is substituted for that sentence, the court which determines the appeal must (as soon as reasonably practicable) arrange—

(a)   for notice of the quashing of the conviction or the substituting of the sentence to be sent to the relevant licensing authority, and

(b)   for a copy of the notice to be sent to the relevant person.

(4)   Where the case is referred to the Court of Appeal under section 36 of the Criminal Justice Act 1988 (c 33) (review of lenient sentence), the court must cause—

(a)   notice of any action it takes under subsection (1) of that section to be sent to the relevant licensing authority, and

(b)   a copy of the notice to be sent to the relevant person.

(5)   For the purposes of subsection (2) "the appropriate officer" is—

(a)   in the case of a magistrates' court, the designated officer for the court, and

(b)   in the case of the Crown Court, the appropriate officer;

and section 141 of the Magistrates' Courts Act 1980 (c 43) (meaning of "clerk of a magistrates' court") applies in relation to this subsection as it applies in relation to that section.

[Licensing Act 2003, s 131 as amended by the Courts and Tribunals (Judiciary and Functions of Staff) Act 2018, Sch.]

7.7812   132. Licence holder's duty to notify licensing authority of convictions etc
(1)   Subsection (2) applies where the holder of a personal licence—

(a) is convicted of a relevant offence, in a case where section 131(1) does not apply, or

(b) is convicted of a foreign offence.

(2) The holder must—

(a) as soon as reasonably practicable after the conviction, give the relevant licensing authority a notice containing details of the nature and date of the conviction, and any sentence imposed on him in respect of it, and

(b) as soon as reasonably practicable after the determination of any appeal against the conviction or sentence, or of any reference under section 36 of the Criminal Justice Act 1988 (c 33) in respect of the case, give the relevant licensing authority a notice containing details of the determination.

(2A) Subsection (2B) applies where the holder of a personal licence is required to pay an immigration penalty.

(2B) The holder must, as soon as reasonably practicable after being required to pay the penalty, give the relevant licensing authority a notice containing details of the penalty, including the date of the notice by which the penalty was imposed.

(3) A notice under subsection (2) or (2B) must be accompanied by the personal licence or, if that is not practicable, a statement of the reasons for the failure to provide the licence.

(4) A person commits an offence if he fails, without reasonable excuse, to comply with this section.

(5) A person guilty of an offence under subsection (4) is liable on summary conviction to a fine not exceeding level 2 on the standard scale.

[Licensing Act 2003, s 132 as amended by the Immigration Act 2016, Sch 4.]

7.7813   132A.   Convictions etc of licence-holder: powers of licensing authority   (1)   This section applies where a licensing authority has granted a personal licence and it becomes aware (whether by virtue of section 123(1), 131 or 132 or otherwise) that the holder of the licence ("the licence holder") has been, at any time before or after the grant of the licence—

(a) convicted of any relevant offence or foreign offence, or

(b) required to pay an immigration penalty.

(2) But this section does not apply at any time when in the case of a licence holder who has been convicted of any relevant offence or foreign offence—

(a) the licence holder has appealed against a conviction for, or any sentence imposed in relation to, a relevant offence or foreign offence and that appeal has not been disposed of, or

(b) the time limit for appealing against such a conviction or sentence has not expired.

(3) The relevant licensing authority may—

(a) suspend the licence for a period not exceeding six months, or

(b) revoke the licence.

(4) If the relevant licensing authority is considering whether to suspend or revoke the licence, the authority must give notice to the licence holder.

(5) A notice under subsection (4) must invite the licence holder to make representations regarding—

(a) the relevant offence, foreign offence or immigration penalty that has caused the relevant licensing authority to issue the notice,

(b) any decision of a court under section 129 or 130 in relation to the licence, and

(c) any other relevant information (including information regarding the licence holder's personal circumstances).

(6) The licence holder may make representations under subsection (5) to the relevant licensing authority within the period of 28 days beginning with the day the notice was issued.

(7) Before deciding whether to suspend or revoke the licence the relevant licensing authority must take into account—

(a) any representations made by the licence holder under this section,

(b) any decision of a court under section 129 or 130 of which the licensing authority is aware, and

(c) any other information which the authority considers relevant.

(8) Having taken into account the matters described in subsection (7) the relevant licensing authority may make a decision whether to suspend or revoke a licence, unless subsection (9) applies.

(9) This subsection applies where the relevant licensing authority has taken into account the matters described in subsection (7) and proposes not to revoke the licence.

(10) Where subsection (9) applies the authority must—

(a) give notice to the chief officer of police for its area that it proposes not to revoke the licence, and

(b) invite the officer to make representations regarding the issue of whether the licence should be suspended or revoked having regard to the crime prevention objective.

(11) The chief officer of police may make representations under subsection (10)(b) to the relevant licensing authority within the period of 14 days beginning with the day the notice was received.

(12) Where the relevant licensing authority has given notice to the chief officer of police under subsection (10)(a), the authority must take into account—

(a)   any representations from the officer, and

(b)   the matters described in subsection (7),

and then make a decision whether to suspend or revoke the licence.

(13)   The relevant licensing authority must give notice of any decision made under subsection (8) or (12) to the licence holder and the chief officer of police, including reasons for the decision.

(14)   A decision under this section does not have effect—

(a)   until the end of the period given for appealing against the decision, or

(b)   if the decision is appealed against, until the appeal is disposed of.

(15)   A decision under subsection (8) or (12) may be appealed (see paragraph 17(5A) of Part 3 of Schedule 5 (appeals: personal licences)).

[Licensing Act 2003, s 132A as inserted by the Policing and Crime Act 2017, s 138.]

General provision

7.7814   133.   Form etc of applications and notices under Part 6   *Form of application or notice, manner in which it is to be made or give and information and documents to accompany it and any fee payable to be prescribed by regulations[1].*

---

[1]   The Licensing Act 2003 (Personal Licences) Regulations 2005, SI 2005/41 (for amending instruments, see note to s 120, ante), the Licensing Act 2003 (Fees) Regulations 2005, SI 2005/79 (for amending instruments, see note to s 100, ante) and the Welsh Language (Gambling and Licensing Forms) Regulations 2010, SI 2010/2440 have been made.

7.7815   134.   Licensing authority's duty to update licence document   (1)   Where—

(*a*)   the relevant licensing authority makes a determination under section 124(4),

(*b*)   it receives a notice under section 123(1), 127, 131 or 132, or

(*c*)   an appeal against a decision under this Part is disposed of,

in relation to a personal licence, the authority must make the appropriate amendments (if any) to the licence.

(2)   Where, under section 131, notice is given of the making of an order under section 129, the relevant licensing authority must make an endorsement on the licence stating the terms of the order.

(3)   Where, under section 131, notice is given of the quashing of such an order, any endorsement previously made under subsection (2) in respect of it must be cancelled.

(4)   Where a licensing authority is not in possession of a personal licence, it may, for the purposes of discharging its obligations under this section, require the holder of the licence to produce it to the authority within 14 days beginning with the day on which he is notified of the requirement.

(5)   A person commits an offence if he fails, without reasonable excuse, to comply with a requirement under subsection (4).

(6)   A person guilty of an offence under subsection (5) is liable on summary conviction to a fine not exceeding level 2 on the standard scale.

[Licensing Act 2003, s 134 as amended by the Deregulation Act 2015, Sch 18.]

Production of licence

7.7816   135.   Licence holder's duty to produce licence   (1)   This section applies where the holder of a personal licence is on premises to make or authorise the supply of alcohol, and such supplies—

(*a*)   are authorised by a premises licence in respect of those premises, or

(*b*)   are a permitted temporary activity on the premises by virtue of a temporary event notice given under Part 5 in respect of which he is the premises user.

(2)   Any constable or authorised officer may require the holder of the personal licence to produce that licence for examination.

(3)   An authorised officer exercising the power conferred by subsection (2) must, if so requested, produce evidence of his authority to exercise the power.

(4)   A person who fails, without reasonable excuse, to comply with a requirement under subsection (2) is guilty of an offence.

(5)   A person guilty of an offence under subsection (4) is liable on summary conviction to a fine not exceeding level 2 on the standard scale.

(6)   In this section "authorised officer" means an officer of a licensing authority authorised by the authority for the purposes of this Act.

[Licensing Act 2003, s 135.]

PART 7[1]
OFFENCES

Unauthorised licensable activities

7.7817   136.   Unauthorised licensable activities[2]   (1)   A person commits an offence[3] if—

(*a*)   he carries on or attempts to carry on[4] a licensable activity[5] on or from any premises otherwise than under and in accordance with an authorisation, or

(*b*)   he knowingly allows a licensable activity[5] to be so carried on.

(2)   Where the licensable activity[5] in question is the provision of regulated entertainment, a

person does not commit an offence under this section if his only involvement in the provision of the entertainment is that he—

- (a)   performs in a play,
- (b)   participates as a sportsman in an indoor sporting event,
- (c)   boxes or wrestles in a boxing or wrestling entertainment,
- (d)   performs live music,
- (e)   plays recorded music,
- (f)   performs dance, or
- (g)   does something coming within paragraph 2(1)(h) of Schedule 1 (entertainment similar to music, dance, etc).

(3)   Subsection (2) is to be construed in accordance with Part 3 of Schedule 1.

(4)   A person guilty of an offence under this section is liable on summary conviction to imprisonment for a term not exceeding six months or to a fine, or to both.

(5)   In this Part "authorisation" means—

- (a)   a premises licence,
- (b)   a club premises certificate, or
- (c)   a temporary event notice in respect of which the conditions of section 98(2) to (4) are satisfied.*

[Licensing Act 2003, s 136 as amended by SI 2015/664.]

---

* **Amended by the Deregulation Act 2015, s 67 from a date to be appointed.**
[1] Part 7 comprises ss 136–159.
[2] See **para 7.7643 Offences – unauthorised licensable activities** ante, for liability under this provision.
[3] For defence of due diligence, see s 139, post.
[4] In *Hall v Woodhouse Ltd v Borough and County of the Town of Poole* [2009] EWHC 1587 (Admin) the convictions under this provision of a business which let a public house in which the tenant and his manager conducted unauthorised licensable activities were quashed:

> "17. In my judgment, s 136(1)(a) is directed at persons who, as a matter of fact, actually carry on or attempt to carry on a licensable activity on or from premises. That is the natural meaning of the language used. The matters referred to in subs (2), namely performing a play, participating as a sportsman and so on, also suggest that the focus is on actual conduct. So does s 139(1) which gives a person a defence where his act was due to a mistake etc and he took all reasonable precautions and exercised all due diligence to avoid committing the offence.
>
> 18. Section 136(1)(a) is not directed at holders of premises licences as such. An offence may be committed by carrying on a licensable activity when no premises licence exists at all. Where there is a premises licence but a licensable activity is carried on outside the scope of that licence or in breach of the conditions of the licence, it must, in my view, be a question of fact whether it is carried on by the holder of the licence. The mere fact that he is the holder of a licence does not make him automatically liable in respect of the carrying of a licensable activity on or from the premises to which the licence relates (per Richards LJ)."

[5] For meaning of "licensing activity", see s 1(1).

7.7818   137.   Exposing alcohol for unauthorised sale   (1)   A person commits an offence[1] if, on any premises, he exposes for sale by retail any alcohol in circumstances where the sale by retail of that alcohol on those premises would be an unauthorised licensable activity.

(2)   For that purpose a licensable activity is unauthorised unless it is under and in accordance with an authorisation.

(3)   A person guilty of an offence under this section is liable on summary conviction to imprisonment for a term not exceeding six months or to a fine, or to both.

(4)   The court by which a person is convicted of an offence under this section may order the alcohol in question, and any container for it, to be forfeited and either destroyed or dealt with in such other manner as the court may order.

[Licensing Act 2003, s 137 as amended by SI 2015/664.]

---

[1] For defence of due diligence, see s 139, post.

7.7819   138.   Keeping alcohol on premises for unauthorised sale etc   (1)   A person commits an offence[1] if he has in his possession or under his control alcohol which he intends to sell by retail or supply in circumstances where that activity would be an unauthorised licensable activity.

(2)   For that purpose a licensable activity is unauthorised unless it is under and in accordance with an authorisation[2].

(3)   In subsection (1) the reference to the supply of alcohol is a reference to the supply of alcohol by or on behalf of a club to, or to the order of, a member of the club.

(4)   A person guilty of an offence under this section is liable on summary conviction to a fine not exceeding level 2 on the standard scale.

(5)   The court by which a person is convicted of an offence under this section may order the alcohol in question, and any container for it, to be forfeited and either destroyed or dealt with in such other manner as the court may order.

[Licensing Act 2003, s 138.]

---

[1] For defence of due diligence, see s 139, post.
[2] For meaning of "authorisation", see s 136(5), post.

7.7820   139.   Defence of due diligence   (1)   In proceedings against a person for an offence to which subsection (2) applies, it is a defence that—

   (a)   his act was due to a mistake, or to reliance on information given to him, or to an act or omission by another person, or to some other cause beyond his control, and

   (b)   he took all reasonable precautions and exercised all due diligence to avoid committing the offence.

  (2)   This subsection applies to an offence under—

   (a)   section 136(1)(a) (carrying on unauthorised licensable activity),

   (b)   section 137 (exposing alcohol for unauthorised sale), or

   (c)   section 138 (keeping alcohol on premises for unauthorised sale).

[Licensing Act 2003, s 139.]

Drunkenness and disorderly conduct

7.7821   140.   Allowing disorderly conduct on licensed premises etc   (1)   A person to whom subsection (2) applies commits an offence if he knowingly allows disorderly conduct on relevant premises.

  (2)   This subsection applies—

   (a)   to any person who works at the premises in a capacity, whether paid or unpaid, which authorises him to prevent the conduct,

   (b)   in the case of licensed premises, to—

      (i)   the holder of a premises licence in respect of the premises, and

      (ii)   the designated premises supervisor (if any) under such a licence,

   (c)   in the case of premises in respect of which a club premises certificate has effect, to any member or officer of the club which holds the certificate who at the time the conduct takes place is present on the premises in a capacity which enables him to prevent it, and

   (d)   in the case of premises which may be used for a permitted temporary activity by virtue of Part 5, to the premises user in relation to the temporary event notice in question.

  (3)   A person guilty of an offence under this section is liable on summary conviction to a fine not exceeding level 3 on the standard scale. *

[Licensing Act 2003, s 140.]

---

* **Amended by the Deregulation Act 2015, s 67 from a date to be appointed.**

7.7822   141.   Sale of alcohol to a person who is drunk   (1)   A person to whom subsection (2) applies commits an offence if, on relevant premises, he knowingly—

   (a)   sells or attempts to sell alcohol to a person who is drunk, or

   (b)   allows alcohol to be sold to such a person.

  (2)   This subsection applies—

   (a)   to any person who works at the premises in a capacity, whether paid or unpaid, which gives him authority to sell the alcohol concerned,

   (b)   in the case of licensed premises, to—

      (i)   the holder of a premises licence in respect of the premises, and

      (ii)   the designated premises supervisor (if any) under such a licence,

   (c)   in the case of premises in respect of which a club premises certificate has effect, to any member or officer of the club which holds the certificate who at the time the sale (or attempted sale) takes place is present on the premises in a capacity which enables him to prevent it, and

   (d)   in the case of premises which may be used for a permitted temporary activity by virtue of Part 5, to the premises user in relation to the temporary event notice in question.

  (3)   This section applies in relation to the supply of alcohol by or on behalf of a club to or to the order of a member of the club as it applies in relation to the sale of alcohol.

  (4)   A person guilty of an offence under this section is liable on summary conviction to a fine not exceeding level 3 on the standard scale. *

[Licensing Act 2003, s 141.]

---

* **Amended by the Deregulation Act 2015, s 67 from a date to be appointed.**

7.7823   142.   Obtaining alcohol for a person who is drunk   (1)   A person commits an offence if, on relevant premises, he knowingly obtains or attempts to obtain alcohol for consumption on those premises by a person who is drunk.

  (2)   A person guilty of an offence under this section is liable on summary conviction to a fine not exceeding level 3 on the standard scale.

[Licensing Act 2003, s 142.]

7.7824   143.   Failure to leave licensed premises etc   (1)   A person who is drunk or disorderly commits an offence if, without reasonable excuse—

   (a)   he fails to leave relevant premises when requested to do so by a constable or by a person to whom subsection (2) applies, or

   (b)   he enters or attempts to enter relevant premises after a constable or a person to whom subsection (2) applies has requested him not to enter.

  (2)   This subsection applies—

   (a)   to any person who works at the premises in a capacity, whether paid or unpaid, which authorises him to make such a request,

(*b*)   in the case of licensed premises, to—
    (i)   the holder of a premises licence in respect of the premises, or
    (ii)   the designated premises supervisor (if any) under such a licence,
(*c*)   in the case of premises in respect of which a club premises certificate has effect, to any member or officer of the club which holds the certificate who is present on the premises in a capacity which enables him to make such a request, and
(*d*)   in the case of premises which may be used for a permitted temporary activity by virtue of Part 5, to the premises user in relation to the temporary event notice in question.

(3)   A person guilty of an offence under subsection (1) is liable on summary conviction to a fine not exceeding level 1 on the standard scale.

(4)   On being requested to do so by a person to whom subsection (2) applies, a constable must—
(*a*)   help to expel from relevant premises a person who is drunk or disorderly;
(*b*)   help to prevent such a person from entering relevant premises[1].*

[Licensing Act 2003, s 143.]

---

* **Amended by the Deregulation Act 2015, s 67 from a date to be appointed.**
[1] Although no provision is made in this section for the use of force, the right of the licence holder to eject a customer arises from common law and he may use at least reasonable force. The licensee may use an agent to assist. Subsection (4) merely requires a constable to assist. Accordingly, a constable exercises a common law power in using reasonable force to eject a customer when required to assist a licence holder. Implicit in a landlord's request for help to eject a customer, is a request to stop him immediately coming back into that public house: *Semple v Luton and South Bedfordshire Magistrates' Court* [2009] EWHC 3241 (Admin), [2010] 2 All ER 353.

Smuggled goods

7.7825   144.   Keeping of smuggled goods   (1)   A person to whom subsection (2) applies commits an offence if he knowingly keeps or allows to be kept, on any relevant premises, any goods which have been imported without payment of duty or which have otherwise been unlawfully imported.

(2)   This subsection applies—
(*a*)   to any person who works at the premises in a capacity, whether paid or unpaid, which gives him authority to prevent the keeping of the goods on the premises,
(*b*)   in the case of licensed premises, to—
    (i)   the holder of a premises licence in respect of the premises, and
    (ii)   the designated premises supervisor (if any) under such a licence,
(*c*)   in the case of premises in respect of which a club premises certificate has effect, to any member or officer of the club which holds the certificate who is present on the premises at any time when the goods are kept on the premises in a capacity which enables him to prevent them being so kept, and
(*d*)   in the case of premises which may be used for a permitted temporary activity by virtue of Part 5, to the premises user in relation to the temporary event notice in question.

(3)   A person guilty of an offence under this section is liable on summary conviction to a fine not exceeding level 3 on the standard scale.

(4)   The court by which a person is convicted of an offence under this section may order the goods in question, and any container for them, to be forfeited and either destroyed or dealt with in such other manner as the court may order.*

[Licensing Act 2003, s 144.]

---

* **Amended by the Deregulation Act 2015, s 67 from a date to be appointed.**

Children and alcohol

7.7826   145.   Unaccompanied children prohibited from certain premises   (1)   A person to whom subsection (3) applies commits an offence if—
(*a*)   knowing that relevant premises are within subsection (4), he allows an unaccompanied child to be on the premises at a time when they are open for the purposes of being used for the supply of alcohol for consumption there, or
(*b*)   he allows an unaccompanied child to be on relevant premises at a time between the hours of midnight and 5 a.m. when the premises are open for the purposes of being used for the supply of alcohol for consumption there.

(2)   For the purposes of this section—
(*a*)   "child" means an individual aged under 16,
(*b*)   a child is unaccompanied if he is not in the company of an individual aged 18 or over.

(3)   This subsection applies—
(*a*)   to any person who works at the premises in a capacity, whether paid or unpaid, which authorises him to request the unaccompanied child to leave the premises,
(*b*)   in the case of licensed premises, to—
    (i)   the holder of a premises licence in respect of the premises, and
    (ii)   the designated premises supervisor (if any) under such a licence,
(*c*)   in the case of premises in respect of which a club premises certificate has effect, to any member or officer of the club which holds the certificate who is present on the premises in a capacity which enables him to make such a request, and

(d)　　　in the case of premises which may be used for a permitted temporary activity by virtue of Part 5, to the premises user in relation to the temporary event notice in question.

(4)　Relevant premises are within this subsection if—

(a)　　　they are exclusively or primarily used for the supply of alcohol for consumption on the premises, or

(b)　　　they are open for the purposes of being used for the supply of alcohol for consumption on the premises by virtue of Part 5 (permitted temporary activities) and, at the time the temporary event notice in question has effect, they are exclusively or primarily used for such supplies.

(5)　No offence is committed under this section if the unaccompanied child is on the premises solely for the purpose of passing to or from some other place to or from which there is no other convenient means of access or egress.

(6)　Where a person is charged with an offence under this section by reason of his own conduct it is a defence that—

(a)　　　he believed that the unaccompanied child was aged 16 or over or that an individual accompanying him was aged 18 or over, and

(b)　　　either—

　　　(i)　　　he had taken all reasonable steps to establish the individual's age, or

　　　(ii)　　nobody could reasonably have suspected from the individual's appearance that he was aged under 16 or, as the case may be, under 18.

(7)　For the purposes of subsection (6), a person is treated as having taken all reasonable steps to establish an individual's age if—

(a)　　　he asked the individual for evidence of his age, and

(b)　　　the evidence would have convinced a reasonable person.

(8)　Where a person ("the accused") is charged with an offence under this section by reason of the act or default of some other person, it is a defence that the accused exercised all due diligence to avoid committing it.

(9)　A person guilty of an offence under this section is liable on summary conviction to a fine not exceeding level 3 on the standard scale.

(10)　In this section "supply of alcohol" means—

(a)　　　the sale by retail of alcohol, or

(b)　　　the supply of alcohol by or on behalf of a club to, or to the order of, a member of the club.

[Licensing Act 2003, s 145.]

7.7827　146.　Sale of alcohol to children　(1)　A person commits an offence if he sells alcohol to an individual aged under 18.

(2)　A club commits an offence if alcohol is supplied by it or on its behalf—

(a)　　　to, or to the order of, a member of the club who is aged under 18, or

(b)　　　to the order of a member of the club, to an individual who is aged under 18.

(3)　A person commits an offence if he supplies alcohol on behalf of a club—

(a)　　　to, or to the order of, a member of the club who is aged under 18, or

(b)　　　to the order of a member of the club, to an individual who is aged under 18.

(4)　Where a person is charged with an offence under this section by reason of his own conduct it is a defence that—

(a)　　　he believed that the individual was aged 18 or over, and

(b)　　　either—

　　　(i)　　　he had taken all reasonable steps to establish the individual's age, or

　　　(ii)　　nobody could reasonably have suspected from the individual's appearance that he was aged under 18.

(5)　For the purposes of subsection (4), a person is treated as having taken all reasonable steps to establish an individual's age if—

(a)　　　he asked the individual for evidence of his age, and

(b)　　　the evidence would have convinced a reasonable person.

(6)　Where a person ("the accused") is charged with an offence under this section by reason of the act or default of some other person, it is a defence that the accused exercised all due diligence to avoid committing it.

(7)　A person guilty of an offence under this section is liable on summary conviction to a fine not exceeding level 5 on the standard scale.

[Licensing Act 2003, s 146.]

7.7828　147.　Allowing the sale of alcohol to children　(1)　A person to whom subsection (2) applies commits an offence if he knowingly allows the sale of alcohol on relevant premises to an individual aged under 18.

(2)　This subsection applies to a person who works at the premises in a capacity, whether paid or unpaid, which authorises him to prevent the sale.

(3)　A person to whom subsection (4) applies commits an offence if he knowingly allows alcohol to be supplied on relevant premises by or on behalf of a club—

(a)　　　to or to the order of a member of the club who is aged under 18, or

(b)   to the order of a member of the club, to an individual who is aged under 18.

(4)   This subsection applies to—

(a)   a person who works on the premises in a capacity, whether paid or unpaid, which authorises him to prevent the supply, and

(b)   any member or officer of the club who at the time of the supply is present on the relevant premises in a capacity which enables him to prevent it.

(5)   A person guilty of an offence under this section is liable on summary conviction to a fine not exceeding level 5 on the standard scale.

[Licensing Act 2003, s 147.]

7.7829   147A.   Persistently selling alcohol to children   (1)   A person is guilty of an offence if—

(a)   on 2 or more different occasions within a period of 3 consecutive months alcohol is unlawfully sold on the same premises to an individual aged under 18;

(b)   at the time of each sale the premises were either licensed premises or premises authorised to be used for a permitted temporary activity by virtue of Part 5; and

(c)   that person was a responsible person in relation to the premises at each such time.

(2)   For the purposes of this section alcohol sold to an individual aged under 18 is unlawfully sold to him if—

(a)   the person making the sale believed the individual to be aged under 18; or

(b)   that person did not have reasonable grounds for believing the individual to be aged 18 or over.

(3)   For the purposes of subsection (2) a person has reasonable grounds for believing an individual to be aged 18 or over only if—

(a)   he asked the individual for evidence of his age and that individual produced evidence that would have convinced a reasonable person; or

(b)   nobody could reasonably have suspected from the individual's appearance that he was aged under 18.

(4)   A person is, in relation to premises and a time, a responsible person for the purposes of subsection (1) if, at that time, he is—

(a)   the person or one of the persons holding a premises licence in respect of the premises; or

(b)   the person or one of the persons who is the premises user in respect of a temporary event notice by reference to which the premises are authorised to be used for a permitted temporary activity by virtue of Part 5.

(5)   The individual to whom the sales mentioned in subsection (1) are made may, but need not be, the same in each case.

(6)   The same sale may not be counted in respect of different offences for the purpose—

(a)   of enabling the same person to be convicted of more than one offence under this section; or

(b)   of enabling the same person to be convicted of both an offence under this section and an offence under section 146 or 147.

(7)   In determining whether an offence under this section has been committed, the following shall be admissible as evidence that there has been an unlawful sale of alcohol to an individual aged under 18 on any premises on any occasion—

(a)   the conviction of a person for an offence under section 146 in respect of a sale to that individual on those premises on that occasion;

(b)   the giving to a person of a caution (within the meaning of Part 5 of the Police Act 1997) in respect of such an offence; or

(c)   the payment by a person of a fixed penalty under Part 1 of the Criminal Justice and Police Act 2001 in respect of such a sale.

(8)   A person guilty of an offence under this section shall be liable, on summary conviction, to a fine.

(9)   The Secretary of State may by order amend subsection (8) to increase the maximum fine for the time being specified in that subsection.*

[Licensing Act 2003, s 147A as inserted by the Violent Crime Reduction Act 2006, s 23 and amended by the Policing and Crime Act 2009, s 28, the Police Reform and Social Responsibility Act 2011, s 118 and SI 2015/664.]

---

*   **Amended by the Deregulation Act 2015, s 67 from a date to be appointed.**

7.7830   147B.   Order suspending a licence in respect of offence under section 147A

(1)   Where the holder of a premises licence is convicted of an offence under section 147A in respect of sales on the premises to which the licence relates, the court may order that so much of the licence as authorises the sale by retail of alcohol on those premises is suspended for a period not exceeding three months.

(2)   Where more than one person is liable for an offence under section 147A relating to the same sales, no more than one order under subsection (1) may be made in relation to the premises in question in respect of convictions by reference to those sales.

(3)   Subject to subsections (4) and (5), an order under subsection (1) comes into force at the

time specified by the court that makes it.

(4)   Where a magistrates' court makes an order under subsection (1), it may suspend its coming into force pending an appeal.

(5)   Section 130 (powers of appellate court to suspend section 129 order) applies (with the omission of subsection (9)) where an order under subsection (1) is made on conviction of an offence under section 147A as it applies where an order under section 129 is made on conviction of a relevant offence in Part 6.

[Licensing Act 2003, s 147B as inserted by the Violent Crime Reduction Act 2006, s 23.]

7.7831 149. Purchase of alcohol by or on behalf of children (1) An individual aged under 18 commits an offence if—

(a)   he buys or attempts to buy alcohol, or

(b)   where he is a member of a club—

      (i)   alcohol is supplied to him or to his order by or on behalf of the club, as a result of some act or default of his, or

      (ii)   he attempts to have alcohol supplied to him or to his order by or on behalf of the club.

(2)   But subsection (1) does not apply where the individual buys or attempts to buy the alcohol at the request of—

(a)   a constable, or

(b)   a weights and measures inspector,

who is acting in the course of his duty.

(3)   A person commits an offence if—

(a)   he buys or attempts to buy alcohol on behalf of an individual aged under 18, or

(b)   where he is a member of a club, on behalf of an individual aged under 18 he—

      (i)   makes arrangements whereby alcohol is supplied to him or to his order by or on behalf of the club, or

      (ii)   attempts to make such arrangements.

(4)   A person ("the relevant person") commits an offence if—

(a)   he buys or attempts to buy alcohol for consumption on relevant premises by an individual aged under 18, or

(b)   where he is a member of a club—

      (i)   by some act or default of his, alcohol is supplied to him, or to his order, by or on behalf of the club for consumption on relevant premises by an individual aged under 18, or

      (ii)   he attempts to have alcohol so supplied for such consumption.

(5)   But subsection (4) does not apply where—

(a)   the relevant person is aged 18 or over,

(b)   the individual is aged 16 or 17,

(c)   the alcohol is beer, wine or cider,

(d)   its purchase or supply is for consumption at a table meal on relevant premises, and

(e)   the individual is accompanied at the meal by an individual aged 18 or over.

(6)   Where a person is charged with an offence under subsection (3) or (4) it is a defence that he had no reason to suspect that the individual was aged under 18.

(7)   A person guilty of an offence under this section is liable on summary conviction—

(a)   in the case of an offence under subsection (1), to a fine not exceeding level 3 on the standard scale, and

(b)   in the case of an offence under subsection (3) or (4), to a fine not exceeding level 5 on the standard scale.

[Licensing Act 2003, s 149.]

7.7832 150. Consumption of alcohol by children (1) An individual aged under 18 commits an offence if he knowingly consumes alcohol on relevant premises.

(2)   A person to whom subsection (3) applies commits an offence if he knowingly allows the consumption of alcohol on relevant premises by an individual aged under 18.

(3)   This subsection applies—

(a)   to a person who works at the premises in a capacity, whether paid or unpaid, which authorises him to prevent the consumption, and

(b)   where the alcohol was supplied by a club to or to the order of a member of the club, to any member or officer of the club who is present at the premises at the time of the consumption in a capacity which enables him to prevent it.

(4)   Subsections (1) and (2) do not apply where—

(a)   the individual is aged 16 or 17,

(b)   the alcohol is beer, wine or cider,

(c)   its consumption is at a table meal on relevant premises, and

(d)   the individual is accompanied at the meal by an individual aged 18 or over.

(5)   A person guilty of an offence under this section is liable on summary conviction—

(a)   in the case of an offence under subsection (1), to a fine not exceeding level 3 on the standard scale, and

(b)   in the case of an offence under subsection (2), to a fine not exceeding level 5 on the standard scale.

[Licensing Act 2003, s 150.]

7.7833   151.   Delivering alcohol to children   (1)   A person who works on relevant premises in any capacity, whether paid or unpaid, commits an offence if he knowingly delivers to an individual aged under 18—

(a)   alcohol sold on the premises, or

(b)   alcohol supplied on the premises by or on behalf of a club to or to the order of a member of the club.

(2)   A person to whom subsection (3) applies commits an offence if he knowingly allows anybody else to deliver to an individual aged under 18 alcohol sold on relevant premises.

(3)   This subsection applies to a person who works on the premises in a capacity, whether paid or unpaid, which authorises him to prevent the delivery of the alcohol.

(4)   A person to whom subsection (5) applies commits an offence if he knowingly allows anybody else to deliver to an individual aged under 18 alcohol supplied on relevant premises by or on behalf of a club to or to the order of a member of the club.

(5)   This subsection applies—

(a)   to a person who works on the premises in a capacity, whether paid or unpaid, which authorises him to prevent the supply, and

(b)   to any member or officer of the club who at the time of the supply in question is present on the premises in a capacity which enables him to prevent the supply.

(6)   Subsections (1), (2) and (4) do not apply where—

(a)   the alcohol is delivered at a place where the buyer or, as the case may be, person supplied lives or works, or

(b)   the individual aged under 18 works on the relevant premises in a capacity, whether paid or unpaid, which involves the delivery of alcohol, or

(c)   the alcohol is sold or supplied for consumption on the relevant premises.

(7)   A person guilty of an offence under this section is liable on summary conviction to a fine not exceeding level 5 on the standard scale.

[Licensing Act 2003, s 151.]

7.7834   152.   Sending a child to obtain alcohol   (1)   A person commits an offence if he knowingly sends an individual aged under 18 to obtain—

(a)   alcohol sold or to be sold on relevant premises for consumption off the premises, or

(b)   alcohol supplied or to be supplied by or on behalf of a club to or to the order of a member of the club for such consumption.

(2)   For the purposes of this section, it is immaterial whether the individual aged under 18 is sent to obtain the alcohol from the relevant premises or from other premises from which it is delivered in pursuance of the sale or supply.

(3)   Subsection (1) does not apply where the individual aged under 18 works on the relevant premises in a capacity, whether paid or unpaid, which involves the delivery of alcohol.

(4)   Subsection (1) also does not apply where the individual aged under 18 is sent by—

(a)   a constable, or

(b)   a weights and measures inspector,

who is acting in the course of his duty.

(5)   A person guilty of an offence under this section is liable on summary conviction to a fine not exceeding level 5 on the standard scale.

[Licensing Act 2003, s 152.]

7.7835   153.   Prohibition of unsupervised sales by children   (1)   A responsible person commits an offence if on any relevant premises he knowingly allows an individual aged under 18 to make on the premises—

(a)   any sale of alcohol, or

(b)   any supply of alcohol by or on behalf of a club to or to the order of a member of the club,

unless the sale or supply has been specifically approved by that or another responsible person.

(2)   But subsection (1) does not apply where—

(a)   the alcohol is sold or supplied for consumption with a table meal,

(b)   it is sold or supplied in premises which are being used for the service of table meals (or in a part of any premises which is being so used), and

(c)   the premises are (or the part is) not used for the sale or supply of alcohol otherwise than to persons having table meals there and for consumption by such a person as an ancillary to his meal.

(3)   A person guilty of an offence under this section is liable on summary conviction to a fine not exceeding level 1 on the standard scale.

(4)   In this section "responsible person" means—

(a)   in relation to licensed premises—

(i)   the holder of a premises licence in respect of the premises,

(ii)   the designated premises supervisor (if any) under such a licence, or

        (iii)   any individual aged 18 or over who is authorised for the purposes of this section by such a holder or supervisor,

   (b)   in relation to premises in respect of which there is in force a club premises certificate, any member or officer of the club present on the premises in a capacity which enables him to prevent the supply in question, and

   (c)   in relation to premises which may be used for a permitted temporary activity by virtue of Part 5—

        (i)   the premises user, or

        (ii)   any individual aged 18 or over who is authorised for the purposes of this section by the premises user.*

[Licensing Act 2003, s 153.]

---

* **Amended by the Deregulation Act 2015, s 67 from a date to be appointed.**

7.7836   154.   Enforcement role for weights and measures authorities   (1)   It is the duty of every local weights and measures authority in England and Wales to enforce within its area the provisions of sections 146 and 147, so far as they apply to sales of alcohol made on or from premises to which the public have access.

(2)   A weights and measures inspector may make, or authorise any person to make on his behalf, such purchases of goods as appear expedient for the purpose of determining whether those provisions are being complied with.

[Licensing Act 2003, s 154.]

Confiscation of alcohol

7.7837   155.   Confiscation of sealed containers of alcohol   *Confiscation of Alcohol (Young Persons) Act 1997 amended to remove the requirement for the alcohol to be in a sealed container in certain circumstances.*

Vehicles and trains

7.7838   156.   Prohibition on sale of alcohol on moving vehicles   (1)   A person commits an offence under this section if he sells by retail alcohol on or from a vehicle at a time when the vehicle is not permanently or temporarily parked.

(2)   A person guilty of an offence under this section is liable on summary conviction to imprisonment for a term not exceeding three months or to a fine, or to both.

(3)   In proceedings against a person for an offence under this section, it is a defence that—

   (a)   his act was due to a mistake, or to reliance on information given to him, or to an act or omission by another person, or to some other cause beyond his control, and

   (b)   he took all reasonable precautions and exercised all due diligence to avoid committing the offence.

[Licensing Act 2003, s 156 as amended by SI 2015/664.]

7.7839   157.   Power to prohibit sale of alcohol on trains   (1)   A magistrates' court acting for the local justice area may make an order prohibiting the sale of alcohol, during such period as may be specified, on any railway vehicle—

   (a)   at such station or stations as may be specified, being stations in that area, or

   (b)   travelling between such stations as may be specified, at least one of which is in that area.

(2)   A magistrates' court may make an order under this section only on the application of a senior police officer.

(3)   A magistrates' court may not make such an order unless it is satisfied that the order is necessary to prevent disorder.

(4)   Where an order is made under this section, the responsible senior police officer must, forthwith, serve a copy of the order on the train operator (or each train operator) affected by the order.

(5)   A person commits an offence if he knowingly—

   (a)   sells or attempts to sell alcohol in contravention of an order under this section, or

   (b)   allows the sale of alcohol in contravention of such an order.

(6)   A person guilty of an offence under this section is liable on summary conviction to imprisonment for a term not exceeding three months or to a fine, or to both.

(7)   In this section—

"railway vehicle" has the meaning given by section 83 of the Railways Act 1993;

"responsible senior police officer", in relation to an order under this section, means the senior police officer who applied for the order or, if the chief officer of police of the force in question has designated another senior police officer for the purpose, that other officer;

"senior police officer" means a police officer of, or above, the rank of inspector;

"specified" means specified in the order under this section;

"station" has the meaning given by section 83 of the Railways Act 1993 (c 43); and

"train operator" means a person authorised by a licence under section 8 of that Act to operate railway assets (within the meaning of section 6 of that Act).

[Licensing Act 2003, s 157, as amended by SI 2005/886 and SI 2015/664.]

False statement relating to licensing etc

7.7840   158.   False statements made for the purposes of this Act   (1)   A person commits an offence if he knowingly or recklessly makes a false statement in or in connection with—

(a)   an application for the grant, variation, transfer or review of a premises licence or club premises certificate,

(b)   an application for a provisional statement,

(c)   a temporary event notice, an interim authority notice or any other notice under this Act,

(d)   an application for the grant of a personal licence, or

(e)   a notice within section 178(1) (notice by freeholder etc conferring right to be notified of changes to licensing register).

(2)   For the purposes of subsection (1) a person is to be treated as making a false statement if he produces, furnishes, signs or otherwise makes use of a document that contains a false statement.

(3)   A person guilty of an offence under this section is liable on summary conviction to a fine not exceeding level 5 on the standard scale.

[Licensing Act 2003, s 158 as amended by the Deregulation Act 2015, Sch 18.]

Interpretation

7.7841   159.   Interpretation of Part 7   In this Part—

"authorisation" has the meaning given in section 136(5);

"relevant premises" means—

(a)   licensed premises, or

(b)   premises in respect of which there is in force a club premises certificate, or

(c)   premises which may be used for a permitted temporary activity by virtue of Part 5;

"table meal" means a meal eaten by a person seated at a table, or at a counter or other structure which serves the purpose of a table and is not used for the service of refreshments for consumption by persons not seated at a table or structure serving the purpose of a table; and

"weights and measures inspector" means an inspector of weights and measures appointed under section 72(1) of the Weights and Measures Act 1985 (c 72).*

[Licensing Act 2003, s 159.]

---

*   **Amended by the Deregulation Act 2015, s 67 from a date to be appointed.**

PART 8[1]

CLOSURE OF PREMISES

Closure of premises in an identified area

7.7842   160.   Orders to close premises in area experiencing disorder   (1)   Where there is or is expected to be disorder in any local justice area, a magistrates' court acting in the area may make an order requiring all premises—

(a)   which are situated at or near the place of the disorder or expected disorder, and

(b)   in respect of which a premises licence or a temporary event notice has effect,

to be closed for a period, not exceeding 24 hours, specified in the order.

(2)   A magistrates' court may make an order under this section only on the application of a police officer who is of the rank of superintendent or above.

(3)   A magistrates' court may not make such an order unless it is satisfied that it is necessary to prevent disorder.

(4)   Where an order is made under this section, a person to whom subsection (5) applies commits an offence if he knowingly keeps any premises to which the order relates open, or allows any such premises to be kept open, during the period of the order.

(5)   This subsection applies—

(a)   to any manager of the premises,

(b)   in the case of licensed premises, to—

(i)   the holder of a premises licence in respect of the premises, and

(ii)   the designated premises supervisor (if any) under such a licence, and

(c)   in the case of premises in respect of which a temporary event notice has effect, to the premises user in relation to that notice.

(6)   A person guilty of an offence under subsection (4) is liable on summary conviction to a fine not exceeding level 3 on the standard scale.

(7)   A constable may use such force as may be necessary for the purpose of closing premises ordered to be closed under this section.

[Licensing Act 2003, s 160, as amended by SI 2005/886.]

---

[1]   Part 8 comprises ss 160–171.

Closure of identified premises

7.7843   167.   Review of premises licence following closure order   (1)   This section applies where—

    (a)   a magistrates' court has made a closure order under section 80 of the Anti-social Behaviour, Crime and Policing Act 2014, or the Crown Court has made a closure order on appeal under section 84 of that Act, in relation to premises in respect of which a premises licence has effect, and

    (b)   the relevant licensing authority has accordingly received a notice under section 80(9) or 84(7) of that Act.

(1A)   This section also applies where a court has made an illegal working compliance order under Schedule 6 to the Immigration Act 2016 and the relevant licensing authority has accordingly received a notice under that Schedule.

(2)   The relevant licensing authority must review the premises licence.

(3)   The authority must reach a determination on the review no later than 28 days after the day on which it receives the notice mentioned in subsection (1)(b).

(4)   The Secretary of State must by regulations[1]—

    (a)   require the relevant licensing authority to give, to the holder of the premises licence and each responsible authority, notice of the review and of the order mentioned in subsection (1)(a);

    (b)   require the authority to advertise the review and invite representations about it to be made to the authority by responsible authorities and other persons;

    (c)   prescribe the period during which representations may be made by the holder of the premises licence, any responsible authority or any other person;

    (d)   require any notice under paragraph (a) or advertisement under paragraph (b) to specify that period.

(5)   The relevant licensing authority must—

    (a)   hold a hearing to consider the order mentioned in subsection (1)(a) and any relevant representations; and

    (b)   take such of the steps mentioned in subsection (6) (if any) as it considers appropriate for the promotion of the licensing objectives.

(6)   Those steps are—

    (a)   to modify the conditions of the premises licence,

    (b)   to exclude a licensable activity from the scope of the licence,

    (c)   to remove the designated premises supervisor from the licence,

    (d)   to suspend the licence for a period not exceeding three months, or

    (e)   to revoke the licence;

and for this purpose the conditions of a premises licence are modified if any of them is altered or omitted or any new condition is added.

(7)   Subsection (5)(b) is subject to sections 19 to 21 (requirement to include certain conditions in premises licences).

(8)   Where the authority takes a step within subsection (6)(a) or (b), it may provide that the modification or exclusion is to have effect only for a specified period (not exceeding three months).

(9)   In this section "relevant representations" means representations which—

    (a)   are relevant to one or more of the licensing objectives, and

    (b)   meet the requirements of subsection (10).

(10)   The requirements are—

    (a)   that the representations are made by the holder of the premises licence, a responsible authority or any other person within the period prescribed under subsection (4)(c),

    (b)   that they have not been withdrawn, and

    (c)   if they are made by a person who is not a responsible authority, that they are not, in the opinion of the relevant licensing authority, frivolous or vexatious.

(11)   Where the relevant licensing authority determines that any representations are frivolous or vexatious, it must notify the person who made them of the reasons for that determination.

(12)   Where a licensing authority determines a review under this section it must notify the determination and its reasons for making it to—

    (a)   the holder of the licence,

    (b)   any person who made relevant representations, and

    (c)   the chief officer of police for the police area (or each police area) in which the premises are situated.

(13)   Section 168 makes provision about when the determination takes effect.

(14)   In this section "responsible authority" has the same meaning as in Part 3.

[Licensing Act 2003, s 167 as amended by the Policing and Crime Act 2009, Sch 7, the Police Reform and Social Responsibility Act 2011, ss 106, 111, the Anti-social Behaviour, Crime and Policing Act 2014, Sch 11 and the Immigration Act 2016, Sch 6.]

---

[1] See the Licensing Act 2003 (Premises Licences and Club Premises Certificates) Regulations 2005, SI 2005/42 (for amending instruments, see note to s 13, ante) and the Welsh Language (Gambling and Licensing Forms) Regulations 2010, SI 2010/2440.

7.7844   168. Provision about decisions under section 167   (1)   Subject to this section, a decision under section 167 does not have effect until the relevant time.

(2)   In this section "the relevant time", in relation to any decision, means—

    (a)   the end of the period given for appealing against the decision, or

(b)   if the decision is appealed against, the time the appeal is disposed of.

(3)   Subsections (4) and (5) apply where—

(a)   the relevant licensing authority decides on a review under section 167 to take one or more of the steps mentioned in subsection (6)(a) to (d) of that section, and

(b)   the premises to which the licence relates are closed at the time of the decision by virtue of an closure order made under section 80 or 84 of the Anti-social Behaviour, Crime and Policing Act 2014.

(4)   The decision by the relevant licensing authority to take any of the steps mentioned in section 167(6)(a) to (d) takes effect when it is notified to the holder of the licence under section 167(12).

This is subject to subsection (5) and paragraph 18(3) of Schedule 5 (power of magistrates' court to suspend decision pending appeal).

(5)   The relevant licensing authority may, on such terms as it thinks fit, suspend the operation of that decision (in whole or in part) until the relevant time.

(6)   Subsection (7) applies where—

(a)   the relevant licensing authority decides on a review under section 167 to revoke the premises licence, and

(b)   the premises to which the licence relates are closed at the time of the decision by virtue of an closure order made under section 80 or 84 of the Anti-social Behaviour, Crime and Policing Act 2014.

(7)   The premises must remain closed (but the licence otherwise in force) until the relevant time.

This is subject to paragraph 18(4) of Schedule 5 (power of magistrates' court to modify closure order pending appeal).

(8)   A person commits an offence if, without reasonable excuse, he allows premises to be open in contravention of subsection (7).

(9)   A person guilty of an offence under subsection (8) is liable on summary conviction to imprisonment for a term not exceeding three months or to a fine, or to both.

[Licensing Act 2003, s 168 as amended by the Anti-social Behaviour, Crime and Policing Act 2014, Sch 11 and SI 2015/664.]

Closure notices

7.7845   169A.   Closure notices for persistently selling alcohol to children   (1)   A relevant officer may give a notice under this section (a "closure notice") applying to any premises if—

(a)   there is evidence that a person ("the offender") has committed an offence under section 147A in relation to those premises;

(b)   the relevant officer considers that the evidence is such that, if the offender were prosecuted for the offence, there would be a realistic prospect of his being convicted; and

(c)   the offender is still, at the time when the notice is given, the holder of a premises licence in respect of those premises, or one of the holders of such a licence.

(2)   A closure notice is a notice which—

(a)   proposes a prohibition, for the period specified in the notice, on sales of alcohol on the premises in question; and

(b)   offers the opportunity to discharge all criminal liability in respect of the alleged offence by the acceptance of the prohibition proposed by the notice.

(3)   A closure notice must—

(a)   be in the form prescribed by regulations[1] made by the Secretary of State;

(b)   specify the premises to which it applies;

(c)   give such particulars of the circumstances believed to constitute the alleged offence (including the sales to which it relates) as are necessary to provide reasonable information about it;

(d)   specify the length of the period during which it is proposed that sales of alcohol should be prohibited on those premises;

(e)   specify when that period would begin if the prohibition is accepted;

(f)   explain what would be the effect of the proposed prohibition and the consequences under this Act (including the maximum penalties) of a sale of alcohol on the premises during the period for which it is in force;

(g)   explain the right of every person who, at the time of the alleged offence, held or was one of the holders of a premises licence in respect of those premises to be tried for that offence; and

(h)   explain how that right may be exercised and how (where it is not exercised) the proposed prohibition may be accepted.

(4)   The period specified for the purposes of subsection (3)(d) must be at least 48 hours but not more than 336 hours; and the time specified as the time from which that period would begin must be not less than 14 days after the date of the service of the closure notice in accordance with subsection (6).

(5)   The provision included in the notice by virtue of subsection (3)(h) must—

(a)   provide a means of identifying a police officer or trading standards officer to whom notice exercising the option to accept the prohibition may be given;

(b)   set out particulars of where and how that notice may be given to that police officer or trading standards officer;

(c)   require that notice to be given within 14 days after the date of the service of the closure notice; and

(d)   explain that the right to be tried for the alleged offence will be taken to have been exercised unless every person who, at the time of the notice, holds or is one of the holders of the premises licence for the premises in question accepts the proposed prohibition.

(6)   Section 184 (giving of notices) does not apply to a closure notice; but such a notice must be served on the premises to which it applies.

(7)   A closure notice may be served on the premises to which it applies—

(a)   only by being handed by a constable or trading standards officer to a person on the premises who appears to the constable or trading standards officer to have control of or responsibility for the premises (whether on his own or with others); and

(b)   only at a time when it appears to that constable or trading standards officer that licensable activities are being carried on there.

(8)   A copy of every closure notice given under this section must be sent to the holder of the premises licence for the premises to which it applies at whatever address for that person is for the time being set out in the licence.

(9)   A closure notice must not be given more than 3 months after the time of the last of the sales to which the alleged offence relates.

(10)   No more that one closure notice may be given in respect of offences relating to the same sales; nor may such a notice be given in respect of an offence in respect of which a prosecution has already been brought.

(11)   In this section "relevant officer" means—

(a)   a police officer of the rank of superintendent or above; or

(b)   an inspector of weights and measures appointed under section 72(1) of the Weights and Measures Act 1985.

[Licensing Act 2003, s 169A as inserted by the Violent Crime Reduction Act 2006, s 24 and amended by the Police Reform and Social Responsibility Act 2011, s 118.]

---

[1] The Licensing Act 2003 (Persistent Selling of Alcohol to Children) (Prescribed Form of Closure Notice) Regulations 2012, SI 2012/963 have been made.

7.7846   169B.   Effect of closure notices   (1)   This section applies where a closure notice is given under section 169A in respect of an alleged offence under section 147A.

(2)   No proceedings may be brought for the alleged offence or any related offence at any time before the time when the prohibition proposed by the notice would take effect.

(3)   If before that time every person who, at the time of the notice, holds or is one of the holders of the premises licence for the premises in question accepts the proposed prohibition in the manner specified in the notice—

(a)   that prohibition takes effect at the time so specified in relation to the premises in question; and

(b)   no proceedings may subsequently be brought against any such person for the alleged offence or any related offence.

(4)   If the prohibition contained in a closure notice takes effect in accordance with subsection (3)(a) in relation to any premises, so much of the premises licence for those premises as authorises the sale by retail of alcohol on those premises is suspended for the period specified in the closure notice.

(5)   In this section "related offence", in relation to the alleged offence, means an offence under section 146 or 147 in respect of any of the sales to which the alleged offence relates.

(6)   The operation of this section is not affected by any contravention of section 169A(8).

[Licensing Act 2003, s 169B as inserted by the Violent Crime Reduction Act 2006, s 24.]

Interpretation

7.7847   171.   Interpretation of Part 8   (1)   This section has effect for the purposes of this Part.

(2)   Premises are open if a person who is not within subsection (4) enters the premises and—

(a)   he buys or is otherwise supplied with food, drink or anything usually sold on the premises, or

(b)   while he is on the premises, they are used for the provision of regulated entertainment.

(3)   But in determining whether premises are open the following are to be disregarded—

(a)   where no premises licence has effect in respect of the premises, any use of the premises for activities (other than licensable activities) which do not take place during an event period specified in a temporary event notice having effect in respect of the premises,

(b)   any use of the premises for a qualifying club activity under and in accordance with a club premises certificate, and

(c)   any supply exempted under paragraph 3 of Schedule 2 (certain supplies of hot food and drink by clubs, hotels etc not a licensable activity) in circumstances where a person will neither be admitted to the premises, nor be supplied as mentioned in sub-paragraph (1)(*b*) of that paragraph, except by virtue of being a member of a recognised club or a guest of such a member.

(4)   A person is within this subsection if he is—
(*a*)   an appropriate person in relation to the premises,
(*b*)   a person who usually lives at the premises, or
(*c*)   a member of the family of a person within paragraph (*a*) or (*b*).

(5)   The following expressions have the meanings given—
"appropriate person", in relation to any premises, means—
(*a*)   any person who holds a premises licence in respect of the premises,
(*b*)   any designated premises supervisor under such a licence,
(*c*)   the premises user in relation to any temporary event notice which has effect in respect of the premises, or
(*d*)   a manager of the premises;
"closure notice" has the meaning given in section 169A;
"local weights and measures authority' has the meaning given by section 69 of the Weights and Measures Act 1985;
"manager", in relation to any premises, means a person who works at the premises in a capacity, whether paid or unpaid, which authorises him to close them;
"relevant licensing authority", in relation to any licensed premises, has the same meaning as in Part 3;
"trading standards officer", in relation to any premises to which a premises licence relates, means a person authorised by a local weights and measures authority to act in the area where those premises are situated in relation to proposed prohibitions contained in closure notices.

(6)   A temporary event notice has effect from the time it is given in accordance with Part 5 until—
(*a*)   the time it is withdrawn,
(*b*)   the time a counter notice is given under that Part, or
(*c*)   the expiry of the event period specified in the temporary event notice,
whichever first occurs.

[Licensing Act 2003, s 171 as amended by SI 2005/886, the Violent Crime Reduction Act 2006, s 24 and the Anti-social Behaviour, Crime and Policing Act 2014, Sch 11.]

PART 9[1]
MISCELLANEOUS AND SUPPLEMENTARY

Special occasions

7.7848   172.   Relaxation of opening hours for special occasions   *Power of Secretary of State to make a "Licensing Hours Order" for celebration periods marking an occasion of exceptional international, national or local significance.*

[Licensing Act 2003, s 172.]

---

[1]   Part 8 comprises ss 172–201 and Schs 5–8.

7.7849   172A.   Power to make early morning alcohol restriction order   (1)   If a licensing authority considers it appropriate for the promotion of the licensing objectives, it may, subject as follows, make an order under this section.

(2)   An order under this section is an order providing that—
(*a*)   premises licences and club premises certificates granted by the authority, and temporary event notices given to the authority, do not have effect to the extent that they authorise the sale of alcohol during the period specified in the order, and
(*b*)   club premises certificates granted by the authority do not have effect to the extent that they authorise the supply of alcohol by or on behalf of a club to, or to the order of, a member of the club during the period specified in the order.

(3)   For the purposes of subsection (2)(*a*) and (*b*), the period that may be specified in the order must—
(*a*)   begin no earlier than midnight, and
(*b*)   end no later than 6am.

(4)   It is immaterial for the purposes of an order under this section whether a premises licence or club premises certificate is granted, or a temporary event notice is given, before or after the order is made.

(5)   An order under this section may provide that it is to apply—
(*a*)   in relation to the same period of every day on which the order is to apply, or in relation to different periods of different days,
(*b*)   every day or only on particular days (for example, particular days of the week or year),
(*c*)   in relation to the whole or part of a licensing authority's area, or
(*d*)   for a limited or unlimited period.

(6)   An order under this section must specify—
(*a*)   the days on which it is to apply and the period of those days,
(*b*)   the area in relation to which it is to apply,

(c)   if it is to apply for a limited period, that period, and

(d)   the date from which it is to apply.

(7)   An order under this section must—

(a)   be in the prescribed form, and

(b)   have the prescribed content.

[Licensing Act 2003, s 172A as inserted by the Police Reform and Social Responsibility Act 2011, s 119.]

7.7850   172B. Procedural requirements for early morning alcohol restriction order

(1)   A licensing authority proposing to make an order under section 172A must—

(a)   advertise the proposed order in the prescribed manner, and

(b)   hold a hearing to consider any relevant representations, unless the authority and each person who has made such representations agree that a hearing is unnecessary.

(2)   In this section "relevant representations" means representations which—

(a)   are about the likely effect of the making of the proposed order on the promotion of the licensing objectives,

(b)   are made to the licensing authority by an affected person, a responsible authority or any other person,

(c)   are made in the prescribed form and manner and within the prescribed period,

(d)   have not been withdrawn, and

(e)   in the case of representations made by a person who is not a responsible authority, are not, in the opinion of the licensing authority, frivolous or vexatious.

(3)   In subsection (2)(b), "affected person" means—

(a)   the holder of the premises licence or club premises certificate in respect of affected premises,

(b)   the premises user in relation to a temporary event notice in respect of affected premises,

(c)   a person who has applied for a premises licence or club premises certificate in respect of affected premises (where the application has not been determined), and

(d)   a person to whom a provisional statement has been issued in respect of affected premises.

(4)   In subsection (2)(b) and (e), "responsible authority" means—

(a)   the licensing authority and any other licensing authority in whose area part of any affected premises is situated,

(b)   the chief officer of police for a police area any part of which is in the area specified in the order,

(c)   the fire and rescue authority for an area any part of which is in the area specified in the order,

(d)   the Primary Care Trust or Local Health Board for an area any part of which is in the area specified in the order,

(e)   the local weights and measures authority for any such area,

(f)   the enforcing authority within the meaning given by section 18 of the Health and Safety at Work etc Act 1974 for any such area,

(g)   the local planning authority within the meaning given by the Town and Country Planning Act 1990 for any such area,

(h)   the local authority by which statutory functions are exercisable in the area specified in the order in relation to minimising or preventing the risk of pollution of the environment or of harm to human health,

(i)   a body which—

     (i)   represents those who, in relation to the area specified in the order, are responsible for, or interested in, matters relating to the protection of children from harm, and

     (ii)   is recognised by the licensing authority for the purposes of this section as being competent to advise on such matters,

(j)   where affected premises are a vessel—

     (i)   a navigation authority (within the meaning given by section 221(1) of the Water Resources Act 1991) having functions in relation to the waters where the vessel is usually moored or berthed or any waters where it is navigated at a time when it is used for licensable activities to which the proposed order relates,

     (ii)   the Environment Agency,

     (iii) Canal & River Trust, and

     (iv) the Secretary of State, and

(k)   a prescribed person.

(5)   Where a licensing authority determines for the purposes of subsection (2)(e) that any representations are frivolous or vexatious, it must notify the person who made them of its reasons for its determination.

(6)   In this section—

"affected premises", in relation to a proposed order, means premises in respect of which it applies from the date specified in it;

"statutory function" means a function conferred by or under an enactment.

[Licensing Act 2003, s 172B as inserted by the Police Reform and Social Responsibility Act 2011, s 119 and amended by SI 2012/1659.]

7.7851 172C. Making of early morning alcohol restriction order (1) A licensing authority may not make an order under section 172A applying in relation to—

    (*a*)   an area not specified in the proposed order advertised under section 172B,

    (*b*)   a day not specified in that proposed order, or

    (*c*)   a period other than the period specified in that proposed order of any day so specified.

(2) After making an order under section 172A a licensing authority must publish it or otherwise make it available—

    (*a*)   in the prescribed form and manner, and

    (*b*)   within the prescribed period.

[Licensing Act 2003, s 172C as inserted by the Police Reform and Social Responsibility Act 2011, s 119.]

7.7852 172D. Variation and revocation of early morning alcohol restriction order

(1) A licensing authority may vary or revoke an order under section 172A.

(2) Sections 172B and 172C apply in relation to the variation or revocation of an order under section 172A as in relation to the making of such an order.

[Licensing Act 2003, s 172D as inserted by the Police Reform and Social Responsibility Act 2011, s 119.]

7.7853 172E. Exceptions from effect of early morning alcohol restriction order (1) An order under section 172A does not apply in prescribed cases or circumstances.

(2) The cases referred to in subsection (1) may in particular be defined by reference to—

    (*a*)   particular kinds of premises, or

    (*b*)   particular days.

(3) An order under section 172A is subject to an order under section 172 (whether made before or afterwards), unless and to the extent that the order under section 172 provides otherwise.

[Licensing Act 2003, s 172E as inserted by the Police Reform and Social Responsibility Act 2011, s 119.]

Exemptions etc

7.7854 173. Activities in certain locations not licensable (1) An activity is not a licensable activity if it is carried on—

    (*a*)   aboard an aircraft, hovercraft or railway vehicle engaged on a journey,

    (*b*)   aboard a vessel engaged on an international journey,

    (*c*)   at an approved wharf at a designated port or hoverport,

    (*d*)   at an examination station at a designated airport,

    (*e*)   at a royal palace,

    (*f*)   at premises which, at the time when the activity is carried on, are permanently or temporarily occupied for the purposes of the armed forces of the Crown,

    (*g*)   at premises in respect of which a certificate issued under section 174 (exemption for national security) has effect, or

    (*h*)   at such other place as may be prescribed.

(2) For the purposes of subsection (1) the period during which an aircraft, hovercraft, railway vehicle or vessel is engaged on a journey includes—

    (*a*)   any period ending with its departure when preparations are being made for the journey, and

    (*b*)   any period after its arrival at its destination when it continues to be occupied by those (or any of those) who made the journey (or any part of it).

(3) The Secretary of State may by order designate a port, hoverport or airport for the purposes of subsection (1), if it appears to him to be one at which there is a substantial amount of international passenger traffic.

(4) Any port, airport or hoverport where section 86A or 87 of the Licensing Act 1964 (c 26) is in operation immediately before the commencement of this section is, on and after that commencement, to be treated for the purposes of subsection (1) as if it were designated.

(5) But provision may by order be made for subsection (4) to cease to have effect in relation to any port, airport or hoverport.

(6) For the purposes of this section—

"approved wharf" has the meaning given by section 20A of the Customs and Excise Management Act 1979 (c 2);

"designated" means designated by an order under subsection (3);

"examination station" has the meaning given by section 22A of that Act;

"international journey" means—

    (*a*)   a journey from a place in the United Kingdom to an immediate destination outside the United Kingdom, or

    (*b*)   a journey from a place outside the United Kingdom to an immediate destination in the United Kingdom; and

"railway vehicle" has the meaning given by section 83 of the Railways Act 1993 (c 43).

[Licensing Act 2003, s 173.]

7.7855   174.   Certifying of premises on grounds of national security   (1)   A Minister of the Crown may issue a certificate under this section in respect of any premises, if he considers that it is appropriate to do so for the purposes of safeguarding national security.

(2)   A certificate under this section may identify the premises in question by means of a general description.

(3)   A document purporting to be a certificate under this section is to be received in evidence and treated as being a certificate under this section unless the contrary is proved.

(4)   A document which purports to be certified by or on behalf of a Minister of the Crown as a true copy of a certificate given by a Minister of the Crown under this section is evidence of that certificate.

(5)   A Minister of the Crown may cancel a certificate issued by him, or any other Minister of the Crown, under this section.

(6)   The powers conferred by this section on a Minister of the Crown may be exercised only by a Minister who is a member of the Cabinet or by the Attorney General.

(7)   In this section "Minister of the Crown" has the meaning given by the Ministers of the Crown Act 1975 (c 26).

[Licensing Act 2003, s 174.]

7.7856   175.   Exemption for incidental lottery   (1)   The promotion of a lottery to which this section applies shall not constitute a licensable activity by reason only of one or more of the prizes in the lottery consisting of or including alcohol, provided that the alcohol is in a sealed container.

(2)   *Repealed.*

[Licensing Act 2003, s 175 as substituted by the Gambling Act 2005, Sch 16 and amended by SI 2016/124.]

Service areas and garages etc

7.7857   176.   Prohibition of alcohol sales at service areas, garages etc   (1)   No premises licence, club premises certificate or temporary event notice has effect to authorise the sale by retail or supply of alcohol on or from excluded premises.

(2)   In this section "excluded premises" means—

(*a*)   premises situated on land acquired or appropriated by a special road authority, and for the time being used, for the provision of facilities to be used in connection with the use of a special road provided for the use of traffic of class I (with or without other classes); or

(*b*)   premises used primarily as a garage or which form part of premises which are primarily so used[1].

(3)   The Secretary of State may by order amend the definition of excluded premises in subsection (2) so as to include or exclude premises of such description as may be specified in the order.

(4)   For the purposes of this section—

(*a*)   "special road" and "special road authority" have the same meaning as in the Highways Act 1980 (c 66), except that "special road" includes a trunk road to which (by virtue of paragraph 3 of Schedule 23 to that Act) the provisions of that Act apply as if the road were a special road,

(*b*)   "class I" means class I in Schedule 4 to the Highways Act 1980 as varied from time to time by an order under section 17 of that Act, but if that Schedule is amended by such an order so as to add to it a further class of traffic, the order may adapt the reference in subsection (2)(*a*) to traffic of class I so as to take account of the additional class, and

(*c*)   premises are used as a garage if they are used for one or more of the following—

(i)   the retailing of petrol,

(ii)   the retailing of derv,

(iii)   the sale of motor vehicles,

(iv)   the maintenance of motor vehicles.

[Licensing Act 2003, s 176.]

---

[1]   As to the determination of primary use and the entitlement to adjourn to elicit more information and clarification from the applicant, see *R (on the application of Murco Petroleum Ltd) v Bristol City Council* [2010] EWHC 1992 (Admin), 174 JP 425.

Small premises

7.7858   177.   Dancing in certain small premises   (1)   Subsection (2) applies where—

(*a*)   a premises licence authorises—

(i)   the supply of alcohol for consumption on the premises, and

(ii)   dancing, and

(*b*)   the premises—

(i)   are used primarily for the supply of alcohol for consumption on the premises, and

(ii)   have a permitted capacity of not more than 200 persons.

(2)   At any time when—

(*a*)   the premises—

      (i)   are open for the purposes of being used for the supply of alcohol for consumption on the premises, and

      (ii)   are being used for dancing,

  (b)   *repealed*

any licensing authority imposed condition of the premises licence which relates to dancing does not have effect unless it falls within subsection (5) or (6).

(3)   *Repealed.*

(4)   *Repealed.*

(5)   A condition falls within this subsection if the premises licence specifies that the licensing authority which granted the licence considers the imposition of the condition appropriate on one or both of the following grounds—

  (a)   the prevention of crime and disorder,

  (b)   public safety.

(6)   A condition falls within this subsection if, on a review of the premises licence—

  (a)   it is altered so as to include a statement that this section does not apply to it, or

  (b)   it is added to the licence and includes such a statement.

(7)   This section applies in relation to a club premises certificate as it applies in relation to a premises licence except that, in the application of this section in relation to such a certificate, the definition of "licensing authority imposed condition" in subsection (8) has effect as if for "section 18(3)(b)" to the end there were substituted "section 72(3)(b) (but is not referred to in section 72(2)) or which is imposed by virtue of section 85(3)(b) or 88(3)".

(8)   In this section—

"licensing authority imposed condition" means a condition which is imposed by virtue of section 18(3)(b) (but is not referred to in section 18(2)(a)) or which is imposed by virtue of 35(3)(b), 52(3) or 167(5)(b) or in accordance with section 21;

"dancing" means—

  (a)   entertainment of a description falling within, or of a similar description to that falling within, paragraph 2(1)(g) of Schedule 1,

  (b)   *repealed*

"permitted capacity", in relation to any premises, means—

  (a)   *repealed*

  (b)   the limit on the number of persons who may be on the premises at any one time in accordance with a recommendation made by, or on behalf of, the fire and rescue authority for the area in which the premises are situated (or, if the premises are situated in the area of more than one fire and rescue authority, those authorities); and

"supply of alcohol" means

  (a)   the sale by retail of alcohol, or

  (b)   the supply of alcohol by or on behalf of a club to, or to the order of, a member of the club.

[Licensing Act 2003, s 177 as amended by SI 2005/1541, the Police Reform and Social Responsibility Act 2011, s 109 and the Live Music Act 2012, s 1.]

7.7859 177A. Licence review for live and recorded music (1) Subsection (2) applies where—

  (a)   music takes place on premises which are authorised by a premises licence or club premises certificate to be used for the supply of alcohol for consumption on the premises,

  (b)   at the time of the music, the premises are open for the purposes of being used for the supply of alcohol for consumption on the premises,

  (c)   if the music is amplified, it takes place in the presence of an audience of no more than 500 persons, and

  (d)   the music takes place between 8am and 11pm on the same day (or, where an order under section 172 has effect in relation to music, during any times specified under that order).

(2)   Any condition of the premises licence or club premises certificate which relates to live music, recorded music or both does not have effect in relation to the music unless it falls within subsection (3) or is added to the licence in accordance with subsection (4).

(3)   A condition falls within this subsection if, on a review of the premises licence or club premises certificate it is altered so as to include a statement that this section does not apply to it.

(4)   On a review of a premises licence or club premises certificate a licensing authority may (without prejudice to any other steps available to it under this Act) add a condition relating to music as if—

  (a)   the music were regulated entertainment, and

  (b)   the licence or certificate licensed the music.

(4A) This section does not apply to music which, by virtue of a provision other than paragraph 12A or 12C of Schedule 1, is not regarded as the provision of regulated entertainment for the purposes of this Act.

(5)   In this section—

"condition" means a condition—

    (a)   included in a premises licence by virtue of section 18(2)(a) or (3)(b), 35(3)(b), 52(3) or 167(5)(b),

    (b)   included in a club premises certificate by virtue of section 72(2)(a) or (3)(b), 85(3)(b) or 88(3),

    (c)   added to a premises licence by virtue of its inclusion in an application to vary the licence in accordance with section 34 or 41A which is granted under section 35(2) or 41B(3) (as the case may be), or

    (d)   added to a club premises certificate by virtue of its inclusion in an application to vary the certificate in accordance with section 84 or 86A which is granted under section 85(2) or 86B(3) (as the case may be);

"live music" means entertainment of a description falling within, or of a similar description to that falling within, paragraph 2(1)(e) of Schedule 1;

"music" means live music or recorded music or both;

"recorded music" means entertainment of a description falling within, or of a similar description to that falling within, paragraph 2(1)(f) of Schedule 1;

"supply of alcohol" means—

    (a)   the sale by retail of alcohol, or

    (b)   the supply of alcohol by or on behalf of a club to, or to the order of, a member of the club.

[Licensing Act 2003, s 177A as inserted by the Live Music Act 2012, s 1 and amended by SI 2014/3253.]

Rights of freeholders etc

7.7860   178.   Right of freeholder etc to be notified of licensing matters   *Right of person with a property interest in any premises to notify the licensing authority of that interest and then to be told by the licensing authority of any changes to the licensing register affecting that premises.*

Rights of entry

7.7861   179.   Rights of entry to investigate licensable activities   (1)   Where a constable or an authorised person has reason to believe that any premises are being, or are about to be, used for a licensable activity, he may enter the premises with a view to seeing whether the activity is being, or is to be, carried on and in accordance with an authorisation.

(1A)   Where an immigration officer has reason to believe that any premises are being used for a licensable activity within section 1(1)(a) or (d), the officer may enter the premises with a view to seeing whether an offence under any of the Immigration Acts is being committed in connection with the carrying on of the activity.

(2)   An authorised person or an immigration officer exercising a power conferred by this section must, if so requested, produce evidence of his authority to exercise the power.

(3)   A person exercising the power conferred by this section may, if necessary, use reasonable force.

(4)   A person commits an offence if he intentionally obstructs an authorised person or an immigration officer exercising a power conferred by this section.

(5)   A person guilty of an offence under subsection (4) is liable on summary conviction to a fine not exceeding level 3 on the standard scale.

(6)   In this section—

"authorisation" means—

    (a)   a premises licence,

    (b)   a club premises certificate, or

    (c)   a temporary event notice in respect of which the conditions of section 98(2) to (4) are satisfied;

"authorised person" means an authorised person within the meaning of Part 3 or 4 or an authorised officer within the meaning of section 108(5);

"immigration officer" means a person appointed as an immigration officer under paragraph 1 of Schedule 2 to the Immigration Act 1971.

(7)   Nothing in this section applies in relation to premises in respect of which there is a club premises certificate but no other authorisation.

[Licensing Act 2003, s 179 as amended by the Immigration Act 2016, Sch 4.]

7.7862   180.   Right of entry to investigate offences   (1)   A constable may enter and search any premises in respect of which he has reason to believe that an offence under this Act has been, is being or is about to be committed.

(2)   A constable exercising a power conferred by this section may, if necessary, use reasonable force.

[Licensing Act 2003, s 180.]

Appeals

7.7863   181.   Appeals against decisions of licensing authorities   (1)   Schedule 5 (which makes provision for appeals against decisions of licensing authorities) has effect.

(2)   On an appeal in accordance with that Schedule against a decision of a licensing authority, a magistrates' court may—

    (a)   dismiss the appeal,

    (*b*)   substitute for the decision appealed against any other decision which could have been made by the licensing authority, or

    (*c*)   remit the case to the licensing authority to dispose of it in accordance with the direction of the court,

and may make such order as to costs as it thinks fit[1].

[Licensing Act 2003, s 181.]

---

[1] In *Crawley Borough Council v Attenborough* [2006] EWHC 1278 (Admin) it was held that there was no practical distinction between the terms of this section and s 64(1) of the Magistrates' Courts Act 1980 (see para 1.377, in Part I: Magistrates' Courts, Procedure, ante). But in *Prasannan v Royal Borough of Kensington and Chelsea* [2010] EWHC 319 (Admin), 174 JP 418 it was held that the remarks in the *Crawley Borough Council* case were obiter. There was no scope for fettering the power in s 182(2) by construing it in light of the provisions of s 64(1) of the 1980 Act. The two provisions are entirely independent of each other for good reason. In licensing cases the permutations of result may be frequently more complex than simple success or failure. The court has an unfettered power in relation to costs subject to the requirement that in making such order as is just it must take into account all relevant matters and not take into account irrelevant matters. See further *Aldenir v Cornwall Council* [2019] EWHC 2407 (Admin). The power conferred by s 181 is not limited to orders against the parties to the appeal and, in an appropriate case an award of costs can be made against a non-party, but this is subject to procedural fairness:

"23. . . . an application for costs against a non-party is a course of action that is out of the ordinary and can, as was the case here, lead to significant financial consequences. It is important that such an application is heard and determined in accordance with a fair procedure. There is no need for anything elaborate; there are no particular hard and fast rules; but the principles of natural justice must be observed. The person against whom the application is made must have fair notice of the application and the grounds on which it is made, and a fair opportunity to respond to the application." (per Swift J)

Guidance, hearings etc

7.7864   **182. Guidance** (1) The Secretary of State must issue guidance ("the licensing guidance") to licensing authorities on the discharge of their functions under this Act.[1].

---

[1] The "Guidance issued under s 182 of the Licensing Act 2003 and Guidance to Police Officers on the operation of Closure Powers in Part 8 of the Licensing Act 2003" dated July 2004 has been issued by the Secretary of State.

7.7865   **183. Hearings** *Power to make regulations prescribing hearings procedure*[1].

---

[1] The Licensing Act 2003 (Hearings) Regulations 2005, SI 2005/44 have been made. A licensing authority may not award costs in respect of licensing hearings.

7.7866   **184. Giving of notices, etc** (1) This section has effect in relation to any document required or authorised by or under this Act to be given to any person ("relevant document").

    (2) Where that person is a licensing authority, the relevant document must be given by addressing it to the authority and leaving it at or sending it by post to—

    (*a*)   the principal office of the authority, or

    (*b*)   any other office of the authority specified by it as one at which it will accept documents of the same description as that document.

    (3) In any other case the relevant document may be given to the person in question by delivering it to him, or by leaving it at his proper address, or by sending it by post to him at that address.

    (4) A relevant document may—

    (*a*)   in the case of a body corporate (other than a licensing authority), be given to the secretary or clerk of that body;

    (*b*)   in the case of a partnership, be given to a partner or a person having the control or management of the partnership business;

    (*c*)   in the case of an unincorporated association (other than a partnership), be given to an officer of the association.

    (5) For the purposes of this section and section 7 of the Interpretation Act 1978 (c 30) (service of documents by post) in its application to this section, the proper address of any person to whom a relevant document is to be given is his last known address, except that—

    (*a*)   in the case of a body corporate or its secretary or clerk, it is the address of the registered office of that body or its principal office in the United Kingdom,

    (*b*)   in the case of a partnership, a partner or a person having control or management of the partnership business, it is that of the principal office of the partnership in the United Kingdom, and

    (*c*)   in the case of an unincorporated association (other than a partnership) or any officer of the association, it is that of its principal office in the United Kingdom.

    (6) But if a relevant document is given to a person in his capacity as the holder of a premises licence, club premises certificate or personal licence, or as the designated premises supervisor under a premises licence, his relevant registered address is also to be treated, for the purposes of this section and section 7 of the Interpretation Act 1978 (c 30), as his proper address.

    (7) In subsection (6) "relevant registered address", in relation to such a person, means the address given for that person in the record for the licence or certificate (as the case may be) which is contained in the register kept under section 8 by the licensing authority which granted the licence or certificate.

    (8) The following provisions of the Local Government Act 1972 (c 70) do not apply in relation to the service of a relevant document—

(a)   section 231 (service of notices on local authorities etc),

(b)   section 233 (service of notices by local authorities).

[Licensing Act 2003, s 184.]

7.7867   185.   Provision of information   *Power to share information between responsible authorities and licensing authorities for the purposes of facilitating the exercise of their functions under the Act.*

General provisions about offences

7.7868   186.   Proceedings for offences   (1)   In this section "offence" means an offence under this Act.

(2)   Proceedings for an offence may be instituted—

(a)   except in the case of an offence under section 147A, by a licensing authority,

(b)   by the Director of Public Prosecutions, or

(c)   in the case of an offence under section 146, 147 or 147A (sale of alcohol to children), by a local weights and measures authority (within the meaning of section 69 of the Weights and Measures Act 1985 (c 72)).

(3)   In relation to any offence, section 127(1) of the Magistrates' Courts Act 1980 (information to be laid within six months of offence) is to have effect as if for the reference to six months there were substituted a reference to 12 months.

[Licensing Act 2003, s 186 as amended by the Violent Crime Reduction Act 2006, s 23.]

7.7869   187.   Offences by bodies corporate etc   (1)   If an offence committed by a body corporate is shown—

(a)   to have been committed with the consent or connivance of an officer, or

(b)   to be attributable to any neglect on his part,

the officer as well as the body corporate is guilty of the offence and liable to be proceeded against and punished accordingly.

(2)   If the affairs of a body corporate are managed by its members, subsection (1) applies in relation to the acts and defaults of a member in connection with his functions of management as if he were a director of the body.

(3)   In subsection (1) "officer", in relation to a body corporate, means—

(a)   a director, member of the committee of management, chief executive, manager, secretary or other similar officer of the body, or a person purporting to act in any such capacity, or

(b)   an individual who is a controller of the body.

(4)   If an offence committed by a partnership is shown—

(a)   to have been committed with the consent or connivance of a partner, or

(b)   to be attributable to any neglect on his part,

the partner as well as the partnership is guilty of the offence and liable to be proceeded against and punished accordingly.

(5)   In subsection (4) "partner" includes a person purporting to act as a partner.

(6)   If an offence committed by an unincorporated association (other than a partnership) is shown—

(a)   to have been committed with the consent or connivance of an officer of the association or a member of its governing body, or

(b)   to be attributable to any neglect on the part of such an officer or member,

that officer or member as well as the association is guilty of the offence and liable to be proceeded against and punished accordingly.

(7)   Regulations may provide for the application of any provision of this section, with such modifications as the Secretary of State considers appropriate, to a body corporate or unincorporated association formed or recognised under the law of a territory outside the United Kingdom.

(8)   In this section "offence" means an offence under this Act.

[Licensing Act 2003, s 187.]

7.7870   188.   Jurisdiction and procedure in respect of offences   (1)   A fine imposed on an unincorporated association on its conviction for an offence is to be paid out of the funds of the association.

(2)   Proceedings for an offence alleged to have been committed by an unincorporated association must be brought in the name of the association (and not in that of any of its members).

(3)   Rules of court relating to the service of documents are to have effect as if the association were a body corporate.

(4)   In proceedings for an offence brought against an unincorporated association, section 33 of the Criminal Justice Act 1925 (c 86) and Schedule 3 to the Magistrates' Courts Act 1980 (c 43) (procedure) apply as they do in relation to a body corporate.

(5)   Proceedings for an offence may be taken—

(a)   against a body corporate or unincorporated association at any place at which it has a place of business;

(b)   against an individual at any place where he is for the time being.

(6)   Subsection (5) does not affect any jurisdiction exercisable apart from this section.

(7)   In this section "offence" means an offence under this Act.

[Licensing Act 2003, s 188.]

Vessels, vehicles and moveable structures

7.7871   189.   Vessels, vehicles and moveable structures   (1)   This Act applies in relation to a vessel which is not permanently moored or berthed as if it were premises situated in the place where it is usually moored or berthed.

(2)   Where a vehicle which is not permanently situated in the same place is, or is proposed to be, used for one or more licensable activities while parked at a particular place, the vehicle is to be treated for the purposes of this Act as if it were premises situated at that place.

(3)   Where a moveable structure which is not permanently situated in the same place is, or is proposed to be, used for one or more licensable activities while set in a particular place, the structure is to be treated for the purposes of this Act as if it were premises situated at that place.

(4)   Where subsection (2) applies in relation to the same vehicle, or subsection (3) applies in relation to the same structure, in respect of more than one place, the premises which by virtue of that subsection are situated at each such place are to be treated as separate premises.

(5)   Sections 29 to 31 (which make provision in respect of provisional statements relating to premises licences) do not apply in relation to a vessel, vehicle or structure to which this section applies.

[Licensing Act 2003, s 189.]

Interpretation

7.7872   190.   Location of sales   (1)   This section applies where the place where a contract for the sale of alcohol is made is different from the place where the alcohol is appropriated to the contract.

(2)   For the purposes of this Act the sale of alcohol is to be treated as taking place where the alcohol is appropriated to the contract.

[Licensing Act 2003, s 190.]

7.7873   191.   Meaning of "alcohol"   (1)   In this Act, "alcohol" means spirits, wine, beer, cider or any other fermented, distilled or spirituous liquor (in any state), but does not include—

(a)   alcohol which is of a strength not exceeding 0.5% at the time of the sale or supply in question,

(b)   perfume,

(c)   flavouring essences recognised by the Commissioners of Customs and Excise as not being intended for consumption as or with dutiable alcoholic liquor,

(d)   the aromatic flavouring essence commonly known as Angostura bitters,

(e)   alcohol which is, or is included in, a medicinal product or a veterinary medicinal product,

(f)   denatured alcohol,

(g)   methyl alcohol,

(h)   naphtha, or

(i)   alcohol contained in liqueur confectionery.

(2)   In this section—

"denatured alcohol" has the same meaning as in section 5 of the Finance Act 1995 (c 4);

"dutiable alcoholic liquor" has the same meaning as in the Alcoholic Liquor Duties Act 1979 (c 4);

"liqueur confectionery" means confectionery which—

(a)   contains alcohol in a proportion not greater than 0.2 litres of alcohol (of a strength not exceeding 57%) per kilogram of the confectionery, and

(b)   either consists of separate pieces weighing not more than 42g or is designed to be broken into such pieces for the purpose of consumption;

"medicinal product" has the same meaning as in section 130 of the Medicines Act 1968 (c 67); and

"strength" is to be construed in accordance with section 2 of the Alcoholic Liquor Duties Act 1979

"veterinary medicinal product" has the same meaning as in regulation 2 of the Veterinary Medicines Regulations 2006.

[Licensing Act 2003, s 191 as amended by SI 2006/2407 and the Policing and Crime Act 2017, s 135.]

7.7874   192.   Meaning of "sale by retail"   (1)   For the purposes of this Act "sale by retail", in relation to any alcohol, means a sale of alcohol to any person, other than a sale of alcohol that—

(a)   is within subsection (2),

(b)   is made from premises owned by the person making the sale, or occupied by him under a lease to which the provisions of Part 2 of the Landlord and Tenant Act 1954 (c 56) (security of tenure) apply, and

(c)   is made for consumption off the premises.

(2)   A sale of alcohol is within this subsection if it is—

(a)   to a trader for the purposes of his trade,

    (b)   to a club, which holds a club premises certificate, for the purposes of that club,

    (c)   to the holder of a personal licence for the purpose of making sales authorised by a premises licence,

    (d)   to the holder of a premises licence for the purpose of making sales authorised by that licence, or

    (e)   to the premises user in relation to a temporary event notice for the purpose of making sales authorised by that notice.

[Licensing Act 2003, s 192.]

7.7875 192A. Entitlement to work in the United Kingdom (1) For the purposes of this Act an individual is entitled to work in the United Kingdom if—

    (a)   the individual does not under the Immigration Act 1971 require leave to enter or remain in the United Kingdom, or

    (b)   the individual has been granted such leave and the leave—

        (i)   is not invalid,

        (ii)   has not ceased to have effect (whether by reason of curtailment, revocation, cancellation, passage of time or otherwise), and

        (iii)   is not subject to a condition preventing the individual from doing work relating to the carrying on of a licensable activity within section 1(1)(a) or (d).

    (2) Where an individual is on immigration bail within the meaning of Part 1 of Schedule 10 to the Immigration Act 2016—

    (a)   the individual is to be treated for the purposes of subsection (1) as if the individual had been granted leave to enter the United Kingdom, but

    (b)   any condition as to the individual's work in the United Kingdom to which the individual's immigration bail is subject is to be treated for those purposes as a condition of leave.

[Licensing Act 2003, s 192A as inserted by the Immigration Act 2016, Sch 4.]

7.7876 193. Other definitions (1) In this Act—

"beer" has the same meaning as in the Alcoholic Liquor Duties Act 1979 (c 4);

"cider" has the same meaning as in that Act;

"community premises" means premises that are or form part of—

    (a)   a church hall, chapel hall or other similar building, or

    (b)   a village hall, parish hall, community hall or other similar building;

"crime prevention objective" means the licensing objective mentioned in section 4(2)(a) (prevention of crime and disorder);

"licensed premises" means premises in respect of which a premises licence has effect;

"licensing functions" is to be construed in accordance with section 4(1);

"management committee", in relation to any community premises, means a committee or board of individuals with responsibility for the management of the premises;

"order", except so far as the contrary intention appears, means an order made by the Secretary of State;

"premises" means any place and includes a vehicle, vessel or moveable structure;

"prescribed" means prescribed by regulations;

"recognised club" means a club which satisfies conditions 1 to 3 of the general conditions in section 62;

"regulations" means regulations made by the Secretary of State;

"relevant electronic facility" means—

    (a)   the electronic assistance facility referred to in regulation 38 of the Provision of Services Regulations 2009, or

    (b)   any facility established and maintained by a licensing authority for the purpose of receiving applications, notices or representations electronically;

"vehicle" means a vehicle intended or adapted for use on roads;

"vessel" includes a ship, boat, raft or other apparatus constructed or adapted for floating on water;

"wine" means—

    (a)   "wine" within the meaning of the Alcoholic Liquor Duties Act 1979, and

    (b)   "made-wine" within the meaning of that Act;

"working day" means any day other than a Saturday, a Sunday, Christmas Day, Good Friday or a day which is a bank holiday under the Banking and Financial Dealings Act 1971 (c 80) in England and Wales.

    (2) For the purposes of references in this Act to the prevention of illegal working in licensed premises, a person is working illegally if by doing that work at that time the person is committing an offence under section 24B of the Immigration Act 1971.

[Licensing Act 2003, s 193 as amended by SI 2009/1724, SI 2009/2999 and the Immigration Act 2016, Sch 4.]

7.7877 194. Index of defined expressions In this Act the following expressions are defined or otherwise explained by the provisions indicated—

Expression	Interpretation provision
alcohol	section 191
associate member	section 67(2)
authorised person, in Part 3	section 13
authorised person, in Part 4	section 69
beer	section 193
cider	section 193
club premises certificate	section 60
community premises	section 193
conviction, in Part 6	section 114
crime prevention objective	section 193
designated premises supervisor	section 15
entitled to work in the United Kingdom	section 192A
foreign offence, in Part 6	section 113
given, in relation to a notice, etc	section 184
guest	section 67(1)
immigration offence	section 113
immigration penalty (and required to pay, in relation to an immigration penalty)	section 113
interim authority notice	section 47
late night refreshment	Schedule 2
late temporary event notice	section 100A(1)(b)
licensable activity	section 1(1)
licensed premises	section 193
licensing authority	section 3(1)
licensing authority's area	section 3(2)
licensing functions	sections 4(1) and 193
licensing objectives	section 4(2)
management committee	section 193
order	section 193
permitted temporary activity	section 98
personal licence	section 111(1)
premises	section 193
premises licence	section 11
premises user, in relation to a temporary event notice	section 100(2)
prescribed	section 193
provisional statement	section 29(3)
qualifying club	section 61
qualifying club activity	section 1(2)
recognised club	section 193
regulated entertainment	Schedule 1
regulations	section 193
relevant electronic facility	section 193
relevant licensing authority, in Part 3	section 12
relevant licensing authority, in Part 4	section 68
relevant licensing authority, in Part 5	section 99
relevant licensing authority, in Part 6	section 112
relevant offence, in Part 6	section 113
relevant person, in Part 5	section 99A
responsible authority, in Part 3	section 13
responsible authority, in Part 4	section 69
sale by retail, in relation to alcohol	section 192
secretary, in Part 4	section 70
standard temporary event notice	section 100A(1)(a)
supply of alcohol, in Part 3	section 14
supply of alcohol to members or guests, in relation to a club, in Part 4	section 70
temporary event notice	section 100(1)

Expression	Interpretation provision
vehicle	section 193
vessel	section 193
wine	section 193
working day	section 193
working illegally, in relation to the prevention of illegal working in licensed premises	section 193*

[Licensing Act 2003, s 194 as amended by SI 2009/1724, SI 2009/2999, the Police Reform and Social Responsibility Act 2011, ss 105, 107, 112, 114 and the Immigration Act 2016, Sch 4.]

* **Amended by the Deregulation Act 2015, s 67 from a date to be appointed.**

Supplementary and general

7.7878   195.   Crown application   (1)   This Act binds the Crown and has effect in relation to land in which there is—

    (*a*)   an interest belonging to Her Majesty in right of the Crown,

    (*b*)   an interest belonging to a government department, or

    (*c*)   an interest held in trust for Her Majesty for the purposes of such a department.

    (2)   This Act also applies to—

    (*a*)   land which is vested in, but not occupied by, Her Majesty in right of the Duchy of Lancaster, and

    (*b*)   land which is vested in, but not occupied by, the possessor for the time being of the Duchy of Cornwall.

    (3)   No contravention by the Crown of any provision made by or under this Act makes the Crown criminally liable; but the High Court may declare unlawful any act or omission of the Crown which constitutes such a contravention.

    (4)   Provision made by or under this Act applies to persons in the public service of the Crown as it applies to other persons.

    (5)   But nothing in this Act affects Her Majesty in Her private capacity.

[Licensing Act 2003, s 195.]

7.7879   196.   Removal of privileges and exemptions   No privilege or exemption mentioned in section 199(*a*) or (*b*) of the Licensing Act 1964 (c 26) (University of Cambridge and the Vintners of the City of London) operates to exempt any person from the requirements of this Act.

[Licensing Act 2003, s 196.]

7.7880   197.   Regulations and orders

7.7881   198.   Minor and consequential amendments

7.7882   199.   Repeals

7.7883   200.   Transitional provision etc

7.7884   201.   Short title, commencement and extent   (1)   This Act may be cited as the Licensing Act 2003.

    (2)   The preceding provisions (and the Schedules) come into force in accordance with provision made by order[1].

    (3)   Subject to subsections (4) and (5), this Act extends to England and Wales only.

    (4)   Section 155(1) also extends to Northern Ireland.

    (5)   An amendment or repeal contained in Schedule 6 or 7 has the same extent as the enactment to which it relates.

[Licensing Act 2003, s 201.]

---

[1] For commencement orders made at the date of going to press, see the note to the title of this Act, ante.

SCHEDULE 1

Provision of Regulated Entertainment   Section 1

7.7885

(*Amended by the Gambling Act 2005, Sch 16, the Policing and Crime Act 2009, Sch 7, the Live Music Act 2012, ss 2, 3, SI 2013/1578, SI 2014/3253 and the Deregulation Act 2015, s 76.*)

PART 1

GENERAL DEFINITIONS

The provision of regulated entertainment

1.   (1)   For the purposes of this Act, the "provision of regulated entertainment" means the provision of entertainment of a description falling within paragraph 2 where the conditions in sub-paragraphs (2) and (3) are satisfied.

    (2)   The first condition is that the entertainment is provided—

    (*a*)   to any extent for members of the public or a section of the public,

    (b)   exclusively for members of a club which is a qualifying club in relation to the provision of regulated entertainment, or for members of such a club and their guests, or

    (c)   in any case not falling within paragraph (a) or (b), for consideration and with a view to profit.

  (3)   The second condition is that the premises on which the entertainment is provided are made available for the purpose, or for purposes which include the purpose, of enabling the entertainment concerned to take place.

  (4)   For the purposes of sub-paragraph (2)(c), entertainment is to be regarded as provided for consideration only if any charge—

    (a)   is made by or on behalf of any person concerned in the organisation or management of that entertainment, and

    (b)   is paid by or on behalf of some or all of the persons for whom that entertainment is provided.

  (5)   In sub-paragraph (4), "charge" includes any charge for the provision of goods or services.

  (6)   For the purposes of sub-paragraph (4)(a), where the entertainment consists of the performance of live music or the playing of recorded music, a person performing or playing the music is not concerned in the organisation or management of the entertainment by reason only that he does one or more of the following—

    (a)   chooses the music to be performed or played,

    (b)   determines the manner in which he performs or plays it,

    (c)   *repealed.*

  (7)   This paragraph is subject to Part 2 of this Schedule (exemptions).

Entertainment

2. (1)   The descriptions of entertainment are—

    (a)   a performance of a play,

    (b)   an exhibition of a film,

    (c)   an indoor sporting event,

    (d)   a boxing or wrestling entertainment,

    (e)   a performance of live music,

    (f)   any playing of recorded music,

    (g)   a performance of dance,

    (h)   entertainment of a similar description to that falling within paragraph (e), (f) or (g),

the following conditions are satisfied (so far as relevant).

  (1A)   The first condition is that the entertainment—

    (a)   takes place in the presence of an audience, and

    (b)   is provided for the purpose, or for purposes which include the purpose, of entertaining that audience.

  (1B)   The second condition is relevant only to a performance of a play, and is that one or more of the following applies—

    (a)   the audience consists of more than 500 persons;

    (b)   the entertainment takes place before 8am on any day;

    (c)   the entertainment takes place after 11pm on any day.

  (1C)   The third condition is relevant only to an indoor sporting event, and is that one or more of the following applies—

    (a)   the audience consists of more than 1000 persons;

    (b)   the entertainment takes place before 8am on any day;

    (c)   the entertainment takes place after 11pm on any day.

  (1D)   The fourth condition is relevant only to a performance of dance, and is that one or more of the following applies—

    (a)   the audience consists of more than 500 persons;

    (b)   the entertainment takes place before 8am on any day;

    (c)   the entertainment takes place after 11pm on any day;

    (d)   the entertainment is relevant entertainment within the meaning of paragraph 2A of Schedule 3 to the Local Government (Miscellaneous Provisions) Act 1982 (meaning of "sexual entertainment venue").

  (1E)   So much of any entertainment of a description specified in paragraphs (a) to (h) of sub-paragraph (1) as does not satisfy the conditions in sub-paragraphs (1A) to (1D) (so far as relevant) is not to be regarded as falling within sub-paragraph (1).

  (2)   Any reference in this paragraph to an audience includes a reference to spectators.

  (3)   This paragraph is subject to Part 3 of this Schedule (interpretation).

3. *Repealed.*

Power to amend Schedule

4.   The Secretary of State may by order amend this Schedule for the purposes of modifying the descriptions of entertainment specified in paragraph 2, and for this purpose "modify" includes adding, varying or removing any description.

PART 2
EXEMPTIONS
Film exhibitions for the purposes of advertisement, information, education, etc

5.   The provision of entertainment consisting of the exhibition of a film is not to be regarded as the provision of regulated entertainment for the purposes of this Act if its sole or main purpose is to—

    (a)   demonstrate any product,

    (b)   advertise any goods or services, or

    (c)   provide information, education or instruction.

Film exhibitions: museums and art galleries

6.   The provision of entertainment consisting of the exhibition of a film is not to be regarded as the provision of regulated entertainment for the purposes of this Act if it consists of or forms part of an exhibit put on show for any purposes of a museum or art gallery.

Film exhibitions: community premises

6A. (1) The provision of entertainment consisting of the exhibition of a film at community premises is not to be regarded as the provision of regulated entertainment for the purposes of this Act if the following conditions are satisfied.

(2) The first condition is that prior written consent for the entertainment to take place at the community premises has been obtained, by or on behalf of a person concerned in the organisation or management of the entertainment—

    (a)   from the management committee of the community premises, or

    (b)   where there is no management committee, from—

        (i)   a person who has control of the community premises (as occupier or otherwise) in connection with the carrying on by that person of a trade, business or other undertaking (for profit or not), or

        (ii)   where there is no such person, an owner of the community premises.

(3) The second condition is that the entertainment is not provided with a view to profit.

(4) The third condition is that the entertainment takes place in the presence of an audience of no more than 500 persons.

(5) The fourth condition is that the entertainment takes place between 8am and 11pm on the same day.

(6) The fifth condition is that the film classification body or the relevant licensing authority has made a recommendation concerning the admission of children to an exhibition of the film and—

    (a)   where a recommendation has been made only by the film classification body, the admission of children is subject to such restrictions (if any) as are necessary to comply with the recommendation of that body;

    (b)   where a recommendation has been made only by the relevant licensing authority, the admission of children is subject to such restrictions (if any) as are necessary to comply with the recommendation of that authority;

    (c)   where recommendations have been made both by the film classification body and the relevant licensing authority, the admission of children is subject to such restrictions (if any) as are necessary to comply with the recommendation of the relevant licensing authority.

(7) In sub-paragraph (6) the reference to the "relevant licensing authority", in relation to the exhibition of a film at particular community premises, is a reference to—

    (a)   the licensing authority in whose area the premises are situated, or

    (b)   where the premises are situated in the areas of two or more licensing authorities, those authorities or (as the context requires) such of those authorities as have made a recommendation.

(8) In this paragraph—

"children" and "film classification body" have the same meaning as in section 20;

"owner", in relation to community premises, means—

    (a)   a person who is for the time being entitled to dispose of the fee simple in the premises, whether in possession or in reversion, or

    (b)   a person who holds or is entitled to the rents and profits of the premises under a lease which (when granted) was for a term of not less than 3 years.

Music and film incidental to certain other activities

7. The provision of entertainment consisting of the performance of live music, the playing of recorded music or the exhibition of a film is not to be regarded as the provision of regulated entertainment for the purposes of this Act to the extent that it is incidental to some other activity which is not itself a description of entertainment falling within paragraph 2.

Use of television or radio receivers

8. The provision of any entertainment is not to be regarded as the provision of regulated entertainment for the purposes of this Act to the extent that it consists of the simultaneous reception and playing of a programme included in a programme service within the meaning of the Broadcasting Act 1990 (c 42).

Religious services, places of worship etc

9. The provision of any entertainment—

    (a)   for the purposes of, or for purposes incidental to, a religious meeting or service, or

    (b)   at a place of public religious worship,

is not to be regarded as the provision of regulated entertainment for the purposes of this Act.

Garden fêtes, etc

10. (1) The provision of any entertainment at a garden fête, or at a function or event of a similar character, is not to be regarded as the provision of regulated entertainment for the purposes of this Act.

(2) But sub-paragraph (1) does not apply if the fête, function or event is promoted with a view to applying the whole or part of its proceeds for purposes of private gain.

(3) In sub-paragraph (2) "private gain", in relation to the proceeds of a fête, function or event, is to be construed in accordance with section 19(3) of the Gambling Act 2005.

Morris dancing etc

11. The provision of any entertainment is not to be regarded as the provision of regulated entertainment for the purposes of this Act to the extent that it consists of the provision of—

    (a)   a performance of morris dancing or any dancing of a similar nature or the playing of live or recorded music that forms an integral part of such a performance, or

    (b)   repealed.

Sexual entertainment venues

11A. (1) The provision of relevant entertainment—

    (a)   at premises for which a licence for a sexual entertainment venue is required (or the requirement has been waived) by virtue of Schedule 3 to the Local Government (Miscellaneous Provisions) Act 1982, and

    (*b*)   of a kind, and in a way, by virtue of which the premises qualify as such a venue,
is not to be regarded as the provision of regulated entertainment for the purposes of this Act.

    (2)   The provision of relevant entertainment—

    (*a*)   at premises which are subject to a licence for a sexual entertainment venue but are not such a venue merely because of the operation of paragraph 2A(3)(*b*) of Schedule 3 to the Act of 1982, and

    (*b*)   of a kind, and in a way, by virtue of which the premises would qualify as such a venue but for the operation of that paragraph,
is not to be regarded as the provision of regulated entertainment for the purposes of this Act.

    (3)   The provision of entertainment consisting of the performance of live music or the playing of recorded music is not to be regarded as the provision of regulated entertainment for the purposes of this Act to the extent that it is an integral part of such provision of relevant entertainment as falls within sub-paragraph (1) or (2).

    (4)   *Repealed*

    (5)   In this paragraph—

"premises" has the meaning given by paragraph 2A(14) of Schedule 3 to the Act of 1982;

"relevant entertainment" has the meaning given by paragraph 2A(2) of that Schedule to that Act;

"sexual entertainment venue" has the meaning given by paragraph 2A(1) of that Schedule to that Act.

Vehicles in motion

12.   The provision of any entertainment—

    (*a*)   on premises consisting of or forming part of a vehicle, and

    (*b*)   at a time when the vehicle is not permanently or temporarily parked,
is not to be regarded as the provision of regulated entertainment for the purposes of this Act.

Entertainment provided by health care providers, local authorities and school proprietors

12ZA.   (1)   The provision of any entertainment by or on behalf of a health care provider, local authority or school proprietor is not to be regarded as the provision of regulated entertainment for the purposes of this Act if the conditions in sub-paragraphs (2) to (5) are satisfied.

    (2)   The first condition is that the entertainment takes place—

    (*a*)   if it is provided by or on behalf of a health care provider, on any premises forming part of a hospital—

        (i)   in which that provider has a relevant property interest, or

        (ii)   which are lawfully occupied by that provider,

    (*b*)   if it is provided by or on behalf of a local authority, on any premises in which that authority has a relevant property interest or which are lawfully occupied by that authority, and

    (*c*)   if it is provided by or on behalf of a school proprietor, on the premises of the school.

    (3)   The second condition is that the premises are not domestic premises.

    (4)   The third condition is that the entertainment takes place between 8am and 11pm on the same day (or, where an order under section 172 has effect in relation to that entertainment, during any times specified under that order).

    (5)   The fourth condition is that the entertainment is not relevant entertainment within the meaning of paragraph 2A(2) of Schedule 3 to the Local Government (Miscellaneous Provisions) Act 1982 (meaning of "sexual entertainment venue").

    (6)   For the purposes of this paragraph, a person has a relevant property interest in premises if that person—

    (*a*)   is for the time being entitled to dispose of the fee simple in the premises, whether in possession or in reversion, or

    (*b*)   holds or is entitled to the rents and profits of the premises under a lease which (when granted) was for a term of not less than 3 years.

    (7)   In sub-paragraph (3), "domestic premises" means premises occupied as a private dwelling, including any garden, yard, garage, outhouse or other appurtenance of such premises whether or not used in common by the occupants of more than one such dwelling.

Music at community premises etc.

12ZB.   (1)   The provision of entertainment consisting of one or both of the following is not to be regarded as the provision of regulated entertainment for the purposes of this Act if the conditions in sub-paragraphs (2) to (6) are satisfied—

    (*a*)   a performance of live music,

    (*b*)   the playing of recorded music.

    (2)   The first condition is that the entertainment takes place at—

    (*a*)   community premises that are not authorised, by a premises licence or club premises certificate, to be used for the supply of alcohol for consumption on the premises,

    (*b*)   the premises of a hospital,

    (*c*)   premises in which a local authority has a relevant property interest or which are lawfully occupied by a local authority, or

    (*d*)   the premises of a school.

    (3)   The second condition is that the premises are not domestic premises (within the meaning of paragraph 12ZA(7)).

    (4)   The third condition is that the entertainment takes place in the presence of an audience of no more than 500 persons.

    (5)   The fourth condition is that the entertainment takes place between 8am and 11pm on the same day (or, where an order under section 172 has effect in relation to that entertainment, during any times specified under that order).

    (6)   The fifth condition is that a person concerned in the organisation or management of the entertainment has obtained the prior written consent of a relevant person for the entertainment to take place.

    (7)   In sub-paragraph (6), "relevant person" means—

    (*a*)   where the entertainment takes place at community premises—

        (i)   the management committee of the premises, or

(ii)　　if there is no management committee, a person who has control of the premises (as occupier or otherwise) in connection with the carrying on by that person of a trade, business or other undertaking (for profit or not) or (in the absence of such a person) a person with a relevant property interest in the premises;

(b)　　where the entertainment takes place at the premises of a hospital, a health care provider which has a relevant property interest in or lawfully occupies those premises;

(c)　　where the entertainment takes place at premises in which a local authority has a relevant property interest or which are lawfully occupied by a local authority, that authority;

(d)　　where the entertainment takes place at the premises of a school, the school proprietor.

(8)　　Paragraph 12ZA(6) (meaning of "relevant property interest") applies for the purposes of this paragraph as it applies for the purposes of paragraph 12ZA.

Music in licensed venues

12A.　(1)　The provision of entertainment consisting of one or both of the following is not to be regarded as the provision of regulated entertainment for the purposes of this Act if the conditions in sub-paragraph (2) are satisfied—

(a)　　a performance of live music;

(b)　　the playing of recorded music.

(2)　　The conditions referred to in sub-paragraph (1) are that—

(a)　　the requirements of section 177A(1) are satisfied, and

(b)　　conditions are not included in the premises licence or club premises certificate referred to in section 177A(1)(a) by virtue of section 177A(3) or (4).

Live music in workplaces

12B.　The provision of entertainment consisting of a performance of live music is not to be regarded as the provision of regulated entertainment for the purposes of this Act, provided that—

(a)　　the place where the performance is provided is not licensed under this Act (or is so licensed only for the provision of late night refreshment) but is a workplace as defined in regulation 2(1) of the Workplace (Health, Safety and Welfare) Regulations 1992,

(b)　　the performance takes place in the presence of an audience of no more than 500 persons, and

(c)　　the performance takes place between 8am and 11pm on the same day.

Live unamplified music

12C.　The provision of entertainment consisting of a performance of live music is not (subject to section 177A(3) and (4)) to be regarded as the provision of regulated entertainment for the purposes of this Act provided that the music—

(a)　　is unamplified; and

(b)　　takes place between 8am and 11pm on the same day.

Circuses

12D.　(1)　The provision of any entertainment that consists of or forms part of a performance by a travelling circus is not to be regarded as the provision of regulated entertainment for the purposes of this Act if the conditions in sub-paragraphs (2) to (5) are satisfied.

(2)　　The first condition is that the entertainment is not of a description falling within paragraph 2(1)(b) (exhibition of a film) or paragraph 2(1)(d) (boxing or wrestling entertainment).

(3)　　The second condition is that the entertainment takes place between 8am and 11pm on the same day.

(4)　　The third condition is that—

(a)　　the entertainment takes place wholly within a moveable structure, and

(b)　　the audience present is accommodated wholly inside that moveable structure.

(5)　　The fourth condition is that the travelling circus has not been located on the same site for more than 28 consecutive days.

(6)　　In this paragraph, "travelling circus" means a circus which travels from site to site for the purpose of giving performances.

Boxing or wrestling entertainment: certain forms of wrestling

12E.　The provision of entertainment consisting of a boxing or wrestling entertainment is not to be regarded as the provision of regulated entertainment for the purposes of this Act if—

(a)　　it is a contest, exhibition or display of Greco-Roman wrestling, or of freestyle wrestling, between two participants (regardless of their sex),

(b)　　it takes place in the presence of no more than 1000 spectators,

(c)　　it takes place between 8am and 11pm on the same day,

(d)　　it takes place wholly inside a building, and

(e)　　the spectators present at that entertainment are accommodated wholly inside that building.

PART 3

INTERPRETATION

General

13.　This Part has effect for the purposes of this Schedule.

Plays

14.　(1)　A "performance of a play" means a performance of any dramatic piece, whether involving improvisation or not,—

(a)　　which is given wholly or in part by one or more persons actually present and performing, and

(b)　　in which the whole or a major proportion of what is done by the person or persons performing, whether by way of speech, singing or action, involves the playing of a role.

(2)　　In this paragraph, "performance" includes rehearsal (and "performing" is to be construed accordingly).

Film exhibitions

15. An "exhibition of a film" means any exhibition of moving pictures.

Indoor sporting events

16. (1) An "indoor sporting event" is a sporting event—
   (a) which takes place wholly inside a building, and
   (b) at which the spectators present at the event are accommodated wholly inside that building.
   (2) In this paragraph—
"building" means any roofed structure (other than a structure with a roof which may be opened or closed) and includes a vehicle, vessel or moveable structure,
"sporting event" means any contest, exhibition or display of any sport, and
"sport" other than a boxing or wrestling entertainment includes—
   (a) any game in which physical skill is the predominant factor, and
   (b) any form of physical recreation which is also engaged in for purposes of competition or display.

Boxing or wrestling entertainments

17. A "boxing or wrestling entertainment" is any contest, exhibition or display of boxing or wrestling, or which combines boxing or wrestling with one or more martial arts.

Music

18. "Music" includes vocal or instrumental music or any combination of the two.

Health care providers and hospitals

19. (1) "Health care provider" means a person providing any form of health care services for individuals.
   (2) In sub-paragraph (1), "health care" means all forms of health care provided for individuals, whether relating to physical or mental health, and the reference to health care services is to be read accordingly.
   (3) "Hospital"—
   (a) in England, has the same meaning as in section 275 of the National Health Service Act 2006, and
   (b) in Wales, has the same meaning as in section 206 of the National Health Service (Wales) Act 2006.

Local authorities

20. "Local authority" means—
   (a) a local authority within the meaning of section 270 of the Local Government Act 1972;
   (b) the Greater London Authority;
   (c) the Common Council of the City of London;
   (d) the Council of the Isles of Scilly;
   (e) a National Park authority established by an order under section 63(1) of the Environment Act 1995 for an area in England or Wales;
   (f) the Broads Authority; and
   (g) the Sub-Treasurer of the Inner Temple or the Under-Treasurer of the Middle Temple

Schools, school proprietors and school premises

21. (1) "School" means—
   (a) a maintained school as defined by section 20(7) of the School Standards and Framework Act 1998;
   (b) an independent school as defined by section 463 of the Education Act 1996 entered on a register of independent schools kept under section 158 of the Education Act 2002;
   (c) an independent educational institution within section 92(1)(b) of the Education and Skills Act 2008 entered on a register of independent educational institutions kept under section 95 of that Act;
   (d) a pupil referral unit as defined by section 19 of the Education Act 1996;
   (e) an alternative provision Academy within the meaning of section 1C(3) of the Academies Act 2010, other than an independent school as defined by section 463 of the Education Act 1996;
   (f) a school approved under section 342 of the Education Act 1996 (non-maintained special schools);
   (g) a 16 to 19 Academy within the meaning of section 1B(3) of the Academies Act 2010;
   (h) a sixth form college as defined by section 91(3A) of the Further and Higher Education Act 1992;
   (i) a maintained nursery school as defined by section 22(9) of the Schools Standards and Framework Act 1998.
   (2) "School proprietor" means—
   (a) in relation to a school (other than a pupil referral unit or a sixth form college), the person or body of persons responsible for the management of the school,
   (b) in relation to a pupil referral unit—
     (i) the committee which is established to act as the management committee for that unit by virtue of paragraph 15 of Schedule 1 to the Education Act 1996, or
     (ii) if there is no such committee, the local authority (as defined by section 579(1) of that Act) which maintains that unit,
   (c) in relation to a sixth form college, the sixth form college corporation as defined in section 90(1) of the Further and Higher Education Act 1992.
   (3) In relation to a school, "premises" includes any detached playing fields.

SCHEDULE 2
Provision of Late Night Refreshment

(As amended by the Charities Act 2011, Sch 7 and the Deregulation Act 2015, s 71) Section 1

The provision of late night refreshment

7.7886 1. (1) For the purposes of this Act, a person "provides late night refreshment" if—
   (a) at any time between the hours of 11.00 p.m. and 5.00 a.m., he supplies hot food or hot drink to members of the public, or a section of the public, on or from any premises, whether for consumption on or off the premises, or

(b)   at any time between those hours when members of the public, or a section of the public, are admitted to any premises, he supplies, or holds himself out as willing to supply, hot food or hot drink to any persons, or to persons of a particular description, on or from those premises, whether for consumption on or off the premises,

unless the supply is an exempt supply by virtue of paragraph 2A, 3, 4 or 5.

(2)   References in this Act to the "provision of late night refreshment" are to be construed in accordance with sub-paragraph (1).

(3)   This paragraph is subject to the following provisions of this Schedule.

Hot food or hot drink

2.   Food or drink supplied on or from any premises is "hot" for the purposes of this Schedule if the food or drink, or any part of it,—

(a)   before it is supplied, is heated on the premises or elsewhere for the purpose of enabling it to be consumed at a temperature above the ambient air temperature and, at the time of supply, is above that temperature, or

(b)   after it is supplied, may be heated on the premises for the purpose of enabling it to be consumed at a temperature above the ambient air temperature.

Exempt supplies: designated areas, descriptions of premises and times

2A.   (1)   The supply of hot food or hot drink is an exempt supply for the purposes of paragraph 1(1) if it takes place—

(a)   on or from premises which are wholly situated in an area designated by the relevant licensing authority;

(b)   on or from premises which are of a description designated by the relevant licensing authority; or

(c)   during a period (beginning no earlier than 11.00 pm and ending no later than 5.00 am) designated by the relevant licensing authority.

(2)   A licensing authority may designate a description of premises under sub-paragraph (1)(b) only if the description is one that is prescribed by regulations[1].

(3)   A designation under sub-paragraph (1) may be varied or revoked by the licensing authority that made it.

(4)   A licensing authority that makes, varies or revokes a designation under sub-paragraph (1) must publish the designation, variation or revocation.

(4)   In sub-paragraph (1) references to the "relevant licensing authority", in relation to a supply of hot food or hot drink, are references to—

(a)   the licensing authority in whose area the premises on or from which the food or drink is supplied are situated, or

(b)   where those premises are situated in the areas of two or more licensing authorities, any of those authorities.

---

[1] The Licensing Act 2003 (Late Night Refreshment) Regulations 2015, SI 2015/1781 have been made.

Exempt supplies: clubs, hotels etc and employees

3.   (1)   The supply of hot food or hot drink on or from any premises at any time is an exempt supply for the purposes of paragraph 1(1) if, at that time, a person will neither—

(a)   be admitted to the premises, nor

(b)   be supplied with hot food or hot drink on or from the premises,

except by virtue of being a person of a description falling within sub-paragraph (2).

(2)   The descriptions are that—

(a)   he is a member of a recognised club,

(b)   he is a person staying at a particular hotel, or at particular comparable premises, for the night in question,

(c)   he is an employee of a particular employer,

(d)   he is engaged in a particular trade, he is a member of a particular profession or he follows a particular vocation,

(e)   he is a guest of a person falling within any of paragraphs (a) to (d).

(3)   The premises which, for the purposes of sub-paragraph (2)(b), are comparable to a hotel are—

(a)   a guest house, lodging house or hostel,

(b)   a caravan site or camping site, or

(c)   any other premises the main purpose of maintaining which is the provision of facilities for overnight accommodation.

Exempt supplies: premises licensed under certain other Acts

4.   The supply of hot food or hot drink on or from any premises is an exempt supply for the purposes of paragraph 1(1) if it takes place during a period for which—

(a)   the premises may be used for a public exhibition of a kind described in section 21(1) of the Greater London Council (General Powers) Act 1966 (c xxviii) by virtue of a licence under that section, or

(b)   the premises may be used as near beer premises within the meaning of section 14 of the London Local Authorities Act 1995 (c x) by virtue of a licence under section 16 of that Act.

Miscellaneous exempt supplies

5.   (1)   The following supplies of hot food or hot drink are exempt supplies for the purposes of paragraph 1(1)—

(a)   the supply of hot drink which consists of or contains alcohol,

(b)   the supply of hot drink by means of a vending machine,

(c)   the supply of hot food or hot drink free of charge,

(d)   the supply of hot food or hot drink by a registered charity or a person authorised by a registered charity,

(e)   the supply of hot food or hot drink on a vehicle at a time when the vehicle is not permanently or temporarily parked.

(2)   Hot drink is supplied by means of a vending machine for the purposes of sub-paragraph (1)(b) only if—

(a)   the payment for the hot drink is inserted into the machine by a member of the public, and

(b)   the hot drink is supplied directly by the machine to a member of the public.

(3)   Hot food or hot drink is not to be regarded as supplied free of charge for the purposes of sub-paragraph (1)(c) if, in order to obtain the hot food or hot drink, a charge must be paid—

(a)   for admission to any premises, or

(b)   for some other item.

(4)   In sub-paragraph (1)(d) "registered charity" means—

(a)   a charity which is registered in accordance with section 30 of the Charities Act 2011, or

(b)   a charity which by virtue of subsection (2) of that section is not required to be so registered.

Clubs which are not recognised clubs: members and guests

6.   For the purposes of this Schedule—

(a)   the supply of hot food or hot drink to a person as being a member, or the guest of a member, of a club which is not a recognised club is to be taken to be a supply to a member of the public, and

(b)   the admission of any person to any premises as being such a member or guest is to be taken to be the admission of a member of the public.

SCHEDULE 4
Personal Licence: Relevant Offences   Section 113

(Amended by SI 2005/2366, the Gambling Act 2005, Sch 16, the Fraud Act 2006, Sch 1, SI 2007/2075, SI 2008/1277, the Police Reform and Social Responsibility Act 2011, s 123, the Psychoactive Substances Act 2015, Sch 5, the Immigration Act 2016, Sch 4 and the Policing and Crime Act 2017, s 139)

7.7887 **1.**   An offence under this Act.

2.   An offence under any of the following enactments—

(a)   Schedule 12 to the London Government Act 1963 (c 33) (public entertainment licensing);

(b)   the Licensing Act 1964 (c 26);

(c)   the Private Places of Entertainment (Licensing) Act 1967 (c 19);

(d)   section 13 of the Theatres Act 1968 (c 54);

(e)   the Late Night Refreshment Houses Act 1969 (c 53);

(f)   section 6 of, or Schedule 1 to, the Local Government (Miscellaneous Provisions) Act 1982 (c 30);

(g)   the Licensing (Occasional Permissions) Act 1983 (c 24);

(h)   the Cinemas Act 1985 (c 13);

(i)   the London Local Authorities Act 1990 (c vii).

3.   An offence under the Firearms Act 1968 (c 27).

4.   An offence under section 1 of the Trade Descriptions Act 1968 (c 29) (false trade description of goods) in circumstances where the goods in question are or include alcohol.

5.   An offence under any of the following provisions of the Theft Act 1968 (c 60)—

(a)   section 1 (theft);

(b)   section 8 (robbery);

(c)   section 9 (burglary);

(d)   section 10 (aggravated burglary);

(e)   section 11 (removal of articles from places open to the public);

(f)   section 12A (aggravated vehicle-taking), in circumstances where subsection (2)(b) of that section applies and the accident caused the death of any person;

(g)   section 13 (abstracting of electricity);

(h)   section 15 (obtaining property by deception);

(i)   section 15A (obtaining a money transfer by deception);

(j)   section 16 (obtaining pecuniary advantage by deception);

(k)   section 17 (false accounting);

(l)   section 19 (false statements by company directors etc);

(m)   section 20 (suppression, etc of documents);

(n)   section 21 (blackmail);

(o)   section 22 (handling stolen goods);

(p)   section 24A (dishonestly retaining a wrongful credit);

(q)   section 25 (going equipped for stealing etc).

6.   An offence under section 7(2) of the Gaming Act 1968 (c 65) (allowing child to take part in gaming on premises licensed for the sale of alcohol).

7.   An offence under any of the following provisions of the Misuse of Drugs Act 1971 (c 38)—

(a)   section 4(2) (production of a controlled drug);

(b)   section 4(3) (supply of a controlled drug);

(c)   section 5(3) (possession of a controlled drug with intent to supply);

(d)   section 8 (permitting activities to take place on premises).

7A.   An offence under any of the Immigration Acts.

8.   An offence under either of the following provisions of the Theft Act 1978 (c 31)—

(a)   section 1 (obtaining services by deception);

(b)   section 2 (evasion of liability by deception).

9.   An offence under either of the following provisions of the Customs and Excise Management Act 1979 (c 2)—

(a)   section 170 (disregarding subsection (1)(a)) (fraudulent evasion of duty etc);

(b)   section 170B (taking preparatory steps for evasion of duty).

10.   An offence under either of the following provisions of the Tobacco Products Duty Act 1979 (c 7)—

(a)   section 8G (possession and sale of unmarked tobacco);

(b)   section 8H (use of premises for sale of unmarked tobacco).

11.   An offence under the Forgery and Counterfeiting Act 1981 (c 45) (other than an offence under section 18 or 19 of that Act).

12.   An offence under the Firearms (Amendment) Act 1988 (c 45).

13.   An offence under any of the following provisions of the Copyright, Designs and Patents Act 1988 (c 48)—

(a)   section 107(1)(d)(iii) (public exhibition in the course of a business of article infringing copyright);

(b)   section 107(3) (infringement of copyright by public performance of work etc);

(c)   section 198(2) (broadcast etc of recording of performance made without sufficient consent);
(d)   section 297(1) (fraudulent reception of transmission);
(e)   section 297A(1) (supply etc of unauthorised decoder).
14.   An offence under any of the following provisions of the Road Traffic Act 1988 (c 52)—
(a)   section 3A (causing death by careless driving while under the influence of drink or drugs);
(b)   section 4 (driving etc a vehicle when under the influence of drink or drugs);
(c)   section 5 (driving etc a vehicle with alcohol concentration above prescribed limit);
(d)   section 6(6) (failing to co-operate with a preliminary test).
15.   An offence under either of the following provisions of the Food Safety Act 1990 (c 16) in circumstances where the food in question is or includes alcohol—
(a)   section 14 (selling food or drink not of the nature, substance or quality demanded);
(b)   section 15 (falsely describing or presenting food or drink).
16.   An offence under section 92(1) or (2) of the Trade Marks Act 1994 (c 26) (unauthorised use of trade mark, etc in relation to goods) in circumstances where the goods in question are or include alcohol.
17.   An offence under the Firearms (Amendment) Act 1997 (c 5).
18.   A sexual offence, being an offence—
(a)   listed in Part 2 of Schedule 15 to the Criminal Justice Act 2003, other than the offence mentioned in paragraph 95 (an offence under section 4 of the Sexual Offences Act 1967 (procuring others to commit homosexual acts));
(aa)   listed in Schedule 3 to the Sexual Offences Act 2003 (sexual offences for the purposes of notification and orders);
(b)   an offence under section 8 of the Sexual Offences Act 1956 (intercourse with a defective);
(c)   an offence under section 18 of the Sexual Offences Act 1956 (fraudulent abduction of an heiress).
19.   A violent offence, being any offence which leads, or is intended or likely to lead, to a person's death or to physical injury to a person, including an offence which is required to be charged as arson (whether or not it would otherwise fall within this definition).
19A.   An offence listed in Part 1 of Schedule 15 to the Criminal Justice Act 2003 (specified violent offences).
20.   An offence under section 3 of the Private Security Industry Act 2001 (c 12) (engaging in certain activities relating to security without a licence).
21.   An offence under section 46 of the Gambling Act 2005 if the child or young person was invited, caused or permitted to gamble on premises in respect of which a premises licence under this Act had effect.
22.   An offence under the Fraud Act 2006.
22ZA.   An offence under any of the following provisions of the Violent Crime Reduction Act 2006—
(a)   section 28 (using someone to mind a weapon);
(b)   section 36 (manufacture, import and sale of realistic imitation firearms).
22A.   An offence under regulation 6 of the Business Protection from Misleading Marketing Regulations 2008 (offence of misleading advertising) in circumstances where the advertising in question relates to alcohol or to goods that include alcohol.
23.   An offence under regulation 8, 9, 10, 11 or 12 of the Consumer Protection from Unfair Trading Regulations 2008 (offences relating to unfair commercial practices) in circumstances where the commercial practice in question is directly connected with the promotion, sale or supply of alcohol or of a product that includes alcohol.
23A.   An offence under any of the following provisions of the Psychoactive Substances Act 2016—
(a)   section 4 (producing a psychoactive substance);
(b)   section 5 (supplying, or offering to supply, a psychoactive substance);
(c)   section 7 (possession of psychoactive substance with intent to supply);
(d)   section 8 (importing or exporting a psychoactive substance).
23B.   An offence listed in section 41 of the Counter-Terrorism Act 2008 (terrorism offences).
24.   An offence under section 1 of the Criminal Attempts Act 1981 of attempting to commit an offence that is a relevant offence.
25.   An offence under section 1 of the Criminal Law Act 1977 of conspiracy to commit an offence that is a relevant offence.
26.   The offence at common law of conspiracy to defraud.

SCHEDULE 5
Appeals

(Amended by SI 2005/886, the Violent Crime Reduction Act 2006, s 22, the Police Reform and Social Responsibility Act 2011, ss 112, 114, the Deregulation Act 2015, Sch 18, the Immigration Act 2016, Sch 4 and the Policing and Crime Act 2017, ss 137, 138.)   Section 181

PART 1
PREMISES LICENCES
Rejection of applications relating to premises licences

7.7888   1.   Where a licensing authority—
(a)   rejects an application for a premises licence under section 18,
(b)   rejects (in whole or in part) an application to vary a premises licence under section 35,
(c)   rejects an application to vary a premises licence to specify an individual as the premises supervisor under section 39, or
(d)   rejects an application to transfer a premises licence under section 44,
the applicant may appeal against the decision.

Decision to grant premises licence or impose conditions etc

2.   (1)   This paragraph applies where a licensing authority grants a premises licence under section 18.
(2)   The holder[1] of the licence may appeal against any decision—
(a)   to impose conditions on the licence under subsection (2)(a) or (3)(b) of that section, or
(b)   to take any step mentioned in subsection (4)(b) or (c) of that section (exclusion of licensable activity or refusal to specify person as premises supervisor).
(3)   Where a person who made relevant representations in relation to the application desires to contend—
(a)   that the licence ought not to have been granted, or

(b) that, on granting the licence, the licensing authority ought to have imposed different or additional conditions, or to have taken a step mentioned in subsection (4)(b) or (c) of that section,

he may appeal against the decision.

(4) In sub-paragraph (3) "relevant representations" has the meaning given in section 18(6).

Issue of provisional statement

3. (1) This paragraph applies where a provisional statement is issued under subsection (3)(c) of section 31.

(2) An appeal against the decision may be made by—

 (a) the applicant, or

 (b) any person who made relevant representations in relation to the application.

(3) In sub-paragraph (2) "relevant representations" has the meaning given in subsection (5) of that section.

Variation of licence under section 35

4. (1) This paragraph applies where an application to vary a premises licence is granted (in whole or in part) under section 35.

(2) The applicant may appeal against any decision to modify the conditions of the licence under subsection (4)(a) of that section.

(3) Where a person who made relevant representations in relation to the application desires to contend—

 (a) that any variation made ought not to have been made, or

 (b) that, when varying the licence, the licensing authority ought not to have modified the conditions of the licence, or ought to have modified them in a different way, under subsection (4)(a) of that section,

he may appeal against the decision.

(4) In sub-paragraph (3) "relevant representations" has the meaning given in section 35(5).

Variation of licence to specify individual as premises supervisor

5. (1) This paragraph applies where an application to vary a premises licence is granted under section 39(2) in a case where a chief officer of police gave a notice under section 37(5) (which was not withdrawn).

(2) The chief officer of police may appeal against the decision to grant the application.

Transfer of licence

6. (1) This paragraph applies where an application to transfer a premises licence is granted under section 44 in a case where a chief officer of police gave a notice under section 42(6) or the Secretary of State gave a notice under section 42(8) (which, in either case, was not withdrawn).

(2) The chief officer of police or the Secretary of State, as the case may be, may appeal against the decision to grant the application.

Interim authority notice

7. (1) This paragraph applies where—

 (a) an interim authority notice is given in accordance with section 47, and

 (b) a chief officer of police gives a notice under section 48(2) or the Secretary of State gives a notice under section 48(2B) (which, in either case, is not withdrawn).

(2) Where the relevant licensing authority decides to cancel the interim authority notice under subsection (3) of section 48, the person who gave the interim authority notice may appeal against that decision.

(3) Where the relevant licensing authority decides not to cancel the interim authority notice under section 48(3) after the giving of a notice by a chief officer of police under section 48(2), the chief officer of police may appeal against that decision.

(3A) Where the relevant licensing authority decides not to cancel the interim authority notice under section 48(3) after the giving of a notice by the Secretary of State under section 48(2B), the Secretary of State may appeal against that decision.

(4) Where an appeal is brought under sub-paragraph (2), the court to which it is brought may, on such terms as it thinks fit, order the reinstatement of the interim authority notice pending—

 (a) the disposal of the appeal, or

 (b) the expiry of the interim authority period,

whichever first occurs.

(5) Where the court makes an order under sub-paragraph (4), the premises licence is reinstated from the time the order is made, and section 47 has effect in a case where the appeal is dismissed or abandoned before the end of the interim authority period as if—

 (a) the reference in subsection (7)(b) to the end of the interim authority period were a reference to the time when the appeal is dismissed or abandoned, and

 (b) the reference in subsection (9)(a) to the interim authority period were a reference to that period disregarding the part of it which falls after that time.

(6) In this paragraph "interim authority period" has the same meaning as in section 47.

Review of premises licence

8. (1) This paragraph applies where an application for a review of a premises licence is decided under section 52.

(2) An appeal may be made against that decision by—

 (a) the applicant for the review,

 (b) the holder[2] of the premises licence, or

 (c) any other person who made relevant representations in relation to the application.

(3) In sub-paragraph (2) "relevant representations" has the meaning given in section 52(7).

Summary review of premises licence

8A. (1) This paragraph applies where a review of a premises licence is decided under section 53A(2)(b) (review of premises licence following review notice).

(2) An appeal may be made against that decision by—

 (a) the chief officer of police for the police area (or each police area) in which the premises are situated,

 (b) the holder[1] of the premises licence, or

    (c)   any other person who made relevant representations in relation to the application for the review.

    (3)   In sub-paragraph (2) "relevant representations" has the meaning given in section 53C(7).

---

[1] For the position where there has been a mistake as to the identity or description of the premises licence holder in the appeal notice, see *R (Essence Bars Ltd) v Wimbledon Magistrates' Court* [2016] EWCA Civ 63, [2016] 1 WLR 3265, 181 JP 297 and the Magistrates' Courts Act 1980, s 123 and para 1.191 **Objection to the information or charge** in PART I: MAGISTRATES' COURTS, PROCEDURE, ante.

Review of interim steps

8B.   (1)   This paragraph applies where a review of interim steps is decided under section 53D (review of interim steps at a summary review of a premises licence).

    (2)   An appeal may be made against that decision by—

    (a)   the chief officer of police for the police area (or each police area) in which the premises are situated, or

    (b)   the holder of the premises licence.

    (3)   An appeal under this paragraph must be heard by the magistrates' court within the period of 28 days beginning with the day on which the appellant commenced the appeal (see paragraph 9(2)).

General provision about appeals under this Part

9.   (1)   An appeal under this Part must be made to a magistrates' court.

    (2)   An appeal under this Part must be commenced by notice of appeal given by the appellant to the designated officer for the magistrates' court within the period of 21 days beginning with the day on which the appellant was notified by the licensing authority of the decision appealed against.

    (3)   On an appeal under paragraph 2(3), 3(2)(b), 4(3), 5(2), 6(2) or 8(2)(a) or (c), the holder of the premises licence is to be the respondent in addition to the licensing authority[1].

    (4)   On an appeal under paragraph 7(3) or (3A), the person who gave the interim authority notice is to be the respondent in addition to the licensing authority.

---

[1] For the position of interested parties and responsible authorities as respondents, see *R (Chief Constable of Nottinghamshire Police) v Nottingham Magistrates' Court* [2009] EWHC 3182 (Admin), [2010] 2 All ER 342, 174 JP 1 and para 7.7636 **Procedure on appeals**, ante.

PART 2
CLUB PREMISES CERTIFICATES
Rejection of applications relating to club premises certificates

10.   Where a licensing authority—

    (a)   rejects an application for a club premises certificate under section 72, or

    (b)   rejects (in whole or in part) an application to vary a club premises certificate under section 85, the club that made the application may appeal against the decision.

Decision to grant club premises certificate or impose conditions etc

11.   (1)   This paragraph applies where a licensing authority grants a club premises certificate under section 72.

    (2)   The club holding the certificate may appeal against any decision—

    (a)   to impose conditions on the certificate under subsection (2) or (3)(b) of that section, or

    (b)   to take any step mentioned in subsection (4)(b) of that section (exclusion of qualifying club activity).

    (3)   Where a person who made relevant representations in relation to the application desires to contend—

    (a)   that the certificate ought not to have been granted, or

    (b)   that, on granting the certificate, the licensing authority ought to have imposed different or additional conditions, or to have taken a step mentioned in subsection (4)(b) of that section,

he may appeal against the decision.

    (4)   In sub-paragraph (3) "relevant representations" has the meaning given in section 72(7).

Variation of club premises certificate

12.   (1)   This paragraph applies where an application to vary a club premises certificate is granted (in whole or in part) under section 85.

    (2)   The club may appeal against any decision to modify the conditions of the certificate under subsection (3)(b) of that section.

    (3)   Where a person who made relevant representations in relation to the application desires to contend—

    (a)   that any variation ought not to have been made, or

    (b)   that, when varying the certificate, the licensing authority ought not to have modified the conditions of the certificate, or ought to have modified them in a different way, under subsection (3)(b) of that section,

he may appeal against the decision.

    (4)   In sub-paragraph (3) "relevant representations" has the meaning given in section 85(5).

Review of club premises certificate

13.   (1)   This paragraph applies where an application for a review of a club premises certificate is decided under section 88.

    (2)   An appeal may be made against that decision by—

    (a)   the applicant for the review,

    (b)   the club that holds or held the club premises certificate, or

    (c)   any other person who made relevant representations in relation to the application.

    (3)   In sub-paragraph (2) "relevant representations" has the meaning given in section 88(7).

Withdrawal of club premises certificate

14.   Where the relevant licensing authority gives notice withdrawing a club premises certificate under section 90, the club which holds or held the certificate may appeal against the decision to withdraw it.

General provision about appeals under this Part

15. (1) An appeal under this Part must be made to a magistrates' court.

(2) An appeal under this Part must be commenced by notice of appeal given by the appellant to the designated officer for the magistrates' court within the period of 21 days beginning with the day on which the appellant was notified by the licensing authority of the decision appealed against.

(3) On an appeal under paragraph 11(3), 12(3) or 13(2)(*a*) or (*c*), the club that holds or held the club premises certificate is to be the respondent in addition to the licensing authority.

PART 3
OTHER APPEALS
Temporary event notices

16. (1) This paragraph applies where—

　(*a*)　a standard temporary event notice is given under section 100, and

　(*b*)　a relevant person gives an objection notice in accordance with section 104(2).

(2) Where the relevant licensing authority gives a counter notice under section 105(3), the premises user may appeal against that decision.

(3) Where that authority decides not to give such a counter notice, the relevant person may appeal against that decision.

(4) An appeal under this paragraph must be made to a magistrates' court.

(5) An appeal under this paragraph must be commenced by notice of appeal given by the appellant to the designated officer for the magistrates' court within the period of 21 days beginning with the day on which the appellant was notified by the licensing authority of the decision appealed against.

(6) But no appeal may be brought later than five working days before the day on which the event period specified in the temporary event notice begins.

(7) On an appeal under sub-paragraph (3), the premises user is to be the respondent in addition to the licensing authority.

(8) In this paragraph—

"objection notice" has the same meaning as in section 104;

"relevant licensing authority" has the meaning given in section 99; and

"relevant person" has the meaning given in section 99A.

Personal licences

17. (1) Where a licensing authority rejects an application for the grant of a personal licence under section 120, the applicant may appeal against that decision.

(2) Where a licensing authority grants an application for a personal licence under section 120(7A) after the giving of a notice under section 120(5), the chief officer of police who gave the notice may appeal against that decision.

(2A) Where a licensing authority grants an application for a personal licence under section 120(7A) after the giving of a notice under section 120(5B), the Secretary of State may appeal against that decision.

(3) *Repealed.*

(4) Where a licensing authority revokes a personal licence under section 124(4), the holder of the licence may appeal against that decision.

(5) Where in a case to which section 124 (convictions coming to light after grant) applies—

　(*a*)　the chief officer of police for the licensing authority's area gives a notice under subsection (3) of that section (and does not later withdraw it), and

　(*b*)　the licensing authority decides not to revoke the licence,

the chief officer of police may appeal against the decision.

(5A) Where in a case to which section 124 applies—

　(*a*)　the Secretary of State gives a notice under subsection (3B) of that section (and does not later withdraw it), and

　(*b*)　the licensing authority decides not to revoke the licence,

the Secretary of State may appeal against the decision.

(5B) Where a licensing authority revokes or suspends a personal licence under section 132A(8) or (12) the holder of the licence may appeal against that decision.

(6) An appeal under this paragraph must be made to a magistrates' court.

(7) An appeal under this paragraph must be commenced by notice of appeal given by the appellant to the designated officer for the magistrates' court within the period of 21 days beginning with the day on which the appellant was notified by the licensing authority of the decision appealed against.

(8) On an appeal under sub-paragraph (2), (2A), (5) or (5A), the holder of the personal licence is to be the respondent in addition to the licensing authority.

(9) *Repealed.*

(10) *Repealed.*

(11) *Repealed.*

Closure orders

18. (1) This paragraph applies where, on a review of a premises licence under section 167, the relevant licensing authority decides under subsection (5)(*b*) of that section—

　(*a*)　to take any of the steps mentioned in subsection (6) of that section, in relation to a premises licence for those premises, or

　(*b*)　not to take any such step.

(2) An appeal may be made against that decision by—

　(*a*)　the holder of the premises licence, or

　(*b*)　any other person who made relevant representations in relation to the review.

(3) Where an appeal is made under this paragraph against a decision to take any of the steps mentioned in section 167(6)(*a*) to (*d*) (modification of licence conditions etc), the magistrates' court may in a case within section 168(3) (premises closed when decision taken)—

(a)   if the relevant licensing authority has not made an order under section 168(5) (order suspending operation of decision in whole or part), make any order under section 168(5) that could have been made by the relevant licensing authority, or

(b)   if the authority has made such an order, cancel it or substitute for it any order which could have been made by the authority under section 168(5).

(4)   Where an appeal is made under this paragraph in a case within section 168(6) (premises closed when decision to revoke made to remain closed pending appeal), the magistrates' court may, on such conditions as it thinks fit, order that section 168(7) (premises to remain closed pending appeal) is not to apply to the premises.

(5)   An appeal under this paragraph must be commenced by notice of appeal given by the appellant to the designated officer for the magistrates' court within the period of 21 days beginning with the day on which the appellant was notified by the relevant licensing authority of the decision appealed against.

(6)   On an appeal under this paragraph by a person other than the holder of the premises licence, that holder is to be the respondent in addition to the licensing authority that made the decision.

(7)   In this paragraph—

"relevant licensing authority" has the same meaning as in Part 3 of this Act; and

"relevant representations" has the meaning given in section 167(9).

PART 4
QUESTIONS ABOUT LEAVE TO ENTER OR REMAIN IN THE UK

19. On an appeal under this Schedule, a magistrates' court is not entitled to entertain any question as to whether—

(a)   an individual should be, or should have been, granted leave to enter or remain in the United Kingdom, or

(b)   an individual has, after the date of the decision being appealed against, been granted leave to enter or remain in the United Kingdom.

Local Democracy, Economic Development and Construction Act 2009[1]
(2009 c 20)

7.7889   47.   Access to information (1) A person appointed under this Chapter in relation to an entity (in this section referred to as an "auditor") has a right of access at all reasonable times to every document relating to the entity which appears to the auditor necessary for the purpose of the exercise of their functions under section 45.

(2)   The right conferred by subsection (1) includes power to inspect, copy or take away the document.

(3)   An auditor may—

(a)   require a person holding or accountable for any document referred to in subsection (1) to give to the auditor such information or explanation as the auditor thinks necessary for the purpose of the exercise of the auditor's functions under section 45, and

(b)   if the auditor thinks it necessary, require the person to attend before the auditor in person to give the information or explanation or to produce the document.

(4)   Without prejudice to subsection (3), an auditor may—

(a)   require any officer or member of the entity to give to the auditor such information or explanation as the auditor thinks necessary for the purpose of the exercise of the auditor's functions under section 45, and

(b)   if the auditor thinks it necessary, require the officer or member to attend before the auditor in person to give the information or explanation.

(5)   In relation to any document kept in electronic form, the power in subsection (3)(b) to require a person to produce a document includes power to require it to be produced in a form in which it is legible and can be taken away.

(6)   In connection with inspecting such a document, an auditor—

(a)   may obtain access to, and inspect and check the operation of, any computer and associated apparatus or material which the auditor considers is or has been used in connection with the document;

(b)   may require a person within subsection (7) to afford the auditor such reasonable assistance as the auditor may require for that purpose.

(7)   The following persons are within this subsection—

(a)   a person by whom or on whose behalf the computer is or has been used;

(b)   a person having charge of, or otherwise concerned with the operation of, the computer, apparatus or material.

(8)   Without prejudice to subsections (1) to (7), the entity must provide the auditor with every facility and all information which the auditor may reasonably require for the purposes of the exercise of the auditor's functions under section 45.

(9)   A person who without reasonable excuse obstructs the exercise of any power conferred by this section or fails to comply with any requirement of an auditor under this section is guilty of an offence.

(10)   A person guilty of an offence under subsection (9) is liable on summary conviction—

(a)   to a fine not exceeding level 3 on the standard scale, and

(b)   to an additional fine not exceeding £20 for each day on which the offence continues after the person has been convicted of it.

(11)   Any expenses incurred by an auditor in connection with proceedings for an offence under this section, so far as not recovered from any other source, are recoverable from the entity in relation to which the auditor is appointed.

(12)   The powers under this section are in addition to any other powers which an auditor has in relation to the exercise of the auditor's functions under or pursuant to this Chapter.

[Local Democracy, Economic Development and Construction Act 2009, s 147.]

---

[1]   Chapter 3 (ss 36–54) of Part 2 (ss 31–54) implements recommendations from Lord Sharman's independent review into the audit and accountability of public money *Holding to Account: The Review of Audit and Accountability for Central Government (2001)* in relation to companies, limited liability partnerships and industrial and provident societies that are connected with local authorities. Provision is made for the appointment of an auditor to an entity connected to a local authority and for the auditor to issue a public interest report where it is in the public interest to do so. The entity must be connected with a local authority and meet other conditions specified in regulations made by the Secretary of State in England or by Welsh Ministers in Wales. Smaller parish councils are excluded from the provisions as they are not required to prepare statements of accounts. At the date of going to press s 147 had not been brought into force.

Police Reform and Social Responsibility Act 2011
(2011 c 13)

Part 2
Licensing

Chapter 1
Amendments of the Licensing Act 2003

Early morning alcohol restriction orders

7.7890 119.   Early morning alcohol restriction orders   (1)   The Licensing Act 2003 is amended as set out in subsections (2) and (3).

(2)   In section 7 (exercise and delegation of functions), in subsection (2), after paragraph (*a*) (but before the final "or") insert—

   "(*aa*)   the functions of making, and varying or revoking, an order under section 172A (early morning alcohol restriction order),".

(3)   For sections 172A to 172E (early morning alcohol restriction order), as inserted by section 55 of the Crime and Security Act 2010, substitute—

"**172A Power to make early morning alcohol restriction order**   (1)   If a licensing authority considers it appropriate for the promotion of the licensing objectives, it may, subject as follows, make an order under this section.

(2)   An order under this section is an order providing that—

   (*a*)   premises licences and club premises certificates granted by the authority, and temporary event notices given to the authority, do not have effect to the extent that they authorise the sale of alcohol during the period specified in the order, and

   (*b*)   club premises certificates granted by the authority do not have effect to the extent that they authorise the supply of alcohol by or on behalf of a club to, or to the order of, a member of the club during the period specified in the order.

(3)   For the purposes of subsection (2)(*a*) and (*b*), the period that may be specified in the order must

   (*a*)   begin no earlier than midnight, and

   (*b*)   end no later than 6am.

(4)   It is immaterial for the purposes of an order under this section whether a premises licence or club premises certificate is granted, or a temporary event notice is given, before or after the order is made.

(5)   An order under this section may provide that it is to apply

   (*a*)   in relation to the same period of every day on which the order is to apply, or in relation to different periods of different days,

   (*b*)   every day or only on particular days (for example, particular days of the week or year),

   (*c*)   in relation to the whole or part of a licensing authority's area, or

   (*d*)   for a limited or unlimited period.

(6)   An order under this section must specify—

   (*a*)   the days on which it is to apply and the period of those days,

   (*b*)   the area in relation to which it is to apply,

   (*c*)   if it is to apply for a limited period, that period, and

   (*d*)   the date from which it is to apply.

(7)   An order under this section must—

   (*a*)   be in the prescribed form, and

   (*b*)   have the prescribed content.

172B Procedural requirements for early morning alcohol restriction order   (1)   A licensing authority proposing to make an order under section 172A must—

   (*a*)   advertise the proposed order in the prescribed manner, and

(b)   hold a hearing to consider any relevant representations, unless the authority and each person who has made such representations agree that a hearing is unnecessary.

(2)   In this section "relevant representations" means representations which—

(a)   are about the likely effect of the making of the proposed order on the promotion of the licensing objectives,

(b)   are made to the licensing authority by an affected person, a responsible authority or any other person,

(c)   are made in the prescribed form and manner and within the prescribed period,

(d)   have not been withdrawn, and

(e)   in the case of representations made by a person who is not a responsible authority, are not, in the opinion of the licensing authority, frivolous or vexatious.

(3)   In subsection (2)(b), "affected person" means—

(a)   the holder of the premises licence or club premises certificate in respect of affected premises,

(b)   the premises user in relation to a temporary event notice in respect of affected premises,

(c)   a person who has applied for a premises licence or club premises certificate in respect of affected premises (where the application has not been determined), and

(d)   a person to whom a provisional statement has been issued in respect of affected premises.

(4)   In subsection (2)(b) and (e), "responsible authority" means—

(a)   the licensing authority and any other licensing authority in whose area part of any affected premises is situated,

(b)   the chief officer of police for a police area any part of which is in the area specified in the order,

(c)   the fire and rescue authority for an area any part of which is in the area specified in the order,

(d)   the Primary Care Trust or Local Health Board for an area any part of which is in the area specified in the order,

(e)   the local weights and measures authority for any such area,

(f)   the enforcing authority within the meaning given by section 18 of the Health and Safety at Work etc Act 1974 for any such area,

(g)   the local planning authority within the meaning given by the Town and Country Planning Act 1990 for any such area,

(h)   the local authority by which statutory functions are exercisable in the area specified in the order in relation to minimising or preventing the risk of pollution of the environment or of harm to human health,

(i)   a body which—

       (i)   represents those who, in relation to the area specified in the order, are responsible for, or interested in, matters relating to the protection of children from harm, and

       (ii)   is recognised by the licensing authority for the purposes of this section as being competent to advise on such matters,

(j)   where affected premises are a vessel—

       (i)   a navigation authority (within the meaning given by section 221(1) of the Water Resources Act 1991) having functions in relation to the waters where the vessel is usually moored or berthed or any waters where it is navigated at a time when it is used for licensable activities to which the proposed order relates,

       (ii)   the Environment Agency,

       (iii)   the British Waterways Board, and

       (iv)   the Secretary of State, and

(k)   a prescribed person.

(5)   Where a licensing authority determines for the purposes of subsection (2)(e) that any representations are frivolous or vexatious, it must notify the person who made them of its reasons for its determination.

(6)   In this section—

"affected premises", in relation to a proposed order, means premises in respect of which it applies from the date specified in it;

"statutory function" means a function conferred by or under an enactment.

172C Making of early morning alcohol restriction order (1)   A licensing authority may not make an order under section 172A applying in relation to—

(a)   an area not specified in the proposed order advertised under section 172B,

(b)   a day not specified in that proposed order, or

(c)   a period other than the period specified in that proposed order of any day so specified.

(2)   After making an order under section 172A a licensing authority must publish it or otherwise make it available—

(a)   in the prescribed form and manner, and

(b)   within the prescribed period.

172D Variation and revocation of early morning alcohol restriction order   (1)   A licensing authority may vary or revoke an order under section 172A.

(2)   Sections 172B and 172C apply in relation to the variation or revocation of an order under section 172A as in relation to the making of such an order.

172E Exceptions from effect of early morning alcohol restriction order   (1)   An order under section 172A does not apply in prescribed cases or circumstances.

(2)   The cases referred to in subsection (1) may in particular be defined by reference to—

(a)   particular kinds of premises, or

(b)   particular days.

(3)   An order under section 172A is subject to an order under section 172 (whether made before or afterwards), unless and to the extent that the order under section 172 provides otherwise.".

(4)   Section 55 of the Crime and Security Act 2010 (power to restrict sale and supply of alcohol) is repealed.

[Police Reform and Social Responsibility Act 2011, s 119.]

Fees

7.7891   121.   Power for licensing authorities to set fees   (1)   The Licensing Act 2003 is amended as follows.

(2)   After section 197 insert—

"**197A Regulations about fees**   (1)   Subsection (2) applies where the Secretary of State makes regulations under this Act prescribing the amount of any fee.

(2)   The Secretary of State may, in determining the amount of the fee, have regard, in particular, to—

(a)   the costs of any licensing authority to whom the fee is to be payable which are referable to the discharge of the function to which the fee relates, and

(b)   the general costs of any such licensing authority;

and may determine an amount by reference to fees payable to, and costs of, any such licensing authorities, taken together.

(3)   A power under this Act to prescribe the amount of a fee includes power to provide that the amount of the fee is to be determined by the licensing authority to whom it is to be payable.

(4)   Regulations which so provide may also specify constraints on the licensing authority's power to determine the amount of the fee.

(5)   Subsections (6) and (7)—

(a)   apply where, by virtue of subsection (3), regulations provide that the amount of a fee is to be determined by a licensing authority, and

(b)   are subject to any constraint imposed under subsection (4).

(6)   The licensing authority—

(a)   must determine the amount of the fee (and may from time to time determine a revised amount),

(b)   may determine different amounts for different classes of case specified in the regulations (but may not otherwise determine different amounts for different cases), and

(c)   must publish the amount of the fee as determined from time to time.

(7)   In determining the amount of the fee, the licensing authority must seek to secure that the income from fees of that kind will equate, as nearly as possible, to the aggregate of—

(a)   the licensing authority's costs referable to the discharge of the function to which the fee relates, and

(b)   a reasonable share of the licensing authority's general costs;

and must assess income and costs for this purpose in such manner as it considers appropriate.

197B Regulations about fees: supplementary provision   (1)   Subsections (2) and (3) apply for the purposes of section 197A.

(2)   References to a licensing authority's costs referable to the discharge of a function include, in particular—

(a)   administrative costs of the licensing authority so far as they are referable to the discharge of the function, and

(b)   costs in connection with the discharge of the function which are incurred by the licensing authority acting—

(i)   under this Act, but

(ii)   in a capacity other than that of licensing authority (whether that of local authority, local planning authority or any other authority).

(3)   References to the general costs of a licensing authority are costs of the authority so far as they are referable to the discharge of functions under this Act in respect of which no fee is otherwise chargeable and include, in particular—

(a)   costs referable to the authority's functions under section 5;

(b)   costs of or incurred in connection with the monitoring and enforcement of Parts 7 and 8 of this Act;

(c)   costs incurred in exercising functions conferred by virtue of section 197A.

(4)   To the extent that they prescribe the amount of a fee or include provision made by virtue of section 197A(3) or (4), regulations may—

(a)   make provision which applies generally or only to specified authorities or descriptions of authority, and

(b)   make different provision for different authorities or descriptions of authority.

(5)   Subsection (4) is not to be taken to limit the generality of section 197.".

(3)   In section 10(4) (sub-delegation of functions by licensing committee etc)—

(a)   omit "or" at the end of paragraph (c), and

(b)   after paragraph (d) insert

"or

(e)   any function conferred by virtue of section 197A (regulations about fees).".

[Police Reform and Social Responsibility Act 2011, s 121.]

CHAPTER 2
LATE NIGHT LEVY

Application of late night levy requirement in licensing authority's area

125.   *Chapter 2 (ss 125–139) makes provision for licensing authorities to apply a light night levy requirement in its area in accordance with regulations having regard to the costs of policing and other arrangements for the reduction or prevention of crime and disorder, in connection with the supply of alcohol between midnight and 6 am.*

Localism Act 2011
(2011 c 20)

CHAPTER 7
STANDARDS

7.7892   *Chapter 7 (26–37) makes further provision for standards relating to the conduct of local government members and employees. A relevant authority (which includes county, district and parish councils and fire and rescue authorities) must promote and maintain high standards of conduct by members and co-opted members of the authority. In particular, an authority must adopt a code dealing with the conduct that is expected of members and co-opted members of the authority when they are acting in that capacity (27–28). The monitoring officer of a relevant authority must establish and maintain a register of interests of members and co-opted members of the authority (28).*

7.7893   30.   Disclosure of pecuniary interests on taking office   (1)   A member or co-opted member of a relevant authority must, before the end of 28 days beginning with the day on which the person becomes a member or co-opted member of the authority, notify the authority's monitoring officer of any disclosable pecuniary interests which the person has at the time when the notification is given.

(2)   Where a person becomes a member or co-opted member of a relevant authority as a result of re-election or re-appointment, subsection (1) applies only as regards disclosable pecuniary interests not entered in the authority's register when the notification is given.

(3)   For the purposes of this Chapter, a pecuniary interest is a "disclosable pecuniary interest" in relation to a person ("M") if it is of a description specified in regulations made by the Secretary of State and either—

(a)   it is an interest of M's, or

(b)   it is an interest of—

(i)   M's spouse or civil partner, or

(ii)   *repealed*

(iii)   a person with whom M is living as if they were a married couple or civil partners, and M is aware that that other person has the interest.

(4)   Where a member or co-opted member of a relevant authority gives a notification for the purposes of subsection (1), the authority's monitoring officer is to cause the interests notified to be entered in the authority's register (whether or not they are disclosable pecuniary interests).[1]

[Localism Act 2011, s 30 as amended by SI 2019/1458.]

---

[1]   The Localism Act 2011 (Commencement No 6 and Transitional, Savings and Transitory Provisions) Order 2012, SI 2012/1463, brought into force on 7 June 2012 s 31(10) so far as it enables a relevant authority to make standing orders that will take effect on or after 1 July 2012; and s 33 so far as it enables a relevant authority to grant a dispensation which will take effect on or after 1 July 2012; s 34 on 1 July 2012; ss 30–34 fully in force 1 July 2012.

7.7894   31.   Pecuniary interests in matters considered at meetings or by a single member

(1)   Subsections (2) to (4) apply if a member or co-opted member of a relevant authority—

(a)   is present at a meeting of the authority or of any committee, sub-committee, joint committee or joint sub-committee of the authority,

(b)   has a disclosable pecuniary interest in any matter to be considered, or being considered, at the meeting, and

(c)   is aware that the condition in paragraph (b) is met.

(2)   If the interest is not entered in the authority's register, the member or co-opted member must disclose the interest to the meeting, but this is subject to section 32(3).

(3)   If the interest is not entered in the authority's register and is not the subject of a pending notification, the member or co-opted member must notify the authority's monitoring officer of the interest before the end of 28 days beginning with the date of the disclosure.

(4)   The member or co-opted member may not—

(a)   participate, or participate further, in any discussion of the matter at the meeting, or

(b)   participate in any vote, or further vote, taken on the matter at the meeting,

but this is subject to section 33.

(5)   In the case of a relevant authority to which Part 1A of the Local Government Act 2000 applies and which is operating executive arrangements, the reference in subsection (1)(a) to a committee of the authority includes a reference to the authority's executive and a reference to a committee of the executive.

(6)   Subsections (7) and (8) apply if—

(a)   a function of a relevant authority may be discharged by a member of the authority acting alone,

(b)   the member has a disclosable pecuniary interest in any matter to be dealt with, or being dealt with, by the member in the course of discharging that function, and

(c)   the member is aware that the condition in paragraph (b) is met.

(7)   If the interest is not entered in the authority's register and is not the subject of a pending notification, the member must notify the authority's monitoring officer of the interest before the end of 28 days beginning with the date when the member becomes aware that the condition in subsection (6)(b) is met in relation to the matter.

(8)   The member must not take any steps, or any further steps, in relation to the matter (except for the purpose of enabling the matter to be dealt with otherwise than by the member).

(9)   Where a member or co-opted member of a relevant authority gives a notification for the purposes of subsection (3) or (7), the authority's monitoring officer is to cause the interest notified to be entered in the authority's register (whether or not it is a disclosable pecuniary interest).

(10)   Standing orders of a relevant authority may provide for the exclusion of a member or co-opted member of the authority from a meeting while any discussion or vote takes place in which, as a result of the operation of subsection (4), the member or co-opted member may not participate.

(11)   For the purpose of this section, an interest is "subject to a pending notification" if—

(a)   under this section or section 30, the interest has been notified to a relevant authority's monitoring officer, but

(b)   has not been entered in the authority's register in consequence of that notification.

[Localism Act 2011, s 31.]

7.7895 32. Sensitive interests   (1)   Subsections (2) and (3) apply where—

(a)   a member or co-opted member of a relevant authority has an interest (whether or not a disclosable pecuniary interest), and

(b)   the nature of the interest is such that the member or co-opted member, and the authority's monitoring officer, consider that disclosure of the details of the interest could lead to the member or co-opted member, or a person connected with the member or co-opted member, being subject to violence or intimidation.

(2)   If the interest is entered in the authority's register, copies of the register that are made available for inspection, and any published version of the register, must not include details of the interest (but may state that the member or co-opted member has an interest the details of which are withheld under this subsection).

(3)   If section 31(2) applies in relation to the interest, that provision is to be read as requiring the member or co-opted member to disclose not the interest but merely the fact that the member or co-opted member has a disclosable pecuniary interest in the matter concerned.

[Localism Act 2011, s 32.]

7.7896 33. Dispensations from section 31(4)   (1)   A relevant authority may, on a written request made to the proper officer of the authority by a member or co-opted member of the authority, grant a dispensation relieving the member or co-opted member from either or both of the restrictions in section 31(4) in cases described in the dispensation.

(2)   A relevant authority may grant a dispensation under this section only if, after having had regard to all relevant circumstances, the authority—

(a)   considers that without the dispensation the number of persons prohibited by section 31(4) from participating in any particular business would be so great a proportion of the body transacting the business as to impede the transaction of the business,

(b)   considers that without the dispensation the representation of different political groups on the body transacting any particular business would be so upset as to alter the likely outcome of any vote relating to the business,

(c)   considers that granting the dispensation is in the interests of persons living in the authority's area,

(d)   if it is an authority to which Part 1A of the Local Government Act 2000 applies and is operating executive arrangements, considers that without the dispensation each member of the authority's executive would be prohibited by section 31(4) from participating in any particular business to be transacted by the authority's executive, or

(e)   considers that it is otherwise appropriate to grant a dispensation.

(3)   A dispensation under this section must specify the period for which it has effect, and the period specified may not exceed four years.

(4)   Section 31(4) does not apply in relation to anything done for the purpose of deciding whether to grant a dispensation under this section.

[Localism Act 2011, s 33.]

7.7897 34. Offences (1) A person commits an offence if, without reasonable excuse, the person—

(a)   fails to comply with an obligation imposed on the person by section 30(1) or 31(2), (3) or (7),

(b)   participates in any discussion or vote in contravention of section 31(4), or

(c)   takes any steps in contravention of section 31(8).

(2)   A person commits an offence if under section 30(1) or 31(2), (3) or (7) the person provides information that is false or misleading and the person—

(a)   knows that the information is false or misleading, or

(b)   is reckless as to whether the information is true and not misleading.

(3)   A person who is guilty of an offence under this section is liable on summary conviction to a fine not exceeding level 5 on the standard scale.

(4)   A court dealing with a person for an offence under this section may (in addition to any other power exercisable in the person's case) by order disqualify the person, for a period not exceeding five years, for being or becoming (by election or otherwise) a member or co-opted member of the relevant authority in question or any other relevant authority.

(5)   A prosecution for an offence under this section is not to be instituted except by or on behalf of the Director of Public Prosecutions.

(6)   Proceedings for an offence under this section may be brought within a period of 12 months beginning with the date on which evidence sufficient in the opinion of the prosecutor to warrant the proceedings came to the prosecutor's knowledge.

(7)   But no such proceedings may be brought more than three years—

(a)   after the commission of the offence, or

(b)   in the case of a continuous contravention, after the last date on which the offence was committed.

(8)   A certificate signed by the prosecutor and stating the date on which such evidence came to the prosecutor's knowledge is conclusive evidence of that fact; and a certificate to that effect and purporting to be so signed is to be treated as being so signed unless the contrary is proved.

(9)   The Local Government Act 1972 is amended as follows.

(10)   In section 86(1)(b) (authority to declare vacancy where member becomes disqualified otherwise than in certain cases) after "2000" insert "or section 34 of the Localism Act 2011".

(11)   In section 87(1)(ee) (date of casual vacancies)—

(a)   after "2000" insert "or section 34 of the Localism Act 2011 or", and

(b)   after "decision" insert "or order".

(12)   The Greater London Authority Act 1999 is amended as follows.

(13)   In each of sections 7(b) and 14(b) (Authority to declare vacancy where Assembly member or Mayor becomes disqualified otherwise than in certain cases) after sub-paragraph (i) insert—

"(ia)   under section 34 of the Localism Act 2011,".

(14)   In section 9(1)(f) (date of casual vacancies)—

(a)   before "or by virtue of" insert "or section 34 of the Localism Act 2011", and

(b)   after "that Act" insert "of 1998 or that section".

[Localism Act 2011, s 34.]

Local Audit and Accountability Act 2014

(2014 c 2)

Part 2[1]

Basic Concepts and Requirements

---

[1] Part 2 comprises ss 2–6 and Sch 2. For commencement, see s 49, post.

7.7898 2. Relevant authorities (1) In this Act "relevant authority" means a person or body listed in Schedule 2.

(2)   The application of this Act to a relevant authority is subject to any note forming part of the entry for that authority in Schedule 2.

(3)   The Secretary of State may by regulations amend Schedule 2 by adding, modifying or removing an entry relating to a relevant authority.

(4)   Regulations under subsection (3) may add an entry relating to a person or body to Schedule 2 only if that person or body exercises functions of a public nature in relation to an area which is—

(a)   wholly in England, or

(b)   partly in England and partly in Wales.

(5)   The Secretary of State may by regulations or order make provision about the application of this Act or provision made under it to a person or body that comes to fall within Schedule 2 (whether or not as a result of regulations under subsection (3)).

(6)   The power in subsection (5) includes power—

(a)   to amend this Act or provision made under it in its application to that person or body, or

(b)   to make provision for this Act or provision made under it to apply to that person or body with modifications.

[Local Audit and Accountability Act 2014, s 2.]

7.7899 3. General requirements for accounts (1) A relevant authority, other than a health service body, must keep adequate accounting records.

(2)   "Adequate accounting records" means records that are sufficient—

(a)   to show and explain the relevant authority's transactions,

(b)   to disclose at any time, with reasonable accuracy, the financial position of the authority at that time, and

(c)   to enable the authority to ensure that any statements of accounts required to be prepared by the authority comply with the requirements imposed by or under this Act.

(3)   A relevant authority, other than a health service body, must prepare a statement of accounts in respect of each financial year.

(4)   In this Act "financial year" means a period of 12 months ending with 31 March.

(5)   The Secretary of State may by regulations—

(a)   make provision for the financial year of a relevant authority, other than a health service body, for the purposes of this Act to be such period as is specified in the regulations;

(b)   make provision for any requirement in this section not to apply, or to apply with modifications, in relation to the relevant authorities, other than health service bodies, specified or described in the regulations.

(6)   Regulations under subsection (5)(a) may—

(a)   amend this Act or provision made under it in its application to a relevant authority to which the regulations apply, or

(b)   provide for this Act or provision made under it to apply in relation to such a relevant authority with modifications.

(7)   Regulations under subsection (5)(a) may make provision in relation to—

(a)   all relevant authorities (other than health service bodies);

(b)   the relevant authorities specified or described in the regulations.

(8)   Section 32 enables the Secretary of State by regulations to make further provision about accounting records and statements of accounts.

(9)   In this Act "health service body" means

(a)   a clinical commissioning group;

(b)   special trustees appointed as mentioned in section 212(1) of the National Health Service Act 2006 (special trustees for a university hospital or teaching hospital) for a hospital in England (referred to in this Act as "special trustees for a hospital").*

[Local Audit and Accountability Act 2014, s 3.]

---

* Amended by the NIIS (Charitable Trusts Etc) Act 2016, Sch 1 from a date to be appointed.

7.7900 4. General requirements for audit (1) The accounts of a relevant authority for a financial year must be audited—

(a)   in accordance with this Act and provision made under it, and

(b)   by an auditor (a "local auditor") appointed in accordance with this Act or provision made under it.

(2)   In this Act, references to accounts are to be construed in accordance with the following subsections.

(3)   In relation to a relevant authority which is not a health service body, "accounts" means—

(a)   the authority's accounting records, and

(b)   the authority's statement of accounts.

(4)   In relation to a clinical commissioning group, "accounts" means—

(a)   the annual accounts of the group prepared under paragraph 17(2) of Schedule 1A to the National Health Service Act 2006 (accounts and audit of clinical commissioning groups);

(b)   any accounts of the group prepared under paragraph 17(3) of that Schedule in respect of which a direction has been given under paragraph 17(5) of that Schedule.

(5)   In relation to special trustees for a hospital, "accounts" means the annual accounts of the trustees prepared under paragraph 3 of Schedule 15 to the National Health Service Act 2006.*

[Local Audit and Accountability Act 2014, s 4.]

---

* Amended by the NHS (Charitable Trusts Etc) Act 2016, Sch 1 from a date to be appointed.

7.7901 5. Modification of Act in relation to smaller authorities (1) The Secretary of State may by regulations[1] make provision about the audit of the accounts of smaller authorities.

(2)   Regulations under subsection (1) may, in particular, provide for any provision of or made under this Act not to apply, or to apply with modifications, in relation to smaller authorities.

(3)   Subsection (2) applies to a provision of or made under this Act even if it makes specific provision about a smaller authority to which the regulations apply.

(4)   Regulations under subsection (1) may, in particular—

(a)   provide for the appointment, by a person specified by the Secretary of State, of a local auditor in relation to the audit of the accounts of a smaller authority;

(b)   make provision about the persons that may be specified by the Secretary of State;

(c)   make provision about the procedure for specifying a person and for a person's specification to come to an end in specified circumstances;

(d)   make provision about the consequences of a person's specification coming to an end, including for the exercise of functions by the Secretary of State and the transfer of the person's rights and liabilities arising by virtue of the regulations to the Secretary of State or another specified person;

(e)   confer functions on a specified person, including in relation to—
 (i)   the appointment of local auditors under the regulations,
 (ii)   the activities of such auditors, and
 (iii) the resignation or removal from office of such auditors;

(f)   require a specified person to consult such persons as are specified in the regulations before exercising specified functions;

(g)   make provision for the appointment of a local auditor in relation to the accounts of a smaller authority to which arrangements within paragraph (a) apply where the specified person does not make an appointment under the regulations (and in particular for such an appointment to be made by the authority or the Secretary of State).

(5)   Regulations under subsection (1) may, in particular—

(a)   make provision about the smaller authorities to which arrangements within subsection (4)(a) apply, including provision for them to apply to an authority that has opted into them or has not opted out of them;

(b)   make provision about the procedures to be followed in relation to opting into or out of those arrangements;

(c)   impose duties on smaller authorities to which those arrangements apply, including duties as to—
 (i)   the payment of fees to a specified person, and
 (ii)   the provision of information to a specified person;

(d)   make provision for the making of payments, in specified circumstances and by the smaller authorities to which those arrangements apply, to a fund of a specified kind for the purposes of meeting local auditors' costs of a specified kind.

(6)   Provision made by regulations under subsection (1) by virtue of subsection (5)(c)(i) may, in particular—

(a)   provide for fees to be paid in accordance with a scale or scales of fees determined by a specified person, and

(b)   provide for the payment in specified circumstances of a larger or smaller fee than is set out in the appropriate scale.

(7)   Regulations under subsection (1) may, in particular—

(a)   make provision about the eligibility of a person to be appointed as a local auditor of the accounts of a smaller authority;

(b)   make provision about the functions of a local auditor in relation to the accounts of a smaller authority.

(8)   Regulations under subsection (1) may, in particular—

(a)   provide that, in specified circumstances, the accounts of a smaller authority of a specified description are to be exempt from specified audit requirements;

(b)   make provision for an exemption under paragraph (a) not to apply or to cease to apply to an authority in specified circumstances.

(9)   In this section "specified" (except in the expressions "person specified by the Secretary of State" and "specified person") means specified in regulations under subsection (1).

[Local Audit and Accountability Act 2014, s 5.]

---

[1] The Local Audit (Smaller Authorities) Regulations 2015, SI 2015/184 have been made.

7.7902   6. Meaning of "smaller authority"   (1)   For the purposes of section 5, a relevant authority is a "smaller authority" for a financial year if—

(a)   where that year is the year in which the authority was established, the qualifying condition is met for that year,

(b)   where that year is the year following that in which the authority was established, the qualifying condition is met for that year or the previous year, and

(c)   where that year is the second or any subsequent year following that in which the authority was established, the qualifying condition is met for that year or either of the two previous years.

(2)   The qualifying condition is met for a relevant authority and a financial year if the higher of the authority's gross income for the year and its gross expenditure for the year does not exceed £6.5 million.

(3)   For the purpose of determining, at a time when a relevant authority's gross income or expenditure for a financial year cannot be accurately determined, whether subsection (2) applies or will apply to the authority, that subsection is to be read as referring to the authority's estimated gross income or expenditure (as the case may be).

(4)   The Secretary of State may by regulations[1] make provision about the application of this Act (including in its application by virtue of section 5) or any provision made under it in a case where—

(a)   an authority is treated as a smaller authority for a financial year, and

(b)   the authority was not in fact a smaller authority for that year.

(5)   The Secretary of State may by regulations amend this section.

[Local Audit and Accountability Act 2014, s 6.]

---

[1] The Local Audit (Smaller Authorities) Regulations 2015, SI 2015/184 have been made.

PART 3[1]
APPOINTMENT ETC OF LOCAL AUDITORS

---

[1] Part 3 comprises ss 17–17 and Schs 3 4.

7.7903   7.   Appointment of local auditor   (1)   A relevant authority must appoint a local auditor to audit its accounts for a financial year not later than 31 December in the preceding financial year.

(2)   A relevant authority may appoint a local auditor to audit its accounts for more than one financial year; and in such a case—

(a)   subsection (1) does not apply in relation to the second or any subsequent year for which the appointment is made, but

(b)   the authority must make a further appointment of a local auditor at least once every 5 years.

(3)   Subsection (2)(b) does not prevent the relevant authority from re-appointing a local auditor.

(4)   The Secretary of State may by regulations amend subsection (2)(b) so as to alter the period for the time being specified in it.

(5)   A local auditor appointed under this section—

(a)   must be eligible for appointment as a local auditor (see Part 4), and

(b)   must not be prohibited from acting as a local auditor of the accounts of the relevant authority by virtue of section 1214 of the Companies Act 2006 (independence requirement) as it has effect by virtue of Schedule 5.

(6)   Two or more local auditors may be appointed to audit the accounts of a relevant authority, and those auditors may be appointed—

(a)   to act jointly in relation to some or all parts of the accounts;

(b)   to act separately in relation to different parts of the accounts;

(c)   to carry out different functions in relation to the audit.

(7)   If, as a result of an appointment under subsection (6)(b) or (c), a function under this Act may be exercised by two or more local auditors—

(a)   it may be exercised by both or all of them acting jointly or by such one or more of them as they may determine, and

(b)   references (however expressed) to the local auditor by whom the function is or has been exercised are to the auditors by whom it is or has been exercised.

(8)   Schedule 3 makes further provision about the appointment of local auditors, and this section is subject to that Schedule and provision made under it.

[Local Audit and Accountability Act 2014, s 7.]

PART 5[1]
CONDUCT OF LOCAL AUDIT

Codes of practice and guidance

7.7904   19 Codes of audit practice and guidance

General powers and duties of auditors

7.7905   20.   General duties of auditors   (1)   In auditing the accounts of a relevant authority other than a health service body, a local auditor must, by examination of the accounts and otherwise, be satisfied—

(a)   that the accounts comply with the requirements of the enactments that apply to them,

(b)   that proper practices have been observed in the preparation of the statement of accounts, and that the statement presents a true and fair view, and

(c)   that the authority has made proper arrangements for securing economy, efficiency and effectiveness in its use of resources.

(2)   Subject as follows, when a local auditor has completed an audit of the accounts of a relevant authority other than a health service body, the auditor must enter on the statement of accounts—

    (a)   a certificate that the auditor has completed the audit in accordance with this Act, and

    (b)   the auditor's opinion on the statement.

(3)   If, for any part of the period for which a relevant authority is required to prepare a statement of accounts, the authority is required to maintain a pension fund under regulations under section 1 of the Public Service Pensions Act 2013 as they relate to local government workers (within the meaning of that Act), the authority's local auditor must give a separate opinion on the part of the statement that relates to the accounts of that pension fund.

(4)   A local auditor may enter an opinion on the statement of accounts on that statement before the audit is completed if—

    (a)   the audit has not been completed because an objection has been made under section 27 and that objection has not been disposed of, and

    (b)   the auditor thinks that, if the objection were resolved in the objector's favour, this would not affect the accuracy of the statement of accounts.

(5)   A local auditor must, in carrying out the auditor's functions in relation to the accounts of a relevant authority, comply with the code of audit practice applicable to the authority that is for the time being in force.

(6)   A local auditor must, in carrying out functions under this Act, have regard to guidance issued by the Comptroller and Auditor General under paragraph 9 of Schedule 6.

[Local Audit and Accountability Act 2014, s 20.]

---

[1] Part 5 comprises ss 19–32 and Schs 6–8.

7.7906   21.   General duties of auditors of accounts of health service bodies   (1) In auditing the accounts of a clinical commissioning group, a local auditor must, by examination of the accounts and otherwise, be satisfied—

    (a)   that the accounts present a true and fair view, and comply with the requirements of the enactments that apply to them,

    (b)   that proper practices have been observed in the preparation of the accounts,

    (c)   that the group has made proper arrangements for securing economy, efficiency and effectiveness in its use of resources,

    (d)   that money provided by Parliament has been expended for the purposes intended by Parliament,

    (e)   that resources authorised by Parliament to be used have been used for the purposes in relation to which the use was authorised, and

    (f)   that the financial transactions of the group are in accordance with any authority which is relevant to the transactions.

(2)   In subsection (1)(e) use of resources means their expenditure, consumption or reduction in value.

(3)   In auditing the accounts of special trustees for a hospital, a local auditor must, by examination of the accounts and otherwise, be satisfied—

    (a)   that the accounts present a true and fair view, and comply with the requirements of the enactments that apply to them,

    (b)   that proper practices have been observed in the preparation of the accounts, and

    (c)   that the special trustees have made proper arrangements for securing economy, efficiency and effectiveness in their use of resources.

(4)   When a local auditor has completed an audit of the accounts of a health service body, the auditor must—

    (a)   enter on the accounts a certificate that the auditor has completed the audit in accordance with this Act, and

    (b)   make a report in accordance with subsection (5).

(5)   A report under subsection (4)(b)—

    (a)   must contain the auditor's opinion on the accounts, including on the matters in subsection (1) or, as the case may be, subsection (3), but

    (b)   must not contain the auditor's opinion on the matter in subsection (1)(c) or (3)(c) if the auditor is satisfied as to that matter.*

[Local Audit and Accountability Act 2014, s 21.]

---

* Amended by the NHS (Charitable Trusts Etc) Act 2016, Sch 1 from a date to be appointed.

7.7907   22.   Auditors' right to documents and information   (1) A local auditor has a right of access at all reasonable times to every document (an "audit document") that—

    (a)   relates to a relevant authority or an entity connected with a relevant authority, and

    (b)   the auditor thinks is necessary for the purposes of the auditor's functions under this Act.

(2)   This includes power to inspect, copy or take away an audit document.

(3)   A local auditor may—

    (a)   require a person holding or accountable for, or who has at any time held or been accountable for, an audit document to provide such information or explanation as the auditor thinks is necessary for the purposes of this Act, and

    (b)   if the auditor thinks it necessary, require the person to meet the auditor to give the information or explanation or (if the person holds or is accountable for the document) to produce the document.

    (4)   Where an audit document is in an electronic form, the power to require a person to produce the document includes power to require it to be produced in a form in which it is legible and can be taken away.

    (5)   For the purpose of inspecting an audit document which is in an electronic form, a local auditor—

    (a)   may have access to, and inspect and check the operation of, any computer and associated apparatus or material which the auditor thinks is or has been used in connection with the document, and

    (b)   may require a person within subsection (6) to give the auditor the reasonable assistance that the auditor needs for that purpose.

    (6)   A person is within this subsection who—

    (a)   is the person by whom or on whose behalf the computer is or has been used, or

    (b)   is a person in charge of, or otherwise involved in operating, the computer, apparatus or material.

    (7)   A local auditor may—

    (a)   require any person to whom this subsection applies to provide such information or explanation as the auditor thinks is necessary for the purposes of this Act, and

    (b)   if the auditor thinks it necessary, require the person to meet the auditor to give the information or explanation.

    (8)   Subsection (7) applies to—

    (a)   a member or officer of a relevant authority,

    (b)   where a relevant authority is a corporation sole, the holder of that office,

    (c)   a person elected or appointed—

        (i)   as an entity connected with a relevant authority,

        (ii)   to such an entity, or

        (iii)   to an office of such an entity,

    (d)   an employee of such an entity,

    (e)   an auditor of the accounts of such an entity, or

    (f)   a person who fell within any of paragraphs (a) to (d) at a time to which the information or explanation required by the local auditor relates.

    (9)   A local auditor of the accounts of a parish meeting may only exercise the function in subsection (7), so far as it applies to a person who is or was a member or officer of a relevant authority, in relation to a person who is or was the chairman of the parish meeting or the proper officer of the district council within whose area the parish lies.

    (10)   A relevant authority or an entity connected with a relevant authority must provide a local auditor with the facilities and information that the auditor reasonably requires for the purposes of the auditor's functions under this Act.

    (11)   A statement made by a person in response to a requirement under this section may not be used in evidence against that person in criminal proceedings other than proceedings for an offence under section 23.

    (12)   Nothing in this section compels a person to disclose information in respect of which a claim to legal professional privilege could be maintained in legal proceedings.

[Local Audit and Accountability Act 2014, s 22.]

7.7908   **23. Offences relating to section 22**   (1)   A person is guilty of an offence if, without reasonable excuse, the person—

    (a)   obstructs the exercise of any power conferred by section 22, or

    (b)   fails to comply with any requirement of a local auditor under that section.

    (2)   A person guilty of an offence under subsection (1) is liable on summary conviction—

    (a)   to a fine not exceeding level 3 on the standard scale, and

    (b)   to an additional fine of not more than £20 for each day on which the offence continues after conviction for that offence.

    (3)   The reasonable expenses incurred by a local auditor in connection with proceedings for an offence under subsection (1) alleged to have been committed by a person within subsection (4) in relation to the audit of the accounts of a relevant authority are recoverable from that authority so far as they are not recovered from any other source.

    (4)   The persons within this subsection are—

    (a)   a member or officer of the relevant authority,

    (b)   a person elected or appointed—

        (i)   as an entity connected with the relevant authority,

        (ii)   to such an entity, or

        (iii)   to an office of such an entity, and

(c)   an employee of such an entity.

(5)   Subsection (3) does not apply in relation to a parish meeting unless the offence is alleged to have been committed by the chairman of the parish meeting or the proper officer of the district council within whose area the parish lies.

(6)   In subsection (4)(*a*) the reference to a member of the relevant authority, in relation to a corporation sole, is to the holder of that office.

[Local Audit and Accountability Act 2014, s 23.]

Public inspection etc and action by auditor

7.7909   **25.   Inspection of statements of accounts etc**   (1)   A relevant authority other than a health service body must ensure that a local government elector for its area may inspect and make copies of—

(a)   the statement of accounts prepared by the authority,

(b)   the local auditor's certificate that the audit of the authority's accounts including that statement has been completed,

(c)   the local auditor's opinion on the statement of accounts,

(d)   any public interest report relating to the authority or an entity connected with it, and

(e)   any recommendation relating to the authority or an entity connected with it.

(2)   A relevant authority other than a health service body must ensure that a local government elector for its area may have copies of any document within subsection (1) supplied to the elector at the elector's request on payment of a reasonable sum for each copy.

(3)   The relevant authority must ensure that a local government elector may inspect a document within subsection (1) at all reasonable times and without payment.

(4)   This section applies in relation to a document only if the relevant authority has prepared the document or it has been made available to the authority.

(5)   References in this section to copies of a document include a reference to copies of any part of it.

[Local Audit and Accountability Act 2014, s 25.]

7.7910   **26.   Inspection of documents etc**   (1)   At each audit of accounts under this Act, other than an audit of accounts of a health service body, any persons interested or any journalist may—

(a)   inspect the accounting records for the financial year to which the audit relates and all books, deeds, contracts, bills, vouchers, receipts and other documents relating to those records, and

(b)   make copies of all or any part of those records or documents.

(1A)   In subsection (1) "journalist" means any person who produces for publication journalistic material (whether paid to do so or otherwise).

(2)   At the request of a local government elector for any area to which the accounts relate, the local auditor must give the elector, or any representative of the elector, an opportunity to question the auditor about the accounting records.

(3)   The local auditor's reasonable costs of complying with subsection (2) are recoverable from the relevant authority to which the accounts relate.

(4)   This section does not entitle a person—

(a)   to inspect or copy any part of any record or document containing information which is protected on the grounds of commercial confidentiality, or

(b)   to require any such information to be disclosed in answer to any question.

(5)   Information is protected on the grounds of commercial confidentiality if—

(a)   its disclosure would prejudice commercial confidentiality, and

(b)   there is no overriding public interest in favour of its disclosure.

(6)   This section does not entitle a person—

(a)   to inspect or copy any part of any record or document containing personal information, or

(b)   to require any personal information to be disclosed in answer to any question.

(7)   Information is personal information if it identifies a particular individual or enables a particular individual to be identified (but see subsection (8)).

(8)   Information is not personal information merely because it relates to a business carried on by an individual as a sole trader.

(9)   Information is personal information if it is information about an officer of the relevant authority which relates specifically to a particular individual and is available to the authority because—

(a)   the individual holds or has held an office or employment with that authority, or

(b)   payments or other benefits in respect of an office or employment under any other person are or have been made or provided to that individual by that authority.

(10)   For the purposes of subsection (9)—

(a)   "the relevant authority" means the relevant authority whose accounts are being audited, and

(b)   payments made or benefits provided to an individual in respect of an office or employment include any payment made or benefit provided in respect of the individual ceasing to hold the office or employment.

[Local Audit and Accountability Act 2014, s 26 as amended by the Local Audit (Public Access to Documents) Act 2017, s 1.]

7.7911   27.   Right to make objections at audit   (1)   This section applies if, at an audit of accounts under this Act other than an audit of accounts of a health service body, a local government elector for an area to which the accounts relate makes an objection to the local auditor which meets the requirements in subsection (2) and which—

(a)   concerns a matter in respect of which the auditor could make a public interest report, or

(b)   concerns a matter in respect of which the auditor could apply for a declaration under section 28.

(2)   The requirements are that—

(a)   the objection is made in writing, and

(b)   a copy of the objection is sent to the relevant authority whose accounts are being audited.

(3)   The local auditor must decide—

(a)   whether to consider the objection, and

(b)   if the auditor does so, whether to take action within paragraph (a) or (b) of subsection (1) in response.

(4)   The local auditor may decide not to consider the objection if, in particular, the auditor thinks that—

(a)   the objection is frivolous or vexatious,

(b)   the cost of the auditor considering the objection would be disproportionate to the sums to which the objection relates, or

(c)   the objection repeats an objection already considered—

(i)   under this section by a local auditor of the authority's accounts, or

(ii)   under section 16 of the Audit Commission Act 1998 by an auditor appointed under that Act in relation to those accounts.

(5)   Subsection (4)(b) does not entitle the local auditor to refuse to consider an objection which the auditor thinks might disclose serious concerns about how the relevant authority is managed or led.

(6)   If the local auditor decides not to take action within paragraph (a) or (b) of subsection (1), the auditor may recommend that the relevant authority should instead take action in response to the objection.

(7)   The local auditor's reasonable costs of exercising functions under this section are recoverable from the relevant authority.

[Local Audit and Accountability Act 2014, s 27.]

PART 7

MISCELLANEOUS AND SUPPLEMENTARY[1]

Supplementary

7.7912   44.   Interpretation of Act   (1)   In this Act (unless the context otherwise requires)—

"accounts" is to be construed in accordance with section 4(3) to (5);

"area"—

(a)   in relation to a chief constable, means the police area of the chief constable's police force;

(b)   in relation to a clinical commissioning group, means the area specified in the group's constitution (see Schedule 1A to the National Health Service Act 2006);

"charter trustees" means charter trustees constituted—

(a)   under section 246 of the Local Government Act 1972,

(b)   by the Charter Trustees Regulations 1996 (SI 1996/263), or

(c)   under Part 1 of the Local Government and Public Involvement in Health Act 2007;

"chief constable" means a chief constable for a police force for a police area;

"code of audit practice" means a code of audit practice under Schedule 6;

"combined authority" means a combined authority established under section 103 of the Local Democracy, Economic Development and Construction Act 2009;

"the Common Council" means the Common Council of the City of London;

"costs", in relation to anything done by a local auditor, means the costs of the auditor's time to do that thing, whether or not the auditor charges on the basis of the time taken to do it;

"enactment" includes an enactment contained in subordinate legislation as defined in section 21(1) of the Interpretation Act 1978;

"executive" and "executive arrangements" have the same meaning as in Part 1A of the Local Government Act 2000;

"expenses", in relation to anything done by a local auditor, means the expenses incurred by the auditor in doing that thing, including the auditor's costs of doing it;

"financial year" has the meaning given by section 3(4) (subject to provision made under section 3(5));

"functional body" has the same meaning as in the Greater London Authority Act 1999 (see section 424(1) of that Act);

"health service body" has the meaning given by section 3(9);

"item of account" has the meaning given by section 28(9);

"local auditor" has the meaning given by section 4(1)(*b*);

"local government elector" means a person registered as a local government elector in the register of electors in accordance with the Representation of the People Acts (but see subsection (6));

"officer", in relation to a relevant authority—

    (*a*)   includes a member of the staff of the authority, but

    (*b*)   does not include a local auditor appointed to audit the authority's accounts;

"parish meeting" means a parish meeting of a parish which does not have a separate parish council;

"police area" means a police area listed in Schedule 1 to the Police Act 1996 (police areas outside London);

"public interest report" has the meaning given by paragraph 1(2) of Schedule 7;

"recognised qualifying body" has the meaning given by 1219(12) of the Companies Act 2006 as it has effect by virtue of Schedule 5 to this Act;

"recognised supervisory body" is to be construed in accordance with section 1217(4) of and Schedule 10 to the Companies Act 2006 as they have effect by virtue of Schedule 5 to this Act;

"recommendation" means a recommendation under paragraph 2(1) of Schedule 7;

"related authority" has the meaning given by paragraph 2(6) of Schedule 7;

"relevant authority" has the meaning given by section 2(1);

"special trustees for a hospital" has the meaning given by section 3(9)(*b*);

"sub-national transport body" means a sub-national transport body established under section 102E of the Local Transport Act 2008.

(2)   References in this Act to a function under this Act or a Part of this Act include a function under regulations under this Act or that Part.

(3)   References in this Act to provision made under it include provision made under Part 42 of the Companies Act 2006 as it has effect by virtue of Schedule 5.

(4)   References in this Act to an entity connected with a relevant authority or to a connected entity are to be construed in accordance with paragraph 8 of Schedule 4.

(5)   References in this Act to persons for whom a clinical commissioning group is responsible are to be construed in accordance with section 3 of the National Health Service Act 2006 (duties of clinical commissioning groups as to commissioning certain health services).

(6)   A reference in this Act to a local government elector for any area—

    (*a*)   in relation to a Passenger Transport Executive, is a reference to a local government elector for the area of the Integrated Transport Authority or combined authority for the area for which the Executive is established;

    (*b*)   in relation to the Broads Authority, is a reference to a local government elector for the area of any participating authority (as defined by section 25 of the Norfolk and Suffolk Broads Act 1988);

    (*c*)   in relation to a National Park authority which is the local planning authority for a National Park, is a reference to a local government elector for any area the whole or any part of which is comprised in that Park.

(7)   Any function conferred or imposed on the Greater London Authority under or by virtue of this Act is exercisable by the Mayor of London acting on behalf of the Authority.

(8)   Subsection (7) does not apply in relation to any function expressly conferred on—

    (*a*)   the London Assembly, or

    (*b*)   the Mayor of London and the London Assembly acting jointly on behalf of the Greater London Authority.

(9)   Any function conferred or imposed on a parish meeting under or by virtue of this Act, other than a function expressly conferred on the parish meeting itself, is exercisable by the chairman of the parish meeting acting on behalf of the authority.

(10)   References in this Act to accounts, accounting records or statements of account in relation to the Common Council are to its accounts, accounting records or statements of account so far as relating to—

    (*a*)   the collection fund of the Common Council,

    (*b*)   the City Fund, or

    (*c*)   a pension fund maintained and administered by the Common Council under regulations under section 1 of the Public Service Pensions Act 2013.*

[Local Audit and Accountability Act 2014, s 44 as amended by the Cities and Local Government Devolution Act 2016, Sch 5.]

---

* **Amended by the NHS (Charitable Trusts Etc) Act 2016, Sch 1 from a date to be appointed.**
¹ Part 7 comprises ss 34–50 and Schs 10–13.

7.7913 48. Extent

7.7914 49. Commencement   (1)   The provisions of this Act come into force on such day as the

Secretary of State may by order[1] appoint, subject to subsections (2) to (4).

(2)   Sections 39 and 40 come into force at the end of the period of 2 months beginning with the day on which this Act is passed.

(3)   If this Act is passed before 5 February 2014, section 41 comes into force on the day on which this Act is passed; otherwise that section comes into force on such day as the Secretary of State may by order appoint.

(4)   The following provisions come into force on the day on which this Act is passed—

    (a)   section 43;

    (b)   section 44;

    (c)   section 46;

    (d)   section 48;

    (e)   this section;

    (f)   section 50.

(5)   An order under this section may—

    (a)   appoint different days for different purposes or different areas;

    (b)   make transitional, transitory or saving provision.

(6)   Provision under subsection (5)(b) may, in particular, enable a function of the Audit Commission under—

    (a)   a provision that is amended or repealed by this Act, or

    (b)   any of sections 139A to 139C of the Social Security Administration Act 1992,

to be exercised by a person or body, or by the persons or bodies, specified in the order for a period specified in or determined under the order.

(7)   Where provision under subsection (5)(b) made by virtue of subsection (6) enables a function to be exercised by a Minister of the Crown, an order under this section may enable the Minister to delegate the exercise of that function to another person or body or other persons or bodies.

(8)   An order under this section which makes provision under subsection (5)(b) by virtue of subsection (6) or (7) may in particular provide for references in an enactment to the Audit Commission to be read as references to the person or body or persons or bodies by whom the function may be exercised.

(9)   Provision under subsection (5)(b) may, in particular, provide for the first local auditor appointed by a relevant authority under subsection (1) of section 7 to be appointed on a date later than that specified in that subsection.

(10)   In this section "the Audit Commission" means the Audit Commission for Local Authorities and the National Health Service in England.

[Local Audit and Accountability Act 2014, s 49.]

---

[1] All the provisions reproduced in this Manual have been brought fully into force. The following commencement orders had been made: (No 1) SI 2014/900; (No 2) SI 2014/940; (No 3) SI 2014/1596; (No 4) SI 2014/3319; (No 5) SI 2015/179; (No 6) SI 2015/223; (No 7, Transitional Provisions and Savings) SI 2015/841; and (Commencement No 8 and Commencement No 7, Transitional Provisions and Savings (Amendment)) SI 2016/675.

7.7915   50.   Short title

Non-Domestic Rating (Collection and Enforcement) (Local Lists) Regulations 1989[1]

(SI 1989/1058 amended by SI 1990/145 and 156, SI 1991/141, SI 1992/474 and 1512, SI 1993/616, 774, 894 and 1493, the Statute Law (Repeals) Act 1995, Sch 1, SI 1996/675 and 1880, SI 1998/3089, SI 2000/2026, SI 2001/362 and 1076, the Courts Act 2003, Sch 8, SI 2003/1714 (W), 2210 (E), 2604 (E) and 3052 (F), SI 2006/237 (E) and 3396 (E), SI 2007/501 (E) and 502 (W), SI 2008/428 (E), SI 2009/204 (E), 1597 (E), 2154 (W), 2706 (W) and SI 2010/187 (E), 752 (E), 1507 (E), 1656 (E), 2222 (W), SI 2011/113 (E), 528 (W), 966 (W), 1665 (E), SI 2012/24 (E), 466 (W) and 994 (E), SI 2014/379 (W), 479 (E) and 600 and SI 2017/39 and 113 (W))

PART I   GENERAL

7.7916   *1.   Citation, commencement and interpretation*   (1)   *Citation, commencement.*

(2)   In these Regulations—

"the Act" means the Local Government Finance Act 1988;

"the BRS Act" means the Business Rate Supplements Act 2009;

"address" in relation to electronic communications, includes any number or address used for the purposes of such communications;

"business day" means any day except a Saturday or Sunday, Christmas Day, Good Friday or a day which is a bank holiday under the Banking and Financial Dealings Act 1971 in England and Wales;

"demand notice regulations" means the Council Tax and Non-Domestic Rating (Demand Notices) (England) Regulations 1993 or, as the case may be, the Council Tax and Non-Domestic Rating (Demand Notices) (England) Regulations 2003;

"electronic communication" means a communication transmitted (whether from one person to another, from one device to another or from a person to a device or vice versa)—

    (a)   by means of a telecommunications system (within the meaning of section 32(1) of the Communications Act 2003); or

(b)   by other means but while in electronic form.*

"non-domestic rate" includes a business rate supplement within the meaning of section 1(1) of the BRS Act.

---

* **Reproduced as in force in England.**
¹ These Regulations made under ss 63, 143(1) and (2) and 146(6) of, and paras 1–4 of Sch 9 to, the Local Government Finance Act 1988, are practically identical in form to the Community Charges (Administration and Enforcement) Regulations, ante. So far as non-domestic ratepayers appearing on central lists are concerned, see the Local Government Finance Act 1988, ss 52 to 54, ante in Part IV: Local Government.

7.7917 *2.   Service of notices** (1)   *Common Council notices to be served as under s 233 Local Government Act 1972.*
(2)   Without prejudice to section 233 of the Local Government Act 1972 and paragraph (1) above, where any notice which is required or authorised by these Regulations to be given to or served on a person relates to a hereditament which is (or, where such a notice relates to more than one hereditament, one or more of which is) a place of business of that person, it may be given or served by leaving it at, or by sending it by post to him at, the place of business (or, as the case may be, one of those places of business).
(3)   Without prejudice to section 233 of the Local Government Act 1972 and paragraphs (1) and (2) above and subject to paragraphs (4) to (7) below, any notice required or authorised to be given to or served by a billing authority on any person by a provision of Part II of these Regulations, is served:
(a)   may be so given or served by sending the notice to that person by electronic communication to such address as may be notified by that person for that purpose; or
(b)   shall be treated as given or served to that person where—
   (i)   the billing authority and that person have agreed for that purpose that any documents containing the notice may be accessed by that person on a website;
   (ii)   the document is a document to which that agreement applies;
   (iii)   the billing authority has published the document on a website; and
   (iv)   that person is notified, in a manner for the time being agreed for those purposes between him and the billing authority, of—
       (*aa*) the publication of the document on a website;
       (*bb*) the address of that website; and
       (*cc*) the place on the website where the document may be accessed.
(3A)   Without prejudice to section 233 of the Local Government Act 1972 and subject to paragraphs (5) and (6) below, any information required by the demand notice regulations to be supplied to any person when a demand notice (within the meaning of Part II of these Regulations) is served—
(a)   may be so supplied by sending the information to that person by electronic communication to such address as may be notified by that person for that purpose; or
(b)   subject to paragraph (3B) is treated as supplied to that person where the billing authority has published the information on a website and has notified that person by way of the demand notice of—
   (i)   the publication of the information on a website;
   (ii)   the address of that website; and
   (iii)   the place on the website where the information may be accessed.
(3B)   Where a person requests a hard copy of the information, the authority must supply the information in hard copy as soon as practicable following the request.
(4)   For the purpose of any legal proceedings, a notice given by a means described in paragraph (3) shall, unless the contrary is proved, be treated as served on the second business day after—
(a)   it was sent in accordance with paragraph (3)(*a*); or
(b)   notification of its publication was given in accordance with paragraph (3)(*b*)(iv).
(5)   A person who has notified an address for the purpose of paragraphs (3)(*a*) or (3A)(*a*) shall, by notice in writing to the billing authority, advise the billing authority of any change in that address; and the change shall take effect on the third business day after the date on which the notice is received by the billing authority.
(6)   A person who has notified an address for the purpose of paragraphs (3)(*a*) or (3A)(*a*) may, by notice in writing to the billing authority, withdraw that notification; and the withdrawal shall take effect on the third business day after the date on which the notice is received by the billing authority.
(7)   A person who has entered into an agreement with the billing authority under paragraph (3)(*b*)(i) may, by notice in writing to the billing authority, inform the authority that he no longer wishes to be a party to the agreement; and where such notice is given, the agreement shall be treated as revoked on the third business day after the date on which the notice is received by the billing authority.

---

* **Reproduced as in force in England.**

PART II   BILLING

7.7918 *3.   Interpretation and application of Part II** (1)   In this Part—
   "the amount payable" for a chargeable financial year or part of a chargeable financial year in relation to a ratepayer, a billing authority and a hereditament means—
       (a)   the amount the ratepayer is liable to pay to the authority as regards the hereditament in respect of the year or part under—

    (i)   section 43 or 45 of the Act, whether calculated by reference to section 43(4) to (6) or 45(4) or (4A) of the Act (as those provisions are amended or substituted in any case by or under Schedule 7A to the Act) or by reference to an amount or rules determined or prescribed under section 47(1)(*a*), 57A(3)(*a*) or 58(3)(*a*) of the Act; and

    (ii)   section 11 of the BRS Act, whether calculated by reference to section 13 of the BRS Act (chargeable amount) or determined in accordance with rules set by the levying authority under section 15 of the BRS Act (BRS relief); or(*b*) where an amount falls to be credited by the billing authority against the ratepayer's liability in respect of the year or part, the amount (if any) by which the amount referred to in sub-paragraph (*a*) above exceeds the amount falling to be so credited;

"demand notice" means the notice required to be served by regulation 4(1);

"ratepayer" in relation to a chargeable financial year and a billing authority means a person liable to pay an amount under section 43 or 45 of the Act to the authority in respect of the year; and

"relevant year" in relation to a notice means the chargeable financial year to which the notice relates;

"the 1992 Act" means the Non-Domestic Rating Act 1992;

"the 1993 Act" means the Non-Domestic Rating Act 1993;

"transitional adjustment notice" has the meaning given by paragraph 7A(2)(*b*) of Schedule 1.

(2)   For the purposes of this Part the conditions mentioned in section 43(1) or 45(1) of the Act are not to be treated as fulfilled as regards a hereditament on any day on which the chargeable amount for the day in respect of it is 0 under section 45A of the Act or by virtue of a determination to that effect under section 47(1)(*a*) of the Act.

(3)   Where references are made in this Part to the day on which a notice is issued, they shall be taken to be references—

(*a*)   if the notice is served in the manner described in regulation 2(2) or section 233(2) of the Local Government Act 1972 by being left at, or sent by post to, a person's place of business or proper address, to the day on which it is so left or posted, or

(*b*)   in any other case, to the day on which it is served.

(4)   The provisions of this Part which provide for the repayment or crediting of any amount or the adjustment of payments due under a notice (including in particular paragraph 7 of Schedule 1) shall have effect subject to paragraph 10(4) of Schedule 7 to the Act.

---

  * **Reproduced as in force in England.**

7.7919 *4. The requirement for demand notices* (1) For each chargeable financial year a billing authority shall, in accordance with regulations 5 to 7, serve a notice in writing on every person who is a ratepayer of the authority in relation to the year.

(2)   Different demand notices shall be served for different chargeable financial years.

(3)   A demand notice shall be served with respect to the amount payable for every hereditament as regards which a person is a ratepayer of the authority, though a single notice may relate to the amount payable with respect to more than one such hereditament.

(3A) *Revoked.*

(4)   If a single demand notice relates to the amount payable with respect to more than one hereditament, subject to paragraphs 5 and 8 of Schedule 1 the amounts due under it, and the times at which they fall due, shall be determined as if separate notices were issued in respect of each hereditament.

(5)   *Revoked.*

7.7920 *5. Service of demand notices*[1] (1) Subject to paragraph (2), a demand notice shall be served on or as soon as practicable[2] after—

(*a*)   except in a case falling within sub-paragraph (*b*), 1st April in the relevant year, or

(*b*)   if the conditions mentioned in section 43(1) or 45(1) of the Act are not fulfilled in respect of that day as regards the ratepayers and the hereditament concerned, the first day after that day in respect of which such conditions are fulfilled as regards them.

(2)   Subject to paragraph (3), a demand notice may, if the non-domestic multiplier for the relevant year has been determined or set under Schedule 7 to the Act, be served before the beginning of the relevant year on a person with respect to whom on the day it is issued it appears to the billing authority that the conditions mentioned in section 43(1) or 45(1) of the Act are fulfilled (or would be fulfilled if a list sent under section 41(5) of the Act were in force) as regards the hereditament to which it relates; and if it is so served, references in this Part to a ratepayer shall, in relation to that notice and so far as the context permits, be construed as references to that person.

(3)   A demand notice shall not be served before the authority has set amounts for the relevant year under section 30 of the Local Government Finance Act 1992.

---

  [1] Where a boundary order changes the charging authority to that of another one, this regulation is modified by SI 1991/242.

  [2] There are limited challenges that can be advanced to resist liability once a demand notice has been served. However, one matter that the billing authority must establish is that the demand notice was served "as soon as practicable". There are conflicting opinions as to whether this requirement is absolute or whether the respondent must also establish that they have suffered some prejudice as a result of any delay in serving the notice: see *Encon Insulation Ltd v Nottingham City Council* [1999] All ER (D) 58, *North Somerset District Council v Honda* [2010] EWHC 1505 (QB), and *R (on the application of LB Waltham Forest) v Waltham Forest Magistrates Court* [2008] EWHC 2579 (Admin).

7.7921 *6. Payments under demand notices*[1] (1) If a demand notice is issued before or during the relevant year and it appears to the billing authority that the conditions mentioned in section 43(1) or 45(1) of the Act are fulfilled (or would be fulfilled if a list sent under section 41(5) of the Act were in force) in respect of the day on which the notice is issued as regards the ratepayer and the hereditament to which it relates, the notice shall require payment of an amount equal to the billing authority's estimate of the amount payable for the year, made as respects periods after the issue of the notice on the assumption that the conditions concerned will continue to be fulfilled on every day after that day.

(1A)   Where, as a result of the application of article 7 of the Non-Domestic Rating (Small Business Rate Relief) (England) Order 2004 and in accordance with that Order, there is any change to the amount which the ratepayer is liable to pay to the billing authority as regards the hereditament, the authority's estimate under paragraph (1) of the amount payable shall take account of such change.

(1B)   Where, as a result of the application of article 11A of the Non-Domestic Rating (Small Business Relief) (Wales) Order 2008 and in accordance with that Order, there is any change to the amount which the ratepayer is liable to pay to the billing authority as regards the hereditament, the authority's estimate under paragraph (1) of the amount payable is to take account of such change.

(2)   If a demand notice is issued during the relevant year but paragraph (1) does not apply, the notice shall require payment of an amount equal to the amount payable for the period in the year up to the day on which the conditions mentioned in sections 43(1) and 45(1) were last fulfilled as regards the ratepayer and hereditament concerned.

(3)   If, after a notice is served to which paragraph (2) applies, the conditions mentioned in section 43(1) or 45(1) of the Act are fulfilled again in the relevant year as regards the ratepayer and the hereditament concerned, a further notice shall be served on him requiring payments with respect to the amount payable in relation to the hereditament for the period in the relevant year beginning with the day in respect of which the conditions are so fulfilled again; and regulations 5 to 8 (and, so far as applicable, Schedule 1) shall apply to the further notice with respect to that period as if it were a demand notice and the conditions had previously not been fulfilled.

(4)   If a demand notice is issued after the end of the relevant year, it shall require payment of the amount payable for the year.

---

[1] Where a boundary order changes the charging authority to that of another one, this regulation is modified by SI 1991/242.

**7.7922   7.   *Payments under demand notices: further provision*   (1)   Unless an agreement under paragraph (3) in relation to the relevant year has been reached between the ratepayer and the billing authority before the demand notice is issued or paragraph (1A) or paragraph (1B) applies, a notice to which regulation 6(1) applies shall require the estimate of the amount payable to be paid by instalments in accordance with Part I of Schedule 1; and where such instalments are required Part II of the Schedule applies for their cessation or adjustment in the circumstances described in that Part.

(1A)   Unless an agreement under paragraph (3) in relation to the relevant year has been reached between the ratepayer and the billing authority before the demand notice is issued, where—

(*a*)   the chargeable financial year begins on 1st April 2011;

(*b*)   it appears to the billing authority that the estimate of the amount payable for that year would fall to be calculated by reference to section 43(4A) of the Act or by reference to the rules prescribed in regulation 10(6) of the Non-Domestic Rating (Chargeable Amounts) (England) Regulations 2009; and

(*c*)   the rateable value of the hereditament concerned is not more than £12,000, a notice to which regulation 6(1) applies shall require the estimate of the amount payable to be paid in instalments in accordance with Schedule 1E.

(1B)   Unless an agreement under paragraph (3) in relation to the relevant year has been reached between the ratepayer and the billing authority before the demand notice is issued, where—

(*a*)   the chargeable financial year begins on 1 April 2011;

(*b*)   it appears to the billing authority that the estimate of the amount payable for that year would fall to be calculated by reference to section 43(4A) of the Act; and

(*c*)   the rateable value of the hereditament concerned is not more than £12,000,

a notice to which regulation 6(1) applies must require the estimate of the amount payable to be paid in instalments in accordance with Schedule 1F.

(1C)   *Revoked.*

(1D)   In this regulation and in paragraph 1 of Schedule 1, "instalment notice" means a notice given by a ratepayer to a billing authority under paragraph (1E).

(1E)   Paragraphs (1F) to (1K) apply where a ratepayer gives notice in writing to the billing authority that they wish to pay the estimate of the amount payable for each chargeable financial year by 12 monthly instalments until further notice.

(1F)   An instalment notice may be given either before or after a demand notice is issued and may specify that it is to take effect starting in relation to the relevant year or the year following the relevant year.

(1G)   Where an instalment notice relates to the relevant year, a demand notice to which regulation 6(1) applies shall be issued as soon as reasonably practicable after the date on which the instalment notice is received by the billing authority and shall require the estimate of the amount payable to be paid in instalments in accordance with paragraph 1(2C) of Schedule 1.

(1H)   Where an instalment notice relates to the year following the relevant year, as soon as reasonably practicable after the date on which the instalment notice is received by the billing authority, the billing authority shall write to confirm that the estimate of the amount payable for that year is to be paid in instalments in accordance with paragraph 1(2C) of Schedule 1.

(1I)   For each subsequent chargeable financial year for which the billing authority issues a demand notice to the ratepayer in accordance with regulation 6(1) after an instalment notice has been given, the demand notice shall require payment of the estimate of the amount payable for the year in accordance with paragraph 1(2C) of Schedule 1.

(1J)   A ratepayer may give notice in writing to the billing authority that paragraph 1(2C) of Schedule 1 is no longer to apply.

(1K)   Subject to paragraph (3), a notice given under paragraph (1J) takes effect at the expiry of the chargeable financial year in which it was received.

(2)   If an agreement under paragraph (3) in relation to the relevant year has been reached between the billing authority and the ratepayer before the demand notice is issued, a notice to which regulation 6(1) applies shall require the estimate of the amount payable to be paid in accordance with that agreement.

(3)   A billing authority and a ratepayer may agree that the estimate of the amount payable which is required to be paid under a notice to which regulation 6(1) applies should be paid in such manner as is provided by the agreement, rather than in accordance with Schedules 1 or 1E or 1F.

(4)   Notwithstanding anything in the foregoing provisions of this regulation, such an agreement may be entered into either before or after the demand notice concerned is issued, and may make provision for the cessation or adjustment of payments, and for the making of fresh estimates, in the event of the estimate mentioned in regulation 6(1) turning out to be wrong; and if it is entered into after the demand notice has been issued, it may make provision dealing with the treatment for the purposes of the agreement of any sums paid in accordance with Schedules 1 or 1E or 1F before it was entered into.

(5)   A notice to which regulation 6(2) or (4) applies shall require payment of the amount payable on the expiry of such period (being not less than 14 days) after the day of issue of the notice as is specified in it.

(6)   No payment in respect of the amount payable by a ratepayer in relation to a hereditament for any chargeable financial year (whether interim, final or sole) need be made unless a notice served under this Part requires it.

7.7923   *7A. Backdated liability: special provision in relation to 2005 rating lists*   Notwithstanding the requirements of a demand notice issued in accordance with regulation 7, a ratepayer and a billing authority may reach an agreement in accordance with Schedule 1A.

7.7924   *7B. Deferred payments: special provision in relation to financial years beginning on 1st April 2009, 2010 and 2011*   Schedules 1B and 1C, which contain special provision in relation to payments under demand notices relating to financial years beginning on 1st April 2009, 1st April 2010 and 1st April 2011, shall have effect.

7.7925   *7C. Deferred payments: special provision in relation to Wales for the financial years beginning on 1st April 2009, 2010 and 2011*   Schedule 1D which contains special provision in relation to payments under demand notices relating to financial years beginning on 1st April 2009, 1st April 2010 and 1st April 2011, must have effect.

7.7926   *7D. Deferred payments: special provision in relation to England for financial years beginning on 1st April 2012, 2013 and 2014*   Schedules 1G and 1H, which contain special provision in relation to payments under demand notices relating to financial years beginning on 1st April 2012, 1st April 2013 and 1st April 2014, shall have effect.

7.7927   *8. Failure to pay instalments*   (1)   Where

  (a)   a demand notice has been served by a billing authority on a ratepayer,

  (b)   instalments are payable under the notice in accordance with Schedules 1 or 1E or 1F, and

  (c)   any such instalment is not paid in accordance with Schedules 1 or 1E or 1F,

the billing authority shall (unless all the instalments have fallen due) serve a further notice on the ratepayer stating the instalments required to be paid.

(2)   If, after the service of a further notice under paragraph (1), the ratepayer—

  (a)   fails to pay, before the expiry of the period of 7 days beginning with the day of service of the further notice, any instalments which fall due before the expiry of that period under the demand notice concerned, or

  (b)   fails to pay any instalment which falls due after the expiry of that period under the demand notice concerned on or before the day on which it so falls due,

the unpaid balance of the estimated amount shall become payable by him at the expiry of a further period 7 days beginning with the day of the failure.

(3)   If the unpaid balance of the estimated amount has become payable under paragraph (2), and on calculating the amount payable for the relevant year in relation to a hereditament to which the demand notice concerned relates that amount proves to be greater than the estimated amount in relation to the hereditament, an additional sum equal to the difference between the two shall, on the service by the billing authority on the ratepayer of a notice stating the amount payable, be due from the person to the authority on the expiry of such period (being not less than 14 days) after the day of issue of the notice as is specified in it.

(4)   If the unpaid balance of the estimated amount has become payable under paragraph (2), and on calculating the amount payable for the relevant year in relation to a hereditament to which the demand notice concerned relates that amount proves to be less than the estimated amount in relation to the hereditament, the billing authority shall notify the ratepayer in writing of the amount payable; and any overpayment in respect of any liability of the ratepayer under this Part—

  (a)   shall be repaid if the ratepayer so requires, or

  (b)   in any other case shall (as the billing authority determines) either be repaid or be credited against any subsequent liability of the ratepayer to pay anything to it by way of non-domestic rate.

(5)   If any factor or assumption by reference to which the estimated amount was calculated in relation to a hereditament is shown to be false before the amount payable is capable of final

determination for the purposes of paragraphs (3) and (4), the billing authority may, and if so required by the ratepayer shall, make a calculation of the appropriate amount with a view to adjusting the ratepayer's liability in respect of the estimated amount and (as appropriate) to—

(a)   requiring an interim payment from the ratepayer if the appropriate amount is greater than the estimated amount, or

(b)   making an interim repayment to the ratepayer if the appropriate amount is less than the amount of the estimated amount paid.

(6)   The appropriate amount for the purposes of paragraph (5) is the amount which would be required to be paid under a demand notice if such a notice were issued with respect to the relevant year, the ratepayer and the hereditament on the day that the notice under paragraph (7) is issued or the repayment under paragraph (5)(b) is made (as the case may be); and more than one calculation of the appropriate amount and interim payment or repayment may be required or made under paragraph (5) according to the circumstances.

(7)   On calculating the appropriate amount the billing authority shall notify the ratepayer in writing of it; and a payment required under paragraph (5)(a) shall be due from the ratepayer to the billing authority on the expiry of such period (being not less than 14 days) after the day of issue of the notice as is specified in it.

(8)   In this regulation—

"the appropriate amount" has the meaning given in paragraph (6); and

"the estimated amount" means the amount last estimated under regulation 6(1) for the purposes of the demand notice mentioned in paragraph (1)(a) or any subsequent notice given under paragraph 7(2) or, as the case may be, paragraph 7A or paragraph 7B or paragraph 7C or paragraph 7D or paragraph 7E of Schedule 1, or under paragraph 7 of that Schedule as modified by paragraph 5(3) of Schedule 1E or paragraph 5(3) of Schedule 1F, prior to the failure mentioned in paragraph (2) above, save that if in any case an interim adjustment has been required or made under paragraph (5) in relation to a hereditament, it means as regards the next payment, repayment or interim adjustment in relation to the hereditament under this regulation (if any), the appropriate amount by reference to which the previous interim adjustment was so made.

7.7928   9.   Demand notices: final adjustment   (1)   This regulation applies where—

(a)   a notice has been issued by a billing authority under this Part requiring a payment or payments to be made by a ratepayer in respect of the amount payable in relation to a hereditament for a chargeable financial year or part of a chargeable financial year,

(b)   the payment or payments required to be paid are found to be in excess of or less than the amount payable in relation to the hereditament for the year or the part, and

(c)   provision for adjusting the amounts required under the notice and (as appropriate) for the making of additional payments or the repaying or crediting of any amount overpaid is not made by any other provision of this Part, of the Act or of any agreement entered into under regulation 7(3).

(2)   the billing authority shall as soon as practicable after the expiry of the year or the part of a year serve a further notice on the ratepayer stating the amount payable for the year or part in relation to the hereditament, and adjusting (by reference to that amount) the amounts required to be paid under the notice referred to in paragraph (1)(a).

(3)   If the amount stated in the further notice is greater than the amount required to be paid under the notice referred to in paragraph (1)(a), the amount of the difference for which such other provision as is mentioned in paragraph (1)(c) is not made shall be due from the ratepayer to the billing authority on the expiry of such period (being not less than 14 days) after the day of issue of the notice as is specified in it.

(4)   If there has been an overpayment in respect of any liability of the ratepayer under this Part, the amount overpaid for which such other provision as is mentioned in paragraph (1)(c) is not made—

(a)   shall be repaid if the ratepayer so requires, or

(b)   in any other case shall (as the billing authority determines) either be repaid or be credited against any subsequent liability of the ratepayer to pay anything to it by way of non-domestic rate.

7.7929   10.   Interpretation and application of Part III   (1)   In this Part—

"debtor" means a person against whom a liability order has been made;

"liability order" means an order under regulation 12; and

"Schedule 12" means Schedule 12 to the Tribunals, Courts and Enforcement Act 2007, "the Schedule 12 procedure" means the procedure in that Schedule (taking control of goods and selling them to recover a sum of money), and "enforcement agent" has the meaning given in that Schedule.

(2)   A sum which has become payable to a billing authority under Part II and which has not been paid shall be recoverable under a liability order, or in a court of competent jurisdiction, in accordance with regulations 11 to 21.

(3)   References in this Part to a sum which has become payable and which has not been paid include references to a sum forming part of a larger sum which has become payable and the other part of which has been paid.

7.7930   11.   Liability orders: preliminary steps   (1)   Subject to paragraph (3), before a billing authority applies for a liability order it shall serve on the person against whom the application is to be made a notice ("reminder notice"), which is to be in addition to any notice required to be served under Part II and which is to state every amount in respect of which the authority is to make the application.

(2)   A reminder notice may be served in respect of an amount at any time after it has become due.

(3)   A reminder notice need not be served on a person who has been served under regulation 8(1) with a notice in respect of the amount concerned where there has been such a failure as is mentioned in regulation 8(2)(*a*) in relation to the notice.

7.7931   *12.   Application for liability order*[1]   (1)   Subject to paragraph (3), if an amount which has fallen due under regulation 8(2) in consequence of such a failure as is mentioned in sub-paragraph (*a*) of that provision is wholly or partly unpaid, or (in a case where a reminder notice is required under regulation 11) the amount stated in the reminder notice is wholly or partly unpaid at the expiry of the period of 7 days beginning with the day on which the notice was served, the billing authority may, in accordance with paragraph (2), apply to a magistrates' court for an order against the person by whom it is payable.

(2)   The application is to be instituted by making complaint to a justice of the peace, and requesting the issue of a summons[2] directed to that person to appear before the court to show why he has not paid the sum which is outstanding.

(3)   Section 127(1) of the Magistrates' Courts Act 1980 does not apply to such an application; but no application may be instituted in respect of a sum after the period of 6 years beginning with the day on which it became due under Part II.

(4)   A warrant shall not be issued under section 55(2) of the Magistrates' Courts Act 1980 in any proceedings under this regulation.

(5)   The court shall make the order if it is satisfied that the sum has become payable by the defendant and has not been paid.

(6)   An order made pursuant to paragraph (5) shall be made in respect of an amount equal to the aggregate of—

(*a*)   the sum payable, and

(*b*)   a sum of an amount equal to the costs reasonably incurred by the applicant in obtaining the order (which costs, including those of instituting the application under paragraph (2), are not to exceed the prescribed amount of £70).

(7)   Where the sum payable is paid after a liability order has been applied for under paragraph (2) but before it is made, the court shall nonetheless (if so requested by the billing authority) make the order in respect of a sum of an amount equal to the costs reasonably incurred by the authority in making the application (which costs, including those of instituting the application under paragraph (2), are not to exceed the prescribed amount of £70).

---

[1]   There is a general common law provision to set aside an order made by a magistrates' court in its civil jurisdiction, including a liability order if the following grounds are satisfied: there must be a genuine and arguable dispute as to the defendant's liability to the order in question; the order must be made as a result of a substantial procedural error, defect or mishap; and the application to the justices for the order to be set aside is made promptly after a defendant learns that it has been made or has notice that an order may have been made (*R (London Borough of Newham) v Stratford Magistrates' Court* [2008] EWHC 125 (Admin), 173 JP 30). Magistrates have to consider not only whether the dispute is genuine but also whether it is arguable. It is also necessary for magistrates to identify specifically the procedural error referred to. If, for example, the magistrates find that defendant had not been served with any summons and did not know about the liability proceedings at the relevant time, they must make an express finding to that effect, explaining briefly upon what material they have relied to reach the finding. Failure to do so constitutes a substantial defect in the reasoning in support of their decision per Kenneth Parker J in *London Borough of Tower Hamlets v Rahman* [2012] EWHC 3428 (Admin), 177 JP 192. Justices may reopen their decision to make a liability order made in ignorance of the receipt of an application to adjourn so that they may exercise their judicial discretion whether to grant the order or adjourn (*Liverpool City Council v Pleroma Distribution Ltd* [2003] 04 LS Gaz R 33.
[2]   Under Rule 99(3) of the Magistrates' Courts Rules 1981, summonses under these regulations can be served in accordance with Rule 99 of those rules.

7.7932   *13.   Liability orders: further provision*   (1)   A single liability order may deal with one person and one such amount (or aggregate amount) as is mentioned in regulation 12(6) and (7), or, if the court thinks fit, may deal with more than one person and more than one such amount (or aggregate amount).

(2)   A summons issued under regulation 12(2) may be served on a person—

(*a*)   by delivering it to him,

(*b*)   by leaving it as his usual or last known place of abode, or in the case of a company, at its registered office,

(*c*)   by sending it by post to him at his usual or last known place of abode, or in the case of a company, to its registered office,

(*d*)   where all or part of the sum to which it relates is payable with respect to a hereditament which is a place of business of the person, by leaving it at, or by sending it by post to him at, the place of business, or

(*e*)   by leaving it at, or by sending it by post to him at, an address given by the person as an address at which service of the summons will be accepted.

(2A)   No liability order shall be made in pursuance of a summons issued under regulation 12(2) unless fourteen days have elapsed since the day on which the summons was served.

(3)   The amount in respect of which a liability order is made is enforceable in accordance with this part; and accordingly for the purposes of any of the provisions of Part III of the Magistrates' Courts Act 1980 (satisfaction and enforcement) it is not to be treated as a sum adjudged to be paid by order of the court.

7.7933   *14.   Enforcement by taking control of goods*   Where a liability order has been made, payment may be enforced by using the Schedule 12 procedure.

7.7934   *16.   Commitment to prison*[1]   (1)   Where a billing authority has sought to enforce payment by use of the Schedule 12 procedure pursuant to regulation 14, the debtor is an individual, and the enforcement agent reports to the authority that he was unable (for whatever reason) to find any or sufficient goods of the debtor to enforce payment, the authority may apply to a magistrates' court for the issue of a warrant committing the debtor to prison.

(2)   On such application being made the court shall (in the debtor's presence) inquire as to his means and inquire whether the failure to pay which led to the liability order concerned being made against him was due to his wilful refusal or culpable neglect.

(3)   If (and only if) the court is of the opinion that his failure was due to his wilful refusal or culpable neglect it may if it thinks fit—

(a)   issue a warrant of commitment against the debtor, or

(b)   fix a term of imprisonment and postpone the issue of the warrant until such time and on such conditions (if any) as the court thinks just.

(4)   The warrant shall be made in respect of the relevant amount; and the relevant amount for this purpose is the aggregate of—

(a)   the amount outstanding (within the meaning of Schedule 12), and

(b)   a sum of an amount equal to the costs reasonably incurred by the applicant in respect of the application.

(5)   The warrant—

(a)   shall state the relevant amount mentioned in paragraph (4),

(b)   may be directed to the authority making the application and to such other persons (if any) as the court issuing it thinks fit, and

(c)   may be executed anywhere in England and Wales by any person to whom it is directed.

(6)   If—

(a)   before a warrant has been issued, or a term of imprisonment fixed and the issue of a warrant postponed, an amount determined in accordance with paragraph (6A) is paid or tendered to the authority, or

(b)   after a term of imprisonment has been fixed and the issue of a warrant postponed, any amount the court has ordered the debtor to pay is paid or tendered to the authority, or

(c)   after a warrant has been issued, the amount stated in it is paid or tendered to the authority,

the authority shall accept the amount concerned, no further steps shall be taken as regards its recovery, and the debtor, if committed to prison, shall be released.

(6A)   The amount referred to in paragraph (6)(a) above is the aggregate of—

(a)   the amount outstanding (within the meaning of Schedule 12), and

(b)   subject to sub-paragraph (6B) below, the authority's reasonable costs incurred up to the time of payment or tender in making one or more of the applications referred to in Schedule 4.

(6B)   For the purposes of paragraph (6A)(b) above, the authority's reasonable costs in respect of any application shall not exceed the amount specified in relation to that application in Schedule 4.

(7)   The order[2] in the warrant shall be that the debtor be imprisoned for a time specified[3] in the warrant which shall not exceed 3 months, unless the amount stated in the warrant is sooner paid; but—

(a)   where a warrant is issued after a postponement under paragraph (3)(b) and, since the term of imprisonment was fixed but before the issue of the warrant, the amount mentioned in paragraph (4)(a) with respect to which the warrant would (but for the postponement) have been made has been reduced by a part payment, the period of imprisonment ordered under the warrant shall be the term (a) the appropriate amount mentioned in regulation 14(2) (or so much of it as remains outstanding), and

(b)   subject to sub-paragraph (6B) below, the authority's reasonable costs incurred up to the time of payment or tender in making one or more of the applications referred to in Schedule 4 fixed under paragraph (3) reduced by such number of days as bears to the total number of days in that term less one day the same proportion as the part paid bears to that amount, and

(b)   where, after the issue of a warrant, a part payment of the amount stated in it is made, the period of imprisonment shall be reduced by such number of days as bears to the total number of days in the term of imprisonment specified in the warrant less one day the same proportion as the part paid bears to the amount so stated.

(8)   In calculating a reduction required under paragraph (7) any fraction of a day shall be left out of account; and rule 55(1), (2) and (3) of the Magistrates' Courts Rules 1981 applies (so far as is relevant) to a part payment as if the imprisonment concerned were imposed for insufficient recovery by way of the Schedule 12 procedure to satisfy a sum adjudged to be paid by a magistrates' court.

---

[1]   For the general principles concerning commitment applicable to this regulation and the next, see the notes to Regulation 47 of the Council Tax (Administration and Enforcement) Regulations 1992 below.

[2]   Schedule 2 of the regulations originally prescribed a form for a liability order, however the schedule was revoked in Wales by SI 2003/1714 and in England by SI 2003/2210. The magistrates' court register is now the definitive record of the order.

[3]   When determining the period of imprisonment to be specified in the warrant, the justices must have regard to the principle of proportionality. The more serious the case, whether in terms of the amount outstanding or in terms of the degree of culpability or blame to be attached to the debtor for his non-payment, the closer will any period imposed approach the maximum. A finding of wilful refusal, in this respect, represents a more serious state of affairs than culpable neglect (*R v Highbury Corner Magistrates' Court, ex p Uchendu* (1994) 158 JP 409).

7.7935   **17.   *Commitment to prison: further provision***   (1)   A single warrant may not be issued under regulation 16 against more than one person.

(2)   Where an application under regulation 16 has been made, and after the making of the inquiries mentioned in paragraph (2) of that regulation no warrant is issued or term of imprisonment fixed, the court may remit all or part of the appropriate amount mentioned in

regulation 14(2) to which the application relates.

(3)   Where an application under regulation 16 has been made but no warrant is issued or term of imprisonment fixed, the application may be renewed (except so far as regards any sum remitted under paragraph (2)) on the ground that the circumstances of the debtor have changed.

(4)   A statement in writing to the effect that wages of any amount have been paid to the debtor during any period, purporting to be signed by or on behalf of his employer, shall in any proceedings under regulation 16 be evidence of the facts there stated.

(5)   For the purpose of enabling enquiry to be made as to the debtor's conduct and means under regulation 16(2), a justice of the peace may—

(a)   issue a summons to him to appear before a magistrates' court and (if he does not obey the summons) issue a warrant for his arrest, or

(b)   issue a warrant for the debtor's arrest without issuing a summons.

(6)   A warrant issued under paragraph (5) may be executed anywhere in England and Wales by any person to whom it is directed or by any constable acting within his police area; and section 125(3) of the Magistrates' Courts Act 1980 applies to such a warrant.

(7)   Regulation 16 and this regulation have effect subject to Part I of the Criminal Justice Act 1982 (treatment of young offenders).

7.7936   18.   *Insolvency* (1)   Where a liability order has been made and the debtor against whom it was made is an individual, the amount due shall be deemed to be a debt for the purposes of section 267 of the Insolvency Act 1986 (grounds of creditor's petition).

(2)   Where a liability order has been made and the debtor against whom it was made is a company, the amount due shall be deemed to be a debt for the purpose of section 122(1)(*f*) (winding up of companies by the court) or, as the case may be, section 221(5)(*b*) (winding up of unregistered companies) of that Act.

(3)   The amount due for the purposes of this regulation is an amount equal to any outstanding sum which is or forms part of the amount in respect of which the liability order was made.

7.7937   19.   *Relationship between remedies under a liability order* (1)   Where a warrant of commitment is issued against (or a term of imprisonment is fixed in the case of) a person under regulation 16(3), no steps, or no further steps, may be taken under this Part by way of the Schedule 12 procedure or bankruptcy in relation to the relevant amount mentioned in regulation 16(4).

(2)   Steps under this Part by way of the Schedule 12 procedure, commitment, bankruptcy or winding up may not be taken against a person under a liability order while steps by way of another of those methods are being taken against him under it.

(3)   Subject to paragraphs (1) and (2) the Schedule 12 procedure may be resorted to more than once.

(4)   Where a step is taken by way of the Schedule 12 procedure for the recovery of an outstanding sum which is or forms part of an amount in respect of which a liability order has been made, any sum recovered thereby which is less than the aggregate of the amount outstanding and any charges arising under Schedule 3 shall be treated as discharging first the charges, the balance (if any) being applied towards the discharge of the outstanding sum.

7.7938   20.   *Recovery in court of competent jurisdiction* (1)   A sum which has become payable to a billing authority under Part II, which has not been paid, and in respect of which a liability order has not been made may (as an alternative to recovery under a liability order) be recovered in the court of competent jurisdiction.

(2)   A liability order may not be made in respect of any amount in relation to which proceedings have been instituted under paragraph (1) above.

7.7939   21.   *Magistrates' courts* (1)   *Revoked*.

(1A)   *Revoked*.

(2)   Subject to any other enactment authorising a District Judge (Magistrates' Courts) or other person to act by himself, a magistrates' court shall not under this Part hear a summons, entertain an application for a warrant or hold an inquiry as to means on such an application except when composed of at least two justices.

(3)   References to a justice of the peace in regulations 12(2) and 15(2) shall be construed subject to rule 3 of the Justices' Clerks Rules 1970 (which authorises certain matters authorised to be done by a justice of the peace to be done by a justices' clerk).

(4)   In any proceedings under regulation 12 (application for liability order) or regulation 16 (commitment to prison), a statement contained in a document constituting or forming part of a record compiled by the applicant authority or an authorised person[1] shall be admissible as evidence of any fact stated in it of which direct oral evidence would be admissible.

(5)   In proceedings where the applicant authority or an authorised person[1] desires to give a statement in evidence in accordance with paragraph (4), and the document containing that statement is produced by a computer, a certificate—

(a)   identifying the document containing the statement and the computer by which it was produced;

(b)   containing a statement that at all material times the computer was operating properly, or if not, that any respect in which it was not operating properly or was out of operation was not such as to affect the production of the document or the accuracy of its contents;

(c)   giving such explanation as may be appropriate of the content of the document; and

(d)   purporting to be signed by a person occupying a responsible position in relation to the operation of the computer,

shall be admissible as evidence of anything which is stated in it to the best of the signatory's information and belief.

(6) In paragraph (4) above, "statement" includes any representation of fact, whether made in words or otherwise; and the reference to an application under regulation 16 includes a reference to an application made in the circumstances mentioned in regulation 17(3).

(7) In this regulation and in regulation 23(3), "authorised person" means any person authorised by a billing authority to exercise any functions relating to the collection and enforcement of non-domestic rates[1].

---

[1] A billing authority may authorise another person, or that person's employees, to exercise functions relating to the administration and enforcement of non-domestic rates: see the Local Authorities (Contracting Out of Tax Billing, Collection and Enforcement Functions) Order 1996, SI 1996/1880.

7.7940 **22. Repayments** A sum which has become payable (by way of repayment) under Part II to a person other than a billing authority but which has not been paid shall be recoverable in a court of competent jurisdiction.

7.7941 **23. Miscellaneous provisions** (1) Any matter which could be the subject of an appeal under regulations under section 55 of the Act may not be raised in proceedings under this Part.

(2) The contents of a local non-domestic rating list or an extract from such a list may be proved in proceedings under this Part by production of a copy of the list or relevant part of the list purporting to be certified by the proper officer of the billing authority to which the list or extract relates to be a true copy.

(3) If a liability order has been made and by virtue of—

(a) a notification which is given by the billing authority or an authorised person under regulation 8(4) or (7) or 9(2) or paragraph 6(3) or 7(2)(a) of Schedule 1 or sub-paragraph (2) of paragraph 7A of that Schedule (including a notification given under that sub-paragraph pursuant to paragraph 7B(2) of that Schedule), or

(b) paragraph 10(4) or Schedule 7 to the Act applying in any case,

any part of the amount mentioned in regulation 12(6)(a) in respect of which the order was made would (if paid) fall to be repaid or credited against any subsequent liability, that part shall be treated for the purposes of this Part as paid on the day the notification is given or the multiplier in substitution is set under paragraph 10 of Schedule 7 to the Act (as the case may be) and accordingly as no longer outstanding.

(4) If, after a warrant is issued or term of imprisonment is fixed under regulation 16(3), and before the term of imprisonment has begun or been fully served, a billing authority gives such a notification as is mentioned in paragraph (3)(a) in the case in question, or sets a multiplier in substitution so that paragraph 10(4) of Schedule 7 to the Act applies in the case in question, it shall forthwith notify accordingly the designated officer for the court which issued the warrant and (if the debtor is detained) the governor or keeper of the prison or place where he is detained or such other person as has lawful custody of him.

PART IV MISCELLANEOUS

7.7942 **24. Outstanding liabilities on death*** (1) This regulation applies where a person dies and at any time before his death he was (or is alleged to have been) subject to a non-domestic rate.

(2) Where—

(a) before the deceased's death a sum has become payable by him under Part II or by way of relevant costs in respect of a non-domestic rate but has not been paid, or

(b) after the deceased's death a sum would, but for his death (and whether or not on the service of a notice) become payable by him under Part II in respect of a non-domestic rate,

his executor or administrator shall, subject to paragraph (3) and to the extent that it is not in excess of the deceased's liability under the Act or the BRS Act (including relevant costs payable by him) in respect of the rate, be liable to pay the sum and may deduct out of the assets and effects of the deceased any payments made (or to be made).

(3) Where paragraph (2)(b) applies, the liability of the executor or administrator does not arise until the service on him of a notice requiring payment of the sum.

(4) Where before the deceased's death a sum in excess of his liability under the Act or the BRS Act (including relevant costs payable by him) in respect of a non-domestic rate has been paid (whether the excess arises because of his death or otherwise) and has not been repaid or credited under Part II, his executor or administrator shall be entitled to the sum.

(5) Costs are relevant costs for the purposes of paragraphs (2) and (4) if—

(a) an order or warrant (as the case may be) was made by the court in respect of them under regulation 12(6)(b) or (7) or 16(4)(b), or in proceedings under regulation 20, or

(b) they are charges connected with the use of the Schedule 12 procedure which may be recovered pursuant to regulations under paragraph 62 of Schedule 12.

(6) A sum payable under paragraph (2) shall be enforceable in the administration of the deceased's estate as a debt of the deceased and accordingly—

(a) no liability order need be applied for in respect of it after the deceased's death under regulation 12, and

(b) the liability of the executor or administrator is a liability in his capacity as such.

(7) Regulation 23(1) and (2) applies to proceedings to enforce a liability arising under this regulation as it applies to proceedings under Part III.

(8) Insofar as is relevant to his liability under this regulation in the administration of the deceased's estate, the executor or administrator may institute, continue or withdraw proceedings (whether by way of appeal under regulations under section 55 of the Act or otherwise).

---

* Reproduced as in force in England.

SCHEDULE 1 Non-Domestic Rate Instalment Scheme	Regulation 7(1)
SCHEDULE 1A Backdated Liability: Special Provision in Relation to 2005 Rating Lists	Regulation 7A
SCHEDULE 1B	Regulation 7B
SCHEDULE 1C (Form of application)	Regulation 7B
SCHEDULE 4 Costs Connected with Committal	Regulation 16(6A) and (6B)

Council Tax (Administration and Enforcement) Regulations 1992[1]

(SI 1992/613 amended by SI 1992/3008, SI 1993/196 and 773, SI 1994/505, SI 1995/22, the Statute Law (Repeals) Act 1995, Sch 1, SI 1996/675 and 1880, SI 1997/393, SI 1998/295, SI 1999/534, SI 2000/2026, SI 2001/1076 and 2237, SI 2003/552 (W) and 768 (E), 1715 (W), 2211 (E) and 2604 (E), SI 2004/927 (E), 785 (W) and 1013 (W), SI 2005/2866 (E) and 3302 (W), SI 2006/237 (E) and 3395 (E), SI 2007/501 (E) and 582 (W), SI 2009/2706 (W), SI 2010/752 (E), SI 2011/528 (W), SI 2012/672 and 3086 (E), SI 2013/62(W), 570 (W), 590 (E), 630 (E) and 2977 (E), 2014/129 (W) and 600 and SI 2017/41 (W) and SI 2019/220)

Part I

General

7.7943   1.   *Citation, commencement and interpretation*   (1)   *Citation and commencement.*
(2)   In these Regulations—
"the Act" means the Local Government Finance Act 1992;
"address" in relation to electronic communications, includes any number or address used for the purposes of such communications;
"business day" means any day except a Saturday or Sunday, Christmas Day, Good Friday or a day which is a bank holiday under the Banking and Financial Dealings Act 1971 in England and Wales;
"council tax offence" has the same meaning as in the Detection of Fraud Regulations;
"demand notice regulations" means regulations under paragraph 1(1) of Schedule 2 to the Act making such provision as is mentioned in paragraph 2(4)(e) or 2(4)(j) of that Schedule; and
"Detection of Fraud Regulations" means the Council Tax Reduction Schemes (Detection of Fraud and Enforcement) (England) Regulations 2013;
"discount" means—
    (a)   a discount under section 11 or section 11A of the Act;
    (b)   a reduction in the amount of council tax payable for a dwelling under the Council Tax (Reductions for Annexes) (England) Regulations 2013; or (c) a reduction under section 13A(1)(a) or
    (c)   where—
        (i)   a scheme under section 13A(2) of the Act provides, or
        (ii)   the billing authority has determined under section 13A(7) of the Act,
that liability shall be reduced otherwise than to nil;
"electronic communication" means a communication transmitted (whether from one person to another, from one device to another or from a person to a device or vice versa)—
    (a)   by means of an electronic communications network within the meaning of section 32(1) of the Communications Act 2003;
    (b)   by other means but while in an electronic form;
"exempt dwelling" means a dwelling which is exempt from council tax under the Exempt Dwellings Order or a dwelling in relation to which no council tax is payable by virtue of a reduction under section 13A(1)(a) or section 13A(1)(c) of the Act where—
    (a)   a scheme under section 13A(2) of the Act provides; or
    (b)   the billing authority has determined under section 13A(7) of the Act;
that liability shall be reduced otherwise than to nil;
"Exempt Dwellings Order" means the Council Tax (Exempt Dwellings) Order 1992;
"managing agent", in relation to a dwelling, means any person authorised to arrange lettings of the dwelling;
"premium" means an increase in the amount of council tax payable in respect of a dwelling under section 11B(1) of the Act; and
"universal credit" means universal credit under Part 1 of the Welfare Reform Act 2012".

---

[1] Made by the Secretary of State for the Environment, as respects England, and the Secretary of State for Wales, as respects Wales, in exercise of the powers conferred on them by ss 16(3) and 113(1) and (2) of, and paragraphs 1(1), 2(2), (3), (4)(a) to (c) and (5), 3–11, 13(1)(a) and (3), 16 and 18 of Sch 2, paras 1 and 6 of Sch 3 and paras 1–15, and 17–19 of Sch 4 to, the Local Government Finance Act 1992.

7.7944   2.   *Service of notices*   (1)   Where any notice which is required or authorised by these Regulations to be given to or served on any person falls to be given or served by or on behalf of the Common Council it may be given or served in any manner in which it might be given or served under section 233 of the Local Government Act 1972 if the Common Council were a local authority within the meaning of that section.

(2) If the name of any person on whom a notice is to be served in accordance with regulation 3 (information from residents etc) or regulation 12 (information relating to exempt dwellings etc) cannot after reasonable inquiry be ascertained, the notice may be served by addressing it to "The Resident" or, as the case may be, "The Owner" or "The Managing Agent" of the dwelling concerned (naming the dwelling) without further name or description.

(3) If the name of any person to whom a notice is to be given or on whom a notice is to be served in accordance with any provision of Part V (billing) of these Regulations cannot after reasonable inquiry be ascertained, the notice may be given or served by addressing it to "The Council Tax Payer" of the dwelling concerned (naming the dwelling) without further name or description.

(4) Without prejudice to section 233 of the Local Government Act 1972 and paragraphs (1), (2) and (3) above and subject to paragraphs (5) to (8) below, any notice required or authorised to be given to or served by a billing authority on any person by a provision of Part II, III or V of these Regulations:

(a)   may be so given, served or supplied by sending the notice or information to that person by electronic communication to such address as may be notified by that person for that purpose; or

(b)   shall be treated as given, served or supplied to that person where—

    (i)   the billing authority and that person have agreed for that purpose that any document containing that notice or information may be accessed by that person on a website;

    (ii)   the document is a document to which that agreement applies;

    (iii)   the billing authority has published the document on a website; and

    (iv)   that person is notified, in a manner for the time being agreed for that purpose between him and the billing authority, of—

        (aa) the publication of the document on a website;

        (bb) the address of that website; and

        (cc) the place on the website where the document may be accessed.

(4A) Without prejudice to section 233 of the Local Government Act 1972(b) and subject to paragraphs (6) and (7) below, any information required by the demand notice regulations to be supplied to any person when a demand notice (within the meaning of Part V of these Regulations) is served:

(a)   may be so supplied by sending the information to that person by electronic communication to such address as may be notified by that person for that purpose; or

(b)   subject to paragraph (4B) shall be treated as supplied to that person where the billing authority has published the information on a website and that person is notified by way of the demand notice of—

    (i)   the publication of the information on a website;

    (ii)   the address of that website; and

    (iii)   the place on the website where the information may be accessed;

(4B) Sub-paragraph (b) of paragraph (4A) shall not apply where that person has requested a hard copy of the information.

(4C) Where a person requests a hard copy of the information referred to in paragraph (4A) in writing either before or after the demand notice is issued the authority must supply it as soon as reasonably practicable following receipt of the request.

(5) For the purpose of any legal proceedings, a notice given by a means described in paragraph (4), shall, unless the contrary is proved, be treated as served on the second business day after—

(a)   it was sent in accordance with sub-paragraph (a); or

(b)   notification of its publication was given in accordance with sub-paragraph (b)(iv).

(6) A person who has notified an address for the purposes of paragraph (4)(a) or (4A)(a) shall, by notice in writing to the billing authority, advise the billing authority of any change in that address; and the change shall take effect on the third business day after the date on which the notice is received by the billing authority.

(7) A person who has notified an address for the purposes of paragraph (4)(a) or (4A)(a) may, by notice in writing to the billing authority, withdraw that notification; and the withdrawal shall take effect on the third business day after the date on which the notice is received by the billing authority.

(8) A person who has entered into an agreement with the billing authority under paragraph (4)(b)(i) may, by notice in writing to the billing authority, inform the authority that he no longer wishes to be party to the agreement; and where such notice is given, the agreement shall be treated as revoked on the third business day after the date on which the notice is received by the billing authority.

PART II

Information: General

PART III

Exempt Dwellings, Etc

PART IV

Discounts

PART V

Billing

7.7945　*17. Interpretation and application of Part V*　(1)　In this Part—

"demand notice" means the notice required to be served by regulation 18(1);

"joint taxpayers" means two or more persons who are, or in the opinion of the billing authority will be, jointly and severally liable to pay to the authority an amount in respect of council tax in respect of a particular dwelling and a day (whether such liability arises by virtue of section 6(3) or (4)(*b*), 7(4) or (5), 8(4) or (5) or 9(1) of the Act);

"joint taxpayers' notice" means a notice served in accordance with regulation 28;

"Part II scheme" means a scheme for the payment of the chargeable amount by instalments in accordance with a scheme complying with the requirements of Part II of Schedule 1 to these Regulations;

"the relevant year", in relation to a notice, means the financial year to which the notice relates.

(1A)　Any reference in this Part to the relevant valuation band in relation to a dwelling is a reference to the valuation band shown as applicable to the dwelling—

(*a*)　　in the billing authority's valuation list; or

(*b*)　　if no such list is in force—

　　(i)　　except in a case to which paragraph (1B) applies, in the copy of the proposed list supplied to the authority under section 22(5)(*b*) of the Act;

　　(ii)　　in a case to which paragraph (1B) applies, in information which for the purposes of this paragraph is relevant information.

(1B)　This paragraph applies where the listing officer supplies the authority with information relating to property shown in the proposed list (including information relating to the application to such property of article 3 or 4 of the Council Tax (Chargeable Dwellings) Order 1992); and such information is relevant information for the purposes of paragraph (1A)(*b*)(ii) to the extent that it differs from information contained in the proposed list.

(2)　Except where the context otherwise requires, and subject to paragraph (5), any reference in this Part to the liable person (however expressed) is a reference—

(*a*)　　to a person who is, or in the opinion of the billing authority will be, solely liable to pay to the authority, an amount in respect of council tax in respect of a particular dwelling and a day; or

(*b*)　　where persons are joint taxpayers, to those persons.

(3)　Any reference in this Part to the chargeable amount is a reference to the amount the liable person is or will be liable to pay.

(4)　Any reference in this Part to the day on or time at which a notice is issued, is a reference—

(*a*)　　if the notice is served in the manner described in section 233(2) of the Local Government Act 1972 by being left at, or sent by post to, a person's proper address, to the day on or time at which it is so left or posted, or

(*b*)　　in any other case, to the day on or time at which the notice is served.

(5)　This Part applies (amongst other matters) for the making of payments in relation to the chargeable amount for a financial year; but its application as regards persons who are joint taxpayers is subject to the provisions of regulations 27 to 28A.

(6)　The provisions of this Part which provide for the repayment or crediting of any amount or the adjustment of payments due under a notice shall have effect subject to section 31(4) of the Act.

7.7946　*18. The requirement for demand notices*　(1)　Subject to paragraph (2), for each financial year a billing authority shall serve a notice in writing[1] on every liable person in accordance with regulations 19 to 21.

(2)　Where, but for this paragraph, notices would fall to be served in accordance with this Part—

(*a*)　　at the same time; and

(*b*)　　in respect of the same dwelling,

in relation to a financial year not then ended and any preceding financial year, nothing in paragraph (1) shall require a billing authority to serve more than one notice.

(3)　If a person is liable in any financial year to pay to the same billing authority different chargeable amounts in respect of different dwellings, a demand notice shall be served in respect of each chargeable amount.

---

[1]　The Council Tax and Non-Domestic Rating (Demand Notices) (England) Regulations 1993, SI 1993/191 provide for the content of Council Tax notices and for the information to be supplied with such notices in the financial year beginning on 1 April 1993.

7.7947　*19. Service of demand notices*　(1)　The demand notice is to be served on or as soon as practicable after the day the billing authority first sets an amount of council tax for the relevant year for the category of dwellings which includes the chargeable dwelling to which the notice relates.

(2)   For the purposes of paragraph (1), "category" shall be construed in accordance with section 30(4) of the Act; and where a demand notice is served before 1st April 1993, a dwelling shall be treated as included in the category in which, in the opinion of the billing authority, it will be included on 1st April 1993.

7.7948   20.   *Demand notices: payments required*   (1)   If the demand notice is issued before or during the relevant year, the notice shall require the making of payments on account of the amount referred to in paragraph (2).

(2)   The amount is—

(a)   the billing authority's estimate of the chargeable amount, made as respects the relevant year or part, as the case may be, on the assumptions referred to in paragraph (3); or

(b)   subject to paragraph (2A), where an amount falls to be credited by the billing authority against the chargeable amount, the amount (if any) by which the amount estimated as mentioned in sub-paragraph (a) exceeds the amount falling to be so credited.

(2A)   Where the billing authority has made a determination under—

(a)   paragraph 118(1)(c) of the scheme prescribed in the Schedule to the Council Tax Reduction Schemes (Default Scheme) (England) Regulations 2012; or

(b)   a provision contained in an authority's scheme under section 13A(2) of the Act by virtue of paragraph 14(1)(c) of Schedule 8 to the Council Tax Reduction Schemes (Prescribed Requirements) (England) Regulations 2012

paragraph (2)(b) shall not apply in relation to that amount.

(3)   The assumptions are—

(a)   that the person will be liable to pay the council tax to which the notice relates on every day after the issue of the notice;

(b)   that, as regards the dwelling concerned, the relevant valuation band on the day the notice is issued will remain the relevant valuation band for the dwelling as regards every day after the issue of the notice;

(c)   if on the day the notice is issued the person satisfies conditions prescribed for the purposes of regulations under section 13 of the Act (and consequently the chargeable amount in his case is less than it would otherwise be), that he will continue to satisfy those conditions as regards every day after the issue of the notice;

(d)   if, by virtue of regulation 9(1), the dwelling to which the notice relates is assumed to be a chargeable dwelling on the day the notice is issued, that it will continue to be a chargeable dwelling as regards every day after the issue of the notice;

(e)   if, by virtue of regulation 15(1), the chargeable amount is assumed not to be subject to a discount on the day the notice is issued, that it will not be subject to a discount as regards any day after the issue of the notice;

(f)   if, by virtue of regulation 15(2), the chargeable amount is assumed to be subject to a discount on the day the notice is issued, that it will continue to be subject to the same rate of discount as regards every day after the issue of the notice;

(fa)   if, by virtue of regulation 15(3) it is assumed that the chargeable amount is not subject to a discount, that it will not be subject to a discount as regards any day after the issue of the notice; and

(g)   if on the day the notice is issued a determination as to council tax benefit to which the person is entitled is in effect, and by virtue of regulations under section 138(1) of the Social Security Administration Act 1992 the benefit allowed as regards that day takes the form of a reduction in the amount the person is liable to pay in respect of council tax for the relevant year, that as regards every day after that day he will be allowed the same reduction in that amount.

(4)   If the demand notice is issued during the relevant year and the liable person is not liable to pay an amount by way of council tax in respect of the day on which the notice is issued, the demand notice shall require payment of—

(a)   the chargeable amount for the period in the year up to the last day in respect of which he was so liable; or

(b)   where an amount falls to be credited by the billing authority against that chargeable amount, an amount equal to the amount (if any) by which that chargeable amount exceeds the amount falling to be so credited.

(5)   If the demand notice is issued after the end of the relevant year, it shall require payment of—

(a)   the chargeable amount; or

(b)   where an amount falls to be credited by the billing authority against the chargeable amount, an amount equal to the amount (if any) by which the chargeable amount exceeds the amount falling to be so credited.

7.7949   21.   *Council tax: payments*   (1)   Unless—

(a)   an agreement under paragraph (5) in relation to the relevant year has been reached between the billing authority and the liable person before the demand notice is issued, or

(b)   the authority has resolved that a Part II scheme shall have effect for the relevant year as regards dwellings of a class which includes the dwelling in respect of which the chargeable amount falls to be paid,

a notice to which paragraph (1) of regulation 20 applies shall require the amount mentioned in paragraph (2) of that regulation to be paid by instalments in accordance with Part I of Schedule 1 hereto.

(1A) Where a liable person requests by notice in writing to the billing authority to pay the amount mentioned in regulation 20(2) by 12 monthly instalments paragraphs (1B), (1C) and (1D) apply.

(1B) Such a request may be made either before or after the demand notice is issued and may be made in relation to the relevant year or the year following the relevant year.

(1C) Where the request relates to the relevant year, a notice to which paragraph (1) of regulation 20 applies shall be issued as soon as reasonably practicable after the date on which the notice in paragraph (1A)is received by the billing authority and shall require the amount mentioned in paragraph (2) of regulation 20 to be paid by instalments in accordance with paragraph 2(3A) of Schedule 1 to these Regulations.

(1D) Where the request relates to the year following the relevant year, as soon as reasonably practicable after the date on which the notice is received by the billing authority, the billing authority shall write to confirm that from such date as is requested in the notice in paragraph (1A) the amount mentioned in paragraph (2) of regulation 20 for that year shall be paid by instalments in accordance with paragraph 2(3A) of Schedule 1 to these Regulations.

(2) Where a billing authority has resolved as mentioned in paragraph (1)(*b*), a notice to which paragraph (1) of regulation 20 applies shall require the amount mentioned in paragraph (2) of that regulation to be paid by instalments in accordance with the provisions of the authority's Part II scheme.

(3) Where instalments are required to be paid in accordance with a Part II scheme or under Part I of Schedule 1, Part III of that Schedule applies for their cessation or adjustment in the circumstances described in that Part (subject, in the case of payments in accordance with a Part II scheme, to provision included in the scheme pursuant to paragraph 8(6) of Part II of that Schedule).

(4) If an agreement under paragraph (5) in relation to the relevant year has been reached between the billing authority and the liable person before the demand notice is issued, a notice to which paragraph (1) of regulation 20 applies shall require the amount mentioned in paragraph (2) of that regulation to be paid in accordance with that agreement.

(5) A billing authority and a liable person may agree that the amount mentioned in regulation 20(2) which is required to be paid under a notice to which regulation 20(1) applies shall be paid in such manner as is provided by the agreement.

(6) Notwithstanding the foregoing provisions of this regulation, such an agreement may be entered into either before or after the demand notice concerned is issued, and may make provision for the cessation or adjustment of payments, and for the making of fresh estimates, in the event of the estimate mentioned in regulation 20(2) turning out to be wrong; and if it is entered into after the demand notice has been issued, it may make provision dealing with the treatment for the purposes of the agreement of any sums paid in accordance with Part I of Schedule 1 or a Part II scheme before it was entered into.

(7) A notice to which regulation 20(4) or (5) applies shall (as the billing authority determines) require payment of the amount concerned—

(*a*)   on the expiry of such period (being not less than 14 days) after the day of issue of the notice as is specified in it; or

(*b*)   by instalments of such amounts as are specified in the notice, payable at such intervals and on such day in each interval as is so specified.

7.7950   *21A. Referendums relating to council tax increases: excessive amount not approved*

7.7951   *22. Notices: further provision* No payment on account of the chargeable amount (whether interim, final or sole) need be made unless a notice served under this Part requires it.

7.7952   *23. Failure to pay instalments* (1) Subject to paragraph (2), where—

(*a*)   a demand notice has been served by a billing authority on a liable person,

(*b*)   instalments in respect of the council tax to which the notice relates are payable in accordance with Part I of Schedule 1 or, as the case may be, a Part II scheme or a determination under regulation 21(7), and

(*c*)   any such instalment is not paid in accordance with that Schedule or, as the case may be, the relevant scheme or determination

the billing authority shall serve a notice ("reminder notice") on the liable person stating—

(i)   the amount which is the aggregate of the instalments which are due under the demand notice or any subsequent notice given under paragraph 10 of Schedule 1 and which are unpaid and the instalments that will become due within the period of seven days beginning with the day on which the reminder notice is issued;

(ii)   that the amount mentioned in sub-paragraph (i) above is required to be paid by him within the period mentioned in that sub-paragraph;

(iii)   the effect of paragraph (3) below and the amount that will become payable by him in the circumstances mentioned in that paragraph; and

(iv)   where the notice is the second such notice as regards the relevant year, the effect of paragraph (4) below.

(2) Nothing in paragraph (1) shall require the service of a reminder notice—

(*a*)   where all the instalments have fallen due; or

(*b*)   in the circumstances mentioned in paragraphs (3) and (4).

(3) If, within the period of 7 days beginning with the day on which a reminder notice is issued, the liable person fails to pay any instalments which are or will become due before the expiry of that period, the unpaid balance of the estimated amount (or, as the case may be, the chargeable amount) shall become payable by him at the expiry of a further period of 7 days beginning with the

day of the failure.

(4) If, after making a payment in accordance with a reminder notice which is the second such notice as regards the relevant year, the liable person fails to pay any subsequent instalment as regards that year on or before the day on which it falls due, the unpaid balance of the estimated amount (or, as the case may be, the chargeable amount) shall become payable by him on the day following the day of the failure.

7.7953   24.   *Payments: adjustments*

7.7954   25.   *Lump sum payments*

7.7955   26.   *Non-cash payments*

7.7956   27.   *Joint taxpayers*   (1)   This regulation applies in the case of joint taxpayers; but its application to joint taxpayers on whom a joint taxpayers' notice is served is subject to regulation 28A.

(2)   In a case to which this regulation applies—

(*a*)   regulation 18 (the requirement for demand notices) has effect as if in paragraph (1) for the words "every liable person" there were substituted the words "at least one of the joint taxpayers";

(*b*)   regulation 20 (demand notices; payments required) has effect as if—

(i)   the assumption referred to in sub-paragraph (*c*) of paragraph (3) is made as regards such of the joint taxpayers as on the day of issue of the demand notice satisfy the conditions referred to in that sub-paragraph;

(ii)   the assumption referred to in sub-paragraph (*g*) of paragraph (3) is made as regards such of the joint taxpayers in respect of whom on the day of issue of the demand notice a determination has effect as mentioned in that sub-paragraph;

(*c*)   regulation 21 (council tax: payments) has effect as if—

(i)   in paragraphs (1) and (4), for the words "the liable person" there were substituted the words "one or more of the joint taxpayers";

(ii)   in paragraph (3), for the words after "that Part" there were substituted the following—

"subject—

(*a*)   in the case of payments in accordance with a Part II scheme, to provision included in the scheme pursuant to paragraph 8(6) of Part II of that Schedule; and

(*b*)   in the case of joint taxpayers, to regulations 28 and 28A.";

(iii)   in paragraph (5), for the words "a liable person" there were substituted the words "one or more of the joint taxpayers"; and

(iv)   in paragraph (5), there were inserted at the end the words ": but, subject to regulation 28A(1), a billing authority may not enter into an agreement after the issue of the demand notice concerned with a joint taxpayer on whom that notice was not served";

(*d*)   regulation 23 (failure to pay instalments) has effect as if references to the liable person and to an amount becoming payable by the liable person were references to such of the joint taxpayers as have been served with a demand notice and to an amount becoming payable by them, respectively;

(*e*)   regulation 29 (collection of penalties) has effect as if—

(i)   for paragraph (1), there were substituted the following—

"(1)   Subject to paragraphs (2) and (3), where a penalty is payable to a billing authority under any of sub-paragraphs (1) to (3) of paragraph 1 of Schedule 3 to the Act or under any of regulations 11 to 13 of the Detection of Fraud Regulations by a person who is one of joint taxpayers, it may be collected by the service by the authority on the person of a notice requiring payment of the penalty on the expiry of such period (being not less than 14 days) after the issue of the notice as is specified in it."; and

(ii)   paragraph (4) were omitted; and

(*f*)   paragraph 9 (cessation of instalments) of Schedule 1 does not apply unless—

(i)   every person on whom the demand notice was served has ceased to be a joint taxpayer;

(ii)   none of those persons is, as regards any part of the period to which the demand notice relates, solely liable to pay an amount in respect of council tax as regards the dwelling concerned; and

(iii)   no other person who, as regards any part of that period, was jointly and severally liable with any of those persons as regards the dwelling concerned, is a liable person (whether his liability is sole or joint and several) as regards the dwelling concerned.

7.7957   28.   *Joint taxpayers' notice*   (1)   An amount shall not be payable by a person who is one of joint taxpayers and on whom a demand notice has not been served unless a notice ("joint taxpayers' notice") is served on him in accordance with the following provisions of this regulation.

(2)   A joint taxpayers' notice may not be served on a person after the expiry of the period of six years beginning with the first day of the financial year to which the notice relates.

(3)   Where—

(*a*)   a joint taxpayers' notice is served during the relevant year; and

(*b*)   the person on whom (as one of the joint taxpayers) a demand notice for that year was served (or, if more than one person was so served, each of them) is not on the day of issue of the notice one of the joint taxpayers; and

(c)   the unpaid balance of the estimated amount has not become due as mentioned in
         paragraph (3) or (4) of regulation 23,
the notice shall require the payment of the adjusted amount.
(4)   For the purposes of paragraph (3)—
      "the adjusted amount" means an amount equal to the lesser of—
      (a)   the billing authority's estimate of the chargeable amount made as respects the period to
            which the joint taxpayers' notice relates; and regulation 20(3) shall have effect for these
            purposes as it has effect in a case to which regulation 27 applies and as if references in
            regulation 27(2)(b) to the demand notice were references to the joint taxpayers' notice;
            and
      (b)   the relevant sum; and
      "the relevant sum" means an amount equal to the difference between—
      (a)   the amount estimated or last estimated as regards the dwelling concerned—
            (i)   for the purposes of an agreement under regulation 21(5); or
            (ii)   under regulation 20(2) for the purposes of the demand notice or any subsequent
                   notice given under paragraph 10 of Schedule 1; and
      (b)   the aggregate of the amounts paid to the authority under any such agreement or notice
            before the issue of the joint taxpayers' notice.
(5)   Subject to regulation 28A(1), the amount required to be paid under paragraph (3) shall be
payable by instalments of such amounts, and at such intervals and on such days in each interval, as
are specified in the notice; provided that the number of instalments shall not be less than the
number of instalments payable under the agreement, the demand notice or any subsequent notice
given under paragraph 10 of Schedule 1, as the case may be, as regards the period beginning on
the day on which the joint taxpayers' notice is served and ending on the last day of the relevant
year.
(6)   A joint taxpayers' notice which is issued after the end of the relevant year, or after the unpaid
balance of the estimated amount has become due as mentioned in paragraph (3) or (4) of
regulation 23, shall (as the billing authority determines) require payment of the amount
concerned—
(a)   on the expiry of such period (being not less than 14 days) after the issue of the notice as is
         specified in it; or
(b)   by instalments of such amounts as are specified in the notice, payable at such intervals
         and on such day in each interval as is so specified.

7.7958   28A.   *Joint taxpayers' notice: further provision*   (1)   A billing authority and a person on
whom a joint taxpayers' notice is served may agree that the amount required to be paid under the
notice shall be paid in such manner as is provided by the agreement; and paragraph (6) of
regulation 21 shall apply with the necessary modifications in relation to an agreement under this
paragraph as it applies to an agreement under paragraph (5) of that regulation.
(2)   Regulation 23 (failure to pay instalments) shall apply with the necessary modifications in
relation to instalments payable in accordance with a joint taxpayers' notice as it applies to
instalments payable in accordance with Part I of Schedule 1 or a Part II scheme.
(3)   If the amount required to be paid under a joint taxpayers' notice is shown to be incorrect, the
billing authority shall serve a further notice on every person on whom the joint taxpayers' notice
was served stating the revised sum required to be paid.
(4)   If the amount stated in the further notice served under paragraph (3) is greater than the
amount required to be paid under the joint taxpayers' notice, the further notice shall also state the
revised amount of each remaining instalment or, as the case may be, the period (being not less
than 14 days) after the issue of that further notice within which the further sum payable is required
to be paid.
(5)   If the amount stated in the further notice under paragraph (3) is less than the amount required
to be paid under the joint taxpayers' notice, any overpayment—
(a)   shall be repaid if the person on whom the joint taxpayers' notice was served so requires,
         or
(b)   in any other case shall (as the billing authority determines) either be repaid or be credited
         against any subsequent liability of that person to make a payment in respect of council tax
         to the authority.

7.7959   29.   *Collection of penalties*   [Not reproduced]

7.7960   30.   *Appeals in relation to estimates*   Section 16(1) of the Act shall not apply where the
ground on which the person concerned is aggrieved is that any assumption as to the future that is
required by this Part to be made in the calculation of an amount may prove to be inaccurate.

7.7961   31.   *Demand notices: final adjustment*   (1)   This regulation applies where—
(a)   a notice has been issued by a billing authority under this Part requiring a payment or
         payments to be made by a person in respect of his liability to pay council tax for a
         financial year or part of a financial year,
(b)   the payment or payments required to be made are found to be in excess of or less than his
         liability for the year or the part, and
(c)   provision for adjusting the amounts required under the notice and (as appropriate) for the
         making of additional payments or the repaying or crediting of any amount overpaid is not
         made by any other provision of this Part, of the Act or of any agreement entered into
         under regulation 21(5).
(2)   The billing authority shall as soon as practicable after the expiry of the year or the part of a

year serve a further notice on the person stating the amount of his liability for the year or the part, and adjusting (by reference to that amount) the amounts required to be paid under the notice referred to in paragraph (1)(*a*).

(3) If the amount stated in the further notice is greater than the amount required to be paid under the notice referred to in paragraph (1)(*a*), the amount of the difference for which such other provision as is mentioned in paragraph (1)(*c*) is not made shall be due from the person to the billing authority on the expiry of such period (being not less than 14 days) after the day of issue of the notice as is specified in it.

(4) If there has been an overpayment, the amount overpaid for which such other provision as is mentioned in paragraph (1)(*c*) is not made—

(*a*)   shall be repaid if the person so requires, or

(*b*)   in any other case shall (as the billing authority determines) either be repaid or be credited against any subsequent liability of the person to make a payment in respect of any council tax of the authority.

PART VI

Enforcement

7.7962   *32.   Interpretation and application of Part VI*   (1)   In this Part—

"attachment of allowances order" means an order under regulation 44;

"attachment of earnings order" means an order under regulation 37;

"authorised person" means any person authorised by a billing authority to exercise any functions relating to the administration and enforcement of the council tax[1];

"charging order" means an order under regulation 50;

"debtor" means a person against whom a liability order has been made;

"earnings[2]" means sums payable to a person—

(*a*)   by way of wages or salary (including any fees, bonus, commission, overtime pay or other emoluments payable in addition to wages or salary or payable under a contract of service); or

(*b*)   by way of statutory sick pay,

but, in so far as the following would otherwise be treated as earnings, they shall not be treated as such:

(i)   sums payable by any public department of the Government of Northern Ireland or of a territory outside the United Kingdom;

(ii)   pay or allowances payable to the debtor as a member of Her Majesty's forces other than pay or allowances payable by his employer to him as a special member of a reserve force (within the meaning of the Reserve Forces Act 1996);

(iii)   allowances or benefit payable under the Social Security Acts;

(iiia) tax credits within the meaning of the Tax Credits Act 2002;

(iiib) universal credit;

(iv)   allowances payable in respect of disablement or disability; and

(v)   wages payable to a person as a seaman, other than wages payable to him as a seaman of a fishing boat;

(vi)   tax credits within the meaning of the Tax Credits Act 2002.

"the Income Support Regulations" means the Council Tax (Deductions from Income Support) Regulations 1993;

"liability order" means an order under regulation 34 or regulation 36A(5);

"net earnings" in relation to an employment means the residue of earnings payable under the employment after deduction by the employer of—

(*a*)   income tax;

(*b*)   primary Class 1 contributions under Part I of the Social Security Contributions and Benefits Act 1992; and

(*c*)   amounts deductible under any enactment, or in pursuance of a request in writing by the debtor, for the purposes of a superannuation scheme, namely any enactment, rules, deed or other instrument providing for the payment of annuities or lump sum—

(i)   to the persons with respect to whom the instrument has effect on their retirement at a specified age or on becoming incapacitated at some earlier age, or

(ii)   to the personal representatives or the widows, widowers, surviving civil partners, relatives or dependants of such persons on their death or otherwise, whether with or without any further or other benefits; and where an order under regulation 32 (making of attachment of earnings order) of the Community Charges (Administration and Enforcement) Regulations 1989 made before the making of the attachment of earnings order concerned remains in force,

(*d*)   any amount required to be deducted in accordance with that order; and

"Schedule 12" means Schedule 12 to the Tribunals, Courts and Enforcement Act 2007, and "the Schedule 12 procedure" means the procedure in that Schedule (taking control of goods and selling them to recover a sum of money).

(2)   In sub-paragraph (v) of the definition of "earnings" in paragraph (1) above expressions used in the Merchant Shipping Act 1894 have the same meanings as in that Act.

(3)   Regulations 33 to 53 apply for the recovery of a sum which has become payable to a billing authority under Part V and which has not been paid; but their application in relation to a sum for which persons are jointly and severally liable under that Part is subject to the provisions of

regulation 54 (joint and several liability).

(4) References in this Part to a sum which has become payable and which has not been paid include references to a sum forming part of a larger sum which has become payable and the other part of which has been paid.

(5) Any reference in this Part to the day on or time at which a notice is issued, is a reference—

(a)   if the notice is served in the manner described in section 233(2) of the Local Government Act 1972 by being left at, or sent by post to, a person's proper address, to the day on or time at which it is so left or posted, or

(b)   in any other case, to the day on or time at which the notice is served.

---

[1] A billing authority may authorise another person, or that person's employees, to exercise functions relating to the administration and enforcement of the council tax: see the Local Authorities (Contracting Out of Tax Billing, Collection and Enforcement Functions) Order 1996, SI 1996/1880.

[2] There is a significant contrast between the definition of "earnings" in s 24 of the Attachment of Earnings Act 1971 and the definition in reg 32(1). The latter does not refer to a "pension", and this omission must be taken to be deliberate. Therefore, a local authority is not required to consider proceedings under the 1971 Act as an alternative method of recovering unpaid council tax from a person in receipt of a police pension; nor is a liability order a 'judgment debt' within the meaning of s 2(c) of the 1971 Act: *Powys CC v Hurst* [2018] EWHC 1684 (Admin), [2018] PTSR 1940.

7.7963   *33. Liability orders: preliminary steps*   (1) Subject to paragraph (3), before a billing authority applies for a liability order it shall serve on the person against whom the application is to be made a notice ("final notice"), and which is to state every amount in respect of which the authority is to make the application.

(2) A final notice may be served in respect of an amount at any time after it has become due.

(3) Nothing in paragraph (1) shall require the service of a final notice in the circumstances mentioned in paragraph (3) of regulation 23 (including that paragraph as applied as mentioned in regulation 28A(2)).

7.7964   *34. Application for liability order*   (1) If an amount which has fallen due under paragraph (3) or (4) of regulation 23 (including those paragraphs as applied as mentioned in regulation 28A(2)) is wholly or partly unpaid, or (in a case where a final notice is required under regulation 33) the amount stated in the final notice is wholly or partly unpaid at the expiry of the period of 7 days beginning with the day on which the notice was issued, the billing authority may, in accordance with paragraph (2), apply to a magistrates' court for an order against the person by whom it is payable.

(2) The application is to be instituted by making complaint to a justice of the peace, and requesting the issue of a summons[1] directed to that person to appear before the court to show why he has not paid the sum which is outstanding[1].

(3) Section 127(1) of the Magistrates' Courts Act 1980 does not apply to such an application; but no application may be instituted in respect of a sum after the period of six years beginning with the day on which it became due[2] under Part V.

(4) A warrant shall not be issued under section 55(2) of the Magistrates' Courts Act 1980 in any proceedings under this regulation.

(5) If, after a summons has been issued in accordance with paragraph (2) but before the application is heard, there is paid or tendered to the authority an amount equal to the aggregate of—

(a)   the sum specified in the summons as the sum outstanding or so much of it as remains outstanding (as the case may be); and

(b)   a sum of an amount equal to the costs reasonably incurred by the authority in connection with the application up to the time of the payment or tender,

the authority shall accept the amount and the application shall not be proceeded with.

(6) The court shall[3] make the order[4] if it is satisfied that the sum has become payable by the defendant and has not been paid.

(7) An order made pursuant to paragraph (6) shall be made in respect of an amount equal to the aggregate of—

(a)   the sum payable, and

(b)   a sum of an amount equal to the costs reasonably incurred by the applicant in obtaining the order[4] <u>(which costs, including those of instituting the application under paragraph (2), are not to exceed the prescribed amount of £70)</u>[*].

(8) Where the sum payable is paid after a liability order has been applied for under paragraph (2) but before it is made, the court shall nonetheless (if so requested by the billing authority) make the order in respect of a sum of an amount equal to the costs reasonably incurred by the authority in making the application <u>(which costs, including those of instituting the application under paragraph (2), are not to exceed the prescribed amount of £70)</u>[*].

---

[*] **Words underlined in paras (7), (8) inserted in relation to Wales only by SI 2011/528.**

[1] Under Rule 99(3) of the Magistrates' Courts Rules 1981, summonses under these regulations can be served in accordance with Rule 99 of those rules.

[2] A procedure by which a legal adviser, designated to issue summonses, issued 248 summonses by deciding to issue them, and transmitted that decision to the council, followed by their digital signature being affixed to the summonses by the council was a proper and sensible procedure *R (on the application of Banfield) v Harrow Magistrates Court* [2012] EWHC 3801 (Admin).

[3] Liability to pay council tax arises when the demand is served and not when the amount of tax was set by the billing authority (*Regentford v Thanet District Council* [2004] TLR 143 (whether procedural or substantial prejudice precluded a claim did not arise on the facts where the payer had allowed the proceedings to go by default, see also *Encon Insulation Ltd v Nottingham City Council* [1999] RA 382)).

Schedule 2 of the regulations originally prescribed a form for a liability order, however the schedule was revoked in Wales by SI 2003/1715 and in England by SI 2003/2211. The magistrates' court register is now the definitive record of the order.

[4] Regulation 34(7) means that the court must be satisfied:

   (i)   that the local authority has actually incurred those costs;

   (ii) that the costs in question were incurred in obtaining the liability order; and

   (iii) that it was reasonable for the local authority to incur them.

Once the court is satisfied that the costs have been reasonably incurred, it has no discretion, but must award costs in that amount, and that the ability of a particular respondent to pay those costs is not a relevant consideration.

The provisions in reg 34(7) were considered in *R (on the application of Reverend Nicolson) v Tottenham Magistrates* [2015] EWHC 1252 (Admin), [2015] PTSR 1045, 179 JP 421 and the findings and observations of Andrews J are summarised in what follows.

For the court to be satisfied that the costs were reasonably incurred it is insufficient for the court to rely on general and vague assertions with no supporting particulars. The focus must be not on whether the costs claimed was a reasonable amount but whether those costs were reasonably incurred in obtaining the liability order. There must be a sufficient link between the costs in question and the process of obtaining the liability order. It will be impermissible to include in the costs claimed any element referable to the costs of executing the order after it was obtained, or to the overall administration of council tax in the area concerned.

Costs incurred in obtaining the order encompass costs incurred in connexion with the application for a summons and encompass, but are not confined to, the fee for issuing the summons. In principle the intention in the Regulations is to enable the local authority to recover the actual cost to it of utilising the enforcement process under reg 34, which will include some administrative costs, as well as any legal fees and out of pocket expenses. The Regulations should be construed in such a way as to ensure that the costs recovered are only those which are genuinely attributable to the enforcement process.

Costs do not necessarily have to be incurred on or after the date on which the summons was issued. Once the decision to enforce has been taken there may still need to be checks carried out to ensure that the summons is issued in the correct amount and against the right person. But the costs of taking the decision to exercise the discretion to enforce would appear to fall on the wrong side of the line.

Given the large number of summonses issued, it will not be practical for the local authority to carry out and provide a detailed calculation of the actual costs incurred in each and every case (save possibly where the actual costs are well in excess of the norm, for example if the local authority has to instruct counsel to turn up and argue specific points of law raised by the taxpayer in defence). In principle, therefore, provided that the right types of costs and expenses are taken into account, and provided that due consideration is given to the dangers of double-counting, or of artificial inflation of costs, it may be a legitimate approach for a local authority to calculate and aggregate the relevant costs it has incurred in the previous year, and divide that up by the previous (or anticipated) number of summonses over 12 months so as to provide an average figure which could be levied across the board in "standard" cases, but could be amplified in circumstances where there was justification for incurring additional legal and/or administrative costs. If that approach is adopted, however, it is essential that the magistrates and their clerk are equipped with sufficient readily available information to enable the magistrates to check for themselves without too much difficulty, and relatively swiftly, that a legitimate approach has been taken, and to furnish a respondent with that information on request.

If the necessary causal link is established to the satisfaction of the court then the next question is whether the costs claimed have been "reasonably" incurred. It may be that the method by which the costs are calculated demonstrates this without the need for further evidence; but there may be individual cases in which it will be open to the respondent to argue that the costs were not reasonably incurred, for example, if it is not reasonable for the local authority to take steps to enforce payment, or if the costs which were incurred are excessive – eg if the local authority sends a QC along to argue a simple point of law in the magistrates' court.

Establishing that the costs are reasonably incurred is not the same thing as establishing that the costs are reasonable in amount. The latter may have a bearing on the former, since if the costs appear to be excessive, or disproportionate, there may be legitimate grounds for querying whether it was reasonable of the local authority to incur costs in that amount. So far as proportionality is concerned, in the context where the recoverable sums are relatively small it is inherently likely that there will be a disparity between those sums and the costs of recovering them. On the other hand, the practice of processing applications in bulk could drive the average costs of obtaining liability orders down rather than up.

There is nothing to prevent a summons from stating on its face the amount of costs claimed by the local authority in connection with the complaint: *Williams v East Northamptonshire DC* [2016] EWHC 470 (Admin), [2016] RA 191. However, in *Ewing v Highbury Corner Magistrates' Court* [2015] EWHC 3788 (Admin), [2016] RVR 174 an order for costs was quashed. The court had not had sufficient relevant information to reach a proper determination of whether the costs claimed represented costs reasonably incurred by the local authority in obtaining the liability order.

7.7965 **35.** *Liability orders: further provision* (1) A single liability order may deal with one person and one such amount (or aggregate amount) as is mentioned in regulation 34(7) and (8), or, if the court thinks fit, may deal with more than one person and more than one such amount.

(2) A summons issued under regulation 34(2) may be served on a person—

  (a)   by delivering it to him, or

  (b)   by leaving it at his usual or last known place of abode, or in the case of a company, at its registered office, or

  (c)   by sending it by post to him at his usual or last known place of abode, or in the case of a company, to its registered office, or

  (d)   by leaving it at, or by sending it by post to him at, an address given by the person as an address at which service of the summons will be accepted.

(2A) No liability order shall be made in pursuance of a summons issued under regulation 34(2) unless 14 days have elapsed since the day on which the summons was served.

(3) The amount in respect of which a liability order[1] is made is enforceable in accordance with this Part; and accordingly for the purposes of any of the provisions of Part III of the Magistrates' Courts Act 1980 (satisfaction and enforcement) it is not to be treated as a sum adjudged to be paid by order of the court.

---

[1] In addition to the remedies available under this Part, where a liability order has been made and the debtor is entitled to income support the billing authority concerned may apply to the Secretary of State asking him to deduct sums from any amounts payable to the debtor by way of income support in order to secure the payment of any outstanding sum which is or forms part of the amount in respect of which the liability order was made (Council Tax (Deductions from Income Support) Regulations 1993, SI 1993/494, reg 2).

7.7966 **36.** *Duties of debtors subject to liability order* (1) Where a liability order has been made, the debtor against whom it was made shall, during such time as the amount in respect of which the order was made remains wholly or partly unpaid, be under a duty to supply relevant information to the billing authority on whose application it was made.

(2) For the purposes of paragraph (1), relevant information is such information as fulfils the following conditions—

  (a)   it is in the debtor's possession or control;

  (b)   the billing authority requests him by notice given in writing to supply it; and

(c)   it falls within paragraph (3).

(3)   Information falls within this paragraph if it is specified in the notice mentioned in paragraph (2)(b) and it falls within one or more of the following descriptions—

(a)   information as to the name and address of an employer of the debtor;

(b)   information as to earnings or expected earnings of the debtor;

(c)   information as to deductions and expected deductions from such earnings in respect of the matters referred to in paragraphs (a) to (c) of the definition of "net earnings" in regulation 32 or attachment of earnings orders made under this Part, regulation 32 of the Community Charges (Administration and Enforcement) Regulations 1989, the Attachment of Earnings Act 1971 or the Child Support Act 1991;

(d)   information as to the debtor's work or identity number in an employment, or such other information as will enable an employer of the debtor to identify him;

(e)   information as to sources of income of the debtor other than an employer of his;

(f)   information as to whether another person is jointly and severally liable with the debtor for the whole or any part of the amount in respect of which the order was made.

(4)   Information is to be supplied within 14 days of the day on which the request is made.

7.7967   36A.   *Quashing of liability orders*[1]   (1)   Where—

(a)   a magistrates' court has made a liability order pursuant to regulation 34(6), and

(b)   the authority on whose application the liability order was made considers that the order should not have been made,

the authority may apply to a magistrates' court to have the liability order quashed.

(2)   Where, on an application by an authority in accordance with paragraph (1) above, the magistrates' court is satisfied that the liability order should not have been made, it shall quash the order.

(3)   Where an authority makes an application under paragraph (1) for a liability order ("the original order") to be quashed, and a lesser amount than the amount for which the original order was made has fallen due under paragraph (3) or (4) of regulation 23 (including those paragraphs as applied as mentioned in regulation 28A(2)) and is wholly or partly unpaid or (in a case where a final notice is required under regulation 33) the amount stated in the final notice is wholly or partly unpaid at the expiry of the period of seven days beginning with the day on which the notice was issued, the billing authority may also apply to the magistrates' court for an order against the person by whom the lesser amount was payable.

(4)   Paragraphs (2) to (5) of regulation 34 shall apply to applications under paragraph (3) above.

(5)   Where, having quashed a liability order in accordance with paragraph (2) above, the magistrates' court is satisfied that, had the original application for the liability order been for a liability order in respect of a lesser sum payable, such an order could properly have been made, it shall make a liability order in respect of the aggregate of—

(a)   that lesser sum payable, and

(b)   any sum included in the quashed order in respect of the costs reasonably incurred by the authority in obtaining the quashed order.

---

[1]   Apart from this provision, there is a general common law provision to set aside an order made by a magistrates' court in its civil jurisdiction, including a liability order if the following grounds are satisfied: there must be a genuine and arguable dispute as to the defendant's liability to the order in question; the order must be made as a result of a substantial procedural error, defect or mishap; and the application to the justices for the order to be set aside is made promptly after a defendant learns that it has been made or has notice that an order may have been made (R (*London Borough of Newham*) v *Stratford Magistrates' Court* [2008] EWHC 125 (Admin), 173 JP 30) Magistrates have to consider not only whether the dispute is genuine but also whether it is arguable. It is also necessary for magistrates to identify specifically the procedural error referred to. If, for example, the magistrates find that defendant had not been served with any summons and did not know about the liability proceedings at the relevant time, they must make an express finding to that effect, explaining briefly upon what material they have relied to reach the finding. Failure to do so constitutes a substantial defect in the reasoning in support of their decision per Kenneth Parker J in *London Borough of Tower Hamlets* v *Rahman* [2012] EWHC 3428 (Admin), 177 JP 192. Justices may reopen their decision to make a liability order made in ignorance of the receipt of an application to adjourn so that they may exercise their judicial discretion whether to grant the order or adjourn (*Liverpool City Council* v *Pleroma Distribution Ltd* [2003] 04 LS Gaz R 33.

7.7968   37.   *Making of attachment of earnings order*   (1)   Where a liability order has been made and the debtor against whom it was made is an individual, the authority which applied for the order may, subject to paragraph (4), make an order under this regulation to secure the payment of the appropriate amount.

(1A)   For the purposes of this regulation the appropriate amount is the aggregate of—

(a)   any outstanding sum which is or forms part of the amount in respect of which the liability order was made.

(b)   revoked.

(2)   An order under this regulation—

(a)   shall be in the form specified in (and accordingly contain the matters specified in) Schedule 3; and

(b)   shall remain in force until discharged under regulation 41(2) or the whole amount to which it relates has been paid (whether by attachment of earnings or otherwise).

(3)   The authority may serve a copy of the order on a person who appears to the authority to have the debtor in his employment; and a person on whom it is so served who has the debtor in his employment shall comply with it.

(4)   No order may be made under this regulation by an authority if the effect would be that the number of orders for the time being in force made by that authority in relation to the debtor in question exceeded two.

7.7969   *38.*   *Deductions under attachment of earnings order* (1) Subject to paragraphs (2) and (3), the sum to be deducted by an employer under an attachment of earnings order on any pay-day shall be—

(a)   where the debtor's earnings from the employer are payable weekly, a sum equal to the appropriate percentage of the net earnings otherwise payable on that pay-day; and for this purpose the appropriate percentage is the percentage (or percentages) specified in column 2 of Table A in Schedule 4 in relation to the band in column 1 of that Table within which the net earnings fall;

(b)   where his earnings from the employer are payable monthly, a sum equal to the appropriate percentage of the net earnings otherwise payable on that pay-day; and for this purpose the appropriate percentage is the percentage (or percentages) specified in column 2 of Table B in that Schedule 4 in relation to the band in column 1 of Table within which the net earnings fall;

(c)   where his earnings from the employer are payable at regular intervals of a whole number of weeks or months, the sum arrived at by—

      (i)   calculating what would be his weekly or monthly net earnings by dividing the net earnings payable to him by the employer on the pay-day by that whole number (of weeks or months, as the case may be),

      (ii)   ascertaining the percentage (or percentages) specified in column 2 of Table A (if the whole number is of weeks) or of Table B (if the whole number is of months) in Schedule 4 opposite the band in column 1 of that Table within which the notional net earnings calculated under paragraph (i) fall, and

      (iii)   calculating the sum which equals the appropriate percentage (or percentages) of the notional net earnings for any of those weeks or months and multiplying that sum by the whole number of weeks or months, as appropriate.

(2)   Where paragraph (1) applies and the amount to be paid to the debtor on any pay-day includes an advance in respect of future pay, the sum to be deducted on that pay-day shall be the aggregate of the amount which would otherwise fall to be deducted under paragraph (1) and—

(a)   where the amount advanced would otherwise have been paid on a single pay-day, the sum which would have been deducted on that pay-day in accordance with paragraph (1) if the amount advanced had been the amount of net earnings on that day; or

(b)   where the amount advanced would otherwise have been paid on more than one pay-day, the sums which would have been deducted on each of the relevant pay-days in accordance with paragraph (1) if—

      (i)   an equal proportion of the amount advanced had been paid on each of those days; and

      (ii)   the net earnings of the debtor on each of those days had been an amount equal to that proportion.

(3)   Where the amount payable to the debtor on any pay-day is reduced by reason of an earlier advance of pay, the net earnings of the debtor on that day shall, for the purposes of paragraph (1), be the amount defined in regulation 32(1) less the amount of the deduction.

(4)   Subject to paragraphs (5) and (6), where the debtor's earnings from the employer are payable at regular intervals other than at intervals to which paragraph (1) applies, the sum to be deducted on any pay-day shall be arrived at by—

(a)   calculating what would be his daily net earnings by dividing the net earnings payable to him by the employer on the pay-day by the number of days in the interval,

(b)   ascertaining the percentage (or percentages) specified in column 2 of Table C in Schedule 4 opposite the band in column 1 of that Table within which the notional net earnings calculated under sub-paragraph (a) fall, and

(c)   calculating the sum which equals the appropriate percentage (or percentages) of the notional daily net earnings and multiplying that sum by the number of days in the interval.

(5)   Where the debtor's earnings are payable as mentioned in paragraph (4), and the amount to be paid to the debtor on any pay-day includes an amount advanced in respect of future pay, the amount of the debtor's notional net earnings under sub-paragraph (a) of that paragraph shall be calculated in accordance with the formula—

$$\frac{A+B}{C+D}$$

where—

    A is the amount of net earnings payable to him on that pay-day (exclusive of the amount advanced);

    B is the amount advanced;

    C is the number of days in the period for which the amount of net earnings is payable; and

    D is the number of days in the period for which, but for the agreement to pay in advance, the amount advanced would have been payable.

(6)   Paragraph (3) applies in relation to paragraph (4) as it applies in relation to paragraph (1).

(7)   Where earnings are payable to a debtor by the employer by 2 or more series of payments at regular intervals—

(a)   if some or all of the intervals are of different lengths—

      (i)   for the purpose of arriving at the sum to be deducted, whichever of paragraphs (1), (2), (3), (4), (5) and (6) is appropriate shall apply to the series with the shortest interval (or, if there is more than one series with the shortest interval, such one of those series as the employer may choose), and

    (ii)   in relation to the earnings payable in every other series, the sum to be deducted shall be 20 per cent of the net earnings or, where on any pay-day an amount advanced is also paid, 20 per cent of the aggregate of the net earnings and the amount advanced;

  (b)   if all of the intervals are of the same length, whichever of paragraphs (1), (2), (3), (4), (5) and (6) is appropriate shall apply to such series as the employer may choose and sub-paragraph (a)(ii) shall apply to every other series,

and paragraph (3) shall apply in relation to sub-paragraph (a)(ii) above as it applies in relation to paragraph (1).

(8)   Subject to paragraphs (9) and (10), where the debtor's earnings from the employer are payable at irregular intervals, the sums to be deducted on any pay-day shall be arrived at by—

  (a)   calculating what would be his daily net earnings by dividing the net earnings payable to him by the employer on the pay-day—

    (i)   by the number of days since earnings were last payable by the employer to him, or

    (ii)   if the earnings are the first earnings to be payable by the employer to him with respect to the employment in question, by the number of days since he began the employment;

  (b)   ascertaining the percentage (or percentages) specified in column 2 of Table C of Schedule 4 opposite the band in column 1 of that Table within which the notional net earnings calculated under sub-paragraph (a) fall; and

  (c)   calculating the sum which equals the appropriate percentage (or percentages) of the daily net earnings and multiplying that sum by the same number as that of the divisor for the purposes of the calculation mentioned in sub-paragraph (a).

(9)   Where on the same pay-day there are payable to the debtor by the employer both earnings payable at regular intervals and earnings payable at irregular intervals, for the purpose of arriving at the sum to be deducted on the pay-day under the foregoing provisions of this regulation all the earnings shall be aggregated and treated as earnings payable at the regular interval.

(10)   Where there are earnings payable to the debtor by the employer at regular intervals on the pay-day, and earnings are payable by the employer to him at irregular intervals on a different pay-day, the sum to be deducted on each of the pay-days on which the earnings which are payable at irregular intervals are so payable shall be 20 per cent of the net earnings payable to him on the day.

7.7970 *39. Attachment of earnings orders: ancillary powers and duties of employers and others served* (1)   An employer who deducts and pays amounts under an attachment of earnings order may, on each occasion that he makes such a deduction, also deduct from the debtor's earnings the sum of one pound towards his administrative costs.

(2)   An employer who deducts and pays amounts under an attachment of earnings order shall, in accordance with paragraph (3), notify the debtor in writing of—

  (a)   the total amount of the sums (including sums deducted under paragraph (1)) deducted under the order up to the time of the notification; or

  (b)   the total amount of the sums (including sums deducted under paragraph (1)) that will fall to be so deducted after that time.

(3)   A notification under paragraph (2) must be given at the time that the pay statement given by the employer to the debtor next after a deduction has been made is so given, or if no such statements are usually issued by the employer, as soon as practicable after a deduction has been made.

(4)   A person on whom a copy of an attachment of earnings order has been served shall, in accordance with paragraph (5), notify in writing the authority which made the order if he does not have the debtor against whom it was made in his employment or the debtor subsequently ceases to be in his employment.

(5)   A notification under paragraph (4) must be given within 14 days of the day on which the copy of the order was served on him or the debtor ceased to be in his employment (as the case may be).

(6)   While an attachment of earnings order is in force, any person who becomes the debtor's employer and knows that the order is in force and by what authority it was made shall notify that authority in writing that he is the debtor's employer.

(7)   A notification under paragraph (6) must be given within 14 days of the day on which the debtor became the person's employee or of the day on which the person first knows that the order is in force and the identity of the authority by which it was made, whichever is the later.

7.7971 *40. Attachment of earnings orders: duties of debtor* (1)   While an attachment of earnings order is in force, the debtor in respect of whom the order has been made shall notify in writing the authority which made it of each occasion when he leaves an employment or becomes employed or re-employed, and (in a case where he becomes so employed or re-employed) shall include in the notification a statement of—

  (a)   his earnings and (so far as he is able) expected earnings from the employment concerned,

  (b)   the deductions and (so far as he is able) expected deductions from such earnings—

    (i)   in respect of income tax;

    (ii)   in respect of primary Class 1 contributions under Part I of the Social Security Contributions and Benefits Act 1992;

    (iii) for the purposes of such a superannuation scheme as is mentioned in the definition of "net earnings" in regulation 32(1),

  (c)   the name and address of the employer, and—

(*d*)   his work or identity number in the employment (if any).

(2)   A notification under paragraph (1) must be given within 14 days of the day on which the debtor leaves or commences (or recommences) the employment (as the case may be), or (if later) the day on which he is informed by the authority that the order has been made.

7.7972   *41.*   *Attachment of earnings orders: ancillary powers and duties of authority*   (1)   Where the whole amount to which an attachment of earnings order relates has been paid (whether by attachment of earnings or otherwise), the authority by which it was made shall give notice of the fact to any person who appears to it to have the debtor in his employment and who has been served with a copy of the order.

(2)   The authority by which an attachment of earnings order was made may, on its own account or on the application of the debtor or an employer of the debtor, make an order discharging the attachment of earnings order; and if it does so it shall give notice of that fact to any person who appears to it to have the debtor in his employment and who has been served with a copy of the order.

(3)   If an authority serves a copy of an attachment of earnings order in accordance with regulation 37(3), it shall (unless it has previously done so) also serve a copy of the order on the debtor.

7.7973   *42.*   *Priority as between orders*   (1)   Where an employer would, but for this paragraph, be obliged to make deductions on any pay-day under more than one attachment of earnings order, he shall—

(*a*)   deal with the orders according to the respective dates on which they were made, disregarding any later order until an earlier one has been dealt with; and

(*b*)   deal with any later order as if the earnings to which it relates were the residue of the debtor's earnings after the making of any deduction to comply with any earlier order.

(2)   Subject to paragraph (3), where an employer would, but for this paragraph, be obliged to comply with one or more attachment of earnings order and with one or more deduction order, he shall deal with the orders according to the respective dates on which they were made in like manner as under paragraph (1).

(3)   An employer shall not deal with a deduction order made either wholly or in part in respect of the payment of a judgment debt or payments under an administration order until he has dealt with the attachment of earnings order or orders and any other deduction order.

(4)   In this regulation "deduction order" means an order under the Attachment of Earnings Act 1971 or section 31(2) (deductions from earnings orders) of the Child Support Act 1991.

7.7974   *43.*   *Attachment of earnings orders: persons employed under the Crown*   (1)   Where a debtor is in the employment of the Crown and an attachment of earnings order is made in respect of him, for the purposes of this Part—

(*a*)   the chief officer for the time being of the department, office or other body in which the debtor is employed shall be treated as having the debtor in his employment (any transfer of the debtor from one department, office or body to another being treated as a change of employment); and

(*b*)   any earnings paid by the Crown or a Minister of the Crown, or out of the public revenue of the United Kingdom, shall be treated as paid by that chief officer.

(2)   If any question arises as to what department, office or other body is concerned for the purposes of this regulation, or as to who for those purposes is its chief officer, the question shall be referred to and determined by the Minister for the Civil Service.

(3)   A document purporting to set out a determination of the Minister under paragraph (2) and to be signed by an official of the Office of that Minister shall, in any proceedings arising in relation to an attachment of earnings order, be admissible in evidence and be deemed to contain an accurate statement of such a determination unless the contrary is shown.

(4)   This Part shall have effect in relation to attachment of earnings orders notwithstanding any enactment passed before 29th May 1970 and preventing or avoiding the attachment or diversion of sums due to a person in respect of services under the Crown; whether by way of remuneration, pension or otherwise.

7.7975   *44.*   *Attachment of allowances orders*   (1)   This regulation applies in relation to an elected member of a relevant billing authority or a relevant precepting authority.

(2)   For the purposes of this regulation—

(*a*)   a relevant billing authority is a billing authority other than the Common Council;

(*b*)   a relevant precepting authority is a major precepting authority other than the Receiver for the Metropolitan Police District;

(*c*)   a person is an elected member of a relevant precepting authority other than a county council if he is appointed to the authority by a constituent council of which he is an elected member; and

(*d*)   references to attachable allowances are references to the allowances referred to in paragraph (7)(*b*).

(3)   Where a liability order has been made and the debtor against whom it was made is a person in relation to whom this regulation applies, the authority which applied for the order may make an order under this regulation to secure the payment of any outstanding sum which is or forms part of the amount in respect of which the liability order was made.

(4)   An order under this regulation shall be expressed to be directed to the authority of whom the debtor is an elected member and shall operate as an instruction to the authority to make deductions from attachable allowances payable to the debtor and to pay the sums so deducted to the authority by which the order was made.

(5)   An order under this regulation shall remain in force until discharged or the whole sum to

which it relates has been paid (whether by attachment of allowances or otherwise).

(6)   The sum to be deducted by an authority under an order under this regulation on any day shall be a sum equal to 40 per cent of the aggregate of attachable allowances payable to the debtor on that day.

(7)   Paragraph (3) of regulation 37, paragraphs (1) to (5) of regulation 39 and paragraphs (1) and (2) of regulation 41 shall apply to orders under this regulation as they apply to attachment of earnings orders as if any reference in those paragraphs—

(a)   to an employer or a person having the debtor in his employment, were a reference to such an authority as is mentioned in paragraph (1) above having the debtor as an elected member;

(b)   to the debtor's earnings, were a reference to allowances—

(i)   payable to the debtor in accordance with a scheme under regulations under section 18 (schemes for basic, attendance and special responsibility allowances for local authority members) of the Local Government and Housing Act 1989; or

(ii)   in the nature of an attendance allowance, payable to the debtor under section 175 (allowances for attending conferences and meetings) of the Local Government Act 1972;

(c)   to an attachment of earnings order, were a reference to an order under this regulation.

7.7976   45.   *Enforcement by taking control of goods*   Where a liability order has been made, payment may be enforced by using the Schedule 12 procedure.

7.7977   47.   *Commitment to prison*[1]   (1)   Where a billing authority in England has sought to enforce payment by use of the Schedule 12 procedure pursuant to regulation 45, the debtor is an individual who has attained the age of 18 years, and the enforcement agent reports to the authority that he was unable (for whatever reason) to find any or sufficient goods of the debtor to enforce payment[2], the authority may apply to a magistrates' court for the issue of a warrant committing the debtor to prison[3].

(2)   On such application being made the court shall (in the debtor's presence[4]) inquire as to his means and inquire whether the failure to pay which has led to the application is due to his wilful refusal or culpable neglect[5].

(3)   If (and only if) the court is of the opinion that his failure is due to his wilful refusal or culpable neglect[6] it may if it thinks fit[7]—

(a)   issue a warrant of commitment against the debtor, or

(b)   fix a term of imprisonment and postpone[8] the issue of the warrant until such time and on such conditions[9] (if any) as the court thinks just.

(4)   The warrant shall be made in respect of the relevant amount; and the relevant amount for this purpose is the aggregate of—

(a)   an amount equal to the amount outstanding (within the meaning of Schedule 12), and

(b)   a sum of an amount equal to the costs reasonably incurred by the applicant in respect of the application.

(5)   The warrant—

(a)   shall state the relevant amount mentioned in paragraph (4),

(b)   may be directed to the authority making the application and to such other persons (if any) as the court issuing it thinks fit, and

(c)   may be executed anywhere in England and Wales by any person to whom it is directed.

(6)   If—

(a)   before a warrant has been issued, or a term of imprisonment fixed and the issue of a warrant postponed, an amount determined in accordance with paragraph (6A) below is paid or tendered to the authority, or

(b)   after a term of imprisonment has been fixed and the issue of a warrant postponed, the amount (if any) the court has ordered the debtor to pay is paid or tendered to the authority, or

(c)   after a warrant has been issued, the amount stated in it is paid or tendered to the authority,

the authority shall accept the amount concerned, no further steps shall be taken as regards its recovery, and the debtor, if committed to prison, shall be released.

(6A)   The amount referred to in paragraph (6)(a) above is the aggregate of—

(a)   the amount outstanding (within the meaning of Schedule 12), and

(b)   subject to paragraph (6B) below, the authority's reasonable costs incurred up to the time of payment or tender in making one or more of the applications referred to in Schedule 6.

(6B)   For the purposes of paragraph (6A)(b) above, the authority's reasonable costs in respect of any application shall not exceed the amount specified for that application in Schedule 6.

(7)   The order in the warrant shall be that the debtor be imprisoned for a time specified[10] in the warrant which shall not exceed 3 months, unless the amount stated in the warrant is sooner paid; but—

(a)   where a warrant is issued after a postponement under paragraph (3)(b) and, since the term of imprisonment was fixed but before the issue of the warrant, the amount mentioned in paragraph (4)(a) with respect to which the warrant would (but for the postponement) have been made has been reduced by a part payment, the period of imprisonment ordered under the warrant shall be the term fixed under paragraph (3) reduced by such number of days as bears to the total number of days in that term less one day the same proportion as the part paid bears to that amount, and

(b)   where, after the issue of a warrant, a part payment of the amount stated in it is made, the
period of imprisonment shall be reduced by such number of days as bears to the total
number of days in the term of imprisonment specified in the warrant less one day the
same proportion as the part paid bears to the amount so stated.

(8)   In calculating a reduction required under paragraph (7) any fraction of a day shall be left out
of account; and rule 55(1), (2) and (3) of the Magistrates' Courts Rules 1981 applies (so far as is
relevant) to a part payment as if the imprisonment concerned were imposed for want of sufficient
distress to satisfy a sum adjudged to be paid by a magistrates' court.

---

[1] Cases decided under the similarly worded reg 41 of the Community Charge etc Regulations 1989 are still useful
sources of reference and have, therefore, been included in the footnotes to this regulation. "The power to commit is
coercive: it is intended to be used to extract payment of the debt from those who are able to pay, not to punish the debtor"
(*R (on the application of Woolcock) v Secretary of State for Communities and Local Government and others* [2018] EWHC
17 (Admin) and is a perfectly proper means of extracting payment from a person possessed of income or assets who has
been guilty of wilful refusal (*R v Oldbury Justices, ex p Smith* (1994) 159 JP 316). Justices retain a discretion and the
Regulations do not limit the power to commit to prison to those cases in which every other possibility has been
exhaustively explored (*R v Newcastle-under-Lyme Justices, ex p K.A Massey* (26 May 1993, unreported). Nevertheless,
before committing a debtor to prison, it is incumbent upon justices to consider all available alternatives to effect the
recovery of the sum due (*R v Middleton Magistrates, ex p Phillips* (29 October 1993, unreported).
[2] It is unnecessary for the justices to determine the existence of these preconditions to the local authority's decision to
apply for a warrant of commitment; the procedure adopted by the local authority, however, may be challenged on
proceedings for judicial review (*R v Dudley Justices, ex p Blatchford* (1992) 156 JP 846).
[3] The application need not be by way of complaint and therefore would not be subject to the time limit contained in
s 127 of the Magistrates' Court Act 1980 (*R v Wolverhampton Magistrates' Court* (1992) 157 JP 1017).
[4] While the defaulter must be present for the means inquiry to take place, this is not a requirement when any
subsequent postponed committal order is made or warrant of commitment issued. However, the court must ensure that
he has been put on proper notice of the hearing and, if he fails to attend, the court will usually wish to make inquiries as
to why he is not present and consider steps to encourage or require his attendance. A summons or warrant may be issued.
If he fails to obey a summons, the court should make inquiries as to why he has not attended, including inquiries to ensure
that notice of the hearing was properly served, and take reasonable steps to ensure or at least encourage his attendance,
but, if the court is satisfied that he has received notice of the hearing and has chosen not to attend, it may then proceed in
his absence: *R (Woodcock) v The Secretary of State for Communities and Local Government, The Secretary of State for
Justice and The Welsh Ministers* [2018] EWHC 17 (Admin) (disagreeing with the view expressed in *R v Doncaster Justices,
ex p Jack* (1999) 164 JP 52 that it would be 'very difficult to conceive of circumstances that would justify a committal in the
absence of a defendant' (per Collins J at page 164). Each case will depend on its own facts, but the enforcement history
may show that the defendant has deliberately absented himself to avoid committal, and that the time and cost in issuing
processor further process to compel his attendance would not be reasonable, proportionate or warranted.
[5] This must be a separate inquiry into the circumstances relevant under reg 47 for each separate year of liability: *R (on
the application of Aldous) v Dartford Magistrates' Court and Gravesham Borough Council* [2011] EWHC 1919 (Admin),
(2011) 175 JP 445.
[6] If the basis of the decision is that the defaulter had earning capacity which he chose not to use, there must at least be
clear evidence that gainful employment for which he was fit was on offer to the defaulter which he had rejected; the proper
date for assessing his means is when the court hears the application for commitment (See *R v Poole Justices, ex p Benham*
(1991) 156 JP 177).
[7] Justices must consider the issue of wilful refusal or culpable neglect separately from the question of the appropriate
disposal. Accordingly, where justices find that the debtor has wilfully refused to pay, it does not follow that the court has
no alternative other than to order the immediate issue of the warrant of commitment. It is incumbent on the justices, in
such circumstances, to consider any offer to pay and if they deem it inappropriate to fix a term of imprisonment and
postpone the issue of the warrant on terms, they must give reasons for so deciding (*R v Middleton Magistrates, ex p
Phillips* (29 October 1993, unreported)). See also *R v Alfreton Justices, ex p Gratton* (1993) Times, 7 December.
[8] The court may take into account the attitude of a spouse where the charge payer is financially dependent upon that
spouse (*R v Ramsgate Magistrates' Court, ex p Haddow* (1992) 157 JP 545). In proceedings for recovery of the Community
Charge under the Community Charges (Administration and Enforcement) Regulations 1989, SI 1989/712, it was held that
the principles governing the exercise of discretion under reg 41(3)(a) and (b) of the 1989 regs were different; justices were
not obliged to exhaust all possibilities of recovering unpaid community charge before making a postponed committal
order (*R v Preston Justices, ex p McCosh* (1995) Times, 30 January). We would suggest that this reasoning remains
applicable to reg 47(3)(a) and (b) of the 1992 regulations. Where the court postpones the issue of the warrant of
commitment, it will not be lawful for the warrant to be issued without there being a further hearing, on the application of
the local authority, of which the debtor must be given notice of the date and purpose of the hearing, and an opportunity
of attending. The magistrates must be satisfied that the council tax payer has received notice of the hearing and must carry
out an appropriate inquiry to make sure that the notice must have come into his hands. At that hearing the debtor is
entitled to put the local authority to proof of non-payment and non-compliance with the conditions of postponement; and
to draw the court's attention to any change of circumstances since the decision to fix the terms of imprisonment which
renders it inexpedient for the warrant to issue (*R v Faversham and Sittingbourne Magistrates' Court, ex p Ursell* (1992) 156
JP 765). See also *R v Northampton Justices, ex p Newell* (1992) 157 JP 869. Before it can activate the committal order, the
court must be satisfied that the debtor has had the ability to pay the instalment order, or otherwise comply with the
conditions on which the issue of the warrant was postponed, but has failed to do so; see *R v Felixstowe Justices, ex p
Herridge* [1993] RA 83.
[9] When postponing a warrant on repayment of the sum due by instalments, the court must observe the principles set
out in *R (Woolcock) v The Secretary of State for Communities and Local Government, The Secretary of State for Justice
and The Welsh Ministers*[2018] EWHC 17 (Admin). Giving the judgment of the court, Hickinbottom LJ added:

'23 Whilst I emphasise that the assessment of a reasonable instalment period for the payment of council tax arrears
is an exercise of judgment for the magistrates' court on the facts of a particular case, in my view the cases clearly
indicate that a period of two or three years will normally be entirely appropriate. We were referred to no case in which
a period of five years has been found to be appropriate and, in my view, such cases will be vanishingly rare, and would
require very considerable and clear justification.
24. As I have indicated ... once the magistrates' court has assessed appropriate instalments, in amount and duration,
then it is incumbent on the court to remit the arrears to the extent that they exceed the sum of the instalments. This is
particularly important because it is doubtful whether the court can remit arrears once any committal order (including a
suspended order) has been made...'

This principle does not apply where a court reduces the amount of the instalments, as the court has no power to remit
the arrears following the imposition of a postponed commitment (*R (Woolcock)* above, paragraph 24.
[10] In an application for judicial review of a decision under reg 16 of the Non-Domestic Rating (Collection etc)
Regulations 1989, post, the High Court held that, when determining the period of imprisonment to be specified in the
warrant, the justices must have regard to the principle of proportionality. The more serious the case, whether in terms of
the amount outstanding or in terms of the degree of culpability or blame to be attached to the debtor for his non-payment,
the closer will any period imposed approach the maximum. A finding of wilful refusal, in this respect, represents a more
serious state of affairs than culpable neglect; see *R v Highbury Corner Magistrates' Court, ex p Uchendu* (1994) 158 JP 409.
It follows that, to fix the appropriate term, the court must decide which of culpable neglect or wilful refusal led to the failure

to pay: *R (on the application of Aldous) v Dartford Magistrates' Court and Gravesham Borough Council* (supra).

7.7978   48.   *Commitment to prison: further provision*   (1)   A single warrant may not be issued under regulation 47 against more than one person.

(2)   Where an application under regulation 47 has been made, and after the making of the inquiries mentioned in paragraph (2) of that regulation no warrant is issued or term of imprisonment fixed, the court may remit[1] all or part of the appropriate amount mentioned in regulation 45(2) with respect to which the application related.

(3)   Where an application under regulation 47 has been made but no warrant is issued or term of imprisonment fixed, the application may be renewed (except so far as regards any sum remitted under paragraph (2)) on the ground that the circumstances of the debtor have changed.

(4)   A statement in writing to the effect that wages of any amount have been paid to the debtor during any period, purporting to be signed by or on behalf of his employer, shall in any proceedings under regulation 47 be evidence of the facts there stated.

(5)   For the purpose of enabling inquiry to be made as to the debtor's conduct and means under regulation 47, a justice of the peace may—

(a)   issue a summons to him to appear before a magistrates' court and (if he does not obey the summons) issue a warrant for his arrest, or

(b)   issue a warrant for the debtor's arrest without issuing a summons.

(6)   A warrant issued under paragraph (5) may be executed anywhere in England and Wales by any person to whom it is directed or by any constable acting within his police area; and section 125(3) of the Magistrates' Courts Act 1980 applies to such a warrant.

(7)   Regulation 47 and this regulation have effect subject to Part I of the Criminal Justice Act 1982 (treatment of young offenders).

---

[1] Once the magistrates' court has assessed appropriate instalments, in amount and duration, then it is incumbent upon the court to remit the arrears to the extent that they exceed the sum of the instalments. That is particularly important because it is doubtful in light of paragraph (2) of this regulation that the court can remit arrears once any committal order has been made (*R (Woodcock) v The Secretary of State for Communities and Local Government, The Secretary of State for Justice and The Welsh Ministers* [2018] EWHC 17 (Admin). This view is supported in a case decided under the similarly worded reg 42 of the Community Charge etc Regulations 1989 (*Harrogate Borough Council v Barker* (1995) 159 JP 809). Contrary to cases under the Community Charge regulations, the court in *Woolcock* held that, having remitted arrears, the court could impose a commitment order.

7.7979   49.   *Insolvency*   (1)   Where a liability order has been made and the debtor against whom it was made is an individual, the amount due shall be deemed to be a debt for the purposes of section 267 of the Insolvency Act 1986 (grounds of creditor's petition).

(2)   Where a liability order has been made and the debtor against whom it was made is a company, the amount due shall be deemed to be a debt for the purposes of section 122(1)(*f*) (winding up of companies by the court) or, as the case may be, section 221(5)(*b*) (winding up of unregistered companies) of that Act.

(3)   For the purposes of this regulation the amount due is an amount equal to any outstanding sum which is or forms part of the amount in respect of which the liability order was made.

7.7980   50.   *Charging orders*   (1)   An application to the appropriate court may be made under this regulation where—

(a)   a magistrates' court has made one or more liability orders pursuant to either regulation 34(6) or 36A(5);

(b)   the amount mentioned in regulation 34(7)(*a*) or 36A(5)(*a*) in respect of which the liability order was made, or, where more than one liability order was made, the aggregate of the amounts mentioned in regulation 34(7)(*a*) or 36A(5)(*a*) in respect of which each such liability order was made, is an amount the debtor is liable to pay under Part V; and

(c)   at the time that the application under this regulation is made at least £1000 of the amount in respect of which the liability order was made, or, where more than one liability order was made, the aggregate of the amounts in respect of which those liability orders were made, remains outstanding.

(2)   The application which may be made to the appropriate court under this regulation is an application by the authority concerned for an order imposing, on any interest held by the debtor beneficially in the relevant dwelling, a charge for securing the due amount; and the court may make such an order on such application.

(3)   For the purposes of paragraph (2)—

(a)   the authority concerned is the authority which applied for the one or more liability orders referred to in paragraph (1)(*a*);

(b)   the relevant dwelling is the dwelling in respect of which, at the time the application for the liability order was made, or, where more than one liability order was made, at the time the applications for the liability orders were made, the debtor was liable to pay council tax;

(c)   the due amount is the aggregate of—

(i)   an amount equal to any outstanding sum which is or forms part of the amount in respect of which the one or more liability orders were made; and

(ii)   a sum of an amount equal to the costs reasonably incurred by the applicant in obtaining the charging order;

(d)   the appropriate court is the county court for the area in which the relevant dwelling is situated.

7.7981   51.   *Charging orders: further provision*   (1)   In deciding whether to make a charging order, the court shall consider all the circumstances of the case, and in particular any evidence before it as to—

(a)   the personal circumstances of the debtor, and

(b)   whether any other person would be likely to be unduly prejudiced by the making of the order.

(2)   A charging order—

(a)   shall specify the dwelling concerned and the interest held by the debtor beneficially in it, and

(b)   may, as the court thinks fit, be made absolutely or subject to conditions as to the time when the charge is to become enforceable or as to other matters.

(3)   A charge imposed by a charging order shall have the like effect and shall be enforceable in the same courts and in the same manner as an equitable charge created by the debtor by writing under his hand.

(4)   The court by which a charging order was made may at any time, on the application of the debtor, the authority on whose application the order was made or any person interested in the dwelling, make an order discharging or varying the charging order.

(5)   The Land Charges Act 1972 and the Land Registration Act 1925 shall apply in relation to charging orders as they apply in relation to orders or writs issued or made for the purposes of enforcing judgments; and in section 49(1)(g) of the Land Registration Act 1925, after the words "Local Government Finance Act 1988" there are inserted the words ", or regulations under paragraph 11 of Schedule 4 to the Local Government Finance Act 1992".

(6)   Where a charging order has been protected by an entry registered under the Land Charges Act 1972 or the Land Registration Act 1925, an order under paragraph (4) discharging the charging order may direct that the entry be cancelled.

7.7982   52.   *Relationship between remedies*   (1)   Where a warrant of commitment is issued against (or a term of imprisonment is fixed in the case of) a person under regulation 47(3), no steps, or no further steps, may be taken under this Part by way of attachment of allowances, attachment of earnings, the Schedule 12 procedure, bankruptcy or charging, or under the Income Support Regulations in relation to the relevant amount mentioned in regulation 47(4).

(2)   Steps under this Part by way of attachment of allowances, attachment of earnings, the Schedule 12 procedure, commitment, bankruptcy, winding up or charging may not be taken in relation to a person against whom a liability order has been made while—

(a)   steps by way of another of those methods are being taken against him under it; or

(b)   deductions are being made under the Income Support Regulations from any amount payable to him by way of income support, universal credit or jobseeker's allowance; or

(c)   an application under regulation 2 of the Income Support Regulations has been made in respect of him to the Secretary of State and remains undetermined.

(2A)   An application under regulation 2 of the Income Support Regulations may not be made in respect of a person against whom a liability order has been made while steps under this Part are being taken against him for the recovery of an amount equal to any outstanding sum which is or forms part of the amount in respect of which the liability order was made.

(3)   Subject to paragraphs (1) and (2)—

(a)   attachment of allowances, attachment of earnings, deductions under the Income Support Regulations or the Schedule 12 procedure may be resorted to more than once, and

(b)   attachment of allowances, attachment of earnings, deductions under the Income Support Regulations or the Schedule 12 procedure may be resorted to in any order or alternately (or both).

(4)   Where a step is taken for the recovery of an outstanding sum which is or forms part of an amount in respect of which a liability order has been made and under which additional costs or charges with respect to the step are also recoverable in accordance with this Part, any sum recovered thereby which is less than the aggregate of the amount outstanding and such additional costs and charges shall be treated as discharging first the costs and charges, the balance (if any) being applied towards the discharge of the outstanding sum.

7.7983   53.   *Magistrates' courts*   (1)   *Revoked.*

(1A)   *Revoked.*

(2)   Subject to any other enactment authorising a District Judge (Magistrates' Courts) or other person to act by himself, a magistrates' court shall not under this Part hear a summons, entertain an application for a warrant or hold an inquiry as to means on such an application except when composed of at least two justices.

(3)   References to a justice of the peace in regulations 34(2) and 46(2) shall be construed subject to rule 3 of the Justices' Clerks Rules 1970 (which authorises certain matters authorised to be done by a justice of the pace to be done by a justices' clerk).

(4)   In any proceedings under regulation 34 (application for liability order) or regulation 47 (commitment to prison), a statement contained in a document constituting or forming part of a record compiled by the applicant authority or an authorised person[1] shall be admissible as evidence of any fact stated in it of which direct oral evidence would be admissible.

(5)   In proceedings where the applicant authority or an authorised person[1] desires to give a statement in evidence in accordance with paragraph (4), and the document containing that statement is produced by a computer, a certificate—

(a)   identifying the document containing the statement and the computer by which it was produced;

(b)   containing a statement that at all material times the computer was operating properly, or if not, that any respect in which it was not operating properly or was out of operation was not such as to affect the production of the document or the accuracy of its contents;

(c)   giving such explanation as may be appropriate of the content of the document; and (*d*)   purporting to be signed by a person occupying a responsible position in relation to the operation of the computer,

shall be admissible as evidence of anything which is stated in it to the best of the signatory's information and belief.

(6)   In paragraph (4) above, "statement" includes any representation of fact, whether made in words or otherwise; and the reference to an application under regulation 47 includes a reference to an application made in the circumstances mentioned in regulation 48(3).

---

[1] A billing authority may authorise another person, or that person's employees, to exercise functions relating to the administration and enforcement of the council tax: see the Local Authorities (Contracting Out of Tax Billing, Collection and Enforcement Functions) Order 1996, SI 1996/1880.

7.7984 **54.** *Joint and several liability: enforcement*   (1)   This regulation has effect with respect to the application of regulations 33 to 53 to a sum for which persons are jointly and severally liable under Part V.

(2)   In this regulation, "joint taxpayers" means two or more individuals who are jointly and severally liable to pay an amount in respect of council tax.

(3)   A final notice served in accordance with regulation 33 on every person against whom the application for a liability order is to be made may be addressed to two or more joint taxpayers in joint names.

(3A)   A summons under regulation 34(2) may be addressed to two or more joint taxpayers in joint names.

(4)   A liability order may be made against one or more joint taxpayers in respect of an amount for which they are jointly and severally liable.

(5)   Where a liability order has been made against two or more joint taxpayers, subject to paragraphs (6) and 6(A)—

(*a*)   an attachment of allowances order or an attachment of earnings order may be made against one of them, or different such orders may be made against more than one;

(*b*)   the Schedule 12 procedure may be used against one or more of them;

(*c*)   a charging order may be made against one of them, or against more than one jointly, or different such orders may be made against more than one of them (as the circumstances require); and

(*d*)   deductions may be made under the Income Support Regulations from any amount payable to one or more of them by way of income support or universal credit.

(6)   Where a liability order has been made against two or more joint taxpayers in respect of an amount, steps by way of any method specified in paragraph (5)—

(*a*)   may not be taken under it in respect of one of them while steps by way of that or another of those methods are being taken under it in respect of another of them; and

(*b*)   may be taken under it in respect of one of them notwithstanding that no steps by way of that or another of those methods have been taken under it in respect of another of them.

(6A)   Where a liability order has been made against two or more joint taxpayers and an amount is payable to one of them by way of income support or universal credit and—

(*a*)   deductions are being made under the Income Support Regulations from any such amount; or

(*b*)   an application under regulation 2 of those Regulations has been made in respect of him to the Secretary of State and remains undetermined.

no steps, or no further steps, by way of attachment of allowances or earnings, distress, commitment, bankruptcy or charging may be taken, under that or any other liability order, against him or any other of those joint taxpayers who is a member of his family.

(6B)   In paragraph (6A) above—

"income support" means income support within the meaning of the Social Security Contributions and Benefits Act 1992; and

"family" has the same meaning as in section 137(1) of that Act.

(7)   Where the Schedule 12 procedure has been used against two or more joint taxpayers in respect of an amount, a billing authority in England may, subject to paragraph (8), apply for a warrant of commitment at any time against one of them or different warrants may be applied for against more than one of them: but no such application may be made in respect of any of them who has not attained the age of 18 years.

(8)   Where a liability order has been made against two or more joint taxpayers in respect of an amount, a warrant of commitment may not be applied for unless—

(*a*)   distress has been made against all of them; and

(*b*)   the person making the distress reports to the authority that, in relation to each of them, he was unable (for whatever reason) to find any or sufficient goods.

(9)   Where a liability order has been made against two or more joint taxpayers in respect of an amount, and a warrant of commitment is issued against (or a term of imprisonment is fixed in the case of) one of them under regulation 47(3), no steps, or no further steps, may be taken against any of them by way of attachment of allowances or earnings, the Schedule 12 procedure, bankruptcy or charging in relation to the amount mentioned in regulation 47(4).

(9A)   Where a liability order has been made against persons who are joint taxpayers, and a warrant of commitment is issued against (or a term of imprisonment is fixed in the case of) one of them under regulation 47(3), no steps, or further steps, may be taken under the Income Support Regulations in respect of any of them in relation to the amount mentioned in regulation 47(4).

(10)   Where a liability order has been made against two or more joint taxpayers in respect of an amount and in using the Schedule 12 procedure against one of them goods jointly owned by both or all of them are found, control may be taken of those goods with respect to that amount; but in

any subsequent proceedings under regulation 47 (commitment), charges arising under the Taking Control of Goods (Fees) Regulations 2014 from the use of the Schedule 12 procedure shall be treated as charges relating to the person against whose goods the Schedule 12 procedure was intended to be used when the joint goods were found, and not as charges relating to the other or others.

(11)   Where—

(a)   a liability order has been made against more than one person in respect of an amount; and

(b)   a charge has arisen against one of them for the enforcement stage within the meaning of regulation 5 of the Taking Control of Goods (Fees) Regulations 2014 in respect of that amount,

no further charge for the enforcement stage or compliance stage (within the meaning of regulation 5 of the Taking Control of Goods (Fees) Regulations 2014) in consequence of any further use or attempted use of the Schedule 12 procedure in respect of that amount may be recovered from any of them; and a charge for the compliance stage shall be treated for those purposes as a charge with respect to the others as well as that one.

7.7985   *55. Repayments*   A sum which has become payable (by way of repayment) under Part V to a person other than a billing authority but which has not been paid shall be recoverable in a court of competent jurisdiction.

7.7986   *56. Offences*   (1)   A person shall be guilty of an offence if, following a request under paragraph (2)(b) of regulation 36, he is under a duty to supply information and—

(a)   he fails without reasonable excuse to supply the information in accordance with that regulation, or

(b)   in supplying information in purported compliance with that regulation he makes a statement which is false in a material particular or recklessly makes a statement which is false in a material particular.

(2)   Subject to paragraph (3), a person shall be guilty of an offence if, following the service on him of a copy of an attachment of allowances order or an attachment of earnings order, he is under a duty to comply with the order by virtue of regulation 37(3) (including that provision as applied for the purposes of attachment of allowances orders by regulation 44(7)) and he fails to do so.

(3)   It shall be a defence for a person charged with an offence under paragraph (2) to prove that he took all reasonable steps to comply with the order.

(4)   A person shall be guilty of an offence if he is under a duty to notify another person under regulation 39(2) and (3) or (4) and (5) (including those provisions as applied for the purposes of attachment of allowances orders by regulation 44(7)), regulation 39(6) and (7) or regulation 40 and—

(a)   he fails without reasonable excuse to notify the other person in accordance with the provision concerned, or

(b)   in notifying the other person in purported compliance with the provision concerned he makes a statement which he knows to be false in a material particular or recklessly makes a statement which is false in a material particular.

(5)   A person guilty of an offence under paragraph (1)(a) or (4)(a) shall be liable on summary conviction to a fine not exceeding level 2 on the standard scale.

(6)   A person guilty of an offence under paragraph (1)(b), (2) or (4)(b) shall be liable on summary conviction to a fine not exceeding level 3 on the standard scale.

7.7987   *57. Miscellaneous provisions*   (1)   Any matter which could be the subject of an appeal under section 16 of the Act or regulations under section 24 of the Act may not be raised in proceedings under this Part[1].

(2)   If a liability order has been made and by virtue of—

(a)   a notification which is given by the billing authority or an authorised person under regulation 24(2) or (5), 25(5) or (8), 28(3) or (4) or 31(2), or paragraph 9(3) or 10(2)(a) of Schedule 1, or

(b)   section 31(4) of the Act applying in any case,

any part of the amount mentioned in regulation 34(5)(a) in respect of which the order was made would (if paid) fall to be repaid or credited against any subsequent liability, that part shall be treated for the purposes of this Part as paid on the day the notification is given or the amount in substitution is set under section 31(2) of the Act and accordingly is no longer outstanding.

(3)   If, after a warrant is issued or term of imprisonment is fixed under regulation 47(3), and before the term of imprisonment has begun or been fully served, a billing authority gives such a notification as is mentioned in paragraph (2)(a) in the case in question, or sets an amount in substitution so that section 31(4) of the Act applies in the case in question, it shall forthwith notify accordingly the designated officer for the court which issued the warrant and (if the debtor is detained) the governor or keeper of the prison or place where he is detained or such other person as has lawful custody of him.

(4)   If the debtor is treated as having paid an amount under paragraph (2) on any day, and

(a)   that day falls after the completion of the service of a term of imprisonment imposed under regulation 47 in respect of the amount he is treated as having paid, or

(b)   the debtor is serving a term of imprisonment imposed under regulation 47 on that day and the amount he is treated as having paid exceeds the amount of any part payment which, if made, would cause the expiry of the term of imprisonment pursuant to paragraph (7)(b) of that regulation on that day,

the amount mentioned in sub-paragraph (a) or excess mentioned in sub-paragraph (b) shall be paid to the debtor or credited against any subsequent liability of his, as the debtor requires.

[1] The substantial merits of a billing authority's decision regarding an individual's liability are matters for a valuation tribunal and cannot be raised before the magistrates' court in enforcement proceedings; where an issue as to liability is raised it may be sensible to adjourn the enforcement application to await the decision of the valuation tribunal: *Wiltshire Council v Piggin* [2014] EWHC 4386 (Admin), [2015] RVR 45.

PART VII

Miscellaneous

7.7988   58.   *Outstanding liabilities on death*   (1)   This regulation applies where a person dies and at any time before his death—

(a)   he was (or is alleged to have been) liable to pay council tax under section 6, 7 or 8 of the Act, or

(b)   he was (or is alleged to have been) so liable, as spouse or civil partner, under section 9 of the Act, or

(c)   a penalty was imposed on him under any of sub-paragraphs (1) to (3) of paragraph 1 of Schedule 3 to the Act or under any of regulations 11 to 13 of the Detection of Fraud Regulations.

(2)   Where—

(a)   before the deceased's death a sum has become payable by him under Part V or by way of relevant costs in respect of one of the matters mentioned in paragraph (1) but has not been paid, or

(b)   after the deceased's death a sum would, but for his death (and whether or not on the service of a notice), become payable by him under Part V in respect of one of those matters,

his executor or administrator shall, subject to paragraph (3) and to the extent that it is not in excess of the deceased's liability under the Act (including relevant costs payable by him) in respect of the matter, be liable to pay the sum and may deduct out of the assets and effects of the deceased any payments made (or to be made).

(3)   Where paragraph (2)(b) applies, the liability of the executor or administrator does not arise until the service on him of a notice requiring payment of the sum.

(4)   Where before the deceased's death a sum in excess of his liability under the Act (including relevant costs payable by him) in respect of one of the matters mentioned in paragraph (1) has been paid (whether the excess arises because of his death or otherwise) and has not been repaid or credited under Part V, his executor or administrator shall be entitled to the sum.

(5)   Costs are relevant costs for the purposes of paragraphs (2) and (4) if—

(a)   an order or warrant (as the case may be) was made by the court in respect of them before the deceased's death under regulation 34(7)(b) or (8), 36A(5)(b), 47(4)(b) or 50(3)(c)(ii), or

(b)   they are charges which may be recovered pursuant to the Taking Control of Goods (Fees) Regulations 2014.

(6)   A sum payable under paragraph (2) shall be enforceable in the administration of the deceased's estate as a debt of the deceased and accordingly—

(a)   no liability order need be applied for in respect of it after the deceased's death under regulation 34, and

(b)   the liability of the executor or administrator is a liability in his capacity as such.

(7)   Regulation 57(1) applies to proceedings to enforce a liability arising under this regulation as it applies to proceedings under Part VI.

(8)   Insofar as is relevant to his liability under this regulation in the administration of the deceased's estate, the executor or administrator may institute, continue or withdraw proceedings (whether by way of appeal under section 16 of the Act or otherwise).

SCHEDULE 1
COUNCIL TAX INSTALMENT SCHEMES   Regulation 21

SCHEDULE 3
FORM OF ATTACHMENT OF EARNINGS ORDER   Regulation 37

SCHEDULE 4
DEDUCTIONS TO BE MADE UNDER ATTACHMENT OF EARNINGS ORDER

SCHEDULE 6
COSTS CONNECTED WITH COMMITTAL   Regulation 47(6A) and (6B)

7.7989

(1) Application	(2) Maximum costs
For making an application for a warrant of commitment:	£305.00.
For making an application for a warrant of arrest:	£145.00.

Non-Domestic Rating (Unoccupied Property) (England) Regulations 2008[1]
(SI 2008/386 amended by SI 2009/353, SI 2010/408, SI 2015/1641 and SI 2017/102)

7.7990   *1. Citation, application and commencement*   These Regulations, which apply in relation to England only, may be cited as the Non-Domestic Rating (Unoccupied Property) (England) Regulations 2008 and shall come into force on 1st April 2008.

---

[1] Made by the Secretary of State, in exercise of the powers conferred by ss 45(1)(*d*), (9) and (10), 143(2) and 146(6) of the Local Government Finance Act 1988.

7.7991   *2. Interpretation*   In these Regulations—

"qualifying industrial hereditament" means any hereditament other than a retail hereditament in relation to which all buildings comprised in the hereditament are—

    (*a*)   constructed or adapted for use in the course of a trade or business; and

    (*b*)   constructed or adapted for use for one or more of the following purposes, or one or more such purposes and one or more purposes ancillary thereto—

        (i)   the manufacture, repair or adaptation of goods or materials, or the subjection of goods or materials to any process;

        (ii)   storage (including the storage or handling of goods in the course of their distribution);

        (iii)   the working or processing of minerals; and

        (iv)   the generation of electricity;

"relevant non-domestic hereditament" means any non-domestic hereditament consisting of, or of part of, any building, together with any land ordinarily used or intended for use for the purposes of the building or part;

"retail hereditament" means any hereditament where any building or part of a building comprised in the hereditament is constructed or adapted for the purpose of the retail provision of—

    (*a*)   goods, or

    (*b*)   services, other than storage for distribution services, where the services are to be provided on or from the hereditament; and

"the Act" means the Local Government Finance Act 1988.

7.7992   *3. Hereditaments prescribed for the purposes of section 45(1)(d) of the Act*   The class of non-domestic hereditaments prescribed for the purposes of section 45(1)(*d*) of the Act consists of all relevant non-domestic hereditaments other than those described in regulation 4.

7.7993   *4. Hereditaments not prescribed for the purposes of section 45(1)(d) of the Act*   The relevant non-domestic hereditaments described in this regulation are any hereditament—

(*a*)   which, subject to regulation 5, has been unoccupied for a continuous period not exceeding three months;

(*b*)   which is a qualifying industrial hereditament that, subject to regulation 5, has been unoccupied for a continuous period not exceeding six months;

(*c*)   whose owner is prohibited by law from occupying it or allowing it to be occupied;

(*d*)   which is kept vacant by reason of action taken by or on behalf of the Crown or any local or public authority with a view to prohibiting the occupation of the hereditament or to acquiring it;

(*e*)   which is the subject of a building preservation notice within the meaning of the Planning (Listed Buildings and Conservation Areas) Act 1990 or is included in a list compiled under section 1 of that Act;

(*f*)   which is included in the Schedule of monuments compiled under section 1 of the Ancient Monuments and Archaeological Areas Act 1979;

(*g*)   whose rateable value is less than—

    (i)   in relation to the financial year beginning on 1st April 2008, £2,200;

    (ii)   in relation to the financial year beginning on 1st April 2009, £15,000;

    (iii)   in relation to the financial year beginning on 1st April 2010, £18,000;

    (iv)   in relation to the financial years beginning on 1st April 2011, 1st April 2012, 1st April 2013, 1st April 2014, 1st April 2015 and 1st April 2016, £2,600;

    (v)   in relation to financial years beginning on or after 1st April 2017, £2,900.

(*h*)   whose owner is entitled to possession only in his capacity as the personal representative of a deceased person;

(*i*)   where, in respect of the owner's estate, there subsists a bankruptcy order within the meaning of section 381(2) of the Insolvency Act 1986;

(*j*)   revoked

(*k*)   whose owner is a company which is subject to a winding-up order made under the Insolvency Act 1986 or which is being wound up voluntarily under that Act;

(*l*)   whose owner is a company in administration within the meaning of paragraph 1 of Schedule B1 to the Insolvency Act 1986 or is subject to an administration order made under the former administration provisions within the meaning of article 3 of the Enterprise Act 2002 (Commencement No 4 and Transitional Provisions and Savings) Order 2003;

(*m*)   whose owner is entitled to possession of the hereditament in his capacity as liquidator by virtue of an order made under section 112 or section 145 of the Insolvency Act 1986.

7.7994   *5.   Continuous occupation*   A hereditament which has been unoccupied and becomes occupied on any day shall be treated as having been continuously unoccupied for the purposes of regulation 4(*a*) and (*b*) if it becomes unoccupied again on the expiration of a period of less than six weeks beginning with that day.

7.7995   *6.   Hereditaments not previously occupied*   For the purposes of regulation 4(*a*) and (*b*), a hereditament which has not previously been occupied shall be treated as becoming unoccupied—

(*a*)   on the day determined under paragraph 8 of Schedule 1 to the General Rate Act 1967, or on the day determined under Schedule 4A to the Act, whichever day first occurs; or

(*b*)   where paragraph (*a*) does not apply, on the day for which the hereditament is first shown in a local rating list.

   7.   Revocation and saving

Licensing Act 2003 (Mandatory Licensing Conditions) Order 2010[1]
(SI 2010/860 amended by SI 2014/2440)

7.7996   *1.   Citation and commencement*   (1)   This Order may be cited as the Licensing Act 2003 (Mandatory Licensing Conditions) Order 2010.
(2)   This Order shall come into force on 6th April 2010 other than paragraphs 4 and 5 of the Schedule which shall come into force on 1st October 2010.

---

[1] Made by the Secretary of State in exercise of the powers conferred by ss 19A, 73B and 197(2) of the Licensing Act 2003.

7.7997   *2.   Interpretation*   In this Order—
   "the Act" means the Licensing Act 2003;
   "anti-social behaviour" has the meaning given in section 36 of the Anti-social Behaviour Act 2003;
   "disability" has the meaning given in section 1 of the Disability Discrimination Act 1995;
   "relevant premises" has the meaning given in paragraphs (*a*) and (*b*) of the definition in section 159 of the Act;
   "responsible person" has the meaning given in paragraphs (*a*) and (*b*) of the definition in section 153(4) of the Act.

7.7998   *3.   Mandatory conditions*   (1)   Subject to paragraph (3), in relation to an existing or future relevant premises licence, the conditions set out in the Schedule are specified for the purposes of section 19(4) of the Act (mandatory conditions where licence authorises supply of alcohol).
(2)   Subject to paragraph (3), in relation to an existing or future relevant club premises certificate, the conditions set out in the Schedule are specified for the purposes of section 73A of the Act (mandatory conditions relating to the supply of alcohol to members or guests).
(3)   The conditions in paragraphs 1, 2 and 4 of the Schedule do not apply where the licence or certificate authorises the sale by retail or supply of alcohol only for consumption off the premises.

SCHEDULE
MANDATORY LICENSING CONDITIONS   Article 3
7.7999   *1.*   (1)   The responsible person must ensure that staff on relevant premises do not carry out, arrange or participate in any irresponsible promotions in relation to the premises.
(2)   In this paragraph, an irresponsible promotion means any one or more of the following activities, or substantially similar activities, carried on for the purpose of encouraging the sale or supply of alcohol for consumption on the premises—

(*a*)   games or other activities which require or encourage, or are designed to require or encourage, individuals to—
             (i)   drink a quantity of alcohol within a time limit (other than to drink alcohol sold or supplied on the premises before the cessation of the period in which the responsible person is authorised to sell or supply alcohol), or
             (ii)   drink as much alcohol as possible (whether within a time limit or otherwise);
(*b*)   provision of unlimited or unspecified quantities of alcohol free or for a fixed or discounted fee to the public or to a group defined by a particular characteristic in a manner which carries a significant risk of undermining a licensing objective;
(*c*)   provision of free or discounted alcohol or any other thing as a prize to encourage or reward the purchase and consumption of alcohol over a period of 24 hours or less in a manner which carries a significant risk of undermining a licensing objective;
(*d*)   selling or supplying alcohol in association with promotional posters or flyers on, or in the vicinity of, the premises which can reasonably be considered to condone, encourage or glamorise anti-social behaviour or to refer to the effects of drunkenness in any favourable manner;
(*e*)   dispensing alcohol directly by one person into the mouth of another (other than where that other person is unable to drink without assistance by reason of disability).
2.   The responsible person must ensure that free potable water is provided on request to customers where it is reasonably available.
3.   (1)   The premises licence holder or club premises certificate holder must ensure that an age verification policy is adopted in respect of the premises in relation to the sale or supply of alcohol.
(2)   The designated premises supervisor in relation to the premises licence must ensure that the supply of alcohol at the premises is carried on in accordance with the age verification policy.
(3)   The policy must require individuals who appear to the responsible person to be under 18 years of age (or such older age as may be specified in the policy) to produce on request, before being served alcohol, identification bearing their photograph, date of birth and either—
(*a*)   a holographic mark, or
(*b*)   an ultraviolet feature.
4.   he responsible person must ensure that—
(*a*)   where any of the following alcoholic drinks is sold or supplied for consumption on the premises (other than alcoholic drinks sold or supplied having been made up in advance ready for sale or supply in a securely closed container) it is available to customers in the following measures—

      (i)   beer or cider: ½ pint;

      (ii)   gin, rum, vodka or whisky: 25 ml or 35 ml; and

      (iii)   still wine in a glass: 125 ml;

(b)   these measures are displayed in a menu, price list or other printed material which is available to customers on the premises; and

(c)   where a customer does not in relation to a sale of alcohol specify the quantity of alcohol to be sold, the customer is made aware that these measures are available.

Licensing Act 2003 (Mandatory Conditions) Order 2014[1]
(SI 2014/1252)

7.8000   *1. Citation and commencement*   This Order may be cited as the Licensing Act 2003 (Mandatory Conditions) Order 2014 and comes into force 14 days after the day on which it is made.

---

[1] Made by the Secretary of State in exercise of the powers conferred by ss 19A, 73B and 197(2) of the Licensing Act 2003.

7.8001   *2. Mandatory licensing condition*   (1)   In relation to an existing or future relevant premises licence, the condition set out in the Schedule is specified for the purposes of section 19(4) of the Licensing Act 2003.

(2)   In relation to an existing or future relevant club premises certificate, the condition set out in the Schedule is specified for the purposes of section 73A of the Licensing Act 2003.

SCHEDULE

MANDATORY LICENSING CONDITION   Article 2

7.8002   *1.*   A relevant person shall ensure that no alcohol is sold or supplied for consumption on or off the premises for a price which is less than the permitted price.

2.   For the purposes of the condition set out in paragraph 1—

(a)   "duty" is to be construed in accordance with the Alcoholic Liquor Duties Act 1979;

(b)   "permitted price" is the price found by applying the formula—

$$P = D + (D \times V)$$

where—

      (i)   P is the permitted price,

      (ii)   D is the amount of duty chargeable in relation to the alcohol as if the duty were charged on the date of the sale or supply of the alcohol, and

      (iii)   V is the rate of value added tax chargeable in relation to the alcohol as if the value added tax were charged on the date of the sale or supply of the alcohol;

(c)   "relevant person" means, in relation to premises in respect of which there is in force a premises licence—

      (i)   the holder of the premises licence,

      (ii)   the designated premises supervisor (if any) in respect of such a licence, or

      (iii)   the personal licence holder who makes or authorises a supply of alcohol under such a licence;

(d)   "relevant person" means, in relation to premises in respect of which there is in force a club premises certificate, any member or officer of the club present on the premises in a capacity which enables the member or officer to prevent the supply in question; and

(e)   "value added tax" means value added tax charged in accordance with the Value Added Tax Act 1994.

3.   Where the permitted price given by Paragraph (b) of paragraph 2 would (apart from this paragraph) not be a whole number of pennies, the price given by that sub-paragraph shall be taken to be the price actually given by that sub-paragraph rounded up to the nearest penny.

4.   (1)   Sub-paragraph (2) applies where the permitted price given by Paragraph (b) of paragraph 2 on a day ("the first day") would be different from the permitted price on the next day ("the second day") as a result of a change to the rate of duty or value added tax.

(2)   The permitted price which would apply on the first day applies to sales or supplies of alcohol which take place before the expiry of the period of 14 days beginning on the second day.

LONDON

Contents

Public order

PUBLIC ORDER

Metropolitan Police Act 1839

(2 and 3 Vict c 47)

7.8003   54.   Offences in thoroughfares or public places   Every person shall be liable to a penalty not more than **level 2** on the standard scale, who, within the limits of the metropolitan police district shall in any thoroughfare or public place[1], commit any of the following offences; (that is to say,)

1.   very person who shall, to the annoyance[2] of the inhabitants or passengers expose for show or sale (except in a market lawfully appointed for that purpose) or feed or fodder any horse or other animal, or show any caravan containing any animal or any other show or public entertainment, or shoe, bleed, or farry any horse or animal (except in cases of accident), or clean, dress, exercise, train, or break any horse or animal, or clean, make, or repair any part of any cart or carriage, except in cases of accident where repair on the spot is necessary:

2.   Every person who shall turn loose any horse or cattle, or suffer to be at large any unmuzzled ferocious[3] dog, or set on or urge any dog or other animal to attack, worry, or put in fear any person, horse, or other animal:

3.   Every person who by negligence or ill-usage in driving cattle shall cause any mischief to be done by such cattle, or who shall in anywise misbehave himself in the driving, care, or management of such cattle, and also every person not being hired or employed to drive such cattle who shall wantonly and unlawfully, pelt, drive, or hunt any such cattle:

4.   Every person having the care of any cart or carriage who shall ride on any part thereof, on the shafts, or on any horse or other animal drawing the same, without having and holding the reins, or who shall be at such a distance from such cart or carriage as not to have the complete control over every horse or other animal drawing the same[4]:

5.   Every person who shall ride or drive furiously, or so as to endanger the life or limb of any person, or to the common danger of the passengers in any thoroughfare[5]:

6.   Every person who shall cause any cart, public carriage, sledge, truck, or barrow, with or without horses, to stand longer than may be necessary for loading or unloading or for taking up or setting down passengers, except hackney carriages standing for hire in any place not forbidden by law, or who, by means of any cart, carriage, sledge, truck, or barrow or any horse or other animal, shall wilfully interrupt[6] any public crossing, or wilfully cause any obstruction in any thoroughfare:

7.   Every person who shall lead or ride any horse or other animal, or draw or drive any cart or carriage, sledge, truck, or barrow, upon any footway or curbstone, or fasten any horse or other animal so that it can stand across or upon any footway:

8.   Every person who shall roll or carry any cask, tub, hoop, or wheel, or any ladder, plank, pole, showboard, or placard, upon any footway[7], except for the purpose of loading or unloading any cart or carriage, or of crossing the footway:

9.   Every person who, after being made acquainted with the regulations or directions which the commissioners of police shall have made for regulating the route of horses, carts, carriages, and persons for preventing obstructions during public processions and on other occasions herein-before specified, shall wilfully disregard or not conform himself thereunto:

10.   Every person who, without the consent of the owner or occupier, shall affix any posting bill or other paper against or upon any building, wall, fence, or pale, or write upon, soil, deface, or mark any such building, wall, fence, or pale with chalk or paint, or in any other way whatsoever, or wilfully break, destroy, or damage any part of any such building, wall, fence, or pale, or any fixture or appendage thereunto, or any tree, shrub, or seat in any public walk park, or garden:

11.   *Repealed.*

12.   Every person who shall sell or distribute or offer for sale or distribution, or exhibit to public view, any profane, book, paper, print, drawing, painting or representation, or sing any profane, indecent, or obscene song or ballad, or use any profane, indecent or obscene language to the annoyance[8] of the inhabitants or passengers:

13.   *Repealed.*

14.   Every person except the guards and postmen belonging to her Majesty's Post Office in the performance of their duty, who shall blow any horn or use any other noisy instrument[9] for the purpose of calling persons together, or of announcing any show or entertainment, or for the purpose of hawking, selling, distributing, or collecting any article whatsoever, or of obtaining money or alms:

15.   Every person who shall wantonly discharge any fire-arm or throw or discharge[10] any stone or other missile, to the damage or danger of any person, or make any bonfire, or throw or set fire to any firework:

16.   Every person who shall wilfully and wantonly disturb any inhabitant by pulling or ringing any door-bell[11] or knocking at any door without lawful excuse, or who shall wilfully and unlawfully extinguish the light of any lamp:

17.   Every person who shall fly any kite or play at any game to the annoyance of the inhabitants or passengers[12], or who shall make or use any slide upon ice or snow in any street or other thoroughfare, to the common danger of the passengers.

[Metropolitan Police Act 1839, s 54 as amended by Street Offences Act 1959, Criminal Justice Act 1967, Statute Law (Repeals) Act 1973, Criminal Law Act 1977, Sch 6, the Indecent Displays (Control) Act 1981, Sch, the Criminal Justice Act 1982, s 46, the Police and Criminal Evidence Act 1984, Sch 7 and the Public Order Act 1986, Sch 3.]

---

[1] There is no definition of "public place" in this Act. However, this section can be compared with the Town Police Clauses Act 1847, s 28, to which the definition of "public place" contained in the Public Health Amendment Act 1907, s 81, as amended (post) is expressly extended. Some of the offences created by the following subsections can, it is submitted, be committed on private property adjacent to public places and in view of persons thereon.

[2] To constitute an offence there must have been some annoyance in fact, or something necessarily calculated to be so (*Allen v Baldock* (1867) 31 JP 311). See also *Innes v Newman* [1894] 2 QB 292, 58 JP 543, where it was held, in respect of a prosecution under a byelaw, that as the act complained of was such as was calculated to annoy the inhabitants generally, it was sufficient to prove that one inhabitant was annoyed.

[3] It should be noted that there is no necessity for knowledge of the dog's ferocious nature to be proved.

[4] A similar provision appears in s 78 of the Highway Act 1835, ante.

[5] See also s 35 of the Offences Against the Person Act 1861, and s 28 of the London Hackney Carriages Act 1843.

[6] See note 1 to s 28 of the Town Police Clauses Act 1847, post.

[7] This subsection is wider in its application than similar provisions in s 72 of the Highway Act 1835, which is restricted to footpaths at the road side; see the words "thoroughfare or public place" in the opening sentence of this section.

[8] On a prosecution under s 54(12), where indecent or obscene language is alleged, it is sufficient to show that the words were calculated to annoy; proof of actual annoyance is not required (*Myers v Garrett* [1972] Crim LR 232). See also note 2 to s 54(1), supra.

[9] The Control of Pollution Act 1974, s 62 (see title PUBLIC HEALTH, post) prohibits the use of loudspeakers in streets otherwise than for certain specified purposes and between certain specified hours.

[10] There is a similar provision in the Explosives Act 1875, s 80, in relation to fireworks.

[11] See note 3, to the Town Police Clauses Act 1847, s 28, post.

[12] The playing of football or any game on a highway "to the annoyance of a user" is an offence against the Highways Act 1980, s 161, title HIGHWAYS, ante.

7.8004   58.   Indecent behaviour[1]   Every person who shall be guilty of any violent or indecent behaviour in any police station house, shall be liable to a penalty of not more than **level 1** on the standard scale for every such offence or may be committed, if the magistrate[2] before whom he shall be convicted shall think fit instead of inflicting on him any pecuniary penalty, [to a term of imprisonment not exceeding one month].
[Metropolitan Police Act 1839, s 58 as amended by the Penalties for Drunkenness Act 1962, the Criminal Justice Act 1967, Sch 7 and the Criminal Justice Act 1982, ss 38 and 46.]

---

[1]   The Criminal Justice Act 1967, s 91 in PART I: MAGISTRATES' COURTS, PROCEDURE, ante, has effect in place of this section where a person is guilty whilst drunk of disorderly behaviour (Criminal Justice Act 1967, s 91(2)).
[2]   Lay justices in the Inner London area have jurisdiction by virtue of the Justices of the Peace Act 1979, s 33, ante.

Police Reform and Social Responsibility Act 2011
(2011 c 13)

PART 3
PARLIAMENT SQUARE ETC

Repeal of SOCPA 2005 provisions

7.8005   141.   Demonstrations in vicinity of Parliament: repeal of SOCPA 2005 provisions
   (1)   Sections 132 to 138 of the Serious Organised Crime and Police Act 2005 (which regulate demonstrations and use of loudspeakers in the vicinity of Parliament) are repealed.
   (2)   The public assemblies in relation to which section 14 of the Public Order Act 1986 applies, as a consequence of the repeal of section 132(6) of the Serious Organised Crime and Police Act 2005, include public assemblies which started, or were being organised, before this section comes into force.
[Police Reform and Social Responsibility Act 2011, s 141.]

Controls on activities in Parliament Square etc

7.8006   142.   Controlled area of Parliament Square[1]   (1)   For the purposes of this Part, the "controlled area of Parliament Square" means the area of land that is comprised in—
   (*a*)   the central garden of Parliament Square, and
   (*b*)   the footways that immediately adjoin the central garden of Parliament Square.
   (2)   In subsection (1)—
   "the central garden of Parliament Square" means the site in Parliament Square on which the Minister of Works was authorised by the Parliament Square (Improvements) Act 1949 to lay out the garden referred to in that Act as "the new central garden";
   "footway" has the same meaning as in the Highways Act 1980 (see section 329(1) of that Act).
[Police Reform and Social Responsibility Act 2011, s 142.]

---

[1]   An existing authorisation under s 135 of the Serious Organised Crime and Police Act 2005 did not make unlawful the decision of the authority to enforce Part 3 of this Act. The provisions of Part 3 are compatible with the European Convention on Human Rights as they are limited and proportionate: *R (Gallastegui) v Westminster City Council* [2012] EWHC 1123 (Admin); affd *R (on the application of Gallastegui) v Westminster City Council* [2013] EWCA Civ 28, [2013] 2 All ER 579, [2013] 1 WLR 2377.

7.8007   142A.   Other controlled areas in vicinity of the Palace of Westminster

7.8008   143.   Prohibited activities in controlled area of Parliament Square or in Palace of Westminster controlled area   (1)   A constable or authorised officer who has reasonable grounds for believing that a person is doing, or is about to do, a prohibited activity may[1] direct the person—
   (*a*)   to cease doing that activity, or
   (*b*)   (as the case may be) not to start doing that activity.
   (2)   For the purposes of this Part, a "prohibited activity" is any of the following—
   (*a*)   operating any amplified noise equipment in the controlled area of Parliament Square or in the Palace of Westminster controlled area;
   (*b*)   erecting or keeping erected in the controlled area of Parliament Square—
      (i)   any tent, or
      (ii)   any other structure that is designed, or adapted, (solely or mainly) for the purpose of facilitating sleeping or staying in a place for any period;
   (*c*)   using any tent or other such structure in the controlled area of Parliament Square for the purpose of sleeping or staying in that area;
   (*d*)   placing or keeping in place in the controlled area of Parliament Square any sleeping equipment with a view to its use (whether or not by the person placing it or keeping it in place) for the purpose of sleeping overnight in that area;
   (*e*)   using any sleeping equipment in the controlled area of Parliament Square for the purpose of sleeping overnight in that area.
   (3)   But an activity is not to be treated as a "prohibited activity" within subsection (2) if it is done—
   (*a*)   for police, fire and rescue authority or ambulance purposes,
   (*b*)   by or on behalf of a relevant authority, or

(c)   by a person so far as authorised under section 147 to do it (authorisation for operation of amplified noise equipment).

(4)   In subsection (2)(a) "amplified noise equipment" means any device that is designed or adapted for amplifying sound, including (but not limited to)—

(a)   loudspeakers, and

(b)   loudhailers.

(5)   In subsection (3)(b) "relevant authority" means any of the following—

(a)   a Minister of the Crown or a government department,

(b)   the Greater London Authority, or

(c)   Westminster City Council.

(6)   It is immaterial for the purposes of a prohibited activity—

(a)   in the case of an activity within subsection (2)(b) or (c) of keeping a tent or similar structure erected or using a tent or similar structure, whether the tent or structure was first erected before or after the coming into force of this section;

(b)   in the case of an activity within subsection (2)(d) or (e) of keeping in place any sleeping equipment or using any such equipment, whether the sleeping equipment was first placed before or after the coming into force of this section.

(7)   In this section "sleeping equipment" means any sleeping bag, mattress or other similar item designed, or adapted, (solely or mainly) for the purpose of facilitating sleeping in a place.

(8)   A person who fails without reasonable excuse to comply with a direction under subsection (1) commits an offence and is liable on summary conviction to a fine not exceeding level 5 on the standard scale.

[Police Reform and Social Responsibility Act 2011, s 143 as amended by the Anti-social Behaviour, Crime and Policing Act 2014, s 153.]

---

[1] This creates a discretion not a duty and the discretion should be exercised so as to promote the policy and objectives of the 2011 Act. The discretion not to exercise the power must have been intended by Parliament to be exercised only in exceptional circumstances: *R (on the application of Gallestegui) v Westminster City Council* [2013] EWCA Civ 28, [2013] 2 All ER 579, [2013] 1 WLR 2377

7.8009   144.   Directions under section 143: further provision   (1) A direction requiring a person to cease doing a prohibited activity may include a direction that the person does not start doing that activity again after having ceased it.

(2)   A direction requiring a person not to start doing a prohibited activity continues in force until—

(a)   the end of such period beginning with the day on which the direction is given as may be specified by the constable or authorised officer giving the direction, or

(b)   if no such period is specified, the end of the period of 90 days beginning with the day on which the direction is given.

(3)   A period specified under subsection (2)(a) may not be longer than 90 days.

(4)   A direction may be given to a person to cease operating, or not to start operating, any amplified noise equipment only if it appears to the constable or authorised officer giving the direction that the following condition is met.

(5)   The condition is that the person is operating, or is about to operate, the equipment in such a manner as to produce sound that other persons in or in the vicinity of the controlled area of Parliament Square, or the Palace of Westminster controlled area, can hear or are likely to be able to hear.

(6)   A direction—

(a)   may be given orally,

(b)   may be given to any person individually or to two or more persons together, and

(c)   may be withdrawn or varied by the person who gave it.

(7)   In this section—

"amplified noise equipment" has the meaning given by section 143(4);

"direction" means a direction given under section 143(1).

[Police Reform and Social Responsibility Act 2011, s 144 as amended by the Anti-social Behaviour, Crime and Policing Act 2014, s 153.]

7.8010   145.   Power to seize property   (1) A constable or authorised officer may seize and retain a prohibited item that is on any land in the controlled area of Parliament Square if it appears to that constable or officer that the item is being, or has been, used in connection with the commission of an offence under section 143 in that area.

(1A)   A constable or authorised officer may seize and retain a prohibited item that is on any land in the Palace of Westminster controlled area if it appears to that constable or officer that the item is being, or has been, used in connection with the commission of an offence under section 143 in that area.

(2)   A constable may seize and retain a prohibited item that is on any land outside of the controlled area of Parliament Square if it appears to the constable that the item has been used in connection with the commission of an offence under section 143 in that area.

(2A)   A constable may seize and retain a prohibited item that is on any land outside of the Palace of Westminster controlled area if it appears to the constable that the item has been used in connection with the commission of an offence under section 143 in that area.

(3)   A "prohibited item" is any item of a kind mentioned in section 143(2).

(4)   A constable may use reasonable force, if necessary, in exercising a power of seizure under this section.

(5)   An item seized under this section must be returned to the person from whom it was seized—

(a)   no later than the end of the period of 28 days beginning with the day on which the item was seized, or

(b)   if proceedings are commenced against the person for an offence under section 143 before the return of the item under paragraph (a), at the conclusion of those proceedings.

(6)   If it is not possible to return an item under subsection (5) because the name or address of the person from whom it was seized is not known—

(a)   the item may be returned to any other person appearing to have rights in the property who has come forward to claim it, or

(b)   if there is no such person, the item may be disposed of or destroyed at any time after the end of the period of 90 days beginning with the day on which the item was seized.

(7)   Subsections (5)(b) and (6) do not apply if a court makes an order under section 146(1)(a) for the forfeiture of the item.

(8)   The references in this section to an item that is "on" any land include references to an item that is in the possession of a person who is on any such land.

[Police Reform and Social Responsibility Act 2011, s 145 as amended by the Anti-social Behaviour, Crime and Policing Act 2014, s 153.]

7.8011   146.   Power of court on conviction   (1)   The court may do either or both of the following on the conviction of a person ("P") of an offence under section 143—

(a)   make an order providing for the forfeiture of any item of a kind mentioned in subsection (2) of that section that was used in the commission of the offence;

(b)   make such other order as the court considers appropriate for the purpose of preventing P from engaging in any prohibited activity in a relevant area.

(2)   An order under subsection (1)(b) may (in particular) require P not to enter a relevant area for such period as may be specified in the order.

(2A)   In this section "relevant area" means an area consisting of either or both of the following areas—

(a)   the controlled area of Parliament Square, and

(b)   the Palace of Westminster controlled area.

(3)   Power of the court to make an order under this section is in addition to the court's power to impose a fine under section 143(8).

[Police Reform and Social Responsibility Act 2011, s 146 as amended by the Anti-social Behaviour, Crime and Policing Act 2014, s 153.]

7.8012   147.   Authorisation for operation of amplified noise equipment   (1)   The responsible authority for any land in the controlled area of Parliament Square or the Palace of Westminster controlled area may authorise a person in accordance with this section to operate on that land (or any part of it) any amplified noise equipment (as defined by section 143(4)).

(2)   An application for authorisation must be made to the responsible authority by or on behalf of the person (or persons) seeking the authorisation.

(3)   The responsible authority may—

(a)   determine the form in which, and the manner in which, an application is to be made;

(b)   specify the information to be supplied in connection with an application;

(c)   require a fee to be paid for determining an application.

(4)   If an application is duly made to a responsible authority, the authority must—

(a)   determine the application, and

(b)   give notice in writing to the applicant of the authority's decision within the period of 21 days beginning with the day on which the authority receives the application.

(5)   The notice must specify—

(a)   the person (or persons) authorised (whether by name or description),

(b)   the kind of amplified noise equipment to which the authorisation applies,

(c)   the period to which the authorisation applies, and

(d)   any conditions to which the authorisation is subject.

(6)   The responsible authority may at any time—

(a)   withdraw an authorisation given to a person under this section, or

(b)   vary any condition to which an authorisation is subject.

(7)   Variation under subsection (6)(b) includes—

(a)   imposing a new condition,

(b)   removing an existing condition, or

(c)   altering any period to which a condition applies.

(8)   The exercise of a power under subsection (6) to withdraw an authorisation or to vary a condition is effected by the responsible authority giving notice in writing to the applicant.

[Police Reform and Social Responsibility Act 2011, s 147 as amended by the Anti-social Behaviour, Crime and Policing Act 2014, s 153.]

7.8013   148.   Meaning of "authorised officer" and "responsible authority"   (1)   This section applies for the purposes of this Part.

(2)   "Authorised officer", in relation to any land in the controlled area of Parliament Square, or in relation to any land in the Palace of Westminster controlled area other than Royal Park land, means—

(*a*)   an employee of the responsible authority for that land who is authorised in writing by the authority for the purposes of this Part, and

(*b*)   any other person who, under arrangements made with the responsible authority (whether by that or any other person), is so authorised for the purposes of this Part.

(3)   "Responsible authority", in relation to any land in the controlled area of Parliament Square, means—

(*a*)   the Greater London Authority, for any land comprised in the central garden of Parliament Square (as defined by section 142(2)), and

(*b*)   Westminster City Council, for any other land.

(4)   "Responsible authority", in relation to any land in the Palace of Westminster controlled area, means—

(*a*)   the Secretary of State, for any land comprised in Royal Park land;

(*b*)   Westminster City Council, for any other land.

(5)   In this section "Royal Park land" means any land of a description specified in Schedule 1 to the Royal Parks and Other Open Spaces Regulations 1997 (S.I. 1997/1639), as that Schedule has effect on the day on which the Anti-social Behaviour, Crime and Policing Act 2014 is passed

[Police Reform and Social Responsibility Act 2011, s 148 as amended by the Anti-social Behaviour, Crime and Policing Act 2014, s 153.]

149.   *Byelaws not to be made in respect of prohibited activity within the meaning of this Part.*

LICENSING

Greater London Council (General Powers) Act 1978
(1978 c xiii)
PART II
PROVISIONS RELATING TO THE COUNCIL

Licensing of public entertainments

7.8014   5.   Licensing of entertainments booking offices   (1)   No premises in a borough shall, on or after 1st October, 1978, be used as a booking office except under and in accordance with the terms of a licence (hereafter in this section referred to as a "booking office licence") granted by the borough council in pursuance of the provisions of this section.

(2)   Subject to the next following subsection, the provisions of sub-paragraphs (2), (3) and (5) of paragraph 1, sub-paragraphs (1) and (2) of paragraph 2 and paragraphs 3, 6A, 6B, 7 to 10, 12, 12A, 12B, 12C and 17 to 20 of Schedule 12[1] to the Act of 1963 shall apply to a booking office licence as they apply in relation to a licence under paragraph 1 of that Schedule and as if the booking office licence had been granted under the said paragraph 1.

(3)   For the purposes of the application of the provisions of the said Schedule 12, referred to in the foregoing subsection, to a booking office licence—

(*a*)   for sub-paragraph (1) of paragraph 10 of the said Schedule there shall be substituted the following—

"(1)   If any premises are used as a booking office, as defined in subsection (4) of section 5 (Licensing of entertainments booking offices) of the Greater London Council (General Powers) Act 1978, without a licence being held in respect thereof under the said section 5, then—

(*a*)   any person concerned in the organisation or management of that booking office; and

(*b*)   any other person who, knowing or having reasonable cause to suspect that those premises would be so used as a booking office—

(i)   allowed the premises to be so used; or

(ii)   let the premises, or otherwise made the premises available to any person by whom an offence in connection with that use of the premises has been committed;

shall be guilty of an offence.";

(*b*)   in sub-paragraph (2) of the said paragraph 10, for the words "for any entertainment" there shall be substituted the words "as a booking office (as defined in subsection (4) of section 5 of the said Act of 1978)"; and

(*c*)   in sub-paragraph (1) of paragraph 12 of the said Schedule 12, for the words "at which he has reason to believe that an entertainment to which either of those paragraphs applies is being given or is about to be given" there shall be substituted the words "which he has reason to believe are being used as a booking office (as defined in subsection (4) of section 5 of the said Act of 1978)" and for the word "entertainment", where it occurs for the second time, there shall be substituted the word "use".

(4)

(a)   In this section "booking office" means any premises, not being premises exempted in accordance with paragraph (b) of this subsection or premises in use at the time in question for any of the following purposes, that is to say—

    (i)   public dancing or music or any other public entertainment of the like kind;

    (ii)   *repealed*

whose principal function at that time is to serve as premises at which members of the public may by the purchase of tickets or vouchers, or, on payment, by any other means, secure admission (whether or not on payment of a further charge) to any other premises (not being premises to which paragraph (c) of this subsection applies) used for any of the purposes mentioned in sub-paragraph (i) of this paragraph.

(b)

    (i)   If, in the opinion of the borough council, it is inappropriate that any premises or any class of premises should remain subject as booking offices to the provisions of this section, they may by resolution determine that as from a date to be fixed by the resolution those premises or that class of premises shall be exempted from such provisions.

    (ii)   If, in the opinion of the borough council, after the date fixed by a resolution passed under the foregoing sub-paragraph and having regard to any relevant circumstances, any premises or any class of premises exempted as booking offices from the provisions of this section by virtue of such a resolution should again become subject to the said provisions, they may by a further resolution determine that those premises or that class of premises shall again become subject as booking offices to the said provisions as from a date to be fixed by such further resolution.

(c)   This paragraph applies (for the purposes of paragraph (a) of this subsection) to—

    (i)   the Theatre Royal Drury Lane, the Royal Covent Garden Opera House, the Theatre Royal Haymarket and the Royal Albert Hall;

    (ii)   premises which may be used for the performance of plays without a licence under the Theatres Act 1968 by virtue of any letters patent of the Crown; and

    (iii)   any other premises specified by resolution of the borough council from time to time for the purposes of this paragraph.

(5)   In this section "borough" includes the City of London and "borough council" includes the Common Council.

[Greater London Council (General Powers) Act 1978, s 5 as amended by the Greater London Council (General Powers) Act 1984, s 4 and the Local Government Act 1985, Sch 8 and the Licensing Act 2003, Sch 6.]

---

[1] *Ante.*

London Local Authorities Act 1990
(1990 c vii)
PART III
STREET TRADING

7.8015 **21. Interpretation of Part III** (1) In this Part of this Act—

"grant", unless the context otherwise requires, includes renew and renewal, and cognate words shall be construed accordingly;

"ice cream trading" means the selling, exposing or offering for sale of goods consisting wholly or mainly of ice cream, frozen confectionery or other similar commodities from a vehicle;

"itinerant ice cream trading" means ice cream trading from a vehicle which goes from place to place remaining in any one location in the course of trading for periods of 15 minutes or less and not returning to that location or any other location in the same street on the same day;

"licence street" means a street designated under section 24 (Designation of licence streets) of this Act;

"receptacle" includes a vehicle or stall and any basket, bag, box, vessel, stand, easel, board, tray or thing which is used (whether or not constructed or adapted for such use) as a container for or for the display of any article or thing or equipment used in the provision of any service;

"street" includes—

    (a)   any road or footway;

    (b)   any other area, not being within permanently enclosed premises, within 7 metres of any road or footway, to which the public obtain access without payment—

        (i)   whether or not they need the consent of the owner or occupier; and

        (ii)   if they do, whether or not they have obtained it;

    (c)   any part of such road, footway or area;

    (d)   any part of any housing development provided or maintained by a local authority under Part II of the Housing Act 1985;

"street trading"[1] means subject to subsections (1ZA), (1) and (2) below—

    (a)   the selling or the exposure or offer for sale of any article (including a living thing); and

    (b)   the purchasing of or offering to purchase any ticket; and

(c)   the supplying of or offering to supply any service,

in a street for gain or reward (whether or not the gain or reward accrues to the person actually carrying out the trading);

"street trading licence" means a licence granted under this Part of this Act and valid for the period specified therein being not less than six months and not more than three years;

"temporary licence" means a licence granted under this Part of this Act valid for a single day or for such period as may be specified in the licence not exceeding six months.

(1ZA)   In this Part of this Act "street trading" shall also include the selling or exposure or offer for sale of any motor vehicle in the course of a business if the vehicle is—

(a)   exposed or offered for sale on the internet; and

(b)   kept on a street during the period when it is so exposed or offered for sale.

(1A)   In determining whether activity amounts to street trading for the purposes of this Act, the fact that—

(a)   a transaction was completed elsewhere than in a street in the case where the initial offer or display of the articles in question or the offer of services, as the case may be, took place in a street;

(b)   either party to the transaction was not in a street at the time it was completed;

(c)   the articles actually sold or services actually supplied, as the case may be, were different from those offered,

shall be disregarded.

(2)   The following are not street trading for the purposes of this Part of this Act—

(a)   trading by a person acting as a pedlar under the authority of a Pedlar's Certificate granted under the Pedlars Act 1871, if the trading is carried out only be means of visits from house to house;

(b)   anything done in a market or fair the right to hold which was acquired by virtue of a grant (including a presumed grant) or acquired or established by virtue of any enactment or order;

(c)   trading in a trunk road picnic area provided by the Secretary of State under section 112 of the Highways Act 1980;

(d)   trading as a news-vendor provided that the only articles sold or exposed or offered for sale are current newspapers or periodicals and they are sold or exposed or offered for sale without a receptacle for them or, if with a receptacle for them such receptacle does not—

(i)   exceed 1 metre in length or width or 2 metres in height; or

(ii)   occupy a ground area exceeding 0.25 square metre; or

(iii)   stand on the carriageway of a street; or

(iv)   cause undue interference or inconvenience to persons using the street;

(e)   selling articles or things to occupiers of premises adjoining any street, or offering or exposing them for sale from a vehicle which is used only for the regular delivery of milk or other perishable goods to those persons;

(f)   *repealed*

(g)   *repealed*

(h)   the doing of anything authorised by regulations made under section 5 of the Police, Factories, etc (Miscellaneous Provisions) Act 1916 or by permit or order made under Part III of the Charities Act 1992 (c 41);*

(i)   trading in a highway in relation to which a control order under section 7 of the Local Government (Miscellaneous Provisions) Act 1976 is in force, other than trading to which the control order does not apply; and

(j)   the selling or the exposure or offer for sale of articles or the provision of services on private land adjacent to a shop provided that the selling or the exposure or offer for sale of the articles or the provision of the services—

(i)   forms part of the business of the owner[2] of the shop or a person assessed for uniform business rate in respect of the shop; and

(ii)   takes place during the period during which the shop is open to the public for business.

[London Local Authorities Act 1990, s 21 as amended by the London Local Authorities Act 1994, s 6, the London Local Authorities Act 2004, Sch 4 , the London Local Authorities Act 2007, s 38 and the London Local Authorities Act 2012, s 9.]

---

*   **Substituted by the London Local Authorities Act 1996, s 26 from a date to be appointed.**

1   Exposing goods for sale on a pavement outside a shop for payment within the shop is street trading for the purposes of this Act (*Wandsworth London Borough Council v Rosenthal* (1996) Times, 28 March).

2   Prior to its amendment, this subsection referred to the "owner or occupier", and the phrase "owner or occupier" did not limit the person concerned to freeholder or possessor of the land; it was a question of fact and degree whether a person was the owner or occupier (*O'Gorman v Brent London Borough Council* (1993) 91 LGR 555).

7.8016 22. Application of Part III   This Part of this Act applies to the borough of a participating council[1] as from the appointed day[2].

[London Local Authorities Act 1990, s 22.]

---

¹ The participating councils are listed in Sch 1 to the Act and include Inner and Outer London Boroughs. Subsections 23–33 of the Act make provision for the designation of licence streets, applications for licences, succession on death or retirement, conditions, revocation or variation, appeals, temporary licences, fees and charges, receptacles and containers.
² See the note to s 5 ante as to appointed day.

7.8017 30. Part III appeals: refusal to grant a licence etc (1) Any person aggrieved—

(*aa*) by the refusal of a borough council to renew a licence because they are not satisfied as mentioned in subsection (4)(*b*) of section 25 (Application for street trading licences) of this Act;

(*a*) by the refusal of a borough council to grant or renew a licence on any of the grounds mentioned in subsection (6)(*a*) to (*e*) of section 25 (Application for street trading licences); or

(*b*) by a decision of a borough council under subsection (7) of the said section 25 to grant him a licence either on terms mentioned in that subsection different from those on the licence which he previously held or different from those for which he applied; or

(*c*) by any further condition attached by a borough council under subsection (8) of section 27 (Conditions of street trading licences) of this Act in addition to the standard conditions; or

(*d*) by a decision of the borough council either—
(i) to vary the conditions of a licence under subsection (2) of section 28 (Revocation or variation of licences under Part III) of this Act; or
(ii) to revoke a licence under subsection (1) of the said section 28; or

(*e*) by a resolution of a borough council under section 37 (Ice cream trading) of this Act;

may appeal to a magistrates' court acting for the area in which the licence street is situated.

(2) An appeal under subsection (1) above may be brought—

(*a*) in the case of an appeal under paragraph (*aa*), (*a*), (*b*), (*c*) or (*d*) of that subsection, at any time before the expiration of the period of 21 days beginning with the date upon which notification in writing is given of the refusal or decision;

(*b*) in the case of an appeal under paragraph (*e*) of that subsection, at any time before the expiration of the period of 21 days beginning with the date of the second publication of the notice required by subsection (10) of section 24 (Designation of licence streets) as applied by the said section 37.

(3) A person desiring to appeal against such refusal or decision as is mentioned in subsection (1) above shall give a written notice to the magistrates' court and to the borough council specifying the refusal or decision against which he wishes to appeal and the grounds upon which such appeal is made.

(4) An appeal by either party against the decision of the magistrates' court under this section may be brought to the Crown Court.

(5) On an appeal to the magistrates' court or to the Crown Court under this section, the court may make such order as it thinks fit.

(6) subject to subsections (7) to (9) below, it shall be the duty of the borough council to give effect to the order of the magistrates' court or the Crown Court.

(7) A borough council need not give effect to the order of the magistrates' court until the time for bringing an appeal under subsection (4) above has expired and, if such an appeal is duly brought, until the determination or abandonment of the appeal.

(8) Where a licence holder applies for renewal of his licence, his existing licence shall remain valid—

(*a*) until the grant by the borough council of a new licence with the same conditions; or

(*b*) if the borough council refuse renewal of the licence or decide to grant a licence with conditions different from those of the existing licence and he has a right of appeal under this section, until the time for bringing an appeal has expired or where an appeal is duly brought, until the determination or abandonment of the appeal; or

(*c*) if he has no right of appeal under this section until the borough council either grant him a new licence with conditions different from those of the existing licence or notify him of their decision to refuse his application.

(9) Where—

(*a*) a borough council decide
(i) to vary the conditions of a licence under subsection (2) of the said section 28; or
(ii) to revoke a licence under subsection (1) of the said section 28; and

(*b*) a right of appeal is available to the licence holder under this section;

the variation or revocation shall not take effect until the time for bringing an appeal has expired or where an appeal is duly brought, until the determination or abandonment of the appeal.

(10) For the avoidance of doubt, it is hereby declared that an application under section 31 of the Senior Courts Act 1981 (application for judicial review) or under the Rules of the Supreme Court 1965 in respect of any matter which is or could be the subject of an appeal to the magistrates' court or to the Crown Court under this section shall not be treated as an appeal for the purposes of subsection (8) or (9) above.

(11)   *Repealed.*
(12)   *Repealed.*

[London Local Authorities Act 1990, s 30, as amended by the London Local Authorities Act 1994, s 6, the Constitutional Reform Act 2005, Sch 11 and the Deregulation Act 2015, s 91.]

7.8018   30A.   Other Part III appeals   (1)   Any person aggrieved—

(a)   by a resolution rescinding or varying a designating resolution;

(b)   by a resolution under subsection (1)(b) of section 24 (Designation of licence streets) of this Act;

(c)   by a standard condition prescribed by regulations under subsection (3) of section 27 (Conditions of street trading licences) of this Act; or

(d)   by the amount of a fee or charge under section 32 (Fees and charges) of this Act;

may appeal to a magistrates' court acting for the area of the borough council which passed the resolution, prescribed the condition or determined the amount of the fee or charge (as the case may be).

(2)   An appeal under subsection (1) may be brought—

(a)   in the case of an appeal under paragraph (a) or (b) of that subsection, at any time before the expiration of the period of three months beginning with the date on which notice of the passing of the resolution is published for the second time in accordance with subsection (10) of section 24 (Designation of licence streets) of this Act;

(b)   in the case of an appeal under paragraph (c) of that subsection, at any time before the expiration of the period of three months beginning with the date upon which the licence holders or a body or bodies representative of them were notified of the making of the regulations;

(c)   in the case of an appeal under paragraph (d) of that subsection—

(i)   if it relates to the amount of a fee payable under subsection (1) of section 32 (Fees and charges) of this Act, at any time before the expiration of the period of three months beginning with the date on which the fee payable is notified to the licence holders or a body or bodies representative of them;

(ii)   if it relates to the amount of a charge under subsection (2) of section 32 (Fees and charges) of this Act, at any time before the expiration of the period of three months beginning with the date on which notice of the determination of the charge has been given to the licence holders or a body or bodies representative of them.

(3)   A person desiring to appeal under subsection (1) shall give written notice to the magistrates' court and to the borough council specifying the matter about which the person is aggrieved and the grounds upon which the appeal is made.

(4)   On an appeal to a magistrates' court under this section, the court may make such order as it thinks fit.

[London Local Authorities Act 1990, s 30A as inserted by the Deregulation Act 2015, s 91.]

7.8019   34.   Offences   Any person who without reasonable excuse—

(1)   contravenes any of the conditions of a street trading licence or a temporary licence; or

(2)   in connection with an application for a street trading licence or a temporary licence makes a statement which he knows to be false in a material particular; or

(3)   resists or intentionally obstructs any authorised officer of a borough council in the execution of his duties under this Part of this Act; or

(4)   fails on demand without reasonable excuse in the case of an individual licence holder to produce his licence bearing his photograph, and, in the case of an individual carrying on ice cream trading under a licence granted to a company incorporated under the Companies Acts or to a partnership, to produce the photograph required by subsection (2) of section 27 (Conditions of street trading licences) of this Act to an authorised officer of the borough council or to a constable;

shall be guilty of an offence and shall be liable on summary conviction to a fine not exceeding level 3 on the standard scale.

[London Local Authorities Act 1990, s 34 as amended by the London Local Authorities Act 1994, s 6 and the London Local Authorities Act 2007, s 42.]

7.8020   36.   Employment of assistants   Subject to the provisions of this section a person holding a street trading licence or a temporary licence may employ any other person to assist him in the conduct of street trading authorised by the licence but if any person employed by a licence holder during the temporary absence of the licence holder fails to comply with the conditions of the licence held by his employer such failure shall be deemed to be a failure by the licence holder.

[London Local Authorities Act 1990, s 36 as amended by the London Local Authorities Act 2007, s 43.]

7.8021   37.   Ice cream trading   (1)   Nothing in this Part of this Act shall apply to itinerant ice cream trading in any street unless—

(a)   that street is a licence street; or

(b)   the street has been designated as a prohibited street under the following provisions of this section.

(2)–(4)   *Designation of prohibited street.*

[London Local Authorities Act 1990, s 37 as amended by the London Local Authorities Act 1994, s 6.]

7.8022 38.   Unlicensed street trading   (1)   A person who—

(a)   is not the holder of a street trading licence or a temporary licence and who engages in street trading[1] in a borough whether or not from a stationary position; or

(b)   is the holder of a street trading licence or a temporary licence and who, without the borough council's specific permission in writing engages in street trading[1] in a borough on a day or in a place not specified in that licence;

shall be guilty of an offence and shall be liable on summary conviction to a fine not exceeding **level 3** on the standard scale.

(2)   In any proceedings for an offence under this section or for an offence of aiding, abetting, counselling or procuring the commission of an offence under this section where it is shown that—

(a)   any article or thing was displayed (whether or not in or on any receptacle) in any street; or

(b)   any receptacle or equipment used in the provision of any service was available in any street in such circumstances that a service was being offered;

the article, thing, receptacle or equipment concerned shall be presumed to have been exposed or offered for sale and the receptacle or equipment shall be deemed to have been used for the purposes for which a street trading licence was required unless it can be proved to the satisfaction of the court that the article or thing or receptacle or equipment was brought into that street for some purpose other than street trading[2].

(3)   Where an offence under this section committed by a body corporate is proved to have been committed with the consent or connivance of, or to be attributable to any neglect on the part of, any director, manager, secretary or other similar officer of the body corporate, or any person who was purporting to act in any such capacity, he, as well as the body corporate, shall be guilty of the offence and liable to the same maximum penalty as the body corporate.

(4)   Subject to section 38A (seizure of perishable items) of this Act if an authorised officer or a constable has reasonable grounds for suspecting that a person has committed an offence under this section he may seize—

(a)   any article or thing being offered for sale, displayed or exposed for sale; or

(b)   any other article or thing of a similar nature to that being offered or exposed for sale which is in the possession of or under the control of any person who is displaying an article or thing; or

(c)   any receptacle or equipment being used by that person.

(4A)   An authorised officer or constable may also seize, for examination purposes, any article or thing which he has reasonable cause to suspect may be an article or thing which is prohibited by a specifying resolution made under subsection (1)(b) of section 24 (Designation of licence streets) of this Act.

Unless the article or thing is required for evidential purposes it shall be returned as soon as possible to the person from whom it was seized.

(4B)   An authorised officer shall produce his authority if required to do so by the person having control or possession of anything seized in pursuance of the powers in subsections (4) and (4A) above.

(4C)

(a)   Subject to section 38B (motor vehicles) of this Act, the following provisions of this subsection shall have effect where any article or thing (including any receptacle or equipment) is seized under subsection (4) above or is seized and retained because it is required for evidential purposes under subsection (4A) above and references in those provisions to proceedings are to proceedings in respect of the alleged offence in relation to which the article or thing is seized.

(b)   Subject to paragraph (e) below, following the conclusion of the proceedings the article or thing shall be returned to the person from whom it was seized unless—

(i)   the court orders it to be forfeited under subsection (5) below; or

(ii)   any award of costs to the council by the court, which may include removal, return and storage costs, have not been paid within 28 days of the making of the order.

(ba)   Where after 28 days any costs awarded by the court to the council have not been paid to the council in full—

(i)   the article or thing may be disposed of in any way the council thinks fit; and

(ii)   any sum obtained by the council in excess of the costs awarded by the court shall be returned to the person to whom the article or thing belongs.

(bb)   When any article or thing is disposed of by the council under this subsection the council shall have a duty to secure the best possible price which can reasonably be obtained for that article or thing.

(c)   Subject to paragraph (d) below, where a receptacle seized under subsection (4) above is a motor vehicle used for ice cream trading, the borough council or the Commissioner of Police of the Metropolis (as the case may be) shall, within three days of the receipt of an application in writing by the owner or registered keeper of the vehicle, permit him to remove it.

(d)   Paragraph (c) above shall not apply where—

    (i)   the owner or registered keeper of the vehicle has been convicted of an offence under this Part of this Act or under the City of Westminster Act 1999; or

    (ii)   the owner or registered keeper of the vehicle is being prosecuted for a previous alleged offence under this Part of this Act or the said Act of 1999; or

    (iii)   the vehicle has been used in the commission of such an offence or previous alleged offence;

if the offence or previous alleged offence was committed or is alleged to have been committed no more than three years before the seizure and (in the case of an alleged offence) the proceedings are continuing.

(e)   If no proceedings are instituted before the expiration of a period of 28 days beginning with the date of seizure, or any proceedings instituted within that period are discontinued, at the expiration of that period or, as the case may be, on the discontinuance of the proceedings, the article or thing shall be returned to the person from whom it was seized unless it has not proved possible, after diligent enquiry, to identify that person or ascertain his address.

(f)   paragraph (g) below applies where the article, thing, receptacle or equipment is not returned because—

    (i)   it has not proved possible to identify the person from whom it was seized or ascertain his address; or

    (ii)   the person from whom it was seized and the owner (if different) have disclaimed or refused to accept it.

(g)   where this paragraph applies, the council may make a complaint to the magistrates' court for a disposal order under section 38C (disposal orders) of this Act (whether or not proceedings for an offence under this section have been commenced).

(5)   Subject to subsection (6) below the court by or before which a person is convicted of an offence under this section or for an offence of aiding, abetting, counselling or procuring the commission of an offence under this section may order anything produced to the court[3], and shown to the satisfaction of the court to relate to the offence, to be forfeited and dealt with in such manner as the court may order.

(6)   The court shall not order anything to be forfeited under subsection (5) above where a person claiming to be the owner of or otherwise interested in it applies to be heard by the court, unless an opportunity has been given to him to show cause why the order should not be made and in considering whether to make such an order a court shall have regard—

    (i)   to the value of the property; and

    (ii)   to the likely financial and other effects on the offender of the making of the order (taken together with any other order that the court contemplates making).

(6A)   For the avoidance of doubt the court may order forfeiture notwithstanding that the value of the article, thing, receptacle or equipment exceeds the maximum penalties referred to in this section.

(7)   An authorised officer shall produce his authority if required to do so by the person having care or control of anything seized in pursuance of the powers in subsection (4) above.

(8)

(a)   This subsection shall have effect where—

    (i)   an article, thing or receptacle is seized under subsection (4) above; and

    (ii)

      (A)   not less than six months have passed since the date of the seizure and no information has been laid against any person for an offence under this section in respect of the acts or circumstances which occasioned the seizure; or

      (B)   proceedings for such an offence have been brought and either the person charged has been acquitted (whether or not on appeal) and the time for appealing against or challenging the acquittal (where applicable) has expired without an appeal or challenge being brought, or the proceedings (including any appeal) have been withdrawn by, or have failed for want of prosecution by, the person by whom the original proceedings were brought.

(b)   When this subsection has effect a person who has or at the time of seizure had a legal interest in the article, thing or receptacle seized may recover compensation from the borough council or (where it is seized by a constable) the Commissioner of Police of the Metropolis by civil action in the County Court in respect of any loss suffered by him as a result of the seizure and any such compensation shall not be included in the computation for calculating charges under section 22 (Fees and charges) of this Act.

(c)   The court may not make an order for compensation under paragraph (b) above unless it is satisfied that seizure was not lawful under subsection (4) or (4A) above.

[London Local Authorities Act 1990, s 38 as amended by the London Local Authorities Act 1994, s 6, the London Local Authorities Act 2004, Sch 4 and the London Local Authorities 2007, Sch 4.]

[1] The term "street trading" is apt to cover the sale of one motor vehicle offered for sale in a street with a notice that it was for sale, the price and a telephone number: *Haringey London Borough Council v Michniewicz* [2004] TLR 354.

[2] The issue for the court is not whether the article was in the street entirely for a purpose unrelated to street trading but whether an article was "brought into that street for some purpose other than street trading" ie why was it in "that street" and nowhere else at the material time. Whilst there might be a duality of purpose, that does not mean that wherever that is so s 38(2) would not avail a defendant: *Onasanya v Newham London Borough Council* [2006] EWHC 1775 (Admin), [2006] 4 All ER 459 (defendant wrongly convicted where he had left a "for sale" sign and contact number in the window of his car when he was visiting his doctor).

[3] The items must be physically present or treated as being produced by virtue of being exhibited by a statement served under s 9 of the Criminal Justice Act 1967; but if there is a late objection to non-production in either of the aforementioned ways of the items it is open to the justices to adjourn for the items to be produced, or to make arrangements to view the items on some convenient occasion on the same or a future date (*R (on the application of London Borough of Islington) v Jordan* [2002] EWHC 2645 (Admin), 167 JP 1).

7.8023   38A.   Seizure of perishable items   (1)   No item which is of a perishable nature (in this section referred to as a "perishable item") shall be seized under the provisions of subsection (4) of section 38 (unlicensed street trading) of this Act unless the authorised officer or constable gives a certificate under subsection (2) below to the person from whom the item is seized.

(2)   Where a perishable item is seized under the said section 38, the person from whom it is seized must be given a certificate—

(a)   stating the effect of subsection (4) below and subsection (6) of the said section 38;

(b)   giving the address from which the item may be collected;

(c)   informing the recipient that if he is not the owner of the item, then he should give the owner the information referred to in paragraphs (a) and (b) above.

(3)   The council or the police shall store any perishable item seized under the said section 38 at an appropriate temperature.

(4)   If the person from whom a perishable item was so seized fails to collect it within 48 hours of the seizure the council or the police may dispose of it.

(5)   When any perishable item is disposed of by the council under subsection (4) above, the council shall have a duty to secure the best possible price which can reasonably be obtained for it.

(6)   Paragraphs (a) to (d) of subsection (4C), and subsections (5) and (6) of the said section 38 shall apply to perishable items seized under that section only in cases where the item concerned has not been disposed of by the council at the conclusion of the proceedings in respect of the alleged offence in relation to which the item was seized.

(7)   Paragraphs (e) and (f) of subsection (4C) of the said section 38 shall apply to perishable items seized under that section only in cases where the item concerned has not been disposed of by the council at the expiration of the period mentioned in the said paragraph (e); otherwise subsections (9) to (12) below shall apply.

(8)   Subsection (8) of the said section 38 shall apply with the omission of paragraph (c) in respect of perishable items seized under that section only in cases where the item concerned has not been disposed of by the council by the time the circumstances mentioned in paragraph (a)(ii)(a) or (b) arise; otherwise subsections (9) to (12) below shall apply.

(9)   Subsection (12) below shall have effect where the council have disposed of a perishable item under subsection (4) above and any of the following conditions apply.

(10)   The first condition is that no proceedings in respect of the alleged offence in relation to which the item was seized are instituted before the expiration of a period of 28 days beginning with the date of seizure of the item, or any such proceedings instituted within that period are discontinued.

(11)   The second condition is that—

(a)   not less than six months have passed since the date of the seizure and no information has been laid against any person for an offence under the said section 38 in respect of the acts or circumstances which occasioned the seizure; or

(b)   proceedings for such an offence have been brought and either the person charged has been acquitted (whether or not on appeal) and the time for appealing against or challenging the acquittal (where applicable) has expired without an appeal or challenge being brought, or the proceedings (including any appeal) have been withdrawn by, or have failed for want of prosecution by, the person by whom the original proceedings were brought.

(12)   When this subsection has effect a person who has, or at the time of seizure had, a legal interest in the item seized may recover compensation from the borough council or (where it is seized by a constable) the Commissioner of Police of the Metropolis by civil action in the County Court in respect of any loss suffered by him as a result of the seizure and any such compensation shall not be included in the computation for calculating charges under section 32 (fees and charges) of this Act.

[London Local Authorities Act 1990, s 38A as inserted by the London Local Authorities 2007, s 45.]

7.8024   38B.   Motor vehicles   (1)   Subsection (4) below applies where the following conditions are met.

(2)   The first condition is that where, in ascertaining the identity of the person from whom a vehicle was seized under subsection (4) or (4A) of section 38 (unlicensed street trading) of this Act, a borough council has, before the expiry of 14 days from the date of the seizure, made a request to

the Secretary of State for the supply of relevant particulars.

(3)   The second condition is that those particulars have not been supplied to the council before the date after which that council would, but for this section, have to return the vehicle in accordance with subsection (4C)(*e*) of that section.

(4)   Where this subsection applies, the council must return the vehicle to its owner if—

(*a*)   no proceedings are instituted in respect of the alleged offence in respect of which the vehicle was seized before the expiry of the period of 14 days beginning with the date on which the relevant particulars are supplied; or

(*b*)   any such proceedings instituted within that period are discontinued,

at the expiry of that period or on the discontinuance of the proceedings, as the case may be.

(5)   If the council seeks to return a vehicle in accordance with the said subsection (4C)(*e*) or subsection (4), but the person to whom the council seeks to return the vehicle cannot be found or disclaims or refuses to accept the vehicle, the council may make a complaint for a disposal order in respect of the vehicle under section 38C (disposal orders) of this Act.

(6)   In this section, "relevant particulars" are particulars relating to the identity of the owner of the vehicle contained in the register of mechanically propelled vehicles maintained by the Secretary of State under the Vehicle Excise and Registration Act 1994 (c 22).

(7)   The owner of a vehicle for the purposes of this section shall be taken to be the person by whom the vehicle is kept.

(8)   In determining who was the owner of a motor vehicle at any time, it shall be presumed that the owner is the person in whose name the vehicle is at that time registered under the Vehicle Excise and Registration Act 1994.]

[London Local Authorities Act 1990, s 38B as inserted by the London Local Authorities 2007, s 46.]

7.8025   38C.   Disposal orders   (1)   This section applies in respect of a complaint made by a borough council for a disposal order in respect of—

(*a*)   an article or thing under subsection (4C)(*f*)(ii) of section 38 (unlicensed street trading) of this Act; or

(*b*)   a motor vehicle under subsection (5) of section 38B (motor vehicles) of this Act,

and such articles, things and motor vehicles are together referred to as "seized items" in this section.

(2)   In respect of a complaint to which this section applies, a magistrates' court may, if it is satisfied that the council has made reasonable efforts to identify the person from whom the seized item was seized or its owner, as the case may be, or has made reasonable efforts to return the seized item, it may make an order authorising the complainant council—

(*a*)   to dispose of the seized item in question; and

(*b*)   after payment out of any proceeds arising from the disposal of the expenses incurred in the seizure, storage and disposal, to apply the balance, if any, towards the costs of the council as mentioned in paragraphs (*a*) to (*d*) of subsection (2) of section 32 (fees and charges) of this Act.

(3)   The court shall not make a disposal order under subsection (2) above where a person claiming to be the owner of or otherwise interested in the seized item in question applies to be heard by the court, unless an opportunity has been given to him to show cause why the order should not be made.

(4)   Subsection (5) below applies where—

(*a*)   a person appears before the court under subsection (3) above to show why the order should not be made; and

(*b*)   the court makes an order under subsection (2) above authorising the council to dispose of the item; and

(*c*)   the seized item in question is not of sufficient value to defray the expenses of seizing and storing it; and

(*d*)   the court is satisfied that the person mentioned in paragraph (*a*) above was the owner of the seized item in question or was the person from whom it was seized, as the case may be.

(5)   Where this section applies, the court may order that the person mentioned in subsection (4)(*a*) above pay the expenses, or the balance of the expenses, reasonably incurred by the council in seizing and storing the seized item in question.

(6)   In considering whether to make an order under subsection (2) above a court shall have regard—

(*a*)   to the value of the seized item;

(*b*)   to the likely financial and other effects on the offender of the making of the order (taken together with any other order that the court contemplates making); and

(*c*)   any other circumstances considered to be relevant.

(7)   The court may make a disposal order under this section notwithstanding that the value of the seized item would exceed the maximum penalty for the offence in respect of which the seized item had originally been seized had the said offence been prosecuted to conviction.

(8)   For the purposes of this section, "owner" in respect of a vehicle, has the same meaning as it has for the purposes of the said section 38B.

[London Local Authorities Act 1990, s 38C as inserted by the London Local Authorities 2007, s 47.]

7.8026   39.   Savings   (1)   Nothing in this Part of this Act shall affect—

    (a)   section 13 of the Markets and Fairs Clauses Act 1847 (prohibition of sales elsewhere than in a market or in shops etc) as applied by any other Acts;

    (b)   section 56 of the Food Act 1984 (prohibition of certain sales during market hours);

    (c)   the sale or exposure or offer for sale by Transport for London or any or its subsidiaries (within the meaning of the Greater London Authority Act 1999) of refreshments at any shelter or other accommodation provided by either of them under section 65 (refreshment shelters etc) of the London Passenger Transport Act 1938.

    (2)   Nothing in this Part of this Act shall afford a defence to a charge in respect of any offence at common law or under an enactment other than this Part of this Act.

[London Local Authorities Act 1990, s 39, as amended by SI 2003/1615.]

Traffic and Transport

Port of London Act 1968
(1968 c 32)

[7.8027]

This Act makes provision for numerous offences relating to the operation of the Port of London. The penalties were substantially increased by the Port of London Act 1982 (c ix), Schedule 1. The 1982 Act also supplied a new s 199 to the 1968 Act which provides for traffic offences on dock roads and applies provisions in the (now) Road Traffic Regulation Act 1984 and the Road Traffic Act 1988 to those roads.

London Local Authorities and Transport for London Act 2003
(2003 c iii)

Part 1
Preliminary

7.8028   **1. Citation and commencement**   (1)   This Act may be cited as the London Local Authorities and Transport for London Act 2003 and, except for—

    section 4 (Penalty charges for road traffic contraventions);

    section 5 (Contraventions of lorry ban order: supplementary);

    section 7 (Disapplication of offences); and

    section 16 (Vehicle crossings over footways and verges),

shall come into operation at the end of the period of two months beginning with the date on which it is passed.

    (2)   The said sections 4, 5, 7 and 16 shall come into operation on the appointed day.

    (3)   This Act and the London Local Authorities Acts 1990 to 2000 may be cited together as the London Local Authorities Acts 1990 to 2003.

[London Local Authorities and Transport for London Act 2003, s 1.]

7.8029   **2. Interpretation**   (1)   In this Act—

    "the Act of 1984" means the Road Traffic Regulation Act 1984 (c 27);

    "borough council" means London borough council and includes the Common Council of the City of London in its capacity as a local authority and "borough" and "council" shall be construed accordingly.

    (2)   Subject to paragraph 1(8) of Schedule 1 to this Act, the owner of a vehicle for the purposes of this Act, shall be taken to be the person by whom the vehicle is kept.

    (3)   Subject to the said paragraph 1(8), in determining, for the purposes of this Act, who was the owner of a vehicle at any time, it shall be presumed that the owner was the person in whose name the vehicle was at that time registered under the Vehicle Excise and Registration Act 1994 (c 22).

[London Local Authorities and Transport for London Act 2003, s 2.]

7.8030   **3. Appointed day**   (1)   In subsection (2) of section 1 (Citation and commencement) of this Act "the appointed day" means such day as may be fixed—

    (a)   in relation to a borough by resolution of the borough council; or

    (b)   in relation to a GLA road or a GLA side road by a decision of Transport for London, subject to and in accordance with the provisions of this section.

    (2)   Different days may be fixed under this section for the purpose of the application of different provisions of this Act to a borough.

    (3)   Different days may be fixed under this section for the purpose of the application of the provisions of this Act to different GLA roads or GLA side roads.

    (4)   But no day fixed under this section may be before the end of the period of two months beginning with the date on which this Act is passed.

    (5)   The borough council or Transport for London shall cause to be published in a local newspaper circulating in their area and in the London Gazette notice—

(a)   of the passing of any such resolution or taking of any such decision and of a day fixed
thereby; and

(b)   the general effect of the provisions of this Act coming into operation as from that day,
and the day so fixed shall not be earlier than the expiration of three months from the publication of
the said notice.

(6)   Either a photostatic or other reproduction certified by the officer appointed for that purpose
by the borough council or by Transport for London to be a reproduction of a page or part of a page
of any such newspaper or the London Gazette bearing the date of its publication and containing any
such notice shall be evidence of the publication of the notice, and of the date of publication.

(7)   In subsection (5) above, "their area" in relation to Transport for London means the area of
any borough council in which the GLA road or GLA side road to which the resolution or decision
relates is situated.

[London Local Authorities and Transport for London Act 2003, s 3.]

PART 2
ROAD TRAFFIC AND HIGHWAYS

Penalty charges

7.8031 **4. Penalty charges for road traffic contraventions** (1) This section applies
where—

(a)   in relation to a GLA road or GLA side road, Transport for London or, subject to
subsection (3) below, the relevant borough council; or

(b)   in relation to any other road in the area of a borough council, the relevant borough
council or, subject to subsection (4) below, Transport for London,

have reason to believe (whether or not on the basis of information provided by a camera or other
device) that a penalty charge is payable under this section with respect to a motor vehicle.

(2)   Transport for London or, as the case may be, the relevant borough council may serve a
penalty charge notice—

(a)   in relation to a penalty charge payable by virtue of subsection (5) below, on the person
appearing to them to be the owner of the vehicle; and

(b)   in relation to a penalty charge payable by virtue of subsection (7) below, on either or
both of the following—

(i)   the person appearing to them to be the operator of the vehicle; and

(ii)   the person appearing to them to be the person who was in control of the vehicle
at the time of the contravention.

(3)   The relevant borough council shall not exercise the power exercisable by virtue of
subsection (1)(a) above unless they have obtained the consent in writing of Transport for London.

(4)   Transport for London shall not exercise the power exercisable by virtue of subsection (1)(b)
above unless they have obtained the consent in writing of the relevant borough council.

(5)   Subject to subsection (6) below, for the purposes of this section, a penalty charge is payable
with respect to a motor vehicle by the owner of the vehicle if the person driving or propelling the
vehicle—

(a)   acts in contravention of a prescribed order; or

(b)   fails to comply with an indication given by a scheduled section 36 traffic sign.

(6)   No penalty charge shall be payable under subsection (5)(a) above where—

(a)   the person acting in contravention of the prescribed order also fails to comply with an
indication given by a scheduled section 36 traffic sign; or

(b)   the contravention of the prescribed order would also give rise to a liability to pay a
penalty charge under section 77 of the Road Traffic Act 1991 (c 40).

(7)   For the purposes of this section, a penalty charge is payable with respect to a vehicle by—

(a)   the operator of the vehicle; and

(b)   the person in control of the vehicle,

if the person in control of the vehicle acts in contravention of the lorry ban order.

(8)   A penalty charge notice under this section must—

(a)   state—

(i)   the grounds on which the council or, as the case may be, Transport for London
believe that the penalty charge is payable with respect to the vehicle;

(ii)   the amount of the penalty charge which is payable;

(iii) that the penalty charge must be paid before the end of the period of 28 days
beginning with the date of the notice;

(iv)   that if the penalty charge is paid before the end of the period of 14 days
beginning with the date of the notice, the amount of the penalty charge will be
reduced by the specified proportion;

(v)   that, if the penalty charge is not paid before the end of the 28 day period, an
increased charge may be payable;

(vi)   the amount of the increased charge;

(vii) the address to which payment of the penalty charge must be sent; and

    (viii) that the person on whom the notice is served may be entitled to make representations under paragraph 1 of Schedule 1 to this Act; and

    (b)   specify the form in which any such representations are to be made.

(9)   The Secretary of State may by regulations prescribe additional matters which must be dealt with in any penalty charge notice.

(10)   In subsection (8)(a)(iv) above, "specified proportion" means such proportion, applicable in all cases, as may be determined for the purposes of this section by the borough councils and Transport for London acting through the Joint Committee.

(11)   Schedule 1 to this Act shall have effect with respect to representations against penalty charge notices, and other matters supplementary to the provisions of this section.

(12)   Subject to subsection (13) below, sections 74 and 74A of the Road Traffic Act 1991 (c 40) shall apply in relation to the levels of penalty charges under this section as they apply in relation to the levels of (among other charges) penalty charges under Part II of that Act.

(13)   Before setting the level of any charges under the said section 74 as applied by subsection (12) above, the borough councils and Transport for London shall consult such bodies as in their opinion are sufficiently representative of such road users as would be affected by the imposition of such charges.

(14)   No provision in this section shall apply to any vehicle on an occasion when it is being used for fire brigade, ambulance or police purposes.

(15)   Schedule 2 to this Act shall have effect with respect to financial provisions relating to the provisions of this section.

(16)   In this section—

"Joint Committee" means the Joint Committee established under section 73 of the Road Traffic Act 1991;

"motor vehicle" means a mechanically propelled vehicle intended or adapted for use on roads;

"prescribed order" means an order under section 6 or 9 of the Act of 1984 which makes provision for a relevant traffic control;

"relevant traffic control" means any requirement, restriction or prohibition (other than a requirement, restriction or prohibition under the lorry ban order) which is or may be conveyed by a scheduled traffic sign;

"road" has the same meaning as in the Act of 1984;

"scheduled section 36 traffic sign" means—

    (a)   a scheduled traffic sign of a type to which section 36 (Drivers to comply with traffic signs) of the Road Traffic Act 1988 (c 52) applies by virtue of regulations made under section 64(5) of the Act of 1984; but

    (b)   does not include a traffic sign which indicates any prohibition or restriction imposed by the lorry ban order;

"scheduled traffic sign" means a traffic sign of a type described in Schedule 3 to this Act;

"traffic sign" has the meaning given by section 64(1) of the Act of 1984.

(17)   In this section and section 5 (Contraventions of lorry ban order: supplementary) of this Act—

"driver's notice" means a penalty charge notice served under subsection (2)(b)(ii) above on the person appearing to have been the person in control of the vehicle at the time of the alleged contravention of the lorry ban order;

"the lorry ban order" means the Greater London (Restriction of Goods Vehicles) Traffic Order 1985 made by the Greater London Council under section 6 of the Act of 1984, as amended, replaced or substituted by any subsequent order;

"operator of a vehicle" means the holder of any operator's licence in respect of that vehicle under section 2 of the Goods Vehicles (Licensing of Operators) Act 1995 (c 23);

"operator's notice" means a penalty charge notice served under subsection (2)(b)(i) above on the person appearing to be the operator of a vehicle;

"relevant borough council" means the borough council in whose area the alleged contravention or failure occurred.

(18)   In determining, for the purposes of any provision of this Act, whether a penalty charge has been paid before the end of a particular period, it shall be taken to be paid when it is received by the council concerned, or as the case may be, Transport for London.

(19)   The Secretary of State may, by regulations, amend Schedule 3 to this Act by—

    (a)   adding any traffic signs to the list of traffic signs in the Schedule; or

    (b)   making any other amendments to the Schedule as may be necessary as a consequence of any amendment, replacement or substitution of the Traffic Signs Regulations and General Directions 2002 (SI 2002/3113).* **

[London Local Authorities and Transport for London Act 2003, s 4, as amended by the London Local Authorities and Transport for London Act 2008, s 27.]

---

*   **Repealed by the Traffic Management Act 2004, s 98, Sch 12, Pt 1, from a date to be appointed.**

**   **Amended for a transitional period only beginning 31 March 2008 by SI 2007/2053 (itself amended by SI 2008/757).**

7.8032   5.   Contraventions of lorry ban order: supplementary   (1)   An operator's notice shall state that before the end of the period of 14 days beginning with the date of the notice, the operator of the vehicle must provide the relevant borough council, or as the case may be, Transport for London, with the name and address of the person who was in control of the vehicle when the alleged contravention of the lorry ban order took place.

(2)   Any person who in response to a requirement stated in a penalty charge notice by virtue of subsection (1) above fails to comply with the requirement shall be guilty of an offence unless he shows to the satisfaction of the court that—

    (a)   he was not the operator of the vehicle at the time the alleged contravention of the lorry ban order took place; or

    (b)   he did not know, and could not with reasonable diligence have ascertained, who was the person in control of the vehicle.

(3)   Any person who in response to a requirement stated in a penalty charge notice by virtue of subsection (1) above gives information which is false in a material particular and does so recklessly or knowing it to be false in that particular shall be guilty of an offence.

(4)   Any person guilty of an offence under subsection (2) or (3) above shall be liable on summary conviction—

    (a)   in the case of subsection (2) to a fine not exceeding level 3 on the standard scale; and

    (b)   in the case of subsection (3) to a fine not exceeding level 5 on the standard scale.

(5)   In the case where an operator's notice is served on the person appearing to be the operator of the vehicle, the provisions of this Act mentioned below shall have effect as follows—

    (a)   for paragraph 1(4)(a) of Schedule 1 there shall be substituted—

    "(a)   that the recipient was not the operator of the vehicle at the time the alleged contravention of the order took place;";

    (b)   paragraph 1(4)(c) and (d), (5) and (6) of Schedule 1 shall be omitted; and

    (c)   after paragraph 1(4) of Schedule 1 the following sub-paragraph shall be inserted—

    "(4A)   Where the ground mentioned in sub-paragraph (4)(a) above is relied on in any representations made under this paragraph, those representations must include a statement of the name and address of the operator of the vehicle at the time of the alleged contravention or failure to comply (if that information is in his possession).".

(6)   In the case where a driver's notice is served on the person appearing to have been in control of the vehicle at the time of the alleged contravention, the provisions of this Act mentioned below shall have effect as follows—

    (a)   for paragraph 1(4)(a) of Schedule 1 there shall be substituted—

    "(a)   that the recipient was not the person in control of the vehicle at the time the alleged contravention of the lorry ban order took place;";

    (b)   paragraph 1(4)(c) and (d), (5) and (6) of Schedule 1 shall be omitted; and

    (c)   after paragraph 1(4) of Schedule 1 the following sub-paragraph shall be inserted—

    "(4A)   Where the ground mentioned in sub-paragraph (4)(a) above is relied on in any representations made under this paragraph, those representations must include a statement of the name and address of the person in control of the vehicle at the time of the alleged contravention or failure to comply (if that information is in his possession).".

(7)   In the case where, under paragraph 1(4) of Schedule 1 to this Act as so applied and having effect in accordance with subsections (5) or (6) above the relevant borough council or as the case may be Transport for London is provided with the name and address of—

    (a)   the operator of the vehicle; or

    (b)   the person who was in control of the vehicle at the time of the alleged contravention of the lorry ban order,

they may serve a fresh penalty charge notice in accordance with paragraph 2(2) of that Schedule on either of those persons, or both.*

[London Local Authorities and Transport for London Act 2003, s 5.]

---

* **Repealed by the Traffic Management Act 2004, s 98, Sch 12, Pt 1, from a date to be appointed.**

7.8033   **6.   Limitation on service of penalty charge notice**   (1)   Subject to the provisions of this section, no penalty charge notice may be served under this Act after the expiry of the period of 28 days beginning with the date on which the alleged contravention or failure to comply occurred.

(2)   Subsection (2A) below applies where—

    (a)   a penalty charge notice has been cancelled under paragraph 2 of Schedule 1 to this Act; or

    (b)   a penalty charge notice has been cancelled in compliance with a direction given by a traffic adjudicator under paragraph 4(2) of the said Schedule; or

    (c)   a penalty charge notice is deemed to have been cancelled under paragraph 7(8)(c) of the said Schedule (deemed cancellation where a statutory declaration under paragraph 7(2)(a) of that Schedule is served under paragraph 7(1)(c)),

    (d)   payment of the penalty charge has been made or has purportedly been made before the expiry of the period mentioned in subsection (1) above but the payment or purported payment is subsequently cancelled or withdrawn.

(2A)   Subject to subsection (3) below, the borough council or Transport for London, as the case may be, may not serve a fresh penalty charge notice after the expiry of the period of 28 days from—

    (a)   the date of the cancellation of the penalty charge notice; or

(b)   in a case falling within subsection (2)(c) above, the date on which the council or body are served with notice under paragraph 7(8)(d) of the said Schedule; or

(c)   in a case falling within subsection (2)(d) above, the date on which the council or body received notification that the payment or purported payment had been cancelled or withdrawn.

(3)   Subsection (6) below applies where the following conditions are met.

(4)   The first condition is that where a borough council or Transport for London, as the case may be, has before the expiry of 14 days from—

(a)   the date on which the alleged contravention or failure to comply occurred; or

(b)   the date of the cancellation of the penalty charge notice in the case where a penalty charge notice has been cancelled—

(i)   under paragraph 2 of the said Schedule; or

(ii)   in compliance with a direction given by a traffic adjudicator under paragraph 4(2) of the said Schedule; or

(c)   the date on which the borough council or Transport for London, as the case may be, are served with notice under paragraph 7(8)(d) of the said Schedule where the penalty charge notice is deemed to have been cancelled under paragraph 7(8)(c), or

(d)   the date on which the council or body receives a notification that the payment or purported payment has been cancelled or withdrawn in the circumstances mentioned in subsection (2)(d) above,

made a request to the Secretary of State for the supply of relevant particulars.

(5)   The second condition is that those particulars have not been supplied to the borough council or Transport for London, as the case may be, before the date after which that council or body would not be entitled to serve a penalty charge notice or a fresh penalty charge notice by virtue of subsection (1) or (2A) above.

(6)   Where this subsection applies, the borough council or Transport for London, as the case may be, shall continue to be entitled to serve a penalty charge notice or a fresh penalty charge notice for a further period of 6 months beginning with the date mentioned in subsection (5) above.

(7)   In this section, "relevant particulars" are particulars relating to the identity of the owner of the vehicle contained in the register of mechanically propelled vehicles maintained by the Secretary of State under the Vehicle Excise and Registration Act 1994 (c 22).*

[London Local Authorities and Transport for London Act 2003, s 6, as amended by the London Local Authorities and Transport for London Act 2008, s 7.]

---

* Repealed by the Traffic Management Act 2004, s 98, Sch 12, Pt 1, from a date to be appointed.

7.8034 7. Disapplication of offences (1) This section applies to the following roads—

(a)   GLA roads and GLA side roads; and

(b)   any other road in the area of a borough council.

(2)   Section 8 of the Act of 1984 shall apply in respect of a road to which this section applies as if after subsection (1A), the following subsection were inserted—

"(1B) Subsection (1) above does not apply in relation to any person who acts in contravention of or fails to comply with

(a)   an order under section 6 of this Act; or

(b)   the lorry ban order within the meaning of section 4 of the London Local Authorities and Transport for London Act 2003 (penalty charges for road traffic contraventions),

if as a result a penalty charge is payable under subsection (5) or, as the case may be, subsection (7) of section 4 of that Act.".

(3)   Section 11 of the Act of 1984 shall apply in respect of a road to which this section applies as if after subsection (2), the following subsection were inserted—

"(2A) This section does not apply in relation to any person who acts in contravention of or fails to comply with an experimental traffic order if as a result a penalty charge is payable under section 4(5) of the London Local Authorities and Transport for London Act 2003 (penalty charges for road traffic contraventions).".

(4)   Section 36 of the Road Traffic Act 1988 (c 52) shall apply in respect of a road to which this section applies as if after subsection (1), the following subsection were inserted—

"(1A) Subsection (1) above does not apply in relation to any such person who fails to comply with the indication given by the sign if as a result a penalty charge is payable under section 4(5) of the London Local Authorities and Transport for London Act 2003 (penalty charges for road traffic contraventions).".*

[London Local Authorities and Transport for London Act 2003, s 7.]

---

* Repealed by the Traffic Management Act 2004, s 98, Sch 12, Pt 1, from a date to be appointed.

Fixed penalties

7.8035 8. Fixed penalty offences (1) Where on any occasion an authorised officer of a borough council or Transport for London finds a person who he has reason to believe has on that occasion committed an offence under any of the enactments—

(a)   mentioned in columns (1) and (2) of the table set out in Schedule 4 to this Act; and

(b)   described in column (3) of that table;

the officer may give that person a notice offering him the opportunity of discharging any liability to conviction for that offence by payment of a fixed penalty.

(2)   The powers of an authorised officer of a borough council under subsection (1) above may be exercised only in relation to offences alleged to have been committed in respect of a highway in respect of which the council is highway authority.

(3)   The powers of an authorised officer of Transport for London under subsection (1) above may be exercised only in relation to offences alleged to have been committed in respect of a GLA road or a GLA side road.

(4)   Sections 9 (Fixed penalty notices), 10 (Levels of fixed penalties) and 11 (Fixed penalties: reserve powers of Secretary of State) of this Act shall apply in respect of fixed penalty notices under this section.

(5)   Schedule 2 to this Act shall have effect with respect to financial provisions relating to the administration and enforcement of this section and sections 9 to 11 (Fixed penalties) of this Act.

(6)   The Secretary of State may, by regulations, amend Schedule 4 to this Act by the addition of further offences to the list of offences therein described.

[London Local Authorities and Transport for London Act 2003, s 8.]

7.8036   9.   Fixed penalty notices   (1)   The provisions of this section shall have effect in relation to notices ("fixed penalty notices") which may be given under section 8 (Fixed penalty offences) of this Act.

(2)   Where a person is given a fixed penalty notice in respect of an offence—

    (*a*)   no proceedings shall be instituted for that offence before the expiration of 28 days following the date of the notice; and

    (*b*)   he shall not be convicted of that offence if he pays the fixed penalty before the expiration of that period.

(3)   A fixed penalty notice under this section shall give such particulars of the circumstances alleged to constitute the offence as are necessary for giving reasonable information of the offence and shall state—

    (*a*)   the period during which, by virtue of subsection (2) above, proceedings will not be taken for the offence;

    (*b*)   the amount of the fixed penalty;

    (*ba*)   that if the fixed penalty is paid before the end of the period of 14 days beginning with the date of the notice, the amount of the fixed penalty will be reduced by the specified proportion; and

    (*c*)   the name of the person to whom and the address at which the fixed penalty may be paid; and, without prejudice to payment by any other method, payment of the fixed penalty may be made by pre-paying and posting to that person at that address a letter containing the amount of the penalty (in cash or otherwise).

(4)   Where a letter is sent in accordance with subsection (3) above, payment shall be regarded as having been made at the time at which that letter would be delivered in the ordinary course of post.

(5)   The form of notices under this section shall be such as the Secretary of State may by regulations prescribe.

(6)   The fixed penalty payable in pursuance of a fixed penalty notice under this section shall be paid to the borough council or Transport for London, as the case may be.

(7)   In any proceedings a certificate which—

    (*a*)   purports to be signed by or on behalf of the chief finance officer of the council, or as the case may be, Transport for London; and

    (*b*)   states that payment of a fixed penalty was or was not received by a date specified in the certificate,

shall be evidence of the facts stated.

(8)   In this section—

    (*a*)   "chief finance officer" in relation to a borough council or Transport for London means the person having responsibility for the financial affairs of the council or Transport for London, as the case may be;

    (*b*)   "specified proportion" means such proportion, applicable in all cases, as may be determined for the purposes of this section by the borough councils acting through the Joint Committee as defined in section 4(16) of this Act.

[London Local Authorities and Transport for London Act 2003, s 9, as amended by the London Local Authorities and Transport for London Act 2008, s 26.]

7.8037   10.   Levels of fixed penalties

7.8038   11.   Fixed penalties: reserve powers of Secretary of State

Parking

7.8039   13.   False applications for parking authorisations   (1)   Insofar as subsection (2) of section 115 of the Act of 1984 (mishandling of parking documents and related offences) relates to any authorisation which may be issued by a borough council or by Transport for London—

    (*a*)   proceedings for an offence under that section may be brought within a period of six months from the date on which evidence sufficient in the opinion of the prosecutor to warrant the proceedings came to his knowledge, but

(b)   no such proceedings shall be brought by virtue of this section more than three years after the commission of the offence.

(2)   For the purposes of subsection (1) above a certificate signed by or on behalf of the prosecutor and stating the date on which evidence such as is mentioned in that subsection came to his knowledge, shall be conclusive evidence of that fact; and a certificate purporting to be so signed shall be deemed to be so signed unless the contrary is proved.

[London Local Authorities and Transport for London Act 2003, s 13.]

Vehicle Crossings

7.8040   16.   Vehicle crossings over footways and verges

Removal notices

7.8041   17.   Removal of things deposited on the highway   (1)   This section applies in respect of any part of—

(a)   any highway for which Transport for London are the highway authority; and

(b)   any highway for which a borough council are the highway authority.

(2)   If the highway authority are satisfied that—

(a)   things are deposited unlawfully and persistently on any part of the highway to which this section applies; and

(b)   the depositing of the things is caused by persons having control of or an interest in a business carried on in premises in the vicinity of the part of the highway concerned,

the highway authority may serve a notice under this subsection ("a subsection (2) removal notice") on any person having control of or an interest in the relevant business.

(3)   A subsection (2) removal notice shall—

(a)   state the date on which it shall come into effect (which shall be no sooner than the date on which the period of 7 days beginning with the date of service of the notice expires);

(b)   state the date on which it shall expire (which shall be no later than the date on which the period of 28 days beginning with the date on which it comes into effect expires);

(c)   give a description of the part of the highway to which the notice relates;

(d)   state that in the period during which the notice has effect, the highway authority may without further notice remove any thing deposited unlawfully on the part of the highway to which the notice relates;

(e)   state the effect of subsections (5) and (12) below.

(4)   Where a subsection (2) removal notice is served under subsection (2) above, a copy of the notice shall be affixed by the highway authority to a conspicuous place in the vicinity of the part of the highway to which the notice relates.

(5)   If any thing is deposited unlawfully on any part of the highway to which a subsection (2) removal notice relates, the highway authority may—

(a)   remove the thing forthwith; and

(b)   no sooner than the relevant date, dispose of the thing.

(6)   If a highway authority remove a thing under section 149(2) of the Highways Act 1980 (c 66) (which makes provision about things deposited on the highway so as to cause a danger), instead of proceeding under subsection (3) of that section, they may proceed in accordance with subsection (7) below.

(7)   No later than 24 hours after the removal of the thing under the said section 149(2), the highway authority shall issue a notice ("a subsection (7) removal notice") and proceed in the manner described in subsection (9) below.

(8)   A subsection (7) removal notice shall—

(a)   give a description of the thing removed;

(b)   state the effect of subsections (10) and (12) below.

(9)   Where a subsection (7) removal notice is issued, the notice or a copy of the notice shall be affixed by the highway authority to a conspicuous place in the vicinity of the part of the highway from which the thing was removed.

(10)   A highway authority may, no sooner than the relevant date, dispose of any thing which they have removed and in respect of which a subsection (7) removal notice has been issued.

(11)   Any person who without reasonable excuse removes, alters or damages a notice affixed to any place under subsection (4) or (9) above shall be guilty of an offence and liable on summary conviction to a fine not exceeding level 3 on the standard scale.

(12)   The authority by whom a thing is removed in pursuance of this section may recover from the person by whom it was deposited on the highway, or from any person claiming to be entitled to it, any expenses reasonably incurred by the authority in removing, storing or disposing of it.

(13)   After payment out of any proceeds arising from the disposal of the thing of the expenses incurred in the removal, storage and disposal of the thing, the highway authority may apply the balance, if any, of the proceeds to the maintenance of the highways maintainable at the public expense by them.

(14)   If the thing in question is not of sufficient value to defray the expenses of removing, storing and disposing of it, the highway authority may recover from the person who deposited it on the highway the expenses, or the balance of the expenses, reasonably incurred by them in removing,

storing and disposing of it.

(15) If, after a thing has been disposed of by a highway authority pursuant to this section, a person claims to have been the owner of the thing at the time when it was removed and the conditions specified in subsection (16) below are fulfilled, there shall be payable to him by the highway authority a sum calculated in accordance with subsection (17) below.

(16) The conditions are that—

    (a)   the person claiming satisfies the highway authority that he was the owner of the thing at the time it was removed; and

    (b)   the claim is made before the expiry of the period of five months beginning with the date on which the thing was removed.

(17) The sum payable under subsection (15) above shall be calculated by deducting from the proceeds of sale the charges reasonably incurred by the highway authority for the removing, storing and disposing of the thing.

(18) In subsections (5) and (10) above, the "relevant date" in respect of a thing is the date on which expires the period of 14 days beginning with the date on which the thing was removed by the highway authority.

(19) For the purposes of this section and section 18 (Removal notices: appeals) of this Act—

    (a)   "the relevant business" means the business referred to in subsection (2) above; and

    (b)   a person having an interest in a relevant business includes a person who—

        (i)   owns the business; or

        (ii)   manages the business; or

        (iii)   employs any person to manage the business; or

        (iv)   is involved in the conduct of the business.

[London Local Authorities and Transport for London Act 2003, s 17, as amended by the London Local Authorities and Transport for London Act 2008, s 27.]

7.8042   18.   Removal notices: appeals

7.8043   19.   Service of removal notices

PART 3
SUPPLEMENTARY

7.8044   20.   Disclosure of information

7.8045   21.   Authorised officers

7.8046   22.   Obstruction of authorised officer   Any person who intentionally obstructs any authorised officer acting in the exercise of his powers under this Act shall be guilty of an offence and liable on summary conviction to a fine not exceeding level 3 on the standard scale.

[London Local Authorities and Transport for London Act 2003, s 22.]

7.8047   23.   Provision of information to authorised officer of Transport for London
(1) This section applies where an authorised officer of Transport for London has reasonable grounds for suspecting that any offence in respect of which that body may prosecute legal proceedings has been committed or attempted, or is being committed or attempted.

(2) If, on being requested by the authorised officer to furnish his name and address for service of a summons or fixed penalty notice the relevant person—

    (a)   fails to furnish a name; or

    (b)   furnishes a false name; or

    (c)   furnishes a false address,

the relevant person shall, unless the authorised officer failed to produce his authorisation on making the request, be guilty of an offence punishable on summary conviction by a fine not exceeding level 5 on the standard scale.

(3) In this section "the relevant person" means any person who the authorised officer has reasonable grounds to suspect of having committed or having attempted to commit the offence or being in the course of committing or attempting to commit it.

[London Local Authorities and Transport for London Act 2003, s 23.]

7.8048   24.   Defence of due diligence   (1) In proceedings for an offence under this Act it shall be a defence for the person charged to prove that he took all reasonable precautions and exercised all due diligence to avoid the commission of the offence.

(2) If in any case the defence provided under subsection (1) above involves the allegation that the commission of the offence was due to the act or default of another person, the person charged shall not, without leave of the court, be entitled to rely on that defence unless, no later than 7 clear days before the hearing, he has served on the prosecutor a notice in writing giving such information as was then in his possession identifying or assisting in the identification of that other person.

[London Local Authorities and Transport for London Act 2003, s 24.]

7.8049   25.   Liability of directors, etc   (1) Where an offence under this Act committed by a body corporate is proved to have been committed with the consent or connivance of, or to be attributable to any neglect on the part of, a director, manager, secretary or other similar officer of the body corporate or any person who was purporting to act in any such capacity, he, as well as the body corporate, shall be guilty of the offence.

(2)   Where the affairs of the body corporate are managed by its members, subsection (1) above shall apply to the acts and defaults of a member in connection with his functions of management as if he were a director of the body corporate.

[London Local Authorities and Transport for London Act 2003, s 25.]

7.8050   26.   Regulations

SCHEDULE 1
PENALTY CHARGE NOTICES ETC UNDER SECTION 4
(PENALTY CHARGES FOR
ROAD TRAFFIC CONTRAVENTIONS) OF THIS ACT   Section 4

Representations against penalty charge notice

7.8051   1.   (1)   Where it appears to a person on whom a penalty charge notice has been served under section 4 (Penalty charges for road traffic contraventions) of this Act (in this Schedule referred to as "the recipient") that one or other of the grounds mentioned in sub-paragraph (4) below is satisfied, he may make representations to that effect to the enforcing authority.

(2)   Any representations under this paragraph must be made in such form as may be specified by the enforcing authority, acting through the Joint Committee (within the meaning of subsection (16) of the said section 4).

(3)   The enforcing authority may disregard any such representations which are received by them after the end of the period of 28 days beginning with the date on which the penalty charge notice in question was served.

(4)   The grounds referred to in sub-paragraph (1) above are—

     (*a*)   that the recipient—
         (i)   never was the owner of the vehicle in question;
         (ii)   had ceased to be its owner before the date on which the penalty charge was alleged to have become payable; or
         (iii)   became its owner after that date;

     (*b*)   that there was no—
         (i)   contravention of a prescribed order; or
         (ii)   failure to comply with an indication; or
         (iii)   contravention of the lorry ban order,
     under subsection (5) or (7) of the said section 4 as the case may be;

     (*c*)   that at the time the alleged contravention or failure took place the person who was in control of the vehicle was in control of the vehicle without the consent of the owner;

     (*d*)   that the recipient is a vehicle-hire firm and—
         (i)   the vehicle in question was at the material time hired from that firm under a vehicle hiring agreement; and
         (ii)   the person hiring it had signed a statement of liability acknowledging his liability in respect of any penalty charge notice issued in respect of the vehicle during the currency of the hiring agreement; or

     (*e*)   that the penalty charge exceeded the amount applicable in the circumstances of the case.

(5)   Where the ground mentioned in sub-paragraph (4)(*a*)(ii) above is relied on in any representations made under this paragraph, those representations must include a statement of the name and address of the person to whom the vehicle was disposed of by the person making the representations (if that information is in his possession).

(6)   Where the ground mentioned in sub-paragraph (4)(*a*)(iii) above is relied on in any representations made under this paragraph, those representations must include a statement of the name and address of the person from whom the vehicle was acquired by the person making the representations (if that information is in his possession).

(7)   It shall be the duty of the enforcing authority to whom representations are duly made under this paragraph—

     (*a*)   to consider them and any supporting evidence which the person making them provides; and
     (*b*)   to serve on that person notice of their decision as to whether they accept that the ground in question has been established.

(8)   Where the ground that is accepted is that mentioned in sub-paragraph (4)(*d*) above, the person hiring the vehicle shall be deemed to be its owner for the purposes of this Act.

(9)   In this paragraph, "vehicle hiring agreement" and "vehicle-hire firm" have the same meanings as in section 66 of the Road Traffic Offenders Act 1988 (c 53) (Hired vehicles).

Cancellation of penalty charge notice

2.   (1)   Where representations are made under paragraph 1 above and the enforcing authority accept that the ground in question has been established they shall—

     (*a*)   cancel the penalty charge notice; and
     (*b*)   state in the notice served under sub-paragraph (7) of paragraph 1 above that the penalty charge notice has been cancelled.

(2)   The cancellation of a penalty charge notice under this paragraph shall not be taken to prevent the enforcing authority serving a fresh penalty charge notice on another person.

Rejection of representations against penalty charge notice

3.   Where any representations are made under paragraph 1 above but the enforcing authority do not accept that a ground has been established, the notice served under sub-paragraph (7) of the said paragraph 1 (in this Schedule referred to as "the notice of rejection") must—

     (*a*)   state that a charge certificate may be served under paragraph 5 below unless before the end of the period of 28 days beginning with the date of service of the notice of rejection—
         (i)   the penalty charge is paid; or

(ii)   the person on whom the notice is served appeals to a traffic adjudicator against the penalty charge; and

(b)   describe in general terms the form and manner in which such an appeal must be made,

and may contain such other information as the enforcing authority consider appropriate.

Adjudication by traffic adjudicator

4. (1)   Where an enforcing authority serve a notice of rejection, the person who made the representations under paragraph 1 above in respect of which that notice was served may, before—

(a)   the end of the period of 28 days beginning with the date of service of that notice; or

(b)   such longer period as a traffic adjudicator may allow,

appeal to a traffic adjudicator against the decision of the enforcing authority.

(2)   On an appeal under this paragraph, the traffic adjudicator shall consider the representations in question and any additional representations which are made by the appellant on any of the grounds mentioned in paragraph 1(4) above and may give the enforcing authority such directions as he considers appropriate.

(3)   It shall be the duty of the enforcing authority to whom a direction is given under sub-paragraph (2) above to comply with it forthwith.

Charge certificates

5. (1)   Where a penalty charge notice is served on any person and the penalty charge to which it relates is not paid before the end of the relevant period, the enforcing authority may serve on that person a statement (in this paragraph referred to as a "charge certificate") to the effect that the penalty charge in question is increased by 50 per cent.

(2)   The relevant period, in relation to a penalty charge notice is the period of 28 days beginning—

(a)   where no representations are made under paragraph 1 above, with the date on which the penalty charge notice is served;

(b)   where such representations are made and a notice of rejection is served by the enforcing authority and no appeal against the notice of rejection is made with the date on which the period within which an appeal could have been made expires; or

(c)   where there has been an unsuccessful appeal against a notice of rejection, with the date on which notice of the adjudicator's decision is served on the appellant.

(3)   Where an appeal against a notice of rejection is made but is withdrawn before the decision of the adjudicator is made the relevant period in relation to a penalty charge notice is the period of 14 days beginning with the date on which the appeal is withdrawn.

Enforcement of charge certificate

6. (1)   Where a charge certificate has been served on any person and the increased penalty charge provided for in the certificate is not paid before the end of the period of 14 days beginning with the date on which the certificate is served, the enforcing authority may, if a county court so orders, recover the increased charge as if it were payable under a county court order.

(2)   Any notice of any county court order made under this paragraph and being served on any person shall be accompanied by a copy of the penalty charge notice to which the penalty charge relates.

(3)   Section 78 of the Road Traffic Act 1991 (c 40) (which makes provision for the recovery of sums that are payable under or by virtue of any provision of Part II of that Act and are recoverable as if they were payable under a county court order) shall have effect as though an increased penalty charge recoverable under sub-paragraph (1) above were a Part II debt for the purposes of that section.

Invalid notices

7. (1)   This paragraph applies where—

(a)   a county court makes an order under paragraph 6 above;

(b)   the person against whom it is made makes a statutory declaration complying with sub-paragraph (2) below; and

(c)   that declaration is, before the end of the period of 21 days beginning with the date on which notice of the county court's order is served on him, served on the county court which made the order.

(2)   The statutory declaration must state that the person making it—

(a)   did not receive the penalty charge notice in question;

(b)   made representations to the enforcing authority under paragraph 1 above but did not receive a notice of rejection from that authority; or

(c)   appealed to a traffic adjudicator under paragraph 4 above against the rejection by that authority of representations made by him under paragraph 1 above but had no response to the appeal.

(3)   A statutory declaration under this paragraph is invalid and sub-paragraph (8) below shall not apply in relation to the declaration if one or more of the following grounds is met—

(a)   the person who made the declaration claims that more than one of the grounds mentioned in sub-paragraph (2) above is met;

(b)   the declaration is not signed by any person purporting to make it;

(c)   the declaration is not signed by or does not contain an address for a person purporting to be a witness to the signature of the person making it.

(4)   The Secretary of State may by regulations amend sub-paragraph (3) above by the addition of further grounds for a statutory declaration to be invalid.

(5)   Sub-paragraph (7) below applies where it appears to a district judge, on the application of a person on whom a charge certificate has been served, that it would be unreasonable in the circumstances of his case to insist on him serving his statutory declaration within the period of 21 days allowed for by sub-paragraph (1) above.

(6)   In considering an application under sub-paragraph (5) above the district judge must take into consideration any representations made by the enforcing authority before the expiry of the period of 14 days beginning on the date on which copies of the application and the statutory declaration are served by the court on the enforcing authority.

(7)   Where this sub-paragraph applies, the district judge may allow such longer period for service of the statutory declaration as he considers appropriate.

(8)   Subject to sub-paragraphs (3) above and (10) below, where a statutory declaration is served under sub-paragraph (1)(c) above—

   (*a*)   the order of the court shall be deemed to have been revoked;

   (*b*)   the charge certificate shall be deemed to have been cancelled;

   (*c*)   in the case of a statutory declaration under sub-paragraph (2)(*a*) above, the penalty charge notice to which the charge certificate relates shall be deemed to have been cancelled; and

   (*d*)   the district judge shall serve written notice of the effect of service of the statutory declaration on the person making it and on the enforcing authority.

   (9)   Service of a declaration under sub-paragraph (2)(*a*) above shall not prevent the enforcing authority serving a fresh penalty charge notice but if, when it was served, the relevant order under paragraph 6 was accompanied by a copy of the penalty charge notice to which the charge certificate relates, a fresh penalty charge notice in the same terms shall be deemed to have been served on the person making the declaration on the same day as the declaration was served.

   (10)   Where—

   (*a*)   sub-paragraph (7) above applies; and

   (*b*)   the order of the court is deemed to have been revoked under sub-paragraph (8) above,

the enforcing authority concerned shall not be liable to pay the person making the declaration any sums other than the increased charge which was payable under the county court order.

   (11)   Where a declaration has been served under sub-paragraph (2)(*b*) or (*c*) above, the enforcing authority shall refer the case to the traffic adjudicator who may give such direction as he considers appropriate.

Offence of giving false information

8.   (1)   A person who, in response to a penalty charge notice served under section 4 (Penalty charges for road traffic contraventions) of this Act makes any representation under paragraph 1 or 4 above which is false in a material particular and does so recklessly or knowing it to be false in that particular is guilty of an offence.

   (2)   Any person guilty of such an offence shall be liable on summary conviction to a fine not exceeding level 5 on the standard scale.

Service by post

9.   Any charge certificate, or notice under section 4 (Penalty charges for road traffic contraventions) of this Act or this Schedule—

   (*a*)   may be served by post; and

   (*b*)   where the person on whom it is to be served is a body corporate, is duly served if it is sent by post to the secretary or clerk of that body.

Traffic Adjudicators

10.   (1)   Functions of traffic adjudicators under this Schedule shall be discharged by the persons who are appointed as parking adjudicators under section 73 of the Road Traffic Act 1991 (c 40).

   (2)   Regulations under section 73(11) of the said Act of 1991 (provision as to procedure to be followed in relation to proceedings before parking adjudicators) may make provision with respect to proceedings before parking adjudicators when exercising the functions of traffic adjudicators under this Schedule; and any regulations under that subsection in force at the coming into operation of section 4 (Penalty charges for road traffic contraventions) of this Act shall, with any necessary modifications, apply in relation to such proceedings.

   (3)   The references to a parking adjudicator or parking adjudicators in section 73(13) to (15) and (17) and (18) of the said Act of 1991 shall include references to a parking adjudicator or parking adjudicators exercising the functions of traffic adjudicators under this Schedule but section 73(15) of that Act shall not apply to a penalty charge under the said section 4 which remains payable following an adjudication under this Schedule.

Interpretation

11.   In this Schedule "the enforcing authority", in relation to any penalty charge notice or charge certificate, means—

   (*a*) where the notice was served by a borough council, or the certificate relates to a notice so served, that council;

   (*b*)   where the notice was served by Transport for London, or the certificate relates to a notice so served, Transport for London.* **

---

* **Repealed by the Traffic Management Act 2004, s 98, Sch 12, Pt 1, from a date to be appointed.**

** **Amended for a transitional period only beginning 31 March 2008 by SI 2007/2053 (itself amended by SI 2008/757).**

SCHEDULE 2
Financial Provisions Relating to Sections 4 (Penalty Charges for Road Traffic Contraventions) and* 8 to 11 (Fixed Penalties) of this Act

---

* **Words repealed by the Traffic Management Act 2004, s 98, Sch 12, Pt 1, from a date to be appointed.**

SCHEDULE 3
Scheduled Traffic Signs for the Purposes of Section 4 (Penalty Charges for Road Traffic Contraventions) of this Act*

---

* **Schedule repealed by the Traffic Management Act 2004, s 98, Sch 12, Pt 1, from a date to be appointed.**

SCHEDULE 4

Offences in Respect of which Fixed Penalty Notices may be Served under Section 8 (Fixed Penalty Offences) of this Act

7.8052

(Amended by the Transport for London Act 2008, s 35.)   Section 8

	(1) *Act*	*(2)* *Section*	*(3)* *Description of Offence*
1	Highways Act 1980 (c 66)	132(1)	Painting or otherwise inscribing or affixing picture etc upon the surface of a highway or upon a tree, structure or works on or in a highway
2		137(1)	Wilful obstruction of highway
3		138	Erecting a building, fence or hedge on highway
4		139(3)	Depositing builder's skip on highway without permission
5		139(4)(*a*)	Failure to secure lighting or other marking of builder's skip
6		139(4)(*b*)	Failure to secure marking of builder's skip with name and address
7		139(4)(*c*)	Failure to secure removal of builder's skip
8		139(4)(*d*)	Failure to comply with conditions of permission
9		140(3)	Failure to remove or reposition builder's skip
10		141(3)	Failure to comply with notice requiring removal of tree or shrub
11		147A(2)	Using of stall etc for road side sales in certain circumstances
12		148(*a*)	Depositing material etc on a made-up carriageway
13		148(*b*)	Depositing material etc within 15 feet from centre of made-up carriageway
14		148(*c*)	Depositing anything on highway to the interruption of user
15		148(*d*)	Pitching of booths, stalls or stands or encamping on highway
16		151(3)	Failure to comply with notice requiring works to prevent soil or refuse escaping onto street or into sewer
17		152(4)	Failure to comply with notice requiring removal of projection from buildings
18		153(5)	Failure to comply with notice requiring alteration of door, gate or bar opening outwards onto street
19		155(2)	Keeping of animals straying or lying on side of highway
20		161(1)	Depositing things on highway which cause injury or danger
21		169(5)	Erecting scaffolding or other structure without licence or failing to comply with terms of licence or perform duty under subsection (4)
22	Transport for London Act 2008 (c i)	35(3)	Failure to comply with notice requiring works to prevent soil or refuse escaping onto street or into sewer

Transport for London Act 2008

(2008 c 1)

PART 1

PRELIMINARY

7.8053   1. Citation and commencement *This Act came into force on 22 July 2008 except ss 17–21, 23–25, 27 and Schs 1 and 2 which have effect from a date appointed by TfL.*

PART 2

ROAD USER CHARGING

7.8054   4.   Interpretation of Part 2   Expressions used in this Part and in Schedule 23 to the 1999 Act have the same meaning in this Part as in that Schedule.

[Transport for London Act 2008, s 4.]

7.8055   5.   Contravention of requirement of TfL scheme   (1)   Subject to subsection (2), a TfL scheme may provide that any person who, without reasonable excuse, contravenes or fails to comply with any specified requirement of the scheme shall be liable on summary conviction to a fine for each offence not exceeding level 2 on the standard scale or not exceeding a lesser amount; but such a provision—

     (a)   shall not have effect unless and until it has been approved by the Secretary of State, and

     (b)   shall not apply in relation to anything done before the provision comes into effect.

     (2)   Subsection (1) shall not authorise the creation of an offence which consists only of—

     (a)   a failure to pay a charge or penalty charge imposed by a TfL scheme, or

     (b)   any other contravention or failure to comply with a requirement of a TfL scheme for which a penalty charge imposed by or under regulations made under paragraph 12 of Schedule 23 to the 1999 Act is payable.

     (3)   Nothing in this section shall affect the operation of section 8 (failure to notify changes in eligibility for exemptions etc) or paragraph 25 or 27 of Schedule 23 to the 1999 Act (specific offences relating to road user charging).

[Transport for London Act 2008, s 5.]

7.8056   6.   Extension of power to include enforcement provisions in TfL scheme   (1)   Notwithstanding paragraph 31 of Schedule 23 to the 1999 Act, a TfL scheme may authorise—

     (a)   the examination, for any purpose relating to or connected with a TfL scheme, of a motor vehicle found in a charging area, or

     (b)   the fitting of an immobilisation device to, or the removal of, a motor vehicle found in such an area,

at a time at which the vehicle is on a public off-street parking place as well as at a time at which the vehicle is on a road.

     (2)   The powers conferred by the Charges and Penalty Charges Regulations on TfL, or for a TfL scheme to make provision for TfL, to examine, enter, immobilise or remove any vehicle which is on a road are also exercisable in respect of any vehicle which is on a public off-street parking place.

     (3)   Accordingly, the Charges and Penalty Charges Regulations, so far as they relate to TfL or a TfL scheme, shall have effect as if—

     (a)   the reference in regulation 8(1) to a vehicle which is on a road included a reference to a vehicle which is on a public off-street parking place;

     (b)   the references in regulations 10(1) and 12(1) to a vehicle which is stationary on a road in a charging area included references to a vehicle which is stationary on a public off-street parking place in a charging area;

     (c)   the references in regulations 10(1)(a) and 12(1)(a) to "that road" were references to a road in a charging area; and

     (d)   the reference in regulation 10(2)(b) to "another place on that road or another road" were a reference to another place on a road.

     (4)   TfL may not enter a public off-street parking place for the purpose of exercising any powers conferred on TfL by the Charges and Penalty Charges Regulations, or a TfL scheme, by virtue of this section to examine, enter, immobilise or remove any vehicle there without obtaining the prior consent of the operator.

     (5)   For the purposes of subsection (4) an operator's consent may be given to enter a public off-street parking place—

     (a)   on a specific occasion; or

     (b)   generally.

     (6)   An operator's consent required under subsection (4) is not to be unreasonably withheld but may be given subject to any reasonable conditions.

     (7)   Without prejudice to the generality of subsection (6), it is reasonable for consent to be given subject to conditions requiring TfL to reimburse the operator in respect of any loss of revenue, damage or other liability sustained as a result of the immobilisation or removal of any vehicle by TfL or the taking by TfL of any other action by virtue of this section.

     (8)   The owner, keeper or driver of a vehicle in a public off-street parking place which is immobilised or removed in accordance with the Charges and Penalty Charges Regulations, as they have effect in accordance with this section, shall not be required by the operator to pay any car parking charges or penalty additional to those already paid, or due to be paid, to the operator at the time that the vehicle was immobilised or removed.

     (9)   Where the powers conferred by the Charges and Penalty Charges Regulations are exercised pursuant to this section the notice required by regulation 10(3) shall summarise the effects of subsection (8).

     (10)   Unless the operator and TfL agree otherwise, TfL shall (whether or not conditions are imposed under subsection (6)) reimburse the operator in respect of any losses sustained as a result

of the operation of subsection (8).

(11)   Consent to enter a public off-street parking place on a specific occasion shall be deemed to have been given unconditionally for the purposes of subsection (4) if—

(a)   TfL has served a notice on the operator asking for consent to enter on that occasion and summarising the effect of subsections (8) and (10); and

(b)   the operator fails within 14 days of the service of the notice to give TfL notice of his consent (whether or not subject to conditions) or his refusal to give it.

(12)   At least 7 days before entering a public off-street parking place in accordance with subsection (11) TfL shall take reasonable steps to ascertain whether the operator has received the notice served under subsection (11)(a).

(13)   Any question whether consent is unreasonably withheld or is given subject to reasonable conditions shall be referred to and determined by an arbitrator to be appointed, in default of agreement, by the President of the Chartered Institute of Arbitrators.

(14)   In this section—

(a)   "the Charges and Penalty Charges Regulations" means the Road User Charging (Charges and Penalty Charges) (London) Regulations 2001 (SI 2001/2285);

(b)   "public off-street parking place" means a place, whether above or below ground and whether or not consisting of or including buildings, where off-street parking accommodation is made available by a local authority or any other person to the public (whether or not for payment); and

(c)   any reference to the operator of such a parking place is a reference to the local authority or other person making such parking accommodation at the parking place so available.

[Transport for London Act 2008, s 6.]

7.8057   7.   Power to suspend TfL scheme

7.8058   8.   Failure to notify changes in eligibility for exemptions etc (1)   This section applies where a TfL scheme—

(a)   makes provision for the maintenance of a register of non-chargeable, reduced rate and qualifying person's motor vehicles for the purposes of provisions in the scheme relating to—

(i)   exemptions from charge,

(ii)   the application of reduced rates of charge, or

(iii)   the imposition of limits on the charges payable,

in the case of any particular class of motor vehicles or descriptions of persons; and

(b)   requires the registered keeper of the motor vehicle or qualifying person in relation to whom particulars of the vehicle are entered on the register to notify TfL if the vehicle has ceased to be a non-chargeable vehicle, a reduced rate vehicle or a qualifying person's vehicle for the purposes of those provisions.

(2)   In subsection (1) "qualifying person", in relation to a TfL scheme, means a person who qualifies for an exemption from charge, a reduced rate of charge or a limit on the charge payable.

(3)   Where this section applies, any person who, without reasonable excuse, fails to comply with the requirement referred to in subsection (1)(b) is guilty of an offence and liable on summary conviction to a fine not exceeding level 2 on the standard scale.

(4)   This section shall not apply in relation to anything done before this section comes into force.

[Transport for London Act 2008, s 8.]

PART 3

LONDON CABS AND PRIVATE HIRE VEHICLES

London cabs: general provisions

7.8059   9.   Power to designate directional taxi ranks (1)   TfL may by London cab order designate any standing for hackney carriages appointed under section 4 of the London Hackney Carriages Act 1850 (c 7) to be a directional taxi rank—

(a)   at all times; or

(b)   for such times of the day, days or other periods as may be specified in the order.

(2)   Where TfL designates a directional taxi rank, TfL shall cause a sign to be displayed at the rank clearly indicating—

(a)   the direction or directions in which the drivers of vehicles plying for hire at that rank are required to travel if so requested by any person wishing to hire the vehicle in question; and

(b)   the times, days or other periods for which the rank is designated to be a directional taxi rank.

(3)   Notwithstanding section 35 of the London Hackney Carriage Act 1831 (c 22) and section 17 of the London Hackney Carriage Act 1853 (c 33), the driver of a hackney carriage plying for hire at a directional taxi rank may refuse to drive his vehicle in a direction which is not the specified direction or, where more than one direction is specified, which is not one of the specified directions.

(4)   Where it appears to TfL to be desirable or expedient TfL may suspend the operation of a

designation under this section for such period or periods as TfL thinks fit.

(5)   In this section—

"directional taxi rank" means a standing for hackney carriages whose drivers are plying for hire only for journeys in a specified direction or in one of several specified directions;

"London cab order" means an order made under section 9 of the Metropolitan Public Carriage Act 1869 (c 115); and

"specified direction", in relation to a directional taxi rank, means the direction (or any of the directions) specified in the designation relating to that rank.

[Transport for London Act 2008, s 9.]

7.8060   10.   Power to designate rest ranks   (1)   TfL may by London cab order designate any standing (or part of a standing) for hackney carriages appointed under section 4 of the London Hackney Carriages Act 1850 (c 7) to be a rest rank—

(a)   at all times; or

(b)   for such times of the day, days or other periods as may be specified in the order.

(2)   TfL may by London cab order prescribe the maximum length of time during which a hackney carriage may stand at a rest rank; and different maximum lengths of time may be prescribed—

(a)   for different rest ranks; or

(b)   for different times of the day, days or other periods.

(3)   Where TfL designates a rest rank, TfL shall cause a sign to be displayed at the rank clearly indicating that the rank (or the relevant part of it) is a rest rank.

(4)   Notwithstanding section 35 of the London Hackney Carriage Act 1831 (c 22) and section 17 of the London Hackney Carriage Act 1853 (c 33), the driver of a hackney carriage which is standing at a rest rank shall not be deemed to be plying for hire and, accordingly, may not be compelled to drive his vehicle to any place by any person wishing to hire it.

(5)   Where it appears to TfL to be desirable or expedient TfL may suspend the operation of a designation under this section for such period or periods as TfL thinks fit.

(6)   In this section "London cab order" means an order made under section 9 of the Metropolitan Public Carriage Act 1869 (c 115).

[Transport for London Act 2008, s 10.]

7.8061   15.   Fares for journeys ending outside London   (1)   *Amends the London Cab and Stage Carriage Act 1907, s 1.*

(2)   Nothing in this section shall affect the operation of section 35 of the London Hackney Carriage Act 1831 (c 22), sections 7 and 17 of the London Hackney Carriage Act 1853 (c 33) or any other enactment which makes provision as regards the obligation of drivers of hackney carriages to drive their vehicles on certain journeys if so requested by persons wishing to hire them.

[Transport for London Act 2008, s 15.]

London cabs and private hire vehicles: fixed penalties

7.8062   17.   Fixed penalty cab and private hire vehicle offences   (1)   Where on any occasion an authorised officer finds a person who he has reason to believe has on that occasion committed an offence under any of the enactments—

(a)   specified in columns (1) and (2) of the table set out in Schedule 1 to this Act; and

(b)   described in column (3) of that table;

the authorised officer may give that person a notice offering him the opportunity of discharging any liability to conviction for that offence by payment of a fixed penalty.

(2)   Sections 18 to 21 (fixed penalties) shall apply in respect of fixed penalty notices under this section.

(3)   Schedule 2 to this Act shall have effect with respect to financial provisions relating to the administration and enforcement of this section and sections 18 to 21 (fixed penalties).

(4)   In subsection (1) "authorised officer" means a person authorised in writing by TfL for the purposes of sections 17 to 21 of this Act.

[Transport for London Act 2008, s 17.]

7.8063   18.   Power to amend Schedule 1   (1)   The Secretary of State may, after consulting—

(a)   the Mayor,

(b)   the Greater London Assembly,

(c)   TfL,

(d)   every London borough council,

(e)   the Common Council of the City of London, and

(f)   such bodies or persons as appear to him to be representative of persons who would be affected by the proposed regulations,

by regulations, amend Schedule 1 to this Act by adding a relevant offence to, or removing a relevant offence from, the offences for the time being mentioned in the table set out in that Schedule.

(2)   In subsection (1) "relevant offence" means an offence under an enactment regulating hackney carriages or private hire vehicles in London or the drivers, proprietors or operators of such carriages or vehicles.

[Transport for London Act 2008, s 18.]

7.8064   19.   Fixed penalty notices   (1)   The provisions of this section shall have effect in relation to notices ("fixed penalty notices") which may be given under section 17 (fixed penalty cab and private hire vehicle offences).

(2)   Where a person is given a fixed penalty notice in respect of an offence—

(a)   no proceedings shall be instituted for that offence before the expiration of 28 days following the date of the notice;

(b)   he shall not be convicted of that offence if he pays the fixed penalty before the expiration of that period; and

(c)   in the case of an offence in respect of which (but for this paragraph) section 38 of the London Hackney Carriages Act 1843 (c 86) (which as amended by section 14 (time limit for making complaints) requires complaints for certain offences to be made within 28 days) applies, proceedings may (notwithstanding that section) be instituted for that offence until the expiration of 42 days following the date of the notice.

(3)   A fixed penalty notice under this section shall give such particulars of the circumstances alleged to constitute the offence as are necessary for giving reasonable information of the offence and shall state—

(a)   the period during which, by virtue of subsection (2), proceedings will not be taken for the offence;

(b)   the amount of the fixed penalty;

(c)   the name of the person to whom and the address at which the fixed penalty may be paid; and

(d)   the consequences of not making any payment within the period for payment;

and, without prejudice to payment by any other method, payment of the fixed penalty may be made by pre-paying and posting to that person at that address a letter containing the amount of the penalty (in cash or otherwise).

(4)   Where a letter is sent in accordance with subsection (3) payment shall be regarded as having been made at the time at which that letter would be delivered in the ordinary course of post.

(5)   The form of notices under this section shall be such as the Secretary of State may by regulations prescribe.

(6)   The fixed penalty payable in pursuance of a fixed penalty notice under this section shall be paid to TfL.

(7)   In any proceedings a certificate which—

(a)   purports to be signed by or on behalf of the chief finance officer of TfL; and

(b)   states that payment of a fixed penalty was or was not received by a date specified in the certificate,

shall be evidence of the facts stated.

[Transport for London Act 2008, s 19.]

7.8065   20.   Levels of fixed penalties   (1)   It shall be the duty of TfL to set the levels of fixed penalties payable to TfL.

(2)   Different levels may be set for different cases or classes of case.

(3)   In setting the level of fixed penalty under subsection (1) TfL shall take into account the maximum fine for the particular fixed penalty offence in question and may take account of—

(a)   any reasonable costs or expected costs incurred or to be incurred in connection with the administration of the provisions of the enactment under which the particular fixed penalty offence is created; and

(b)   the cost or expected cost of enforcing the provisions of the relevant enactment.

(4)   Levels of fixed penalties set by TfL in accordance with this section may only come into force in accordance with section 21 (fixed penalties: reserve powers of Secretary of State).

(5)   TfL shall publish, in such manner as the Mayor may determine, the levels of fixed penalties which have been set by TfL in accordance with this section.

[Transport for London Act 2008, s 20.]

7.8066   21.   Fixed penalties: reserve powers of Secretary of State   (1)   Where TfL sets any levels of fixed penalties under subsection (1) of section 20 (levels of fixed penalties), TfL shall notify the Secretary of State of the levels of fixed penalties so set.

(2)   Where notification of any levels of fixed penalties is required to be given under subsection (1), the levels of fixed penalties shall not come into force until after the expiration of—

(a)   the period of one month beginning with the day on which the notification is given; or

(b)   such shorter period as the Secretary of State may allow.

(3)   If, before the expiration of that period, the Secretary of State gives notice to TfL that he objects to the levels of fixed penalties on the grounds that some or all of them are or may be excessive, those levels of fixed penalties shall not come into force unless and until the objection has been withdrawn.

(4)   If, at any time before the levels of fixed penalties required to be notified under subsection (1) to the Secretary of State have come into force, the Secretary of State considers that some or all of them are excessive, he may make regulations setting the levels of fixed penalties.

(5)   Levels of fixed penalties set under subsection (4) must be no higher than those notified

under subsection (1).

(6)   Where the Secretary of State makes any such regulations TfL must not set any further fixed penalties under subsection (1) until after the expiration of the period of 12 months beginning with the day on which the regulations are made.

[Transport for London Act 2008, s 21.]

7.8067   22.   Regulations   Any power to make regulations under section 18, 19 or 21—

(a)   includes power to make provision in respect of such cases only as may be specified in the regulations and to make different provision for different circumstances, and

(b)   shall be exercised by statutory instrument subject to annulment in pursuance of a resolution of either House of Parliament.

[Transport for London Act 2008, s 22.]

Private hire vehicles

7.8068   23.   Production of London PHV driver's badge   (1)   In section 14(3) of the 1998 Act (obligation of driver of London private hire vehicle to wear badge) before "wear the badge in such position and manner as to be plainly and distinctly visible" insert "(*a*)" and after those words insert—

"and—

(b)   at the request of any person, produce the badge for inspection.".

(2)   In section 14(4) of the 1998 Act (power of TfL to exempt a driver from a requirement to wear his badge) for "subsection (3)" insert "subsection (3)(*a*)".[1]

[Transport for London Act 2008, s 23.]

---

[1] The wording above has been reproduced in accordance with the Queen's Printers' Copy. It is understood that there is a drafting error in para (2) and that the word "insert" should actually read "substitute".

7.8069   24.   Return of licences etc on suspension or revocation   (1)   Section 22 of the 1998 Act (return of licences etc) shall be amended as follows.

(2)   In subsection (1), at the beginning insert "Without prejudice to subsection (1A),".

(3)   After subsection (1) insert—

"(1A)   Where the suspension or revocation of a London PHV operator's licence has immediate effect by virtue of section 17(2), the holder of the licence shall, at the request of a constable or authorised officer, forthwith return the licence to the constable or officer.".

(4)   In subsection (2)—

(a)   at the beginning insert "Without prejudice to subsection (2A),";

(b)   for "the plate or disc" substitute "every plate or disc"; and

(c)   after "section 10" insert "or any regulations made under this Act".

(5)   After subsection (2) insert—

"(2A)   Where the suspension or revocation of a London PHV licence has immediate effect by virtue of section 9(3) or 17(2), the owner of the vehicle to which the licence relates shall, at the request of a constable or authorised officer, forthwith return to the constable or officer the licence and every plate or disc which was issued for the vehicle under section 10 or any regulations made under this Act.".

(6)   In subsection (3), at the beginning insert "Without prejudice to subsection (3A),".

(7)   After subsection (3) insert—

"(3A)   Where the suspension or revocation of a London PHV driver's licence has immediate effect by virtue of section 17(2), the holder of the licence shall, at the request of a constable or authorised officer, forthwith return his driver's badge to the constable or officer.".

(8)   In subsection (4)—

(a)   at the beginning insert "Without prejudice to subsections (1A), (2A) and (3A),"; and

(b)   in paragraph (*a*), for "the disc or plate" substitute "every disc or plate" and after "section 10" insert "or any regulations made under this Act".

(9)   In subsection (7), for "the plate or disc" substitute "every disc or plate".

[Transport for London Act 2008, s 24.]

7.8070   25.   Obligation of London operators to keep records   In section 4(3) of the 1998 Act (records to be kept by London operators), for paragraph (*d*) substitute—

"(d)   keep at the specified operating centre or, where more than one operating centre is specified, at one of the operating centres such records as may be prescribed of particulars of the private hire vehicles and drivers which are available to him for carrying out bookings accepted by him at that or, as the case may be, each centre;

(da)   where more than one operating centre is specified—

(i)   give notice to the licensing authority, and

(ii)   display at each specified operating centre a notice,

stating the address of the operating centre at which the records are kept under paragraph (*d*);".

[Transport for London Act 2008, s 25.]

PART 5
STREET MANAGEMENT

7.8071   34.   Power to erect flag poles etc on GLA roads   (1)   Subject to subsection (2), TfL may—

(a)   erect flagpoles, pylons and other structures on any GLA road for the purpose of displaying decorations;

(b)   make slots in any GLA road for the purpose of erecting the structures, and

(c)   remove any structure erected or slot made by TfL in pursuance of paragraph (a) or (b);

and any structures or slots which may be erected or made by virtue of this subsection are hereafter in this section referred to as "relevant works".

(2)   TfL is not entitled to exercise the powers conferred on it by subsection (1) in respect of so much of a GLA road as—

(a)   is carried by a bridge which a body other than TfL has a duty to maintain; or

(b)   forms part of the approaches to such a bridge and is supported or protected by works or materials which a body other than TfL has a duty to maintain,

except with the consent in writing of that body.

(3)   A body may give their consent in pursuance of subsection (2) on such terms as they think fit (including in particular, without prejudice to the generality of the preceding provisions of this subsection, terms providing for the body to remove any of the relevant works and reinstate the bridge or its approaches and to recover the reasonable cost of doing so from TfL).

(4)   TfL shall not exercise any power conferred on it by subsection (1) in relation to a GLA road unless TfL has first obtained the consent of any local authority for the areas in which TfL proposes to exercise the power.

(5)   If TfL erects or makes relevant works by virtue of the preceding provisions of this section TfL shall—

(a)   ensure that the works are erected or made so as to obstruct the GLA road in question as little as is reasonably possible, so as not to obscure or conflict with traffic signs connected with the GLA road and so as to interfere as little as is reasonably possible with the enjoyment of premises adjacent to the GLA road and with, and with access to, any apparatus in or on the GLA road which belongs to or is used or maintained by statutory undertakers; and

(b)   ensure that while the works are retained they are properly maintained and, so far as it is necessary to light them to avoid danger to users of the GLA road, are properly lit.

(6)   A person who without lawful authority interferes with or removes any relevant works is guilty of an offence and liable on summary conviction to a fine not exceeding level 3 on the standard scale.

(7)   In this section—

"bridge" includes a structure which carries a GLA road superimposed over a cutting; and "statutory undertakers" means any of the following, namely, any body which is a statutory undertaker within the meaning provided by section 329(1) of the 1980 Act, any universal service provider in connection with the provision of a universal postal service, any licensee under a street works licence and the operator of an electronic communications code network or a driver information system.

(8)   Nothing in this section shall affect the operation of section 144 of the 1980 Act.

[Transport for London Act 2008, s 34.]

7.8072   35.   Prevention of soil etc being washed on to GLA roads   (1)   Subject to subsections (5) and (6), TfL may, by notice to the owner or occupier of any land adjoining a GLA road, require him, within 28 days from the date of service of the notice, to execute such works as will prevent soil or refuse from that land from falling, or being washed or carried, on to the GLA road or into any sewer or gully in it in such quantities as to obstruct the GLA road or choke the sewer or gully.

(2)   A person aggrieved by a requirement under this section may appeal to a magistrate's court.

(3)   Subject to any order made on appeal, if a person on whom a notice is served under this section fails to comply with it within the period specified in subsection (1), he is guilty of an offence and liable on summary conviction to a fine not exceeding level 3 on the standard scale; and if the offence is continued after conviction, he is guilty of a further offence and liable to a fine not exceeding £50 for each day on which the offence is so continued.

(4)   Section 311 of the 1980 Act shall apply to any offence under subsection (3) as it applies to an offence under section 151(3) of that Act.

(5)   Before serving a notice under subsection (1) TfL shall give not less than 7 days notice to the local authority, or each local authority, in whose area the GLA road is situated.

(6)   A notice served under subsection (1) shall not have effect in any case where—

(a)   a notice has been served under section 151 of the 1980 Act on the same person and in respect of the same land, and

(b)   the works required by that notice will, if carried out, prevent the soil or refuse in question from obstructing the GLA road or choking the sewer or gully.

(7)   At the end of Schedule 4 to the London Local Authorities and Transport for London Act 2003 (c iii) (offences in respect of which fixed penalty notices may be served) insert—

| 22 | Transport for London Act 2008 (c i) | 35(3) | Failure to comply with notice requiring works to prevent soil or refuse escaping onto street or into sewer. |

(8)   Nothing in this section shall affect the operation of section 151 of the 1980 Act.

[Transport for London Act 2008, s 35.]

7.8073   36.   Dangerous land adjoining GLA roads   (1)   Subject to subsections (4) to (6), if, in or on any land adjoining a GLA road there is an unfenced or inadequately fenced source of danger to persons using the GLA road, TfL may, by notice to the owner or occupier of that land, require him within such time as may be specified in the notice to execute such works of repair, protection, removal or enclosure as will obviate the danger.

(2)   A person aggrieved by a requirement under subsection (1) may appeal to a magistrate's court.

(3)   Subject to any order made on appeal, if a person on whom a notice is served under this section fails to comply with the notice within the time specified in it, TfL may execute such works as are necessary to comply with the notice and may recover the expenses reasonably incurred by it in so doing from that person.

(4)   Subject to subsection (5), before serving a notice under subsection (1) TfL shall give not less than 7 days notice to the local authority, or each local authority, in whose area the GLA road is situated.

(5)   Where a notice is served under subsection (1) in the case of emergency, TfL shall not be required to give prior notice to the local authority under subsection (4) but shall notify the authority at the same time as, or as soon as reasonably practicable after, the service of the first mentioned notice.

(6)   A notice served under subsection (1) shall not have effect in any case where—

   (a)   a notice has been served under section 165 of the 1980 Act on the same person and in respect of the same land, and

   (b)   the works required by that notice will, if carried out, obviate the danger in question.

(7)   Nothing in this section shall affect the operation of section 165 of the 1980 Act.

[Transport for London Act 2008, s 36.]

7.8074   38.   Powers relating to retaining walls near GLA roads   (1)   This section applies to any length of a retaining wall, being a length—

   (a)   any cross-section of which is wholly or partly within 3.66 metres of a GLA road; and

   (b)   which is at any point of greater height than 1.37 metres above the level of the ground at the boundary of the GLA road nearest that point;

but does not apply to any length of a retaining wall erected on land belonging to any transport undertakers so long as that land is used by them primarily for the purpose of their undertaking or to any length of a retaining wall for the maintenance of which a highway authority are responsible.

(2)   Subject to subsections (6) to (8), if a length of retaining wall to which this section applies is in such condition (whether for want of repair or some other reason) as to be liable to endanger persons using the GLA road, TfL may, by notice served on the owner or occupier of the land on which that length of wall is, require him to execute such works as will obviate the danger.

(3)   Subsections (2) to (7) of section 290 of the Public Health Act 1936 (c 49) (appeals against, and the enforcement of, certain notices under that Act) apply to any notice served under subsection (2) as they apply to such notices as are mentioned in subsection (1) of that section, but subject to the following modifications—

   (a)   references to the local authority are to be construed as including references to TfL;

   (b)   for paragraph (f) of subsection (3) there is substituted the following paragraph—

   "(f)   that some other person ought to contribute towards the expense of executing any works required by the notice".

(4)   Sections 300 to 302 of the Public Health Act 1936 (supplementary provisions relating to appeals under the said section 290) apply, with the necessary modifications, to appeals brought by virtue of subsection (3).

(5)   In this section "retaining wall" means a wall, not forming part of a permanent building, which serves, or is intended to serve, as a support for earth or other material on one side only.

(6)   Subject to subsection (7), before serving a notice under subsection (2) TfL shall give not less than 7 days notice to the local authority, or each local authority, in whose area the GLA road is situated.

(7)   Where a notice is served under subsection (2) in the case of emergency, TfL shall not be required to give prior notice to the local authority under subsection (6) but shall notify the local authority at the same time as, or as soon as reasonably practicable after, the service of the first mentioned notice.

(8)   A notice served under subsection (2) shall not have effect in any case where—

   (a)   a notice has been served under section 167 of the 1980 Act on the same person and in respect of the same land, and

   (b)   the works required by that notice will, if carried out, obviate the danger in question.

(9)   Nothing in this section shall affect the operation of section 167 of the 1980 Act.

[Transport for London Act 2008, s 38.]

SCHEDULE 1
Offences in Respect of Which Fixed Penalty Notices may be Served Under Section 17 (Fixed Penalty Cab and
Private Hire Vehicle Offences) of This Act   Section 17(1)

7.8075

(1) Act/Instrument	(2) Enactment	(3) Description of offence
London Hackney Carriages Act 1843 (c 86)	Section 17	Failure to wear, or to produce, badge.
London Cab Order 1934 (SR&O/1346)	Article 28	Failure to produce copy of licence.
	Article 31(1)(ii)	Plying outside licensed area.
	Article 33(1)	Carrying excess passengers.
Regulations for Enforcing Order at Cab Standings in the Metropolitan Police District made on 11th October 1963	Regulation (1)	Failure to attend cab at cab standing.

HACKNEY CARRIAGES AND PRIVATE HIRE VEHICLES

London Hackney Carriage Act 1831
(1 & 2 Will 4 c 22)

7.8076   35.   Hackney carriage standing in a street or place and not already hired shall be deemed
to be plying for hire; driver refusing hire and unable to adduce evidence to court of hiring shall
forfeit a sum not exceeding **level 1** on the standard scale[1].

[London Hackney Carriage Act 1831, s 35, as amended by the Statute Law Revision (No 2) Act 1888, the Criminal
Justice Act 1967, Sch 3 and the Criminal Justice Act 1982, ss 38 and 46—summarised.]

---

[1] This section, for the purpose of hiring of taxis at separate fares under ss 10 and 11 of the Transport Act 1985, has
been disapplied by the Licensed Taxis (Hiring at Separate Fares) (London) Order 1986, SI 1986/1387.

7.8077   36.   Compensation to be made to drivers improperly summoned for refusing to carry any
person.

[London Hackney Carriage Act 1831, s 36, as amended by the Statute Law Revision (No 2) Act 1888, and the Statute
Law (Repeals) Act 1976—summarised.]

**7.8078   41.   Persons refusing to pay the driver his fare, or in injuring his carriage, to be
liable to make compensation, or to be committed to prison**   If any person shall refuse or omit
to pay the driver of any hackney carriage the sum justly due to him for the hire of such hackney
carriage, or if any person shall deface or in any manner injure any such hackney carriage it shall be
lawful for any justice of the peace, upon complaint thereof made to him, to grant a summons, or if
it shall appear to him necessary, a warrant, for bringing before him or any other justice such
defaulter or defender, and upon proof of the facts made upon oath before any such justice, to award
reasonable satisfaction to the party so complaining for his fare or for his damages and costs, and also
a reasonable compensation for his loss of time in attending to make and establish such complaint.

[London Hackney Carriage Act 1831, s 41 as amended by the Statute Law (Repeals) Act 1976.]

7.8079   47.   Driver may demand deposit when required to wait with carriage—penalty on such
driver refusing to wait, or to account for the deposit, etc **level 1** on the standard scale.

[London Hackney Carriage Act 1831, s 47 as amended by the Statute Law Revision Act 1974, the Statute Law Revision
(No 2) Act 1888, the Criminal Law Act 1977, s 31 and the Criminal Justice Act 1982, s 46—summarised.]

7.8080   56.   Penalty on proprietors or drivers misbehaving   If the proprietor or driver of any
hackney carriage, or any other person having the care thereof, shall, by intoxication, or by wanton
and furious driving or by any other wilful misconduct, injure or endanger any person in his life,
limbs or property, or if any such proprietor or driver shall make use of any abusive or insulting
language, or be guilty of other rude behaviour to or towards any person whatever, or shall assault or
obstruct any officer of police, constable, watchman, or patrole, in the execution of his duty, every
such proprietor, driver or other person so offending in any of the several cases aforesaid, shall forfeit
a sum not exceeding **level 1** on the standard scale[1].

[London Hackney Carriage Act 1831, s 56 as amended by the Summary Jurisdiction Act 1884, s 4, the Statute Law
Revision (No 2) Act 1888, the Statute Law (Repeals) Act 1976, the Criminal Law Act 1977, s 31, the Criminal Justice Act
1982, s 46 and the Statute Law (Repeals) Act 2004.]

---

[1] The wording of the section has been slightly edited to accord with modern circumstances. A conviction under this
section can lead to the proprietor's licence being revoked.

London Hackney Carriages Act 1843[1]
(6 & 7 Vict c 86)

7.8081 10. Lending etc licence or badge Any person transferring or lending a licence or permitting another person to use or wear a badge, or proprietor knowingly suffering unlicensed person to act as driver: penalty not exceeding **level 3** on the standard scale.

[London Hackney Carriages Act 1843, s 10 as amended by the Statute Law Revision Act 1874 (No 2), the Statute Law Revision Act 1891, the Criminal Justice Act 1967, Sch 3, the Statute Law (Repeals) Act 1976, the Criminal Justice Act 1982, ss 35, 38 and 46, the Statute Law (Repeals) Act 1993, Sch 1 and the Transport for London Act 2008, s 11—summarised.]

---

[1] A hackney carriage is defined for the purposes of these Acts by the Metropolitan Public Carriage Act 1869, s 4, as meaning any carriage for the conveyance of passengers which plies for hire (within the Metropolitan Police District or the City of London) and is not a stage carriage. A motor vehicle is included within the definition (Road Traffic Act 1988, s 191).

This Act, to the extent that it is part of the taxi code, except ss 3 and 33, shall apply to the use of taxis to provide local services under a special licence under s 12 of the Transport Act 1985 (Local Services (Operation by Taxis) (London) Regulations 1986, SI 1986/566).

7.8082 14. Persons applying for licences to sign a requisition for the same, etc—Penalty on applicants or referees making false representations Before any such licence shall be granted, a requisition for the same, in such form as Transport for London shall from time to time appoint for that purpose, shall be made and signed by the person by whom such licence shall be required; and in every such requisition all such particulars as Transport for London shall require shall be truly set forth; and every person applying for or attempting to procure any such licence who shall make or cause to be made any false representation in regard to any of the said particulars, or who shall not truly answer all questions which shall be demanded of him in relation to such application for a licence, and also every person to whom reference shall be made who shall, in regard to such application, wilfully and knowingly make any misrepresentation, shall forfeit for every such offence the sum of **level 3** on the standard scale; and it shall be lawful for Transport for London to proceed for recovering of such penalty before any magistrate at any time within one calendar month after the commission of the offence, or during the currency of the licence so improperly obtained.

[London Hackney Carriages Act 1843, s 14, as amended by the Statute Law Revision Act 1891, the Criminal Justice Act 1967, Sch 3, the Forgery and Counterfeiting Act 1981, Sch, the Criminal Justice Act 1982, ss 38 and 46 and the Greater London Authority Act 1999, Sch 20.]

7.8083 17. Badges to be worn by drivers, etc Every licensed driver shall at all times during his employment, and when he shall be required to attend before any justice of the peace, wear his badge conspicuously upon his breast, in such manner that the whole of the writing thereon shall be distinctly legible; and every driver who shall act as such, or who shall attend when required before any justice of the peace, without wearing such badge in manner aforesaid, or who, when thereunto required, shall refuse to produce such badge for inspection, or to permit any person to note the writing thereon, shall for every such offence forfeit a sum not exceeding **level 1** on the standard scale.

[London Hackney Carriages Act 1843, s 17 as amended by the Statute Law Revision Act 1874 (No 2), the Statute Law Revision Act 1891, the Criminal Justice Act 1967, Sch 3, the Statute Law (Repeals) Act 1976, the Criminal Justice Act 1982, ss 38 and 46 and the Transport for London Act 2008, s 11.]

7.8084 18. Licences and badges to be delivered up on the discontinuance of licences Wilful neglect to deliver up within 3 days, or use or wear false badge for purposes of deception; maximum fine **level 1** on the standard scale; limitation period 12 months from expiry of licence.

[London Hackney Carriages Act 1843, s 18 as amended by the Statute Law Revision Act 1891, the Criminal Law Act 1977, s 31, the Criminal Justice Act 1982, s 46, the Transport for London Act 2008, s 11 and the Immigration Act 2016, Sch 5—summarised.]

7.8085 19. New badges to be delivered instead of defaced or lost badges Every person licensed under the authority of this Act who shall use or wear the badge granted to him after the writing thereon shall be obliterated, defaced or obscured so that the same shall not be distinctly legible, shall for every such offence forfeit the sum of **level 1** on the standard scale.

[London Hackney Carriages Act 1843, s 19 as amended by the Statute Law Revision Act 1891, the Criminal Law Act 1977, s 31 and the Criminal Justice Act 1982, s 46 and the Transport for London Act 2008, s 11—summarised.]

7.8086 25. Licences may be revoked or suspended It shall be lawful for any justice of the peace before whom any driver shall be convicted of any offence, whether under this Act or any other Act, if such justice in his discretion shall think fit, to revoke the licence of such driver, and also any other licence he shall hold under the provisions of this Act, or to suspend the same for such time as the justice shall think proper, and for that purpose to require the proprietor (*or*) driver in whose possession such licence and the badge thereunto belonging shall then be to deliver up the same; and every proprietor, (*or*) driver who, being so required, shall refuse or neglect to deliver up such licence and any such ticket, or either of them, shall forfeit[1] so often as he shall be so required and refuse or neglect as aforesaid the sum of **level 1** on the standard scale; and the justice shall forthwith send such licence and badge to Transport for London, who shall cancel such licence if it has been revoked by the justice, or, if it has been suspended shall, at the end of the time for which it shall have been suspended, re-deliver such licence with the badge, to the person to whom it was granted.

A magistrates' court that makes an order revoking or suspending any licence under this section may, if the court thinks fit, suspend the effect of the order pending an appeal against the order.

[London Hackney Carriages Act 1843, s 25 as amended by the Statute Law Revision Act 1874 (No 2), the Statute Law Revision Act 1891, the Statute Law (Repeals) Act 1976, the Criminal Law Act 1977, s 31, the Criminal Justice Act 1982, s 46, the Transport Act 1985, Sch 7, the Greater London Authority Act 1999, Sch 20 and the Transport for London Act 2008, s 11.]

---

[1] Penalty recoverable on summary conviction.

7.8087 27. No person to act as driver etc of any carriage without the consent of the proprietor The person and any driver suffering him to act liable to fine not exceeding **level 1** on the standard scale; driver not revealing name, address and (any) licence number of person he has allowed to act as driver is liable therefor to further penalty not exceeding **level 1** on the standard scale; police constable may take charge of carriage.

[London Hackney Carriages Act 1843, s 27 as amended by the Statute Law Revision Act (No 2), the Statute Law Revision Act 1891, the Statute Law (Repeals) Act 1976, the Criminal Law Act 1977, s 31, the Criminal Justice Act 1982, s 46 and the Police and Criminal Evidence Act 1984, Sch 6 and the Transport for London Act 2008, s 11—summarised.]

7.8088 28. Punishment for furious driving, and wilful misbehaviour—Compensation[1] for injury, etc Proprietor paying compensation may recover from driver, etc.—Every driver of a hackney carriage, who shall be guilty of wanton or furious driving, or who by carelessness or wilful misbehaviour shall cause any hurt or damage to any person or property being in any street or highway, and also every driver, who during his employment shall be drunk, or shall make use of any insulting or abusive language, or shall be guilty of any insulting gesture or any misbehaviour, shall for every such offence forfeit the sum of **level 1** on the standard scale; or it shall be lawful for the justice before whom such complaint shall be brought, if in his discretion he shall think proper, instead of inflicting such penalty, forthwith to commit the offender to prison for any period not exceeding **two calendar months**.*

[London Hackney Carriages Act 1843, s 28 as amended by the Statute Law Revision Act 1872 (No 2), the Statute Law Revision Act 1891, the Statute Law (Repeals) Act 1976, the Criminal Law Act 1977, s 31, the Criminal Justice Act 1982, s 46 and the Statute Law (Repeals) Act 1993, Sch 1.]

---

[1] The provision relating to compensation was repealed by the Statute Law (Repeals) Act 1993, Sch 1.
* **Words repealed by the Criminal Justice Act 2003, Sch 37 from a date to be appointed.**

7.8089 33. Penalty on drivers for loitering or causing any obstruction etc[1].—Every driver of a hackney carriage who shall ply for hire elsewhere than at some standing or place appointed for that purpose, or who by loitering or by any wilful misbehaviour shall cause any obstruction in or upon any public street, road or place, and every driver of a hackney carriage, whether hired or unhired, allowing any person beside himself, not being the hirer or a person employed by such hirer, to ride on the driving box, shall for every such offence forfeit a sum not exceeding **level 1** on the standard scale.

[London Hackney Carriages Act 1843, s 33 as amended by the Statute Law Revision Act 1891, the Criminal Justice Act 1967, Sch 3, the Statute Law (Repeals) Act 1976 and the Criminal Justice Act 1982, ss 38 and 46.]

---

[1] As to disapplication of this section to a taxi being used for local services under a special licence, see note 1 to s 10, ante.

7.8090 38. Complaints to be made within 28 days All complaints under the provisions of the London Hackney Carriage Act 1831, or of this Act, or of the orders and regulations made in pursuance of either of them, shall be made within 28 days next after the day on which the cause of complaint shall have arisen.

[London Hackney Carriages Act 1843, s 38 as amended by the Statute Law Revision Act 1891, the Statute Law (Repeals) Act 1976 and the Transport for London Act 2008, s 14.]

London Hackney Carriages Act 1850
(13 & 14 Vict c 7)

[7.8091]

This Act is to be construed as one with the 1843 Act and the 1853 Act. Section 4 enables Transport for London to appoint standings for hackney carriages and to make regulations therefor. Breach of regulations is punishable under s 19 of the London Hackney Carriage Act 1853.

London Hackney Carriage Act 1853
(16 & 17 Vict c 33)

7.8092 17. Drivers liable to penalties for certain offences[1] The driver of any hackney carriage who shall commit any of the following offences within the limits of this Act, shall be liable to a penalty not exceeding **level 3** on the standard scale for each offence:

(1) Every driver of a hackney carriage[2] who shall demand or take more than the proper fare[3], or who shall refuse to admit and carry in his carriage the number of persons painted or marked on such carriage or specified in the certificate granted by Transport for London in respect of such carriage, or who shall refuse to carry by his carriage a reasonable quantity of luggage for any person hiring or intending to hire such carriage:

(2) Every driver of a hackney carriage who shall refuse to drive such carriage to any place within

the limits of the Act, not exceeding six miles[4] to which he shall be required to drive any person hiring or intending to hire such carriage, or who shall refuse to drive any such carriage for any time not exceeding one hour, if so required by any person hiring or intending to hire such carriage, or who shall not drive the same at a reasonable and proper speed, not less than six miles an hour, except in cases of unavoidable delay, or when required by the hirer thereof to drive at any slower pace:

(3)   Every driver of a hackney carriage who shall ply for hire with any carriage or horse which shall be at the time unfit for public use.

[London Hackney Carriage Act 1853, s 17 as amended by the Summary Jurisdiction Act 1884, the Statute Law Revision Act 1892, the Criminal Justice Act 1967, Sch 3, the Statute Law (Repeals) Act 1973, the Statute Law (Repeals) Act 1976, the Criminal Justice Act 1982, ss 39, 46 and Sch 3 and the Greater London Authority Act 1999, Sch 20.]

---

[1] This section, to the extent that it is part of the taxi code, has been disapplied as regards the use of a taxi to provide local services under a special licence under s 12 of the Transport Act 1985 (Local Services (Operation by Taxis) (London) Regulations 1986, SI 1986/566). Moreover, for the purpose of hiring of taxis at separate fares under ss 10 and 11 of the Transport Act 1985, the provisions of this section relating to obligatory hirings, the number of persons to be carried at the instance of the hirer, and the carriage of luggage have been disapplied by the Licensed Taxis (Hiring of Separate Fares) (London) Order 1986, SI 1986/1387.

[2] A vehicle licensed and commonly used as a hackney carriage which plies for hire within s 4 of the Metropolitan Public Carriage Act 1869 cannot be divested of the attribute of a hackney carriage (*Bassam v Green* [1981] RTR 362).

[3] A driver demands or takes more than the proper fare if he either asks for an excessive fare or asks for the proper fare and in addition for some supplemental payment which is not a fare (*Bassam v Green* [1981] RTR 362).

[4] Now twenty miles (London Cab Order 1972, SI 1972 No 1074). A taxi driver commits no offence by refusing to stop when hailed (*Hunt v Morgan* [1949] 1 KB 233, [1948] 2 All ER 1065). The driver must observe the general law despite the requirements of this section (*Lovinson v Powell* [1967] 3 All ER 796, 132 JP 10).

Metropolitan Public Carriage Act 1869[1]
(32 & 33 Vict c 115)

7.8093   6.   *Grant of hackney carriage licences.*

---

[1] This Act, to the extent that it is part of the taxi code, except ss 2, 9, and 10, shall apply to the use of a taxi to provide local services under a special licence under s 12 of the Transport Act 1985 (Local Services (Operation by Taxis) (London) Regulations 1986, SI 1986/566).

7.8094   7.   Penalty on use of unlicensed carriage   If any unlicensed hackney carriage plies for hire[1], the owner of such carriage shall be liable to a penalty not exceeding **level 4** on the standard scale. And if any unlicensed hackney carriage is found on any stand within the limits of this Act[2], the owner of such carriage shall be liable to a penalty not exceeding **level 4** on the standard scale. The driver also shall in every such case be liable to a like penalty unless he proves that he was ignorant of the fact of the carriage being an unlicensed carriage.

Any hackney carriage plying for hire, and any hackney carriage found on any stand without having such distinguishing mark, or being otherwise distinguished in such manner as may for the time being be prescribed shall be deemed to be an unlicensed carriage.

[Metropolitan Public Carriage Act 1869, s 7 as amended by the Criminal Justice Act 1967, Sch 3, the Statute Law (Repeals) Act 1976, Sch 1, the Criminal Justice Act 1982, ss 35, 39, 46 and Sch 3 and the Greater London Authority Act 1999, Schs 20 and 34.]

---

[1] As to "plying for hire" see note to the Town Police Clauses Act 1847, s 38, in title TOWNS IMPROVEMENT: TOWN POLICE, post.

[2] The Metropolitan Police District and the City of London (Town Police Clauses Act 1847, s 2).

7.8095   8.   Hackney carriage to be driven by licensed drivers   (1)   Transport for London shall have the function of licensing persons to be drivers of hackney carriages.

(2)   No hackney carriage shall ply for hire within the limits of this Act unless under the charge of a driver having a licence under this section from Transport for London.

(3)   If any hackney carriage plies for hire in contravention of this section—

(a)   the person driving the carriage, and

(b)   the owner of the carriage, unless he proves that the driver acted without his privity or consent,

shall each be liable to a penalty not exceeding level 3 on the standard scale.

(4)   Transport for London may send to the Commissioner of Police of the Metropolis or the Commissioner of Police for the City of London—

(a)   details of a person to whom Transport for London is considering granting a licence under this section, and

(b)   a request for the Commissioner's observations;

and the Commissioner shall respond to the request.

(5)   A licence under this section may—

(a)   be granted on such conditions,

(b)   be in such form,

(c)   be subject to revocation or suspension in such event, and

(d)   generally be dealt with in such manner,

as may be prescribed.

(6)   Subsection (5) of this section is subject to the following provisions of this section.

(7)   Subject to section 8A, a licence under this section shall, if not revoked or suspended, be in

force for three years.

(8)   A fee of such amount (if any) as Transport for London may determine shall be paid to Transport for London—

(a)   by any applicant for a licence under this section, on making the application for the licence;

(b)   by any applicant for the taking or re-taking of any test or examination, or any part of a test or examination, with respect to any matter of fitness, on making the application for the taking or re-taking of the test, examination or part; and

(c)   by any person granted a licence under this section, on the grant of the licence.

(9)   In paragraph (b) of subsection (8) of this section "matter of fitness" means—

(a)   any matter as respects which Transport for London must be satisfied before granting a licence under this section; or

(b)   any matter such that, if Transport for London is not satisfied with respect to the matter, they may refuse to grant a licence under this section.

(10)   Different amounts may be determined under subsection (8) of this section for different purposes or different cases.

(11)   Transport for London may remit or refund the whole or part of a fee under subsection (8) of this section.

[Metropolitan Public Carriage Act 1869, s 8 as substituted by the Greater London Authority Act 1999, Sch 20 and amended by the Immigration Act 2016, Sch 5.]

7.8096   8A.   Drivers'   licences   for   persons   subject   to   immigration   control

(1)   Subsection (2) applies if—

(a)   a licence under section 8 is to be granted to a person who has been granted leave to enter or remain in the United Kingdom for a limited period ("the leave period"),

(b)   the person's leave has not been extended by virtue of section 3C of the Immigration Act 1971 (continuation of leave pending variation decision), and

(c)   apart from subsection (2), the period for which the licence would have been in force would have ended after the end of the leave period.

(2)   Transport for London must grant the licence for a period which ends at or before the end of the leave period.

(3)   Subsection (4) applies if—

(a)   a licence under section 8 is to be granted to a person who has been granted leave to enter or remain in the United Kingdom for a limited period, and

(b)   the person's leave has been extended by virtue of section 3C of the Immigration Act 1971 (continuation of leave pending variation decision).

(4)   Transport for London must grant the licence for a period that does not exceed six months.

(5)   A licence under section 8 ceases to be in force if the person to whom it was granted becomes disqualified by reason of the person's immigration status from driving a hackney carriage.

(6)   If a licence granted in accordance with subsection (2) or (4) expires, the person to whom it was granted must, within the period of 7 days beginning with the day after that on which it expired, return to Transport for London—

(a)   the licence,

(b)   the person's copy of the licence (if any), and

(c)   the person's driver's badge.

(7)   If subsection (5) applies to a licence, the person to whom it was granted must, within the period of 7 days beginning with the day after the day on which the person first became disqualified, return to Transport for London—

(a)   the licence,

(b)   the person's copy of the licence (if any), and

(c)   the person's driver's badge.

(8)   A person who, without reasonable excuse, contravenes subsection (6) or (7) is guilty of an offence and liable on summary conviction—

(a)   to a fine not exceeding level 3 on the standard scale, and

(b)   in the case of a continuing offence, to a fine not exceeding ten pounds for each day during which an offence continues after conviction.

(9)   The Secretary of State may by regulations made by statutory instrument amend the amount for the time being specified in subsection (8)(b).

(10)   Regulations under subsection (9) may make transitional, transitory or saving provision.

(11)   A statutory instrument containing regulations under subsection (9) may not be made unless a draft of the instrument has been laid before, and approved by a resolution of, each House of Parliament.

(12)   For the purposes of this section a person is disqualified by reason of the person's immigration status from driving a hackney carriage if the person is subject to immigration control and—

(a)   the person has not been granted leave to enter or remain in the United Kingdom, or

(b)   the person's leave to enter or remain in the United Kingdom—

(i)   is invalid,

(ii) has ceased to have effect (whether by reason of curtailment, revocation, cancellation, passage of time or otherwise), or

(iii) is subject to a condition preventing the person from driving a hackney carriage.

(13) Where a person is on immigration bail within the meaning of Part 1 of Schedule 10 to the Immigration Act 2016—

(a) the person is to be treated for the purposes of this section as if the person had been granted leave to enter the United Kingdom, but

(b) any condition as to the person's work in the United Kingdom to which the person's immigration bail is subject is to be treated for those purposes as a condition of leave.

(14) For the purposes of this section a person is subject to immigration control if under the Immigration Act 1971 the person requires leave to enter or remain in the United Kingdom.

[Metropolitan Public Carriage Act 1869, s 8A as inserted by the Immigration Act 2016, Sch 5.]

7.8097 9. *Regulations as to hackney and stage carriages[1].*

[1] Various London Cab Orders have been made: see SR & O 1934 No 1346. Penalty for contravention is fine not exceeding £20.

London Cab Act 1896
(59 & 60 Vict c 27)

7.8098 1. Penalties for defrauding cabmen If any person commits any of the following offences with respect to a cab[1] namely:

(a) hires a cab[1] knowing or having reason to believe that he cannot pay the lawful fare, or with intent to avoid payment of the lawful fare; or

(b) fraudulently endeavours to avoid payment of a fare lawfully due from him; or

(c) having failed or refused to pay a fare lawfully due from him, either refuses to give to the driver an address at which he can be found, or, with intent to deceive, gives a false address,

he shall be liable on summary conviction to pay, in addition to the fare, a fine not exceeding level 1 on the standard scale, or in the discretion of the court, to be imprisoned for a term not exceeding fourteen days; and the whole or any part of any fine imposed may be applied in compensation to the driver.

[London Cab Act 1896, s 1, as amended by the Criminal Justice Act 1967, Sch 3 and the Criminal Justice Act 1982, ss 38 and 46.]

[1] A "cab" means a hackney carriage within the meaning of the Metropolitan Public Carriage Act 1869.

Transport Act 1985
(1985 c 67)

7.8099 17. London taxi and taxi driver licensing: appeals

(1) In this section—

"licence" means a licence under section 6 of the Metropolitan Public Carriage Act 1869 (taxi licences) or under section 8 of that Act (taxi driver licences); and

"licensing authority" means the person empowered to grant a licence. (2) Where the licensing authority has refused to grant, or has suspended or revoked, a licence the applicant for, or (as the case may be) holder of, the licence may, before the expiry of the designated period—

(a) require the authority to reconsider his decision; or

(b) appeal to a magistrates' court.

(3) Any call for a reconsideration under subsection (2) above must be made to the licensing authority in writing.

(4) On any reconsideration under this section the person calling for the decision to be reconsidered shall be entitled to be heard either in person or by his representative.

(5) If the person calling for a decision to be reconsidered under this section is dissatisfied with the decision of the licensing authority on reconsideration, he may, before the expiry of the designated period, appeal to a magistrates' court.

(6) On any appeal to it under this section, the court may make such order as it thinks fit; and any order which it makes shall be binding on the licensing authority.

(7) Where a person holds a licence which is in force when he applies for a new licence in substitution for it, the existing licence shall continue in force until the application for the new licence, or any appeal under this section in relation to that application, is disposed of, but without prejudice to the exercise in the meantime of any power of the licensing authority to revoke the existing licence.

(8) For the purposes of subsection (7) above, where the licensing authority refuses to grant the new licence the application shall not be treated as disposed of—

(a) where no call for a reconsideration of the authority's decision is made under subsection (2) above, until the expiry of the designated period;

(b) where such a reconsideration is called for, until the expiry of the designated period which begins by reference to the decision of the authority on reconsideration.

(9)   Where the licensing authority suspends or revokes a licence, or confirms a decision to do so, he may, if the holder of the licence so requests, direct that his decision shall not have effect until the expiry of the designated period.

(10)   In this section

"designated period" means such period as may be specified for the purpose by London cab order;

"London cab order" means an order made by Transport for London.

(11)   Any power to make a London cab order under this section includes power to vary or revoke a previous such order.

[Transport Act 1985, s 17 as amended by the Greater London Authority Act 1999, Sch 21 and the Courts Act 2003, Sch 8.]

Private Hire Vehicles (London) Act 1998[1]

(1998 c 34)

Introductory

7.8100   **1.   Meaning of "private hire vehicle", "operator" and related expressions**   (1)   In this Act—

(a)   "private hire vehicle" means a vehicle constructed or adapted to seat fewer than nine passengers which is made available with a driver for hire for the purpose of carrying passengers, other than a licensed taxi or a public service vehicle[2];

(b)   "operator" means a person who makes provision for the invitation or acceptance of, or who accepts, private hire bookings; and

(c)   "operate", in relation to a private hire vehicle, means to make provision for the invitation or acceptance of, or to accept, private hire bookings in relation to the vehicle.

(2)   Any reference in this Act to a vehicle being "used as a private hire vehicle" is a reference to a private hire vehicle which—

(a)   is in use in connection with a hiring for the purpose of carrying one or more passengers; or

(b)   is immediately available to an operator to carry out a private hire booking.

(3)   Any reference in this Act to the operator of a vehicle which is being used as a private hire vehicle is a reference to the operator who accepted the booking for the hiring or to whom the vehicle is immediately available, as the case may be.

(4)   In this Act "private hire booking" means a booking for the hire of a private hire vehicle for the purpose of carrying one or more passengers (including a booking to carry out as sub-contractor a private hire booking accepted by another operator).

(5)   In this Act "operating centre" means premises at which private hire bookings are accepted by an operator.

[Private Hire Vehicles (London) Act 1998, s 1 as amended by the Road Safety Act 2006, Sch 7 and the Immigration Act 2016, Sch 5.]

---

[1]   This Act is to be brought into force in accordance with orders made under s 40. At the date of going to press, the Private Hire Vehicles (London) Act 1998 (Commencement No 1) Order 2000, SI 2000/3144; the (No 2) Order 2003, SI 2003/580; and the (No 3) Order 2004, SI 2004/241 had been made.

[2]   For savings in respect of vehicles used for funerals and weddings, see s 29, post.

Regulation of private hire vehicle operators in London

7.8101   **2.   Requirement for London operator's licence**   (1)   No person shall in London make provision for the invitation or acceptance of, or accept, private hire bookings unless he is the holder of a private hire vehicle operator's licence for London (in this Act referred to as a "London PHV operator's licence").

(2)   A person who makes provision for the invitation or acceptance of private hire bookings, or who accepts such a booking, in contravention of this section is guilty of an offence and liable on summary conviction to a fine not exceeding level 4 on the standard scale.

[Private Hire Vehicles (London) Act 1998, s 2.]

7.8102   **3.   London operator's licences**   (1)   Any person may apply to the licensing authority for a London PHV operator's licence.

(2)   An application under this section shall state the address of any premises in London which the applicant proposes to use as an operating centre.

(3)   The licensing authority shall grant a London PHV operator's licence to the applicant if the authority is satisfied that—

(a)   the applicant is a fit and proper person to hold a London PHV operator's licence;

(aa)   if the applicant is an individual, the applicant is not disqualified by reason of the applicant's immigration status from operating a private hire vehicle; and

(b)   any further requirements that may be prescribed (which may include requirements relating to operating centres) are met.

(3A)   In determining for the purposes of subsection (3) whether an applicant is disqualified by reason of the applicant's immigration status from operating a private hire vehicle, the licensing authority must have regard to any guidance issued by the Secretary of State.

(4)   A London PHV operator's licence shall be granted subject to such conditions as may be

prescribed[1] and such other conditions as the licensing authority may think fit.

(5)   Subject to section 3A, a London PHV operator's licence shall be granted for five years or such shorter period as the licensing authority may consider appropriate in the circumstances of the case.

(6)   A London PHV operator's licence shall—

    (a)   specify the address of any premises in London which the holder of the licence may use as an operating centre;

    (b)   be in such form and contain such particulars as the licensing authority may think fit.

(7)   An applicant for a London PHV operator's licence may appeal[2] to a magistrates' court against—

    (a)   a decision not to grant such a licence;

    (b)   a decision not to specify an address proposed in the application as an operating centre; or

    (c)   any condition (other than a prescribed condition) to which the licence is subject.

[Private Hire Vehicles (London) Act 1998, s 3 as amended by the Greater London Authority Act 1999, Sch 21 and the Immigration Act 2016, Sch 5.]

---

  [1] See the Private Hire Vehicles (London) (Operators' Licences) Regulations 2000, SI 2000/3146.

  [2] For provisions relating to appeals, see ss 25–26, post and the Magistrates' Courts Rules 1991, r 34 in PART 1 MAGISTRATES COURT PROCEDURE, ante.

7.8103   3A.   London PHV operator's licences for persons subject to immigration control

(1)   Subsection (2) applies if—

    (a)   a London PHV operator's licence is to be granted to a person who has been granted leave to enter or remain in the United Kingdom for a limited period ("the leave period");

    (b)   the person's leave has not been extended by virtue of section 3C of the Immigration Act 1971 (continuation of leave pending variation decision); and

    (c)   apart from subsection (2), the period for which the licence would have been granted would have ended after the end of the leave period.

(2)   The licence must be granted for a period which ends at or before the end of the leave period.

(3)   Subsection (4) applies if—

    (a)   a London PHV operator's licence is to be granted to a person who has been granted leave to enter or remain in the United Kingdom for a limited period; and

    (b)   the person's leave has been extended by virtue of section 3C of the Immigration Act 1971 (continuation of leave pending variation decision).

(4)   The licence must be granted for a period which does not exceed six months.

(5)   A London PHV operator's licence ceases to be in force if the person to whom it was granted becomes disqualified by reason of the person's immigration status from operating a private hire vehicle.

(6)   If subsection (5) applies to a licence, the person to whom it was granted must, within the period of 7 days beginning with the day after the day on which the person first became disqualified, return it to the licensing authority.

(7)   A person who, without reasonable excuse, contravenes subsection (6) is guilty of an offence and liable on summary conviction—

    (a)   to a fine not exceeding level 3 on the standard scale; and

    (b)   in the case of a continuing offence, to a fine not exceeding ten pounds for each day during which an offence continues after conviction.

(8)   The Secretary of State may by regulations amend the amount for the time being specified in subsection (7)(b).

[Private Hire Vehicles (London) Act 1998, s 3A as inserted by the Immigration Act 2016, Sch 5.]

7.8104   4.   Obligations of London operators   (1)   The holder of a London PHV operator's licence (in this Act referred to as a "London PHV operator") shall not in London accept a private hire booking other than at an operating centre specified in his licence.

(2)   A London PHV operator shall secure that any vehicle which is provided by him for carrying out a private hire booking accepted by him in London is—

    (a)   a vehicle for which a London PHV licence is in force driven by a person holding a London PHV driver's licence; or

    (b)   a London cab driven by a person holding a London cab driver's licence.

(3)   A London PHV operator shall—

    (a)   display a copy of his licence at each operating centre specified in the licence;

    (b)   keep at each specified operating centre a record in the prescribed[1] form of the private hire bookings accepted by him there;

    (c)   before the commencement of each journey booked at a specified operating centre, enter in the record kept under paragraph (b) the prescribed[1] particulars of the booking;

    <u>(d)</u>   <u>keep at each specified operating centre such records as may be prescribed[1] of particulars of the private hire vehicles and drivers which are available to him for carrying out bookings accepted by him at that centre;</u>

    (e)   at the request of a constable or authorised officer, produce for inspection any record required by this section to be kept.

(4) If a London PHV operator ceases to use an operating centre specified in his licence he shall preserve any record he was required by this section to keep there for such period as may be prescribed[1].

(5) A London PHV operator who contravenes any provision of this section is guilty of an offence and liable on summary conviction to a fine not exceeding **level 3** on the standard scale.

(6) It is a defence[2] in proceedings for an offence under this section for an operator to show that he exercised all due diligence to avoid committing such an offence.

[Private Hire Vehicles (London) Act 1998, s 4.]

---

* **Substituted by the Transport for London Act 2008, s 25 from a date to be appointed.**
[1] See the Private Hire Vehicles (London) (Operators' Licences) Regulations 2000, SI 2000/3146.
[2] An accused who raises this defence is not required to establish it beyond reasonable doubt, but on the balance of probabilities: see *R v Carr-Briant* [1943] KB 607, [1943] 2 All ER 156, 107 JP 167.

7.8105 5. Hirings accepted on behalf of another operator (1) A London PHV operator ("the first operator") who has in London accepted a private hire booking may not arrange for another operator to provide a vehicle to carry out that booking as sub-contractor unless—

(a)   the other operator is a London PHV operator and the sub-contracted booking is accepted at an operating centre in London;

(b)   the other operator is licensed under section 55 of the Local Government (Miscellaneous Provisions) Act 1976 (in this Act referred to as "the 1976 Act") by the council of a district and the sub-contracted booking is accepted in that district; or

(c)   the other operator accepts the sub-contracted booking in Scotland.

(2) A London PHV operator who contravenes subsection (1) is guilty of an offence and liable on summary conviction to a fine not exceeding **level 3** on the standard scale.

(3) It is a defence[1] in proceedings for an offence under this section for an operator to show that he exercised all due diligence to avoid committing such an offence.

(4) It is immaterial for the purposes of subsection (1) whether or not sub-contracting is permitted by the contract between the first operator and the person who made the booking.

(5) For the avoidance of doubt (and subject to any relevant contract terms), a contract of hire between a person who made a private hire booking at an operating centre in London and the London PHV operator who accepted the booking remains in force despite the making of arrangements by that operator for another contractor to provide a vehicle to carry out that booking as sub-contractor.

[Private Hire Vehicles (London) Act 1998, s 5.]

---

[1] An accused who raises this defence is not required to establish it beyond reasonable doubt, but on the balance of probabilities: see *R v Carr-Briant* [1943] KB 607, [1943] 2 All ER 156, 107 JP 167.

Regulation of private hire vehicles in London

7.8106 6. Requirement for private hire vehicle licence (1) A vehicle shall not be used as a private hire vehicle on a road in London unless a private hire vehicle licence is in force for that vehicle.

(2) The driver and operator of a vehicle used in contravention of this section are each guilty of an offence.

(3) The owner[1] of a vehicle who permits it to be used in contravention of this section is guilty of an offence.

(4) It is a defence[2] in proceedings for an offence under subsection (2) for the driver or operator to show that he exercised all due diligence to prevent the vehicle being used in contravention of this section.

(5) A person guilty of an offence under this section is liable on summary conviction to a fine not exceeding **level 4** on the standard scale.

(6) In this section "private hire vehicle licence" means—

(a)   except where paragraph (b) or (c) applies, a London PHV licence;

(b)   if the vehicle is in use for the purposes of a hiring the booking for which was accepted outside London in a controlled district, a licence under section 48 of the 1976 Act issued by the council for that district; and

(c)   if the vehicle is in use for the purposes of a hiring the booking for which was accepted in Scotland, a licence under section 10 of the Civic Government (Scotland) Act 1982 (in this Act referred to as "the 1982 Act"),

and for the purposes of paragraph (b) or (c) it is immaterial that the booking in question is a sub-contracted booking.

(7) This section does not apply to a vehicle used for the purposes of a hiring for a journey beginning outside London in an area of England and Wales which is not a controlled district.

[Private Hire Vehicles (London) Act 1998, s 6.]

---

[1] For "owner" see s 35, post.
[2] An accused who raises this defence is not required to establish it beyond reasonable doubt, but on the balance of probabilities: see *R v Carr-Briant* [1943] KB 607, [1943] 2 All ER 156, 107 JP 167.

7.8107 7. London PHV licences (1) The owner[1] of any vehicle constructed or adapted to seat fewer than nine passengers may apply to the licensing authority for a private hire vehicle licence for London (in this Act referred to as a "London PHV licence") for that vehicle.

(2)   The licensing authority shall grant a London PHV licence for a vehicle if the authority is satisfied—

     (*a*)   that the vehicle—

         (i)   is suitable in type, size and design for use as a private hire vehicle;

         (ii)   is safe, comfortable and in a suitable mechanical condition for that use; and

         (iii)   is not of such design and appearance as would lead any person to believe that the vehicle is a London cab;

     (*b*)   that there is in force in relation to the use of the vehicle a policy of insurance or such security as complies with the requirements of Part VI of the Road Traffic Act 1988; and

     (*c*)   that any further requirements that may be prescribed are met.

(3)   A London PHV licence may not be granted in respect of more than one vehicle.

(4)   A London PHV licence shall be granted subject to such conditions as may be prescribed and such other conditions as the licensing authority may think fit.

(5)   A London PHV licence shall be in such form and shall contain such particulars as the licensing authority may think fit.

(6)   A London PHV licence shall be granted for one year or for such shorter period as the licensing authority may consider appropriate in the circumstances of the case.

(7)   An applicant for a London PHV licence may appeal[2] to a magistrates' court against a decision not to grant such a licence or against any condition (other than a prescribed condition) to which the licence is subject.

[Private Hire Vehicles (London) Act 1998, s 7 as amended by the Greater London Authority Act 1999, Sch 21.]

---

   [1]   For "owner" see s 35, post.

   [2]   For provisions relating to appeals see ss 25–26, post and the Magistrates' Court Rules 1981, r 34 in PART 1: MAGISTRATES' COURTS PROCEDURE ante.

7.8108   8.   Obligations of owners of licensed vehicles   (1)   This section applies to the owner of any vehicle to which a London PHV licence relates.

(2)   The owner[1] shall present the vehicle for inspection and testing by or on behalf of the licensing authority within such period and at such place as the authority may by notice reasonably require.

The vehicle shall not be required to be presented under this subsection on more than three separate occasions during any one period of 12 months.

(3)   The owner shall (without prejudice to section 170 of the Road Traffic Act 1988) report any accident to the vehicle materially affecting—

     (*a*)   the safety, performance or appearance of the vehicle, or

     (*b*)   the comfort or convenience of persons carried in the vehicle,

to the licensing authority as soon as reasonably practical and in any case within 72 hours of the accident occurring.

(4)   If the ownership of the vehicle changes, the person who was previously the owner shall within 14 days of the change give notice to the licensing authority of that fact and the name and address of the new owner.

(5)   A person who, without reasonable excuse, contravenes any provision of this section is guilty of an offence and liable on summary conviction to a fine not exceeding **level 3** on the standard scale.

[Private Hire Vehicles (London) Act 1998, s 8 as amended by the Greater London Authority Act 1999, Sch 21.]

---

   [1]   For "owner" see s 35, post.

7.8109   9.   Fitness of licensed vehicles   (1)   A constable or authorised officer has power at all reasonable times to inspect and test, for the purpose of ascertaining its fitness, any vehicle to which a London PHV licence relates.

(2)   If a constable or authorised officer is not satisfied as to the fitness of such a vehicle he may by notice to the owner of the vehicle—

     (*a*)   require the owner[1] to make the vehicle available for further inspection and testing at such reasonable time and place as may be specified in the notice; and

     (*b*)   if he thinks fit, suspend the London PHV licence relating to that vehicle until such time as a constable or authorised officer is satisfied as to the fitness of the vehicle.

(3)   A notice under subsection (2)(*b*) shall state the grounds on which the licence is being suspended and the suspension shall take effect on the day on which it is served on the owner.

(4)   A licence suspended under subsection (2)(*b*) shall remain suspended until such time as a constable or authorised officer by notice to the owner directs that the licence is again in force.

(5)   If a licence remains suspended at the end of the period of two months beginning with the day on which a notice under subsection (2)(*b*) was served on the owner of the vehicle—

     (*a*)   a constable or authorised officer may by notice to the owner direct that the licence is revoked; and

     (*b*)   the revocation shall take effect at the end of the period of 21 days beginning with the day on which the owner is served with that notice.

(6)   An owner[1] may appeal[2] against a notice under subsection (2)(*b*) or (5) to a magistrates' court.

[Private Hire Vehicles (London) Act 1998, s 9.]

¹ For "owner" see s 35, post.
² For provisions relating to appeals see ss 25–26, post and the Magistrates' Court Rules 1981, r 34 in PART 1: MAGISTRATES' COURTS PROCEDURE ante.

7.8110 10. Identification of licensed vehicles (1) The licensing authority shall issue a disc or plate for each vehicle to which a London PHV licence relates which identifies that vehicle as a vehicle for which such a licence is in force.

(2) No vehicle to which a London PHV licence relates shall be used as a private hire vehicle on a road in London unless the disc or plate issued under this section is exhibited on the vehicle in such manner as may be prescribed.

(3) The licensing authority may by notice exempt a vehicle from the requirement under subsection (2) when it is being used to provide a service specified in the notice if the authority considers it inappropriate (having regard to that service) to require the disc or plate in question to be exhibited.

(4) The driver and operator of a vehicle used in contravention of subsection (2) are each guilty of an offence.

(5) The owner¹ of a vehicle who permits it to be used in contravention of subsection (2) is guilty of an offence.

(6) It is a defence² in proceedings for an offence under subsection (4) for the driver or operator to show that he exercised all due diligence to prevent the vehicle being used in contravention of subsection (2).

(7) A person guilty of an offence under this section is liable on summary conviction to a fine not exceeding **level 3** on the standard scale.

[Private Hire Vehicles (London) Act 1998, s 10 as amended by the Greater London Authority Act 1999, Sch 21.]

¹ For "owner" see s 35, post.
² An accused who raises this defence is not required to establish it beyond reasonable doubt, but on the balance of probabilities: see *R v Carr-Briant* [1943] KB 607, [1943] 2 All ER 156, 107 JP 167.

7.8111 11. Prohibition of taximeters (1) No vehicle to which a London PHV licence relates shall be equipped with a taximeter.

(2) If such a vehicle is equipped with a taximeter, the owner¹ of that vehicle is guilty of an offence and liable on summary conviction to a fine not exceeding **level 3** on the standard scale.

(3) In this section "taximeter" means a device for calculating the fare to be charged in respect of any journey by reference to the distance travelled or time elapsed since the start of the journey (or a combination of both).

[Private Hire Vehicles (London) Act 1998, s 11.]

¹ For "owner" see s 35, post.

Regulation of drivers of private hire vehicles in London

7.8112 12. Requirement for private hire vehicle driver's licence (1) No vehicle shall be used as a private hire vehicle on a road in London unless the driver holds a private hire vehicle driver's licence.

(2) The driver and operator of a vehicle used in contravention of this section are each guilty of an offence.

(3) The owner¹ of a vehicle who permits it to be used in contravention of this section is guilty of an offence.

(4) It is a defence² in proceedings against the operator of a vehicle for an offence under subsection (2) for the operator to show that he exercised all due diligence to prevent the vehicle being used in contravention of this section.

(5) A person guilty of an offence under this section is liable on summary conviction to a fine not exceeding **level 4** on the standard scale.

(6) In this section "private hire vehicle driver's licence" means—

   (a)   except where paragraph (b) or (c) applies, a London PHV driver's licence;

   (b)   if the vehicle is in use for the purposes of a hiring the booking for which was accepted outside London in a controlled district in England and Wales, a licence under section 51 of the 1976 Act issued by the council for that district; and

   (c)   if the vehicle is in use for a hiring the booking for which was accepted in Scotland, a licence under section 13 of the 1982 Act,

and for the purposes of paragraph (b) or (c) it is immaterial that the booking in question is a sub-contracted booking.

(7) This section does not apply to the use of a vehicle for the purposes of a hiring for a journey beginning outside London in an area of England and Wales which is not a controlled district.

[Private Hire Vehicles (London) Act 1998, s 12.]

¹ For "owner" see s 35, post.
² An accused who raises this defence is not required to establish it beyond reasonable doubt, but on the balance of probabilities: see *R v Carr-Briant* [1943] KB 607, [1943] 2 All ER 156, 107 JP 167.

7.8113 13. London PHV driver's licences (1) Any person may apply to the licensing authority for a private hire vehicle driver's licence for London (in this Act referred to as a "London

PHV driver's licence").

(2)　　The licensing authority shall grant a London PHV driver's licence to an applicant if the authority is satisfied that—

(*a*)　　　　the applicant has attained the age of 21, is (and has for at least three years been) authorised to drive a motor car and is a fit and proper person to hold a London PHV driver's licence;

(*aa*)　　　the applicant is not disqualified by reason of the applicant's immigration status from driving a private hire vehicle; and

(*b*)　　　　the requirement mentioned in subsection (3), and any further requirements prescribed by the licensing authority, are met.

(2A)　　In determining for the purposes of subsection (2) whether an applicant is disqualified by reason of the applicant's immigration status from driving a private hire vehicle, the licensing authority must have regard to any guidance issued by the Secretary of State.

(3)　　The licensing authority shall require applicants to show to the authority's satisfaction (whether by taking a test or otherwise) that they possess a level—

(*a*)　　　　of knowledge of London or parts of London; and

(*b*)　　　　of general topographical skills,

which appears to the authority to be appropriate.
The licensing authority may impose different requirements in relation to different applicants.

(4)　　The licensing authority may send a copy of an application to the Commissioner of Police of the Metropolis or the Commissioner of Police for the City of London with a request for the Commissioner's observations; and the Commissioner shall respond to the request.

(5)　　A London PHV driver's licence—

(*a*)　　　　may be granted subject to such conditions as the licensing authority may think fit;

(*b*)　　　　shall be in such form and shall contain such particulars as the licensing authority may think fit; and

(*c*)　　　　subject to section 13A, shall be granted for three years or for such shorter period as the Secretary of State may consider appropriate in the circumstances of the particular case.

(6)　　An applicant may appeal[1] to a magistrates' court against a decision not to grant a London PHV driver's licence or against any condition to which such a licence is subject.

(7)　　For the purposes of subsection (2), a person is authorised to drive a motor car if—

(*a*)　　　　he holds a licence granted under Part III of the Road Traffic Act 1988 (other than a provisional licence) authorising him to drive a motor car; or

(*b*)　　　　he is authorised by virtue of section 99A(1) or 109(1) of that Act (Community licences and Northern Ireland licences) to drive a motor car in Great Britain.

[Private Hire Vehicles (London) Act 1998, s 13 as amended by the Greater London Authority Act 1999, Sch 21 and the Immigration Act 2016, Sch 5.]

---

[1] For provisions relating to appeals see ss 25–26, post and the Magistrates' Court Rules 1981, r 34 in PART 1, MAGISTRATES' COURTS PROCEDURE ante.

7.8114　13A.　London PHV driver's licences for persons subject to immigration control

(1)　　Subsection (2) applies if—

(a)　　　a London PHV driver's licence is to be granted to a person who has been granted leave to enter or remain in the United Kingdom for a limited period ("the leave period");

(b)　　　the person's leave has not been extended by virtue of section 3C of the Immigration Act 1971 (continuation of leave pending variation decision); and

(c)　　　apart from subsection (2), the period for which the licence would have been granted would have ended after the end of the leave period.

(2)　　The licence must be granted for a period which ends at or before the end of the leave period.

(3)　　Subsection (4) applies if—

(a)　　　a London PHV driver's licence is to be granted to a person who has been granted leave to enter or remain in the United Kingdom for a limited period; and

(b)　　　the person's leave has been extended by virtue of section 3C of the Immigration Act 1971 (continuation of leave pending variation decision).

(4)　　The licence must be granted for a period which does not exceed six months.

(5)　　A London PHV driver's licence ceases to be in force if the person to whom it was granted becomes disqualified by reason of the person's immigration status from driving a private hire vehicle.

(6)　　If subsection (5) applies to a licence, the person to whom it was granted must, within the period of 7 days beginning with the day after the day on which the person first became disqualified, return the licence and the person's driver's badge to the licensing authority.

(7)　　A person who, without reasonable excuse, contravenes subsection (6) is guilty of an offence and liable on summary conviction—

(a)　　　to a fine not exceeding level 3 on the standard scale; and

(b)　　　in the case of a continuing offence, to a fine not exceeding ten pounds for each day during which an offence continues after conviction.

(8)　　The Secretary of State may by regulations amend the amount for the time being specified in subsection (7)(b).

[Private Hire Vehicles (London) Act 1998, s 13A as inserted by the Immigration Act 2016, Sch 5.]

7.8115   14.   Issue of driver's badges   (1)   The licensing authority shall issue a badge to each person to whom the authority has granted a London PHV driver's licence.

(2)   The licensing authority may prescribe the form of badges issued under this section.

(3)   A person issued with such a badge shall, when he is the driver of a vehicle being used as a private hire vehicle, wear the badge in such position and manner as to be plainly and distinctly visible.

(4)   The licensing authority may by notice exempt a person from the requirement under subsection (3), when he is the driver of a vehicle being used to provide a service specified in the notice if the authority considers it inappropriate (having regard to that service) to require the badge to be worn.

(5)   Any person who without reasonable excuse contravenes subsection (3) is guilty of an offence and liable on summary conviction to a fine not exceeding **level 3** on the standard scale.*

[Private Hire Vehicles (London) Act 1998, s 14 as amended by the Greater London Authority Act 1999, Sch 21.]

---

* **Amended by the Transport for London Act 2008, s 23 from a date to be appointed.**

Licences: general provisions

7.8116   15.   Applications for licences   (1)   An application for the grant of a licence under this Act shall be made in such form, and include such declarations and information, as the licensing authority may require.

(2)   The licensing authority may require an applicant to furnish such further information as the authority may consider necessary for dealing with the application.

(3)   The information which an applicant for a London PHV operator's licence may be required to furnish includes in particular information about—

    (*a*)   any premises in London which he proposes to use as an operating centre;

    (*b*)   any convictions recorded against him;

    (*c*)   any business activities he has carried on before making the application;

    (*d*)   if the applicant is or has been a director or secretary of a company, that company;

    (*e*)   if the applicant is a company, information about the directors or secretary of that company;

    (*f*)   if the applicant proposes to act as an operator in partnership with any other person, information about that person.

(4)   An applicant for a London PHV driver's licence may be required by the licensing authority—

    (*a*)   to produce a certificate signed by a registered medical practitioner to the effect that—

        (i)   he is physically fit to be the driver of a private hire vehicle; and

        (ii)   if any specific requirements of physical fitness have been prescribed for persons holding London PHV licences, that he meets those requirements; and

    (*b*)   whether or not such a certificate has been produced, to submit to examination by a registered medical practitioner selected by the licensing authority as to his physical fitness to be the driver of such a vehicle.

(5)   The provisions of this Act apply to the renewal of a licence as they apply to the grant of a licence.

[Private Hire Vehicles (London) Act 1998, s 15 as amended by the Greater London Authority Act 1999, Sch 21.]

7.8117   16.   Power to suspend or revoke licences   (1)   The licensing authority may suspend or revoke a licence under this Act for any reasonable cause including (without prejudice to the generality of this subsection) any ground mentioned below.

(2)   A London PHV operator's licence may be suspended or revoked where—

    (*a*)   the licensing authority is no longer satisfied that the licence holder is fit to hold such a licence;

    (*aa*)   the licence holder has, since the grant of the licence, been convicted of an immigration offence or required to pay an immigration penalty; or

    (*b*)   the licence holder has failed to comply with any condition of the licence or any other obligation imposed on him by or under this Act.

(2A)   Subsection (2)(aa) does not apply if—

    (*a*)   in a case where the licence holder has been convicted of an immigration offence, the conviction is a spent conviction within the meaning of the Rehabilitation of Offenders Act 1974, or

    (*b*)   in a case where the licence holder has been required to pay an immigration penalty—

        (i)   more than three years have elapsed since the date on which the penalty was imposed, and

        (ii)   the amount of the penalty has been paid in full.

(3)   A London PHV licence may be suspended or revoked where—

    (*a*)   the Secretary of State is no longer satisfied that the vehicle to which it relates is fit for use as a private hire vehicle; or

    (*b*)   the owner has failed to comply with any condition of the licence or any other obligation imposed on him by or under this Act.

(4)   A London PHV driver's licence may be suspended or revoked where—

(a)   the licence holder has, since the grant of the licence, been convicted of an offence involving dishonesty, indecency or violence;

(aa)   the licence holder has, since the grant of the licence, been convicted of an immigration offence or required to pay an immigration penalty;

(b)   the licensing authority is for any other reason no longer satisfied that the licence holder is fit to hold such a licence; or

(c)   the licence holder has failed to comply with any condition of the licence or any other obligation imposed on him by or under this Act.

(5)   Subsection (4)(aa) does not apply if—

(a)   in a case where the licence holder has been convicted of an immigration offence, the conviction is a spent conviction within the meaning of the Rehabilitation of Offenders Act 1974, or

(b)   in a case where the licence holder has been required to pay an immigration penalty—

(i)   more than three years have elapsed since the date on which the penalty was imposed, and

(ii)   the amount of the penalty has been paid in full.

[Private Hire Vehicles (London) Act 1998, s 16 as amended by the Greater London Authority Act 1999, Sch 21 and the Immigration Act 2016, Sch 5.]

7.8118   17.   Suspension and revocation under section 16: procedure (1)   Where the licensing authority has decided to suspend or revoke a licence under section 16—

(a)   the authority shall give notice of the decision and the grounds for the decision to the licence holder or, in the case of a London PHV licence, the owner of the vehicle to which the licence relates; and

(b)   the suspension or revocation takes effect at the end of the period of 21 days beginning with the day on which that notice is served on the licence holder or the owner.

(2)   If the licensing authority is of the opinion that the interests of public safety require the suspension or revocation of a licence to have immediate effect, and the authority includes a statement of that opinion and the reasons for it in the notice of suspension or revocation, the suspension or revocation takes effect when the notice is served on the licence holder or vehicle owner (as the case may be).

(3)   A licence suspended under this section shall remain suspended until such time as the licensing authority by notice directs that the licence is again in force.

(4)   The holder of a London PHV operator's or driver's licence, or the owner of a vehicle to which a PHV licence relates, may appeal[1] to a magistrates' court against a decision under section 16 to suspend or revoke that licence.

[Private Hire Vehicles (London) Act 1998, s 17 as amended by the Greater London Authority Act 1999, Sch 21.]

---

[1]   For provisions relating to appeals see ss 25–26, post and the Magistrates' Court Rules 1981, r 34 in PART 1: MAGISTRATES' COURTS PROCEDURE ante.

7.8119   18.   Variation of operator's licence at the request of the operator (1)   The licensing authority may, on the application of a London PHV operator, vary his licence by adding a reference to a new operating centre or removing an existing reference to an operating centre.

(2)   An application for the variation of a licence under this section shall be made in such form, and include such declarations and information, as the licensing authority may require.

(3)   The licensing authority may require an applicant to furnish such further information as he may consider necessary for dealing with the application.

(4)   The licensing authority shall not add a reference to a new operating centre unless the authority is satisfied that the premises in question meet any requirements prescribed under section 3(3)(b).

(5)   An applicant for the variation of a London PHV operator's licence under this section may appeal[1] to a magistrates' court against a decision not to add a new operating centre to the licence.

[Private Hire Vehicles (London) Act 1998, s 18 as amended by the Greater London Authority Act 1999, Sch 21.]

---

[1]   For provisions relating to appeals see ss 25–26, post and the Magistrates' Court Rules 1981, r 34 in PART 1: MAGISTRATES' COURTS PROCEDURE ante.

7.8120   19.   Variation of operator's licence by the licensing authority (1)   The licensing authority may—

(a)   suspend the operation of a London PHV operator's licence so far as relating to any operating centre specified in the licence; or

(b)   vary such a licence by removing a reference to an operating centre previously specified in the licence,

if the authority is no longer satisfied that the operating centre in question meets any requirements prescribed under section 3(3)(b) or for any other reasonable cause.

(2)   Where the licensing authority has decided to suspend the operation of a licence as mentioned in subsection (1)(a) or vary a licence as mentioned in subsection (1)(b)—

(a)   the authority shall give notice of the decision and the grounds for it to the licence holder; and

(b)   the decision shall take effect at the end of the period of 21 days beginning with the day on which the licence holder is served with that notice.

(3)   If the licensing authority is of the opinion that the interests of public safety require his decision to have immediate effect, and the authority includes a statement of that opinion and the reasons for it in the notice, the authority's decision shall take effect when the notice is served on the licence holder.

(4)   If a licence is suspended in relation to an operating centre, the premises in question shall not be regarded for the purposes of this Act as premises at which the licence holder is authorised to accept private hire bookings, until such time as the licensing authority by notice states that the licence is no longer suspended in relation to those premises.

(5)   The holder of a London PHV operator's licence may appeal[1] to a magistrates' court against a decision under subsection (1).

[Private Hire Vehicles (London) Act 1998, s 19 as amended by the Greater London Authority Act 1999, Sch 21.]

---

[1]   For provisions relating to appeals see ss 25–26, post and the Magistrates' Court Rules 1981, r 34 in PART 1: MAGISTRATES' COURTS PROCEDURE ante.

7.8121   20.   Fees for grant of licences, etc

7.8122   21.   Production of documents   (1)   The holder of a London PHV operator's licence or a London PHV driver's licence shall at the request of a constable or authorised officer produce his licence for inspection.

(2)   The owner[1] of a vehicle to which a London PHV licence relates shall at the request of a constable or authorised officer produce for inspection—

(a)   the London PHV licence for that vehicle;

(b)   the certificate of the policy of insurance or security required in respect of the vehicle by Part VI of the Road Traffic Act 1988.

(3)   A document required to be produced under this section shall be produced either forthwith or—

(a)   if the request is made by a constable, at any police station within London nominated by the licence holder or vehicle owner when the request is made, or

(b)   if the request is made by an authorised officer, at such place as the officer may reasonably require,

before the end of the period of 6 days beginning with the day on which the request is made.

(4)   A person who without reasonable excuse contravenes this section is guilty of an offence and liable on summary conviction to a fine not exceeding **level 3** on the standard scale.

[Private Hire Vehicles (London) Act 1998, s 21.]

---

[1]   For "owner" see s 35, post.

7.8123   22.   Return of licences, etc   (1)   The holder of a London PHV operator's licence shall return the licence to the licensing authority after the expiry or revocation of that licence, within the period of 7 days after the day on which the licence expires or the revocation takes effect.

(2)   The owner[1] of a vehicle to which a London PHV licence relates shall return the licence and the plate or disc which was issued for the vehicle under section 10 to the licensing authority after the expiry or revocation of that licence within the period of 7 days after the day on which the licence expires or the revocation takes effect.

(3)   The holder of a London PHV driver's licence shall return the licence and his driver's badge to the licensing authority after the expiry or revocation of that licence, within the period of 7 days after the day on which the licence expires or the revocation takes effect.

(4)   On the suspension of a licence under this Act, the licensing authority, a constable or an authorised officer may by notice direct the holder of the licence, or the owner of the vehicle, to return the licence to the authority, constable or officer (as the case may be) within the period of 7 days after the day on which the notice is served on that person.

A direction under this subsection may also direct—

(a)   the return by the vehicle owner of the disc or plate which was issued for the vehicle under section 10 (in the case of a London PHV licence); or

(b)   the return by the licence holder of the driver's badge (in the case of a London PHV driver's licence).

(5)   A person who without reasonable excuse fails to comply with any requirement or direction under this section to return a licence, disc, plate or badge is guilty of an offence.

(6)   A person guilty of an offence under this section is liable on summary conviction—

(a)   to a fine not exceeding **level 3** on the standard scale; and

(b)   in the case of a continuing offence, to a fine not exceeding **ten pounds for each day** during which an offence continues after conviction.

(7)   A constable or authorised officer is entitled to remove and retain the plate or disc from a vehicle to which an expired, suspended or revoked London PHV licence relates following—

(a)   a failure to comply with subsection (2) or a direction under subsection (4);

(b)   a suspension or revocation of the licence which has immediate effect by virtue of section 9(3) or 17(2).*

[Private Hire Vehicles (London) Act 1998, s 22 as amended by the Greater London Authority Act 1999, Sch 21.]

---

* Amended by the Transport for London Act 2008, s 24 from a date to be appointed.
1 For "owner" see s 35, post.

7.8124   23.   Register of licences

7.8125   24.   Delegation of functions by the Secretary of State

7.8126   25.   Appeals   (1)   This section applies to any appeal which lies under this Act to a magistrates' court against a decision of the licensing authority, a constable or an authorised officer in relation to, or to an application for, a licence under this Act.

(2)   If the licensing authority has exercised the power to delegate functions under section 24, such an appeal shall be heard by a magistrates' court.

(3)   Any such appeal shall be by way of complaint for an order and the Magistrates' Courts Act 1980 shall apply to the proceedings.

(4)   The time within which a person may bring such an appeal is 21 days from the date on which notice of the decision appealed against is served on him.

(5)   In the case of a decision where an appeal lies, the notice of the decision shall state the right of appeal to a magistrates' court and the time within which an appeal may be brought.

(6)   An appeal against any decision of a magistrates' court in pursuance of an appeal to which this section applies shall lie to the Crown Court at the instance of any party to the proceedings in the magistrates' court.

(7)   Where on appeal a court varies or reverses any decision of the licensing authority, a constable or an authorised officer, the order of the court shall be given effect to by the licensing authority or, as the case may be, a constable or authorised officer.

(8)   On an appeal under this Act to the magistrates' court or the Crown Court, the court is not entitled to entertain any question as to whether—

    (a)   a person should be, or should have been, granted leave to enter or remain in the United Kingdom; or

    (b)   a person has, after the date of the decision being appealed against, been granted leave to enter or remain in the United Kingdom.

[Private Hire Vehicles (London) Act 1998, s 25 as amended by the Greater London Authority Act 1999, Sch 21, SI 2005/886 and the Immigration Act 2016, Sch 5.]

7.8127   26.   Effect of appeal on decision appealed against   (1)   If any decision of the licensing authority against which a right of appeal is conferred by this Act—

    (*a*)   involves the execution of any work or the taking of any action;

    (*b*)   makes it unlawful for any person to carry on a business which he was lawfully carrying on at the time of the decision,

the decision shall not take effect until the time for appealing has expired or (where an appeal is brought) until the appeal is disposed of or withdrawn.

(2)   This section does not apply in relation to a decision to suspend, vary or revoke a licence if the notice of suspension, variation or revocation directs that, in the interests of public safety, the decision is to have immediate effect.

[Private Hire Vehicles (London) Act 1998, s 26 as amended by the Greater London Authority Act 1999, Sch 21.]

7.8128   27.   Obstruction of authorised officers etc   (1)   A person who wilfully obstructs a constable or authorised officer acting in pursuance of this Act is guilty of an offence and liable on summary conviction to a fine not exceeding **level 3** on the standard scale.

(2)   A person who, without reasonable excuse—

    (*a*)   fails to comply with any requirement properly made to such person by a constable or authorised officer acting in pursuance of this Act; or

    (*b*)   fails to give a constable or authorised officer acting in pursuance of this Act any other assistance or information which he may reasonably require of such person for the purpose of performing his functions under this Act,

is guilty of an offence and liable on summary conviction to a fine not exceeding level 3 on the standard scale.

(3)   A person who makes any statement which he knows to be false in giving any information to an authorised officer or constable acting in pursuance of this Act is guilty of an offence and liable on summary conviction to a fine not exceeding **level 5** on the standard scale.

[Private Hire Vehicles (London) Act 1998, s 27.]

7.8129   28.   Penalty for false statements   A person who knowingly or recklessly makes a statement or furnishes information which is false or misleading in any material particular for the purpose of procuring the grant or renewal of a licence under this Act, or the variation of an operator's licence under section 18, is guilty of an offence and liable on summary conviction to a fine not exceeding **level 5** on the standard scale.

[Private Hire Vehicles (London) Act 1998, s 28.]

7.8130   29.   Saving for vehicles used for funerals and weddings   Nothing in this Act applies to any vehicle whose use as a private hire vehicle is limited to use in connection with funerals or weddings.

[Private Hire Vehicles (London) Act 1998, s 29.]

Further controls

7.8131   30.   Prohibition of certain signs, notices etc   (1)   The licensing authority may make regulations prohibiting the display in London on or from vehicles (other than licensed taxis and public service vehicles) of any sign, notice or other feature of a description specified in the regulations.

(2)   Before making the regulations the licensing authority shall consult such bodies appearing to the authority to represent the London cab trade and the private hire vehicle trade in London as the authority considers appropriate.

(3)   Any person who—

    (*a*)   drives a vehicle in respect of which a prohibition imposed by regulations under this section is contravened; or

    (*b*)   causes or permits such a prohibition to be contravened in respect of any vehicle,

is guilty of an offence and liable on summary conviction to a fine not exceeding level 4 on the standard scale.

[Private Hire Vehicles (London) Act 1998, s 30 as amended by the Greater London Authority Act 1999, Sch 21.]

7.8132   31.   Prohibition of certain advertisements   (1)   This section applies to any advertisement—

    (*a*)   indicating that vehicles can be hired on application to a specified address in London;

    (*b*)   indicating that vehicles can be hired by telephone on a telephone number being the number of premises in London; or

    (*c*)   on or near any premises in London, indicating that vehicles can be hired at those premises.

(2)   No such advertisement shall include—

    (*a*)   any of the following words, namely "taxi", "taxis", "cab" or "cabs", or

    (*b*)   any word so closely resembling any of those words as to be likely to be mistaken for it,

(whether alone or as part of another word), unless the vehicles offered for hire are London cabs.

(3)   An advertisement which includes the word "minicab", "mini-cab" or "mini cab" (whether in the singular or plural) does not by reason only of that fact contravene this section.

(4)   Any person who issues, or causes to be issued, an advertisement which contravenes this section is guilty of an offence and liable on summary conviction to a fine not exceeding **level 4** on the standard scale.

(5)   It is a defence for a person charged with an offence under this section to prove[1] that—

    (*a*)   he is a person whose business it is to publish or arrange for the publication of advertisements;

    (*b*)   he received the advertisement in question for publication in the ordinary course of business; and

    (*c*)   he did not know and had no reason to suspect that its publication would amount to an offence under this section.

(6)   In this section—

"advertisement" includes every form of advertising (whatever the medium) and references to the issue of an advertisement shall be construed accordingly;

"telephone number" includes any number used for the purposes of communicating with another by electronic means; and "telephone" shall be construed accordingly.

[Private Hire Vehicles (London) Act 1998, s 31.]

---

[1] An accused who raises this defence is not required to establish it beyond reasonable doubt, but on the balance of probabilities: see *R v Carr-Briant* [1943] KB 607, [1943] 2 All ER 156, 107 JP 167.

Miscellaneous and supplementary

7.8133   32.   Regulations[1]

---

[1] See the Private Hire Vehicles (London) (Operators' Licences) Regulations 2000, SI 2000/3146.

7.8134   33.   Offences due to fault of other person   (1)   Where an offence by any person under this Act is due to the act or default of another person, then (whether proceedings are taken against the first mentioned person or not) that other person is guilty of the offence and is liable to be proceeded against and punished accordingly.

(2)   Where an offence under this Act committed by a body corporate is proved to have been committed with the consent or connivance of, or attributable to any neglect on the part of, any director, manager, secretary or other similar officer of the body corporate (or any person purporting to act in that capacity), he as well as the body corporate is guilty of the offence is liable to be proceeded against and punished accordingly.

[Private Hire Vehicles (London) Act 1998, s 33.]

7.8135   34.   Service of notices   (1)   Any notice authorised or required under this Act to be given to any person may be served by post.

(2)   For the purposes of section 7 of the Interpretation Act 1978 any such notice is properly addressed to a London PHV operator if it is addressed to him at any operating centre of his in London.

(3)   Any notice authorised or required under this Act to be given to the owner of a vehicle shall